CONTENTS

ACKNOWLEDGMENTS

In 2008, I saw the end of my professional IT career and the exciting new beginning of my EFI Connection venture. I've followed my passion for manufacturing and gone all in by pursuing excellence in the work that I've done. With few regrets, I can look back at the many accomplishments and unique opportunities with thankfulness and gratitude. I've been blessed to have countless hours with my father and share many successes largely because of his influence in my life. I've experienced the surprise of wonderful friendships from business owners (even competitors) in the automotive performance industry. My passion for manufacturing has grown far beyond my initial expectations, and my skill set has grown exponentially. There will come a time when this season is over, and I want to always look back at this time knowing that I did my best and that my efforts have been a blessing to many.

In the early summer of 2020, I woke up on a Saturday morning with the idea of writing this book. I turned to my wife and said, "I think I should write another book."

Rather than expressing her time and added stress-related concerns, she gave me the support I needed to move forward with the work ahead. Megan, for all of the missed together time, for the freedom to work countless extra hours, for your encouragement, and for always trusting me to make responsible decisions—thank you. I love you.

My work in the automotive industry has benefited me with several friendships that will carry on into eternity. Bill Hillock (of BP Automotive), your selflessness and obedience to our Lord and Savior, Jesus Christ, keep our work in proper perspective as we each strive to serve our mighty God through the work that we do. Thank you for your time, your advice, and your encouragement. "If anyone speaks, he should speak as one conveying the words of God. If anyone serves, he should serve with the strength God provides, so that in all things God may be glorified through Jesus Christ, to whom be the glory and the power forever and ever. Amen." (1 Peter 4:11).

To Jim Hall (of TPIS), Jamy Lippencott, Bill Adam, Troy Adam, and Mark Noonan, I won't forget your time and contributions toward my learning journey with GM LS-series electrical systems. You've all helped me to shape a niche segment of the performance automotive industry through offering unique products that have brought LS-series technology to early GM engines.

To my employees past and present, your hard work has allowed EFI Connection, LLC to grow in a competitive industry. I hope you can read this book with a sense of pride as your efforts have no doubt shaped my understanding and use of GM's LS-series electrical systems.

To EFI Connection customers, thank you for your interest in GM fuel injection systems. This book wouldn't be possible without the years of support you've provided through the purchase of LS wiring products. I've committed many months of my time toward the content you are about to read. I've challenged myself to create exceptional quality three-dimensional (3-D) models and wiring schematics for you to use to be successful with your projects. There is tremendous value in this book; for your ongoing support, you deserve my very best.

"Whatever your hand finds to do, do it with all your might . . ." (Ecclesiastes 9:10).

LS GEN III ENGINE WIRING SYSTEMS

1997–2007

Mike Noonan

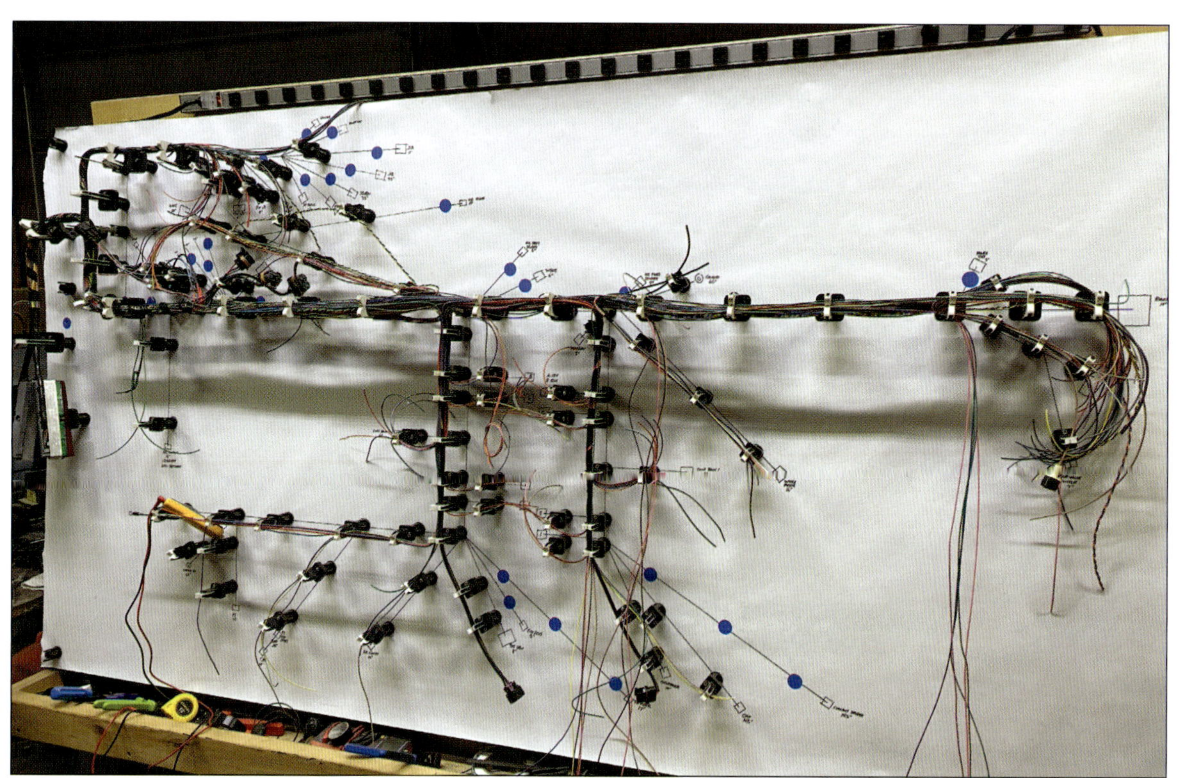

CarTech®

CarTech®

CarTech®, Inc.
6118 Main Street
North Branch, MN 55056
Phone: 651-277-1200 or 800-551-4754
Fax: 651-277-1203
www.cartechbooks.com

Edit by Bob Wilson
Layout by Connie DeFlorin

ISBN 978-1-61325-701-2
Item No. SA516

Library of Congress Cataloging-in-Publication Data Available

Written, edited, designed in the U.S.A. and printed in China

10 9 8 7 6 5 4 3 2

All schematics copyright © 2021 EFI Connection, LLC.

All graphics contained within this document are created by and are property of EFI connection, LLC and may not be copied or distributed without written permission.

GM wire sizes, wire colors, and fuses vary by application—the wire sizes, wire colors, and fuses shown are recommendations for a stand-alone 4-foot-length engine wire harness.

To source materials found within this book, please visit eficonnection.com or lswiring.com.

DISTRIBUTION BY:

Europe
PGUK
63 Hatton Garden
London EC1N 8LE, England
Phone: 020 7061 1980 • Fax: 020 7242 3725
www.pguk.co.uk

Australia
Renniks Publications Ltd.
3/37-39 Green Street
Banksmeadow, NSW 2109, Australia
Phone: 2 9695 7055 • Fax: 2 9695 7355
www.renniks.com

Canada
Login Canada
300 Saulteaux Crescent
Winnipeg, MB, R3J 3T2 Canada
Phone: 800 665 1148 • Fax: 800 665 0103
www.lb.ca

INTRODUCTION

In my first book, *How to Use and Upgrade to GM Gen III LS-series Powertrain Control Systems*, I scratched the surface on some of the wiring details related to the Gen III LS-series powertrain control modules (PCMs). Through reviews and feedback, I quickly discovered that readers wanted more how-to wiring content to help with LS engine conversions. The time is long-overdue to offer a book that covers GM Gen III LS engine wiring.

My first book also presented a few visuals related to PCM programming using EFILive hardware and software. While this book does not go into details about how to custom tune PCMs, there are a few projects presented that provide step-by-step examples of establishing a base calibration and modifications necessary for a starter calibration. Remember that the title of this book states a focus on engine wiring. There are books, message forums, Facebook groups, DVDs, and YouTube content that can assist you in learning how to tune your GM PCM.

The motivating factor behind this book was the obvious lack of an all-in-one documented source about GM LS engine wiring harnesses. Wiring harnesses removed from salvaged vehicles are an overwhelming mystery without easy to read schematics. Aftermarket stand-alone wire harnesses are often evaluated by little more than price. Enthusiasts with little to no experience with wire harness repair are making mistakes that result in safety concerns of which they are not even aware. I will go into detail about all of these areas of LS engine wiring.

You are presented with harness connector illustrations in unmatched stunning detail that can be used as a reference when identifying or repairing your engine wiring harness. I challenged my own CAD skills to meticulously model, feature by feature, every connector used with the LS-series engines and transmissions to present component connector view data with PCM interchange details. These same 3-D models are used throughout the book within the easy-to-read wiring diagrams.

Being limited by page count, there is additional content I would have liked to provide. However, staying true to the title of this book, I think you'll find an excellent mix of content that you would expect related to GM Gen III LS engine wiring systems.

As enthusiasts continue to push the limits of what GM has provided in production vehicles and as government regulations continue to complicate LS engine conversions, new products and solutions are almost guaranteed to be developed and sold by automotive performance vendors. This book serves as a solid foundation on which to support any new advancements in Gen III LS-series electrical systems.

WIRE HARNESS BASICS

I'd like to begin by explaining some of the basic terms surrounding LS wiring so that you can best follow along with the chapters to follow. In the 20-plus years that I've been helping enthusiasts with GM LS-series engine wiring, there are a few conversational disconnects that we should clear up right away. Common disconnects that I experience include the wording used to describe wire harness components that customers are looking for. Common questions often go something like this:

"I'm looking for the connectors that go into the plug for…"

"Do you offer the ends for this connector?"

"Can you help me find the weather pack terminals for . . . ?"

I live and breathe wire harness–related research, design, assembly, instruction, and material sourcing nearly every day. My employees are most efficient in their work when we all speak the same language. By using correct terminology, you will also feel more confident in your work.

Service manuals will be easier to read.

Your search efforts will return better results.

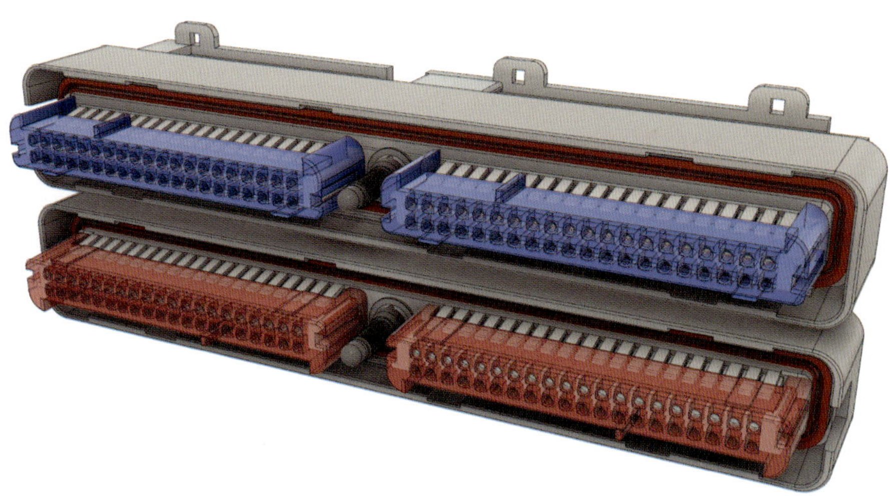

The LS1 PCM uses two 80-way Delphi Micro-Pack 100W connector assemblies. These connectors are secured to the PCM using a captive M6-1.0 threaded bolt. The die-cast aluminum housing contains the white connector, orange silicone seal, and blue or red retainers. Terminated wires are inserted into the back side of each connector. These connectors optionally accept a gray dress cover on the back side for wire protection and wire routing.

You will move more quickly through your project.

The terminology that follows is what you would expect to encounter as you work with GM fuel injection wiring. So, let's get started.

Connectors

A connector is the plastic housing that is designed with a shape that mates with a sensor, device, fuel injector, or opposite gender connector. A connector either has a retaining mechanism or retaining feature that ensures a reliable connection.

A connector is often incorrectly referred to as a "plug." Generally speaking, a plug prevents flow or passage. I'll explain the important role of a plug after clarifying several other wire harness terms. A connector, however, is designed to allow flow or passage. These passages, or cavities, are used to isolate each circuit passing through a connector. Connector

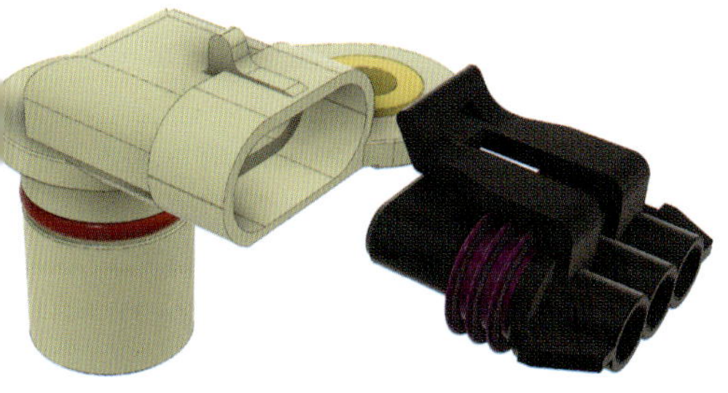

Delphi Metri-Pack 150 sealed female connectors are commonly used within LS-series wire harnesses for engine data sensors, such as this camshaft position (CMP) sensor (left). Notice that this connector allows passage through three cavities to make a connection with the internal pins of the CMP sensor; it does not "plug" the sensor.

cavities are almost always labeled with an alphabetic or numeric designation.

Other types of connectors include:

- Header: the connection soldered to the circuit board of an electronic control module

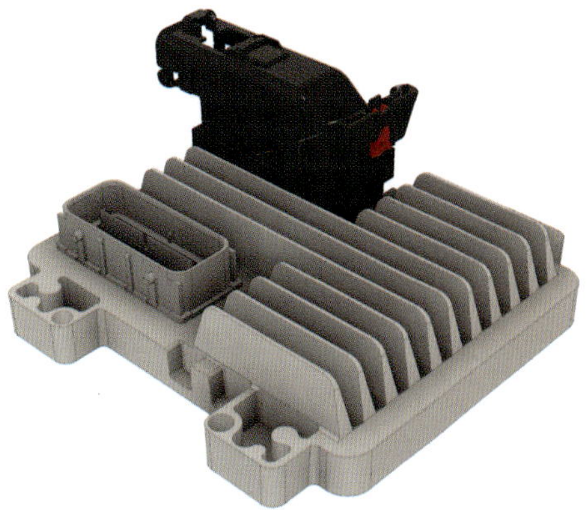

All LS-series PCM, ECM, and TCM harness connectors are "device only." This means there is no other mating harness connector but a circuit board header. Enthusiasts often look for an easy plug-and-play solution to lengthen GM engine harnesses. Unfortunately, the connector manufacturers (Delphi and Molex) never manufactured mating in-line harness connectors for this application. The best solution for an engine harness that is too short is to have a new harness manufactured by a reputable company that has the manufacturing equipment that will meet or exceed OEM specifications.

- Housing: another name for a connector
- Receptacle: another name for a connector

Because mating and disconnecting friction causes minor wear on the contacts, or terminals within a connector, manufacturers sometimes suggest a mating lifecycle. It's very unlikely that you will experience a connector failure due to its mating lifecycle.

The following attributes are important when identifying a connector.

Manufacturer	Family	Applications
Delphi*	Metri-Pack	Sensors, devices
Delphi*	GT	Sensors, devices
Delphi*	Micro-Pack	Gen III LS-series PCMs
* Delphi is now Aptiv		

GM engine wire harnesses are manufactured with a variety of different connectors. Gen III LS-series engine harnesses contain only Delphi connectors, while Gen IV LS-series harnesses contain connectors by other manufacturers, such as Molex, Bosch, Kostal, TE Connectivity, and Yazaki. The addition of new manufacturers and families means additional assembly and disassembly tools are necessary for harness repairs.

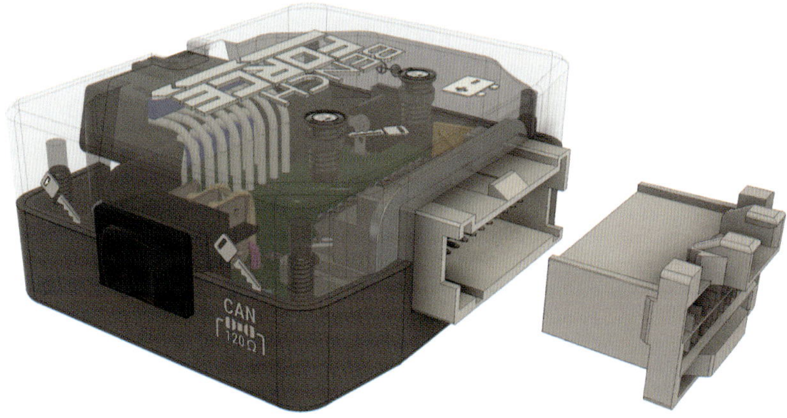

A header is a type of connector with integrated metal pins that are to be soldered to a circuit board. This 24-way gray Delphi Micro-Pack 100 male header is shown attached to this BenchForce PowerBlock II circuit board. The mating 24-way gray Delphi Micro-Pack 100 female connector will contain the terminated wires that make up a harness assembly. The black 16-way Delphi Metri-Pack 150 female unsealed OBD-II diagnostic connector on the opposite side of this circuit board is being used as a header, but because it does not have integrated circuit board pins, it's actually only considered to be a connector. A header is almost always used to connect an electronic module to a wire harness.

Manufacturer, Family, and Series

When identifying a connector, the first attributes in material sourcing are manufacturer, family, and series: Delphi was the manufacturer of the most common connectors within GM LS-series wire harnesses. Metri-Pack is a common family name of Delphi connectors. 150 is the most common series within the Metri-Pack

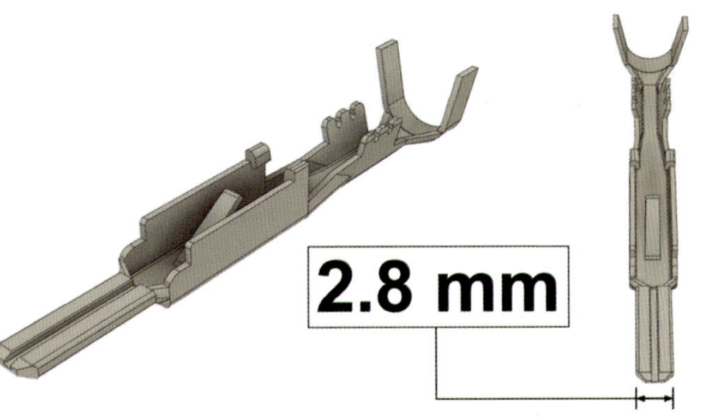

Terminal size is represented by series. Connector manufacturers don't always represent series as a measurement. The easiest way to size up the series of connector(s) that you are working with is to measure the male terminal blade width or the female terminal blade opening. Some manufacturers, such as Delphi, may represent the 2.8-mm series with "280," while others, such as Molex, may just use "2.8." Kostal uses "2,8" to represent 2.8-mm series.

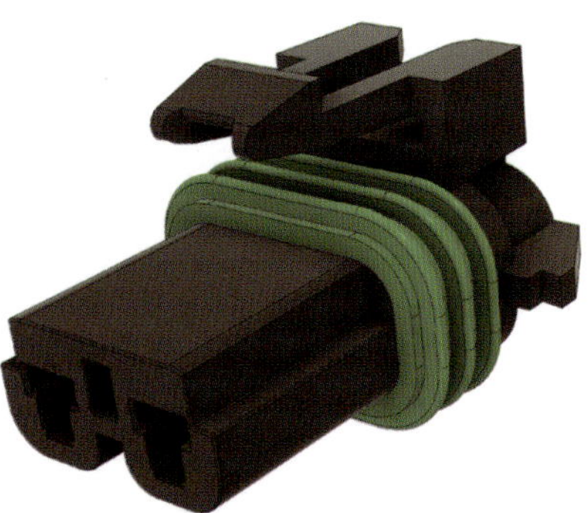

When sourcing replacement connectors, you won't have to look too far to see that what looks like a male connector is actually female. While this may seem confusing, all connector manufacturers determine connector gender by the terminals they receive.

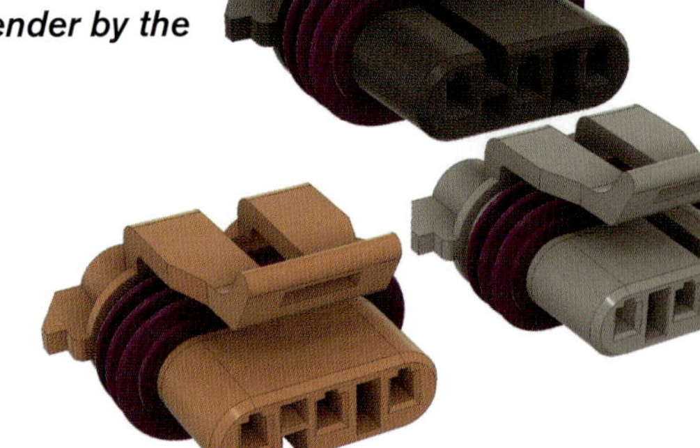

family of connectors used with GM LS-series engine wire harnesses.

Gender

Connectors have gender assignments based on terminal gender—not the general appearance of the connector body. This is so often misunderstood that I try to avoid discussing connector gender with enthusiasts when assisting with their wire harness sourcing needs. More information on gender is provided later in this book.

Sealed or Unsealed

Just as the name implies, connectors that contain a silicone seal are weather resistant and are considered to be sealed. Some sealed connectors have an integrated internal silicone seal for wires to pass through, while other sealed connectors rely on a single wire seal (SWS) on each wire to resist fluids. Sealed connectors also rely on a silicone seal between two connectors to resist fluids.

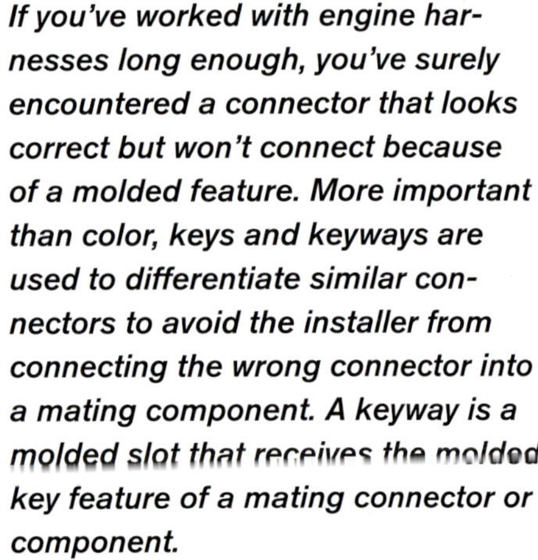

If you've worked with engine harnesses long enough, you've surely encountered a connector that looks correct but won't connect because of a molded feature. More important than color, keys and keyways are used to differentiate similar connectors to avoid the installer from connecting the wrong connector into a mating component. A keyway is a molded slot that receives the molded key feature of a mating connector or component.

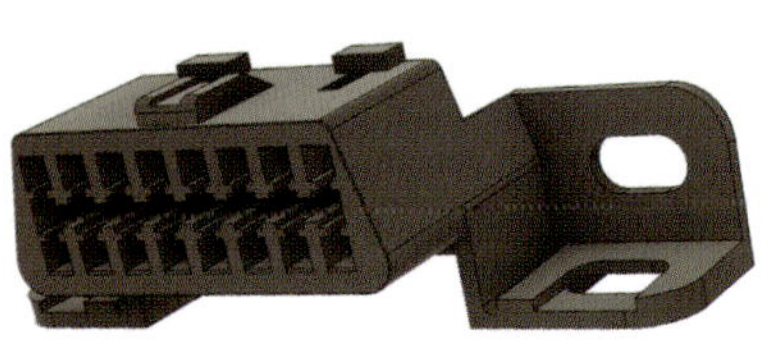

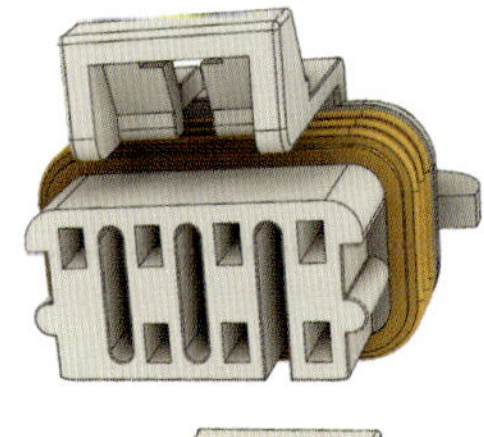

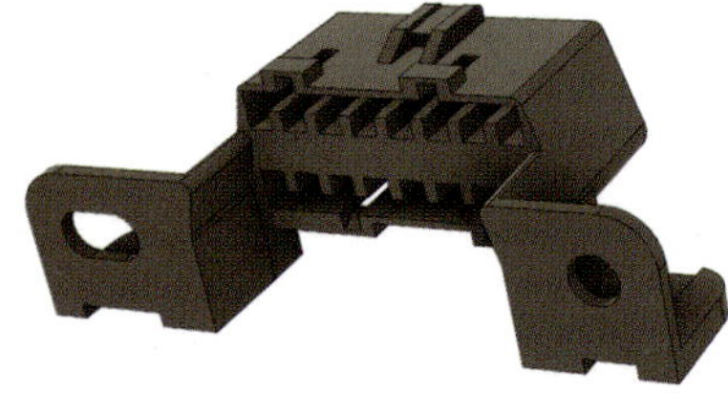

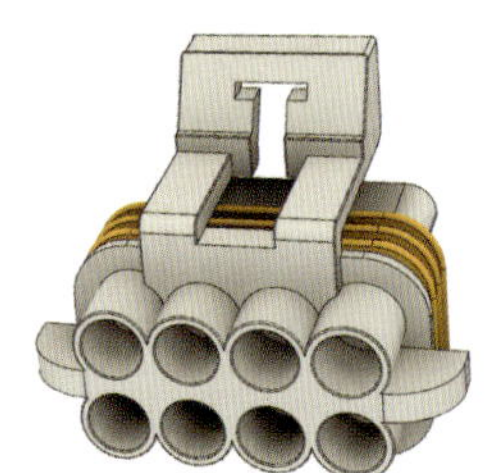

Sealed connectors make up the vast majority of connectors on an LS engine wire harness because the sensors and devices are located in areas of the vehicle that may be exposed to fluids. Unsealed connectors are generally only found at the electrical center and OBD-II diagnostic connector. Sealed connectors are obvious, as they contain a visible connector silicone seal and some sort of silicone seal, cable seal(s), or internal connector seal for the terminated wires. Unsealed connectors are commonly found within the passenger compartment, as they are never exposed to fluids.

Color

I saved this attribute for last because, as you've just read, there are many more important considerations than color when describing a connector. In general, color refers to the connector body color and not its assembly components. Color can also be a deceiving descriptor because some connectors vary only in color.

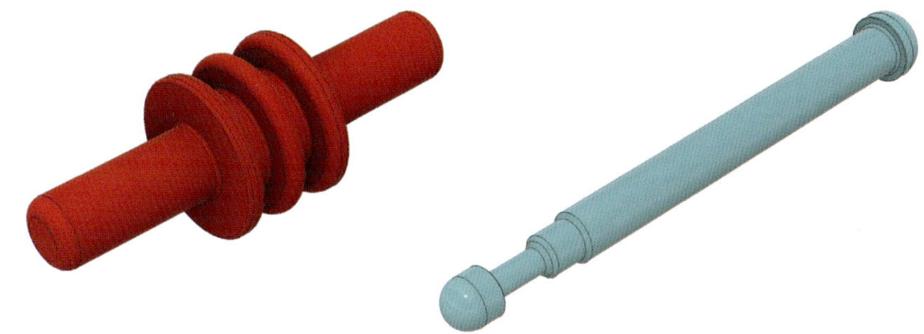

When a sealed connector is assembled with fewer wires than the open cavity count, plugs are inserted into open cavities to prevent fluids from entering the connector assembly. Connectors with an internal cable seal accept plastic plugs, while connectors with no internal seal accept silicone plugs resembling a cable seal.

Wire seals come in many different sizes and colors. These soft silicone seals are designed to prevent fluids from entering a connector cavity. A single wire seal (shown here) is inserted on the end of the wire before a terminal is crimped. The terminal will crimp to the multistrand copper conductor and to the recess in the cable seal.

Cable Seals

Sealed connector systems often require a single wire seal (SWS) to keep fluids out of the connector housing. Cable seals also serve a strain relief function that prevents the stripped end of the cable (or wire) from breaking with repeated movement. To put this another way, if a sealed connector is used in an unsealed environment, such as a vehicle's interior, cable seals are still required.

Cable seals have the following attributes: family, series, and color.

Plugs

As the name implies, a plug is a component used to block passage through a connector housing. Made of silicone, connector cavity plugs are used in sealed environments where a connector has an unused cavity.

Terminals

Connector cavities are populated with formed metal terminals. While the word "pin" is often used synonymously with "terminal," a pin tends to imply a male terminal, while a socket implies a female terminal. You will find manufacturer documentation to use "terminal," so that is the term used throughout this book.

Terminals have the following attributes: family, series, male or female, sealed or unsealed, plated (tin, silver, or gold) or not plated, and tang or tangless.

The proper application of a terminal requires tooling that has been designed to achieve the manufacturer-defined crimp height and width. These tools are necessary for a reliable wire harness solution. A loose connection is often created when a terminal is under- or

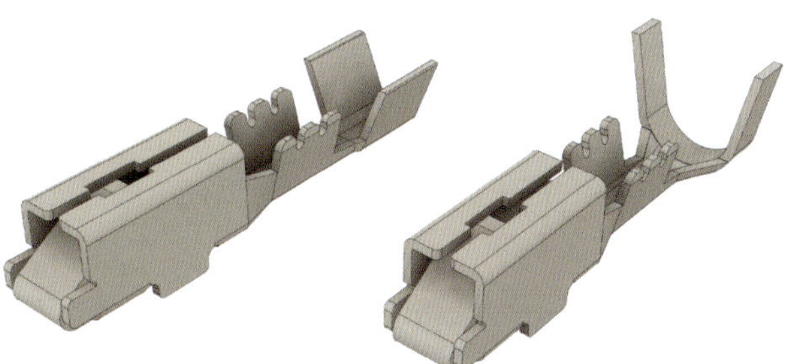

Terminals within a family and series are generally available as sealed and unsealed. Unsealed terminals are only intended for use with unsealed connectors within the same family and series. The same is true for sealed terminals. The most apparent distinguishing feature between a sealed and unsealed terminal is the V or U shape toward the wire end. A single wire seal is installed within the U-shape feature, while the V shape is crimped to the cable insulation.

Electrical centers distribute power across multiple fused circuits by using terminal bus bars. By terminating a bus bar with a power source, the entire bus bar can distribute power to multiple fuses. The other side of each fuse contains a singulated bus bar terminal that is terminated to a wire being used to power a device within the harness. The length of a bus bar, or the terminal count, varies by electrical center design.

Most connectors have a secondary locking mechanism to ensure a good connection. A terminal position assurance (TPA) is a secondary lock that is installed on the back side of a connector as the final step of assembly. The connector body contains features to lock each terminal, but the TPA will absolutely prevent terminated wires from being removed.

over-crimped, as over crimping tends to make the terminal brittle and prone to breaking. Crimps that do not meet manufacturer-defined specifications may not withstand a pull test. I'll go into much more detail about crimp tools, manufacturer specifications, and pull tests later in this book.

Bus Bar Terminals

Fuse blocks and electrical centers are also populated with terminals. A closer look reveals strips of connected terminals. These connected terminals, or a bus bar, are used to share a power source with more than one fused circuit.

Secondary Locks

Connectors are often designed with a few fail-safe features that are referred to as secondary locks. Terminal retention is guaranteed with the use of a terminal position assurance (TPA) lock, while connector-to-connector retention is guaranteed with the use of a connector position assurance (CPA) lock. Some GM connections, such as oxygen sensor connectors, use CPAs that are attached to, or tethered to, the branch of the harness just before the connector.

Dress Covers

High-cavity-count connectors are typically fitted with a protective wire dress cover. Dress covers are also used to route wires neatly while securing a wire bundle with a zip tie. ECU header connectors may rely on the dress cover for a lever locking mechanism with a CPA feature. Some dress covers, such as the 2004-and-newer transmission neutral safety range switch, rely on the dress cover to hold plastic corrugated split loom.

Electrical Centers

Fused circuit protection is contained within the underhood bussed electrical center (UBEC). This UBEC is the place to look for blown fuses, diodes, and relays. It's also a great place for rodents to find a home. A few years into owning my 2003 Sil-

verado SS, I turned off the ignition switch and pulled the key out of the ignition . . . with the engine still running. I had to disconnect the battery to stop the engine from running. I soon found the issue; a mouse had made its home within the UBEC and had been urinating on top of the fuses and relays. A replacement UBEC was necessary to eliminate the excessive corrosion within the electrical center.

The production GM UBEC may be too large and simply overkill for your clean LS engine bay. The best solution is a simple aftermarket electrical center that contains just enough relays and fuses for your powerplant and electric fans. Not only will you be glad you removed all of the unnecessary circuits from your donor LS engine harness but you'll also have a guide to follow while slimming down your used LS harness.

Fusible Link Wire

The electrical center, or fuse block, is protected by one or more fusible links. These short, multistranded, wire segments are ultrasonically welded or crimped to the wire(s) being protected. In the event of an unexpected high-current load, the fusible link wire will melt within its fireproof insulation. In general, a fusible link is four numerical American wire gauge (AWG) sizes smaller than the wire it is protecting. However, the 1982–1992 Camaro and Firebird are examples of where 16 AWG fusible link wire is used to protect 10 AWG wire; that's a difference of six numerical AWG sizes. When replacing a fusible link, it is always best to look at the GM wiring diagrams for the harness you are working with to properly identify the correct fusible link size.

Automotive TXL Wire

The wires found within GM LS-series engine harnesses are made up of multistrand copper conductors wrapped in a high-temperature, chemical-resistant, insulation. This thin-wall, cross-linked polyethylene insulation (TXL) is commonly used in the engine bay of many automobiles. Its small diameter, flexibility, and insulation temperature range of -40°C to 125°C (-40°F to 257°F) make it ideal for use in engine compartments that must experience the effects of winter and summer temperatures.

Every engine wire harness must have fused circuit protection and relays to switch battery power to high-current devices. Electrical centers are used to contain fuses and relays in one convenient location. Unfortunately, the electrical centers used in production LS-equipped vehicles are too large and contain too many extra components for use in a stand-alone engine swap application. An electrical center for a stand-alone LS swap likely includes fuses, an ignition relay, fuel pump relay, electric fan relays, and an air-conditioner (A/C) compressor clutch relay.

Fusible link wire is important for every stand-alone LS engine conversion. Many enthusiasts overlook this detail and run the risk of catastrophic damage. Battery power sources to the electrical center should each be protected by a fusible link. By installing a short length of fusible link wire that is four numerical AWG sizes smaller than the wire it's protecting (e.g., 10 AWG wire protected by a 14 AWG fusible link), the fusible link will safely melt in the event of a circuit overload to sever the battery connection and save the rest of the engine wire harness (and entire vehicle) from meltdown.

Automotive TXL Thin Wall Wire Specifications	
Conductors	Multistranded bare copper
Temperature	-40 to 125°C
Insulation	Crosslinked polyethylene (XLPE)
Colors	GM defined colors with or without single longitudinal stripe
Resistant to	Abrasion, gasoline and oil, moisture
Voltage	Suitable for all 12V DC electrical systems
Specifications	ASTM B3, SAE J1128, Ford ESB-M1L23-A, Chrysler MS-8288
Source: Southwire Company, LLC	

The chart shows the automotive TXL thin wall wire specifications.

Measuring Multistranded Wire

I see it all too often—replacement wire segments that are too small in size. Careless thinking leads some to compare wire sizes by measuring the outside diameter of the insulation. To measure multistranded wire, you must add together the cross sectional measurements of the conductor copper strands. Let's walk through the measurement of a sampled blue wire that has been damaged near the throttle position sensor (TPS) connector.

With the wire cut and insulation stripped to reveal the conductor strands, 7 total conductor strands can be counted. These strands are small and can easily break when stripping away insulation, so careful inspection is important. We will use this number 7 when multiplying the total cross section.

GM engineers have determined appropriate wire sizes based on current draw and wire length. You will find the majority of sensor wire sizes to be 22 and 20 AWG, while high-current circuits, such as the starter, are as large as 10 AWG. GM service manuals represent wire sizes as a cross section measurement in the metric unit millimeters squared (mm²). When repairing or lengthening an engine harness, take caution to use the appropriate wire type and size to avoid the risk of failure and/or injury. Your local auto parts store is not likely to offer automotive TXL wire, so you may want to source this from an online retailer.

Diameter is the distance from one side of the conductor strand to the other. Using a vernier caliper, take a measurement of the diameter of each conductor strand. Ideally, record the averaged measured diameter in the measurement unit millimeters (mm). Here we use the averaged diameter of 0.23 mm. To later calculate area, use the radius value of the measured diameter. Divide the diameter by 2 to record the radius (0.125 mm).

Cross section is an area measurement. The formula for area is A =

Automotive TXL Thin Wall Measurements			
Conductor Size (AWG*)	Conductor Size (mm²)	Nominal Insulation Thickness (inches)	Nominal Outside Diameter (inches)
22	0.35	0.016	0.062
20	0.50	0.016	0.070
18	0.80	0.016	0.078
16	1.00	0.016	0.089
14	2.00	0.016	0.103
12	3.00	0.018	0.127
10	5.00	0.020	0.155

* AWG sizes are nominal numeric values that do not reflect a specific measurement.

When working with the wiring diagrams presented in GM service manuals, you will see wire sizes represented in the measurement unit mm². However, when shopping for wire in North America, you will likely be presented with a selection represented by the numerical AWG. The AWG system is a nominal representation wire size. Being nominal, you won't have to look far to see minor manufacturer variations from AWG to mm².

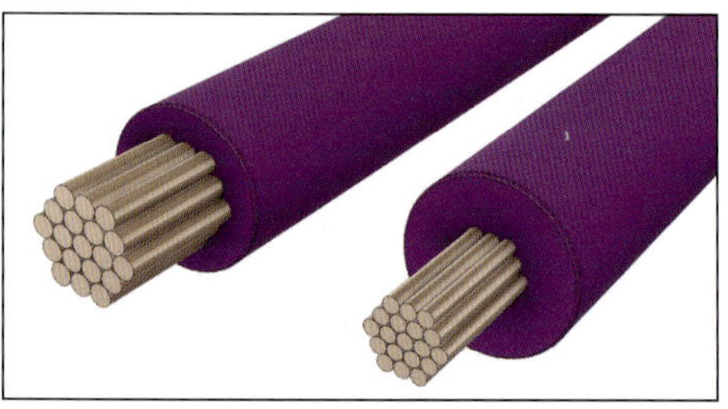

Wire size is important. If, for example, a 10 AWG starter crank circuit is repaired with a 14 AWG wire of the same insulation diameter, the repair is destined to fail. A 14 AWG wire is not adequate to carry the current drawn by the starter. If automotive TXL insulated wire is not among the general repair materials you have on hand, then be sure to calculate the cross sectional area and know the insulation properties of the wire you are using for any repair; the consequences could be catastrophic.

ᴕ r². We know the radius was measured to be 0.125 mm and that pi is approximately 3.14, so we can determine the area with the following multiplication: 0.125 x 0.125 x 3.14. The resulting area is approximately 0.05 mm².

We're not done quite yet. We've only determined the cross section area of each conductor strand to be 0.05 mm². Upon initial inspection of the wire, we counted seven total conductor strands. We must now multiply the recorded cross sectional area of one conductor strand by the total number of conductor strands. Our final math, 0.05 x 7, gives us a total cross sectional area of approximately 0.35 mm².

Looking at our AWG-to-mm² table, we see that the wire we need to use to replace this damaged wire is 22 AWG. While it is true that you can safely substitute a larger wire size, be sure to consider termination, wire splice technique, and tooling; using a terminal and tooling for 22 AWG wire on a larger 20 AWG wire will result in a crushed crimp that may cause the terminal or conductor strands to break.

Service Life of Automotive TXL Wire

While the SAE J1128 automotive wire standard does not state an expected lifespan for automotive primary wires, there surely must be an expected life for the wire harnesses being used with LS-series engines. Being a harness manufacturer, I felt that it was necessary to reach out to the applications engineering department of Southwire Company, LLC to receive an official statement:

"If TXL cable is used and installed as intended, the cable is simulated to approximately 10 years in service. However, like all wire [and] cable products, the life expectancy of TXL cables can be shorter or longer based on the installations, applications, and environment."

The factors impacting the life expectancy of TXL cable include:
- Average number of hours the car is driven or the engine is being utilized per day and the total accumulated hours in a year
- Amount of exposure to fluids including but not limited to engine oil, gasoline, and antifreeze; full immersion of TXL cable in fluids for a long period of time versus minimum contact of TXL cable in fluids will play a significant role in determining the longevity of TXL cables
- Amount of exposure to moisture and salt or deicing agent
- Temperature variations due to the environment (TXL cable is rated for -40 to 125°C); being exposed to large temperature swings from hot to cold or vice versa will enhance the thermal stress of the insulation and eventually oxidizes the XLPE material

When faced with the decision of reworking a used GM engine wire harness or buying a new engine wire harness for your LS-swapped vehicle, the data is strongly in favor of avoiding the use of old, fatigued, or deteriorated wires. Moreover, the condition of the connectors, if not broken, may be delicate or fragile for use. Many enthusiasts take their chances on a used engine wire harness to save a few hundred dollars. Considering the entire LS-swap project costs, is a few hundred dollars savings really worth the risk of failure?

MATERIALS

Many years ago, a customer sent me a competitor's LS engine wire harness for troubleshooting and rework. The first item that caught my attention was the exclusive use of wire with insulation that did not have the same texture or appearance as the TXL wire I knew to be used in original equipment manufacturer (OEM) engine harnesses. Out of curiosity, I applied a flame to the competitor's insulation and was amazed to see that the insulation was an accelerant!

You won't have to look far to find other subpar materials, such as hardware-store PVC tape, that will also accelerate a flame. For many enthusiasts, an LS engine swap project is a once-in-a-lifetime experience that spares no expense. I want to make sure you are choosing and working with the correct materials to ensure quality and safety for your pride and joy.

The following materials are appropriate for use in the engine compartment. This is far from an exhaustive list, so keep in mind that all materials have usage limitations, and those limitations can be obtained through the manufacturer.

Automotive TXL Wire

I don't recommend buying off-the-shelf primary automotive wire from your local auto parts store. The insulation is often too thick and does not compare well to the attributes of the crosslinked polyethylene (XLPE) material that is used with OEM engine wire harnesses. Consider that most terminals and tooling are designed for use with automotive TXL wire.

By applying a terminal to oversized insulation, the crimp will be out of specification (spec) and potentially a failure point. Southwire is a leading manufacturer of automotive TXL wire that meets or exceeds the requirements of OEM engine wire harnesses. Reputable and well established LS engine harness builders should carry and may offer this type of wire in various sizes and color combinations.

Fusible Link Wire

Very simply, fusible link wire is an undersized segment of wire crimped or welded to a circuit that is sized to melt in the event of overcurrent conditions. Fusible link wire insulation prevents the fusible link from catching fire. Your local auto parts store is likely to offer fusible link wire segments. You may also find fusible link wire in by-the-foot segments through an online LS engine harness builder or retailer.

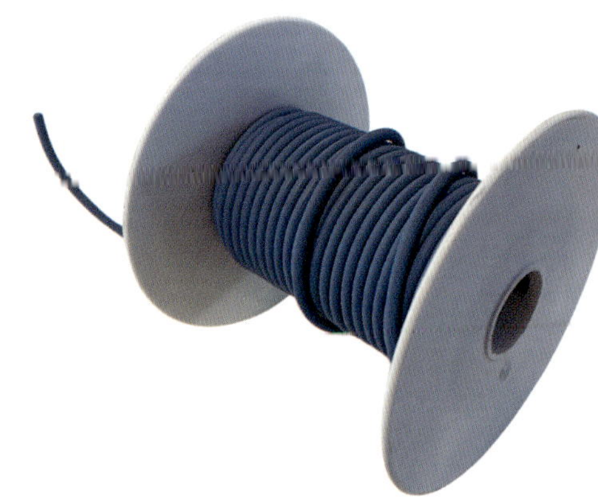

Fuse Holders and Fuses

Whether you are adding electric fans, an electric water pump, or other device to your vehicle, you want to protect the device and the circuit against overcurrent or a short to

ground. In the event of failure, an appropriately sized fuse disconnects the circuit and device from its power source so that troubleshooting and repairs may be performed. Your local auto parts store and online retailer will have many different fuses and fuse holder styles from which to choose.

Relay Bases and Relays

High-current devices may be triggered "on" by a manual toggle switch, temperature switch, ECU, or other controller device. These trigger devices often cannot safely carry the current required for the operation of the new high-current device. By using a 12V automotive relay, battery power can be switched to the device when the switch or trigger energizes the relay coil. Relays are commonly found at your local auto parts store or online retailer. Not all relays are created equal, so be sure to consult the manufacturer of your high-current device to source an appropriate relay for your application.

When splicing wires or adding length to a circuit, solder is commonly used for new work or repairs. In general, you may choose from lead-based or lead-free solder. Soldering with lead may create dust or fumes that are hazardous. Due to its lower melting point, lead-based solder is often preferred because it quickly flows into the workpiece to make a strong and reliable connection. Solder is readily available locally and through many online retailers.

Ring Terminals

Adding a battery circuit, ignition circuit, or ground circuit requires some sort of connection point to its source. That collection point is often attached by a ring terminal to a threaded stud or attaching bolt. Consider having a variety of ring terminal sizes in your toolbox or drawers for this type of work. Ring terminals are inexpensive and easy to find at your local auto parts store or many online retailers.

Butt and Barrel Splice Connectors

My shop does not use or stock butt connectors or barrel splice connectors. In my opinion, these connectors should only be used for temporary repairs. My shop's work is measurable; butt and barrel splice connectors are difficult to measure. Moreover, in many cases, they are a corrosion issue waiting to happen.

Nevertheless, they are handy to have on hand in a pinch. I've not used these types of connectors in more than 20 years; I probably won't add them to my shop drawers anytime soon. You can find these connectors at very low prices almost anywhere that you can buy electronic components.

Heat Shrink Tubing

Keep an assortment of heat shrink tubing in your toolbox so that you can avoid using electrical tape to cover a splice. Adhesive-lined shrink tubing allows adhesive to flow through the splice while sealing the two ends. Nonadhesive shrink tubing is useful for abrasion resistance and as a way to bundle several wires together. Heat shrink tubing will better protect your harness against moisture and engine bay fluids. Assortment packs and individual lengths and sizes are commonly available through many online retailers.

Plastic Split Loom

Slit convoluted plastic tubing, or split loom, is commonly used by OEMs to protect the engine harness from chafing, fluids, and high temperatures. Over time, the engine bay heat causes the plastic to become brittle.

Not all split loom is created equal. Pay careful attention to the colored tracer that runs longitudinally along the loom. No tracer implies a standard loom that will likely melt or lose its form in the engine bay environment. A gray tracer implies high-temperature nylon construction, resisting temperatures up to about 300°F. An orange tracer implies added UV-resistant high-temperature nylon construction. A blue tracer implies high-temperature flame-retardant polypropylene construction. I've yet to see high-temperature split loom at a local auto parts store. Your best bet is to shop online for split loom that meets the environmental needs of your installation.

Expandable Braided Sleeving

Braided sleeving is gaining popularity among enthusiasts. Techflex Flexo polyethylene terephthalate (PET) expandable braided sleeving has a clean and slim look that bundles wires together while providing excellent abrasion resistance. PET construction resists chemicals and UV radiation. An assortment of colors and sizes are available. See techflex.com for additional details and to find an online retailer.

Split Braided Sleeving

When braided expandable sleeving cannot be used, Techflex Flexo F6 split braided sleeving can be applied over existing bundles of wire. When sized appropriately, F6 bends to a tight radius without splitting open. Consider using F6 if you expect

to add wires, remove wires, or be able to service the harness in the future. See techflex.com for additional details and to find an online retailer.

Fiberglass Braided Sleeving

Harness runs near high heat sources may not fare well when using standard expandable braided sleeving. Techflex Insultherm Tru-Fit sleeving is excellent for use with oxygen-sensor harness runs because it offers wire harness protection up to 1,200°F. While made of braided fiberglass with an acrylic binder, it is surprisingly flexible for engine bay use. See techflex.com for additional details and to find an online retailer.

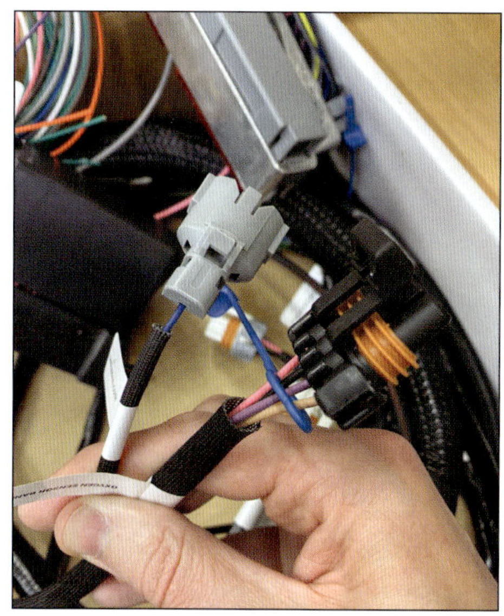

Vinyl Tape

If you've ever serviced a wire harness that was not OEM, you're probably familiar with the dirty excess adhesive that makes disassembly unpleasant. All of the wires remain sticky as you add, remove, or repair the harness. Your local hardware and auto parts stores do not carry vinyl tape designed for use in the automotive engine compartment.

Elliott ETN1000E vinyl tape meets OEM specifications with heat resistance up to 221°F. There's an excellent chance that your online LS engine harness supply retailer offers this tape at an attractive price.

High-Temperature and Medium-Abrasion Cloth Tape

More and more OEM harnesses contain bundled segments with a PET polyester fabric tape that is visibly attractive and comfortable to the touch. The tesa 51025 PET cloth wire harness tape contains a solvent-free rubber-based adhesive, is hand-tearable, and resists heat up to 257°F. I prefer to use this tape for harness segments in the passenger compartment but have also used this tape in appropriate locations in the engine compartment. It is available to purchase through many online retailers.

High-Temperature and High-Abrasion Cloth Tape

A stronger PET cloth wire harness tape (not tearable by hand) was designed for engine-compartment use with resistance to temperatures

up to 302°F. The tesa 51036 PET cloth wire harness tape features an advanced acrylic adhesive with high flag resistance, meaning that the cut end tends not to lift.

Compared to the tesa 51025 tape, the tesa 51036 tape feels thicker and somewhat bulky. Regardless of my preference, the tesa 51036 has proven to be one of EFI Connection's best-selling items. It is available to purchase through many online retailers.

Heat-Reflective Wire Harness Tape

Small engine compartments offer limited harness routing options. In locations where high heat is a concern, an excellent product that can be applied to split loom or braided sleeving is the Polyken 342C aluminum foil laminated fiberglass cloth tape. This high-temperature, flame-retardant tape is resistant to temperatures up to 392°F. Application is easy, as the tape conforms exceptionally well to the harness shape and can be torn by hand. While it is not necessarily easy to source, this tape is available through online retailers and is an excellent final touch to complete an engine harness assembly.

TOOLS OF THE TRADE

You may be surprised to see many of the wire harness–related tools presented in this chapter. I mean, what more is needed than a pair of wire cutters, a generic strip and crimp tool, and a soldering gun? You're about to see that there is a tool or machine designed for just about every step of the wire harness manufacturing process. While some of this equipment is simply too expensive for any enthusiast, my intentions are to satisfy curiosity and get you thinking about quality. I go into further detail about quality in the next chapter.

Cutting Tools

In my shop, wire cutting pliers get a lot of use. They are found almost everywhere and yet nowhere when I'm looking for them. Because all automotive wire harnesses are made with stranded wire, it's important to use cutting pliers that can make a clean and flush cut. Diagonal-cutting pliers feature beveled cutting edges that are ideal for close cutting. I prefer 6-inch diagonal cutters for a comfortable fit in my hand. Anything larger feels too big for 10-22 AWG wire. I still own and use the first two 6-inch diagonal cutters that I purchased in 2002 from Lowes.

Many years later, I found what looked like the same cutters on Amazon for less than $10 each, so I ordered five of them. They were not the same. Rather than cutting the stranded wire, they penetrated the copper strands just enough that I had to rip the wire from the blades. I promptly returned them and purchased several Channellock E336CB 6-inch diagonal-cutting pliers. The cut quality is everything I had expected from a well-known brand that manufactures in the USA.

When cutting larger wire, such as 8 AWG, small diagonal-cutting pliers are noticeably harder to work with. By changing the cut to a shearing action with sharp blades, even 8 AWG wire can be cut with ease. The pinching action of diagonal cutters crush the wire until it is cut, while shearing action cutters produce a cut that is very clean. When used as directed, a long life and ultra clean cuts can be expected. My go-to for larger wire is the Rennsteig Tools cable shears (part number 700 016 36). When using cable shears to cut anything

For less than $30, you can buy a pair of quality 6-inch diagonal cutters. While it's tempting to buy a pair of cutters for less than $10 on Amazon, you are not likely to receive cutters that work well. Buy name-brand cutters from Rennsteig Tools, Channellock, or Klein Tools to receive a tool that performs well and will provide many years of use.

To make a clean cut with larger wire, use a pair of cable shears. While diagonal cutters squeeze wire to make the cut, cable shears perform a shearing action with sharp blades to create a clean cut with nearly no deformation of the wire being cut. Rennsteig Tools part number 700 016 36 is an excellent tool for cutting any size of wire with exceptional results.

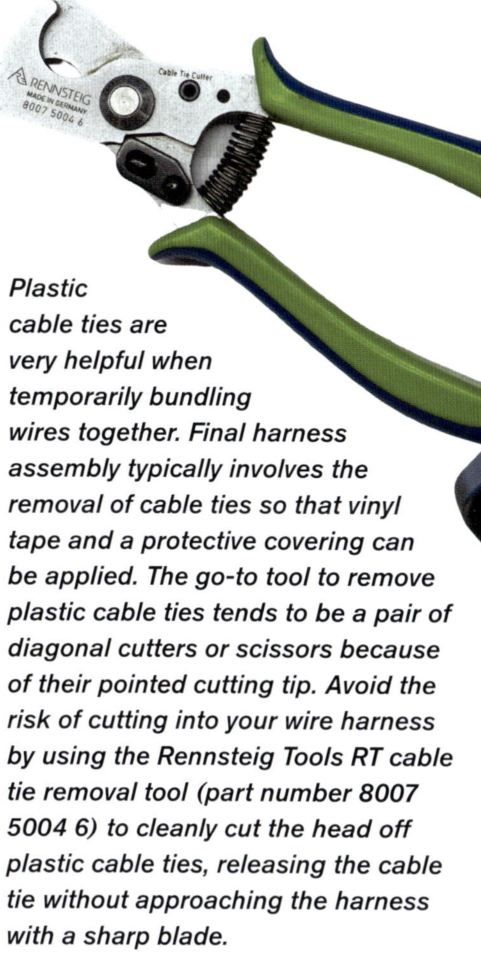

Plastic cable ties are very helpful when temporarily bundling wires together. Final harness assembly typically involves the removal of cable ties so that vinyl tape and a protective covering can be applied. The go-to tool to remove plastic cable ties tends to be a pair of diagonal cutters or scissors because of their pointed cutting tip. Avoid the risk of cutting into your wire harness by using the Rennsteig Tools RT cable tie removal tool (part number 8007 5004 6) to cleanly cut the head off plastic cable ties, releasing the cable tie without approaching the harness with a sharp blade.

Avoid accidentally cutting wire strands while stripping insulation by using the Rennsteig Tools RT MultiStrip 16 Self-Adjusting Insulation Stripper (part number 707 040). By resting the end of any 28-6 AWG-size wire against the adjustable wire stop, insulation is quickly and cleanly removed with the easy pull of the tool's handle. The metal jaws firmly hold the cable's insulation during the stripping process.

The Ideal Stripmaster wire stripper (part number 45-092) cleanly cuts and strips 22-10 AWG-sized cable. The radiused precision ground knife-type blades make this tool an excellent performer when building an engine wire harness. Care must be taken to insert the cable into the correct knife-blade cavity to ensure no copper strands are accidently cut.

harder than what they are designed for, the blades will instantly nick and become dull.

Cable zip ties are sometimes used to temporarily bundle wires together during assembly. Removing zip ties safely involves making a cut that does not touch the wire. The Rennsteig Tools spring-loaded cable tie removal tool (part number 8007 5004 6 RT) uses a shearing action to open the head of plastic zip ties to prevent any harm to the bundled wires. A small investment in one of these tools could save you many hours of rework if you accidentally cut into your near-finished wire harness with a pair of diagonal cutters while removing a zip tie.

Stripping Tools

Once a wire is cut to length, one or both ends must be stripped to remove a small length of insulation prior to termination or a splice. A general repair, an all-in-one wire stripper, crimper, and cutter is highly undesirable because it requires you to tear the wire away from the tool's blades, which often leaves a few copper strands behind. What's missing from the general-repair-type tool is a firm grip on the wire's insulation closest to the strip length. The pulling action by the user causes too much strain on the outer copper strands.

Without a doubt, the easiest and safest tool to remove insulation from the end of a wire is the Rennsteig Tools MultiStrip 16 self-adjusting insulation stripper. After setting the adjustable length stop, the operator simply inserts the end of a wire into the open jaws and then squeezes the handles to perform the cut and strip.

The wire is securely held by the end of the tool to eliminate any strain on the outer copper strands as the radiused blades incise just enough insulation to allow the tool to pull the insulation off the wire with ease.

Those with excellent dexterity may opt for the Ideal Stripmaster wire stripper. For more than 20 years, this has been my go-to tool when stripping a small quantity of wires by hand. There are other similar tools on the shelf at your local hardware store, but I've yet to find one that feels and performs as good as this tool.

The precision-ground blades feature several different radiused locations to best suit various wire sizes ranging from 10 to 22 AWG. The only disappointment I have with this tool is its relatively short life. To be fair, I get many months of frequent

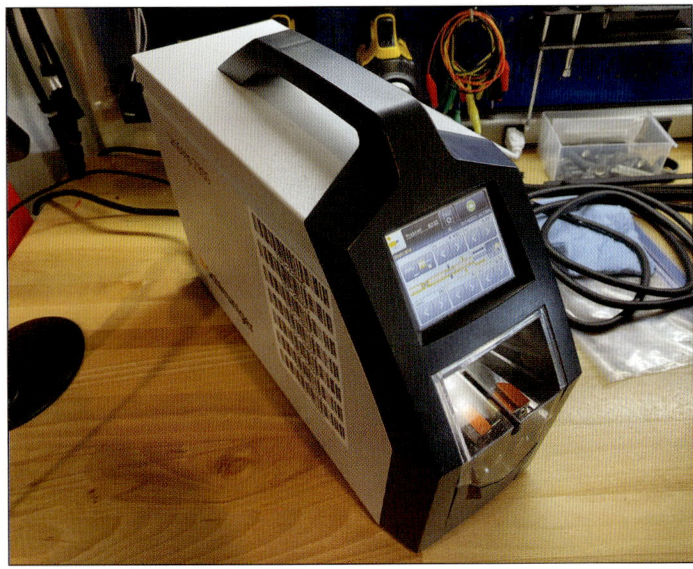

To quickly process batches of precut lengths of wire, the Schleuniger UniStrip 2300 stripping machine is the Cadillac of wire strippers. The operator simply uses an intuitive color touchscreen interface to program many different stripping routines for future use. Being electronic, the operator never has to make mechanical adjustments when changing wire sizes or strip lengths. With a price near $5,000, this machine is not likely for home use.

Automation is key for production efficiency and competitively priced products. Schleuniger's MultiStrip 9480 cut and strip machine can feed, cut, and strip wire at a blazing fast speed. The operator may program the machine through the included color touchscreen display or through the PC-based Cayman software. With unlimited wire list storage capacity, the operator can quickly recall existing programs to minimize setup time. Equipment such as this can be purchased new for about $20,000.

use before the open/close spring mechanism weakens to the point of unacceptable performance. Despite this flaw, the value of this tool is high; everyone should have this tool in their toolbox.

When working with batches of precut wires, nothing outperforms the Schleuniger UniStrip 2300 machine. This programmable stripping machine can strip any wire size found within a GM engine harness. After a small amount of trial and error, wire sizes and strip related parameters are stored in memory to later be accessed via a color touchscreen or quick barcode scan. When the machine's sensitive trigger button senses a wire, the wire is instantly held firmly in place while the V-shaped blades incise, slightly retract, and then pull the insulation from the end of the wire.

Cut and Strip Machine

Professionals reduce labor costs and improve efficiency by using cut and strip machines or cut, strip, and crimp machines. The Schleuniger MultiStrip 9480 machine is a fine example of a high-end cut and strip machine that promotes accuracy and efficiency when performing batch work. After inserting the end of a spool of wire into the machine, the user simply chooses a predefined program to cut and strip the wire to intended lengths.

When paired with Schleuniger's Cayman wire processing software, the machine operator can quickly and easily program and modify stored routines using an attractive graphical user interface.

Unfortunately, custom work is only slower when using this type of equipment because of the time required to program routines, load wire, verify accuracy, and then unload wire. Other inefficient realities of using a cut-and-strip machine for low-volume work include operator error and the occasional "spaghetti" mess created when the wire does not present well into and through the machine. A standard LS engine harness always costs less to produce in batch quantities when compared to a one-off custom LS engine harness because it's simply too inefficient to use a cut-and-strip machine for anything but batch work.

Crimping Tools

Perhaps the most misunderstood aspect of building or repairing an engine wire harness is crimping. I'll touch briefly on this topic here and

As terminals are formed through a progressive die stamping process, they are loaded onto a plastic or cardboard reel that is for sale through approved distributors. When hand-crimping tools are used, terminals must be individually cut from the reel, usually by hand, by separating each terminal from its carrier strip. Crimp presses can process terminals directly from their reel by cycling each carrier strip-fed terminal through a crimping applicator.

Aptiv (formerly Delphi or Packard Electric) offers a variety of hand-crimping tools advertised for popular terminal families and series. These tools are relatively inexpensive and should be used for general-repair purposes only. Many of these tools do not achieve crimps to manufacturer crimp height and crimp width specifications.

go into great detail in the following chapter to drive home the importance of using proper tools. Quite simply, creating an OEM-quality wire harness always requires the use of expensive crimp tooling. As you'll see in the following chapter, there is no room to argue this point.

All terminals found within LS engine harnesses were delivered to the original equipment manufacturer in reel form. Having originated from sheet metal and formed through an automated progressive die stamping process, the terminals are joined by a continuous carrier strip and loaded onto a plastic or cardboard reel. Low-quantity harness production typically involves cutting terminals from their carrier strip for singular use, while high-volume harness production involves the use of semiautomatic applicators and presses.

Singulated Terminals

When manufacturing low volume harness assemblies or performing repairs, terminals are commonly separated, or singulated, from their carrier strip for application by use of a hand tool. With countless general-repair hand-crimping tools flooding the market, I shudder to think about the quality of repair work being performed on used LS engine harnesses. Due to the nature of the manufacturing processes required to make precise hand-crimping tools, the cost to obtain such tooling for the average enthusiast is prohibitive.

Terminal manufacturers often offer general repair hand-crimping tools with prices ranging from about $150 to more than $1,000. The cheaper of these tools use a ratcheting scissor action to close the punch side of the tool to its anvil. The more expensive tools feature a closing

mechanism that performs a parallel movement of the punch to its anvil, creating an even (and typically more accurate) crimp. Whenever possible, I avoid using these tools because they are not always designed for a specific application. In some cases, I recommend carefully applying solder to the resulting crimp—an activity that has the potential to clog the terminal and prevent proper engagement.

Rennsteig Tools is a leading manufacturer of hand-crimp tools. Its modular PEW 12 crimping system offers crimping die sets for just about any terminal you may need to manufacture or repair an LS engine wire harness. The modular PEW 12 crimping system consists of a hand-crimping tool and interchangeable high-precision crimping die sets. Meticulous die set development and manufacturing precision from Rennsteig Tools result in

The Rennsteig Tools PEW 12 crimp tool system is the only handheld crimping tool system designed to crimp all terminals found within any LS engine wire harness. Manufactured in Germany, the PEW 12 crimping hand tool and related crimping die sets are precision manufactured to achieve repeatable results that meet terminal manufacturer crimp height and crimp width specifications.

For crimping at the touch of a button, the Rennsteig Tools RT eForce battery-powered crimping tool (part number 6370 0300 1) takes all the effort out of executing production quality crimps. The eForce tool is compatible with all of the crimping die sets used with the PEW 12 hand-crimping tool.

Good battery and ground connections are critical to the operation of any engine wire harness. Due to the crimping force necessary to use Aptiv's rugged ring terminals, a tool stronger than the PEW 12 tool is necessary. The Rennsteig Tools RT hForce battery-powered hydraulic crimping tool (part number 6320 802 1) works exceptionally well with Rennsteig Tools die sets designed for Aptiv ring terminals.

exceptional-quality crimps that meet terminal manufacturer crimp height and width specifications every time. The PEW 12 hand tool retails for just more than $100, and individual crimping die sets are often in the ballpark of $350 each.

Rennsteig Tools also offers a battery-powered eForce crimping tool that may be held by hand or rested on a tabletop. The eForce crimping tool receives the same crimping die sets as the PEW 12 hand-crimping tool. The push-button operation feature eliminates hand fatigue, but compared to the PEW 12 hand-crimping tool, it results in slower production. The eForce really shines when performing crimping on larger-sized

wires because it requires no extra user effort to crimp a small wire versus a larger wire.

Ring terminals are often used for power and ground circuits and crimped onto heavier-gauge wire. While most would use a basic $15 multi-tool wire stripper/crimper/cutter to squeeze the heck out of ring terminals in efforts to achieve the common "gutentight" (or "good-and-tight") crimp specification, Rennsteig Tools offers a better

solution. The hForce battery-power hydraulic crimping system offers a range of crimping die sets that are compatible with a variety of different ring terminals. By using a die set that has been designed with an appropriate punch and anvil for the terminal and wire size being crimped, you can be sure that the resulting crimp is not only gutentight but also conforms to the terminal manufacturer's measurable crimp specification. In the next chapter, more information is provided on the importance of this.

Unfortunately, the cost to achieve such a quality crimp is prohibitive for the enthusiast. The hForce solution costs several thousand dollars. As the press and applicator alternative is even more expensive, enthusiasts insisting on an OEM-quality harness should seek out a close relationship with a harness builder who uses

OEM-type equipment. The next-best alternative is to cautiously apply solder to the crimp. More information is provided on soldering in the next chapter.

Carrier Strip Terminals

All terminals used within LS engine wire harnesses are manufactured from sheet metal through a progressive die stamping process that creates side-feed front-carrier orientation terminals loaded on a plastic or cardboard reel. Professional harness production shops are able to efficiently apply terminals from a reel to pre-stripped wires by using a press and side-feed applicator that crimps and separates the terminal from its carrier strip in one cycle of the press. After measuring to verify crimp height and width accuracy, the press operator can quickly and consistently apply terminals to wire harness assemblies in a manner that is much faster than using hand-crimping tools.

A crimping applicator is a complex mechanical tool assembly that feeds terminals, one by one, from a reel through a hydraulic press as it applies terminals to pre-stripped wires. The applicator base receives a pair of anvils while the applicator ram receives a pair of punches. With the ram toggled into the press, the operator steps on the foot pedal to perform one cycle. As the punch strikes the terminal against the anvil, the terminated wire is separated from the terminal carrier strip. The operator pulls the terminated wire from the machine and then inserts another wire for termination. The process is repeated until the batch of work is completed.

Heavier wire sizes and thicker terminals sometimes require extra force through the assistance of air pressure. By adding the pneumatic feature to a mechanical crimping applicator, the punch tooling resists premature wear as it forcefully crimps and separates the terminal from its carrier strip. Bus bar terminals are a heavy-duty example of where air pressure is used to perform crimps and singulation. Because bus bars span several connector cavities to share a fused power source, they are not always singulated. An additional applicator feature allows the operator to pull a small handle to disengage the singulation feature as the press is cycled. When the bus bar is to receive its final crimp, the operator simply pushes the small handle forward to engage the singulation feature.

Disassembly Tools

Due to the wide variety of connectors found within the LS-series engine harnesses, disassembly procedures vary. In general, the removal of a terminated wire requires the removal of any secondary lock, or locking features, and the release of the retaining mechanism holding the terminal in its cavity. There are many different types of small blade and pick tools available to remove terminated wires from connector cavities.

Original equipment GM engine wire harnesses are manufactured with the use of terminal crimping applicators. Each applicator is installed in a crimping press that is often cycled through the use of a foot pedal switch. When the operator cycles the press, the applicator's ram moves the precision-machined punch downward to put pressure on the terminal located above the fixed anvil. The terminal's crimp barrel is closed as the terminal is separated from its carrier strip. Completion of the press cycle causes the applicator to automatically feed the next terminal to rest above the anvil. The operator simply removes the terminated wire from the press before inserting another pre-stripped wire for termination.

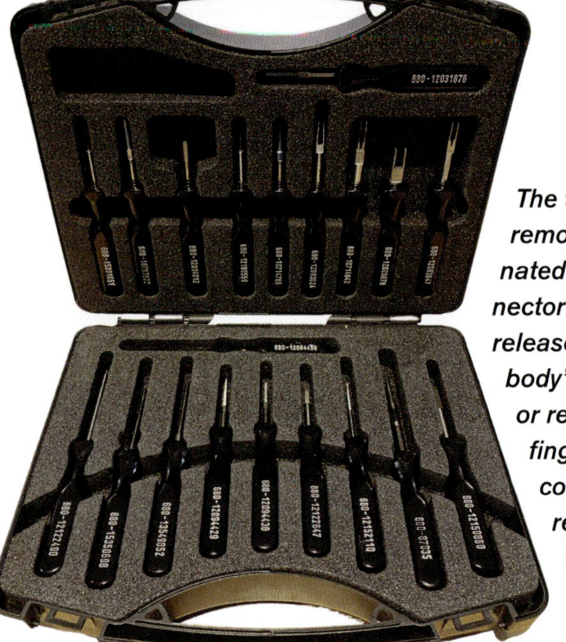

The trick to removing terminated wires from connector cavities is to either release the flexible terminal body's "tang" (if equipped) or release the flexible finger-like feature of the connector cavity. Once the retaining mechanism is temporarily released, the terminated wire will easily pull out of the connector cavity. Rennsteig Tools Terminal Insertion and Removal Tool Kit (part number 680-10502) can be used to remove the terminals from all connectors found within any LS engine wire harness.

An appropriately sized soldering gun makes quick work of soldered splices. The Weller industrial soldering gun (part number D550) quickly heats even the largest splices that are encountered in an LS engine wire harness build. With inexpensive replaceable tips, expect a long life out of this tool.

Soldering Equipment

When it comes to automotive wiring, it's almost guaranteed that soldering will be required at some point in time. Having access to ultrasonic equipment and OEM-quality crimping tools is unlikely, so solder is often necessary to create a reliable splice or connection. For fine detail work, such as applying solder to a crimped terminal, a quality soldering iron's fine conical tip helps make tidy work. For less detailed work, such as soldering a crimped or twisted wire splice, a quality soldering gun adequately gets the workpiece up to temperature quickly and thoroughly so that solder can be adequately applied.

Ultrasonic Welding Machines

Today's OEMs are required to create wire splices through the use of ultrasonic technology. By welding multiple wires together through

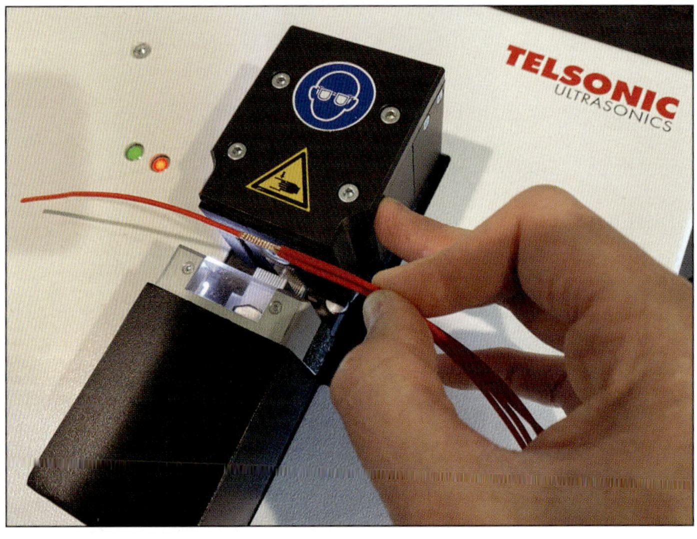

A wire splice nugget is the location where two or more wires have been joined together. The Telsonic TelsoSplice TS3 ultrasonic welding machine compresses pre-stripped wires with a combined cross section from 0.26 mm^2 to 40 mm^2 and vibrates the copper strands at 20 kHz (20,000 times per second) to form a bond. The resulting atomic connection (the copper nugget) resists corrosion and provides lower electrical resistance when compared to other forms of splicing. The splicing action takes only seconds!

frictional heat that is generated by high-frequency sound waves, a secure bond is quickly created. The resulting weld "nugget" can withstand the pull and peel forces established by the SAE/USCAR-45 performance specification for ultrasonically welded wire-to-wire splices.

Ultrasonic welding is not only fast and efficient but it also improves on the old methods of crimp and solder in many ways. Lead-based solder creates a dangerous work environ-

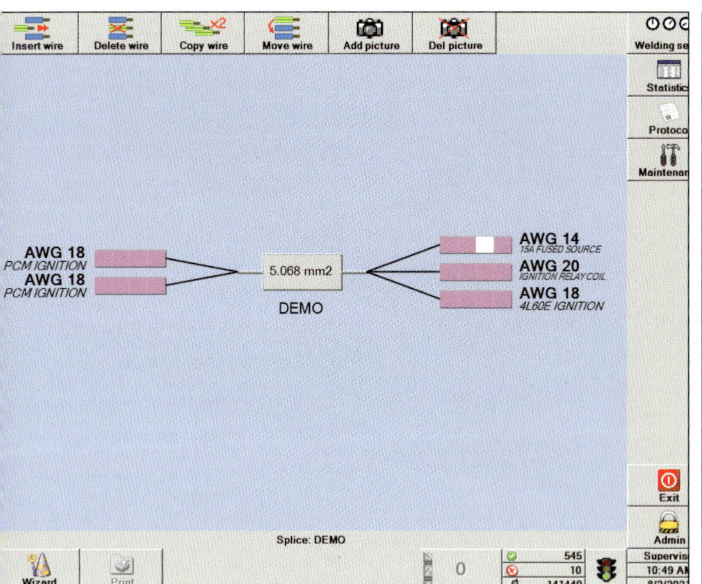

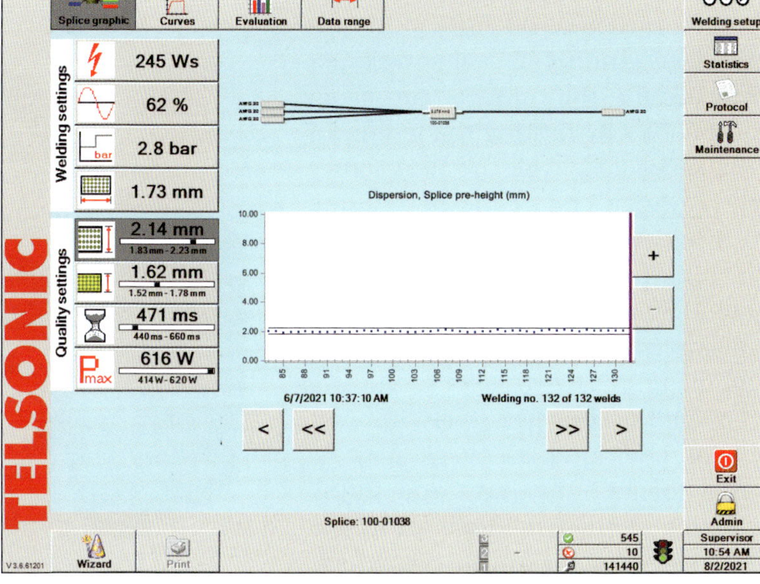

Using the TelsoSplice TS3 intuitive touchscreen interface, the operator simply adds wires to each side of the weld nugget. The machine automatically calculates the total conductor cross section and weld parameters. Each wire can be assigned a color and labeled for identification. The defined splice is stored on the machine's hard drive for future use and can be recalled by scanning a barcode.

Production mistakes are guaranteed, but the TelsoSplice TS3 makes sure that you are aware of any mistakes before moving on to the next splice. The machine compares every weld performance against the stored approved weld parameters. Production managers have the task of initial splice setup, including a measurable pull test. In the event of an error (for example, an undersized wire has been used in the nugget), the machine halts production and requires a supervisor to unlock the machine for continued use.

ment for everyone involved. Ultrasonic welding is not documented to report any known airborne hazards. Perhaps the most important feature of ultrasonic welding machines is the stored history of weld performance, which allows the machine operator or production supervisor to monitor the quality of production. Moreover, a weld that does not meet the established performance thresholds is immediately rejected and machine operation is suspended. Some automotive manufacturers, such as GM, even require that rejected welds are immediately cut by a blade that severs one side of the welded wires.

Heat Gun

Protecting wire splices with adhesive-lined heat shrink tubing requires application by a high heat

When using heat shrink tubing, especially dual-wall, adhesive-lined heat shrink tubing, an electric heat gun is capable of quickly generating the heat necessary to adequately shrink and melt the adhesive to form a protective covering over wire splices. The concentrated heat from a flame (for example, a pocket lighter) does not always perform well and can easily burn through the shrink tubing. Additionally, battery-powered heat guns do not heat as fast or as hot as commercial corded heat guns.

source. Heat guns offer the most control when shrinking heat shrink tubing because the operator can avoid air bubbles by heating the middle of the splice and work the heat source toward each end of the heat shrink tubing. As the tubing reaches its melting point, it will shrink toward its original size as adhesive flows to fill any voids and seal the ends of the tubing.

While conveyer-style hot air ovens and infrared ovens may be used to uniformly heat and shrink the tubing, these methods are far too expensive for the enthusiast. I hesitantly mention the use of a pocket lighter because the concentrated flame has the potential to burn a hole through the tubing. In a pinch, and with careful watch, you may be successful with the use of a flame as a heat source.

Custom Tools

Sometimes the tools we need are not available, too expensive, or don't exist. Do-it-yourselfers have been making or modifying tools to get the job done for the longest time. With a little cutting, grinding, and welding, an existing tool can easily be repurposed. In a similar way, harness-build jigs and templates can be created and used to keep your work organized and easy to work with.

More and more homes and garages have 3-D printing equipment that can quickly take a concept to reality. With a little bit of creativity, you may be able to make a low-cost custom solution to aid with the assembly, disassembly, or installation of your LS engine wiring harness. As harness-related components reach end of life, a 3-D printed alternative may be necessary to apply the final touches to your project.

Sometimes tools don't exist or are out of a project's budget. Get creative with what you have to get the job done. Enthusiasts are often talented and creative to fabricate solutions using metals and plastics. 3D printing has come a long way and has helped me to manufacture assembly fixtures, cable seal insertion tools, and even a unique PEW 12 crimping assembly set to seat the secondary lock on this Molex connector.

QUALITY CONTROL

We live in a world full of regulations; it's no surprise that GM's LS engine wire harnesses are built with the highest standards. The rules surrounding wire harness manufacturing that GM must adhere to ensure safety, reliability, and longevity. Today's LS engine wire harness manufacturers would do well to establish best practices and standards that result in products that meet or exceed OEM-quality standards and regulations. Specifications are measurable indicators of quality: materials are manufactured to withstand limits of temperature and chemical exposures, crimping tools generate measurable crimp heights and widths to meet or exceed pull test requirements, wire sizes are chosen based on length and load, and so on.

If you are building your own LS engine wire harness from scratch, I want you to know that you can source materials designed for engine bay use. Pay attention to manufacturer instructions and specifications. Use proper crimping tools or hire someone who has and knows how to properly work with tools designed for the work. Be willing to take the time to research the work ahead and don't be afraid to ask questions along the way.

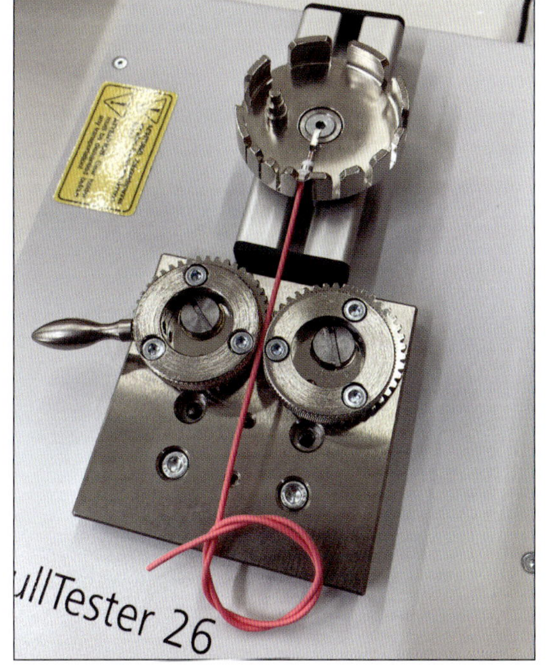

One of the quality checks related to crimped terminals is a pull test. Terminal manufacturers specify a measurable crimp height, crimp width, and pull force. A pull force tester is a motorized benchtop device that holds the end of a terminated wire while pulling on the terminal until a break or slip is detected. In addition to measuring crimp height and crimp width, pull tests are often used to verify crimp quality as part of crimping tool calibration adjustments prior to crimping tool use. You cannot determine the quality of a crimp based on how tight it feels when you simply pull on the wire.

If you are reworking a used GM engine wire harness, take the time to inspect for damage and make repairs where necessary. Use materials that meet or exceed OEM quality to ensure safety and longevity. Automotive TXL wire is not designed to last forever, and corrosion damage is difficult to find prior to failure. Don't compromise but be willing to look beyond your intended budget to carefully consider the viability of the reuse of an old engine wire harness.

If you've already purchased a new engine wire harness assembly, take a closer look at its construction and be willing to ask the manufacturer questions about the materials and tooling that went into its construction. It can be difficult to spot shoddy work. I've gone as far as to carefully remove several terminated wires to observe crimp quality in aftermarket engine harness assemblies. You want your new LS engine wire harness to outlast the usage of your vehicle, so take

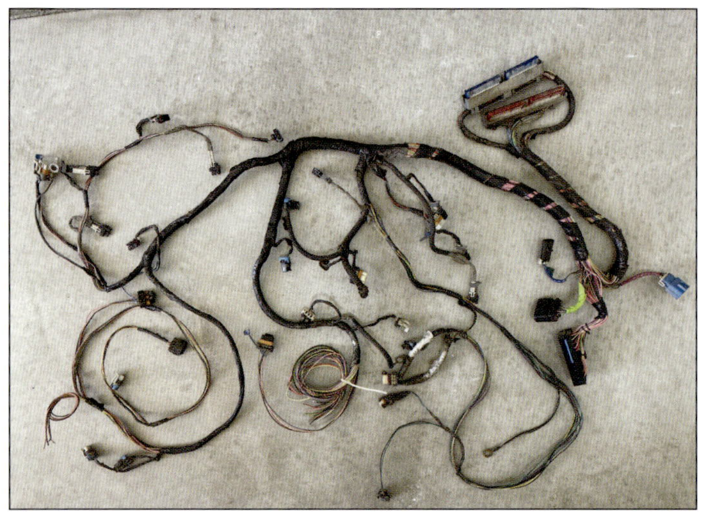 

Many engine and transmission drivetrain pullouts include the original engine and transmission wire harness. It's not uncommon to find missing connectors and/or damaged wire. Be sure to carefully inspect a used vehicle wire harness as you rework it for stand-alone operation. When a damaged wire is found, inspect for corrosion located beyond any broken insulation. Use your best judgment when soldering a replacement pigtail. For example, adding a 4L60E replacement pigtail will mean crimping and/or soldering 13 wires, which introduces the opportunity for corrosion. While the harness is apart for rework, consider replacing missing connectors by pulling out the original connector wires and installing complete wire lengths from PCM to device. Your goal is to make a quality repair and minimize the opportunity for premature wear and failure.

the time to know more about the workmanship of what you are about to install.

To further explain the measurable aspects of engine wire harness production, I provided some examples of the standards and specifications that GM has used to create its LS engine wire harnesses.

Wire Specifications

GM LS engine wire harnesses were manufactured using wire that conforms to SAE J1128 specifications using the AWG nominal size designation. Be aware that there is a metric specification (ISO 6722) for automotive wire that comparatively has a smaller conductor area and thinner insulation wall. Manufacturers using SAE J1128 tooling with the smaller ISO 6722 metric wire may produce crimps that will fail pull test validation.

Wire Size

Most enthusiasts I speak with don't know what wire size to use when requesting custom work. Unfortunately, "whatever size GM used" or "it's just for instrument gauges" is far too vague and not a requirement. For example, the ignition coil control wires in the 2002 Camaro are sized 18 AWG, while the 2002 Corvette wires are sized much smaller at 22 AWG. If you were to build ignition coil relocation extension harnesses, would you use 22 AWG or 18 AWG wire? GM engineers have determined appropriate wire sizes for each vehicle application. My caution here is simply that you should

use the appropriate size wire for its intended use. In cases where you just don't know, it is better to use wire sized larger

Be cautious when stripping insulation from the end of a wire. Stripper blades are sharp and can easily cut several copper strands. It's best to use a stripping tool that holds the insulated wire securely while cutting and removing the insulation in one quick operation. A general multipurpose cut/ strip/crimp tool requires you to bend and pull the wire and/or tool, which is a process that may break copper strands. If you are not careful, an 18 AWG wire could unintentionally be cut down to a cross section measuring that of a 22 AWG wire, which is a mistake that affects the safety of that circuit.

than GM had used; at least that way, you have less chance of a catastrophic failure.

Many years ago, I helped a customer troubleshoot a defective ignition coil sub-harness. After scratching our heads troubleshooting this ignition issue, this customer eventually disassembled the coil connectors and found that only some of the 19 total strands were crimped onto one of the terminals. The assembler clearly stripped the 18 AWG wire incorrectly, breaking most of the strands. This mistake was overlooked and resulted in a poor connection. In addition, the manufacturer's crimp specification was unachievable because what was supposed to be an 18 AWG conductor area resulted in something much smaller.

Wire Insulation

In the early days of GM fuel injection, throttle body injection (TBI) and tuned port injection (TPI) system engine wire harnesses included automotive wire with GXL insulation. Compared to today's engine wire harnesses, these TBI and TPI harnesses look oversized. I began seeing thinner insulation in GM engine harnesses by the late 1980s. The transition from GXL to TXL meant that more wires could be added without the overall bundle size getting excessively large. With multi-port injection and coil-per-cylinder ignition systems, an engine wire harness using GXL wire would be surprisingly heavy and unnecessarily bulky. While GXL insulated wire is still manufactured today, I don't know of any engine harness builders who are using it. Even with its thinner wall of insulation, TXL wire performs exceptionally well in the engine com-

partment environment. With final engine harness assembly including tape and/or a protective loom, there's really no typical need for GXL wire.

When it comes to tooling, you're going to find the most support for TXL wire. Keep in mind that the conductor area, for any given wire size within the same specification, is the same between TXL and GXL. The only variation is insulation thickness. Using a crimping punch and anvil designed for TXL with GXL wire results in an insulation-over-crimp situation that may damage the wire and/or terminal.

Wire Colors

If you were to compare one LS engine wire harness to another, you will notice that GM used many of the same wire colors for similar devices. In fact, I can think of very few wire color differences among all LS-equipped vehicles from 1997 to 2004. Additional wire color variations were introduced by 2005, but the variations are minimal. Whether you are building, repairing, or buying new, choose to use the wire colors that represent the PCM or ECM base calibration. If your PCM was pulled from a 2002 Escalade, then use the wire colors that were used in the 2002 Escalade. In that way, GM's service manuals and online service system will best serve you when troubleshooting is necessary.

Wire Strain

There is an art to building an engine wire harness. When the layout becomes sloppy or there is no build template to follow, it's easy to end up with wire lengths that are too short. If you are building your own

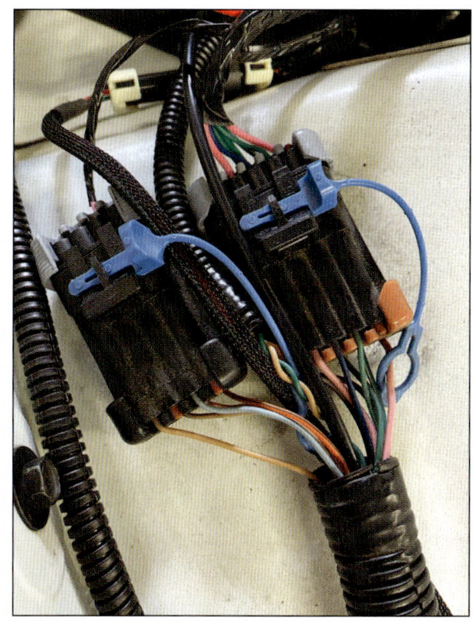

A strained wire is not likely to last the lifetime of the rest of the engine harness. Over time, vibration and movements cause the copper strands to break until the circuit has failed. When making a new harness, take your time to ensure that the harness can be flexed without pulling any one wire too tight.

wire harness, be intentional to bundle the wires together before final assembly in a way that no wires are pulled tight, especially when routing through curves. If you've purchased a new engine wire harness, take some time to check for any wires that are pulled tight. A short, strained wire is likely to be the first failure point in the harness assembly.

Overloaded Terminals

Most terminals are designed for use with only one wire; very few terminals are designed to be used with two wires. It is not good practice to crimp two wires onto a terminal unless the terminal and crimping tool are specifically designed for such an application. It's more common than it should be to see multiple wires crimped onto a battery or ground ring terminal. Take time to plan out spliced circuits so that one

It's poor practice to overload a terminal or crimp more than one wire onto the same terminal. Without tooling designed for this purpose, and for a specific application, overloading a terminal will likely strain the crimp barrel wings and cause cracks that may lead to premature failure. A better solution is to splice multiple wires into one appropriately sized wire and then crimp the terminal to the single wire.

heavy-gauge wire can be used to share power or ground with multiple smaller wires.

Missing Fusible Links

In the event of a shorted circuit or failed device, an appropriately sized fusible link may be the only thing preventing your vehicle from burning to the ground. Installed between your battery source and a battery power circuit, a short segment of appropriately undersized fusible link wire (usually four numerical AWG sizes smaller than the circuit it is protecting) is used so that in the event of an overcurrent situation, the fusible link wire will safely melt and disconnect the circuit before the entire circuit overheats and melts the rest of the bundled wires. For a stand-alone LS engine wire harness, plan to use fusible links for the battery

power to the fuse block and electric fan motors. If you purchased a stand-alone engine harness that does not include fusible link(s), be sure to talk with the manufacturer about this careless oversight.

Spliced Wire

All engine wire harnesses contain spliced wires. Injectors must share a 12V power source, the PCM or ECM share battery and ignition power sources, multiple devices share the same ground, and so on. Some of the custom engine harnesses that I've manufactured include more than 10 splices. Don't be alarmed to see multiple splices within your engine wire harness, but be aware of the methods used to splice wires together because longevity and safety matter.

Production GM engine wire harnesses contain no butt connectors or barrel connectors to join wires together. Let that sink in for a moment. There are better and longer-lasting options to join wires together. To be fair, when done properly with measurable results being verified by manufacturer crimp specifications, these common splice methods can be reliably long lasting. Keep in mind that butt and barrel connectors are only common because they

Fusible links are short lengths of insulated wire (usually 6 to 9 inches) that are attached to a larger circuit to make a battery positive connection. Fusible links are installed on a battery positive stud (sometimes at the starter). In the event of excessive current draw, the fusible link wire safely melts to break the circuit.

Short of an ultrasonic weld, the best splice involves a crimp and solder. Early GM fuel injection wire harnesses joined wires using this method. The crimp ensures a permanent connection, and the solder fills any voids. The splice is a quality connection but has the potential to introduce corrosion if it is not properly protected by adhesive-lined heat shrink tubing. In addition, solder makes the wire undesirably stiff surrounding the crimped splice.

are inexpensive and can be crimped with low-cost tools. You will find a variety of fast splice connectors and doodads anywhere wire supplies are sold. Use these materials with caution. I've not used these materials in more than 20 years.

The next best splice method is to crimp and solder. This sort of splice is

As wire size increases, making a reliable splice becomes more difficult. Ultrasonic welding is the preferred method of creating permanent wire splices. An ultrasonic welder vibrates the loose stripped wire ends into a bonded nugget. Compared to a soldered splice, wire rigidity is minimized to less than 3/4 inch. Ultrasonic welding is the method of splicing found throughout GM LS engine wire harnesses.

seen within early GM fuel injection engine wire harnesses. The wires are bundled together, crimped with a U-shaped splice clip or parallel splice barrel, and then dipped into a pool of molten solder. Alternatively, a solder gun can be used to heat the splice while feeding solder into the splice to fill any air pockets. This method is realistic for enthusiasts as splice clips, solder, and related tools are inexpensive. When a splice clip is not available, wires can be stripped, twisted, and soldered if done correctly—although, this is not my best recommendation.

The best splice is achieved by welding copper conductors together. Through the use of ultrasonic technology, a secure bond can quickly be created and provide long-lasting reliability. Due to their high cost, only harness production shops can justify the purchase and maintenance of an ultrasonic welding machine.

High-end ultrasonic welding involves the use of a computer to define wire bundle sizes and monitor the execution of each weld. Air pockets are eliminated, and the resulting weld, or nugget, is mea-

sured and stored in the computer for quality-control purposes. Operator error is nearly eliminated as the machine can catch (and sometimes destroy) welds that are out of tolerance.

Taped Splices versus Heat Shrink Tubing

I haven't seen a taped splice in a GM engine wire harness in more than 30 years. GM replaced the use of cloth-lined tape with dual-wall, adhesive-lined, heat shrink tubing to protect splices from moisture that leads to premature wire damage due to corrosion. With superior materials being inexpensive and readily available, avoid the use of anything but adhesive-lined heat shrink tubing to cover and protect splices. Your harness manufacturer should also be using adhesive-lined heat shrink tubing.

Inspect the ends of the heat shrink tubing for evidence of clear or white adhesive that has oozed out of the tubing when it was shrunk. If

you see no evidence of adhesive, you can expect premature oxidation that will eventually cause failure. I tend to use nonadhesive-lined heat shrink tubing only when bundling together several wires for a clean look and

Early GM fuel injection wire harnesses protect splice points by wrapping a cloth-lined tape around the spliced wires. The engine bay environment weakens the tape's adhesive bond and causes it to fray. For longevity, avoid taping splice points. Only consider taping a splice as a temporary repair that will soon be corrected with adhesive-lined heat shrink tubing.

GM LS engine wire harnesses feature adhesive-lined heat shrink tubing for a long-lasting and permanent solution to protect splice points. As high heat is applied to the dual wall shrink tubing, the inner adhesive flows throughout the exposed wires and then out the ends of the outer tubing. This is the best method to protect exposed splice points. Be sure to apply heat shrink tubing on the wire to be spliced before crimping and solder as there is no way to apply heat shrink tubing to the harness after the splice has been formed.

---

to prevent the ends of expandable sleeving from fraying. Substituting adhesive-lined heat shrink tubing for these applications is not only a higher cost and additional work but the adhesive also tends to make the harness stiff.

Crimping Tools

Crimping tools are manufactured with the intended use that results in an air-tight seal between the terminal and conductor. Terminals are manufactured via progressive die stamping process that ensures dimensional precision from one to the next.

Terminal precision requires crimping anvil and punch precision to create a crimp that is uniform, strong, and void of air pockets. Just as one terminal type is different from another, the same must be true of crimping tools. A crimping tool for a Metri-Pack 150 terminal cannot be used with a GT 150 terminal and achieve the same results.

Precision manufacturing is an expensive process. Specialized CNC machines, multiple setups, a variety of cutting tools, fixturing, and work-holding add up to make the manufacture of quality crimping tools far too expensive for the average enthusiast. Unfortunately, subpar crimping tools are advertised (for far less cost) to be used in applications where they cannot produce results that meet terminal manufacturer crimp specifications.

It may surprise you to say that a crimping die set designed to crimp (for example, Metri-Pack 100W female terminals by hand using a Rennsteig Tools PEW 12 crimping tool) to manufacturer specifications is in the ballpark of $325. All things considered, that's a good price! The alternative crimping applicator solution (for semiautomatic crimping press) is in the ballpark of $2,500. Now, when you see a $50 tool advertised for the same application, you must pause to ask the seller or manufacturer what sort of results you can expect with such a tool. I've experienced enough of these cheap tools to say that the results will likely be disappointing.

Let's consider the cheaper alternatives. The lowest-cost crimping tools have no terminal locator, meaning that the terminal is not supported in its nest during the crimping process. Making this worse is the scissor-like closing action of the tool. As the crimping punch closes on the terminal, the results include, to one degree or another, terminal rolling, bending, and twisting. Misalignment of the terminal during the crimping process also introduces asymmetrical closing of the conductor and insulation crimp barrels. The crimp quality is often so poor that an accurate measurement of crimp height and width is not possible.

When faced with a visually asymmetrical conductor crimp, the first thought is usually, "I should put some solder on this." Well, at this point, you probably should. However, that introduces other risks. A female terminal makes a good connection with a male terminal because it has a spring-like feature that applies pressure to the male terminal. When the male terminal enters the female terminal, this spring-like feature is depressed from its neutral position. By applying solder to the conductor crimp of a female terminal, you risk the flow of solder into the terminal body, causing this spring-like feature to bond to the solder and terminal body wall. The male terminal is then unable to mate.

Further damage is introduced as the assembled plastic connector is then attempted to mate to a sensor or device. With a good eye and dexterity, a soldered repair can be applied successfully, but I won't go as far as to recommend solder for any terminal you may encounter when working with an LS engine wire harness.

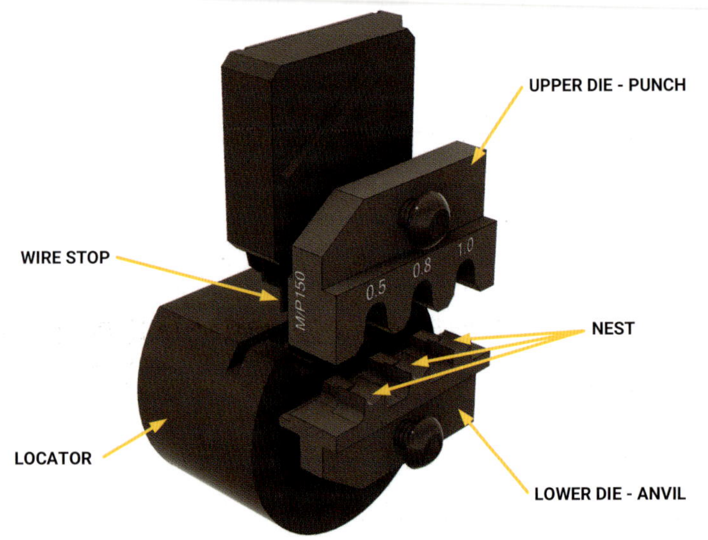

Rennsteig Tools PEW 12 crimping die sets feature an upper crimping die (punch), lower crimping die (anvil), terminal locator, and in many cases a wire stop. Each PEW 12 crimping die set is to be used with a compatible PEW 12 hand tool, bench tool, or toggle press. The operator first inserts a terminal in the locator, then inserts a stripped wire to rest against the wire stop, and then cycles the crimping tool to create an OEM-quality crimp.

Aptiv Crimp Specifications: TXL Thin-Wall Crosslinked Polyethylene (XLPE) Automotive Wire												
					Conductor crimp height (mm)		Conductor crimp width (mm)		Insulation crimp height (mm)		Insulation crimp width (mm)	
Part number	Terminal	Wire Size (mm²)	Wire Size (AWG)	Tear-Out Force (N)	Height (CCH)	Tolerance (+/-)	Width (CCW)	Tolerance (+/-)	Height (ICH)	Tolerance (+/-)	Width (ICW)	Tolerance (+/-)
12084200	Aptiv Metri-Pack 150 Female Sealed 0.35–0.50	0.35	22	55	0.90	0.05	1.80	0.10	3.60	0.10	4.10	0.10
12084200	Aptiv Metri-Pack 150 Female Sealed 0.35–0.50	0.50	20	80	0.95	0.05	1.80	0.10	3.60	0.10	4.10	0.10
12048074	Aptiv Metri-Pack 150 Female Sealed 0.50–1.00	0.50	20	80	1.10	0.05	2.05	0.10	3.70	0.10	4.00	0.10
12048074	Aptiv Metri-Pack 150 Female Sealed 0.50–1.00	0.80	18	90	1.20	0.05	2.05	0.10	3.90	0.10	4.10	0.10
12048074	Aptiv Metri-Pack 150 Female Sealed 0.50–1.00	1.00	16	120	1.35	0.05	2.05	0.10	3.70	0.10	4.00	0.10
12045773	Aptiv Metri-Pack 150 Male Sealed 0.50–1.00	0.50	20	80	1.25	0.05	2.45	0.10	4.20	0.10	4.20	0.10
12045773	Aptiv Metri-Pack 150 Male Sealed 0.50–1.00	0.80	18	90	1.30	0.05	2.50	0.10	4.20	0.10	4.00	0.10
12045773	Aptiv Metri-Pack 150 Male Sealed 0.50–1.00	1.00	16	120	1.40	0.05	2.50	0.10	4.30	0.10	4.20	0.10
12129373	Aptiv Metri-Pack 150 Female Unsealed 0.35–0.50	0.35	22	55	0.85	0.05	1.80	0.10	2.00	0.10	2.50	0.10
12129373	Aptiv Metri-Pack 150 Female Unsealed 0.35–0.50	0.50	20	80	0.95	0.05	1.80	0.10	2.00	0.10	2.50	0.10
12129484	Aptiv Metri-Pack 150 Female Unsealed 0.80–1.00	0.80	18	90	1.20	0.05	2.05	0.10	2.10	0.10	2.50	0.10
12129484	Aptiv Metri-Pack 150 Female Unsealed 0.80–1.00	1.00	16	120	1.35	0.05	2.05	0.10	2.30	0.10	2.60	0.10
12124076	Aptiv Metri-Pack 150.2 Female Unsealed 0.35–0.50	0.35	22	55	0.85	0.05	1.85	0.10	1.90	0.10	2.60	0.10
12124076	Aptiv Metri-Pack 150.2 Female Unsealed 0.35–0.50	0.50	20	80	0.95	0.05	1.80	0.10	2.00	0.10	2.60	0.10

Aptiv Crimp Specifications: TXL Thin-Wall Crosslinked Polyethylene (XLPE) Automotive Wire					Conductor crimp height (mm)		Conductor crimp width (mm)		Insulation crimp height (mm)		Insulation crimp width (mm)	
Part number	Terminal	Wire Size (mm²)	Wire Size (AWG)	Tear-Out Force (N)	Height (CCH)	Tolerance (+/-)	Width (CCW)	Tolerance (+/-)	Height (ICH)	Tolerance (+/-)	Width (ICW)	Tolerance (+/-)
12124075	Aptiv Metri-Pack 150.2 Female Unsealed 0.80–1.00	0.80	18	90	1.20	0.05	2.05	0.10	2.10	0.10	2.60	0.10
12124075	Aptiv Metri-Pack 150.2 Female Unsealed 0.80–1.00	1.00	16	120	1.30	0.05	2.05	0.10	2.20	0.10	2.60	0.10
12077411	Aptiv Metri-Pack 280 Female Sealed 0.50–1.00	0.50	20	80	1.35	0.05	2.50	0.10	4.80	0.10	4.50	0.10
12077411	Aptiv Metri-Pack 280 Female Sealed 0.50–1.00	0.80	18	90	1.40	0.05	2.50	0.10	4.50	0.10	4.50	0.10
12077411	Aptiv Metri-Pack 280 Female Sealed 0.50–1.00	1.00	16	120	1.55	0.05	2.50	0.10	4.50	0.10	4.50	0.10
12077939	Aptiv Metri-Pack 280.1 Female Unsealed 0.50–1.00	0.50	20	80	1.05	0.05	2.40	0.10	2.20	0.10	2.60	0.10
12077939	Aptiv Metri-Pack 280.1 Female Unsealed 0.50–1.00	0.80	18	90	1.10	0.05	2.40	0.10	2.20	0.10	2.60	0.10
12077939	Aptiv Metri-Pack 280.1 Female Unsealed 0.50–1.00	1.00	16	120	1.20	0.05	2.40	0.10	2.30	0.10	2.60	0.10
15356826	Aptiv Micro 0.64 Female Unsealed 0.35	0.35	22	55	0.75	0.03	1.45	0.03	1.60	0.10	1.90	0.10
15356827	Aptiv Micro 0.64 Female Unsealed 0.50–0.80	0.50	20	80	0.95	0.05	1.45	0.10	1.80	0.10	2.00	0.10
15356827	Aptiv Micro 0.64 Female Unsealed 0.50–0.80	0.80	18	90	0.95	0.05	1.65	0.10	2.00	0.10	2.00	0.10
12084913	Aptiv Micro-Pack 100w Female Unsealed 0.35–0.50	0.35	22	55	1.00	0.05	1.45	0.10	1.90	0.10	2.20	0.10
12084913	Aptiv Micro-Pack 100w Female Unsealed 0.35–0.50	0.50	20	80	1.10	0.05	1.45	0.10	2.00	0.10	2.30	0.10

Aptiv Crimp Specifications: TXL Thin-Wall Crosslinked Polyethylene (XLPE) Automotive Wire

Part number	Terminal	Wire Size (mm²)	Wire Size (AWG)	Tear-Out Force (N)	Conductor crimp height (mm)		Conductor crimp width (mm)		Insulation crimp height (mm)		Insulation crimp width (mm)	
					Height (CCH)	Tolerance (+/-)	Width (CCW)	Tolerance (+/-)	Height (ICH)	Tolerance (+/-)	Width (ICW)	Tolerance (+/-)
12084912	Aptiv Micro-Pack 100w Female Unsealed 0.80	0.80	18	90	1.25	0.05	1.85	0.10	2.30	0.10	2.30	0.10
15326266	Aptiv GT 150 3.5mm Female Sealed 0.35–0.50	0.35	22	55	1.05	0.05	1.80	0.10	2.80	0.10	3.00	0.10
15326266	Aptiv GT 150 3.5mm Female Sealed 0.35–0.50	0.50	20	80	1.10	0.05	1.80	0.10	2.90	0.10	3.00	0.10
15326267	Aptiv GT 150 3.5mm Female Sealed 0.80	0.80	18	90	1.25	0.05	2.05	0.10	3.20	0.10	3.00	0.10
12191818	Aptiv GT 150 Female Sealed 0.35–0.50	0.35	22	50	1.05	0.05	1.80	0.10	3.30	0.10	3.40	0.10
12191818	Aptiv GT 150 Female Sealed 0.35–0.50	0.50	20	80	1.10	0.05	1.80	0.10	3.50	0.10	3.40	0.10
12191819	Aptiv GT 150 Female Sealed 0.80–1.00	0.80	18	90	1.25	0.05	2.05	0.10	3.30	0.10	3.50	0.10
12191819	Aptiv GT 150 Female Sealed 0.80–1.00	1.00	16	120	1.40	0.05	2.10	0.10	3.40	0.10	3.50	0.10
15304718	Aptiv GT 280 Female Sealed 0.35–0.50	0.35	22	50	1.05	0.05	1.80	0.10	4.40	0.10	4.80	0.10
15304718	Aptiv GT 280 Female Sealed 0.35–0.50	0.50	20	80	1.10	0.05	1.80	0.10	4.50	0.10	4.80	0.10
15304719	Aptiv GT 280 Female Sealed 0.80–1.00	0.80	18	90	1.25	0.05	2.05	0.10	4.30	0.10	5.00	0.10
15304719	Aptiv GT 280 Female Sealed 0.80–1.00	1.00	16	120	1.40	0.05	2.10	0.10	4.40	0.10	5.00	0.10
12089307	Aptiv Weather-Pack Male Sealed 0.35	0.35	22	55	1.00	0.03	1.80	0.03	3.80	0.10	4.00	0.10
12089040	Aptiv Weather-Pack Male Sealed 0.50–0.80	0.50	20	80	1.10	0.05	2.40	0.10	4.30	0.10	4.40	0.10
12089040	Aptiv Weather-Pack Male Sealed 0.50–0.80	0.80	18	90	1.15	0.05	2.45	0.10	4.50	0.10	4.50	0.10

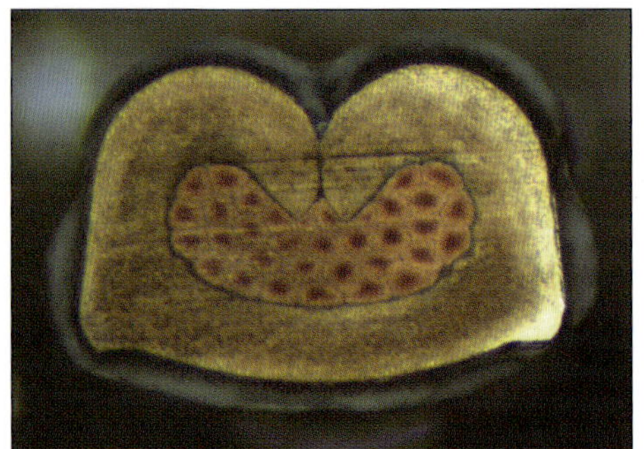

An optimal crimp symmetrically closes the conductor crimp barrel wings, deforming all of the copper strands without creating excessive burrs or cracks on the bottom of the terminal.

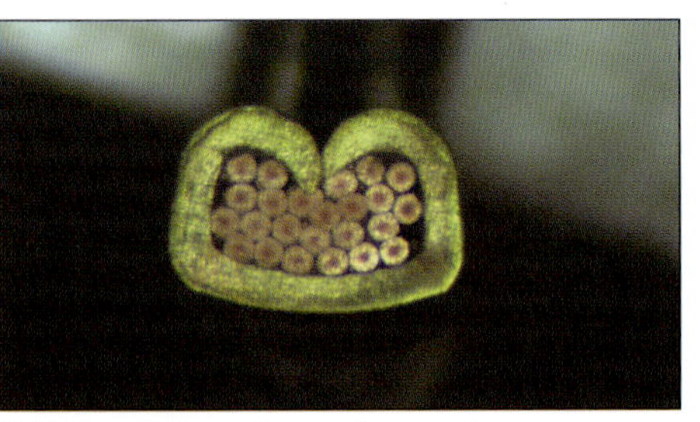

When a crimp is performed in a crimping nest that is too large, the resulting crimp may be symmetrical with no observable burrs, but the copper conductors will not be deformed, and the terminal will likely fail a pull test.

Everyone should have a $15 general-repair stripper/cutter/crimper tool for miscellaneous home and automotive electrical work. However, when it comes to engine wire harness work, leave this in the toolbox and purchase better tools for the job. There is no chance of accomplishing anything close to a proper crimp with this tool.

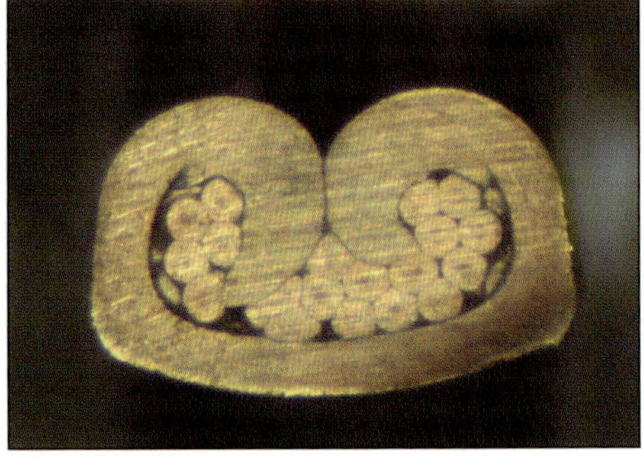

When the wire size is too small, the crimp barrel wings will close slightly asymmetrically, the copper strands will not all deform, and voids can be observed within the crimp barrel. The resulting crimp will not likely pass a pull test.

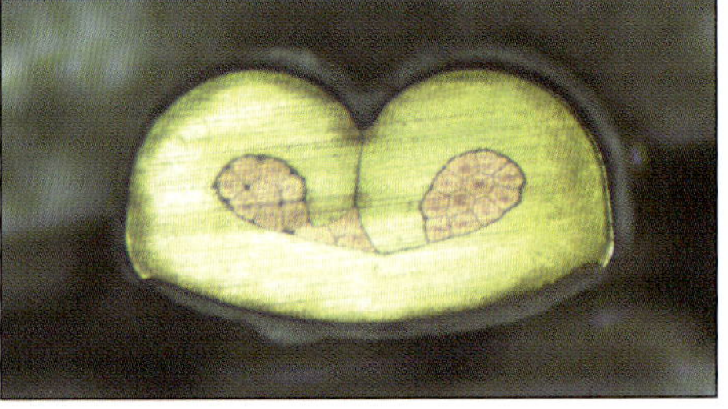

When a crimp is performed in a crimping nest that is too small, the resulting crimp may be symmetrical with no observable burrs, but the crimp barrel wings will touch the bottom of the crimp. While this crimp may pass a pull test, the copper strands are not properly distributed within the crimp barrel. This is a bad crimp.

For less than $50, a variety of generic crimpers with crimp nests of varying sizes are available. Don't expect these low-cost tools to achieve measurable crimps that are within manufacturer specifications. Missing a locator to properly hold the terminal during the crimping process, you will also experience asymmetrical crimp barrel wings and bending and twisting of the terminal body.

When the wire size is too large, the crimp barrel wings will close asymmetrically but not close the crimp barrel. All copper strands will be deformed, but excessive burrs will form on the bottom of the terminal. Burrs lead to stress cracks and the risk of one or both wings falling off the crimp barrel.

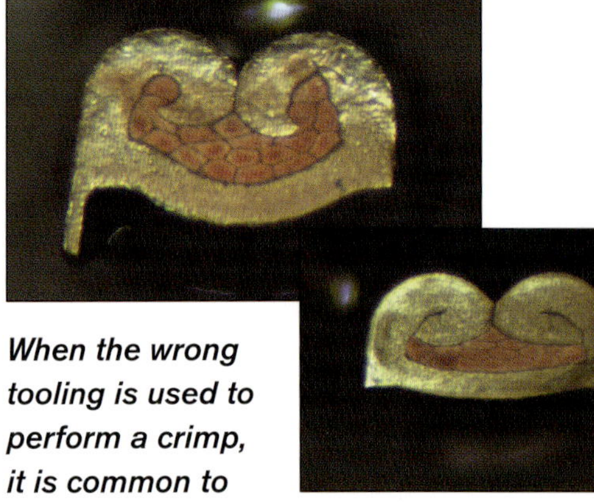

When the wrong tooling is used to perform a crimp, it is common to see excessive burrs at the bottom of the crimp. While the crimp may look intact, the terminal was overly stressed to create one or two burrs. The formation of a burr likely means there are cracks that may not be visible. Don't expect a crimp with one or more burrs to be reliable.

QUALITY CONTROL

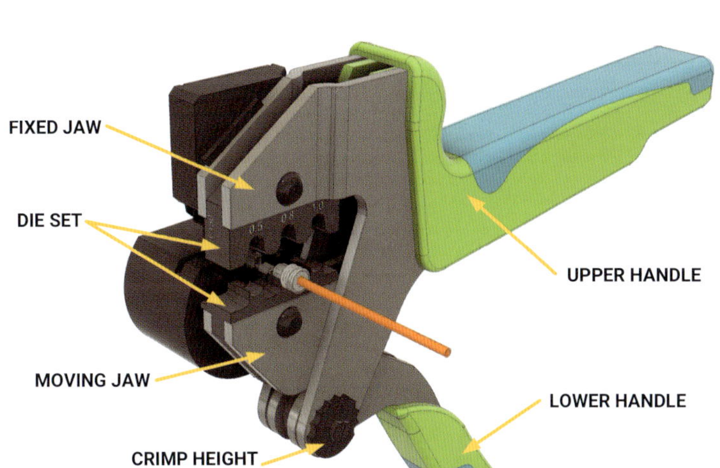

Aptiv (formerly Delphi or Packard Electric) offers a wide variety of crimping tools that are suitable for general repair purposes. Many of these tools feature a locator to hold the terminal body in place during the crimping process to minimize the chance of rolling in the nest that results in bending and twisting of the terminal body. In some cases, only one crimping nest is available for use with multiple sizes of wires and terminals. Without a nest for each wire and terminal size, it's not possible to achieve measurable crimps within manufacturer specifications. When a small-name harness manufacturer advertises that they use Aptiv, Delphi, or Packard Electric tooling, there's a good chance that this is to what they are referring. Expect to pay $100 to $200 for each of these tools.

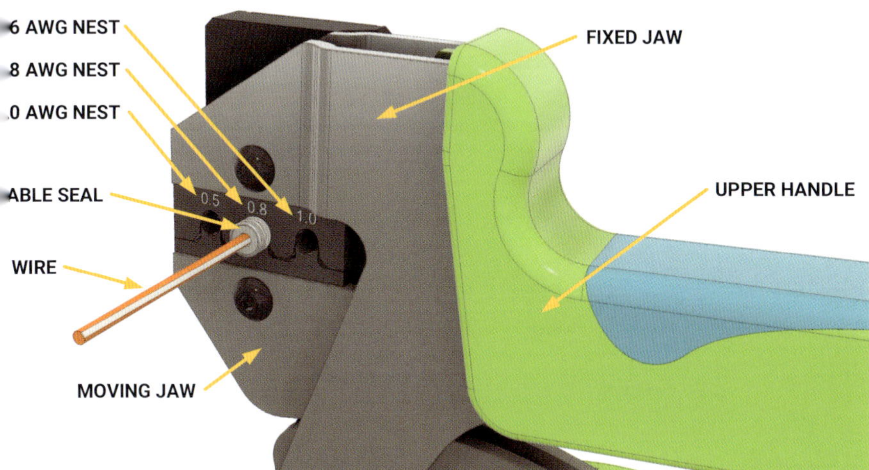

Rennsteig Tools, a German manufacturer of high-quality electrical hand tools, developed crimping die sets for every terminal encountered within an LS engine wire harness. Its PEW 12 crimping solution is based on a hand-crimping tool frame that receives interchangeable crimping die sets for each terminal application. A crimping nest for every wire and terminal size is precision manufactured so that you can achieve measurable crimp heights and widths that are within manufacturer specifications—every time. The PEW 12 crimping tool features crimp height adjustment and parallel jaw movement that delivers 1.2 metric tons of pressure with minimal hand effort. Crimping die sets often include a wire stop and terminal locator to ensure accurate, solderless, electrical connections.

A terminated wire should have a repeatable form. Crimp barrel wings should be symmetrical. A bell mouth flare should be present to provide relief from tension. A brush should extend beyond the crimp barrel and is often flared upward. A cable seal, if applicable, should be firmly held to avoid the cable seal from sliding when the terminated wire is inserted into a connector cavity.

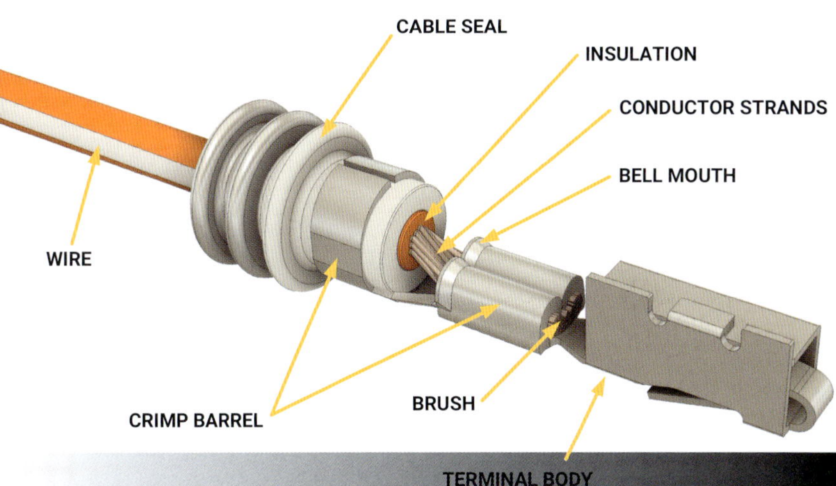

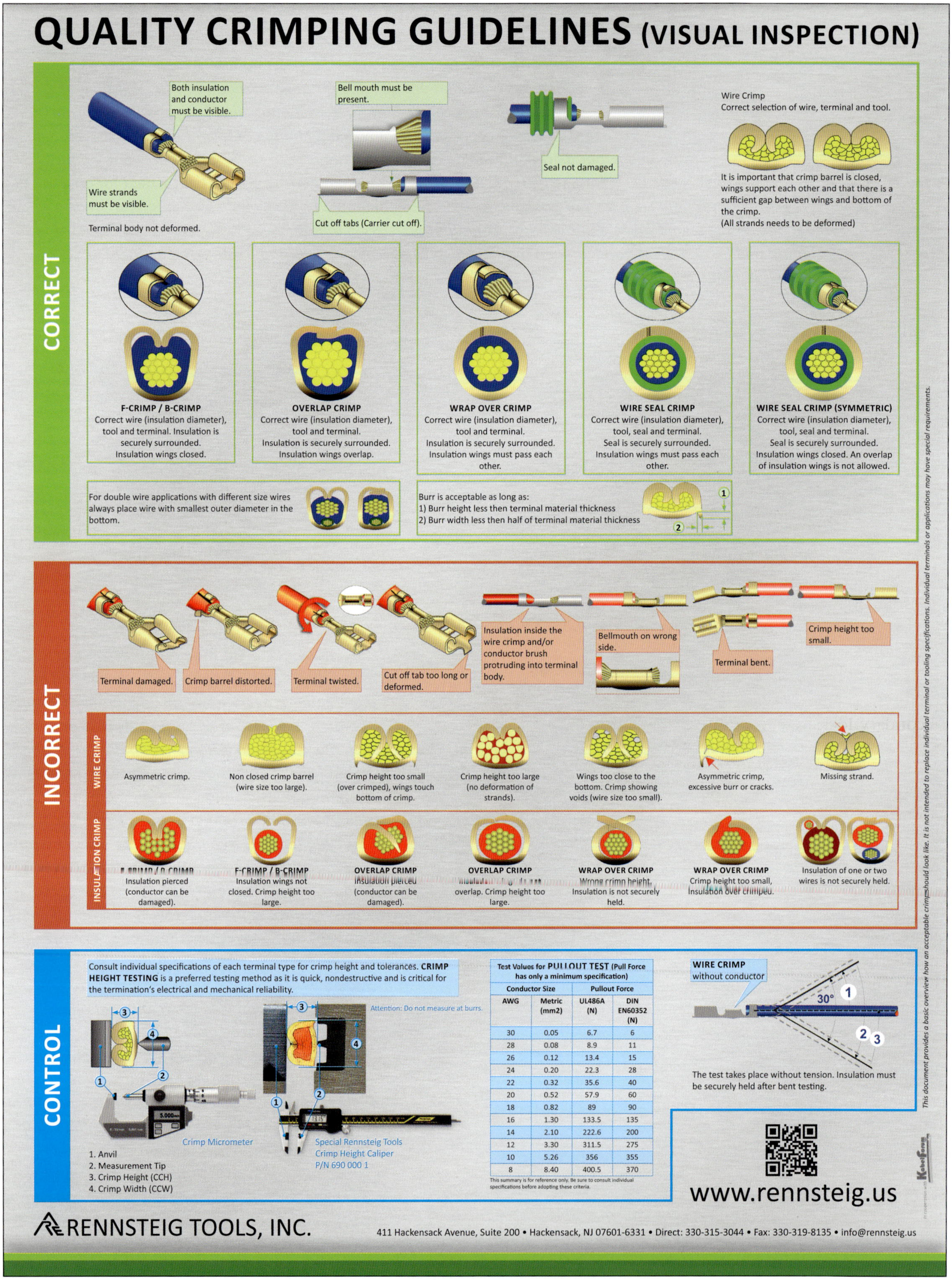

QUALITY CRIMPING GUIDELINES (VISUAL INSPECTION)

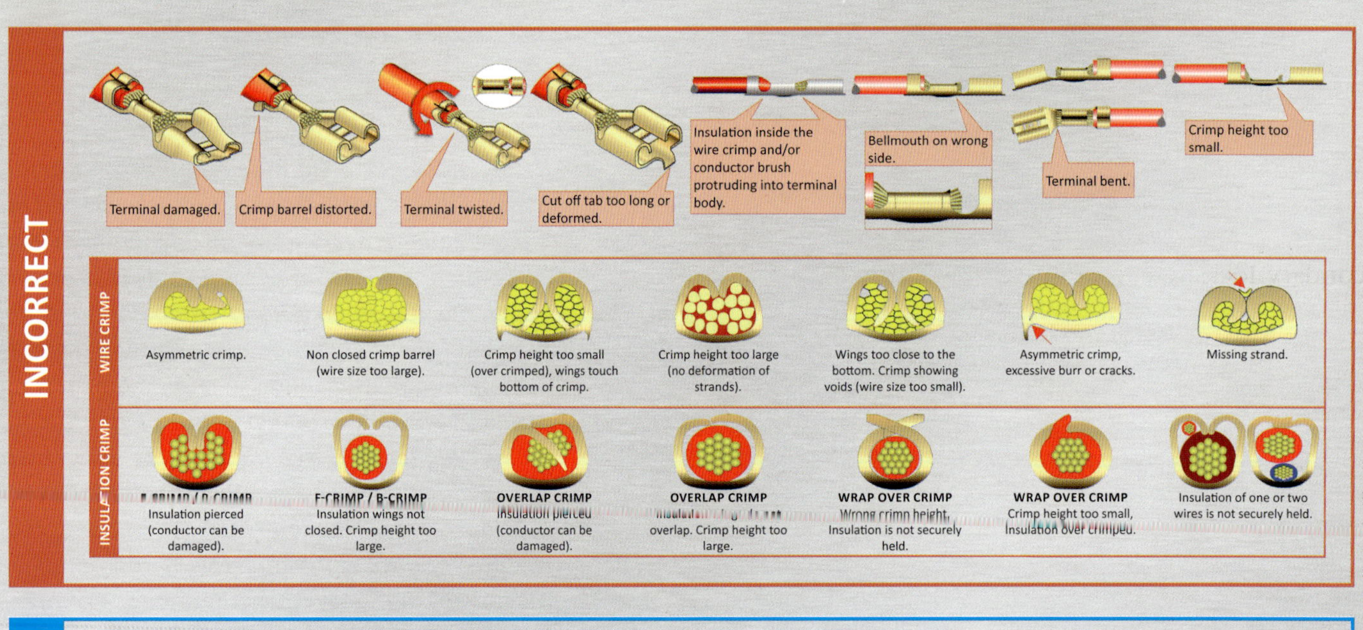

CORRECT

Both insulation and conductor must be visible.

Bell mouth must be present.

Seal not damaged.

Wire Crimp
Correct selection of wire, terminal and tool.

Wire strands must be visible.

Terminal body not deformed.

Cut off tabs (Carrier cut off).

It is important that crimp barrel is closed, wings support each other and that there is a sufficient gap between wings and bottom of the crimp.
(All strands needs to be deformed)

F-CRIMP / B-CRIMP
Correct wire (insulation diameter), tool and terminal. Insulation is securely surrounded. Insulation wings closed.

OVERLAP CRIMP
Correct wire (insulation diameter), tool and terminal. Insulation is securely surrounded. Insulation wings overlap.

WRAP OVER CRIMP
Correct wire (insulation diameter), tool and terminal. Insulation is securely surrounded. Insulation wings must pass each other.

WIRE SEAL CRIMP
Correct wire (insulation diameter), tool, seal and terminal. Seal is securely surrounded. Insulation wings must pass each other.

WIRE SEAL CRIMP (SYMMETRIC)
Correct wire (insulation diameter), tool, seal and terminal. Seal is securely surrounded. Insulation wings closed. An overlap of insulation wings is not allowed.

For double wire applications with different size wires always place wire with smallest outer diameter in the bottom.

Burr is acceptable as long as:
1) Burr height less then terminal material thickness
2) Burr width less then half of terminal material thickness

INCORRECT

Terminal damaged.

Crimp barrel distorted.

Terminal twisted.

Cut off tab too long or deformed.

Insulation inside the wire crimp and/or conductor brush protruding into terminal body.

Bellmouth on wrong side.

Terminal bent.

Crimp height too small.

WIRE CRIMP

Asymmetric crimp.

Non closed crimp barrel (wire size too large).

Crimp height too small (over crimped), wings touch bottom of crimp.

Crimp height too large (no deformation of strands).

Wings too close to the bottom. Crimp showing voids (wire size too small).

Asymmetric crimp, excessive burr or cracks.

Missing strand.

INSULATION CRIMP

F-CRIMP / B-CRIMP
Insulation pierced (conductor can be damaged).

F-CRIMP / B-CRIMP
Insulation wings not closed. Crimp height too large.

OVERLAP CRIMP
Insulation pierced (conductor can be damaged).

OVERLAP CRIMP
Insulation wings no overlap. Crimp height too large.

WRAP OVER CRIMP
Wrong crimp height. Insulation is not securely held.

WRAP OVER CRIMP
Crimp height too small, Insulation over crimped.

Insulation of one or two wires is not securely held.

CONTROL

Consult individual specifications of each terminal type for crimp height and tolerances. **CRIMP HEIGHT TESTING** is a preferred testing method as it is quick, nondestructive and is critical for the termination's electrical and mechanical reliability.

Attention: Do not measure at burrs.

Crimp Micrometer

Special Rennsteig Tools Crimp Height Caliper P/N 690 000 1

1. Anvil
2. Measurement Tip
3. Crimp Height (CCH)
4. Crimp Width (CCW)

Conductor Size		Pullout Force	
AWG	Metric (mm2)	UL486A (N)	DIN EN60352 (N)
30	0.05	6.7	6
28	0.08	8.9	11
26	0.12	13.4	15
24	0.20	22.3	28
22	0.32	35.6	40
20	0.52	57.9	60
18	0.82	89	90
16	1.30	133.5	135
14	2.10	222.6	200
12	3.30	311.5	275
10	5.26	356	355
8	8.40	400.5	370

Test Values for PULLOUT TEST (Pull Force has only a minimum specification)

This summary is for reference only. Be sure to consult individual specifications before adopting these criteria.

WIRE CRIMP without conductor

30°

The test takes place without tension. Insulation must be securely held after bent testing.

This document provides a basic overview how an acceptable crimp should look like. It is not intended to replace individual terminal or tooling specifications. Individual terminals or applications may have special requirements.

RENNSTEIG TOOLS, INC.

411 Hackensack Avenue, Suite 200 • Hackensack, NJ 07601-6331 • Direct: 330-315-3044 • Fax: 330-319-8135 • info@rennsteig.us

www.rennsteig.us

(Photo in Cooperation with Rennsteig Tools, Inc. and Support by Kabelforum)

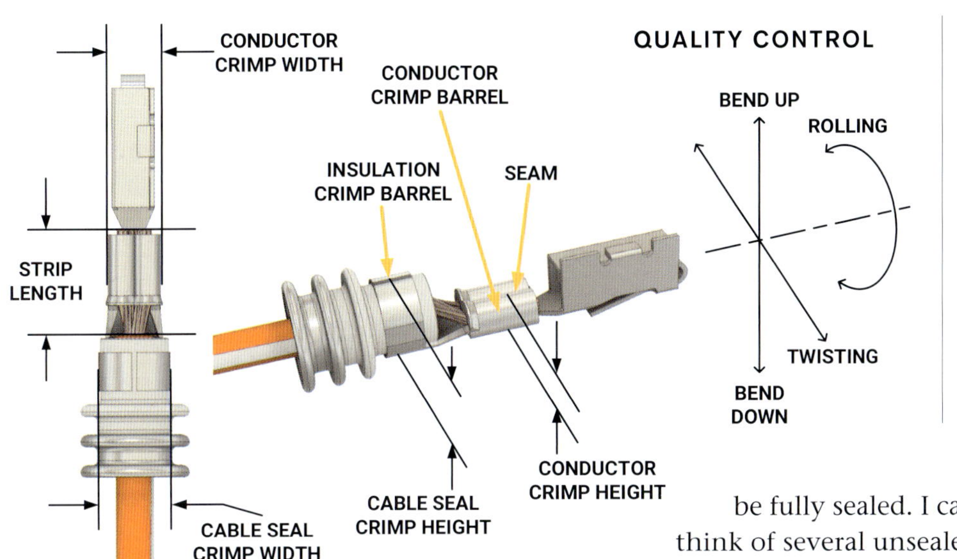

Hand crimping tools lack production efficiency because terminals must be singulated from their carrier strip and then individually handled for insertion into a crimping die set. Wire harness manufacturing facilities often use semiautomatic presses and crimping applicators to quickly apply terminals directly from the reel. With one action of the foot pedal, a press cycles the loaded applicator to feed, crimp, and singulate each terminal. A precision-machined punch and anvil toolset are designed for each wire and terminal size. Insulation and conductor crimp heights are independently adjusted by dials located at the top of the applicator assembly. With crimping presses in the ballpark of $3,500 and applicators starting at closer to $2,500 each, this equipment is best suited for large-scale production work.

Connector Assemblies

My company, EFI Connection, has been selling genuine replacement LS wire harness connectors since the mid-2000s. The company website introduced to the internet a marketplace where customers can shop by connector and simply scroll down the browser page to choose from available assembly-related components, such as terminals, cable seals, secondary locks, etc. It surprised me that many customers choose not to purchase the available secondary locks. I've also wondered why some of the original GM engine harnesses are missing a secondary lock here and there. Regardless of reason, connector manufacturers often design secondary locking components that increase overall quality and reliability of the engine harness assembly. It's simply good practice (and cheap insurance) to assemble connectors as their manufacturers have intended.

Another oversight I see from time to time is the use of a multi-cavity connector with an open cavity. There's no harm to leaving a cavity open in most passenger compartments, but every connector found within the engine bay should ideally be fully sealed. I can think of several unsealed connectors GM has used in the engine compartment through the years, but it's rather uncommon to see an unsealed connector in an LS engine wire harness.

Sealed-type connectors are able to receive either silicone or plastic cavity plugs for unused cavities. Because many replacement connectors contain all open cavities, the most common use of open cavities in the engine bay may be found at the PCM or ECM after a replacement connector repair or because of a sub-par harness builder. Of all places in the engine bay to have open cavities, the ECU is one of the worst. Use appropriate cavity plugs wherever possible.

Verification and Testing

Every time I get myself into an engine swap and/or fuel management system upgrade, I'm reminded at just how time-intensive these projects can be. The rub there is that I don't have time for mistakes—and I bet you don't either. There are several ways you can be reasonably sure that your engine is going to start on the first try.

Be willing to take the time to thoroughly understand your project. Source the correct wiring schematics for your vehicle and the LS-equipped vehicle application with which you are working (the vehicle from which your PCM or ECM came). Ask questions to those who have done similar work. Avoid rework and incompatibilities by establishing a relationship with an ECU tuner prior to getting too deep into your project. If you are unable to accurately explain to someone what you are doing, you probably don't fully understand it yourself and will struggle with implementation and troubleshooting. Having

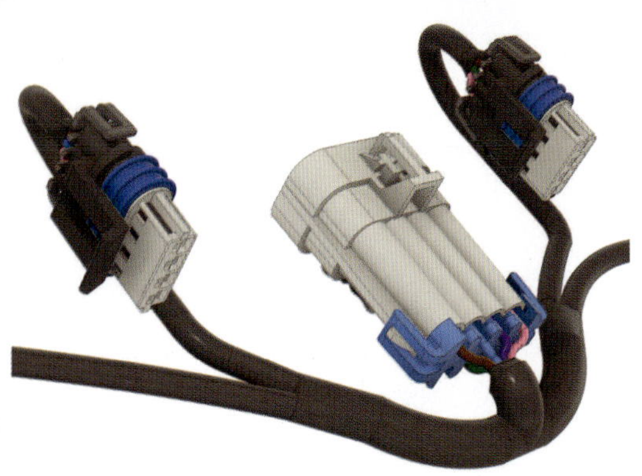

Nearly all Aptiv (formerly Delphi) connectors on an LS engine wire harness are fitted with secondary lock(s). Once a terminated wire is inserted into a connector cavity, its primary retention is accomplished by connector features that hold each terminal in place. Secondary locks ensure terminal retention if the primary retention feature(s) should fail.

To check for continuity from one end of a wire harness to another, use a digital multimeter for quick and accurate results. Turn the dial to continuity test mode (look for a position on the dial with an ohm icon (Ω) and/or buzzer icon). If required, press the continuity button. Insert the black test lead into the "COM" jack and the red test lead into the "VΩ" jack. Apply a test lead to one end of a wire and the other test lead on the other end. If the multimeter produces an audible beep, then the wire has continuity from one end to the other. If the circuit is completely broken, no audible beep will be heard.

notes and schematics to reference helps you with installation and diagnosing any unforeseen problems.

At minimum, continuity-check your work before installing your engine wire harness. A visual inspection can be unreliable because multiples of the same wire colors can be found within the harness and you will never be able to visually see a conductor break in a bundle of wires. Even the cheapest digital multimeter has a continuity setting that features a buzzer to indicate a connection from one end of a circuit to another. A best practice is to continuity-check from the ECU connector(s) to each sensor or device connector while going through the PCM or ECM connector view data. For the enthusiast, this is likely as detailed as costs will allow. Identifying a misplaced wire prior to engine wire harness installation will, in the event of a mistake, save you the time and frustration of removing your installed wire harness for rework. Moreover, it may prevent unnecessarily blown fuses and ruined onboard modules.

Professional wire harness builders use low-voltage harness testing equipment to either detect assembler mistakes as they happen or to test completed harness assemblies. A load is applied to each circuit as the testing device applies resistance to detect any high-resistance connections. Testing software reveals the failed circuit(s) so that corrective action can be taken. Some LS engine harness builders include a copy of the successful test as proof that the harness left the manufacturing facility in good working order. Given the many possibilities for a no-start condition, it's reassuring to be able to at least rule out the wire harness by simply knowing it has been tested prior to installation.

Engine Compartment–Rated Materials

The finishing touches of an engine wire harness deserve the same attention to detail as the rest of the harness construction. When choosing protective tape, cloth, and plastic coverings, be aware of their rated resistance to nearby fluids and temperatures. Your local hardware store is not likely to offer materials designed for engine-compartment use, so shop for these supplies from a trusted engine wire harness material supplier. Assumptions may lead to the installation of combustible materials that could ruin your hard work.

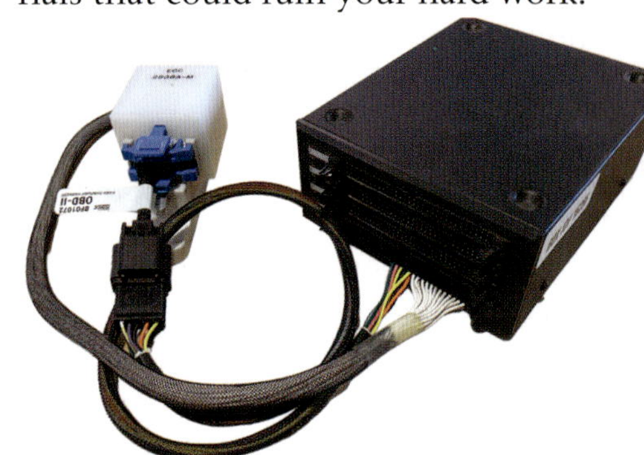

It's good practice for engine harness manufacturers to test finished harness assemblies using a harness tester. Cirris, Inc. offers a compact harness testing system capable of testing up to 32,000 test points. Each CR harness tester is capable of testing up to 256 test points and can be daisy-chain linked to offer up to 32,000 test points. By building a test harness for each engine wire harness assembly and configuring the Cirris Easy-Wire software, an operator can quickly connect each engine harness connection to the tester for a fast and reliable test. Defects are quickly identified so that any necessary repairs can be made. The CR harness tester is fantastic for even the smallest harness assemblies.

The 1997–1998 LS1 PCM

The 1997 Corvette introduced the LS-series engine with engine RPO code LS1. All LS1 (and LS6) Corvette engines are fitted with an electronic, drive-by-wire, throttle system. The LS1 was available in the 1998 Camaro and Firebird but with a cable throttle body. These 1997–1998 LS1-equipped vehicles are controlled by GM PCM service number 16238212.

A brief look at GM schematics reveals many sensor and device similarities compared to the once-popular 1992–1997 LT1 engine management systems. Perhaps the most notable change was the introduction of a coil-per-cylinder ignition system that relies on Hall effect crankshaft and camshaft signals for determining engine position.

Transmission options included the 4L60E 4-speed automatic transmission and Tremec T56 6-speed manual transmission. The PCM is used to control both automatic and manual transmissions but requires a different calibration based on transmission type. PCM control of the 4L60E transmission includes a variety of shift solenoids, torque converter lockup solenoids, and driveshaft speed input. Manual transmissions are fitted with a skip shift solenoid, a fuel-economy feature that forces the driver to shift from first gear to fourth gear during certain driving conditions. Manual transmissions also feature a reverse lockout solenoid that prevents the driver from shifting into reverse based on vehicle speed.

The early LS1 PCM is supported by popular tuning software, such as EFILive and HP Tuners. While this PCM is the oldest of the LS PCMs, it is not considered to be highly desirable. Many enthusiasts have re-pinned their engine wire harness to use the newer P01 or P59 PCM for aftermarket advances, such as custom operating systems and real-time emulation. Moreover, this early LS1 PCM has been known for its unavailability when service replacement is necessary.

The two PCM connectors used with the 1997–1998 LS1 PCM were used through 2007, but the PCM pinout details are unique and are a complete showstopper when attempting to use a newer P01 or P59 PCM. Connector C1 uses two red retainers, and connector C2 uses two blue retainers.

The following schematics are an excellent reference for use when servicing a used engine wire harness or while building your own stand-alone engine wire harness. I went further than the details of GM schematics to show engine data sensor interchangeability. When choosing a newer mass airflow (MAF) sensor, manifold absolute pressure sensor (MAP), or heated oxygen sensor (HO$_2$S), these schematics reveal any variation in pinout details.

Additionally, if you are working with any aftermarket stand-alone engine wire harness, you can expect to have a thorough understanding of the harness by referencing the following schematics.

Quick Reference	
Topic	**Page**
Power, Ground, and Data Communications	42
Charging - Generator Controls	43
Engine Data Sensors - ECT, IAT, MAP, and MAF	44
Engine Data Sensors - HO2S	45
Ignition Controls - CKP, CMP, KS1, and KS2	46
Ignition Controls - Ignition Coils	47
Fuel Controls - EV1 Fuel Injectors	48
Fuel Controls - Fuel Pump and EVAP Purge Solenoid	49
Throttle System - Cable (Camaro/Firebird)	50
Throttle System - Electric (Corvette)	51
Transmission - T56 6-Speed Manual	52
Transmission - 4L60E Automatic	53
Engine Cooling - Electric Fans Low/High Speed	54
Engine Cooling - Electric Fans On/Off	55
HVAC - A/C Compressor Controls	56
Inputs/Outputs	57

1997-1998 LS1 PCM (POWER, GROUND, DATA COMMUNICATION)

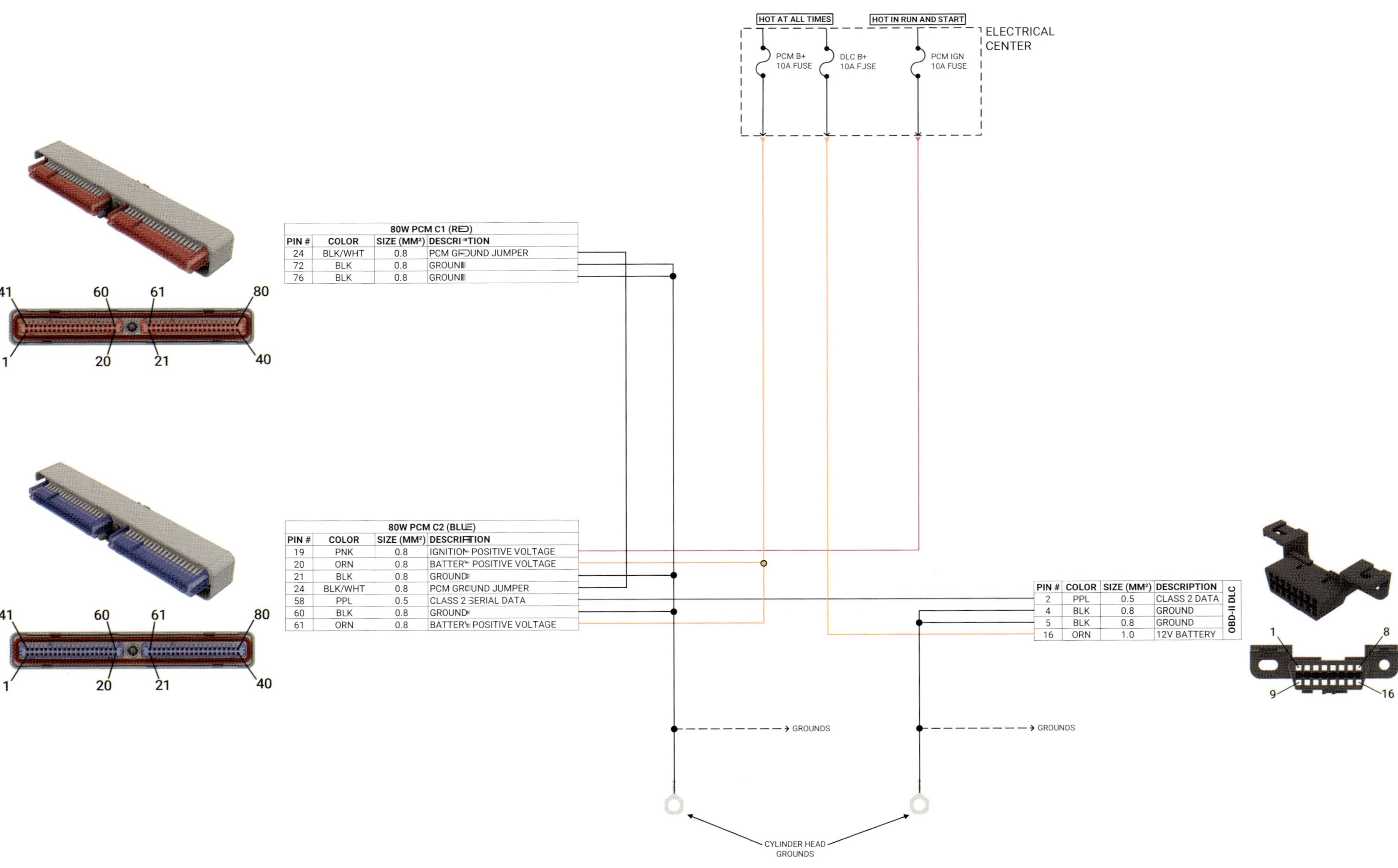

80W PCM C1 (RED)			
PIN #	COLOR	SIZE (MM²)	DESCRIPTION
24	BLK/WHT	0.8	PCM GROUND JUMPER
72	BLK	0.8	GROUND
76	BLK	0.8	GROUND

80W PCM C2 (BLUE)			
PIN #	COLOR	SIZE (MM²)	DESCRIPTION
19	PNK	0.8	IGNITION POSITIVE VOLTAGE
20	ORN	0.8	BATTERY POSITIVE VOLTAGE
21	BLK	0.8	GROUND
24	BLK/WHT	0.8	PCM GROUND JUMPER
58	PPL	0.5	CLASS 2 SERIAL DATA
60	BLK	0.8	GROUND
61	ORN	0.8	BATTERY POSITIVE VOLTAGE

OBD-II DLC			
PIN #	COLOR	SIZE (MM²)	DESCRIPTION
2	PPL	0.5	CLASS 2 DATA
4	BLK	0.8	GROUND
5	BLK	0.8	GROUND
16	ORN	1.0	12V BATTERY

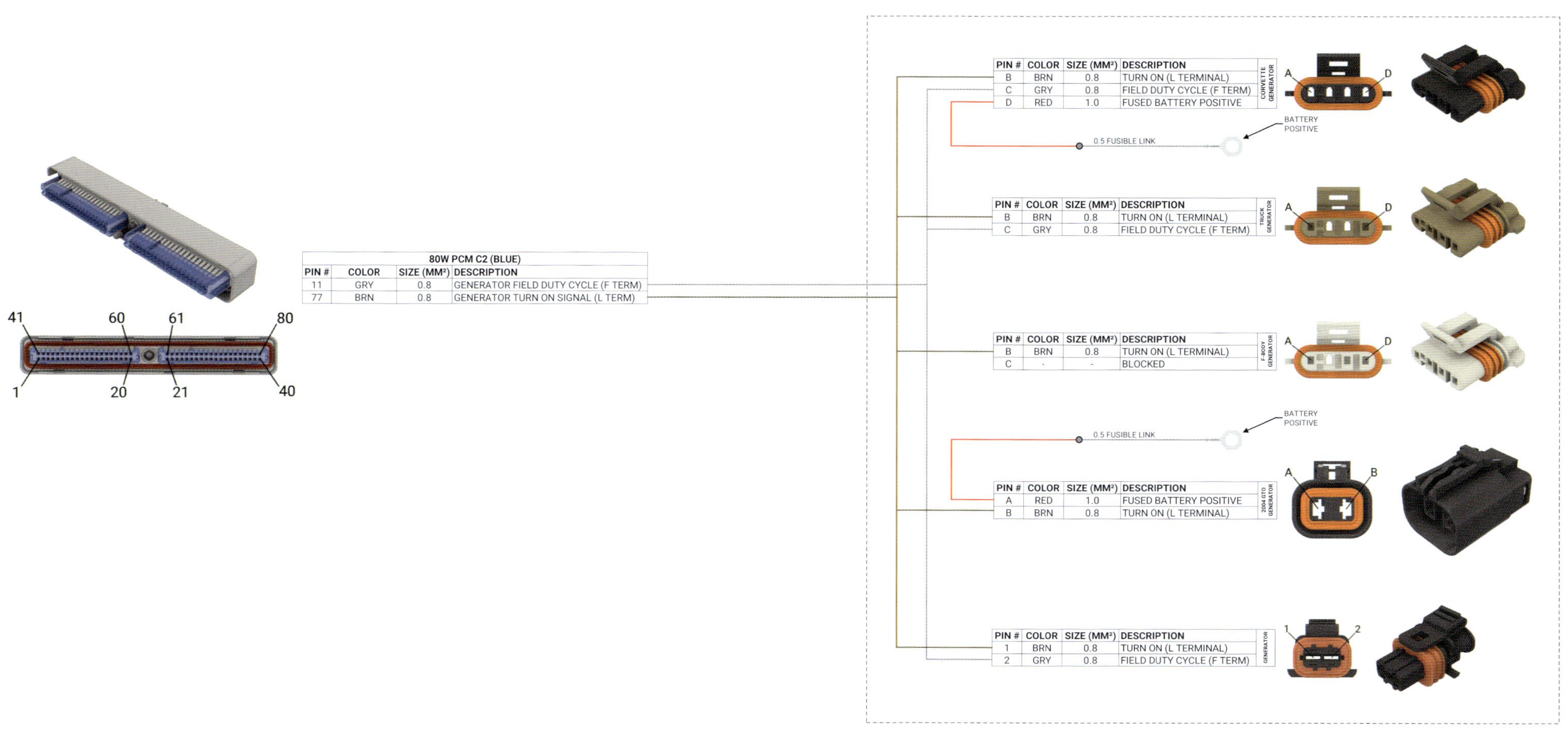

PIN #	COLOR	SIZE (MM²)	DESCRIPTION
B	BRN	0.8	TURN ON (L TERMINAL)
C	GRY	0.8	FIELD DUTY CYCLE (F TERM)
D	RED	1.0	FUSED BATTERY POSITIVE

PIN #	COLOR	SIZE (MM²)	DESCRIPTION
B	BRN	0.8	TURN ON (L TERMINAL)
C	GRY	0.8	FIELD DUTY CYCLE (F TERM)

PIN #	COLOR	SIZE (MM²)	DESCRIPTION
B	BRN	0.8	TURN ON (L TERMINAL)
C	-	-	BLOCKED

PIN #	COLOR	SIZE (MM²)	DESCRIPTION
A	RED	1.0	FUSED BATTERY POSITIVE
B	BRN	0.8	TURN ON (L TERMINAL)

PIN #	COLOR	SIZE (MM²)	DESCRIPTION
1	BRN	0.8	TURN ON (L TERMINAL)
2	GRY	0.8	FIELD DUTY CYCLE (F TERM)

80W PCM C2 (BLUE)			
PIN #	COLOR	SIZE (MM²)	DESCRIPTION
11	GRY	0.8	GENERATOR FIELD DUTY CYCLE (F TERM)
77	BRN	0.8	GENERATOR TURN ON SIGNAL (L TERM)

1997-1998 LS1 PCM (ENGINE DATA SENSORS – ECT, IAT, MAP, MAF)

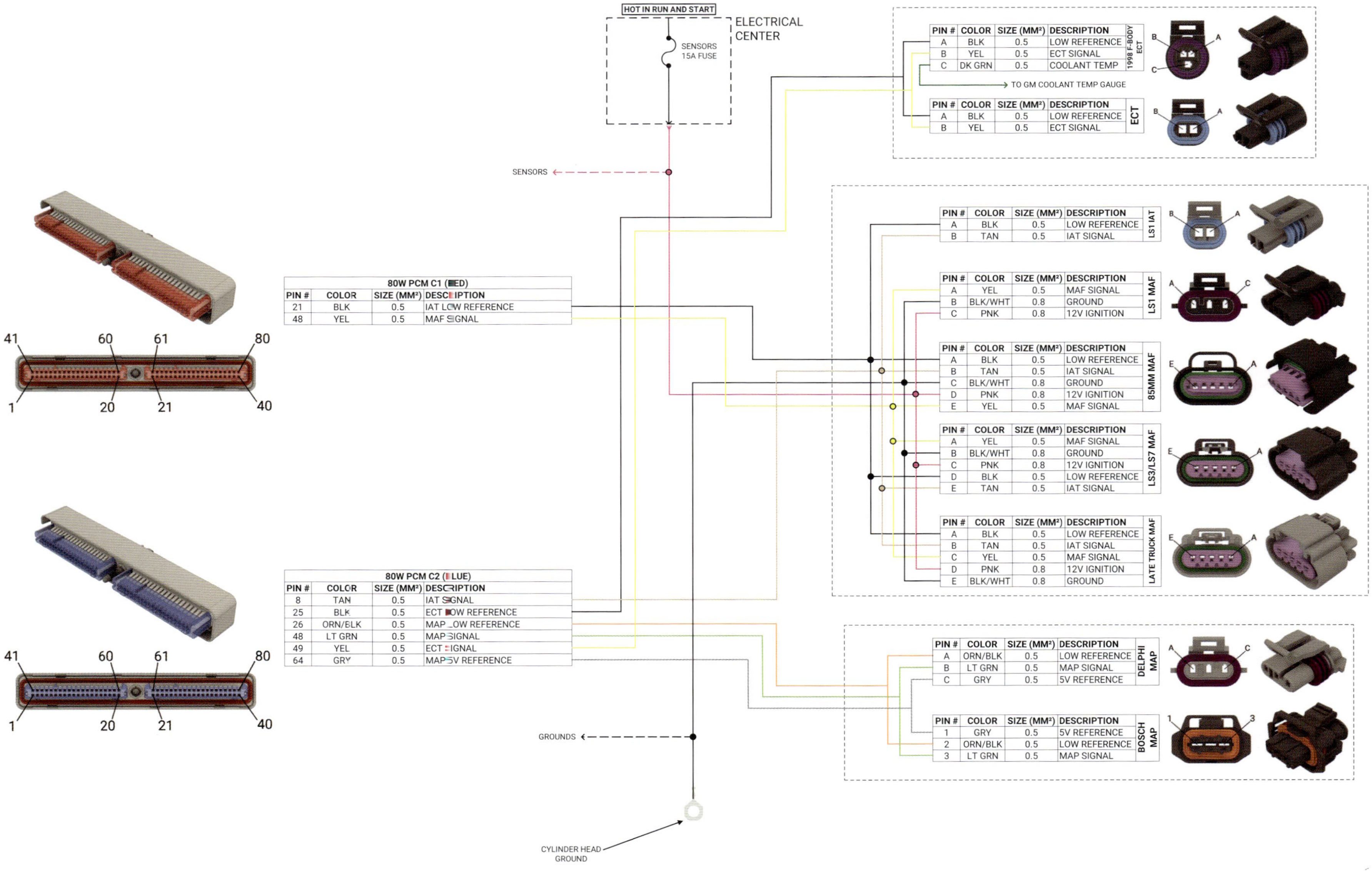

1998 F-BODY ECT

PIN #	COLOR	SIZE (MM²)	DESCRIPTION
A	BLK	0.5	LOW REFERENCE
B	YEL	0.5	ECT SIGNAL
C	DK GRN	0.5	COOLANT TEMP

ECT

PIN #	COLOR	SIZE (MM²)	DESCRIPTION
A	BLK	0.5	LOW REFERENCE
B	YEL	0.5	ECT SIGNAL

LS1 IAT

PIN #	COLOR	SIZE (MM²)	DESCRIPTION
A	BLK	0.5	LOW REFERENCE
B	TAN	0.5	IAT SIGNAL

LS1 MAF

PIN #	COLOR	SIZE (MM²)	DESCRIPTION
A	YEL	0.5	MAF SIGNAL
B	BLK/WHT	0.8	GROUND
C	PNK	0.8	12V IGNITION

85MM MAF

PIN #	COLOR	SIZE (MM²)	DESCRIPTION
A	BLK	0.5	LOW REFERENCE
B	TAN	0.5	IAT SIGNAL
C	BLK/WHT	0.8	GROUND
D	PNK	0.8	12V IGNITION
E	YEL	0.5	MAF SIGNAL

LS3/LS7 MAF

PIN #	COLOR	SIZE (MM²)	DESCRIPTION
A	YEL	0.5	MAF SIGNAL
B	BLK/WHT	0.8	GROUND
C	PNK	0.8	12V IGNITION
D	BLK	0.5	LOW REFERENCE
E	TAN	0.5	IAT SIGNAL

LATE TRUCK MAF

PIN #	COLOR	SIZE (MM²)	DESCRIPTION
A	BLK	0.5	LOW REFERENCE
B	TAN	0.5	IAT SIGNAL
C	YEL	0.5	MAF SIGNAL
D	PNK	0.8	12V IGNITION
E	BLK/WHT	0.8	GROUND

DELPHI MAP

PIN #	COLOR	SIZE (MM²)	DESCRIPTION
A	ORN/BLK	0.5	LOW REFERENCE
B	LT GRN	0.5	MAP SIGNAL
C	GRY	0.5	5V REFERENCE

BOSCH MAP

PIN #	COLOR	SIZE (MM²)	DESCRIPTION
1	GRY	0.5	5V REFERENCE
2	ORN/BLK	0.5	LOW REFERENCE
3	LT GRN	0.5	MAP SIGNAL

80W PCM C1 (RED)

PIN #	COLOR	SIZE (MM²)	DESCRIPTION
21	BLK	0.5	IAT LOW REFERENCE
48	YEL	0.5	MAF SIGNAL

80W PCM C2 (BLUE)

PIN #	COLOR	SIZE (MM²)	DESCRIPTION
8	TAN	0.5	IAT SIGNAL
25	BLK	0.5	ECT LOW REFERENCE
26	ORN/BLK	0.5	MAP LOW REFERENCE
48	LT GRN	0.5	MAP SIGNAL
49	YEL	0.5	ECT SIGNAL
64	GRY	0.5	MAP 5V REFERENCE

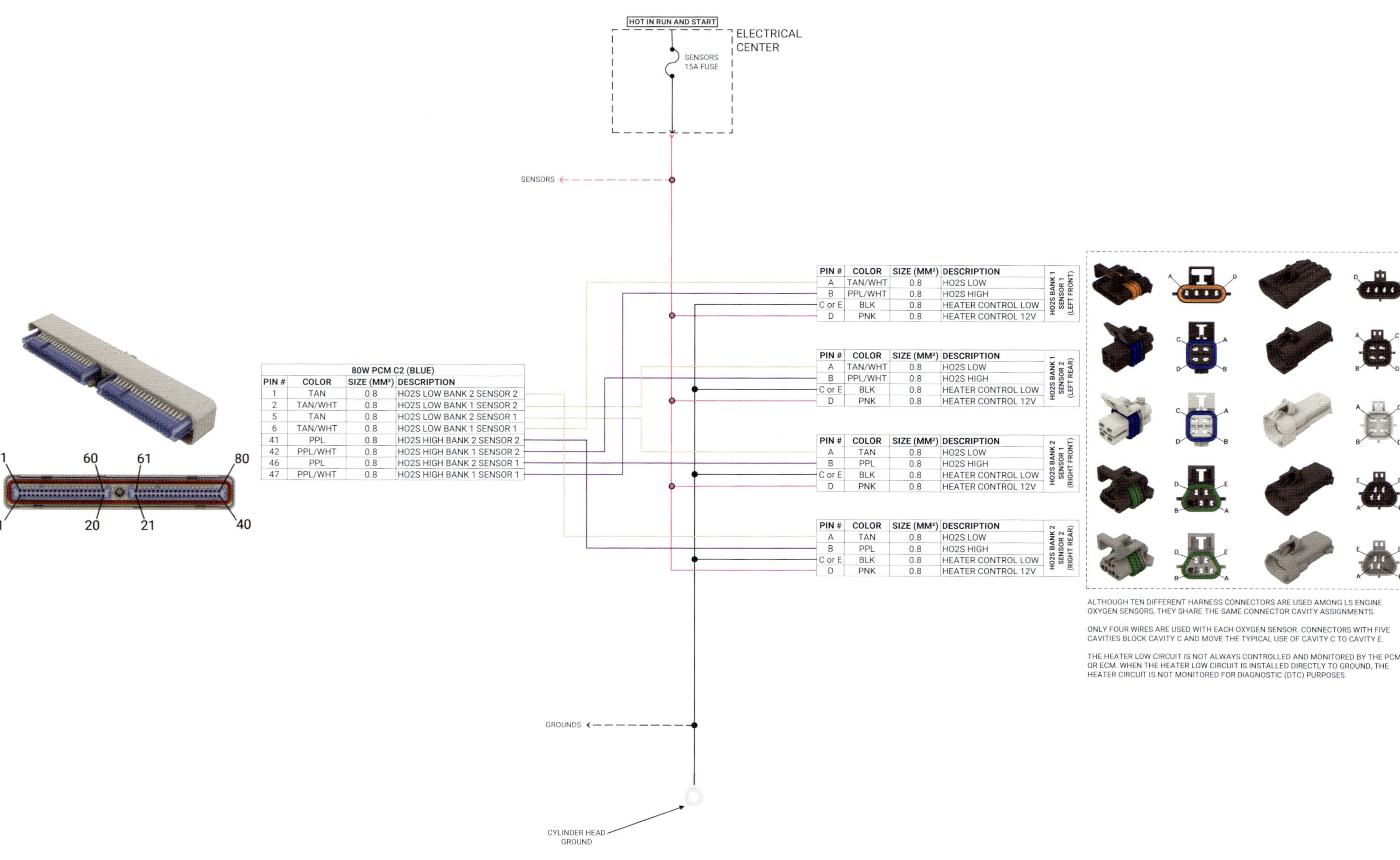

80W PCM C2 (BLUE)			
PIN #	COLOR	SIZE (MM²)	DESCRIPTION
1	TAN	0.8	HO2S LOW BANK 2 SENSOR 2
2	TAN/WHT	0.8	HO2S LOW BANK 1 SENSOR 2
5	TAN	0.8	HO2S LOW BANK 2 SENSOR 1
6	TAN/WHT	0.8	HO2S LOW BANK 1 SENSOR 1
41	PPL	0.8	HO2S HIGH BANK 2 SENSOR 2
42	PPL/WHT	0.8	HO2S HIGH BANK 1 SENSOR 2
46	PPL	0.8	HO2S HIGH BANK 2 SENSOR 1
47	PPL/WHT	0.8	HO2S HIGH BANK 1 SENSOR 1

HO2S BANK 1 SENSOR 1 (LEFT FRONT)

PIN #	COLOR	SIZE (MM²)	DESCRIPTION
A	TAN/WHT	0.8	HO2S LOW
B	PPL/WHT	0.8	HO2S HIGH
C or E	BLK	0.8	HEATER CONTROL LOW
D	PNK	0.8	HEATER CONTROL 12V

HO2S BANK 1 SENSOR 2 (LEFT REAR)

PIN #	COLOR	SIZE (MM²)	DESCRIPTION
A	TAN/WHT	0.8	HO2S LOW
B	PPL/WHT	0.8	HO2S HIGH
C or E	BLK	0.8	HEATER CONTROL LOW
D	PNK	0.8	HEATER CONTROL 12V

HO2S BANK 2 SENSOR 1 (RIGHT FRONT)

PIN #	COLOR	SIZE (MM²)	DESCRIPTION
A	TAN	0.8	HO2S LOW
B	PPL	0.8	HO2S HIGH
C or E	BLK	0.8	HEATER CONTROL LOW
D	PNK	0.8	HEATER CONTROL 12V

HO2S BANK 2 SENSOR 2 (RIGHT REAR)

PIN #	COLOR	SIZE (MM²)	DESCRIPTION
A	TAN	0.8	HO2S LOW
B	PPL	0.8	HO2S HIGH
C or E	BLK	0.8	HEATER CONTROL LOW
D	PNK	0.8	HEATER CONTROL 12V

ALTHOUGH TEN DIFFERENT HARNESS CONNECTORS ARE USED AMONG LS ENGINE OXYGEN SENSORS, THEY SHARE THE SAME CONNECTOR CAVITY ASSIGNMENTS.

ONLY FOUR WIRES ARE USED WITH EACH OXYGEN SENSOR. CONNECTORS WITH FIVE CAVITIES BLOCK CAVITY C AND MOVE THE TYPICAL USE OF CAVITY C TO CAVITY E.

THE HEATER LOW CIRCUIT IS NOT ALWAYS CONTROLLED AND MONITORED BY THE PCM OR ECM. WHEN THE HEATER LOW CIRCUIT IS INSTALLED DIRECTLY TO GROUND, THE HEATER CIRCUIT IS NOT MONITORED FOR DIAGNOSTIC (DTC) PURPOSES.

1997-1998 LS1 PCM (IGNITION CONTROLS – CKP, CMP, KS1, KS2)

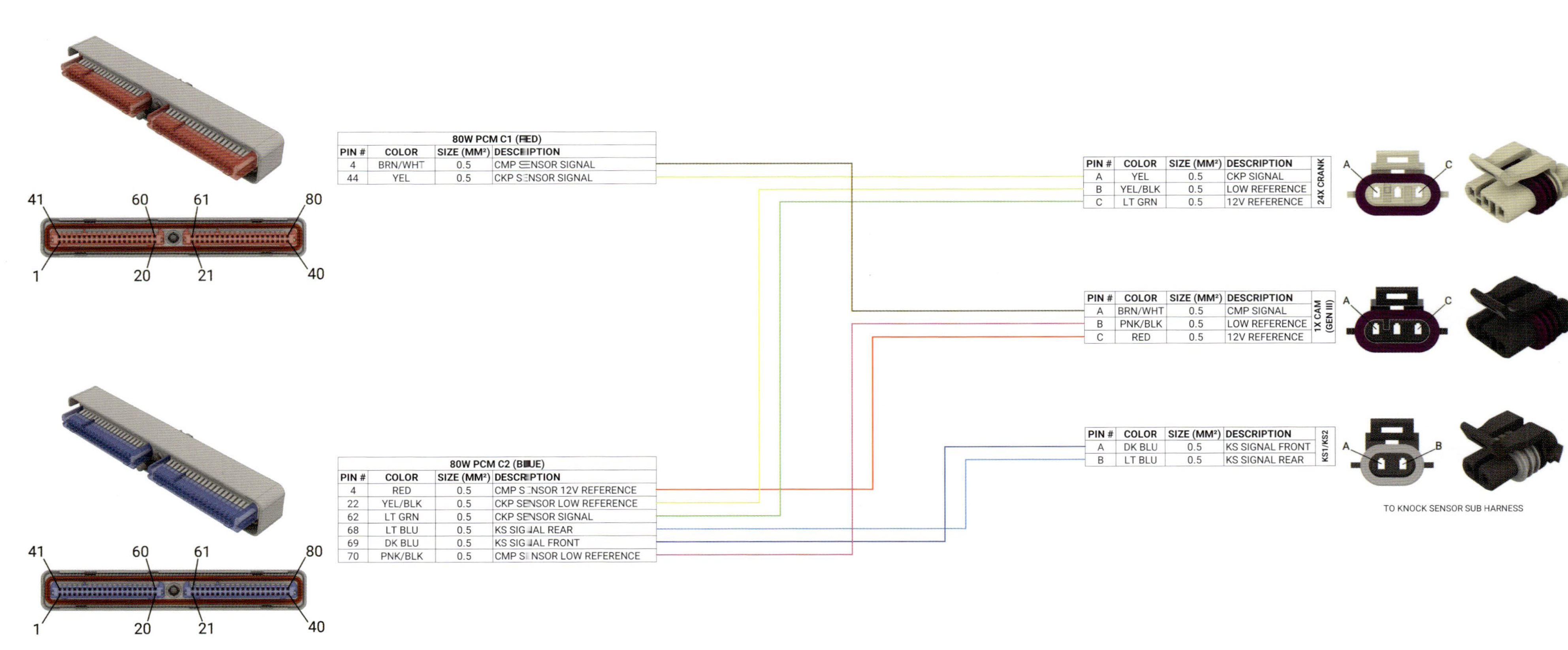

80W PCM C1 (RED)			
PIN #	COLOR	SIZE (MM²)	DESCRIPTION
4	BRN/WHT	0.5	CMP SENSOR SIGNAL
44	YEL	0.5	CKP SENSOR SIGNAL

80W PCM C2 (BLUE)			
PIN #	COLOR	SIZE (MM²)	DESCRIPTION
4	RED	0.5	CMP SENSOR 12V REFERENCE
22	YEL/BLK	0.5	CKP SENSOR LOW REFERENCE
62	LT GRN	0.5	CKP SENSOR SIGNAL
68	LT BLU	0.5	KS SIGNAL REAR
69	DK BLU	0.5	KS SIGNAL FRONT
70	PNK/BLK	0.5	CMP SENSOR LOW REFERENCE

PIN #	COLOR	SIZE (MM²)	DESCRIPTION	24X CRANK
A	YEL	0.5	CKP SIGNAL	
B	YEL/BLK	0.5	LOW REFERENCE	
C	LT GRN	0.5	12V REFERENCE	

PIN #	COLOR	SIZE (MM²)	DESCRIPTION	1X CAM (GEN III)
A	BRN/WHT	0.5	CMP SIGNAL	
B	PNK/BLK	0.5	LOW REFERENCE	
C	RED	0.5	12V REFERENCE	

PIN #	COLOR	SIZE (MM²)	DESCRIPTION	KS1/KS2
A	DK BLU	0.5	KS SIGNAL FRONT	
B	LT BLU	0.5	KS SIGNAL REAR	

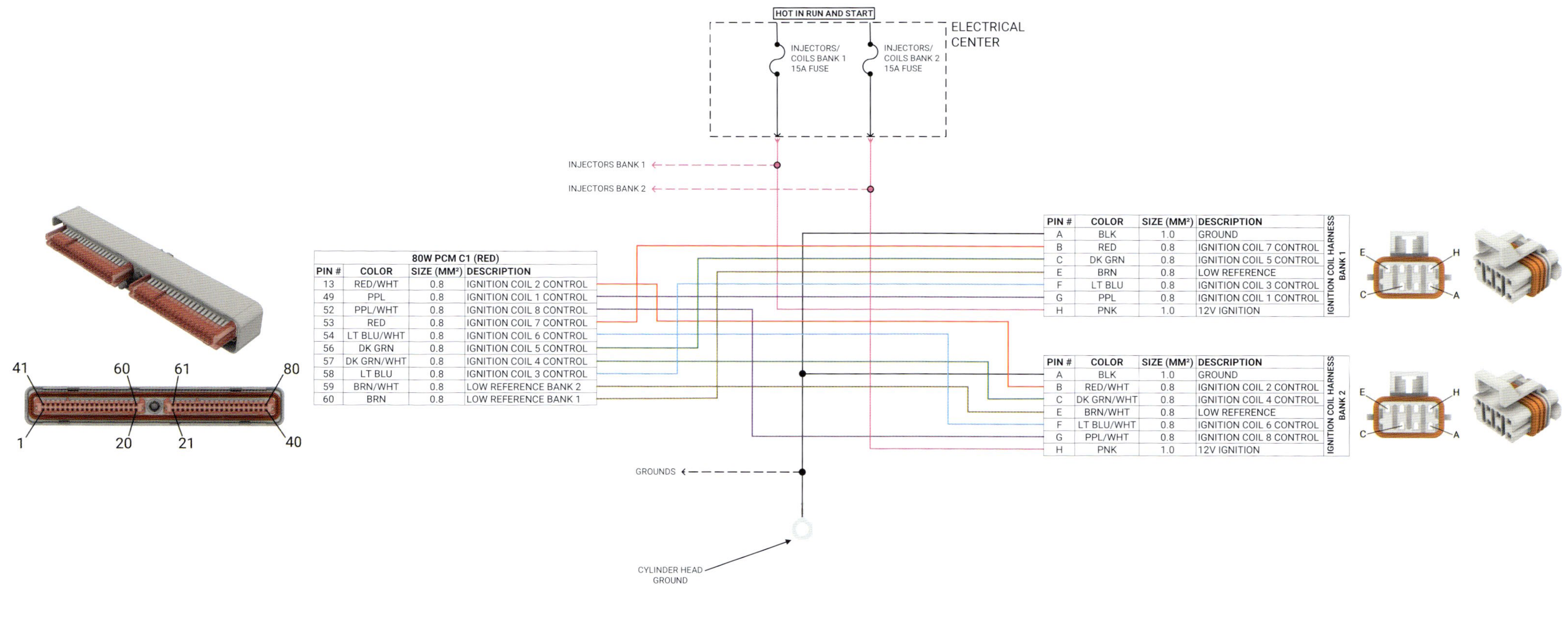

80W PCM C1 (RED)			
PIN #	COLOR	SIZE (MM²)	DESCRIPTION
13	RED/WHT	0.8	IGNITION COIL 2 CONTROL
49	PPL	0.8	IGNITION COIL 1 CONTROL
52	PPL/WHT	0.8	IGNITION COIL 8 CONTROL
53	RED	0.8	IGNITION COIL 7 CONTROL
54	LT BLU/WHT	0.8	IGNITION COIL 6 CONTROL
56	DK GRN	0.8	IGNITION COIL 5 CONTROL
57	DK GRN/WHT	0.8	IGNITION COIL 4 CONTROL
58	LT BLU	0.8	IGNITION COIL 3 CONTROL
59	BRN/WHT	0.8	LOW REFERENCE BANK 2
60	BRN	0.8	LOW REFERENCE BANK 1

IGNITION COIL HARNESS BANK 1

PIN #	COLOR	SIZE (MM²)	DESCRIPTION
A	BLK	1.0	GROUND
B	RED	0.8	IGNITION COIL 7 CONTROL
C	DK GRN	0.8	IGNITION COIL 5 CONTROL
E	BRN	0.8	LOW REFERENCE
F	LT BLU	0.8	IGNITION COIL 3 CONTROL
G	PPL	0.8	IGNITION COIL 1 CONTROL
H	PNK	1.0	12V IGNITION

IGNITION COIL HARNESS BANK 2

PIN #	COLOR	SIZE (MM²)	DESCRIPTION
A	BLK	1.0	GROUND
B	RED/WHT	0.8	IGNITION COIL 2 CONTROL
C	DK GRN/WHT	0.8	IGNITION COIL 4 CONTROL
E	BRN/WHT	0.8	LOW REFERENCE
F	LT BLU/WHT	0.8	IGNITION COIL 6 CONTROL
G	PPL/WHT	0.8	IGNITION COIL 8 CONTROL
H	PNK	1.0	12V IGNITION

LS ENGINES(*) ARE FITTED WITH A PAIR OF IGNITION COIL SUB HARNESSES. EACH IGNITION COIL SUB HARNESS IS ATTACHED TO AN IGNITION COIL BRACKET ON TOP OF THE VALVE COVER. THE MATING 7 CAVITY METRI-PACK 150 FEMALE CONNECTOR CAN BE USED WITH ALL GM LS-SERIES IGNITION COIL SUB HARNESSES. NO REWIRING IS NECESSARY UNLESS THE ENGINE FIRE ORDER HAS CHANGED.

*EXCLUDES LS9 AND LSA ENGINES

TO DIRECTLY WIRE EACH IGNITION COIL TO THE ENGINE HARNESS, EACH 12V IGNITION (PINK WIRE), GROUND (BLACK WIRE), AND LOW REFERENCE WIRE (BROWN & BROWN/WHITE) WILL HAVE TO BE SPLICED TO FOUR ADDITIONAL WIRES TO PROVIDE POWER AND GROUND TO EACH IGNITION COIL.

1997-1998 LS1 PCM (FUEL CONTROLS – EV1 FUEL INJECTORS)

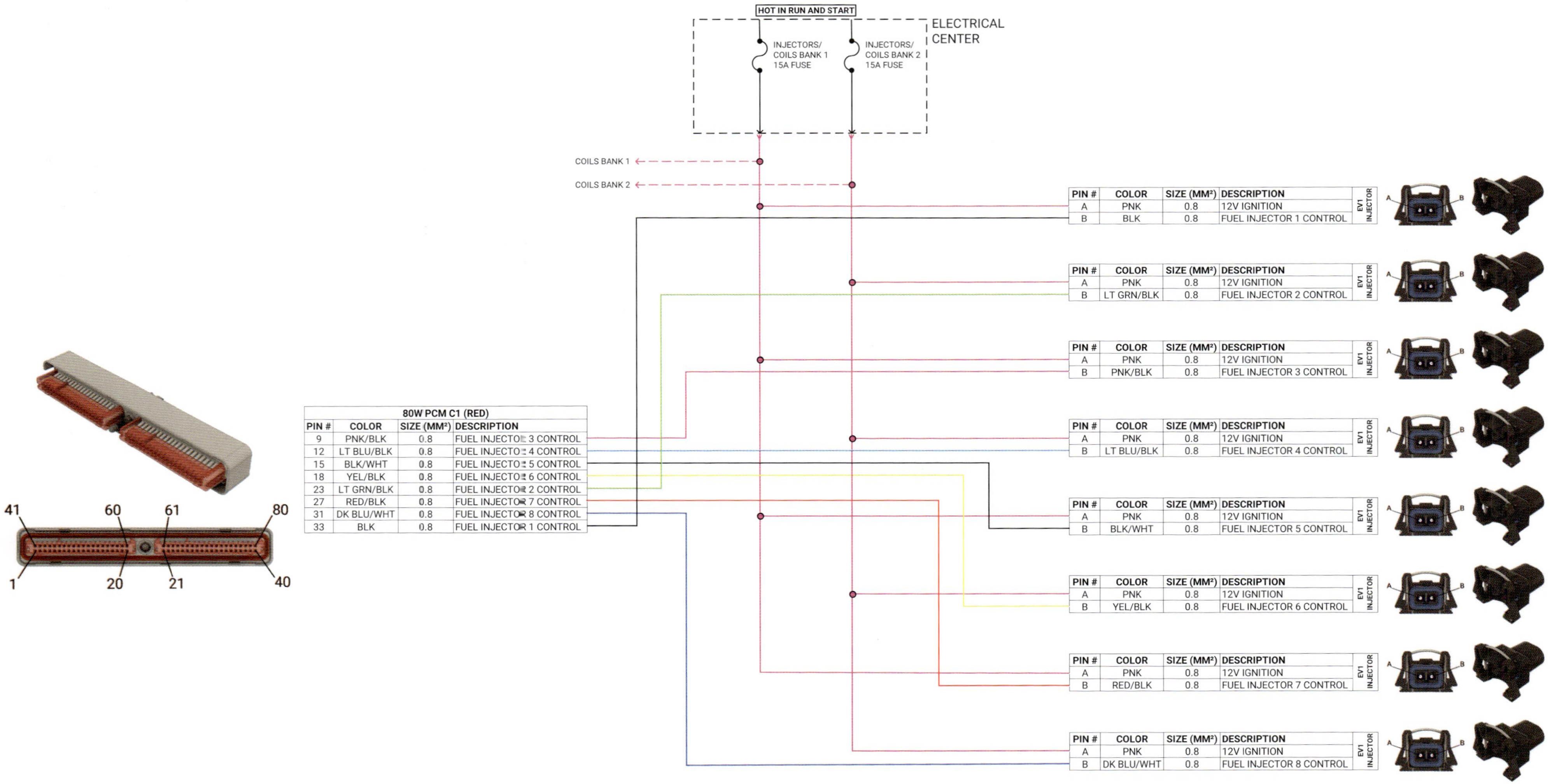

ELECTRICAL CENTER

HOT IN RUN AND START

INJECTORS/ COILS BANK 1 15A FUSE

INJECTORS/ COILS BANK 2 15A FUSE

COILS BANK 1
COILS BANK 2

80W PCM C1 (RED)			
PIN #	COLOR	SIZE (MM²)	DESCRIPTION
9	PNK/BLK	0.8	FUEL INJECTOR 3 CONTROL
12	LT BLU/BLK	0.8	FUEL INJECTOR 4 CONTROL
15	BLK/WHT	0.8	FUEL INJECTOR 5 CONTROL
18	YEL/BLK	0.8	FUEL INJECTOR 6 CONTROL
23	LT GRN/BLK	0.8	FUEL INJECTOR 2 CONTROL
27	RED/BLK	0.8	FUEL INJECTOR 7 CONTROL
31	DK BLU/WHT	0.8	FUEL INJECTOR 8 CONTROL
33	BLK	0.8	FUEL INJECTOR 1 CONTROL

EV1 INJECTOR

PIN #	COLOR	SIZE (MM²)	DESCRIPTION
A	PNK	0.8	12V IGNITION
B	BLK	0.8	FUEL INJECTOR 1 CONTROL

EV1 INJECTOR

PIN #	COLOR	SIZE (MM²)	DESCRIPTION
A	PNK	0.8	12V IGNITION
B	LT GRN/BLK	0.8	FUEL INJECTOR 2 CONTROL

EV1 INJECTOR

PIN #	COLOR	SIZE (MM²)	DESCRIPTION
A	PNK	0.8	12V IGNITION
B	PNK/BLK	0.8	FUEL INJECTOR 3 CONTROL

EV1 INJECTOR

PIN #	COLOR	SIZE (MM²)	DESCRIPTION
A	PNK	0.8	12V IGNITION
B	LT BLU/BLK	0.8	FUEL INJECTOR 4 CONTROL

EV1 INJECTOR

PIN #	COLOR	SIZE (MM²)	DESCRIPTION
A	PNK	0.8	12V IGNITION
B	BLK/WHT	0.8	FUEL INJECTOR 5 CONTROL

EV1 INJECTOR

PIN #	COLOR	SIZE (MM²)	DESCRIPTION
A	PNK	0.8	12V IGNITION
B	YEL/BLK	0.8	FUEL INJECTOR 6 CONTROL

EV1 INJECTOR

PIN #	COLOR	SIZE (MM²)	DESCRIPTION
A	PNK	0.8	12V IGNITION
B	RED/BLK	0.8	FUEL INJECTOR 7 CONTROL

EV1 INJECTOR

PIN #	COLOR	SIZE (MM²)	DESCRIPTION
A	PNK	0.8	12V IGNITION
B	DK BLU/WHT	0.8	FUEL INJECTOR 8 CONTROL

41 60 61 80
1 20 21 40

1997-1998 LS1 PCM (FUEL CONTROLS – FUEL PUMP, EVAP PURGE SOLENOID)

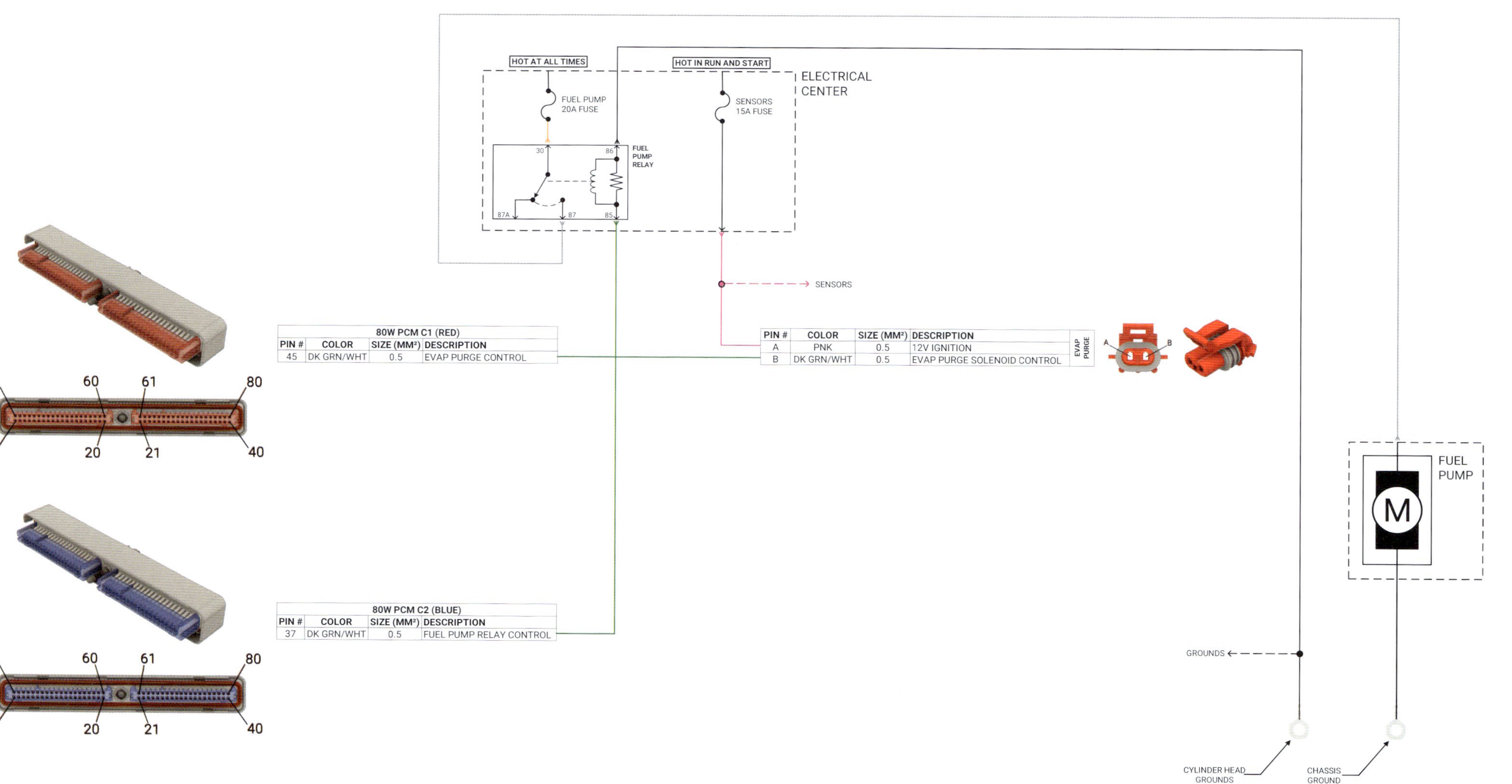

80W PCM C1 (RED)			
PIN #	COLOR	SIZE (MM²)	DESCRIPTION
45	DK GRN/WHT	0.5	EVAP PURGE CONTROL

		PIN #	COLOR	SIZE (MM²)	DESCRIPTION
		A	PNK	0.5	12V IGNITION
		B	DK GRN/WHT	0.5	EVAP PURGE SOLENOID CONTROL

80W PCM C2 (BLUE)			
PIN #	COLOR	SIZE (MM²)	DESCRIPTION
37	DK GRN/WHT	0.5	FUEL PUMP RELAY CONTROL

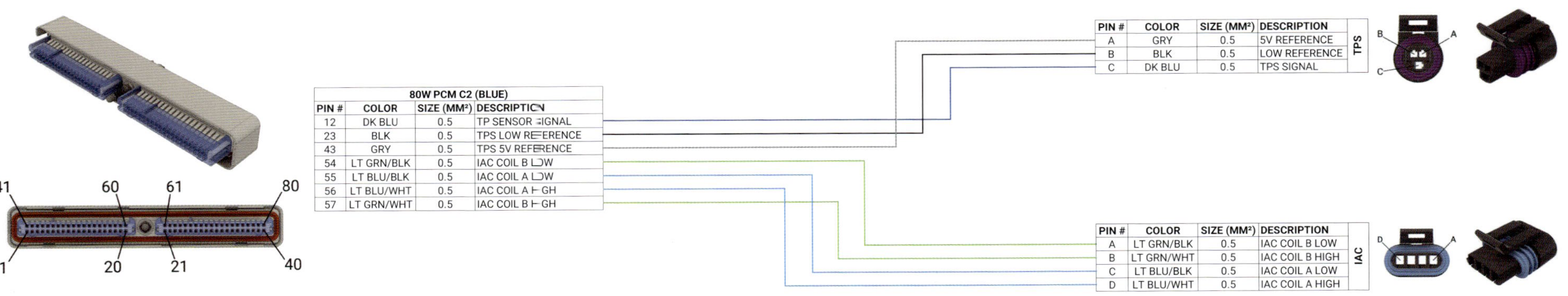

PIN #	COLOR	SIZE (MM²)	DESCRIPTION	
A	GRY	0.5	5V REFERENCE	TPS
B	BLK	0.5	LOW REFERENCE	
C	DK BLU	0.5	TPS SIGNAL	

80W PCM C2 (BLUE)			
PIN #	COLOR	SIZE (MM²)	DESCRIPTION
12	DK BLU	0.5	TP SENSOR SIGNAL
23	BLK	0.5	TPS LOW REFERENCE
43	GRY	0.5	TPS 5V REFERENCE
54	LT GRN/BLK	0.5	IAC COIL B LOW
55	LT BLU/BLK	0.5	IAC COIL A LOW
56	LT BLU/WHT	0.5	IAC COIL A HIGH
57	LT GRN/WHT	0.5	IAC COIL B HIGH

PIN #	COLOR	SIZE (MM²)	DESCRIPTION	
A	LT GRN/BLK	0.5	IAC COIL B LOW	IAC
B	LT GRN/WHT	0.5	IAC COIL B HIGH	
C	LT BLU/BLK	0.5	IAC COIL A LOW	
D	LT BLU/WHT	0.5	IAC COIL A HIGH	

1997-1998 LS1 PCM (THROTTLE SYSTEM – ELECTRONIC (CORVETTE))

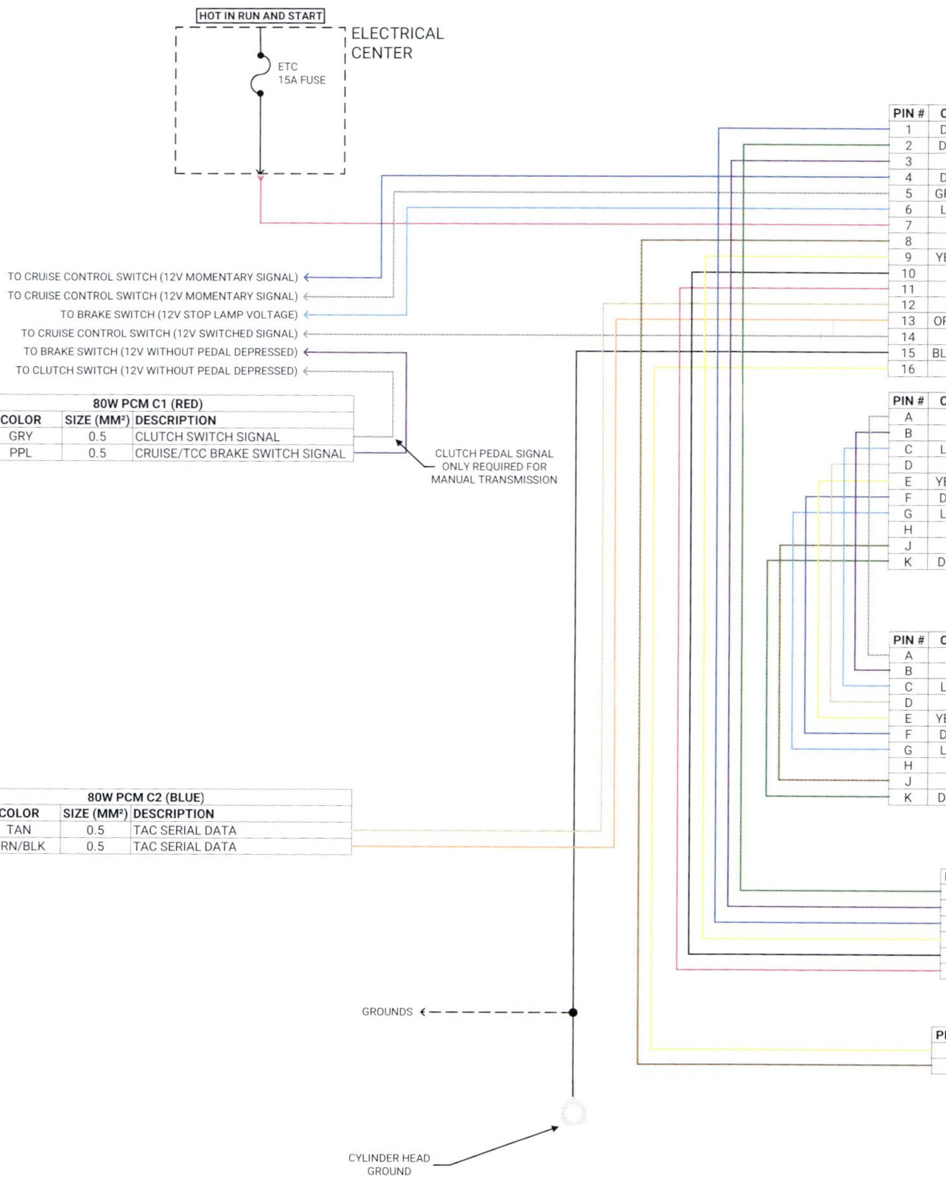

ELECTRICAL CENTER

HOT IN RUN AND START

ETC 15A FUSE

TO CRUISE CONTROL SWITCH (12V MOMENTARY SIGNAL)
TO CRUISE CONTROL SWITCH (12V MOMENTARY SIGNAL)
TO BRAKE SWITCH (12V STOP LAMP VOLTAGE)
TO CRUISE CONTROL SWITCH (12V SWITCHED SIGNAL)
TO BRAKE SWITCH (12V WITHOUT PEDAL DEPRESSED)
TO CLUTCH SWITCH (12V WITHOUT PEDAL DEPRESSED)

CLUTCH PEDAL SIGNAL ONLY REQUIRED FOR MANUAL TRANSMISSION

GROUNDS

CYLINDER HEAD GROUND

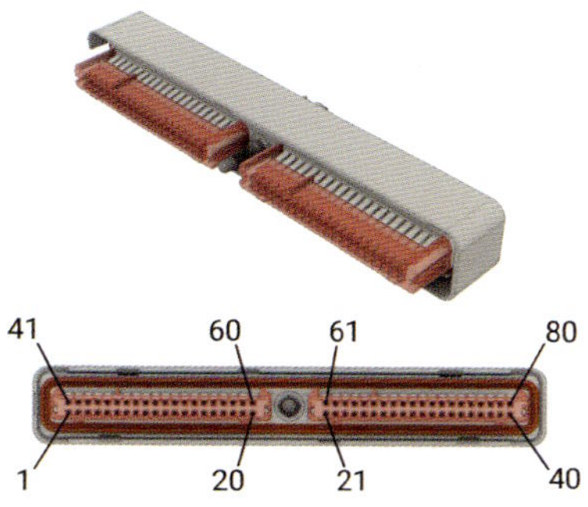

16W THROTTLE ACTUATOR CONTROL (TAC) MODULE

PIN #	COLOR	SIZE (MM²)	DESCRIPTION
1	DK BLU	0.5	TP SENSOR 1 SIGNAL
2	DK GRN	0.5	TP SENSOR 1 5V REFERENCE
3	PPL	0.5	TP SENSOR 1 LOW REFERENCE
4	DK BLU	0.5	CRUISE SET/COAST SIGNAL
5	GRY/BLK	0.5	CRUISE RESUME/ACCEL SIGNAL
6	LT BLU	0.8	STOP LAMP SUPPLY VOLTAGE
7	PNK	0.8	12V IGNITION
8	BRN	0.8	TAC MOTOR CONTROL 2 (CLOSE)
9	YEL/BLK	0.5	TP SENSOR 2 5V REFERENCE
10	WHT	0.5	TP SENSOR 2 LOW REFERENCE
11	PNK	0.5	TP SENSOR 2 SIGNAL
12	TAN	0.5	TAC SERIAL DATA
13	ORN/BLK	0.5	TAC SERIAL DATA
14	GRY	0.5	CRUISE ON/OFF SIGNAL
15	BLK/WHT	0.8	GROUND
16	YEL	0.8	TAC MOTOR CONTROL 1 (OPEN)

10W TAC MODULE

PIN #	COLOR	SIZE (MM²)	DESCRIPTION
A	GRY	0.5	APP 3 LOW REFERENCE
B	PPL	0.5	APP 2 LOW REFERENCE
C	LT BLU	0.5	APP 2 SIGNAL
D	TAN	0.5	APP 2 5V REFERENCE
E	YEL/BLK	0.5	APP 3 5V REFERENCE
F	DK BLU	0.5	APP 1 SIGNAL
G	LT BLU	0.5	APP 1 5V REFERENCE
H	-		NOT USED
J	BRN	0.5	APP 1 LOW REFERENCE
K	DK GRN	0.5	APP 3 SIGNAL

APP SENSOR (ACCELERATOR PEDAL)

PIN #	COLOR	SIZE (MM²)	DESCRIPTION
A	GRY	0.5	APP 3 LOW REFERENCE
B	PPL	0.5	APP 2 LOW REFERENCE
C	LT BLU	0.5	APP 2 SIGNAL
D	TAN	0.5	APP 2 5V REFERENCE
E	YEL/BLK	0.5	APP 3 5V REFERENCE
F	DK BLU	0.5	APP 1 SIGNAL
G	LT BLU	0.5	APP 1 5V REFERENCE
H	-		NOT USED
J	BRN	0.5	APP 1 LOW REFERENCE
K	DK GRN	0.5	APP 3 SIGNAL

TPS

PIN #	COLOR	SIZE (MM²)	DESCRIPTION
A	DK GRN	0.5	TP SENSOR 1 5V REF
B	PPL	0.5	TP SENSOR 1 LOW REF
C	DK BLU	0.5	TP SENSOR 1 SIGNAL
D	YEL/BLK	0.5	TP SENSOR 2 5V REF
E	WHT	0.5	TP SENSOR 2 LOW REF
F	PNK	0.5	TP SENSOR 2 SIGNAL

TAC MOTOR

PIN #	COLOR	SIZE (MM²)	DESCRIPTION
A	YEL	0.8	ACTUATOR CONTROL 1
B	BRN	0.8	ACTUATOR CONTROL 2

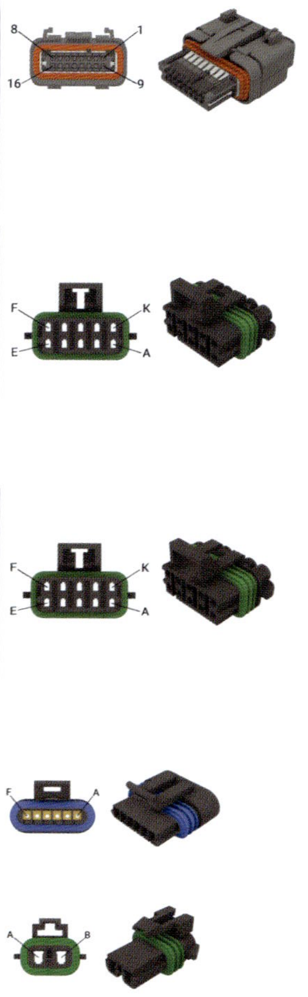

80W PCM C1 (RED)

PIN #	COLOR	SIZE (MM²)	DESCRIPTION
68	GRY	0.5	CLUTCH SWITCH SIGNAL
77	PPL	0.5	CRUISE/TCC BRAKE SWITCH SIGNAL

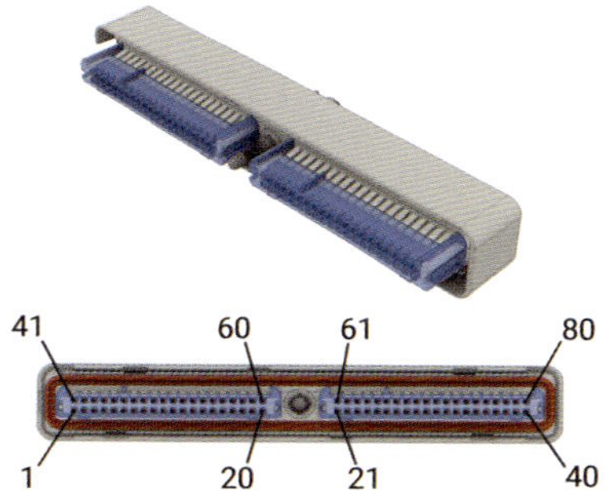

41 60 61 80
1 20 21 40

80W PCM C2 (BLUE)

PIN #	COLOR	SIZE (MM²)	DESCRIPTION
71	TAN	0.5	TAC SERIAL DATA
72	ORN/BLK	0.5	TAC SERIAL DATA

41 60 61 80
1 20 21 40

1997-1998 LS1 PCM (TRANSMISSION – T56 6 SPEED MANUAL)

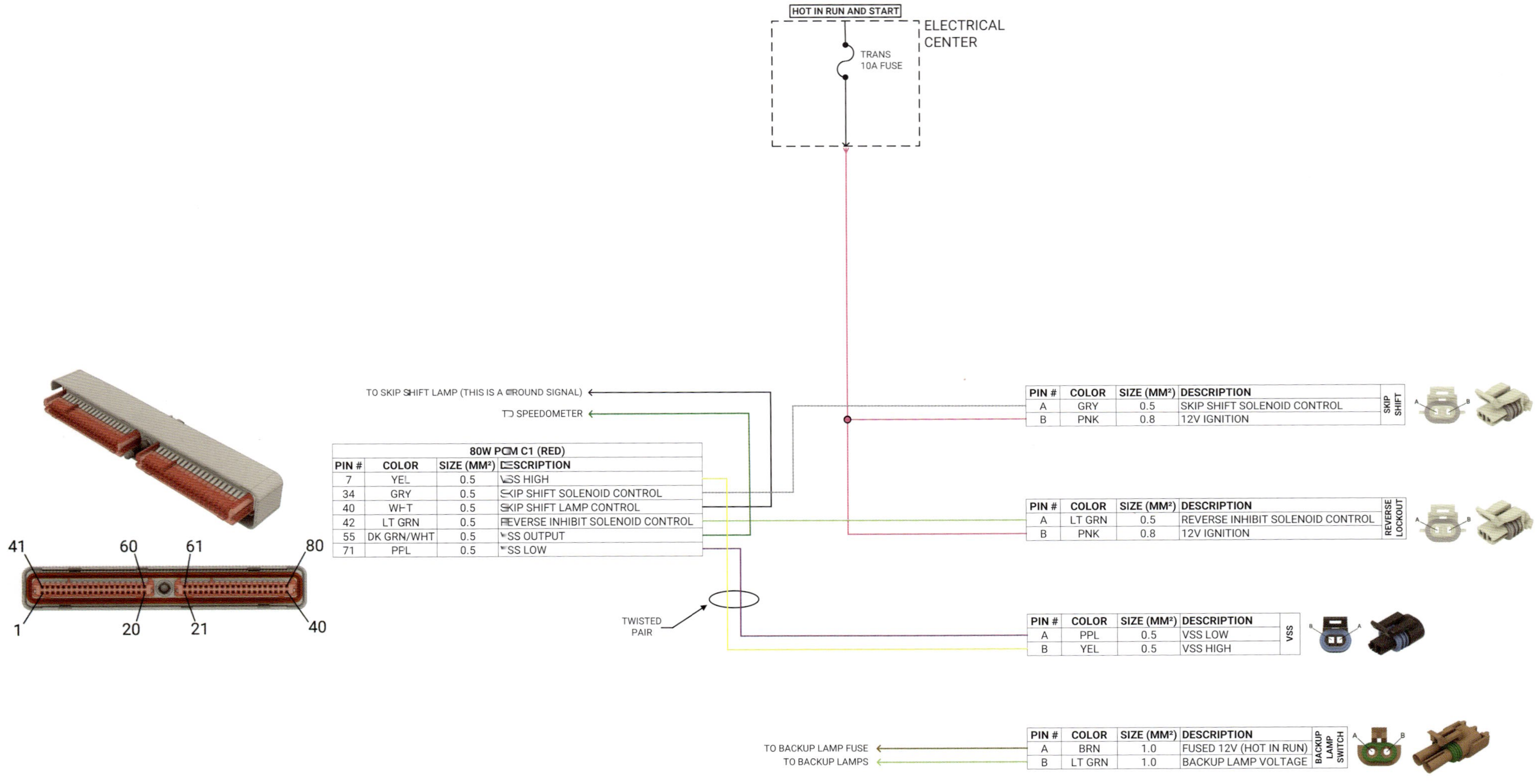

ELECTRICAL CENTER

HOT IN RUN AND START

TRANS 10A FUSE

TO SKIP SHIFT LAMP (THIS IS A GROUND SIGNAL)

TO SPEEDOMETER

TWISTED PAIR

TO BACKUP LAMP FUSE

TO BACKUP LAMPS

80W PCM C1 (RED)			
PIN #	COLOR	SIZE (MM²)	DESCRIPTION
7	YEL	0.5	VSS HIGH
34	GRY	0.5	SKIP SHIFT SOLENOID CONTROL
40	WHT	0.5	SKIP SHIFT LAMP CONTROL
42	LT GRN	0.5	REVERSE INHIBIT SOLENOID CONTROL
55	DK GRN/WHT	0.5	VSS OUTPUT
71	PPL	0.5	VSS LOW

SKIP SHIFT

PIN #	COLOR	SIZE (MM²)	DESCRIPTION
A	GRY	0.5	SKIP SHIFT SOLENOID CONTROL
B	PNK	0.8	12V IGNITION

REVERSE LOCKOUT

PIN #	COLOR	SIZE (MM²)	DESCRIPTION
A	LT GRN	0.5	REVERSE INHIBIT SOLENOID CONTROL
B	PNK	0.8	12V IGNITION

VSS

PIN #	COLOR	SIZE (MM²)	DESCRIPTION
A	PPL	0.5	VSS LOW
B	YEL	0.5	VSS HIGH

BACKUP LAMP SWITCH

PIN #	COLOR	SIZE (MM²)	DESCRIPTION
A	BRN	1.0	FUSED 12V (HOT IN RUN)
B	LT GRN	1.0	BACKUP LAMP VOLTAGE

41 60 61 80

1 20 21 40

1997-1998 LS1 PCM (TRANSMISSION – 4L60E AUTOMATIC)

HOT IN RUN AND START

ELECTRICAL CENTER

TRANS 10A FUSE

VSS OUTPUT (TO SPEEDOMETER)

TO BRAKE SWITCH (12V WITHOUT PEDAL DEPRESSED)

TO PNP SWITCH (GROUND WHEN IN P/N) – CAMARO/FIREBIRD ONLY

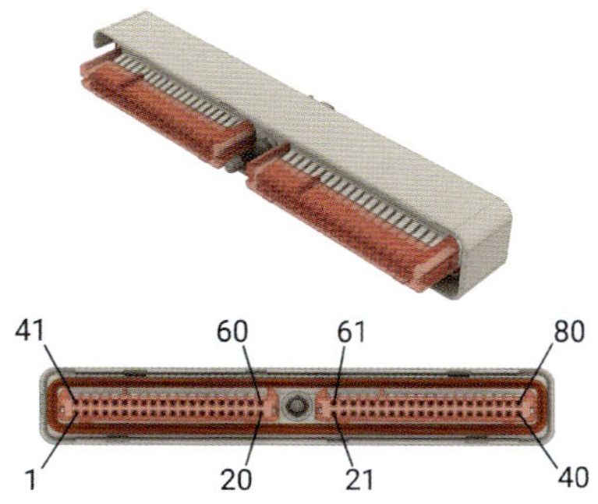

80W PCM C1 (RED)

PIN #	COLOR	SIZE (MM²)	DESCRIPTION
22	DK BLU	0.5	TRANS RANGE SWITCH B INPUT
25	PNK	0.5	TRANS RANGE SWITCH A INPUT
26	BLK/WHT	0.5	PRND A
32	WHT	0.5	PRND P / PNP SWITCH SIGNAL
34	WHT	0.5	3-2 SHIFT SOLENOID CONTROL
35	LT GRN	0.5	1-2 SHIFT SOLENOID CONTROL
40	YEL/BLK	0.5	2-3 SHIFT SOLENOID CONTROL
55	DK GRN/WHT	0.5	VSS OUTPUT
61	RED	0.5	TRANS RANGE SWITCH C INPUT
65	GRY	0.5	PRND C
66	YEL	0.5	PRND B
77	PPL	0.5	TCC BRAKE SWITCH INPUT

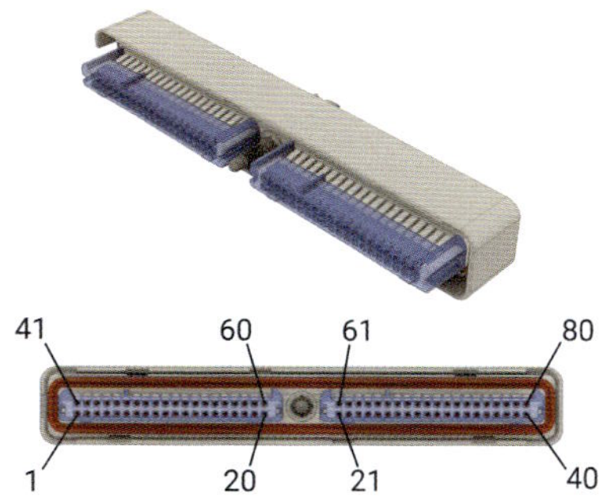

80W PCM C2 (BLUE)

PIN #	COLOR	SIZE (MM²)	DESCRIPTION
7	YEL	0.5	VSS HIGH
13	YEL/BLK	0.5	TFT SENSOR SIGNAL
14	ORN/BLK	0.5	TFT SENSOR LOW REFERENCE
32	TAN/BLK	0.5	TCC SOLENOID CONTROL
33	BRN	0.5	TCC PWM SOLENOID CONTROL
36	LT BLU/WHT	0.5	PC SOLENOID VALVE LOW
39	RED/BLK	0.5	PC SOLENOID VALVE HIGH
71	PPL	0.5	VSS LOW

4L60E TRANSMISSION

PIN #	COLOR	SIZE (MM²)	DESCRIPTION
A	LT GRN	0.5	1-2 SHIFT SOLENOID
B	YEL/BLK	0.5	2-3 SHIFT SOLENOID
C	RED/BLK	0.5	PC SOL VALVE HIGH
D	LT BLU/WHT	0.5	PC SOL VALVE LOW
E	PNK	0.8	12V IGNITION
L	YEL/BLK	0.5	TFT SENSOR SIGNAL
M	ORN/BLK	0.5	TFT SENSOR GROUND
N	PNK	0.5	RANGE SWITCH A SIGNAL
P	RED	0.5	RANGE SWITCH C SIGNAL
R	DK BLU	0.5	RANGE SWITCH B SIGNAL
S	WHT	0.5	3-2 SHIFT SOLENOID
T	TAN/BLK	0.5	TCC SOLENOID VALVE CONTROL
U	BRN	0.5	TCC PWM SOL VALVE CONTROL

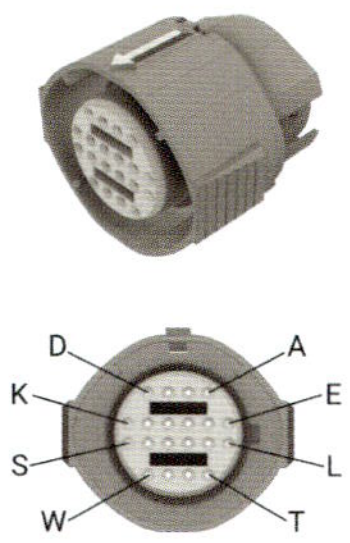

PNP/BACKUP SWITCH

PIN #	COLOR	SIZE (MM²)	DESCRIPTION
A	-	-	VEHICLE SPECIFIC
B	-	-	VEHICLE SPECIFIC
C	-	-	VEHICLE SPECIFIC
D	BLK/WHT	0.8	PNP SIGNAL GROUND
E	-	-	VEHICLE SPECIFIC
F	-	-	VEHICLE SPECIFIC
G	-	-	VEHICLE SPECIFIC

GROUNDS

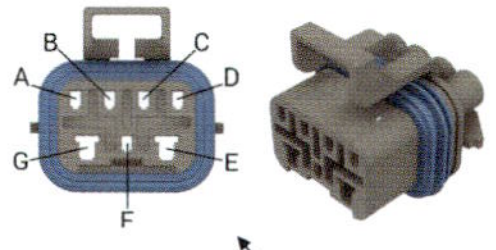

CORVETTE ONLY

PNP

PIN #	COLOR	SIZE (MM²)	DESCRIPTION
A	BLK/WHT	0.5	PRND A
B	GRY	0.5	PRND C
C	WHT	0.5	PRND P
D	YEL	0.5	PRND B

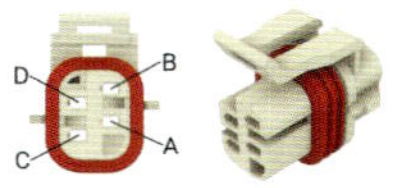

VSS

PIN #	COLOR	SIZE (MM²)	DESCRIPTION
A	PPL	0.5	VSS LOW
B	YEL	0.5	VSS HIGH

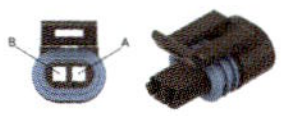

TWISTED PAIR

1997-1998 LS1 PCM (ENGINE COOLING – ELECTRIC FANS (LOW/HIGH SPEED))

LOW/HIGH SPEED OPERATION
PRODUCTION GM VEHICLES WITH TWO ELECTRIC FANS USE THREE RELAYS AND TWO PCM ENABLED "ON" SIGNALS FOR SERIES/PARALLEL OR LOW/HIGH SPEED OPERATION. WHEN THE PCM APPLIES GROUND TO THE LOW SPEED CONTROL, THE TWO FAN MOTORS OPERATE IN SERIES FOR LOW SPEED. WHEN THE PCM THEN APPLIES GROUND TO THE HIGH SPEED CONTROL, THE TWO FAN MOTORS OPERATE IN PARALLEL FOR HIGH SPEED.

ELECTRIC FAN MOTOR WIRE SIZE AND FUSE PROTECTION
IMPORTANT! BE SURE TO ASK YOUR ELECTRIC FAN MANUFACTURER FOR THEIR RECOMMENDED WIRE SIZE AND FUSE SIZE FOR SAFE OPERATION. USE RELAYS THAT ARE RATED FOR FAN MOTOR CURRENT.

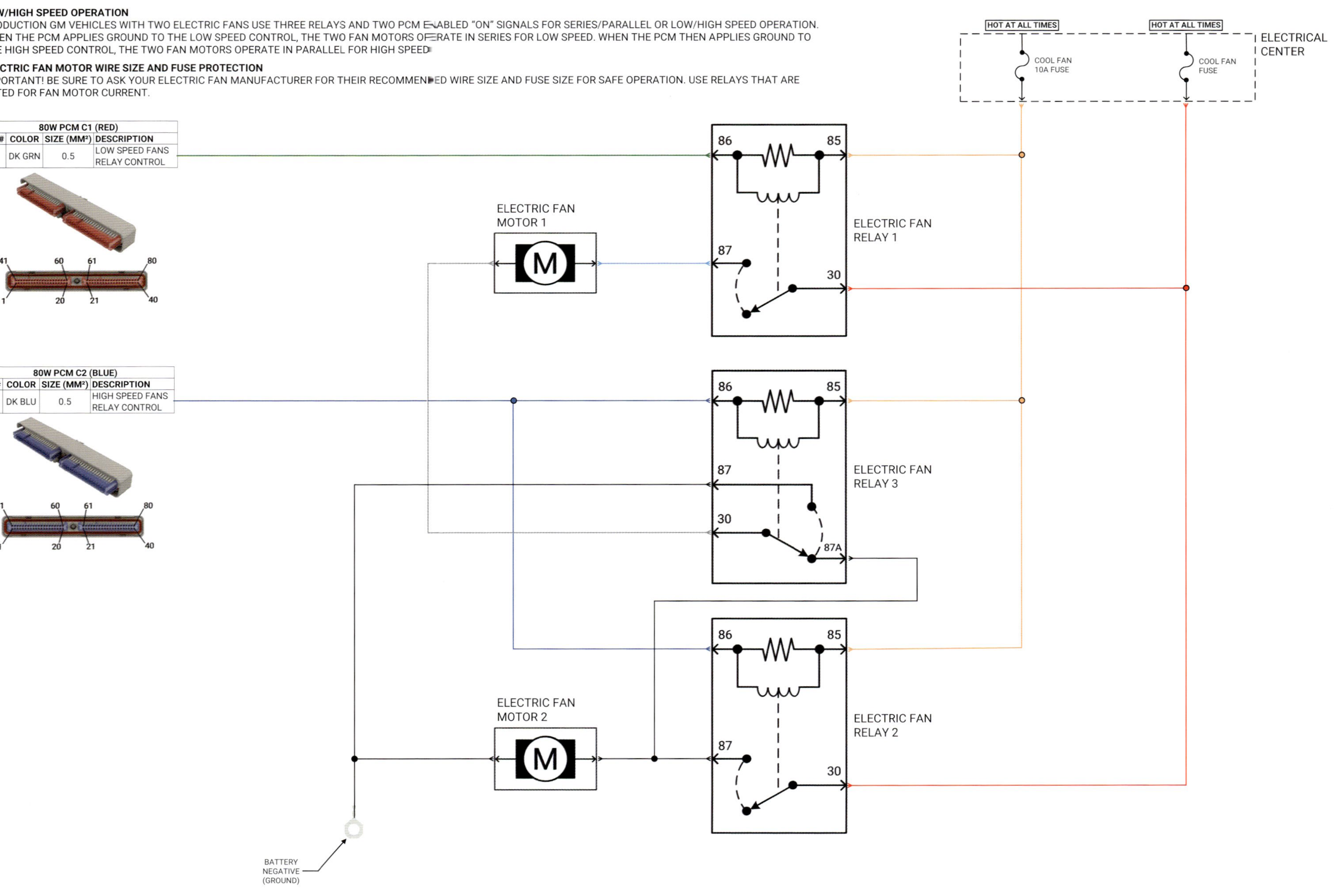

INDEPENDENT ON/OFF OPERATION
TWO ELECTRIC FANS CAN BE INDEPENDENTLY CONTROLLED THROUGH THE USE OF TWO RELAYS FOR ON/OFF (HIGH SPEED) OPERATION.

ELECTRIC FAN MOTOR WIRE SIZE AND FUSE PROTECTION
IMPORTANT! BE SURE TO ASK YOUR ELECTRIC FAN MANUFACTURER FOR THEIR RECOMMENDED WIRE SIZE AND FUSE SIZE FOR SAFE OPERATION. USE RELAYS THAT ARE RATED FOR FAN MOTOR CURRENT.

ELECTRICAL CENTER

HOT AT ALL TIMES

COOL FAN FUSE

COOL FAN 10A FUSE

ELECTRIC FAN RELAY 1

ELECTRIC FAN RELAY 2

ELECTRIC FAN MOTOR 1

ELECTRIC FAN MOTOR 2

BATTERY NEGATIVE (GROUND)

80W PCM C1 (RED)

PIN #	COLOR	SIZE (MM²)	DESCRIPTION
43	DK GRN	0.5	FAN 1 RELAY CONTROL

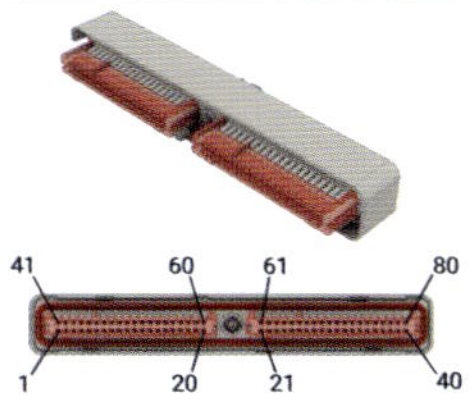

80W PCM C2 (BLUE)

PIN #	COLOR	SIZE (MM²)	DESCRIPTION
28	DK BLU	0.5	FAN 2 RELAY CONTROL

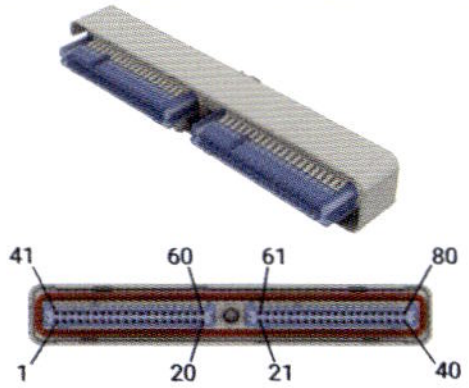

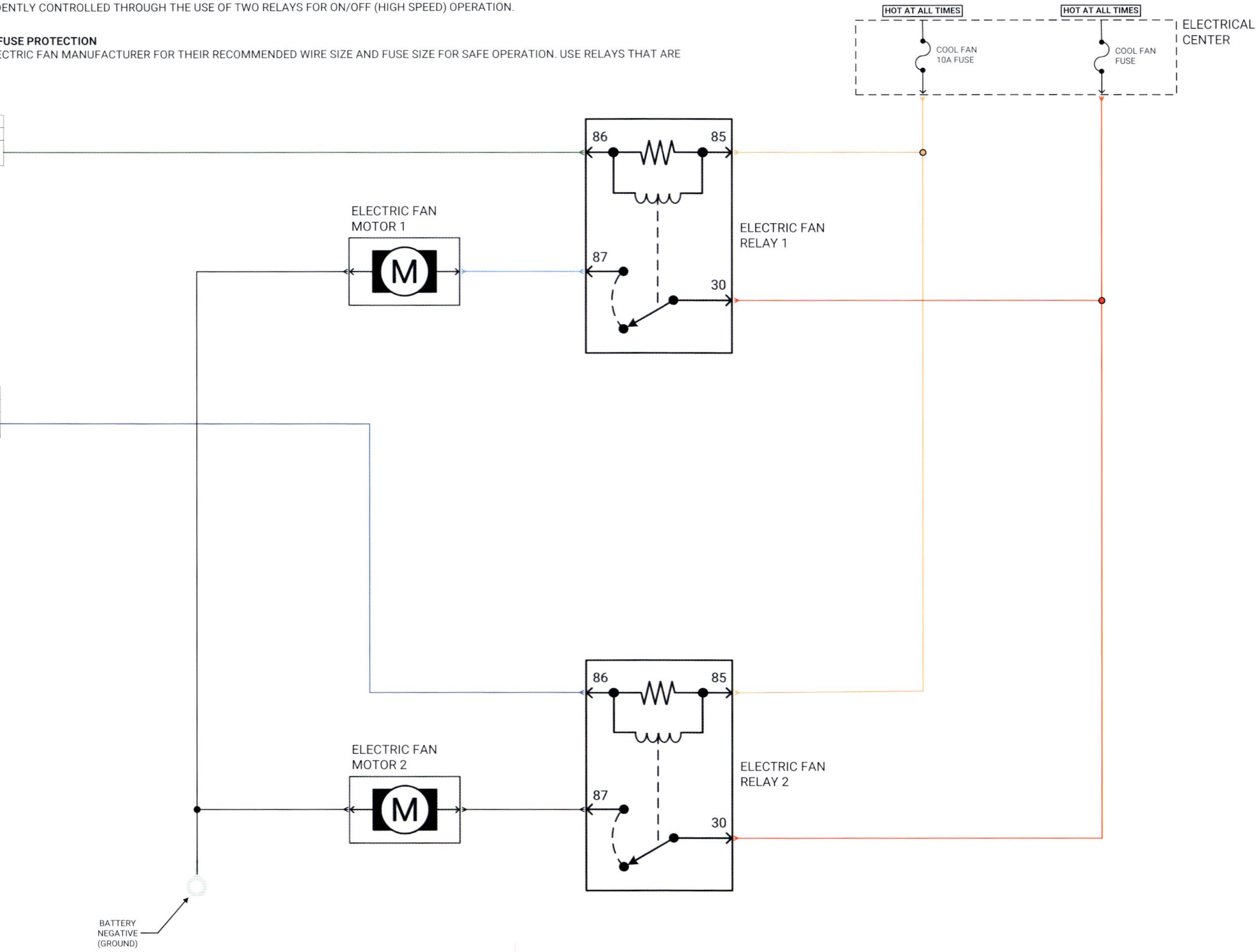

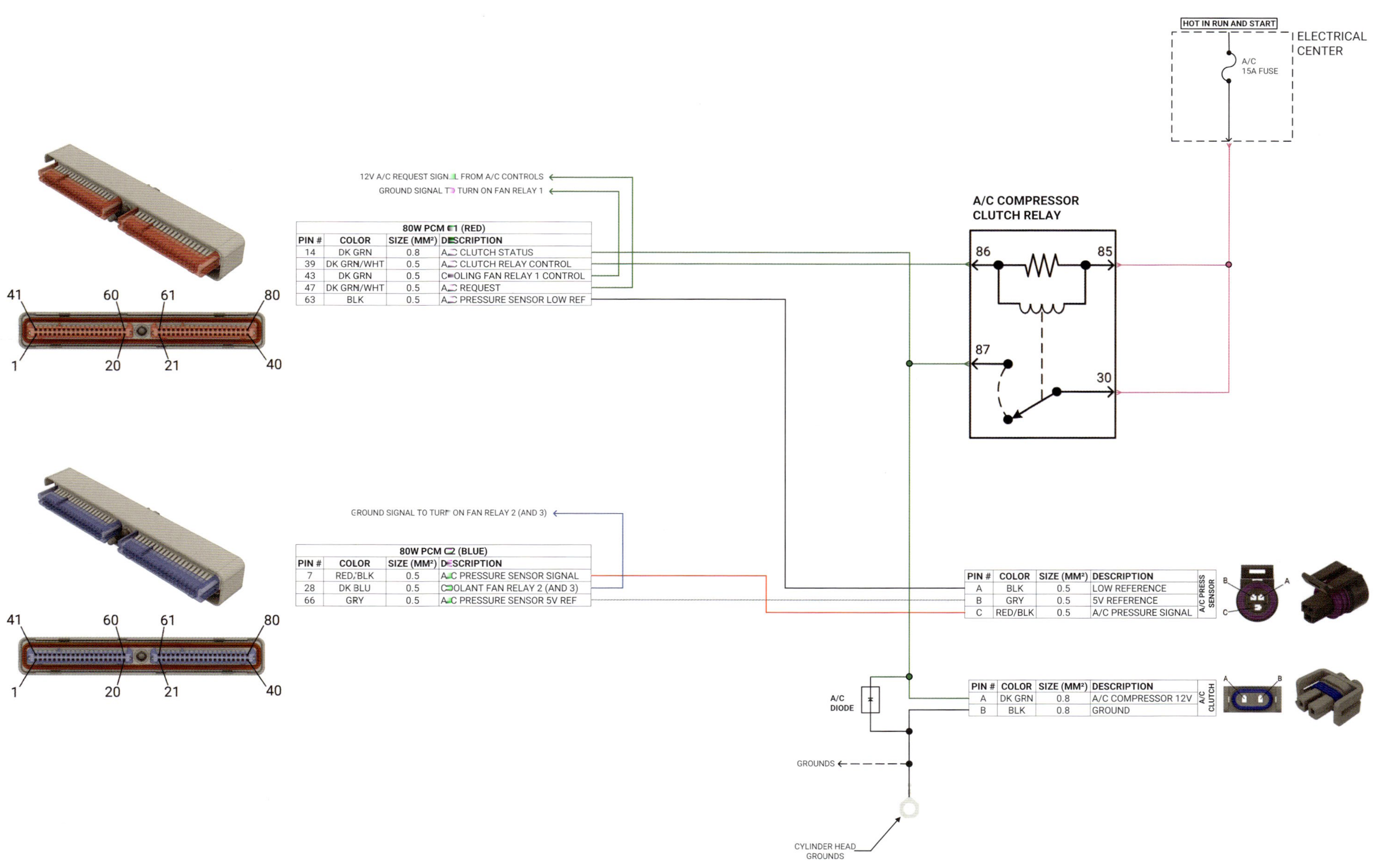

80W PCM C1 (RED)

PIN #	COLOR	SIZE (MM²)	DESCRIPTION
14	DK GRN	0.8	A/C CLUTCH STATUS
39	DK GRN/WHT	0.5	A/C CLUTCH RELAY CONTROL
43	DK GRN	0.5	COOLING FAN RELAY 1 CONTROL
47	DK GRN/WHT	0.5	A/C REQUEST
63	BLK	0.5	A/C PRESSURE SENSOR LOW REF

80W PCM C2 (BLUE)

PIN #	COLOR	SIZE (MM²)	DESCRIPTION
7	RED/BLK	0.5	A/C PRESSURE SENSOR SIGNAL
28	DK BLU	0.5	COOLANT FAN RELAY 2 (AND 3)
66	GRY	0.5	A/C PRESSURE SENSOR 5V REF

A/C PRESS SENSOR

PIN #	COLOR	SIZE (MM²)	DESCRIPTION
A	BLK	0.5	LOW REFERENCE
B	GRY	0.5	5V REFERENCE
C	RED/BLK	0.5	A/C PRESSURE SIGNAL

A/C CLUTCH

PIN #	COLOR	SIZE (MM²)	DESCRIPTION
A	DK GRN	0.8	A/C COMPRESSOR 12V
B	BLK	0.8	GROUND

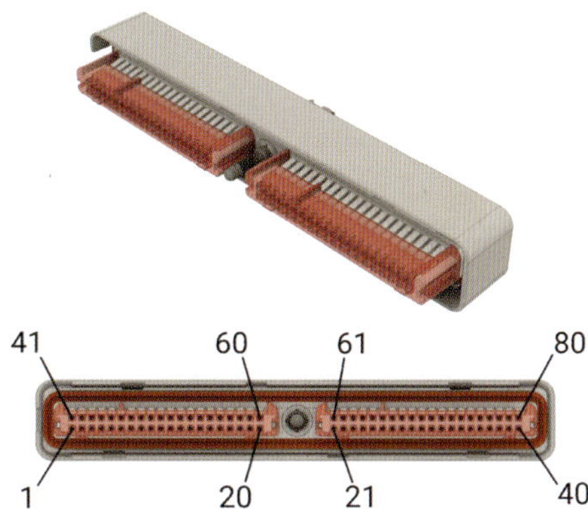

80W PCM C1 (RED)					
PIN #	COLOR	SIZE (MM²)	SIGNAL	I/O	DESCRIPTION
14	DK GRN	0.8	12V	INPUT	A/C STATUS
32	ORN/BLK	0.5	GROUND	INPUT	PARK/NEUTRAL INDICATOR
37	BRN/WHT	0.5	GROUND	OUTPUT	MALFUNCTION INDICATOR LAMP
43	DK GRN	0.5	GROUND	OUTPUT	FAN RELAY 1 CONTROL
47	DK GRN/WHT	0.5	12V	INPUT	A/C REQUEST
55	DK GRN/WHT	0.5	-	OUTPUT	VSS OUTPUT (SPEEDOMETER)
68	GRY	0.5	12V	INPUT	CLUTCH PEDAL SWITCH
77	PPL	0.5	12V	INPUT	TCC/BRAKE SWITCH

12V SIGNAL FROM A/C COMPRESSOR CLUTCH – INDICATES A/C CLUTCH HAS 12V

GROUND SIGNAL FROM P/N SWITCH – INDICATES AUTOMATIC TRANSMISSION IS IN PARK OR NEUTRAL

GROUND SIGNAL TO MIL LAMP – ILLUMINATES 12V LAMP WHEN DTC(S) ARE PRESENT

GROUND SIGNAL TO FAN RELAY COIL

12V SIGNAL FROM A/C CONTROLS – INDICATES A/C IS REQUESTED ON BY OPERATOR

VEHICLE SPEED SIGNAL FOR SPEEDOMETER – PULSE COUNT CONFIGURABLE WITHIN PCM CALIBRATION

12V SIGNAL FROM CLUTCH PEDAL SWITCH – 12V WITHOUT CLUTCH PEDAL DEPRESSED (EXCEPT CAMARO/FIREBIRD)

12V SIGNAL FROM BRAKE SWITCH – 12V TO PCM WITHOUT BRAKE PEDAL DEPRESSED

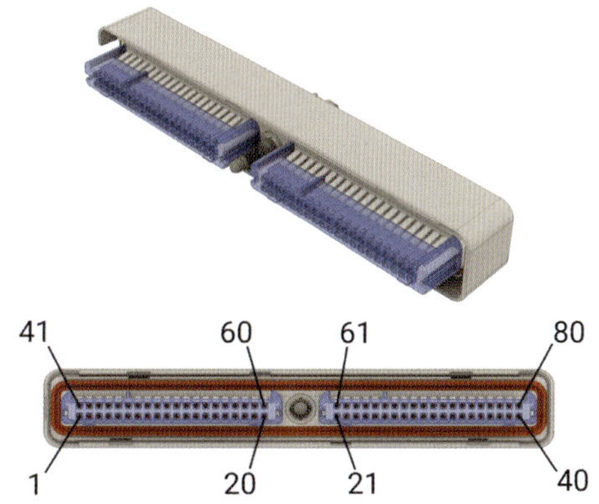

80W PCM C2 (BLUE)					
PIN #	COLOR	SIZE (MM²)	SIGNAL	I/O	DESCRIPTION
28	DK BLU	0.5	GROUND	OUTPUT	FAN RELAY 2 (AND 3) CONTROL
35	WHT	0.8	-	OUTPUT	ENGINE SPEED (TACHOMETER)
37	DK GRN/WHT	0.5	12V	OUTPUT	FUEL PUMP RELAY CONTROL

GROUND SIGNAL TO FAN RELAY COIL (CONTROLS HIGH/LOW SPEED W/ THREE RELAYS)

ENGINE SPEED SIGNAL FOR TACHOMETER – CONFIGURABLE WITHIN PCM CALIBRATION

12V SIGNAL TO FUEL PUMP RELAY COIL – TURNS ON FUEL PUMP

THE 1999–2002 P01 PCM

The LS-series engines gained significant momentum in 1999 with the addition of the 4.8L, 5.3L, and 6.0L engines. The 4L80E transmission and 5-speed manual transmission were also introduced with the new generation bodystyle of GM truck. By 2000, an additional electronic throttle system was available with well-equipped trucks and SUVs.

LS-equipped vehicles from 1999 to 2000 were fitted with the GM number 09354896 PCM. While this PCM shares the same harness connectors as the 1997–1998 LS1 PCM, it is a mistake to use the 1997–1998 harness with the 1999–2000 PCM because the pinouts are completely different.

Additionally, GM now referred to the connector with blue retainers as C1 and the connector with red retainers as C2. The GM number 09354896 PCM was replaced with GM number 12200411 PCM in 2001. The GM number 12200411 PCM has become incredibly popular because it supports 1996-and-newer V-6 and V-8 single-coil and distributor ignition systems as well as the LS coil-per-cylinder ignition system. All 1999–2002 LS PCMs are known as P01 controllers. The only vehicle to receive the GM number 12200411 P01 PCM beyond model year 2002 was the 2003 Corvette.

The LS engine had no significant electrical component changes, so the P01 PCM is fully capable of controlling the 1997–1998 LS1 engines with the correct engine wire harness and PCM calibration. The 4L80E transmission is wired similarly to the 4L60E transmission but not directly interchangeable. Also, be sure to watch out for minor differences between the Corvette and truck electronic throttle systems.

All P01 PCMs are supported by popular tuning software, such as EFILive and HP Tuners. Many enthusiasts choose a P01 PCM when planning an LS engine conversion with cable throttle because the Camaro, Firebird, and many truck calibrations are configured for an idle air motor and throttle position sensor (TPS). While the PCM can easily be reprogrammed for an electronic throttle system, the limited availability of early electronic throttle bodies and throttle actuator control (TAC) modules may be a deterrent.

The following schematics are an excellent reference when servicing a used engine wire harness or while building a stand-alone engine wire harness. I went further than the details of GM schematics to show engine data sensor interchangeability. When choosing a newer MAF, MAP, or HO_2S sensor, these schematics reveal any variation in pinout details.

Additionally, if you are working with any aftermarket stand-alone engine wire harness, you can expect to have a thorough understanding of the harness by referencing the following schematics.

Quick Reference	
Topic	**Page**
Power, Ground, and Data Communications	59
Charging - Generator Controls	60
Engine Data Sensors - ECT, IAT, MAP, and MAF	61
Engine Data Sensors - HO2S	62
Ignition Controls - CKP, CMP, KS1, and KS2	63
Inputs/Outputs	63
Ignition Controls - Ignition Coils	64
Fuel Controls - EV1 Fuel Injectors	65
Fuel Controls - Multec 2 Fuel Injectors	66
Fuel Controls - Fuel Pump and EVAP Purge Solenoid	67
Throttle System - Cable	68
Throttle System - Electric (Corvette)	69
Throttle System - Electric (Truck/SUV)	70
Transmission - T56 6-Speed Manual	71
Transmission - Truck Manual	72
Transmission - 4L60E Automatic	73
Transmission - 4L80E Automatic	74
Engine Cooling - Electric Fans Low/High Speed	75
Engine Cooling - Electric Fans On/Off	76
HVAC - A/C Compressor Controls	77

1999-2002 P01 PCM (POWER, GROUND, DATA COMMUNICATION)

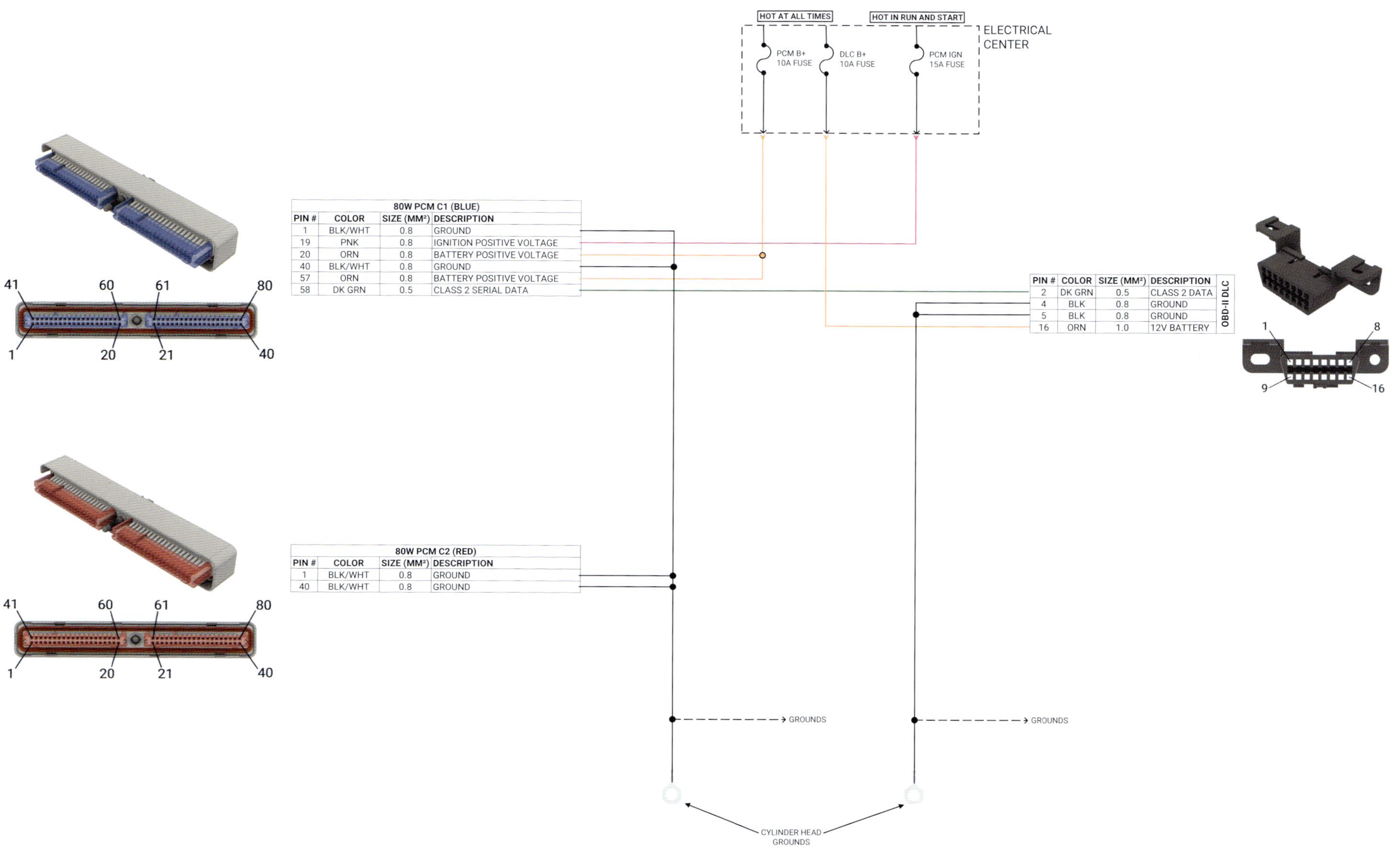

80W PCM C1 (BLUE)			
PIN #	COLOR	SIZE (MM²)	DESCRIPTION
1	BLK/WHT	0.8	GROUND
19	PNK	0.8	IGNITION POSITIVE VOLTAGE
20	ORN	0.8	BATTERY POSITIVE VOLTAGE
40	BLK/WHT	0.8	GROUND
57	ORN	0.8	BATTERY POSITIVE VOLTAGE
58	DK GRN	0.5	CLASS 2 SERIAL DATA

80W PCM C2 (RED)			
PIN #	COLOR	SIZE (MM²)	DESCRIPTION
1	BLK/WHT	0.8	GROUND
40	BLK/WHT	0.8	GROUND

OBD-II DLC			
PIN #	COLOR	SIZE (MM²)	DESCRIPTION
2	DK GRN	0.5	CLASS 2 DATA
4	BLK	0.8	GROUND
5	BLK	0.8	GROUND
16	ORN	1.0	12V BATTERY

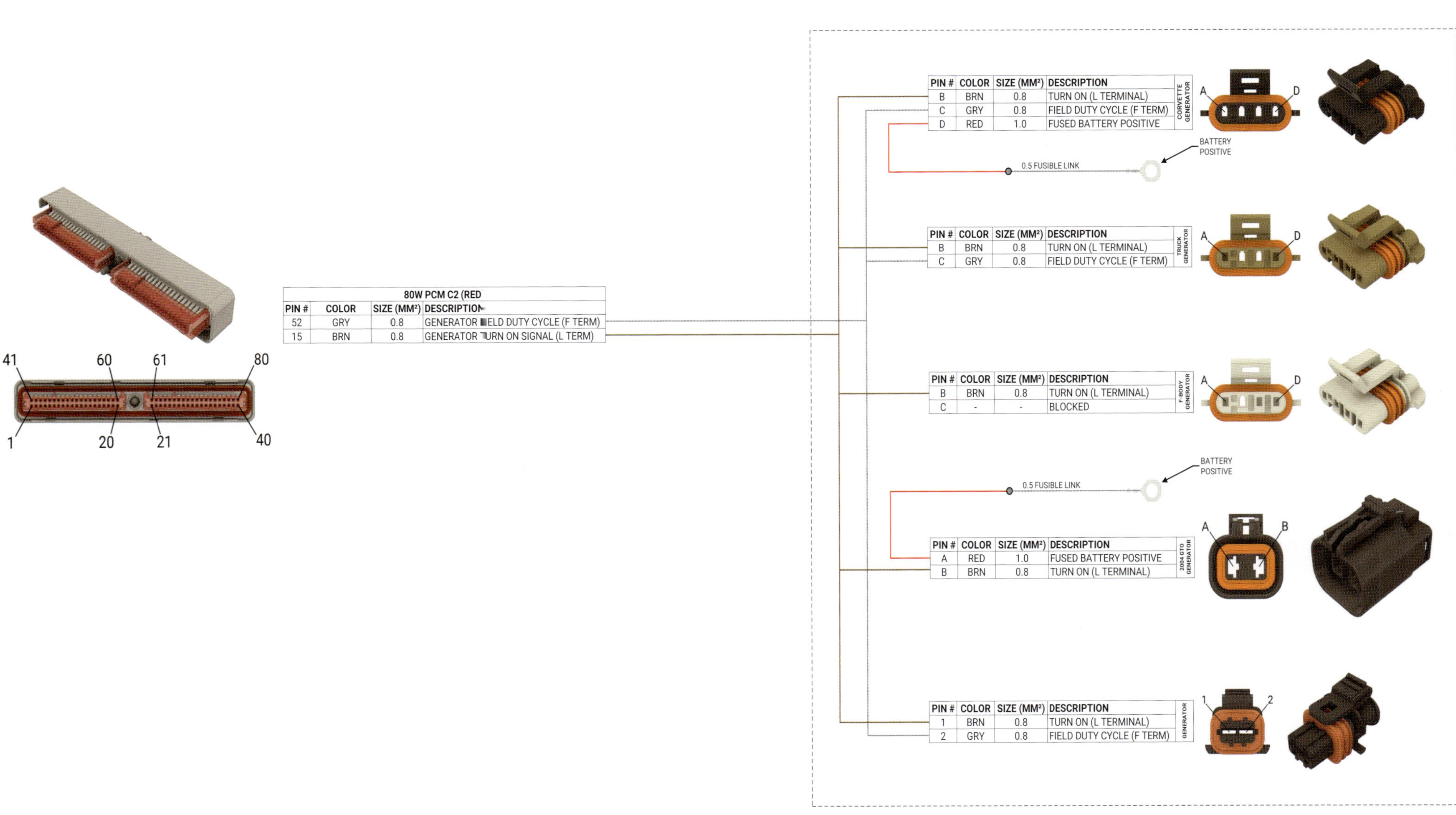

80W PCM C2 (RED

PIN #	COLOR	SIZE (MM²)	DESCRIPTION
52	GRY	0.8	GENERATOR FIELD DUTY CYCLE (F TERM)
15	BRN	0.8	GENERATOR TURN ON SIGNAL (L TERM)

CORVETTE GENERATOR

PIN #	COLOR	SIZE (MM²)	DESCRIPTION
B	BRN	0.8	TURN ON (L TERMINAL)
C	GRY	0.8	FIELD DUTY CYCLE (F TERM)
D	RED	1.0	FUSED BATTERY POSITIVE

TRUCK GENERATOR

PIN #	COLOR	SIZE (MM²)	DESCRIPTION
B	BRN	0.8	TURN ON (L TERMINAL)
C	GRY	0.8	FIELD DUTY CYCLE (F TERM)

F-BODY GENERATOR

PIN #	COLOR	SIZE (MM²)	DESCRIPTION
B	BRN	0.8	TURN ON (L TERMINAL)
C	-	-	BLOCKED

2004 GTO GENERATOR

PIN #	COLOR	SIZE (MM²)	DESCRIPTION
A	RED	1.0	FUSED BATTERY POSITIVE
B	BRN	0.8	TURN ON (L TERMINAL)

GENERATOR

PIN #	COLOR	SIZE (MM²)	DESCRIPTION
1	BRN	0.8	TURN ON (L TERMINAL)
2	GRY	0.8	FIELD DUTY CYCLE (F TERM)

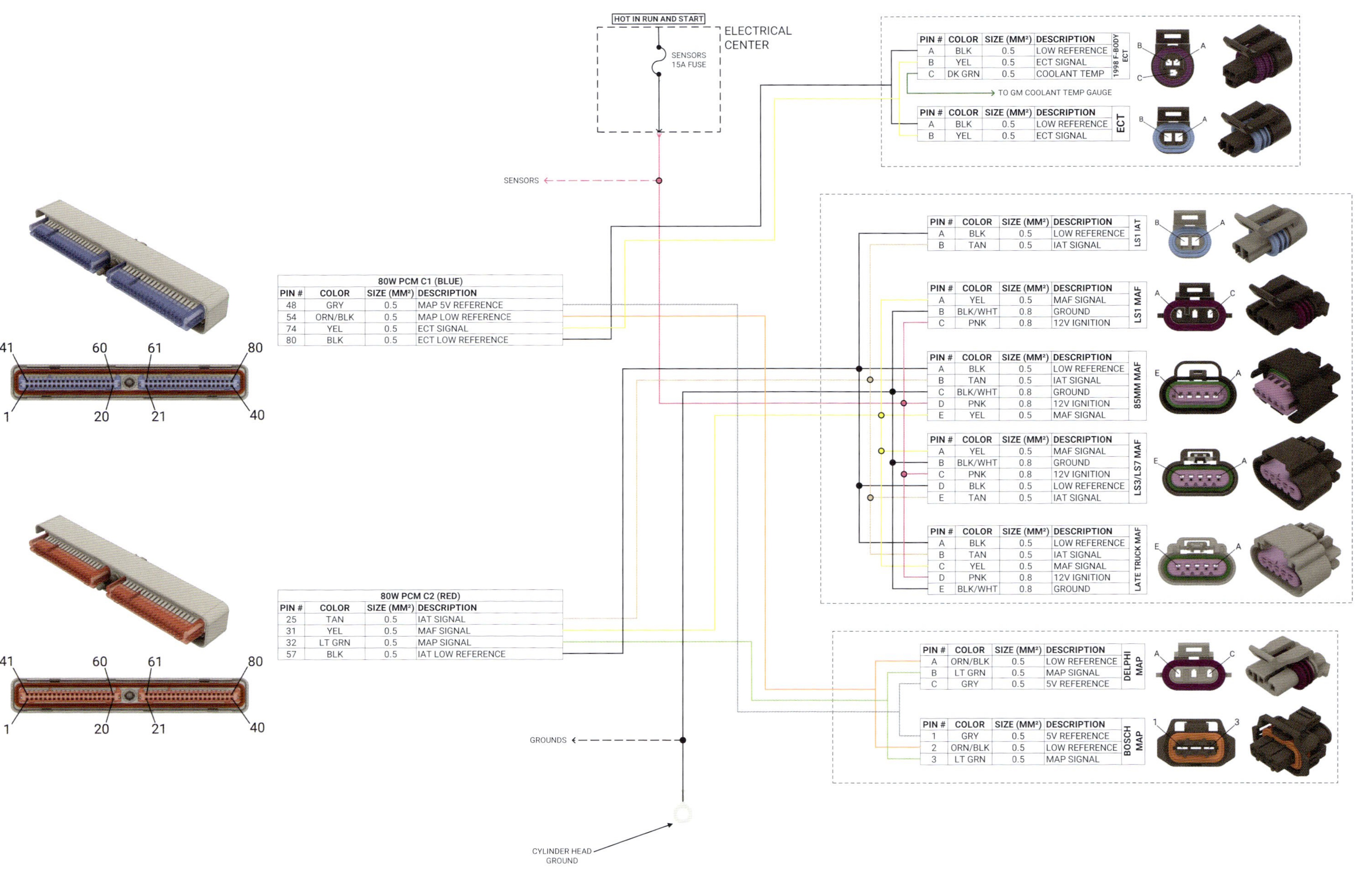

1998 F-BODY ECT

PIN #	COLOR	SIZE (MM²)	DESCRIPTION
A	BLK	0.5	LOW REFERENCE
B	YEL	0.5	ECT SIGNAL
C	DK GRN	0.5	COOLANT TEMP → TO GM COOLANT TEMP GAUGE

ECT

PIN #	COLOR	SIZE (MM²)	DESCRIPTION
A	BLK	0.5	LOW REFERENCE
B	YEL	0.5	ECT SIGNAL

LS1 IAT

PIN #	COLOR	SIZE (MM²)	DESCRIPTION
A	BLK	0.5	LOW REFERENCE
B	TAN	0.5	IAT SIGNAL

LS1 MAF

PIN #	COLOR	SIZE (MM²)	DESCRIPTION
A	YEL	0.5	MAF SIGNAL
B	BLK/WHT	0.8	GROUND
C	PNK	0.8	12V IGNITION

85MM MAF

PIN #	COLOR	SIZE (MM²)	DESCRIPTION
A	BLK	0.5	LOW REFERENCE
B	TAN	0.5	IAT SIGNAL
C	BLK/WHT	0.8	GROUND
D	PNK	0.8	12V IGNITION
E	YEL	0.5	MAF SIGNAL

LS3/LS7 MAF

PIN #	COLOR	SIZE (MM²)	DESCRIPTION
A	YEL	0.5	MAF SIGNAL
B	BLK/WHT	0.8	GROUND
C	PNK	0.8	12V IGNITION
D	BLK	0.5	LOW REFERENCE
E	TAN	0.5	IAT SIGNAL

LATE TRUCK MAF

PIN #	COLOR	SIZE (MM²)	DESCRIPTION
A	BLK	0.5	LOW REFERENCE
B	TAN	0.5	IAT SIGNAL
C	YEL	0.5	MAF SIGNAL
D	PNK	0.8	12V IGNITION
E	BLK/WHT	0.8	GROUND

DELPHI MAP

PIN #	COLOR	SIZE (MM²)	DESCRIPTION
A	ORN/BLK	0.5	LOW REFERENCE
B	LT GRN	0.5	MAP SIGNAL
C	GRY	0.5	5V REFERENCE

BOSCH MAP

PIN #	COLOR	SIZE (MM²)	DESCRIPTION
1	GRY	0.5	5V REFERENCE
2	ORN/BLK	0.5	LOW REFERENCE
3	LT GRN	0.5	MAP SIGNAL

80W PCM C1 (BLUE)

PIN #	COLOR	SIZE (MM²)	DESCRIPTION
48	GRY	0.5	MAP 5V REFERENCE
54	ORN/BLK	0.5	MAP LOW REFERENCE
74	YEL	0.5	ECT SIGNAL
80	BLK	0.5	ECT LOW REFERENCE

80W PCM C2 (RED)

PIN #	COLOR	SIZE (MM²)	DESCRIPTION
25	TAN	0.5	IAT SIGNAL
31	YEL	0.5	MAF SIGNAL
32	LT GRN	0.5	MAP SIGNAL
57	BLK	0.5	IAT LOW REFERENCE

ELECTRICAL CENTER

HOT IN RUN AND START

SENSORS 15A FUSE

SENSORS

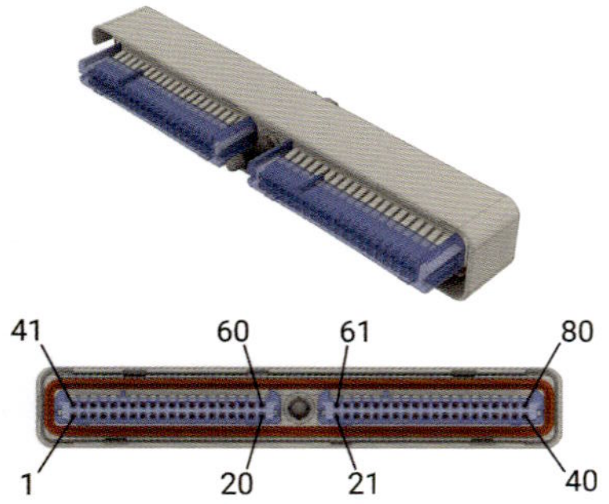

80W PCM C1 (BLUE)			
PIN #	COLOR	SIZE (MM²)	DESCRIPTION
25	TAN	0.8	HO2S LOW BANK 2 SENSOR 2
26	TAN	0.8	HO2S LOW BANK 2 SENSOR 1
28	TAN/WHT	0.8	HO2S LOW BANK 1 SENSOR 2
29	TAN/WHT	0.8	HO2S LOW BANK 1 SENSOR 1
65	PPL	0.8	HO2S HIGH BANK 2 SENSOR 2
66	PPL	0.8	HO2S HIGH BANK 2 SENSOR 1
68	PPL/WHT	0.8	HO2S HIGH BANK 1 SENSOR 2
69	PPL/WHT	0.8	HO2S HIGH BANK 1 SENSOR 1

41 60 61 80
1 20 21 40

PIN #	COLOR	SIZE (MM²)	DESCRIPTION	HO2S BANK 1 SENSOR 1 (LEFT FRONT)
A	TAN/WHT	0.8	HO2S LOW	
B	PPL/WHT	0.8	HO2S HIGH	
C or E	BLK	0.8	HEATER CONTROL LOW	
D	PNK	0.8	HEATER CONTROL 12V	

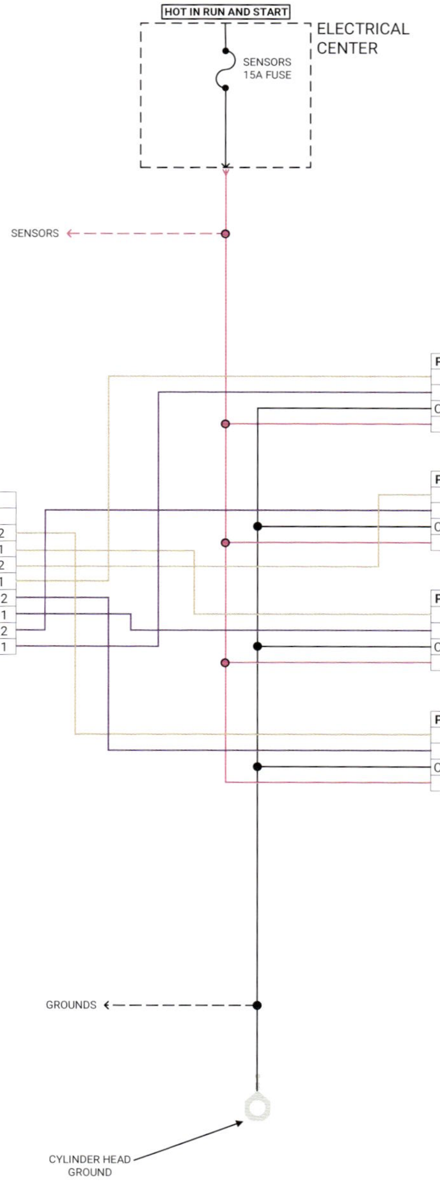

PIN #	COLOR	SIZE (MM²)	DESCRIPTION	HO2S BANK 1 SENSOR 2 (LEFT REAR)
A	TAN/WHT	0.8	HO2S LOW	
B	PPL/WHT	0.8	HO2S HIGH	
C or E	BLK	0.8	HEATER CONTROL LOW	
D	PNK	0.8	HEATER CONTROL 12V	

PIN #	COLOR	SIZE (MM²)	DESCRIPTION	HO2S BANK 2 SENSOR 1 (RIGHT FRONT)
A	TAN	0.8	HO2S LOW	
B	PPL	0.8	HO2S HIGH	
C or E	BLK	0.8	HEATER CONTROL LOW	
D	PNK	0.8	HEATER CONTROL 12V	

PIN #	COLOR	SIZE (MM²)	DESCRIPTION	HO2S BANK 2 SENSOR 2 (RIGHT REAR)
A	TAN	0.8	HO2S LOW	
B	PPL	0.8	HO2S HIGH	
C or E	BLK	0.8	HEATER CONTROL LOW	
D	PNK	0.8	HEATER CONTROL 12V	

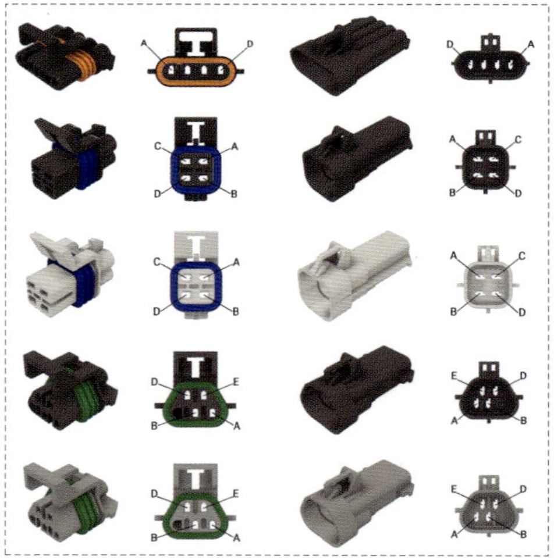

ALTHOUGH TEN DIFFERENT HARNESS CONNECTORS ARE USED AMONG LS ENGINE OXYGEN SENSORS, THEY SHARE THE SAME CONNECTOR CAVITY ASSIGNMENTS.

ONLY FOUR WIRES ARE USED WITH EACH OXYGEN SENSOR. CONNECTORS WITH FIVE CAVITIES BLOCK CAVITY C AND MOVE THE TYPICAL USE OF CAVITY C TO CAVITY E.

THE HEATER LOW CIRCUIT IS NOT ALWAYS CONTROLLED AND MONITORED BY THE PCM OR ECM. WHEN THE HEATER LOW CIRCUIT IS INSTALLED DIRECTLY TO GROUND, THE HEATER CIRCUIT IS NOT MONITORED FOR DIAGNOSTIC (DTC) PURPOSES.

GROUNDS

CYLINDER HEAD GROUND

1999-2002 P01 PCM (IGNITION CONTROLS – CKP, CMP, KS1, KS2)

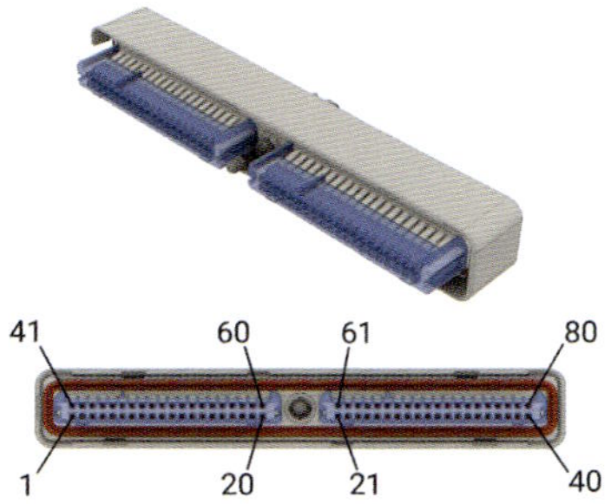

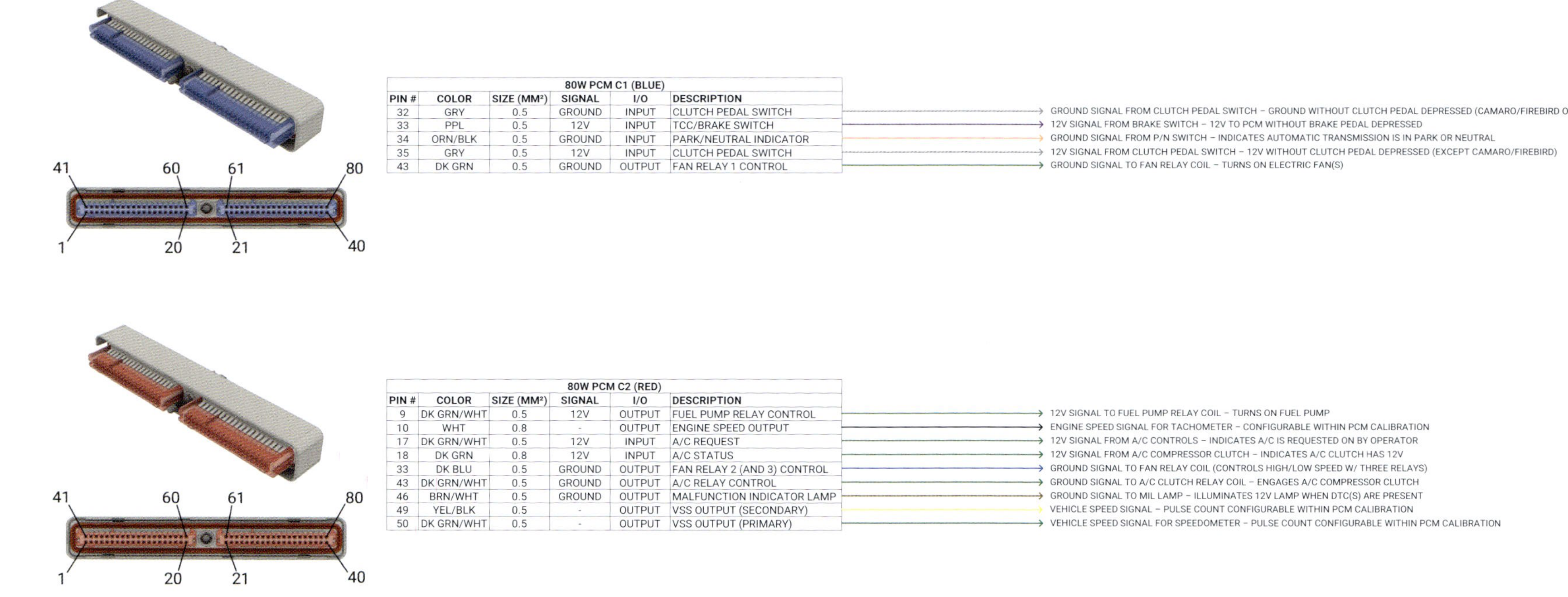

80W PCM C1 (BLUE)			
PIN #	COLOR	SIZE (MM²)	DESCRIPTION
2	LT GRN	0.5	CKP SENSOR 12V REFERENCE
11	LT BLU	0.5	KS SIGNAL REAR
12	DK BLU/WHT	0.5	CKP SENSOR SIGNAL
21	YEL/BLK	0.5	CKP SENSOR LOW REFERENCE
51	DK BLU	0.5	KS SIGNAL FRONT
61	PNK/BLK	0.5	CMP SENSOR LOW REFERENCE
73	BRN/WHT	0.5	CMP SENSOR SIGNAL

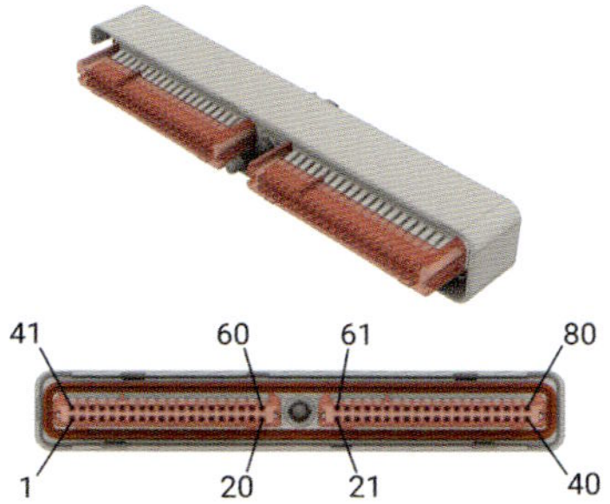

80W PCM C2 (RED)			
PIN #	COLOR	SIZE (MM²)	DESCRIPTION
39	RED	0.5	CMP SENSOR 12V REFERENCE

PIN #	COLOR	SIZE (MM²)	DESCRIPTION	
A	DK BLU/WHT	0.5	CKP SIGNAL	24X CRANK
B	YEL/BLK	0.5	LOW REFERENCE	
C	LT GRN	0.5	12V REFERENCE	

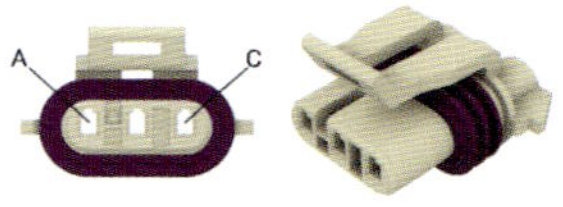

PIN #	COLOR	SIZE (MM²)	DESCRIPTION	
A	BRN/WHT	0.5	CMP SIGNAL	1X CAM (GEN III)
B	PNK/BLK	0.5	LOW REFERENCE	
C	RED	0.5	12V REFERENCE	

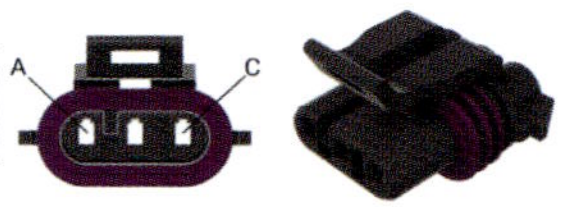

PIN #	COLOR	SIZE (MM²)	DESCRIPTION	
A	DK BLU	0.5	KS SIGNAL FRONT	KS1/KS2
B	LT BLU	0.5	KS SIGNAL REAR	

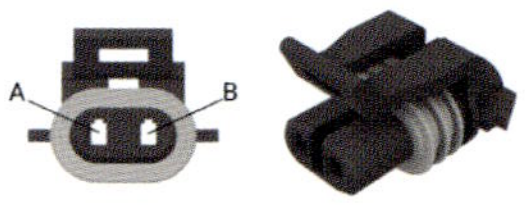

TO KNOCK SENSOR SUB HARNESS

1999-2002 P01 PCM (INPUTS/OUTPUTS)

80W PCM C1 (BLUE)					
PIN #	COLOR	SIZE (MM²)	SIGNAL	I/O	DESCRIPTION
32	GRY	0.5	GROUND	INPUT	CLUTCH PEDAL SWITCH
33	PPL	0.5	12V	INPUT	TCC/BRAKE SWITCH
34	ORN/BLK	0.5	GROUND	INPUT	PARK/NEUTRAL INDICATOR
35	GRY	0.5	12V	INPUT	CLUTCH PEDAL SWITCH
43	DK GRN	0.5	GROUND	OUTPUT	FAN RELAY 1 CONTROL

- GROUND SIGNAL FROM CLUTCH PEDAL SWITCH – GROUND WITHOUT CLUTCH PEDAL DEPRESSED (CAMARO/FIREBIRD ONLY)
- 12V SIGNAL FROM BRAKE SWITCH – 12V TO PCM WITHOUT BRAKE PEDAL DEPRESSED
- GROUND SIGNAL FROM P/N SWITCH – INDICATES AUTOMATIC TRANSMISSION IS IN PARK OR NEUTRAL
- 12V SIGNAL FROM CLUTCH PEDAL SWITCH – 12V WITHOUT CLUTCH PEDAL DEPRESSED (EXCEPT CAMARO/FIREBIRD)
- GROUND SIGNAL TO FAN RELAY COIL – TURNS ON ELECTRIC FAN(S)

80W PCM C2 (RED)					
PIN #	COLOR	SIZE (MM²)	SIGNAL	I/O	DESCRIPTION
9	DK GRN/WHT	0.5	12V	OUTPUT	FUEL PUMP RELAY CONTROL
10	WHT	0.8	-	OUTPUT	ENGINE SPEED OUTPUT
17	DK GRN/WHT	0.5	12V	INPUT	A/C REQUEST
18	DK GRN	0.8	12V	INPUT	A/C STATUS
33	DK BLU	0.5	GROUND	OUTPUT	FAN RELAY 2 (AND 3) CONTROL
43	DK GRN/WHT	0.5	GROUND	OUTPUT	A/C RELAY CONTROL
46	BRN/WHT	0.5	GROUND	OUTPUT	MALFUNCTION INDICATOR LAMP
49	YEL/BLK	0.5	-	OUTPUT	VSS OUTPUT (SECONDARY)
50	DK GRN/WHT	0.5	-	OUTPUT	VSS OUTPUT (PRIMARY)

- 12V SIGNAL TO FUEL PUMP RELAY COIL – TURNS ON FUEL PUMP
- ENGINE SPEED SIGNAL FOR TACHOMETER – CONFIGURABLE WITHIN PCM CALIBRATION
- 12V SIGNAL FROM A/C CONTROLS – INDICATES A/C IS REQUESTED ON BY OPERATOR
- 12V SIGNAL FROM A/C COMPRESSOR CLUTCH – INDICATES A/C CLUTCH HAS 12V
- GROUND SIGNAL TO FAN RELAY COIL (CONTROLS HIGH/LOW SPEED W/ THREE RELAYS)
- GROUND SIGNAL TO A/C CLUTCH RELAY COIL – ENGAGES A/C COMPRESSOR CLUTCH
- GROUND SIGNAL TO MIL LAMP – ILLUMINATES 12V LAMP WHEN DTC(S) ARE PRESENT
- VEHICLE SPEED SIGNAL – PULSE COUNT CONFIGURABLE WITHIN PCM CALIBRATION
- VEHICLE SPEED SIGNAL FOR SPEEDOMETER – PULSE COUNT CONFIGURABLE WITHIN PCM CALIBRATION

1999-2002 P01 PCM (IGNITION CONTROLS – IGNITION COILS)

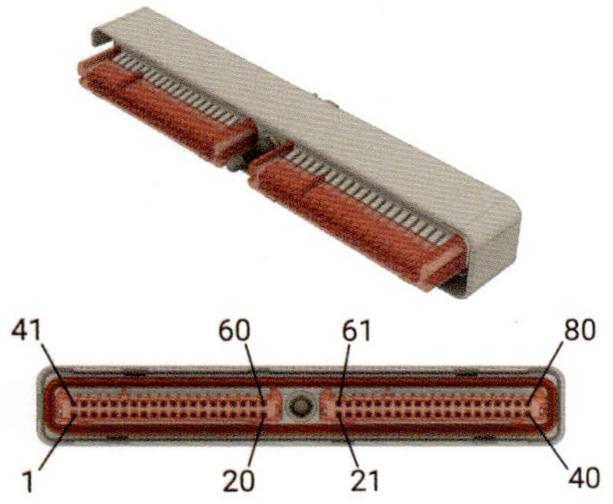

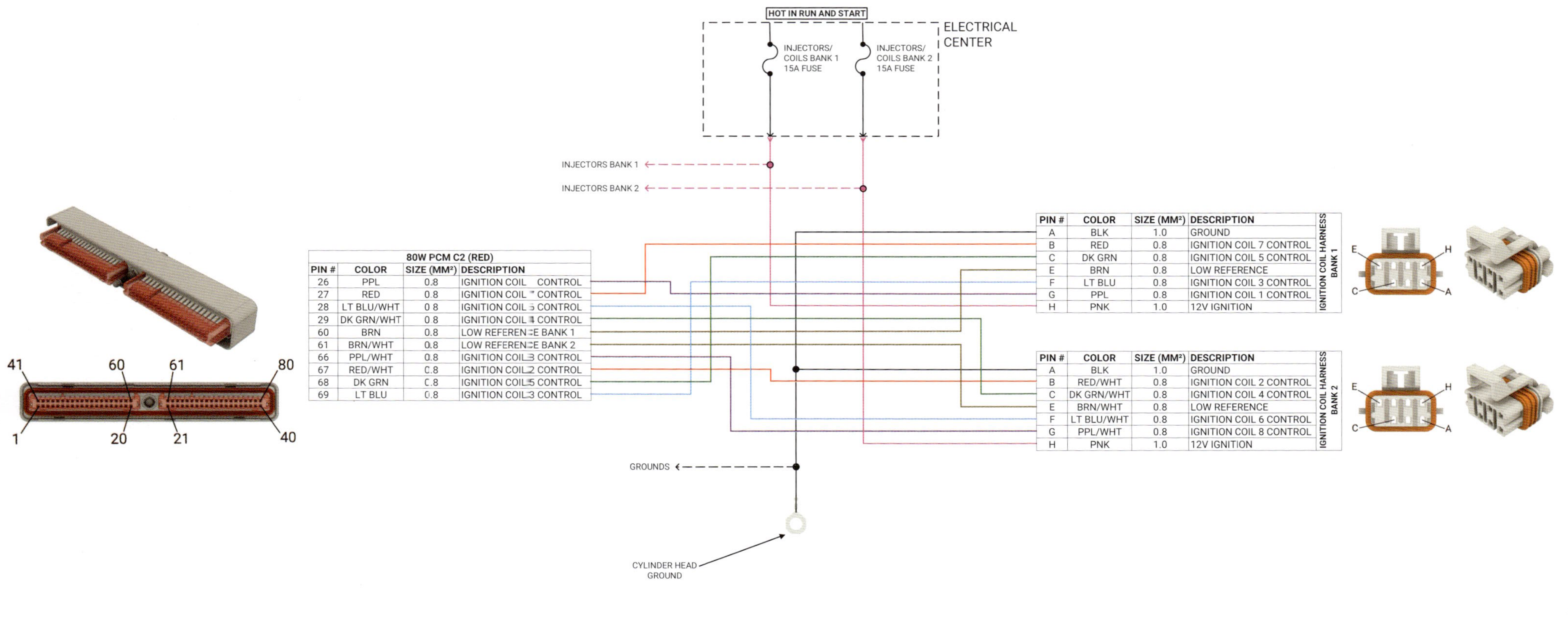

80W PCM C2 (RED)			
PIN #	COLOR	SIZE (MM²)	DESCRIPTION
26	PPL	0.8	IGNITION COIL [illegible] CONTROL
27	RED	0.8	IGNITION COIL [illegible] CONTROL
28	LT BLU/WHT	0.8	IGNITION COIL [illegible] CONTROL
29	DK GRN/WHT	0.8	IGNITION COIL 4 CONTROL
60	BRN	0.8	LOW REFERENCE BANK 1
61	BRN/WHT	0.8	LOW REFERENCE BANK 2
66	PPL/WHT	0.8	IGNITION COIL 3 CONTROL
67	RED/WHT	0.8	IGNITION COIL 2 CONTROL
68	DK GRN	0.8	IGNITION COIL 5 CONTROL
69	LT BLU	0.8	IGNITION COIL 3 CONTROL

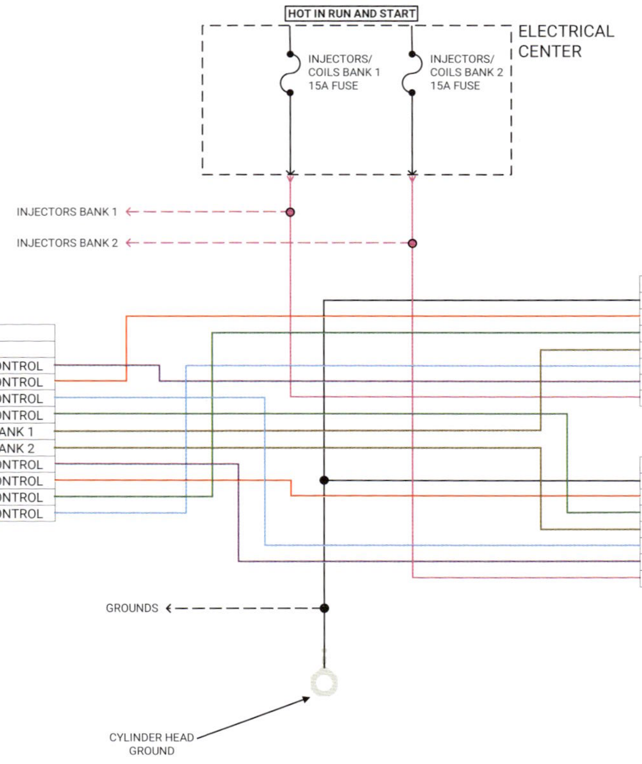

PIN #	COLOR	SIZE (MM²)	DESCRIPTION
A	BLK	1.0	GROUND
B	RED	0.8	IGNITION COIL 7 CONTROL
C	DK GRN	0.8	IGNITION COIL 5 CONTROL
E	BRN	0.8	LOW REFERENCE
F	LT BLU	0.8	IGNITION COIL 3 CONTROL
G	PPL	0.8	IGNITION COIL 1 CONTROL
H	PNK	1.0	12V IGNITION

IGNITION COIL HARNESS BANK 1

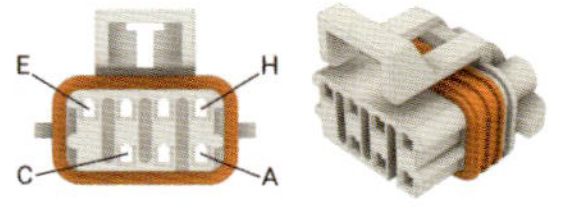

PIN #	COLOR	SIZE (MM²)	DESCRIPTION
A	BLK	1.0	GROUND
B	RED/WHT	0.8	IGNITION COIL 2 CONTROL
C	DK GRN/WHT	0.8	IGNITION COIL 4 CONTROL
E	BRN/WHT	0.8	LOW REFERENCE
F	LT BLU/WHT	0.8	IGNITION COIL 6 CONTROL
G	PPL/WHT	0.8	IGNITION COIL 8 CONTROL
H	PNK	1.0	12V IGNITION

IGNITION COIL HARNESS BANK 2

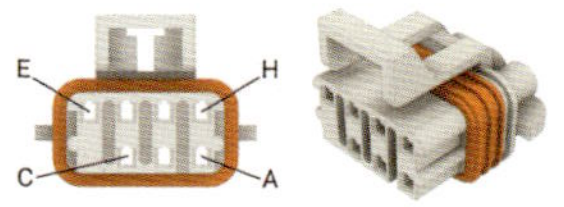

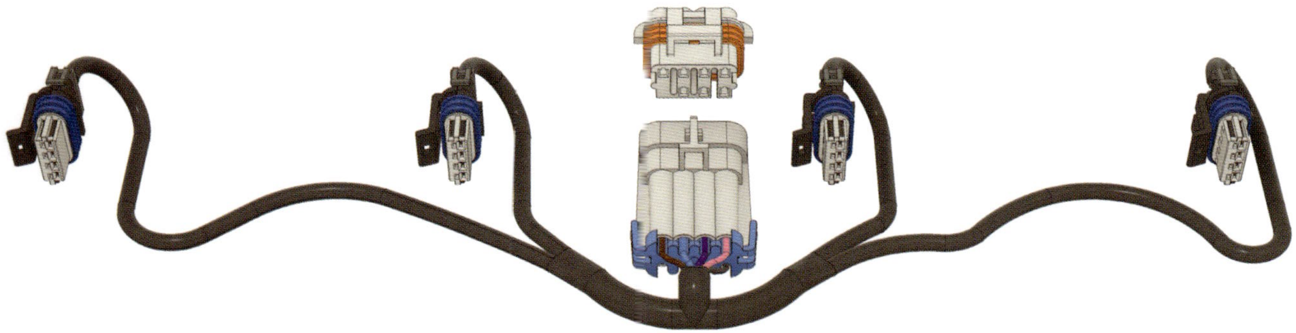

LS ENGINES(*) ARE FITTED WITH A PAIR OF IGNITION COIL SUB HARNESSES. EACH IGNITION COIL SUB HARNESS IS ATTACHED TO AN IGNITION COIL BRACKET ON TOP OF THE VALVE COVER. THE MATING 7 CAVITY METRI-PACK 150 FEMALE CONNECTOR CAN BE USED WITH ALL GM LS-SERIES IGNITION COIL SUB HARNESSES. NO REWIRING IS NECESSARY UNLESS THE ENGINE FIRE ORDER HAS CHANGED.

*EXCLUDES LS9 AND LSA ENGINES

TO DIRECTLY WIRE EACH IGNITION COIL TO THE ENGINE HARNESS, EACH 12V IGNITION (PINK WIRE), GROUND (BLACK WIRE), AND LOW REFERENCE WIRE (BROWN & BROWN/WHITE) WILL HAVE TO BE SPLICED TO FOUR ADDITIONAL WIRES TO PROVIDE POWER AND GROUND TO EACH IGNITION COIL.

INJECTOR EV1 (1)

PIN #	COLOR	SIZE (MM²)	DESCRIPTION
A	PNK	0.8	12V IGNITION
B	BLK	0.8	FUEL INJECTOR 1 CONTROL

INJECTOR EV1 (2)

PIN #	COLOR	SIZE (MM²)	DESCRIPTION
A	PNK	0.8	12V IGNITION
B	LT GRN/BLK	0.8	FUEL INJECTOR 2 CONTROL

INJECTOR EV1 (3)

PIN #	COLOR	SIZE (MM²)	DESCRIPTION
A	PNK	0.8	12V IGNITION
B	PNK/BLK	0.8	FUEL INJECTOR 3 CONTROL

INJECTOR EV1 (4)

PIN #	COLOR	SIZE (MM²)	DESCRIPTION
A	PNK	0.8	12V IGNITION
B	LT BLU/BLK	0.8	FUEL INJECTOR 4 CONTROL

INJECTOR EV1 (5)

PIN #	COLOR	SIZE (MM²)	DESCRIPTION
A	PNK	0.8	12V IGNITION
B	BLK/WHT	0.8	FUEL INJECTOR 5 CONTROL

INJECTOR EV1 (6)

PIN #	COLOR	SIZE (MM²)	DESCRIPTION
A	PNK	0.8	12V IGNITION
B	YEL/BLK	0.8	FUEL INJECTOR 6 CONTROL

INJECTOR EV1 (7)

PIN #	COLOR	SIZE (MM²)	DESCRIPTION
A	PNK	0.8	12V IGNITION
B	RED/BLK	0.8	FUEL INJECTOR 7 CONTROL

INJECTOR EV1 (8)

PIN #	COLOR	SIZE (MM²)	DESCRIPTION
A	PNK	0.8	12V IGNITION
B	DK BLU/WHT	0.8	FUEL INJECTOR 8 CONTROL

ELECTRICAL CENTER

HOT IN RUN AND START

INJECTORS/COILS BANK 2 15A FUSE

INJECTORS/COILS BANK 1 15A FUSE

COILS BANK 1

COILS BANK 2

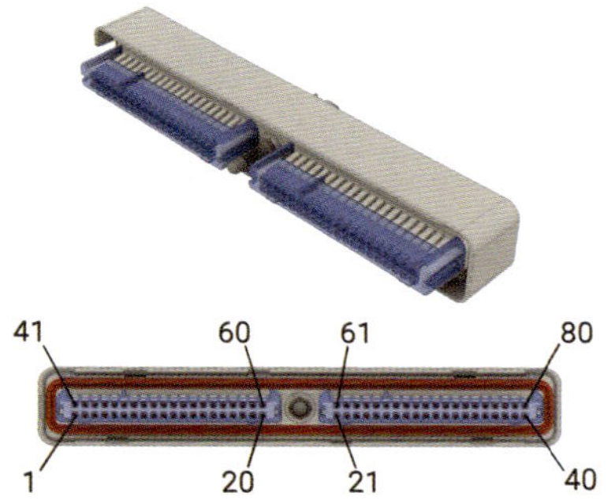

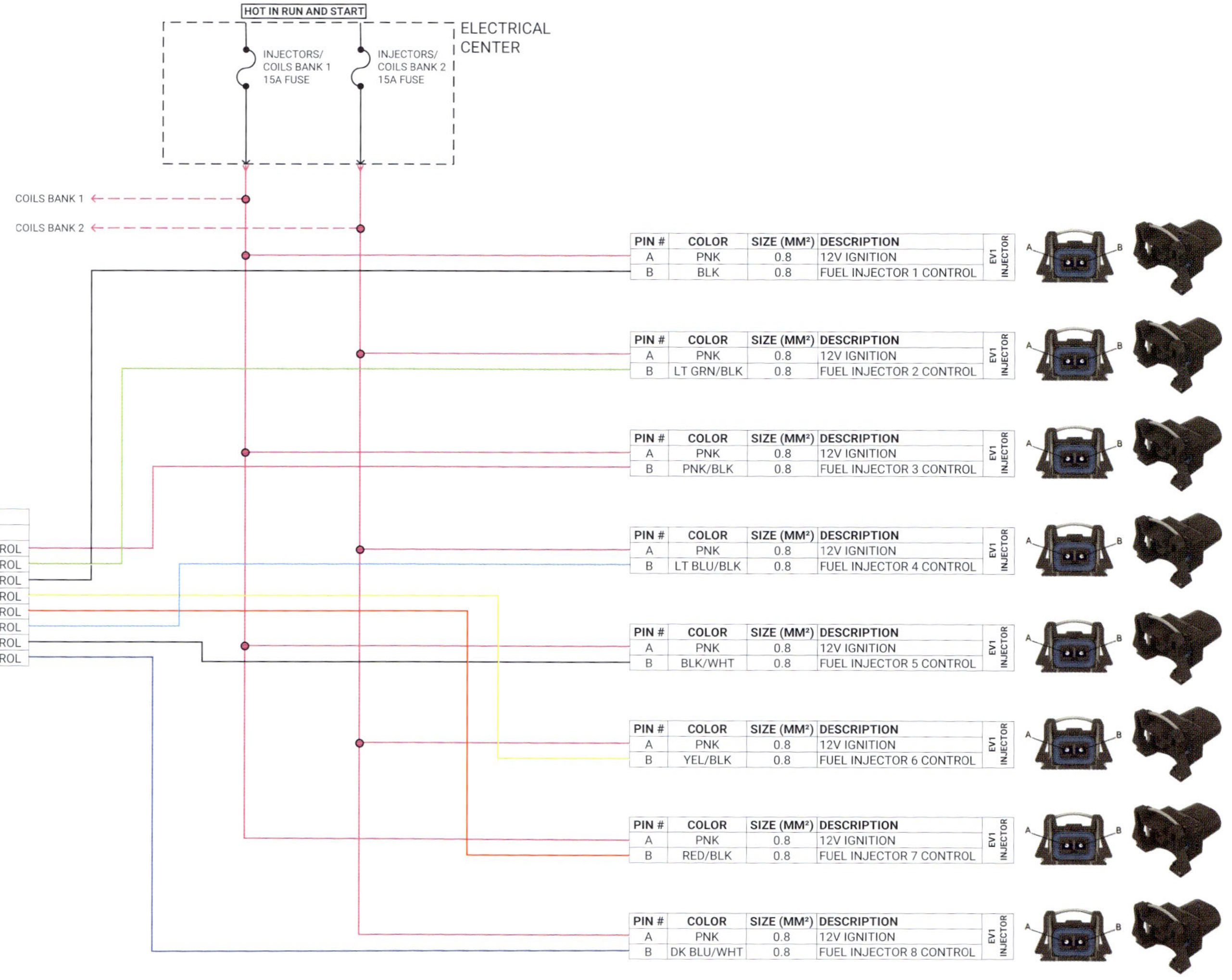

80W PCM C1 (BLUE)

PIN #	COLOR	SIZE (MM²)	DESCRIPTION
3	PNK/BLK	0.8	FUEL INJECTOR 3 CONTROL
4	LT GRN/BLK	0.8	FUEL INJECTOR 2 CONTROL
36	BLK	0.8	FUEL INJECTOR 1 CONTROL
37	YEL/BLK	0.8	FUEL INJECTOR 6 CONTROL
43	RED/BLK	0.8	FUEL INJECTOR 7 CONTROL
44	LT BLU/BLK	0.8	FUEL INJECTOR 4 CONTROL
76	BLK/WHT	0.8	FUEL INJECTOR 5 CONTROL
77	DK BLU/WHT	0.8	FUEL INJECTOR 8 CONTROL

1999-2002 P01 PCM (FUEL CONTROLS – MULTEC 2 FUEL INJECTORS)

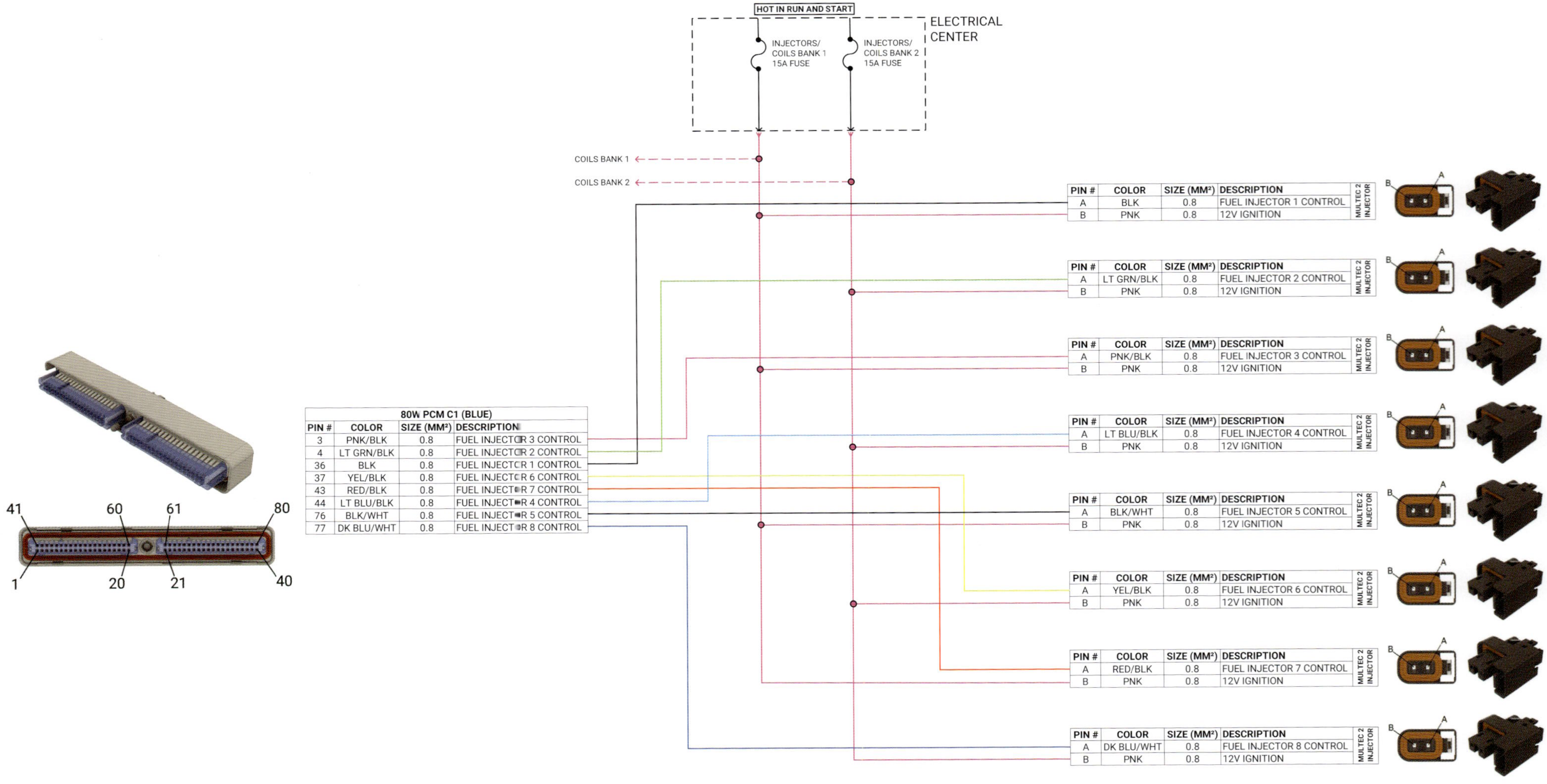

80W PCM C1 (BLUE)

PIN #	COLOR	SIZE (MM²)	DESCRIPTION
3	PNK/BLK	0.8	FUEL INJECTOR 3 CONTROL
4	LT GRN/BLK	0.8	FUEL INJECTOR 2 CONTROL
36	BLK	0.8	FUEL INJECTOR 1 CONTROL
37	YEL/BLK	0.8	FUEL INJECTOR 6 CONTROL
43	RED/BLK	0.8	FUEL INJECTOR 7 CONTROL
44	LT BLU/BLK	0.8	FUEL INJECTOR 4 CONTROL
76	BLK/WHT	0.8	FUEL INJECTOR 5 CONTROL
77	DK BLU/WHT	0.8	FUEL INJECTOR 8 CONTROL

MULTEC 2 INJECTOR

PIN #	COLOR	SIZE (MM²)	DESCRIPTION
A	BLK	0.8	FUEL INJECTOR 1 CONTROL
B	PNK	0.8	12V IGNITION

MULTEC 2 INJECTOR

PIN #	COLOR	SIZE (MM²)	DESCRIPTION
A	LT GRN/BLK	0.8	FUEL INJECTOR 2 CONTROL
B	PNK	0.8	12V IGNITION

MULTEC 2 INJECTOR

PIN #	COLOR	SIZE (MM²)	DESCRIPTION
A	PNK/BLK	0.8	FUEL INJECTOR 3 CONTROL
B	PNK	0.8	12V IGNITION

MULTEC 2 INJECTOR

PIN #	COLOR	SIZE (MM²)	DESCRIPTION
A	LT BLU/BLK	0.8	FUEL INJECTOR 4 CONTROL
B	PNK	0.8	12V IGNITION

MULTEC 2 INJECTOR

PIN #	COLOR	SIZE (MM²)	DESCRIPTION
A	BLK/WHT	0.8	FUEL INJECTOR 5 CONTROL
B	PNK	0.8	12V IGNITION

MULTEC 2 INJECTOR

PIN #	COLOR	SIZE (MM²)	DESCRIPTION
A	YEL/BLK	0.8	FUEL INJECTOR 6 CONTROL
B	PNK	0.8	12V IGNITION

MULTEC 2 INJECTOR

PIN #	COLOR	SIZE (MM²)	DESCRIPTION
A	RED/BLK	0.8	FUEL INJECTOR 7 CONTROL
B	PNK	0.8	12V IGNITION

MULTEC 2 INJECTOR

PIN #	COLOR	SIZE (MM²)	DESCRIPTION
A	DK BLU/WHT	0.8	FUEL INJECTOR 8 CONTROL
B	PNK	0.8	12V IGNITION

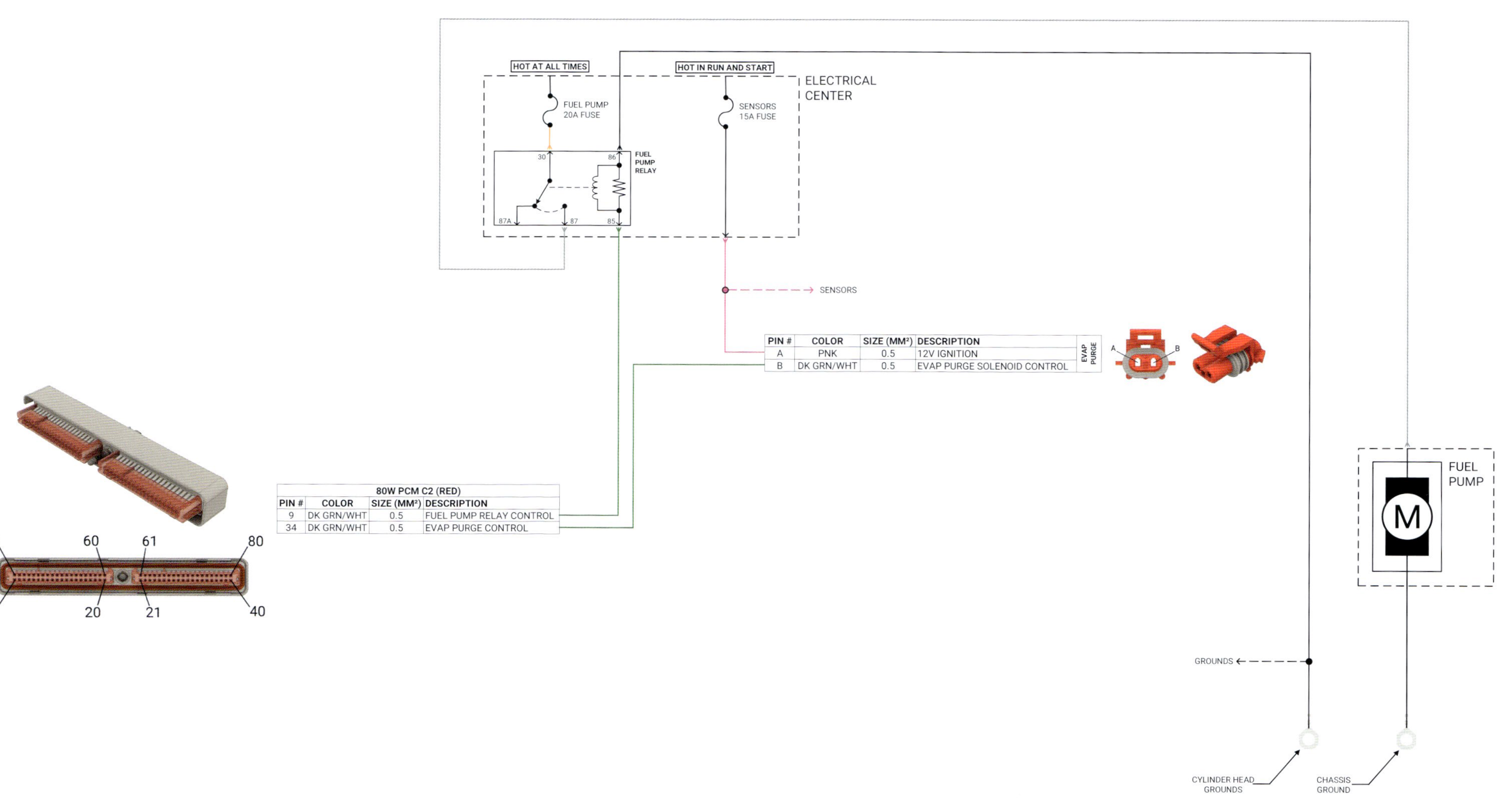

PIN #	COLOR	SIZE (MM²)	DESCRIPTION	EVAP PURGE	
A	PNK	0.5	12V IGNITION		
B	DK GRN/WHT	0.5	EVAP PURGE SOLENOID CONTROL		

80W PCM C2 (RED)			
PIN #	COLOR	SIZE (MM²)	DESCRIPTION
9	DK GRN/WHT	0.5	FUEL PUMP RELAY CONTROL
34	DK GRN/WHT	0.5	EVAP PURGE CONTROL

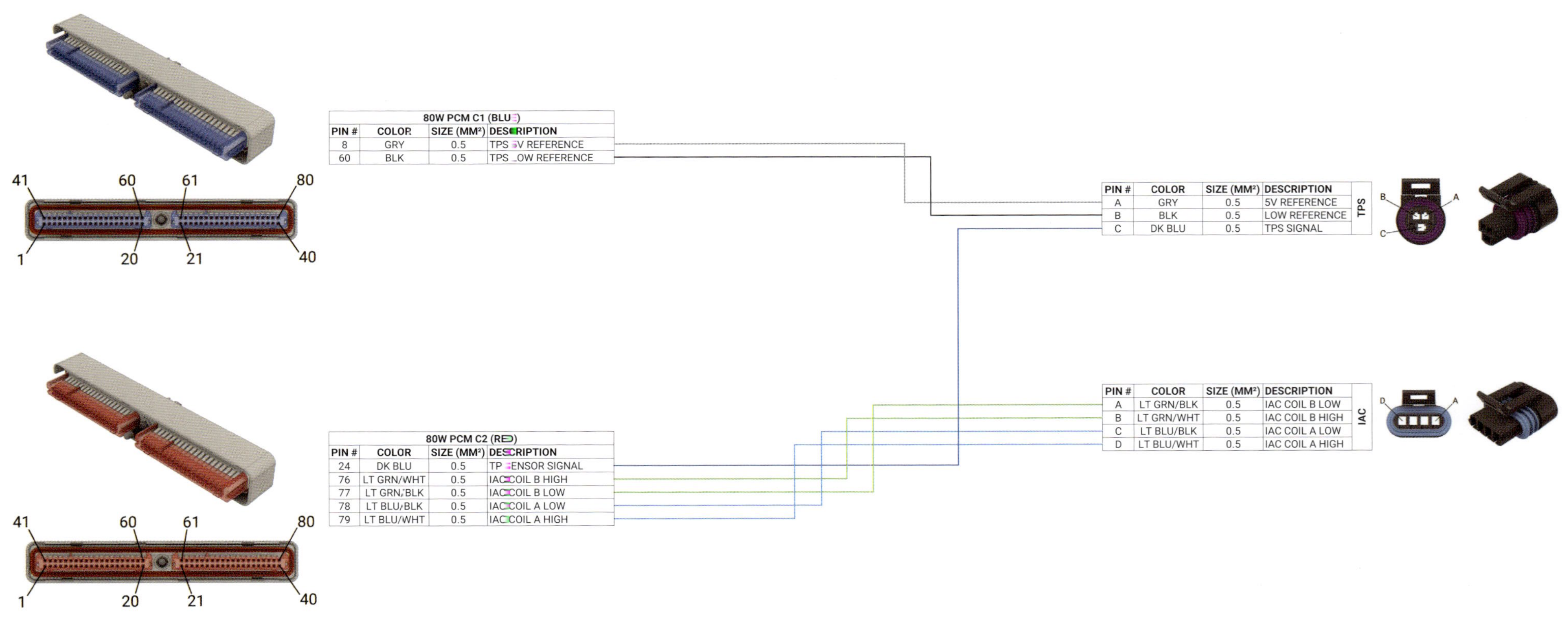

80W PCM C1 (BLUE)			
PIN #	COLOR	SIZE (MM²)	DESCRIPTION
8	GRY	0.5	TPS 5V REFERENCE
60	BLK	0.5	TPS LOW REFERENCE

PIN #	COLOR	SIZE (MM²)	DESCRIPTION
A	GRY	0.5	5V REFERENCE
B	BLK	0.5	LOW REFERENCE
C	DK BLU	0.5	TPS SIGNAL

TPS

80W PCM C2 (RED)			
PIN #	COLOR	SIZE (MM²)	DESCRIPTION
24	DK BLU	0.5	TP SENSOR SIGNAL
76	LT GRN/WHT	0.5	IAC COIL B HIGH
77	LT GRN/BLK	0.5	IAC COIL B LOW
78	LT BLU/BLK	0.5	IAC COIL A LOW
79	LT BLU/WHT	0.5	IAC COIL A HIGH

PIN #	COLOR	SIZE (MM²)	DESCRIPTION
A	LT GRN/BLK	0.5	IAC COIL B LOW
B	LT GRN/WHT	0.5	IAC COIL B HIGH
C	LT BLU/BLK	0.5	IAC COIL A LOW
D	LT BLU/WHT	0.5	IAC COIL A HIGH

IAC

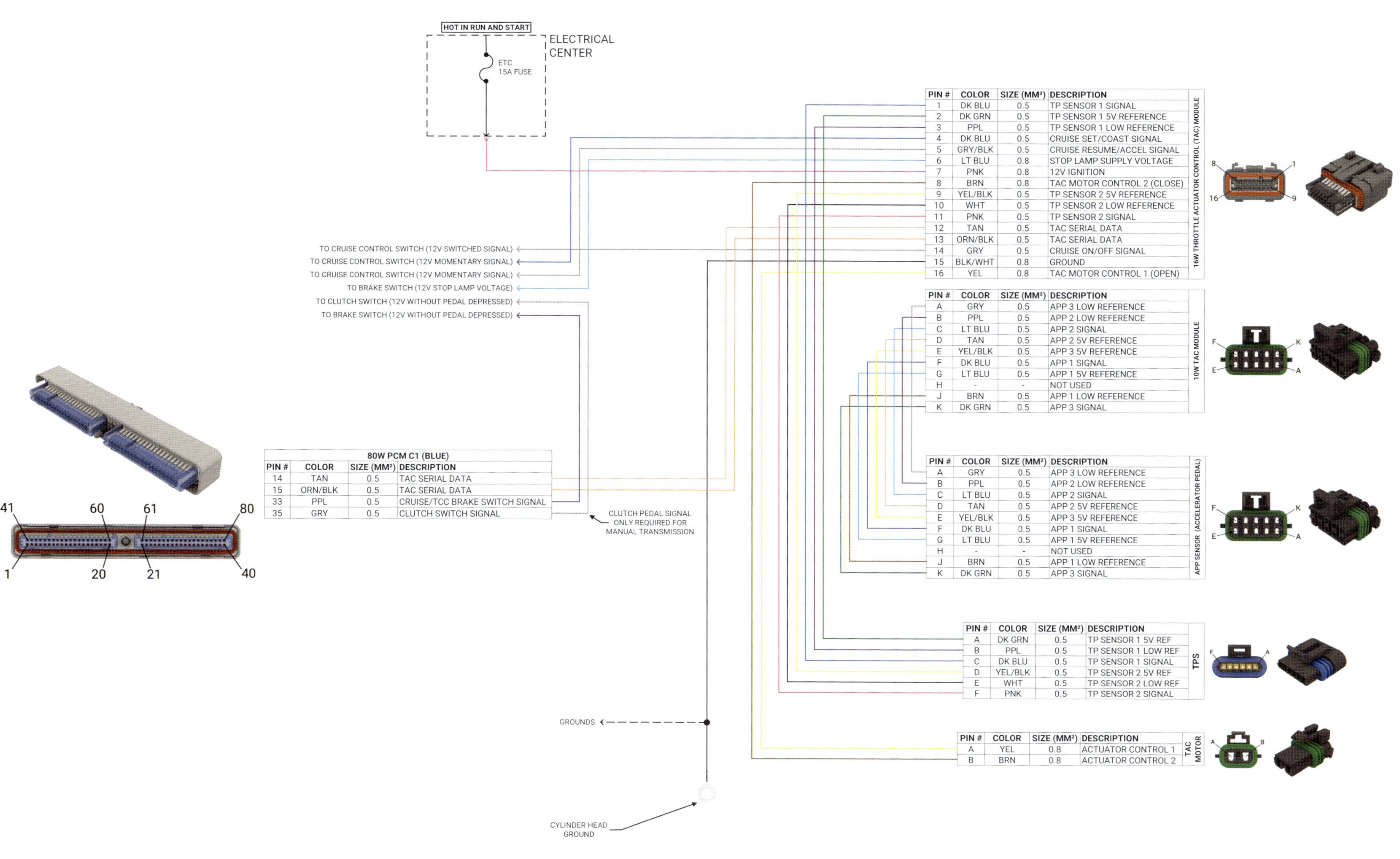

16W THROTTLE ACTUATOR CONTROL (TAC) MODULE

PIN #	COLOR	SIZE (MM²)	DESCRIPTION
1	DK BLU	0.5	TP SENSOR 1 SIGNAL
2	DK GRN	0.5	TP SENSOR 1 5V REFERENCE
3	PPL	0.5	TP SENSOR 1 LOW REFERENCE
4	DK BLU	0.5	CRUISE SET/COAST SIGNAL
5	GRY/BLK	0.5	CRUISE RESUME/ACCEL SIGNAL
6	LT BLU	0.8	STOP LAMP SUPPLY VOLTAGE
7	PNK	0.8	12V IGNITION
8	BRN	0.8	TAC MOTOR CONTROL 2 (CLOSE)
9	YEL/BLK	0.5	TP SENSOR 2 5V REFERENCE
10	WHT	0.5	TP SENSOR 2 LOW REFERENCE
11	PNK	0.5	TP SENSOR 2 SIGNAL
12	TAN	0.5	TAC SERIAL DATA
13	ORN/BLK	0.5	TAC SERIAL DATA
14	GRY	0.5	CRUISE ON/OFF SIGNAL
15	BLK/WHT	0.8	GROUND
16	YEL	0.8	TAC MOTOR CONTROL 1 (OPEN)

10W TAC MODULE

PIN #	COLOR	SIZE (MM²)	DESCRIPTION
A	GRY	0.5	APP 3 LOW REFERENCE
B	PPL	0.5	APP 2 LOW REFERENCE
C	LT BLU	0.5	APP 2 SIGNAL
D	TAN	0.5	APP 2 5V REFERENCE
E	YEL/BLK	0.5	APP 3 5V REFERENCE
F	DK BLU	0.5	APP 1 SIGNAL
G	LT BLU	0.5	APP 1 5V REFERENCE
H	-	-	NOT USED
J	BRN	0.5	APP 1 LOW REFERENCE
K	DK GRN	0.5	APP 3 SIGNAL

APP SENSOR (ACCELERATOR PEDAL)

PIN #	COLOR	SIZE (MM²)	DESCRIPTION
A	GRY	0.5	APP 3 LOW REFERENCE
B	PPL	0.5	APP 2 LOW REFERENCE
C	LT BLU	0.5	APP 2 SIGNAL
D	TAN	0.5	APP 2 5V REFERENCE
E	YEL/BLK	0.5	APP 3 5V REFERENCE
F	DK BLU	0.5	APP 1 SIGNAL
G	LT BLU	0.5	APP 1 5V REFERENCE
H	-	-	NOT USED
J	BRN	0.5	APP 1 LOW REFERENCE
K	DK GRN	0.5	APP 3 SIGNAL

TPS

PIN #	COLOR	SIZE (MM²)	DESCRIPTION
A	DK GRN	0.5	TP SENSOR 1 5V REF
B	PPL	0.5	TP SENSOR 1 LOW REF
C	DK BLU	0.5	TP SENSOR 1 SIGNAL
D	YEL/BLK	0.5	TP SENSOR 2 5V REF
E	WHT	0.5	TP SENSOR 2 LOW REF
F	PNK	0.5	TP SENSOR 2 SIGNAL

TAC MOTOR

PIN #	COLOR	SIZE (MM²)	DESCRIPTION
A	YEL	0.8	ACTUATOR CONTROL 1
B	BRN	0.8	ACTUATOR CONTROL 2

80W PCM C1 (BLUE)

PIN #	COLOR	SIZE (MM²)	DESCRIPTION
14	TAN	0.5	TAC SERIAL DATA
15	ORN/BLK	0.5	TAC SERIAL DATA
33	PPL	0.5	CRUISE/TCC BRAKE SWITCH SIGNAL
35	GRY	0.5	CLUTCH SWITCH SIGNAL

2000-2002 P01 PCM (THROTTLE SYSTEM – ELECTRONIC (TRUCK/SUV))

HOT IN RUN AND START

ELECTRICAL CENTER

ETC
15A FUSE

TO CRUISE CONTROL SWITCH (12V SWITCHED SIGNAL)
TO CRUISE CONTROL SWITCH (12V MOMENTARY SIGNAL)
TO CRUISE CONTROL SWITCH (12V MOMENTARY SIGNAL)
TO BRAKE SWITCH (12V STOP LAMP VOLTAGE)
TO CLUTCH SWITCH (12V WITHOUT PEDAL DEPRESSED)
TO BRAKE SWITCH (12V WITHOUT PEDAL DEPRESSED)

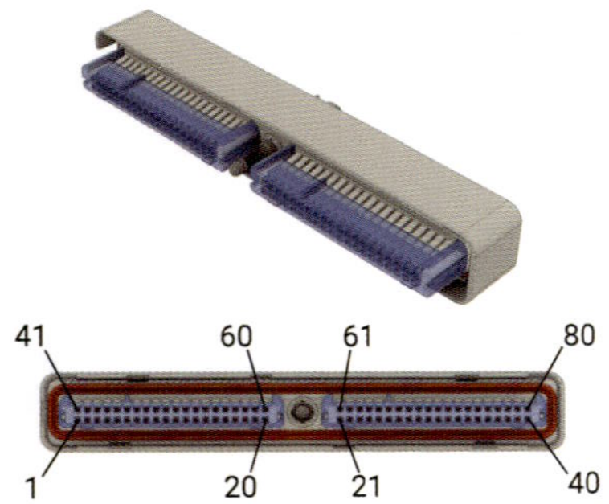

41
60
61
80
1
20
21
40

80W PCM C1 (BLUE)

PIN #	COLOR	SIZE (MM²)	DESCRIPTION
14	ORN/BLK	0.5	TAC SERIAL DATA
15	DK BLU/WHT	0.5	TAC SERIAL DATA
33	PPL	0.5	CRUISE/TCC BRAKE SWITCH SIGNAL
35	GRY	0.5	CLUTCH SWITCH SIGNAL

CLUTCH PEDAL SIGNAL ONLY REQUIRED FOR MANUAL TRANSMISSION

GROUNDS

CYLINDER HEAD GROUND

16W THROTTLE ACTUATOR CONTROL (TAC) MODULE

PIN #	COLOR	SIZE (MM²)	DESCRIPTION
1	DK GRN	0.5	TP SENSOR 1 SIGNAL
2	GRY	0.5	TP SENSOR 1 5V REFERENCE
3	BLK	0.5	TP SENSOR 1 LOW REFERENCE
4	DK BLU	0.5	CRUISE SET/COAST SIGNAL
5	GRY/BLK	0.5	CRUISE RESUME/ACCEL SIGNAL
6	LT BLU	0.8	STOP LAMP SUPPLY VOLTAGE
7	PNK	0.8	12V IGNITION
8	BRN	0.8	TAC MOTOR CONTROL 2 (CLOSE)
9	LT BLU/BLK	0.5	TP SENSOR 2 5V REFERENCE
10	BLK/WHT	0.5	TP SENSOR 2 LOW REFERENCE
11	PPL	0.5	TP SENSOR 2 SIGNAL
12	ORN/BLK	0.5	TAC SERIAL DATA
13	DK BLU/WHT	0.5	TAC SERIAL DATA
14	GRY	0.5	CRUISE ON/OFF SIGNAL
15	BLK/WHT	0.8	GROUND
16	YEL	0.8	TAC MOTOR CONTROL 1 (OPEN)

10W TAC MODULE

PIN #	COLOR	SIZE (MM²)	DESCRIPTION
A	GRY	0.5	APP 3 LOW REFERENCE
B	PPL	0.5	APP 2 LOW REFERENCE
C	LT BLU	0.5	APP 2 SIGNAL
D	TAN	0.5	APP 2 5V REFERENCE
E	YEL/BLK	0.5	APP 3 5V REFERENCE
F	DK BLU	0.5	APP 1 SIGNAL
G	WHT/BLK	0.5	APP 1 5V REFERENCE
H	-	-	NOT USED
J	BRN	0.5	APP 1 LOW REFERENCE
K	DK GRN	0.5	APP 3 SIGNAL

APP SENSOR (ACCELERATOR PEDAL)

PIN #	COLOR	SIZE (MM²)	DESCRIPTION
A	GRY	0.5	APP 3 LOW REFERENCE
B	PPL	0.5	APP 2 LOW REFERENCE
C	LT BLU	0.5	APP 2 SIGNAL
D	TAN	0.5	APP 2 5V REFERENCE
E	BRN	0.5	APP 1 LOW REFERENCE
F	DK BLU	0.5	APP 1 SIGNAL
G	WHT/BLK	0.5	APP 1 5V REFERENCE
H	-	-	NOT USED
J	YEL/BLK	0.5	APP 3 5V REFERENCE
K	DK GRN	0.5	APP 3 SIGNAL

TPS

PIN #	COLOR	SIZE (MM²)	DESCRIPTION
A	GRY	0.5	TP SENSOR 1 5V REF
B	BLK	0.5	TP SENSOR 1 LOW REF
C	DK GRN	0.5	TP SENSOR 1 SIGNAL
D	LT BLU/BLK	0.5	TP SENSOR 2 5V REF
E	BLK/WHT	0.5	TP SENSOR 2 LOW REF
F	PPL	0.5	TP SENSOR 2 SIGNAL

TAC MOTOR

PIN #	COLOR	SIZE (MM²)	DESCRIPTION
A	BRN	0.8	ACTUATOR CONTROL 2
B	YEL	0.8	ACTUATOR CONTROL 1

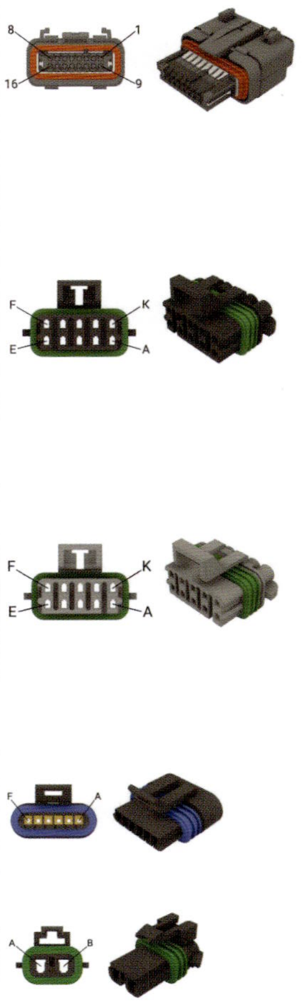

8
1
16
9
F
K
E
A

1999-2002 P01 PCM (TRANSMISSION – T56 6 SPEED MANUAL)

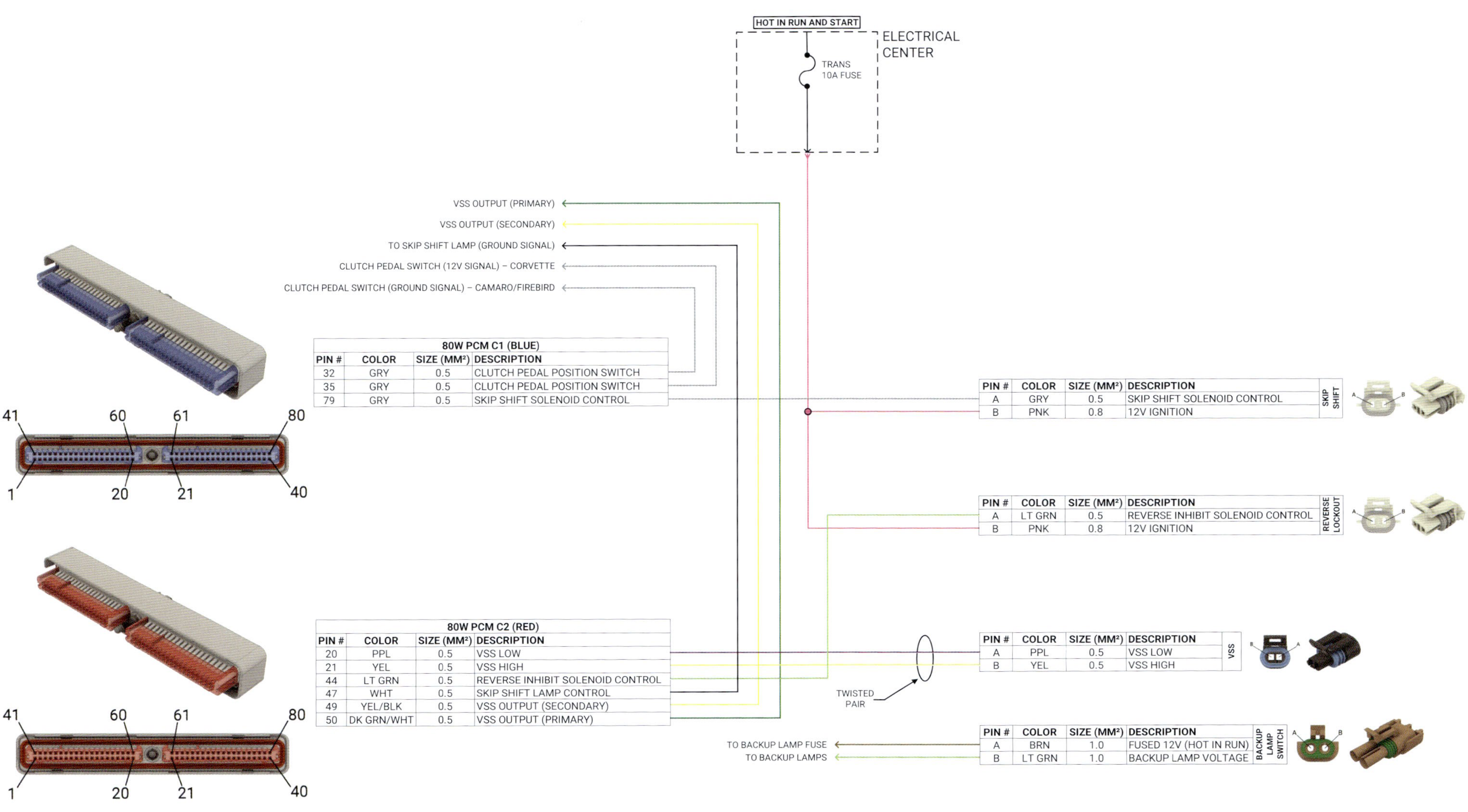

80W PCM C1 (BLUE)			
PIN #	COLOR	SIZE (MM²)	DESCRIPTION
32	GRY	0.5	CLUTCH PEDAL POSITION SWITCH
35	GRY	0.5	CLUTCH PEDAL POSITION SWITCH
79	GRY	0.5	SKIP SHIFT SOLENOID CONTROL

80W PCM C2 (RED)			
PIN #	COLOR	SIZE (MM²)	DESCRIPTION
20	PPL	0.5	VSS LOW
21	YEL	0.5	VSS HIGH
44	LT GRN	0.5	REVERSE INHIBIT SOLENOID CONTROL
47	WHT	0.5	SKIP SHIFT LAMP CONTROL
49	YEL/BLK	0.5	VSS OUTPUT (SECONDARY)
50	DK GRN/WHT	0.5	VSS OUTPUT (PRIMARY)

PIN #	COLOR	SIZE (MM²)	DESCRIPTION	
A	GRY	0.5	SKIP SHIFT SOLENOID CONTROL	SKIP SHIFT
B	PNK	0.8	12V IGNITION	

PIN #	COLOR	SIZE (MM²)	DESCRIPTION	
A	LT GRN	0.5	REVERSE INHIBIT SOLENOID CONTROL	REVERSE LOCKOUT
B	PNK	0.8	12V IGNITION	

PIN #	COLOR	SIZE (MM²)	DESCRIPTION	
A	PPL	0.5	VSS LOW	VSS
B	YEL	0.5	VSS HIGH	

PIN #	COLOR	SIZE (MM²)	DESCRIPTION	
A	BRN	1.0	FUSED 12V (HOT IN RUN)	BACKUP LAMP SWITCH
B	LT GRN	1.0	BACKUP LAMP VOLTAGE	

1999-2002 P01 PCM (TRANSMISSION – TRUCK MANUAL)

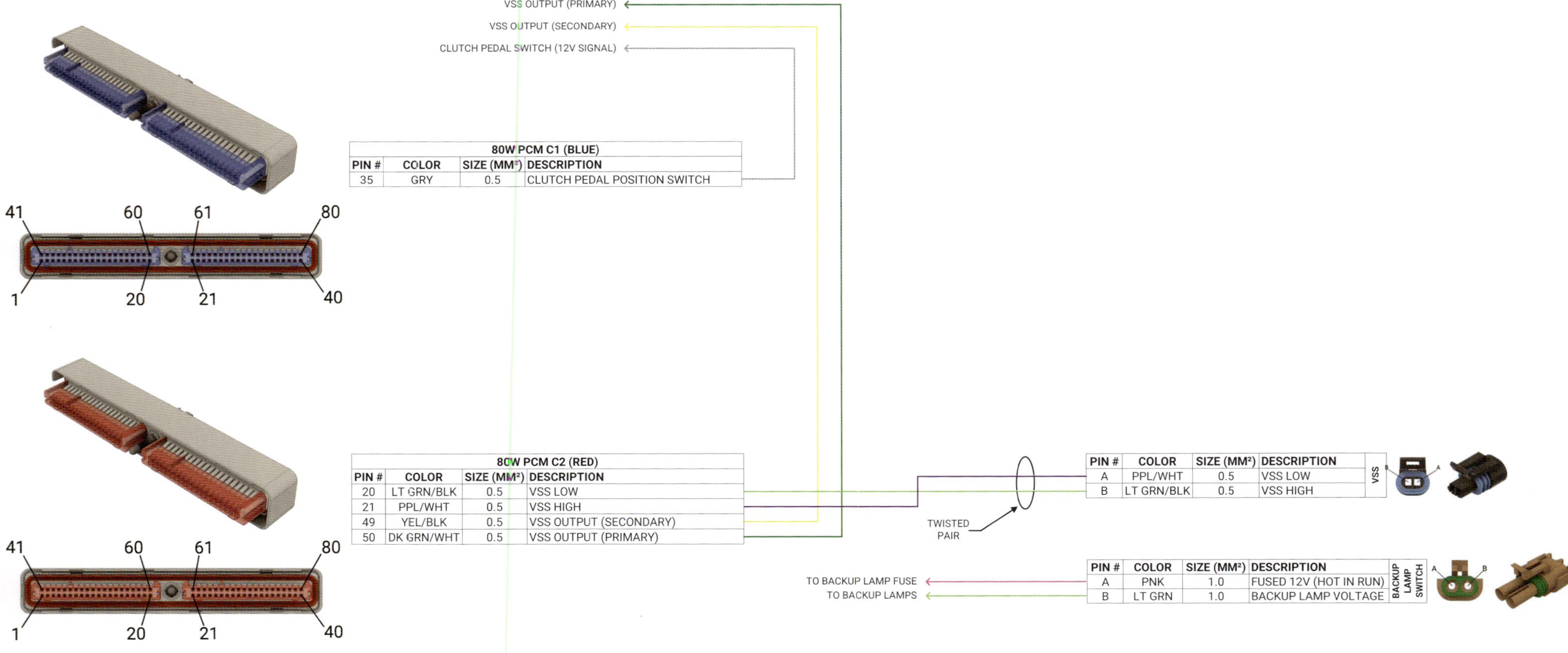

80W PCM C1 (BLUE)			
PIN #	COLOR	SIZE (MM²)	DESCRIPTION
35	GRY	0.5	CLUTCH PEDAL POSITION SWITCH

80W PCM C2 (RED)			
PIN #	COLOR	SIZE (MM²)	DESCRIPTION
20	LT GRN/BLK	0.5	VSS LOW
21	PPL/WHT	0.5	VSS HIGH
49	YEL/BLK	0.5	VSS OUTPUT (SECONDARY)
50	DK GRN/WHT	0.5	VSS OUTPUT (PRIMARY)

PIN #	COLOR	SIZE (MM²)	DESCRIPTION
A	PPL/WHT	0.5	VSS LOW
B	LT GRN/BLK	0.5	VSS HIGH

PIN #	COLOR	SIZE (MM²)	DESCRIPTION
A	PNK	1.0	FUSED 12V (HOT IN RUN)
B	LT GRN	1.0	BACKUP LAMP VOLTAGE

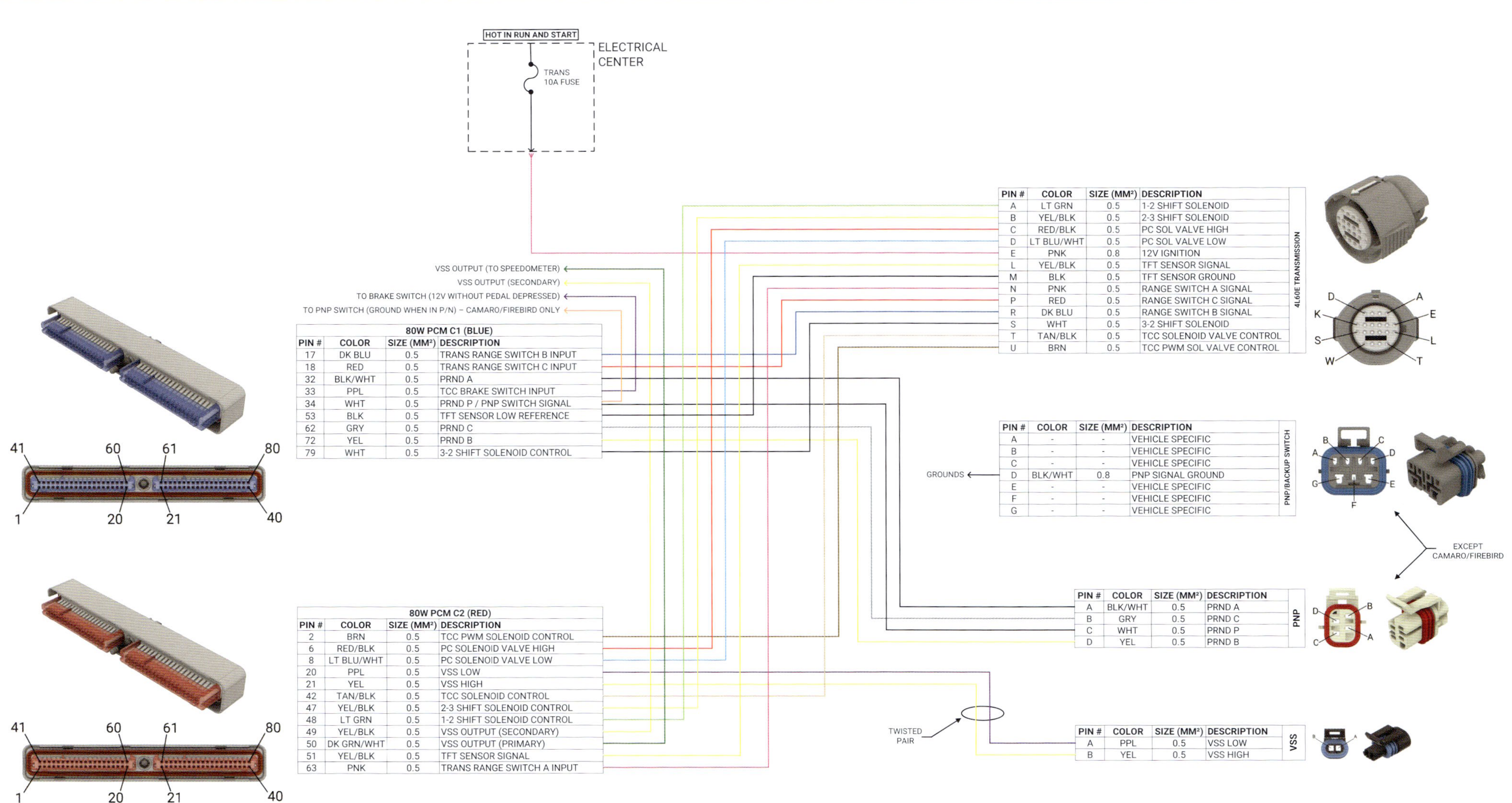

4L60E TRANSMISSION

PIN #	COLOR	SIZE (MM²)	DESCRIPTION
A	LT GRN	0.5	1-2 SHIFT SOLENOID
B	YEL/BLK	0.5	2-3 SHIFT SOLENOID
C	RED/BLK	0.5	PC SOL VALVE HIGH
D	LT BLU/WHT	0.5	PC SOL VALVE LOW
E	PNK	0.8	12V IGNITION
L	YEL/BLK	0.5	TFT SENSOR SIGNAL
M	BLK	0.5	TFT SENSOR GROUND
N	PNK	0.5	RANGE SWITCH A SIGNAL
P	RED	0.5	RANGE SWITCH C SIGNAL
R	DK BLU	0.5	RANGE SWITCH B SIGNAL
S	WHT	0.5	3-2 SHIFT SOLENOID
T	TAN/BLK	0.5	TCC SOLENOID VALVE CONTROL
U	BRN	0.5	TCC PWM SOL VALVE CONTROL

PNP/BACKUP SWITCH

PIN #	COLOR	SIZE (MM²)	DESCRIPTION
A	-	-	VEHICLE SPECIFIC
B	-	-	VEHICLE SPECIFIC
C	-	-	VEHICLE SPECIFIC
D	BLK/WHT	0.8	PNP SIGNAL GROUND
E	-	-	VEHICLE SPECIFIC
F	-	-	VEHICLE SPECIFIC
G	-	-	VEHICLE SPECIFIC

PnP

PIN #	COLOR	SIZE (MM²)	DESCRIPTION
A	BLK/WHT	0.5	PRND A
B	GRY	0.5	PRND C
C	WHT	0.5	PRND P
D	YEL	0.5	PRND B

VSS

PIN #	COLOR	SIZE (MM²)	DESCRIPTION
A	PPL	0.5	VSS LOW
B	YEL	0.5	VSS HIGH

80W PCM C1 (BLUE)

PIN #	COLOR	SIZE (MM²)	DESCRIPTION
17	DK BLU	0.5	TRANS RANGE SWITCH B INPUT
18	RED	0.5	TRANS RANGE SWITCH C INPUT
32	BLK/WHT	0.5	PRND A
33	PPL	0.5	TCC BRAKE SWITCH INPUT
34	WHT	0.5	PRND P / PNP SWITCH SIGNAL
53	BLK	0.5	TFT SENSOR LOW REFERENCE
62	GRY	0.5	PRND C
72	YEL	0.5	PRND B
79	WHT	0.5	3-2 SHIFT SOLENOID CONTROL

80W PCM C2 (RED)

PIN #	COLOR	SIZE (MM²)	DESCRIPTION
2	BRN	0.5	TCC PWM SOLENOID CONTROL
6	RED/BLK	0.5	PC SOLENOID VALVE HIGH
8	LT BLU/WHT	0.5	PC SOLENOID VALVE LOW
20	PPL	0.5	VSS LOW
21	YEL	0.5	VSS HIGH
42	TAN/BLK	0.5	TCC SOLENOID CONTROL
47	YEL/BLK	0.5	2-3 SHIFT SOLENOID CONTROL
48	LT GRN	0.5	1-2 SHIFT SOLENOID CONTROL
49	YEL/BLK	0.5	VSS OUTPUT (SECONDARY)
50	DK GRN/WHT	0.5	VSS OUTPUT (PRIMARY)
51	YEL/BLK	0.5	TFT SENSOR SIGNAL
63	PNK	0.5	TRANS RANGE SWITCH A INPUT

1999-2002 P01 PCM (TRANSMISSION – 4L80E AUTOMATIC)

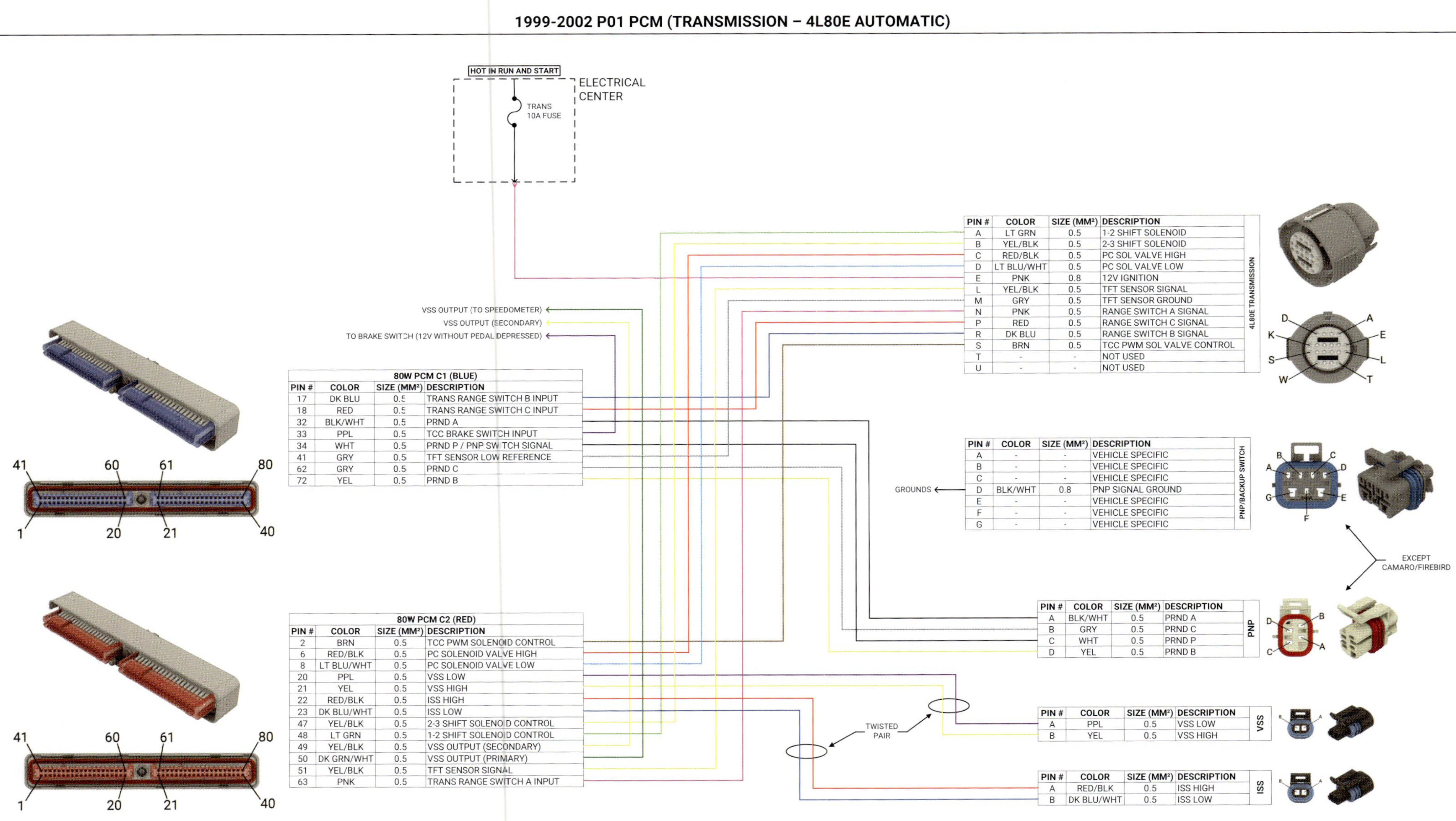

4L80E TRANSMISSION

PIN #	COLOR	SIZE (MM²)	DESCRIPTION
A	LT GRN	0.5	1-2 SHIFT SOLENOID
B	YEL/BLK	0.5	2-3 SHIFT SOLENOID
C	RED/BLK	0.5	PC SOL VALVE HIGH
D	LT BLU/WHT	0.5	PC SOL VALVE LOW
E	PNK	0.8	12V IGNITION
L	YEL/BLK	0.5	TFT SENSOR SIGNAL
M	GRY	0.5	TFT SENSOR GROUND
N	PNK	0.5	RANGE SWITCH A SIGNAL
P	RED	0.5	RANGE SWITCH C SIGNAL
R	DK BLU	0.5	RANGE SWITCH B SIGNAL
S	BRN	0.5	TCC PWM SOL VALVE CONTROL
T	-	-	NOT USED
U	-	-	NOT USED

PNP/BACKUP SWITCH

PIN #	COLOR	SIZE (MM²)	DESCRIPTION
A	-	-	VEHICLE SPECIFIC
B	-	-	VEHICLE SPECIFIC
C	-	-	VEHICLE SPECIFIC
D	BLK/WHT	0.8	PNP SIGNAL GROUND
E	-	-	VEHICLE SPECIFIC
F	-	-	VEHICLE SPECIFIC
G	-	-	VEHICLE SPECIFIC

PNP

PIN #	COLOR	SIZE (MM²)	DESCRIPTION
A	BLK/WHT	0.5	PRND A
B	GRY	0.5	PRND C
C	WHT	0.5	PRND P
D	YEL	0.5	PRND B

VSS

PIN #	COLOR	SIZE (MM²)	DESCRIPTION
A	PPL	0.5	VSS LOW
B	YEL	0.5	VSS HIGH

ISS

PIN #	COLOR	SIZE (MM²)	DESCRIPTION
A	RED/BLK	0.5	ISS HIGH
B	DK BLU/WHT	0.5	ISS LOW

80W PCM C1 (BLUE)

PIN #	COLOR	SIZE (MM²)	DESCRIPTION
17	DK BLU	0.5	TRANS RANGE SWITCH B INPUT
18	RED	0.5	TRANS RANGE SWITCH C INPUT
32	BLK/WHT	0.5	PRND A
33	PPL	0.5	TCC BRAKE SWITCH INPUT
34	WHT	0.5	PRND P / PNP SWITCH SIGNAL
41	GRY	0.5	TFT SENSOR LOW REFERENCE
62	GRY	0.5	PRND C
72	YEL	0.5	PRND B

80W PCM C2 (RED)

PIN #	COLOR	SIZE (MM²)	DESCRIPTION
2	BRN	0.5	TCC PWM SOLENOID CONTROL
6	RED/BLK	0.5	PC SOLENOID VALVE HIGH
8	LT BLU/WHT	0.5	PC SOLENOID VALVE LOW
20	PPL	0.5	VSS LOW
21	YEL	0.5	VSS HIGH
22	RED/BLK	0.5	ISS HIGH
23	DK BLU/WHT	0.5	ISS LOW
47	YEL/BLK	0.5	2-3 SHIFT SOLENOID CONTROL
48	LT GRN	0.5	1-2 SHIFT SOLENOID CONTROL
49	YEL/BLK	0.5	VSS OUTPUT (SECONDARY)
50	DK GRN/WHT	0.5	VSS OUTPUT (PRIMARY)
51	YEL/BLK	0.5	TFT SENSOR SIGNAL
63	PNK	0.5	TRANS RANGE SWITCH A INPUT

LOW/HIGH SPEED OPERATION
PRODUCTION GM VEHICLES WITH TWO ELECTRIC FANS USE THREE RELAYS AND TWO PCM ENABLED "ON" SIGNALS FOR SERIES/PARALLEL OR LOW/HIGH SPEED OPERATION. WHEN THE PCM APPLIES GROUND TO THE LOW SPEED CONTROL, THE TWO FAN MOTORS OPERATE IN SERIES FOR LOW SPEED. WHEN THE PCM THEN APPLIES GROUND TO THE HIGH SPEED CONTROL, THE TWO FAN MOTORS OPERATE IN PARALLEL FOR HIGH SPEED.

ELECTRIC FAN MOTOR WIRE SIZE AND FUSE PROTECTION
IMPORTANT! BE SURE TO ASK YOUR ELECTRIC FAN MANUFACTURER FOR THEIR RECOMMENDED WIRE SIZE AND FUSE SIZE FOR SAFE OPERATION. USE RELAYS THAT ARE RATED FOR FAN MOTOR CURRENT.

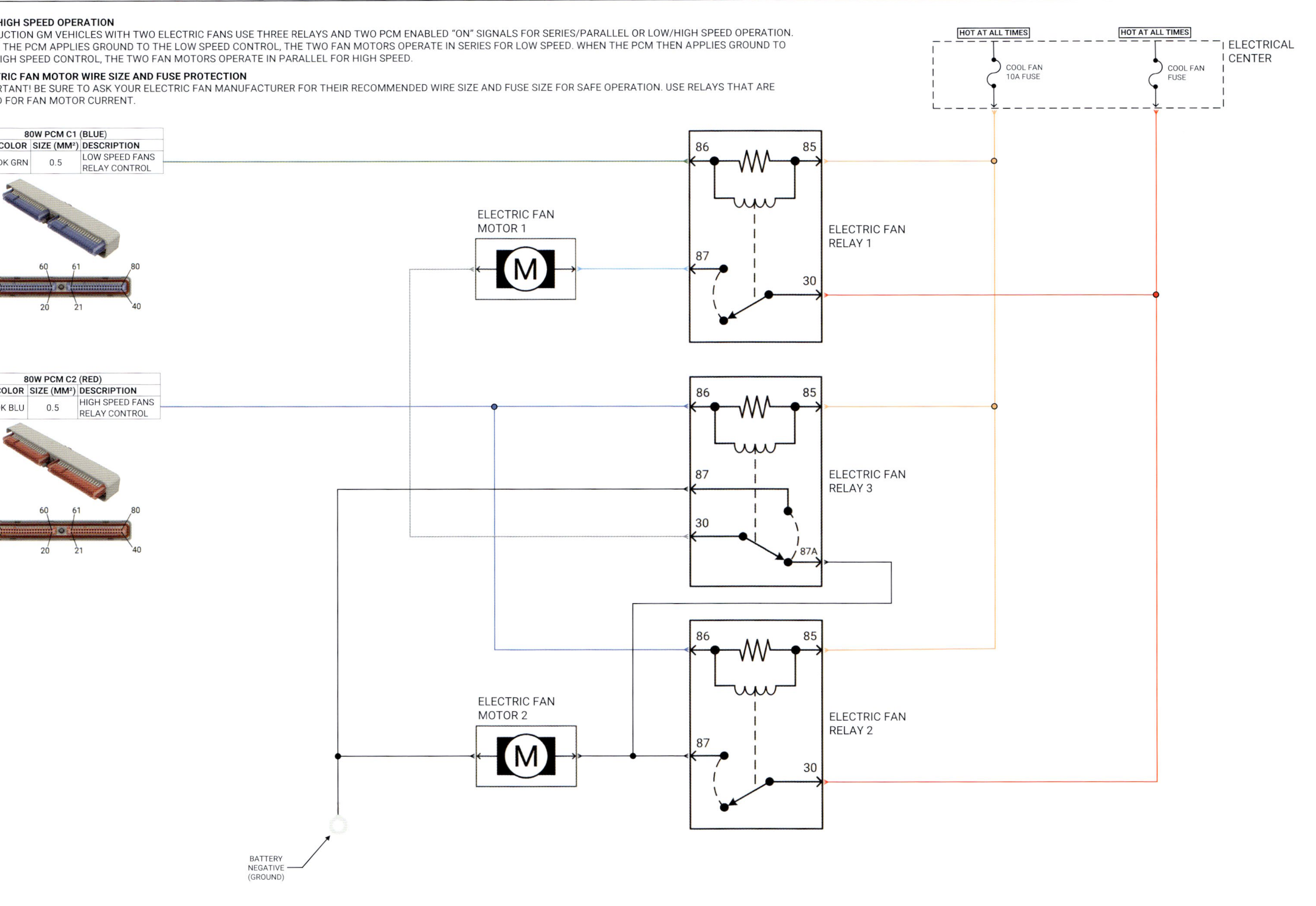

80W PCM C1 (BLUE)			
PIN #	COLOR	SIZE (MM²)	DESCRIPTION
42	DK GRN	0.5	LOW SPEED FANS RELAY CONTROL

80W PCM C2 (RED)			
PIN #	COLOR	SIZE (MM²)	DESCRIPTION
33	DK BLU	0.5	HIGH SPEED FANS RELAY CONTROL

1999-2002 P01 PCM (ENGINE COOLING – ELECTRIC FANS (ON/OFF))

INDEPENDENT ON/OFF OPERATION
TWO ELECTRIC FANS CAN BE INDEPENDENTLY CONTROLLED THROUGH THE USE OF TWO RELAYS FOR ON/OFF (HIGH SPEED) OPERATION.

ELECTRIC FAN MOTOR WIRE SIZE AND FUSE PROTECTION
IMPORTANT! BE SURE TO ASK YOUR ELECTRIC FAN MANUFACTURER FOR THEIR RECOMMENDED WIRE SIZE AND FUSE SIZE FOR SAFE OPERATION. USE RELAYS THAT ARE RATED FOR FAN MOTOR CURRENT.

80W PCM C1 (BLUE)			
PIN #	COLOR	SIZE (MM²)	DESCRIPTION
42	DK GRN	0.5	FAN 1 RELAY CONTROL

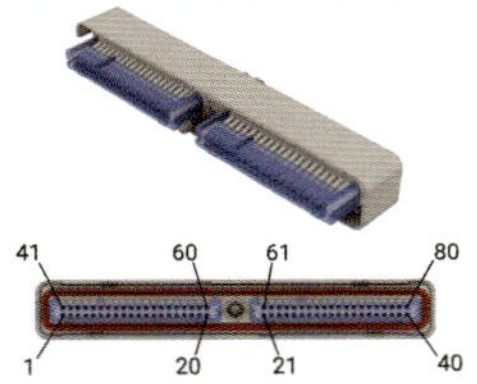

80W PCM C2 (RED)			
PIN #	COLOR	SIZE (MM²)	DESCRIPTION
33	DK BLU	0.5	FAN 2 RELAY CONTROL

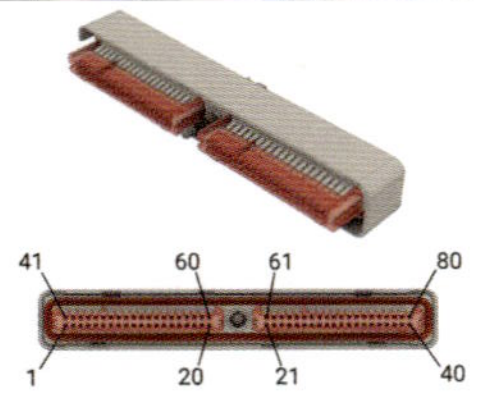

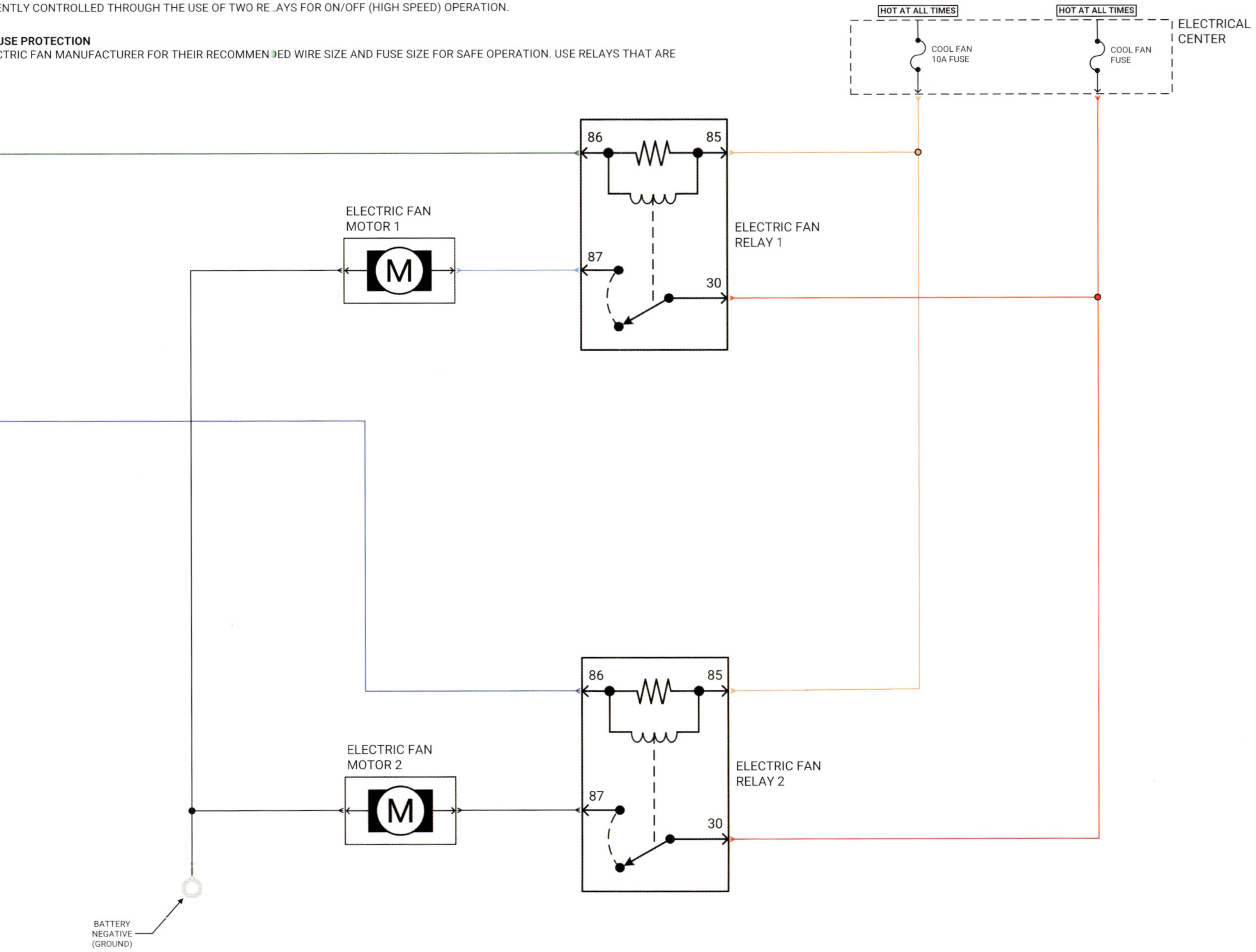

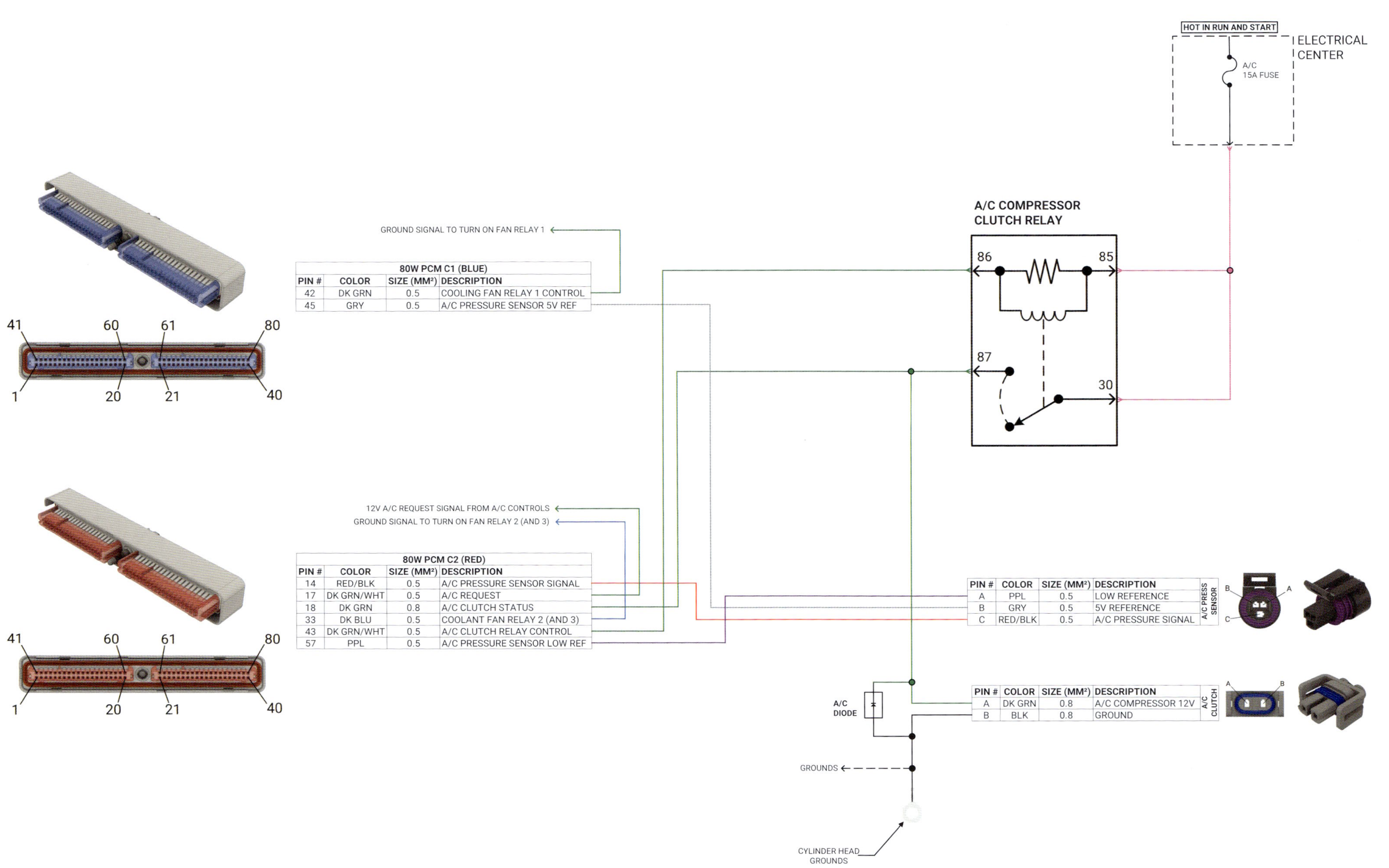

80W PCM C1 (BLUE)			
PIN #	COLOR	SIZE (MM²)	DESCRIPTION
42	DK GRN	0.5	COOLING FAN RELAY 1 CONTROL
45	GRY	0.5	A/C PRESSURE SENSOR 5V REF

80W PCM C2 (RED)			
PIN #	COLOR	SIZE (MM²)	DESCRIPTION
14	RED/BLK	0.5	A/C PRESSURE SENSOR SIGNAL
17	DK GRN/WHT	0.5	A/C REQUEST
18	DK GRN	0.8	A/C CLUTCH STATUS
33	DK BLU	0.5	COOLANT FAN RELAY 2 (AND 3)
43	DK GRN/WHT	0.5	A/C CLUTCH RELAY CONTROL
57	PPL	0.5	A/C PRESSURE SENSOR LOW REF

PIN #	COLOR	SIZE (MM²)	DESCRIPTION	
A	PPL	0.5	LOW REFERENCE	A/C PRESS SENSOR
B	GRY	0.5	5V REFERENCE	
C	RED/BLK	0.5	A/C PRESSURE SIGNAL	

PIN #	COLOR	SIZE (MM²)	DESCRIPTION	
A	DK GRN	0.8	A/C COMPRESSOR 12V	A/C CLUTCH
B	BLK	0.8	GROUND	

THE 2003–2007 P59 PCM

By 2003, most LS engines were fitted with electronic throttle systems. The truck and SUV TAC module and throttle body were updated while the Corvette received the same electronic throttle equipment that was introduced in 1997. Cable-driven throttle systems remained available with the 2003–2006 vans and 2004 GTO. Known as P59 controllers, the 2003–2007 PCMs have much in common with the 1999–2002 P01 PCMs. However, there are several differences of which to be aware.

Using the same external die-cast aluminum case as its predecessor, the P59 uses a slightly different circuit board header that requires the same connectors since 1997 but with connector C1 having two blue retainers and C2 having two green retainers. For stand-alone use, the P01 and P59 engine harnesses are pinned nearly the same. Be careful to notice the generator control circuit differences between the P01 and P59 PCMs.

P59 PCMs have several different service numbers but in some cases may share the same engine wire harness. Watch out for P59 PCMs that do not have idle air motor drivers on their circuit board because those PCMs may only be used with electronic throttle systems. Rather than opening the PCM case to inspect for the idle air motor drivers, simply look at the PCM service number to determine if it can be used with a cable throttle body.

All P59 PCMs are supported by popular tuning software like EFILive and HP Tuners. Due to the number of salvaged vehicles from 2003–2007, the P59 PCM is a very popular choice among enthusiasts for LS engine swaps. Depending on service number, the P59 is the last PCM to support a cable throttle body, as all Gen IV LS ECMs require the use of an electronic throttle body.

The following schematics are an excellent reference for use when servicing a used engine wire harness or while building your own stand-alone engine wire harness. I went further than the details of GM schematics to show engine data sensor interchangeability. When choosing a newer MAF, MAP, or HO_2S sensor, these schematics reveal any variation in pinout details.

Additionally, if you are working with any aftermarket stand-alone engine wire harness, you can expect to have a thorough understanding of the harness by referencing the following schematics.

Quick Reference	
Topic	Page
Power, Ground, and Data Communication	79
Charging - Generator Controls	80
Engine Data Sensors - ECT, IAT, MAP, and MAF	81
Engine Data Sensors - HO2S	82
Ignition Controls - CKP, CMP, KS1, and KS2	83
Ignition Controls - Ignition Coils	84
Fuel Controls - EV1 Fuel Injectors	85
Fuel Controls - Multec 2 Fuel Injectors	86
Fuel Controls - Fuel Pump and EVAP Purge Solenoid	87
Throttle System - Cable	88
Throttle System - Electric (Corvette)	89
Throttle System - Electric (CTS-V)	90
Throttle System - Electric (2003–2004 Truck/SUV)	91
Throttle System - Electric (2005 Truck/SUV)	92
Throttle System - Electric (2006–2007 Truck/SUV)	93
Throttle System - Electric (2004–2006 Van)	94
Throttle System - Electric (2007 Van)	95
Transmission - Truck Manual	96
Transmission - 4L60E Automatic Early PRNDL	97
Transmission - 4L60E Automatic Late PRNDL	98
Transmission - 4L80E Automatic Early PRNDL	99
Transmission - 4L80E Automatic Late PRNDL	100
Engine Cooling - Electric Fans Low/High Speed	101
Engine Cooling - Electric Fans On/Off	102
HVAC - Compressor Controls	103
Inputs/Outputs	104

GM Service Number	With Idle Air Control (IAC) Support (Cable/Electronic Throttle)	Without IAC Support (Electronic Throttle Only)
12576106	X	
12582605		X
12581565	X	
12586242		X
12586243	X	
12589463		X
12589462	X	
12602802		X
12602801	X	

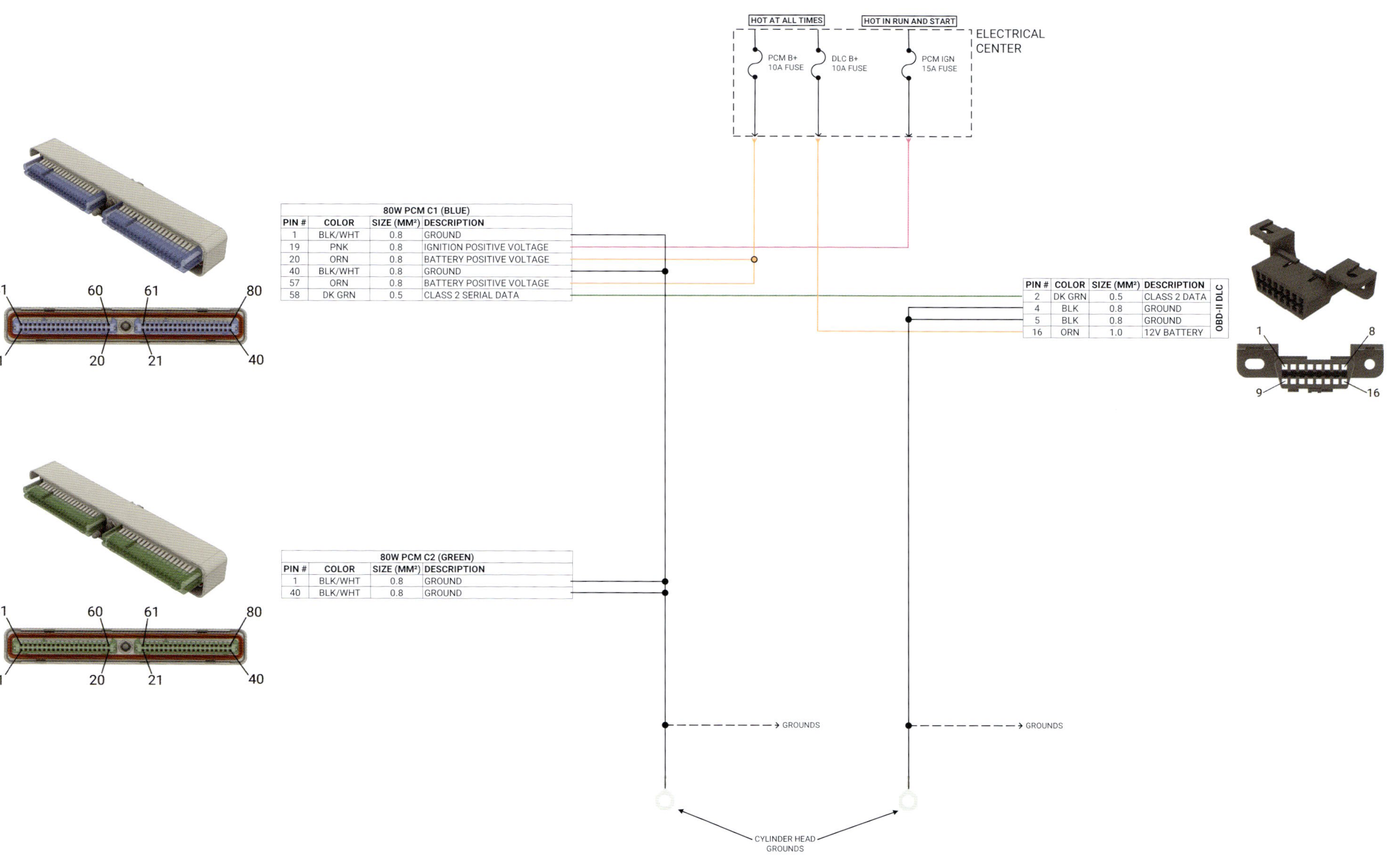

80W PCM C1 (BLUE)			
PIN #	COLOR	SIZE (MM²)	DESCRIPTION
1	BLK/WHT	0.8	GROUND
19	PNK	0.8	IGNITION POSITIVE VOLTAGE
20	ORN	0.8	BATTERY POSITIVE VOLTAGE
40	BLK/WHT	0.8	GROUND
57	ORN	0.8	BATTERY POSITIVE VOLTAGE
58	DK GRN	0.5	CLASS 2 SERIAL DATA

80W PCM C2 (GREEN)			
PIN #	COLOR	SIZE (MM²)	DESCRIPTION
1	BLK/WHT	0.8	GROUND
40	BLK/WHT	0.8	GROUND

OBD-II DLC			
PIN #	COLOR	SIZE (MM²)	DESCRIPTION
2	DK GRN	0.5	CLASS 2 DATA
4	BLK	0.8	GROUND
5	BLK	0.8	GROUND
16	ORN	1.0	12V BATTERY

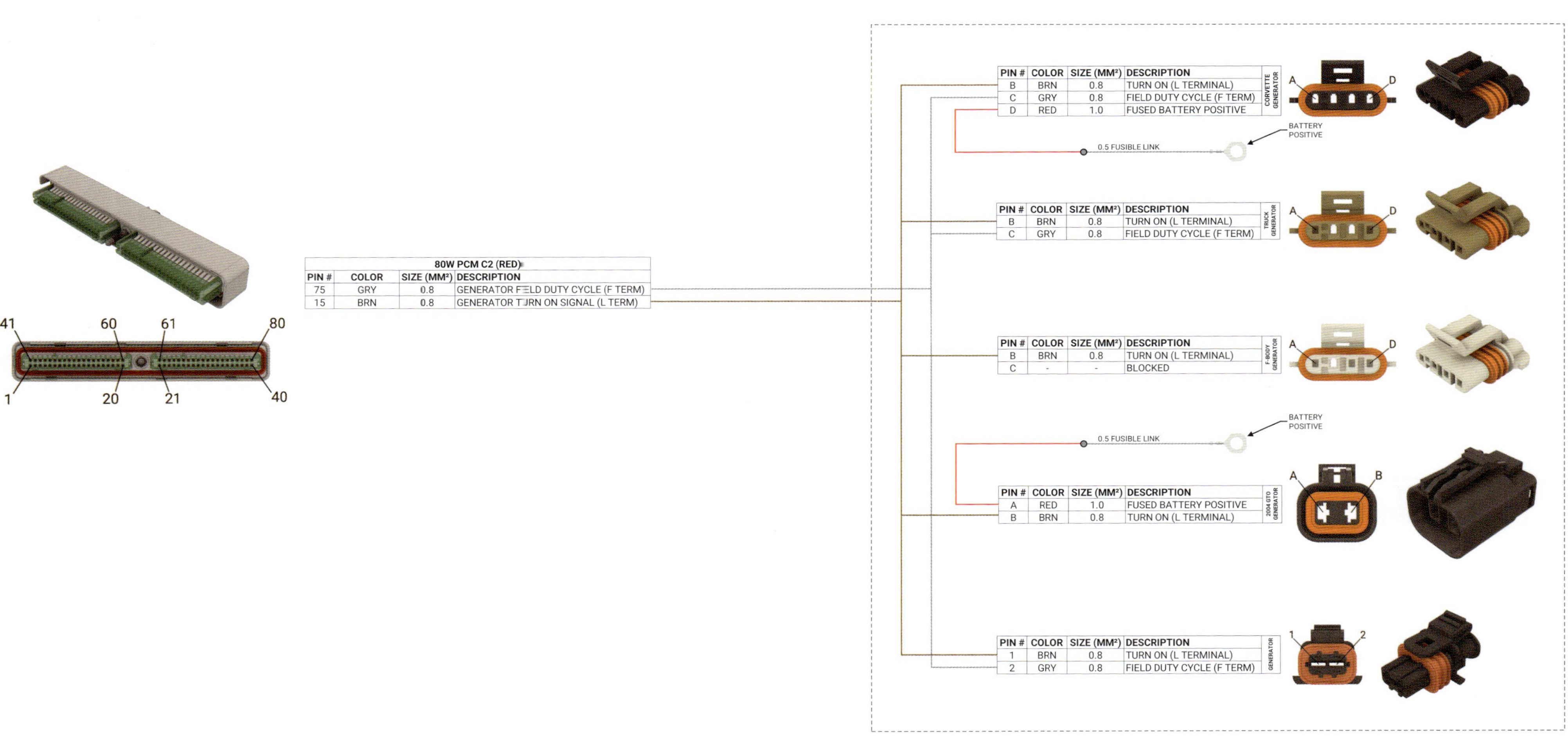

80W PCM C2 (RED)			
PIN #	COLOR	SIZE (MM²)	DESCRIPTION
75	GRY	0.8	GENERATOR FIELD DUTY CYCLE (F TERM)
15	BRN	0.8	GENERATOR TURN ON SIGNAL (L TERM)

PIN #	COLOR	SIZE (MM²)	DESCRIPTION
B	BRN	0.8	TURN ON (L TERMINAL)
C	GRY	0.8	FIELD DUTY CYCLE (F TERM)
D	RED	1.0	FUSED BATTERY POSITIVE

PIN #	COLOR	SIZE (MM²)	DESCRIPTION
B	BRN	0.8	TURN ON (L TERMINAL)
C	GRY	0.8	FIELD DUTY CYCLE (F TERM)

PIN #	COLOR	SIZE (MM²)	DESCRIPTION
B	BRN	0.8	TURN ON (L TERMINAL)
C	-	-	BLOCKED

PIN #	COLOR	SIZE (MM²)	DESCRIPTION
A	RED	1.0	FUSED BATTERY POSITIVE
B	BRN	0.8	TURN ON (L TERMINAL)

PIN #	COLOR	SIZE (MM²)	DESCRIPTION
1	BRN	0.8	TURN ON (L TERMINAL)
2	GRY	0.8	FIELD DUTY CYCLE (F TERM)

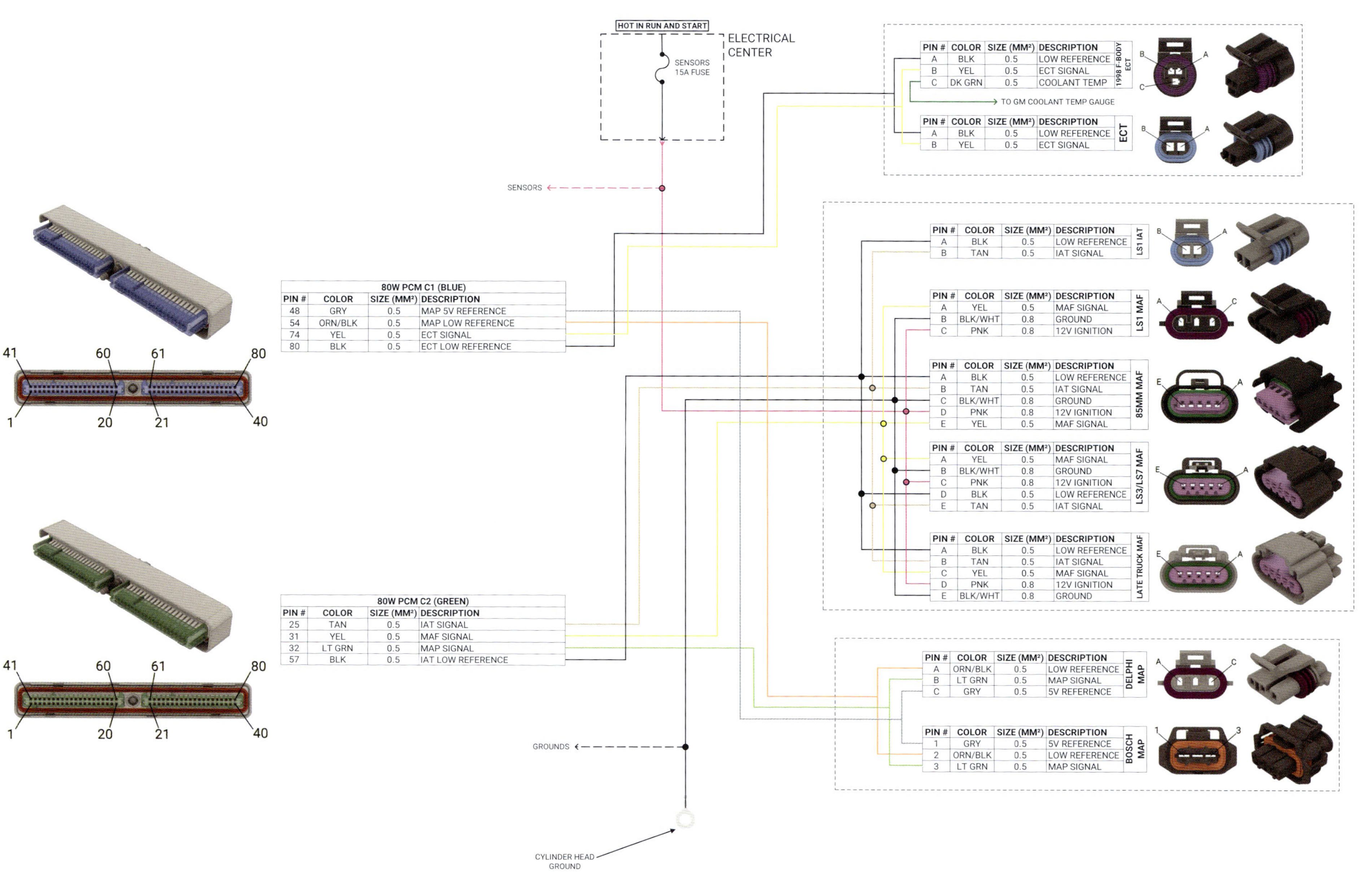

1998 F-BODY ECT

PIN #	COLOR	SIZE (MM²)	DESCRIPTION
A	BLK	0.5	LOW REFERENCE
B	YEL	0.5	ECT SIGNAL
C	DK GRN	0.5	COOLANT TEMP

ECT

PIN #	COLOR	SIZE (MM²)	DESCRIPTION
A	BLK	0.5	LOW REFERENCE
B	YEL	0.5	ECT SIGNAL

LS1 IAT

PIN #	COLOR	SIZE (MM²)	DESCRIPTION
A	BLK	0.5	LOW REFERENCE
B	TAN	0.5	IAT SIGNAL

LS1 MAF

PIN #	COLOR	SIZE (MM²)	DESCRIPTION
A	YEL	0.5	MAF SIGNAL
B	BLK/WHT	0.8	GROUND
C	PNK	0.8	12V IGNITION

85MM MAF

PIN #	COLOR	SIZE (MM²)	DESCRIPTION
A	BLK	0.5	LOW REFERENCE
B	TAN	0.5	IAT SIGNAL
C	BLK/WHT	0.8	GROUND
D	PNK	0.8	12V IGNITION
E	YEL	0.5	MAF SIGNAL

LS3/LS7 MAF

PIN #	COLOR	SIZE (MM²)	DESCRIPTION
A	YEL	0.5	MAF SIGNAL
B	BLK/WHT	0.8	GROUND
C	PNK	0.8	12V IGNITION
D	BLK	0.5	LOW REFERENCE
E	TAN	0.5	IAT SIGNAL

LATE TRUCK MAF

PIN #	COLOR	SIZE (MM²)	DESCRIPTION
A	BLK	0.5	LOW REFERENCE
B	TAN	0.5	IAT SIGNAL
C	YEL	0.5	MAF SIGNAL
D	PNK	0.8	12V IGNITION
E	BLK/WHT	0.8	GROUND

DELPHI MAP

PIN #	COLOR	SIZE (MM²)	DESCRIPTION
A	ORN/BLK	0.5	LOW REFERENCE
B	LT GRN	0.5	MAP SIGNAL
C	GRY	0.5	5V REFERENCE

BOSCH MAP

PIN #	COLOR	SIZE (MM²)	DESCRIPTION
1	GRY	0.5	5V REFERENCE
2	ORN/BLK	0.5	LOW REFERENCE
3	LT GRN	0.5	MAP SIGNAL

80W PCM C1 (BLUE)

PIN #	COLOR	SIZE (MM²)	DESCRIPTION
48	GRY	0.5	MAP 5V REFERENCE
54	ORN/BLK	0.5	MAP LOW REFERENCE
74	YEL	0.5	ECT SIGNAL
80	BLK	0.5	ECT LOW REFERENCE

80W PCM C2 (GREEN)

PIN #	COLOR	SIZE (MM²)	DESCRIPTION
25	TAN	0.5	IAT SIGNAL
31	YEL	0.5	MAF SIGNAL
32	LT GRN	0.5	MAP SIGNAL
57	BLK	0.5	IAT LOW REFERENCE

2003-2007 P59 PCM (ENGINE DATA SENSORS – HO2S)

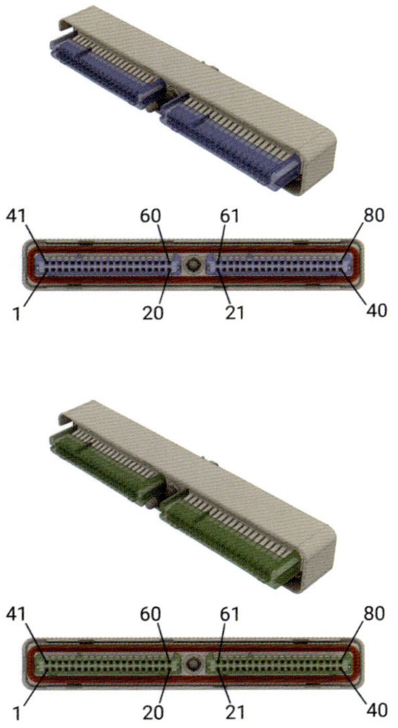

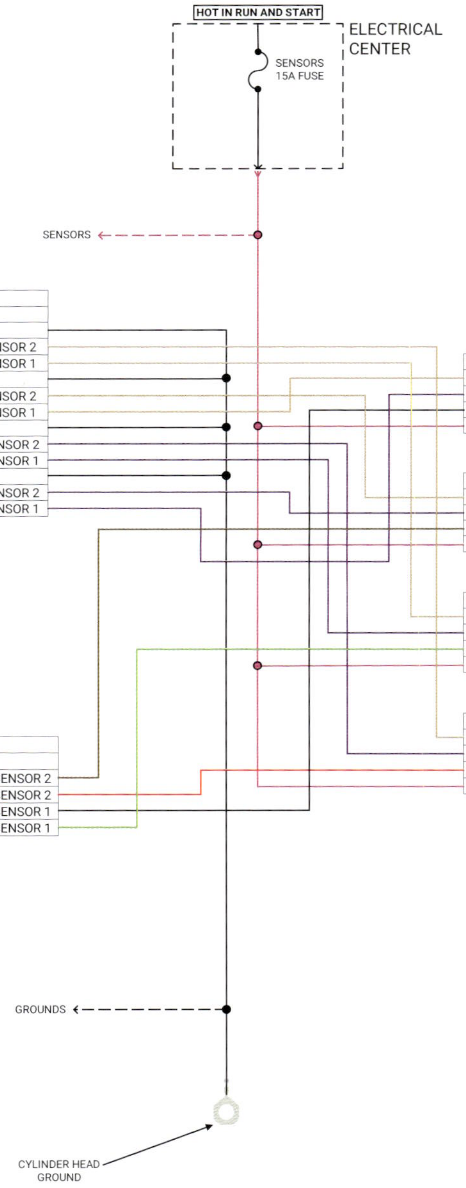

80W PCM C1 (BLUE)

PIN #	COLOR	SIZE (MM²)	DESCRIPTION
24	BLK/WHT	0.8	GROUND
25	TAN	0.8	HO2S LOW BANK 2 SENSOR 2
26	TAN	0.8	HO2S LOW BANK 2 SENSOR 1
27	BLK/WHT	0.8	GROUND
28	TAN/WHT	0.8	HO2S LOW BANK 1 SENSOR 2
29	TAN/WHT	0.8	HO2S LOW BANK 1 SENSOR 1
64	BLK/WHT	0.3	GROUND
65	PPL	0.3	HO2S HIGH BANK 2 SENSOR 2
66	PPL	0.3	HO2S HIGH BANK 2 SENSOR 1
67	BLK/WHT	0.8	GROUND
68	PPL/WHT	0.8	HO2S HIGH BANK 1 SENSOR 2
69	PPL/WHT	0.8	HO2S HIGH BANK 1 SENSOR 1

80W PCM C2 (GREEN)

PIN #	COLOR	SIZE (MM²)	DESCRIPTION
52	BRN	0.8	HEATER LOW BANK 1 SENSOR 2
53	RED/WHT	0.8	HEATER LOW BANK 2 SENSOR 2
72	BLK/WHT	0.8	HEATER LOW BANK 1 SENSOR 1
74	LT GRN	0.8	HEATER LOW BANK 2 SENSOR 1

HO2S BANK 1 SENSOR 1 (LEFT FRONT)

PIN #	COLOR	SIZE (MM²)	DESCRIPTION
A	TAN/WHT	0.8	HO2S LOW
B	PPL/WHT	0.8	HO2S HIGH
C or E	BLK/WHT	0.8	HEATER CONTROL LOW
D	PNK	0.8	HEATER CONTROL 12V

HO2S BANK 1 SENSOR 2 (LEFT REAR)

PIN #	COLOR	SIZE (MM²)	DESCRIPTION
A	TAN/WHT	0.8	HO2S LOW
B	PPL/WHT	0.8	HO2S HIGH
C or E	BRN	0.8	HEATER CONTROL LOW
D	PNK	0.8	HEATER CONTROL 12V

HO2S BANK 2 SENSOR 1 (RIGHT FRONT)

PIN #	COLOR	SIZE (MM²)	DESCRIPTION
A	TAN	0.8	HO2S LOW
B	PPL	0.8	HO2S HIGH
C or E	LT GRN	0.8	HEATER CONTROL LOW
D	PNK	0.8	HEATER CONTROL 12V

HO2S BANK 2 SENSOR 2 (RIGHT REAR)

PIN #	COLOR	SIZE (MM²)	DESCRIPTION
A	TAN	0.8	HO2S LOW
B	PPL	0.8	HO2S HIGH
C or E	RED	0.8	HEATER CONTROL LOW
D	PNK	0.8	HEATER CONTROL 12V

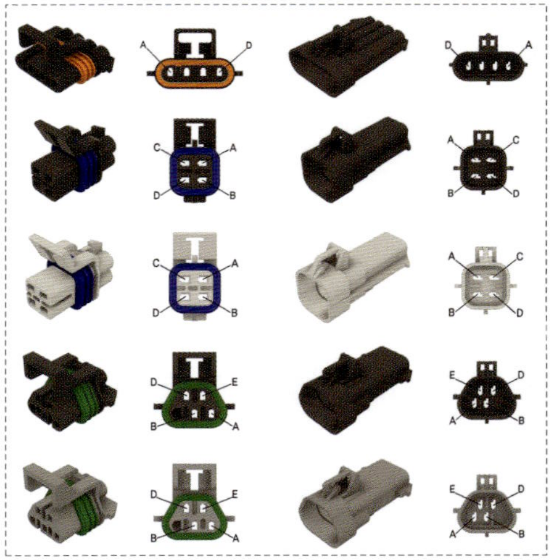

ALTHOUGH TEN DIFFERENT HARNESS CONNECTORS ARE USED AMONG LS ENGINE OXYGEN SENSORS, THEY SHARE THE SAME CONNECTOR CAVITY ASSIGNMENTS.

ONLY FOUR WIRES ARE USED WITH EACH OXYGEN SENSOR. CONNECTORS WITH FIVE CAVITIES BLOCK CAVITY C AND MOVE THE TYPICAL USE OF CAVITY C TO CAVITY E.

THE HEATER LOW CIRCUIT IS NOT ALWAYS CONTROLLED AND MONITORED BY THE PCM OR ECM. WHEN THE HEATER LOW CIRCUIT IS INSTALLED DIRECTLY TO GROUND, THE HEATER CIRCUIT IS NOT MONITORED FOR DIAGNOSTIC (DTC) PURPOSES.

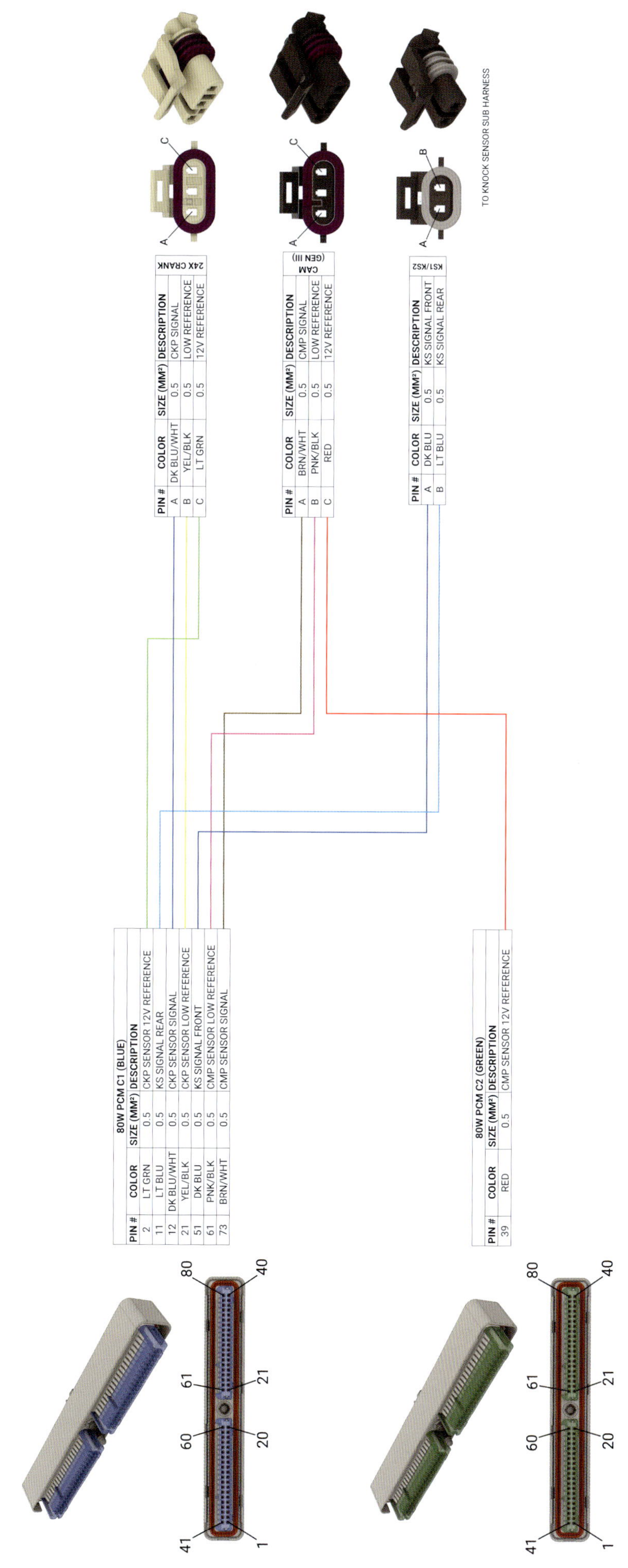

2003-2007 P59 PCM (IGNITION CONTROLS – CKP, CMP, KS1, KS2)
TO KNOCK SENSOR SUB HARNESS

24X CRANK
PIN # | COLOR | SIZE (MM²) | DESCRIPTION
A | DK BLU/WHT | 0.5 | CKP SIGNAL
B | YEL/BLK | 0.5 | LOW REFERENCE
C | LT GRN | 0.5 | 12V REFERENCE

CAM (GEN III)
PIN # | COLOR | SIZE (MM²) | DESCRIPTION
A | BRN/WHT | 0.5 | CMP SIGNAL
B | PNK/BLK | 0.5 | LOW REFERENCE
C | RED | 0.5 | 12V REFERENCE

KS1/KS2
PIN # | COLOR | SIZE (MM²) | DESCRIPTION
A | DK BLU | 0.5 | KS SIGNAL FRONT
B | LT BLU | 0.5 | KS SIGNAL REAR

80W PCM C1 (BLUE)
PIN # | COLOR | SIZE (MM²) | DESCRIPTION
2 | LT GRN | 0.5 | CKP SENSOR 12V REFERENCE
11 | LT BLU | 0.5 | KS SIGNAL REAR
12 | DK BLU/WHT | 0.5 | CKP SENSOR SIGNAL
21 | YEL/BLK | 0.5 | CKP SENSOR LOW REFERENCE
51 | DK BLU | 0.5 | KS SIGNAL FRONT
61 | PNK/BLK | 0.5 | CMP SENSOR LOW REFERENCE
73 | BRN/WHT | 0.5 | CMP SENSOR SIGNAL

80W PCM C2 (GREEN)
PIN # | COLOR | SIZE (MM²) | DESCRIPTION
39 | RED | 0.5 | CMP SENSOR 12V REFERENCE

A B C
80 40 61 21 60 20 41 1

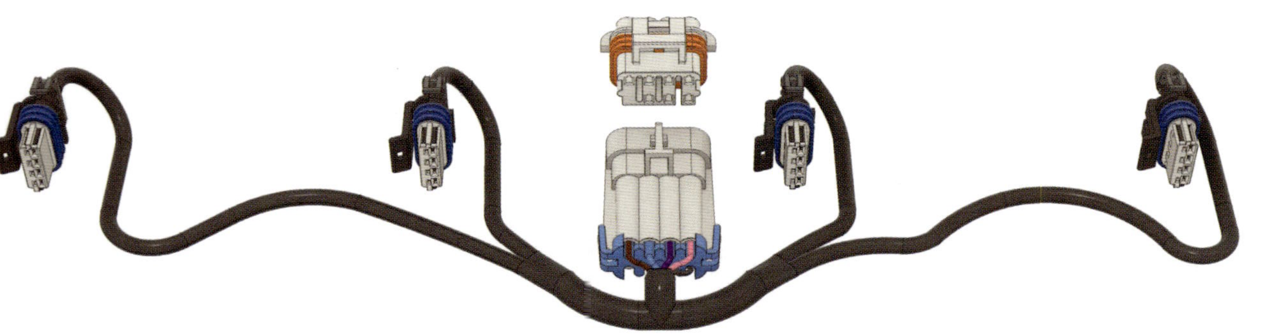

2003-2007 P59 PCM (IGNITION CONTROLS – IGNITION COILS)

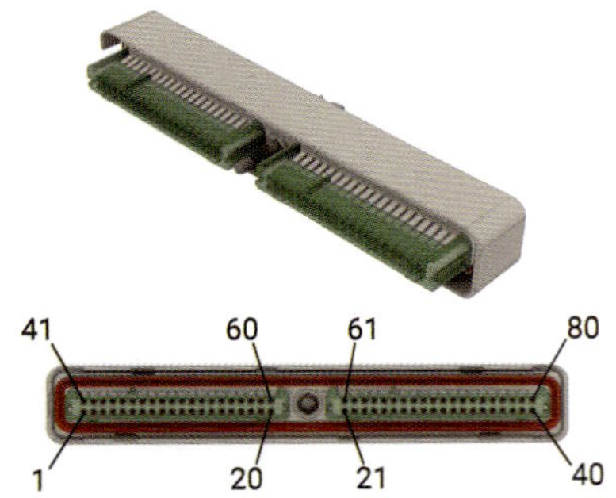

80W PCM C2 (GREEN)			
PIN #	COLOR	SIZE (MM²)	DESCRIPTION
26	PPL	0.8	IGNITION COIL 1 CONTROL
27	RED	0.8	IGNITION COIL 7 CONTROL
28	LT BLU/WHT	0.8	IGNITION COIL 6 CONTROL
29	DK GRN/WHT	0.8	IGNITION COIL 4 CONTROL
60	BRN	0.8	LOW REFERENCE BANK 1
61	BRN/WHT	0.8	LOW REFERENCE BANK 2
66	PPL/WHT	0.8	IGNITION COIL 8 CONTROL
67	RED/WHT	0.8	IGNITION COIL 2 CONTROL
68	DK GRN	0.8	IGNITION COIL 5 CONTROL
69	LT BLU	0.8	IGNITION COIL 3 CONTROL

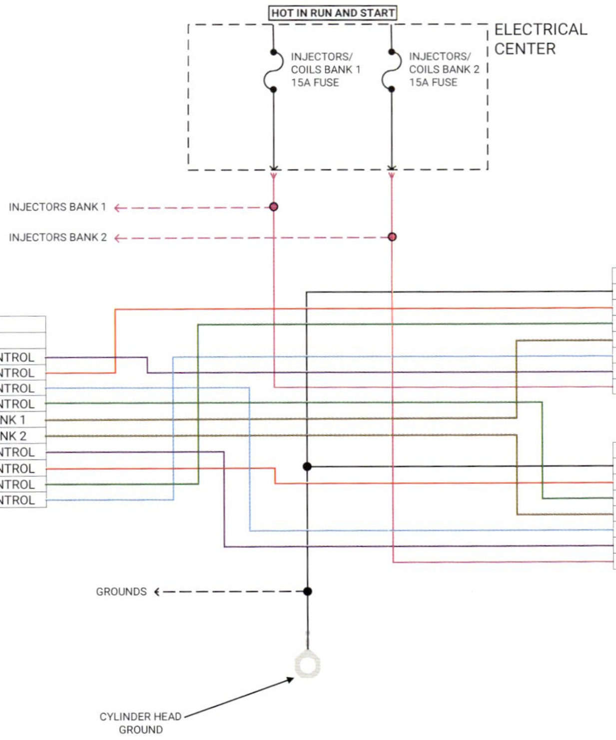

IGNITION COIL HARNESS BANK 1

PIN #	COLOR	SIZE (MM²)	DESCRIPTION
A	BLK	1.0	GROUND
B	RED	0.8	IGNITION COIL 7 CONTROL
C	DK GRN	0.8	IGNITION COIL 5 CONTROL
E	BRN	0.8	LOW REFERENCE
F	LT BLU	0.8	IGNITION COIL 3 CONTROL
G	PPL	0.8	IGNITION COIL 1 CONTROL
H	PNK	1.0	12V IGNITION

IGNITION COIL HARNESS BANK 2

PIN #	COLOR	SIZE (MM²)	DESCRIPTION
A	BLK	1.0	GROUND
B	RED/WHT	0.8	IGNITION COIL 2 CONTROL
C	DK GRN/WHT	0.8	IGNITION COIL 4 CONTROL
E	BRN/WHT	0.8	LOW REFERENCE
F	LT BLU/WHT	0.8	IGNITION COIL 6 CONTROL
G	PPL/WHT	0.8	IGNITION COIL 8 CONTROL
H	PNK	1.0	12V IGNITION

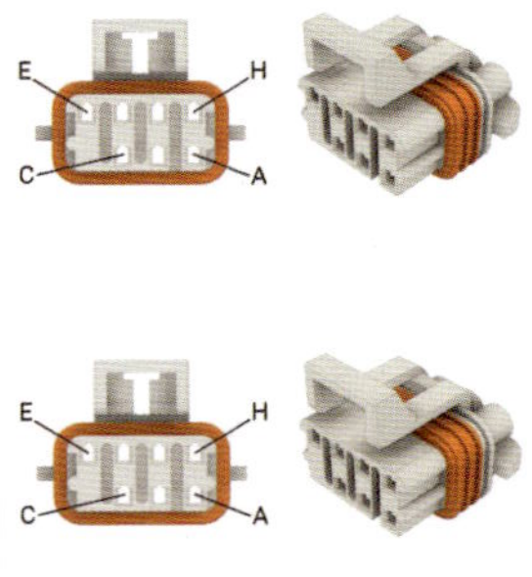

LS ENGINES(*) ARE FITTED WITH A PAIR OF IGNITION COIL SUB HARNESSES. EACH IGNITION COIL SUB HARNESS IS ATTACHED TO AN IGNITION COIL BRACKET ON TOP OF THE VALVE COVER. THE MATING 7 CAVITY METRI-PACK 150 FEMALE CONNECTOR CAN BE USED WITH ALL GM LS-SERIES IGNITION COIL SUB HARNESSES. NO REWIRING IS NECESSARY UNLESS THE ENGINE FIRE ORDER HAS CHANGED.

*EXCLUDES LS9 AND LSA ENGINES

TO DIRECTLY WIRE EACH IGNITION COIL TO THE ENGINE HARNESS, EACH 12V IGNITION (PINK WIRE), GROUND (BLACK WIRE), AND LOW REFERENCE WIRE (BROWN & BROWN/WHITE) WILL HAVE TO BE SPLICED TO FOUR ADDITIONAL WIRES TO PROVIDE POWER AND GROUND TO EACH IGNITION COIL.

2003-2007 P59 PCM (FUEL CONTROLS – EV1 FUEL INJECTORS)

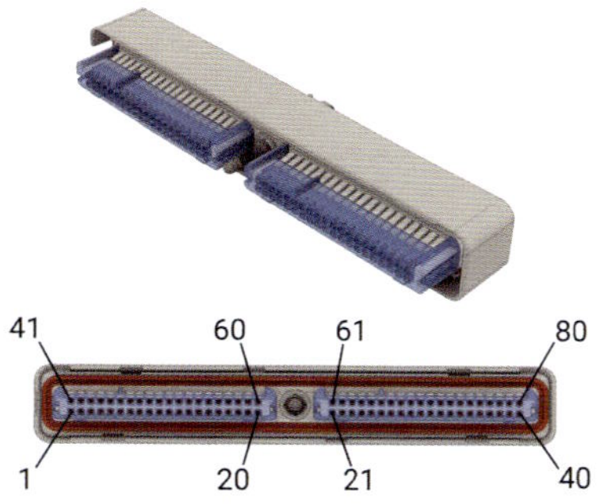

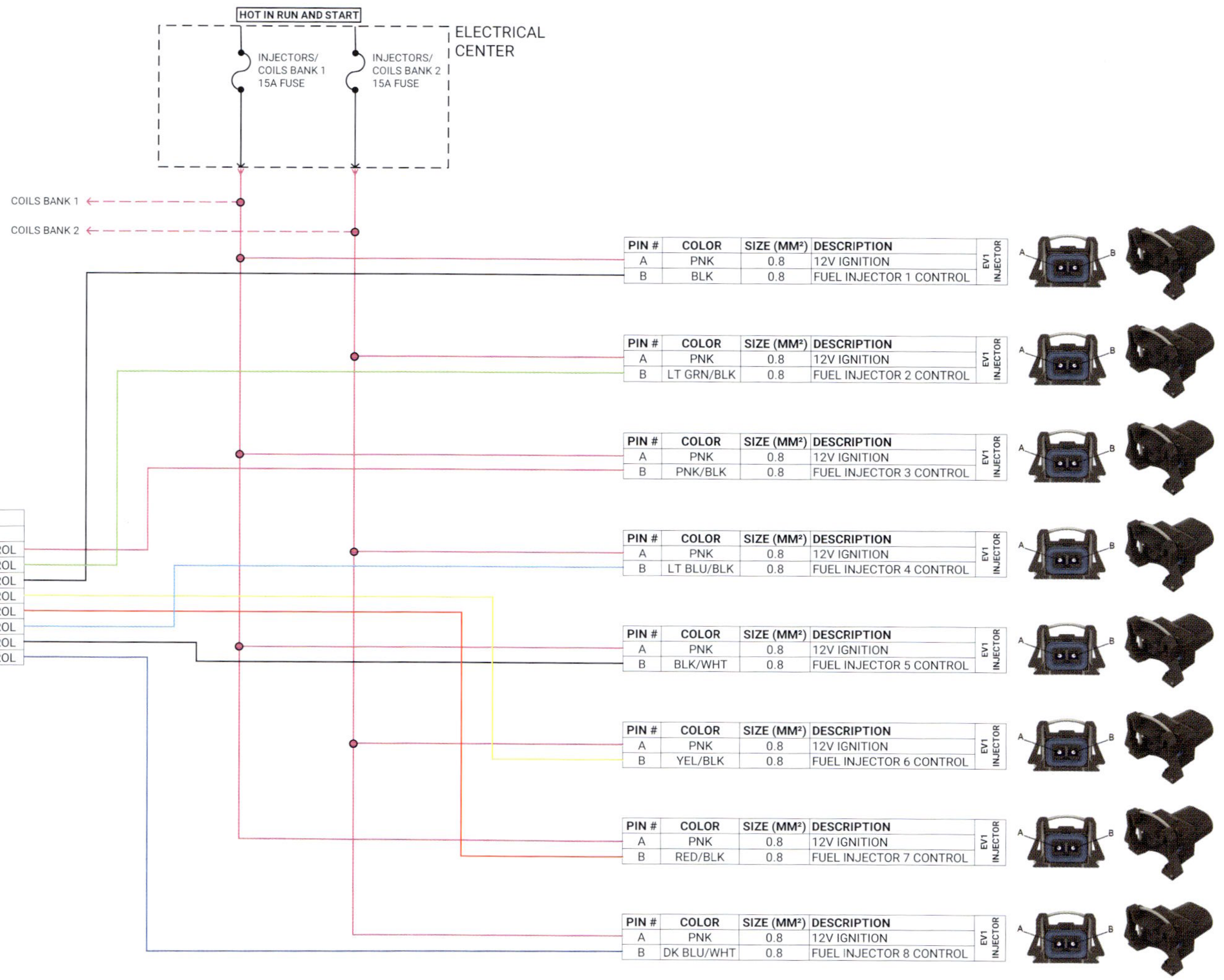

80W PCM C1 (BLUE)			
PIN #	COLOR	SIZE (MM²)	DESCRIPTION
3	PNK/BLK	0.8	FUEL INJECTOR 3 CONTROL
4	LT GRN/BLK	0.8	FUEL INJECTOR 2 CONTROL
36	BLK	0.8	FUEL INJECTOR 1 CONTROL
37	YEL/BLK	0.8	FUEL INJECTOR 6 CONTROL
43	RED/BLK	0.8	FUEL INJECTOR 7 CONTROL
44	LT BLU/BLK	0.8	FUEL INJECTOR 4 CONTROL
76	BLK/WHT	0.8	FUEL INJECTOR 5 CONTROL
77	DK BLU/WHT	0.8	FUEL INJECTOR 8 CONTROL

EV1 INJECTOR

PIN #	COLOR	SIZE (MM²)	DESCRIPTION
A	PNK	0.8	12V IGNITION
B	BLK	0.8	FUEL INJECTOR 1 CONTROL

EV1 INJECTOR

PIN #	COLOR	SIZE (MM²)	DESCRIPTION
A	PNK	0.8	12V IGNITION
B	LT GRN/BLK	0.8	FUEL INJECTOR 2 CONTROL

EV1 INJECTOR

PIN #	COLOR	SIZE (MM²)	DESCRIPTION
A	PNK	0.8	12V IGNITION
B	PNK/BLK	0.8	FUEL INJECTOR 3 CONTROL

EV1 INJECTOR

PIN #	COLOR	SIZE (MM²)	DESCRIPTION
A	PNK	0.8	12V IGNITION
B	LT BLU/BLK	0.8	FUEL INJECTOR 4 CONTROL

EV1 INJECTOR

PIN #	COLOR	SIZE (MM²)	DESCRIPTION
A	PNK	0.8	12V IGNITION
B	BLK/WHT	0.8	FUEL INJECTOR 5 CONTROL

EV1 INJECTOR

PIN #	COLOR	SIZE (MM²)	DESCRIPTION
A	PNK	0.8	12V IGNITION
B	YEL/BLK	0.8	FUEL INJECTOR 6 CONTROL

EV1 INJECTOR

PIN #	COLOR	SIZE (MM²)	DESCRIPTION
A	PNK	0.8	12V IGNITION
B	RED/BLK	0.8	FUEL INJECTOR 7 CONTROL

EV1 INJECTOR

PIN #	COLOR	SIZE (MM²)	DESCRIPTION
A	PNK	0.8	12V IGNITION
B	DK BLU/WHT	0.8	FUEL INJECTOR 8 CONTROL

2003-2007 P59 PCM (FUEL CONTROLS – MULTEC 2 FUEL INJECTORS)

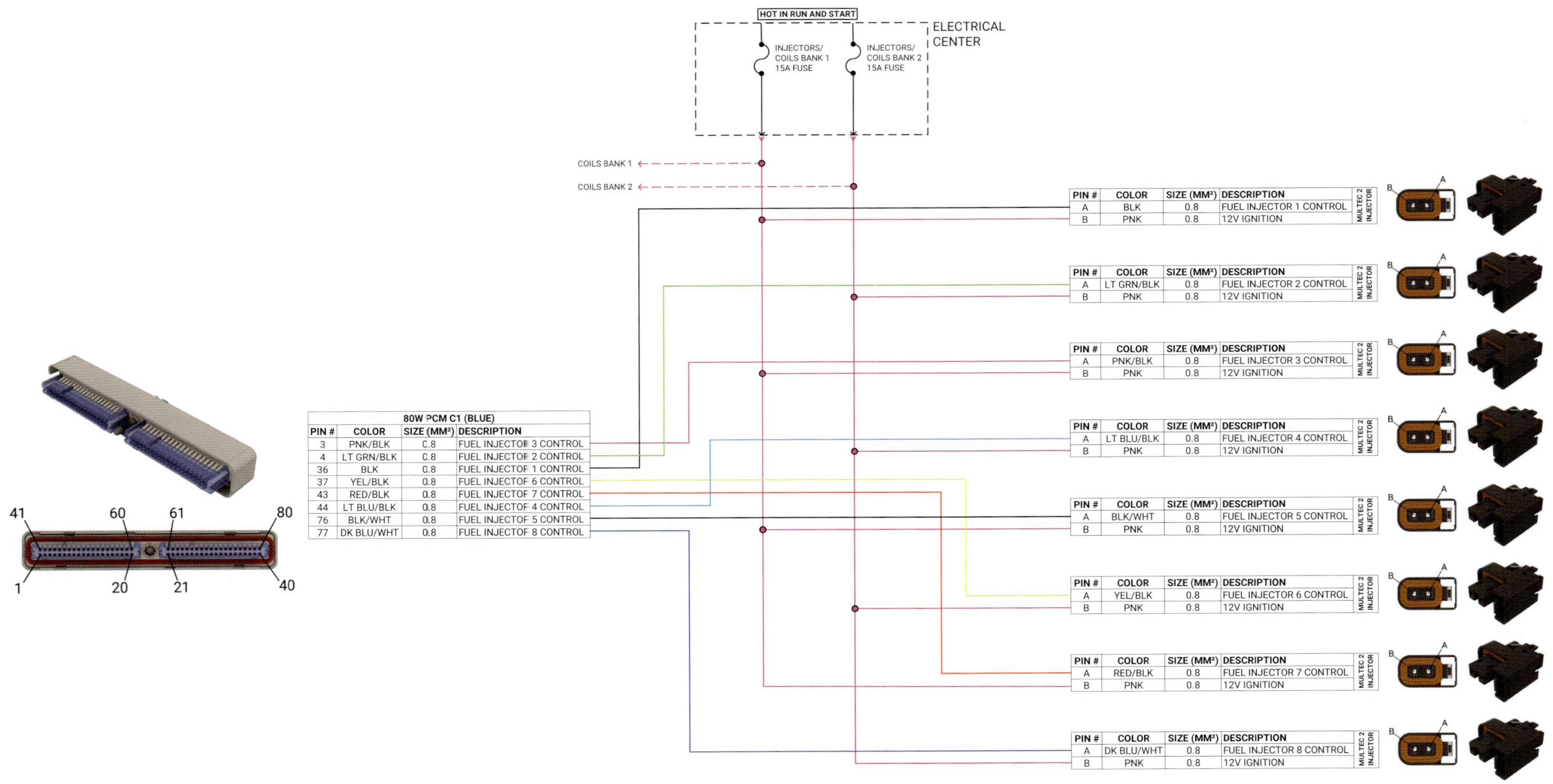

PIN #	COLOR	SIZE (MM²)	DESCRIPTION	
A	BLK	0.8	FUEL INJECTOR 1 CONTROL	MULTEC 2 INJECTOR
B	PNK	0.8	12V IGNITION	

PIN #	COLOR	SIZE (MM²)	DESCRIPTION	
A	LT GRN/BLK	0.8	FUEL INJECTOR 2 CONTROL	MULTEC 2 INJECTOR
B	PNK	0.8	12V IGNITION	

PIN #	COLOR	SIZE (MM²)	DESCRIPTION	
A	PNK/BLK	0.8	FUEL INJECTOR 3 CONTROL	MULTEC 2 INJECTOR
B	PNK	0.8	12V IGNITION	

PIN #	COLOR	SIZE (MM²)	DESCRIPTION	
A	LT BLU/BLK	0.8	FUEL INJECTOR 4 CONTROL	MULTEC 2 INJECTOR
B	PNK	0.8	12V IGNITION	

PIN #	COLOR	SIZE (MM²)	DESCRIPTION	
A	BLK/WHT	0.8	FUEL INJECTOR 5 CONTROL	MULTEC 2 INJECTOR
B	PNK	0.8	12V IGNITION	

PIN #	COLOR	SIZE (MM²)	DESCRIPTION	
A	YEL/BLK	0.8	FUEL INJECTOR 6 CONTROL	MULTEC 2 INJECTOR
B	PNK	0.8	12V IGNITION	

PIN #	COLOR	SIZE (MM²)	DESCRIPTION	
A	RED/BLK	0.8	FUEL INJECTOR 7 CONTROL	MULTEC 2 INJECTOR
B	PNK	0.8	12V IGNITION	

PIN #	COLOR	SIZE (MM²)	DESCRIPTION	
A	DK BLU/WHT	0.8	FUEL INJECTOR 8 CONTROL	MULTEC 2 INJECTOR
B	PNK	0.8	12V IGNITION	

80W PCM C1 (BLUE)			
PIN #	COLOR	SIZE (MM²)	DESCRIPTION
3	PNK/BLK	0.8	FUEL INJECTOR 3 CONTROL
4	LT GRN/BLK	0.8	FUEL INJECTOR 2 CONTROL
36	BLK	0.8	FUEL INJECTOR 1 CONTROL
37	YEL/BLK	0.8	FUEL INJECTOR 6 CONTROL
43	RED/BLK	0.8	FUEL INJECTOR 7 CONTROL
44	LT BLU/BLK	0.8	FUEL INJECTOR 4 CONTROL
76	BLK/WHT	0.8	FUEL INJECTOR 5 CONTROL
77	DK BLU/WHT	0.8	FUEL INJECTOR 8 CONTROL

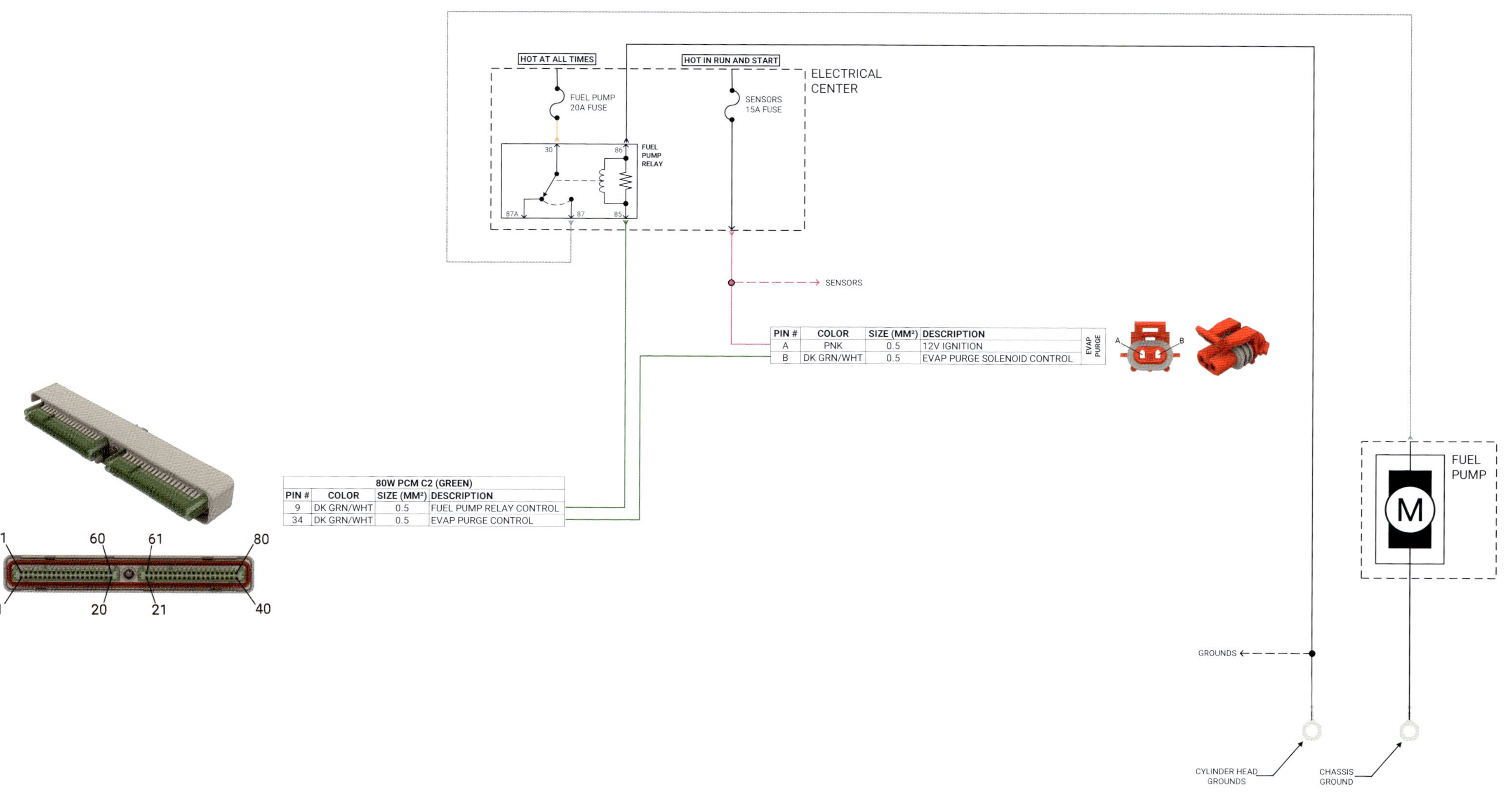

PIN #	COLOR	SIZE (MM²)	DESCRIPTION	
A	PNK	0.5	12V IGNITION	EVAP PURGE
B	DK GRN/WHT	0.5	EVAP PURGE SOLENOID CONTROL	

80W PCM C2 (GREEN)			
PIN #	COLOR	SIZE (MM²)	DESCRIPTION
9	DK GRN/WHT	0.5	FUEL PUMP RELAY CONTROL
34	DK GRN/WHT	0.5	EVAP PURGE CONTROL

2003-2007 P59 PCM (THROTTLE SYSTEM – CABLE)

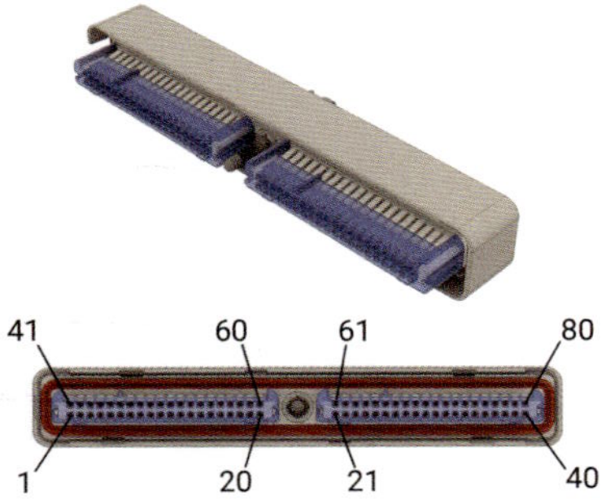

80W PCM C1 (BLUE)			
PIN #	COLOR	SIZE (MM²)	DESCRIPTION
8	GRY	0.5	TPS 5V REFERENCE
60	BLK	0.5	TPS LOW REFERENCE

PIN #	COLOR	SIZE (MM²)	DESCRIPTION	TPS
A	GRY	0.5	5V REFERENCE	
B	BLK	0.5	LOW REFERENCE	
C	DK BLU	0.5	TPS SIGNAL	

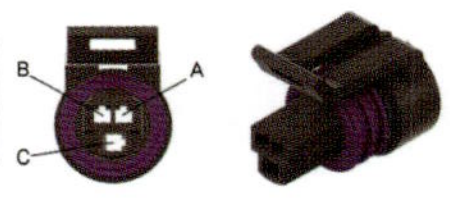

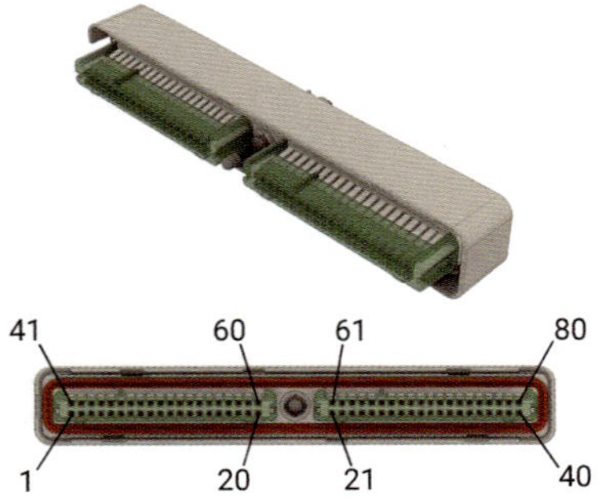

80W PCM C2 (GREEN)			
PIN #	COLOR	SIZE (MM²)	DESCRIPTION
24	DK BLU	0.5	TP SENSOR SIGNAL
76	LT GRN/WHT	0.5	IAC COIL B HIGH
77	LT GRN/BLK	0.5	IAC COIL B LOW
78	LT BLU/BLK	0.5	IAC COIL A LOW
79	LT BLU/WHT	0.5	IAC COIL A HIGH

PIN #	COLOR	SIZE (MM²)	DESCRIPTION	IAC
A	LT GRN/BLK	0.5	IAC COIL B LOW	
B	LT GRN/WHT	0.5	IAC COIL B HIGH	
C	LT BLU/BLK	0.5	IAC COIL A LOW	
D	LT BLU/WHT	0.5	IAC COIL A HIGH	

IMPORTANT!

THE FOLLOWING P59 PCMS CONTAIN AN IAC DRIVER AND CAN BE
USED WITH CABLE THROTTLE AND ELECTRONIC THROTTLE SYSTEMS:
- 12581565
- 12586243
- 12589462
- 12602801

THE FOLLOWING P59 PCMS DO NOT CONTAIN AN IAC DRIVER AND
CAN ONLY BE USED WITH ELECTRONIC THROTTLE SYSTEMS:
- 12582605
- 12586242
- 12589463
- 12602802

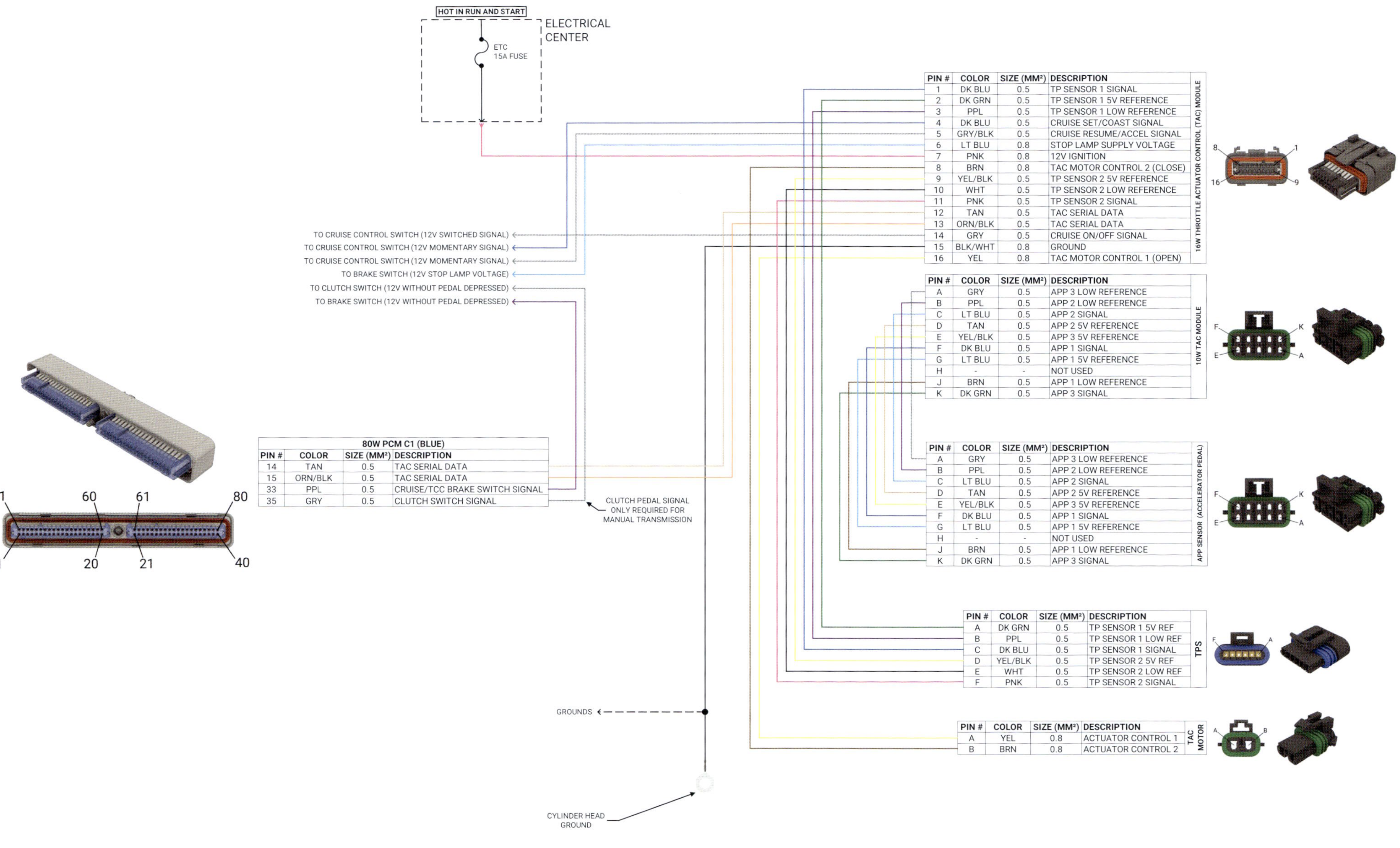

16W THROTTLE ACTUATOR CONTROL (TAC) MODULE

PIN #	COLOR	SIZE (MM²)	DESCRIPTION
1	DK BLU	0.5	TP SENSOR 1 SIGNAL
2	DK GRN	0.5	TP SENSOR 1 5V REFERENCE
3	PPL	0.5	TP SENSOR 1 LOW REFERENCE
4	DK BLU	0.5	CRUISE SET/COAST SIGNAL
5	GRY/BLK	0.5	CRUISE RESUME/ACCEL SIGNAL
6	LT BLU	0.8	STOP LAMP SUPPLY VOLTAGE
7	PNK	0.8	12V IGNITION
8	BRN	0.8	TAC MOTOR CONTROL 2 (CLOSE)
9	YEL/BLK	0.5	TP SENSOR 2 5V REFERENCE
10	WHT	0.5	TP SENSOR 2 LOW REFERENCE
11	PNK	0.5	TP SENSOR 2 SIGNAL
12	TAN	0.5	TAC SERIAL DATA
13	ORN/BLK	0.5	TAC SERIAL DATA
14	GRY	0.5	CRUISE ON/OFF SIGNAL
15	BLK/WHT	0.8	GROUND
16	YEL	0.8	TAC MOTOR CONTROL 1 (OPEN)

10W TAC MODULE

PIN #	COLOR	SIZE (MM²)	DESCRIPTION
A	GRY	0.5	APP 3 LOW REFERENCE
B	PPL	0.5	APP 2 LOW REFERENCE
C	LT BLU	0.5	APP 2 SIGNAL
D	TAN	0.5	APP 2 5V REFERENCE
E	YEL/BLK	0.5	APP 3 5V REFERENCE
F	DK BLU	0.5	APP 1 SIGNAL
G	LT BLU	0.5	APP 1 5V REFERENCE
H	-	-	NOT USED
J	BRN	0.5	APP 1 LOW REFERENCE
K	DK GRN	0.5	APP 3 SIGNAL

APP SENSOR (ACCELERATOR PEDAL)

PIN #	COLOR	SIZE (MM²)	DESCRIPTION
A	GRY	0.5	APP 3 LOW REFERENCE
B	PPL	0.5	APP 2 LOW REFERENCE
C	LT BLU	0.5	APP 2 SIGNAL
D	TAN	0.5	APP 2 5V REFERENCE
E	YEL/BLK	0.5	APP 3 5V REFERENCE
F	DK BLU	0.5	APP 1 SIGNAL
G	LT BLU	0.5	APP 1 5V REFERENCE
H	-	-	NOT USED
J	BRN	0.5	APP 1 LOW REFERENCE
K	DK GRN	0.5	APP 3 SIGNAL

TPS

PIN #	COLOR	SIZE (MM²)	DESCRIPTION
A	DK GRN	0.5	TP SENSOR 1 5V REF
B	PPL	0.5	TP SENSOR 1 LOW REF
C	DK BLU	0.5	TP SENSOR 1 SIGNAL
D	YEL/BLK	0.5	TP SENSOR 2 5V REF
E	WHT	0.5	TP SENSOR 2 LOW REF
F	PNK	0.5	TP SENSOR 2 SIGNAL

TAC MOTOR

PIN #	COLOR	SIZE (MM²)	DESCRIPTION
A	YEL	0.8	ACTUATOR CONTROL 1
B	BRN	0.8	ACTUATOR CONTROL 2

80W PCM C1 (BLUE)

PIN #	COLOR	SIZE (MM²)	DESCRIPTION
14	TAN	0.5	TAC SERIAL DATA
15	ORN/BLK	0.5	TAC SERIAL DATA
33	PPL	0.5	CRUISE/TCC BRAKE SWITCH SIGNAL
35	GRY	0.5	CLUTCH SWITCH SIGNAL

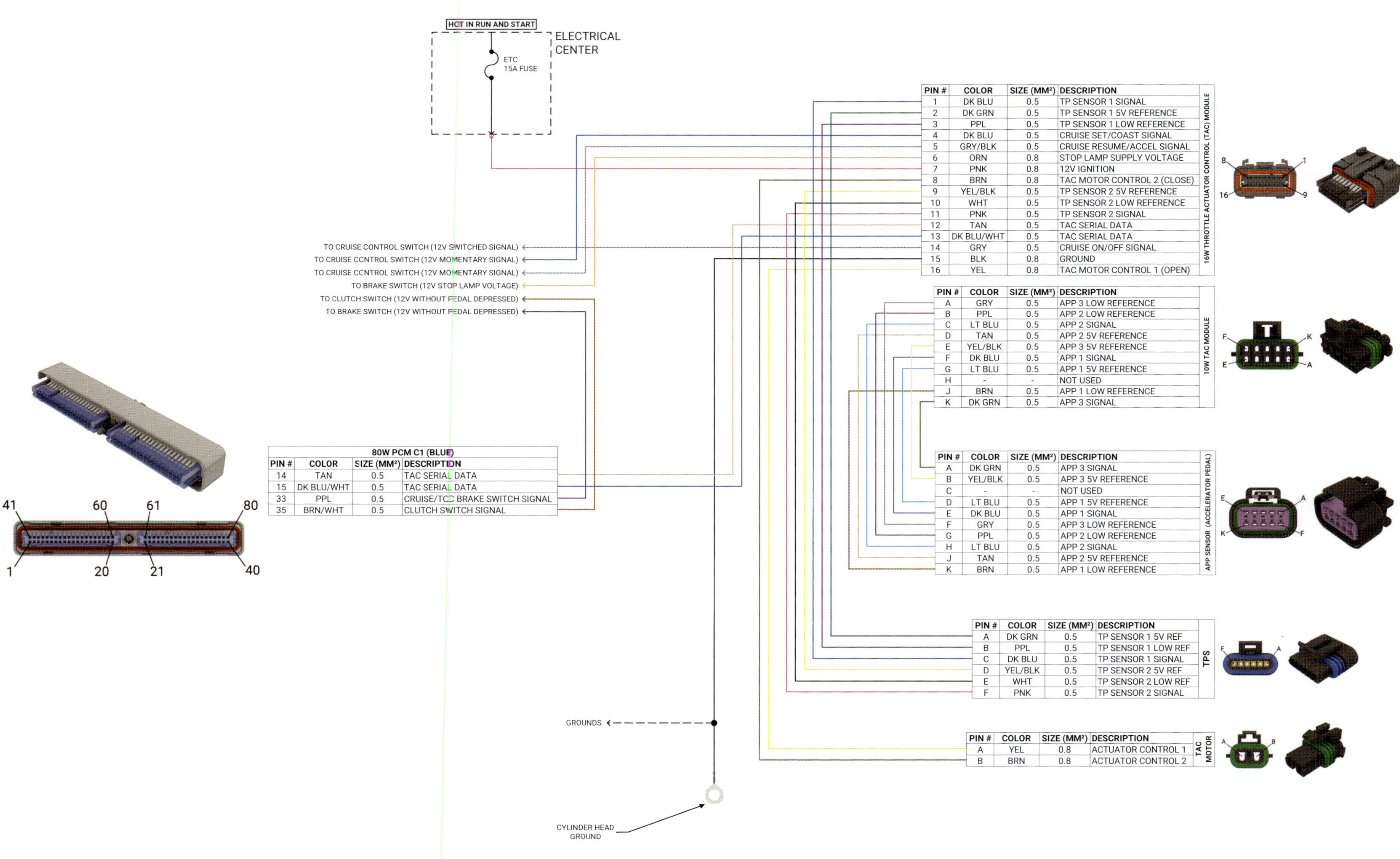

16W THROTTLE ACTUATOR CONTROL (TAC) MODULE

PIN #	COLOR	SIZE (MM²)	DESCRIPTION
1	DK BLU	0.5	TP SENSOR 1 SIGNAL
2	DK GRN	0.5	TP SENSOR 1 5V REFERENCE
3	PPL	0.5	TP SENSOR 1 LOW REFERENCE
4	DK BLU	0.5	CRUISE SET/COAST SIGNAL
5	GRY/BLK	0.5	CRUISE RESUME/ACCEL SIGNAL
6	ORN	0.8	STOP LAMP SUPPLY VOLTAGE
7	PNK	0.8	12V IGNITION
8	BRN	0.8	TAC MOTOR CONTROL 2 (CLOSE)
9	YEL/BLK	0.5	TP SENSOR 2 5V REFERENCE
10	WHT	0.5	TP SENSOR 2 LOW REFERENCE
11	PNK	0.5	TP SENSOR 2 SIGNAL
12	TAN	0.5	TAC SERIAL DATA
13	DK BLU/WHT	0.5	TAC SERIAL DATA
14	GRY	0.5	CRUISE ON/OFF SIGNAL
15	BLK	0.8	GROUND
16	YEL	0.8	TAC MOTOR CONTROL 1 (OPEN)

10W TAC MODULE

PIN #	COLOR	SIZE (MM²)	DESCRIPTION
A	GRY	0.5	APP 3 LOW REFERENCE
B	PPL	0.5	APP 2 LOW REFERENCE
C	LT BLU	0.5	APP 2 SIGNAL
D	TAN	0.5	APP 2 5V REFERENCE
E	YEL/BLK	0.5	APP 3 5V REFERENCE
F	DK BLU	0.5	APP 1 SIGNAL
G	LT BLU	0.5	APP 1 5V REFERENCE
H	-	-	NOT USED
J	BRN	0.5	APP 1 LOW REFERENCE
K	DK GRN	0.5	APP 3 SIGNAL

APP SENSOR (ACCELERATOR PEDAL)

PIN #	COLOR	SIZE (MM²)	DESCRIPTION
A	DK GRN	0.5	APP 3 SIGNAL
B	YEL/BLK	0.5	APP 3 5V REFERENCE
C	-	-	NOT USED
D	LT BLU	0.5	APP 1 5V REFERENCE
E	DK BLU	0.5	APP 1 SIGNAL
F	GRY	0.5	APP 3 LOW REFERENCE
G	PPL	0.5	APP 2 LOW REFERENCE
H	LT BLU	0.5	APP 2 SIGNAL
J	TAN	0.5	APP 2 5V REFERENCE
K	BRN	0.5	APP 1 LOW REFERENCE

80W PCM C1 (BLUE)

PIN #	COLOR	SIZE (MM²)	DESCRIPTION
14	TAN	0.5	TAC SERIAL DATA
15	DK BLU/WHT	0.5	TAC SERIAL DATA
33	PPL	0.5	CRUISE/TCC BRAKE SWITCH SIGNAL
35	BRN/WHT	0.5	CLUTCH SWITCH SIGNAL

TPS

PIN #	COLOR	SIZE (MM²)	DESCRIPTION
A	DK GRN	0.5	TP SENSOR 1 5V REF
B	PPL	0.5	TP SENSOR 1 LOW REF
C	DK BLU	0.5	TP SENSOR 1 SIGNAL
D	YEL/BLK	0.5	TP SENSOR 2 5V REF
E	WHT	0.5	TP SENSOR 2 LOW REF
F	PNK	0.5	TP SENSOR 2 SIGNAL

TAC MOTOR

PIN #	COLOR	SIZE (MM²)	DESCRIPTION
A	YEL	0.8	ACTUATOR CONTROL 1
B	BRN	0.8	ACTUATOR CONTROL 2

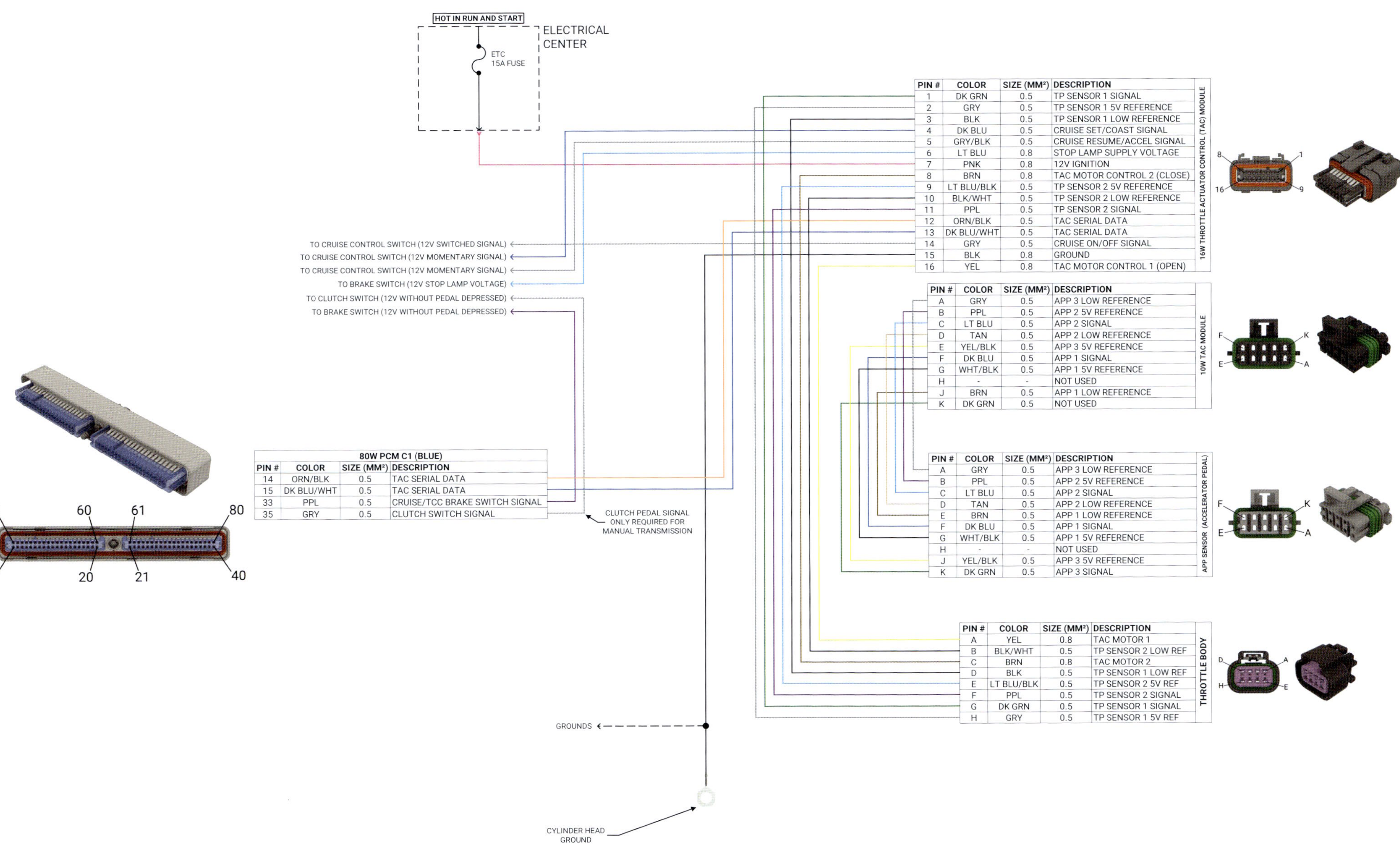

PIN #	COLOR	SIZE (MM²)	DESCRIPTION	
1	DK GRN	0.5	TP SENSOR 1 SIGNAL	16W THROTTLE ACTUATOR CONTROL (TAC) MODULE
2	GRY	0.5	TP SENSOR 1 5V REFERENCE	
3	BLK	0.5	TP SENSOR 1 LOW REFERENCE	
4	DK BLU	0.5	CRUISE SET/COAST SIGNAL	
5	GRY/BLK	0.5	CRUISE RESUME/ACCEL SIGNAL	
6	LT BLU	0.8	STOP LAMP SUPPLY VOLTAGE	
7	PNK	0.8	12V IGNITION	
8	BRN	0.8	TAC MOTOR CONTROL 2 (CLOSE)	
9	LT BLU/BLK	0.5	TP SENSOR 2 5V REFERENCE	
10	BLK/WHT	0.5	TP SENSOR 2 LOW REFERENCE	
11	PPL	0.5	TP SENSOR 2 SIGNAL	
12	ORN/BLK	0.5	TAC SERIAL DATA	
13	DK BLU/WHT	0.5	TAC SERIAL DATA	
14	GRY	0.5	CRUISE ON/OFF SIGNAL	
15	BLK	0.8	GROUND	
16	YEL	0.8	TAC MOTOR CONTROL 1 (OPEN)	

PIN #	COLOR	SIZE (MM²)	DESCRIPTION	
A	GRY	0.5	APP 3 LOW REFERENCE	10W TAC MODULE
B	PPL	0.5	APP 2 5V REFERENCE	
C	LT BLU	0.5	APP 2 SIGNAL	
D	TAN	0.5	APP 2 LOW REFERENCE	
E	YEL/BLK	0.5	APP 3 5V REFERENCE	
F	DK BLU	0.5	APP 1 SIGNAL	
G	WHT/BLK	0.5	APP 1 5V REFERENCE	
H	-	-	NOT USED	
J	BRN	0.5	APP 1 LOW REFERENCE	
K	DK GRN	0.5	NOT USED	

PIN #	COLOR	SIZE (MM²)	DESCRIPTION	
A	GRY	0.5	APP 3 LOW REFERENCE	APP SENSOR (ACCELERATOR PEDAL)
B	PPL	0.5	APP 2 5V REFERENCE	
C	LT BLU	0.5	APP 2 SIGNAL	
D	TAN	0.5	APP 2 LOW REFERENCE	
E	BRN	0.5	APP 1 LOW REFERENCE	
F	DK BLU	0.5	APP 1 SIGNAL	
G	WHT/BLK	0.5	APP 1 5V REFERENCE	
H	-	-	NOT USED	
J	YEL/BLK	0.5	APP 3 5V REFERENCE	
K	DK GRN	0.5	APP 3 SIGNAL	

PIN #	COLOR	SIZE (MM²)	DESCRIPTION	
A	YEL	0.8	TAC MOTOR 1	THROTTLE BODY
B	BLK/WHT	0.5	TP SENSOR 2 LOW REF	
C	BRN	0.8	TAC MOTOR 2	
D	BLK	0.5	TP SENSOR 1 LOW REF	
E	LT BLU/BLK	0.5	TP SENSOR 2 5V REF	
F	PPL	0.5	TP SENSOR 2 SIGNAL	
G	DK GRN	0.5	TP SENSOR 1 SIGNAL	
H	GRY	0.5	TP SENSOR 1 5V REF	

80W PCM C1 (BLUE)			
PIN #	COLOR	SIZE (MM²)	DESCRIPTION
14	ORN/BLK	0.5	TAC SERIAL DATA
15	DK BLU/WHT	0.5	TAC SERIAL DATA
33	PPL	0.5	CRUISE/TCC BRAKE SWITCH SIGNAL
35	GRY	0.5	CLUTCH SWITCH SIGNAL

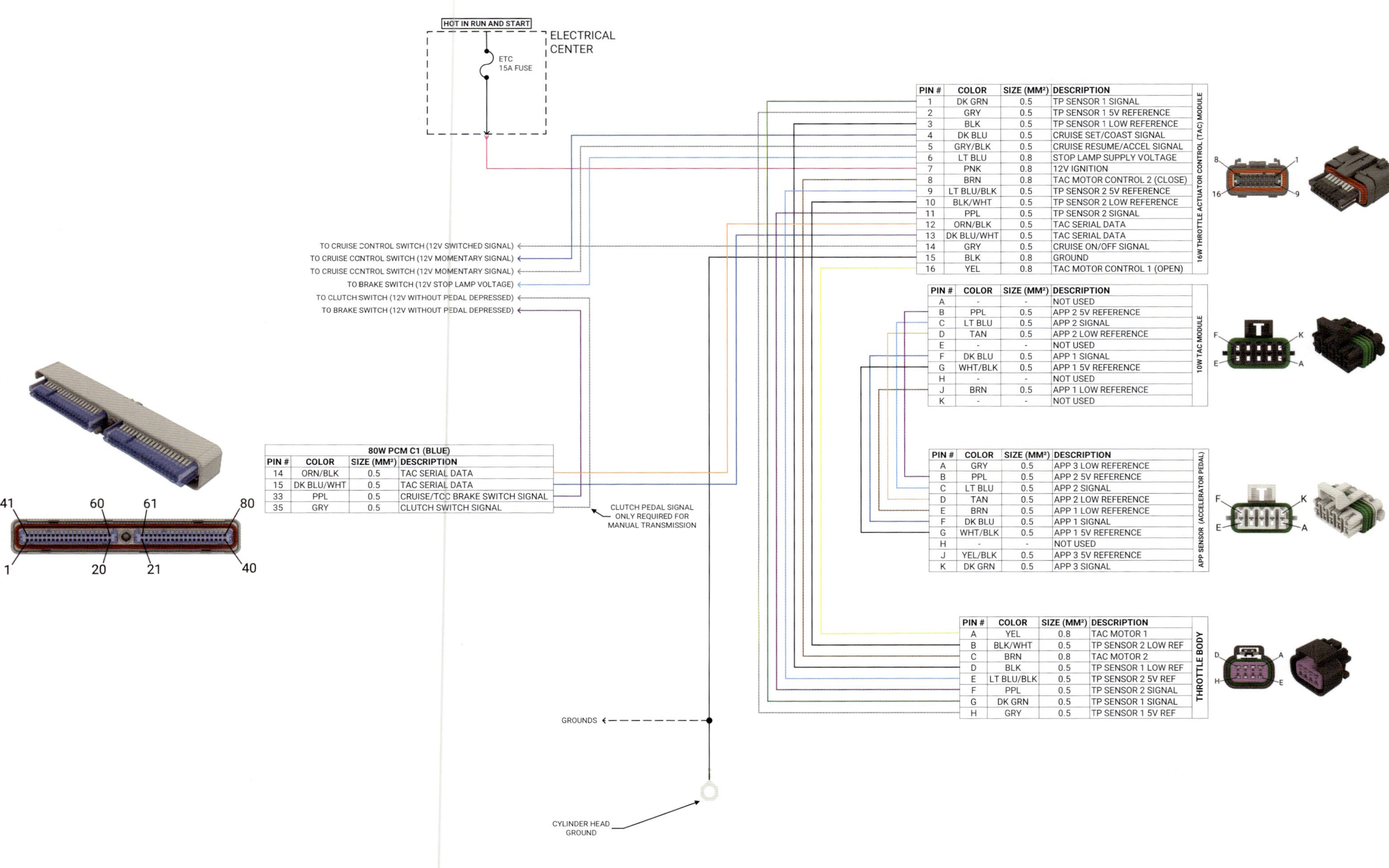

16W THROTTLE ACTUATOR CONTROL (TAC) MODULE

PIN #	COLOR	SIZE (MM²)	DESCRIPTION
1	DK GRN	0.5	TP SENSOR 1 SIGNAL
2	GRY	0.5	TP SENSOR 1 5V REFERENCE
3	BLK	0.5	TP SENSOR 1 LOW REFERENCE
4	DK BLU	0.5	CRUISE SET/COAST SIGNAL
5	GRY/BLK	0.5	CRUISE RESUME/ACCEL SIGNAL
6	LT BLU	0.8	STOP LAMP SUPPLY VOLTAGE
7	PNK	0.8	12V IGNITION
8	BRN	0.8	TAC MOTOR CONTROL 2 (CLOSE)
9	LT BLU/BLK	0.5	TP SENSOR 2 5V REFERENCE
10	BLK/WHT	0.5	TP SENSOR 2 LOW REFERENCE
11	PPL	0.5	TP SENSOR 2 SIGNAL
12	ORN/BLK	0.5	TAC SERIAL DATA
13	DK BLU/WHT	0.5	TAC SERIAL DATA
14	GRY	0.5	CRUISE ON/OFF SIGNAL
15	BLK	0.8	GROUND
16	YEL	0.8	TAC MOTOR CONTROL 1 (OPEN)

10W TAC MODULE

PIN #	COLOR	SIZE (MM²)	DESCRIPTION
A	-	-	NOT USED
B	PPL	0.5	APP 2 5V REFERENCE
C	LT BLU	0.5	APP 2 SIGNAL
D	TAN	0.5	APP 2 LOW REFERENCE
E	-	-	NOT USED
F	DK BLU	0.5	APP 1 SIGNAL
G	WHT/BLK	0.5	APP 1 5V REFERENCE
H	-	-	NOT USED
J	BRN	0.5	APP 1 LOW REFERENCE
K	-	-	NOT USED

APP SENSOR (ACCELERATOR PEDAL)

PIN #	COLOR	SIZE (MM²)	DESCRIPTION
A	GRY	0.5	APP 3 LOW REFERENCE
B	PPL	0.5	APP 2 5V REFERENCE
C	LT BLU	0.5	APP 2 SIGNAL
D	TAN	0.5	APP 2 LOW REFERENCE
E	BRN	0.5	APP 1 LOW REFERENCE
F	DK BLU	0.5	APP 1 SIGNAL
G	WHT/BLK	0.5	APP 1 5V REFERENCE
H	-	-	NOT USED
J	YEL/BLK	0.5	APP 3 5V REFERENCE
K	DK GRN	0.5	APP 3 SIGNAL

THROTTLE BODY

PIN #	COLOR	SIZE (MM²)	DESCRIPTION
A	YEL	0.8	TAC MOTOR 1
B	BLK/WHT	0.5	TP SENSOR 2 LOW REF
C	BRN	0.8	TAC MOTOR 2
D	BLK	0.5	TP SENSOR 1 LOW REF
E	LT BLU/BLK	0.5	TP SENSOR 2 5V REF
F	PPL	0.5	TP SENSOR 2 SIGNAL
G	DK GRN	0.5	TP SENSOR 1 SIGNAL
H	GRY	0.5	TP SENSOR 1 5V REF

80W PCM C1 (BLUE)

PIN #	COLOR	SIZE (MM²)	DESCRIPTION
14	ORN/BLK	0.5	TAC SERIAL DATA
15	DK BLU/WHT	0.5	TAC SERIAL DATA
33	PPL	0.5	CRUISE/TCC BRAKE SWITCH SIGNAL
35	GRY	0.5	CLUTCH SWITCH SIGNAL

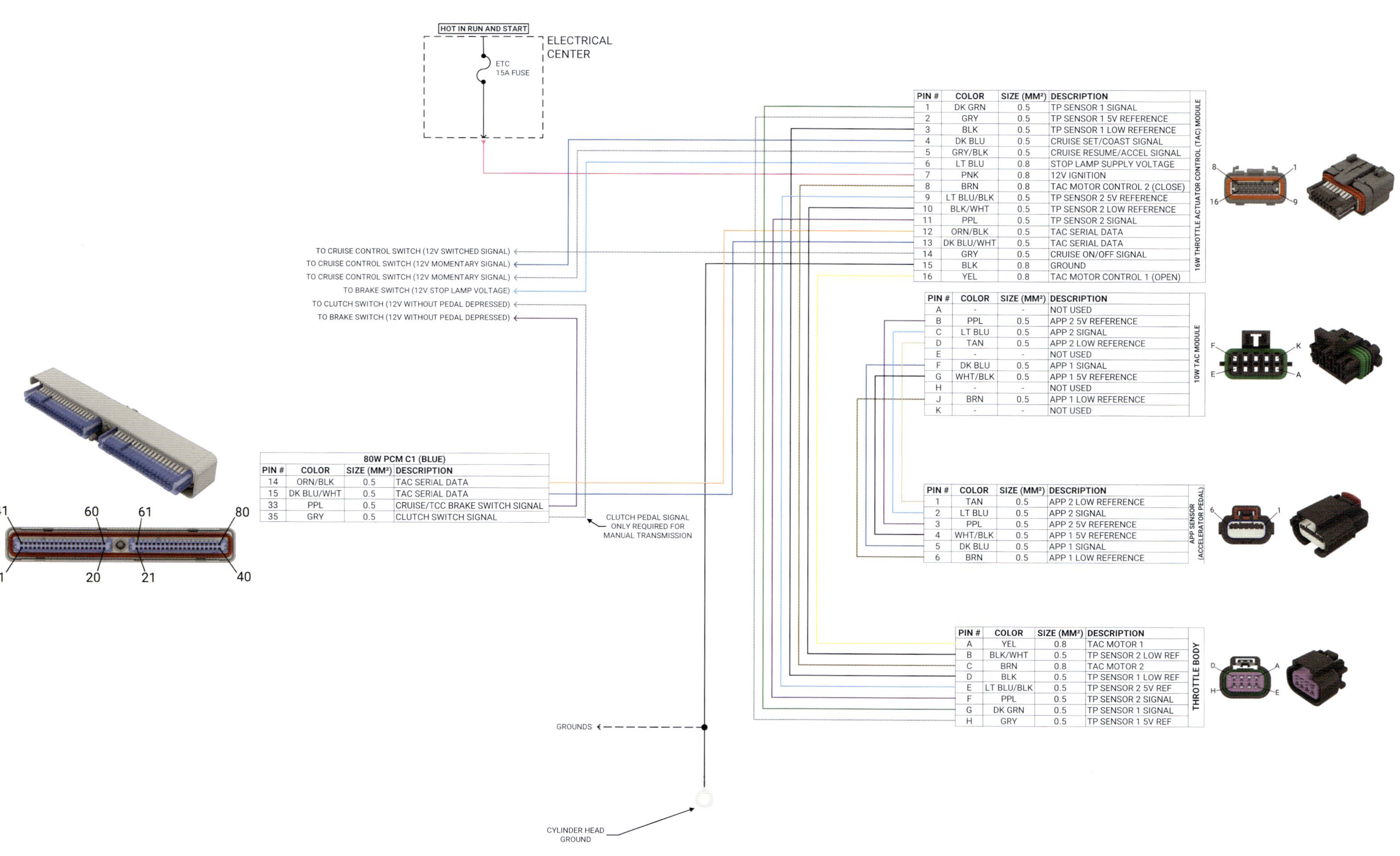

16W THROTTLE ACTUATOR CONTROL (TAC) MODULE

PIN #	COLOR	SIZE (MM²)	DESCRIPTION
1	DK GRN	0.5	TP SENSOR 1 SIGNAL
2	GRY	0.5	TP SENSOR 1 5V REFERENCE
3	BLK	0.5	TP SENSOR 1 LOW REFERENCE
4	DK BLU	0.5	CRUISE SET/COAST SIGNAL
5	GRY/BLK	0.5	CRUISE RESUME/ACCEL SIGNAL
6	LT BLU	0.8	STOP LAMP SUPPLY VOLTAGE
7	PNK	0.8	12V IGNITION
8	BRN	0.8	TAC MOTOR CONTROL 2 (CLOSE)
9	LT BLU/BLK	0.5	TP SENSOR 2 5V REFERENCE
10	BLK/WHT	0.5	TP SENSOR 2 LOW REFERENCE
11	PPL	0.5	TP SENSOR 2 SIGNAL
12	ORN/BLK	0.5	TAC SERIAL DATA
13	DK BLU/WHT	0.5	TAC SERIAL DATA
14	GRY	0.5	CRUISE ON/OFF SIGNAL
15	BLK	0.8	GROUND
16	YEL	0.8	TAC MOTOR CONTROL 1 (OPEN)

10W TAC MODULE

PIN #	COLOR	SIZE (MM²)	DESCRIPTION
A	-	-	NOT USED
B	PPL	0.5	APP 2 5V REFERENCE
C	LT BLU	0.5	APP 2 SIGNAL
D	TAN	0.5	APP 2 LOW REFERENCE
E	-	-	NOT USED
F	DK BLU	0.5	APP 1 SIGNAL
G	WHT/BLK	0.5	APP 1 5V REFERENCE
H	-	-	NOT USED
J	BRN	0.5	APP 1 LOW REFERENCE
K	-	-	NOT USED

80W PCM C1 (BLUE)

PIN #	COLOR	SIZE (MM²)	DESCRIPTION
14	ORN/BLK	0.5	TAC SERIAL DATA
15	DK BLU/WHT	0.5	TAC SERIAL DATA
33	PPL	0.5	CRUISE/TCC BRAKE SWITCH SIGNAL
35	GRY	0.5	CLUTCH SWITCH SIGNAL

APP SENSOR (ACCELERATOR PEDAL)

PIN #	COLOR	SIZE (MM²)	DESCRIPTION
1	TAN	0.5	APP 2 LOW REFERENCE
2	LT BLU	0.5	APP 2 SIGNAL
3	PPL	0.5	APP 2 5V REFERENCE
4	WHT/BLK	0.5	APP 1 5V REFERENCE
5	DK BLU	0.5	APP 1 SIGNAL
6	BRN	0.5	APP 1 LOW REFERENCE

THROTTLE BODY

PIN #	COLOR	SIZE (MM²)	DESCRIPTION
A	YEL	0.8	TAC MOTOR 1
B	BLK/WHT	0.5	TP SENSOR 2 LOW REF
C	BRN	0.8	TAC MOTOR 2
D	BLK	0.5	TP SENSOR 1 LOW REF
E	LT BLU/BLK	0.5	TP SENSOR 2 5V REF
F	PPL	0.5	TP SENSOR 2 SIGNAL
G	DK GRN	0.5	TP SENSOR 1 SIGNAL
H	GRY	0.5	TP SENSOR 1 5V REF

2004-2006 P59 PCM (THROTTLE SYSTEM – ELECTRONIC (VAN))

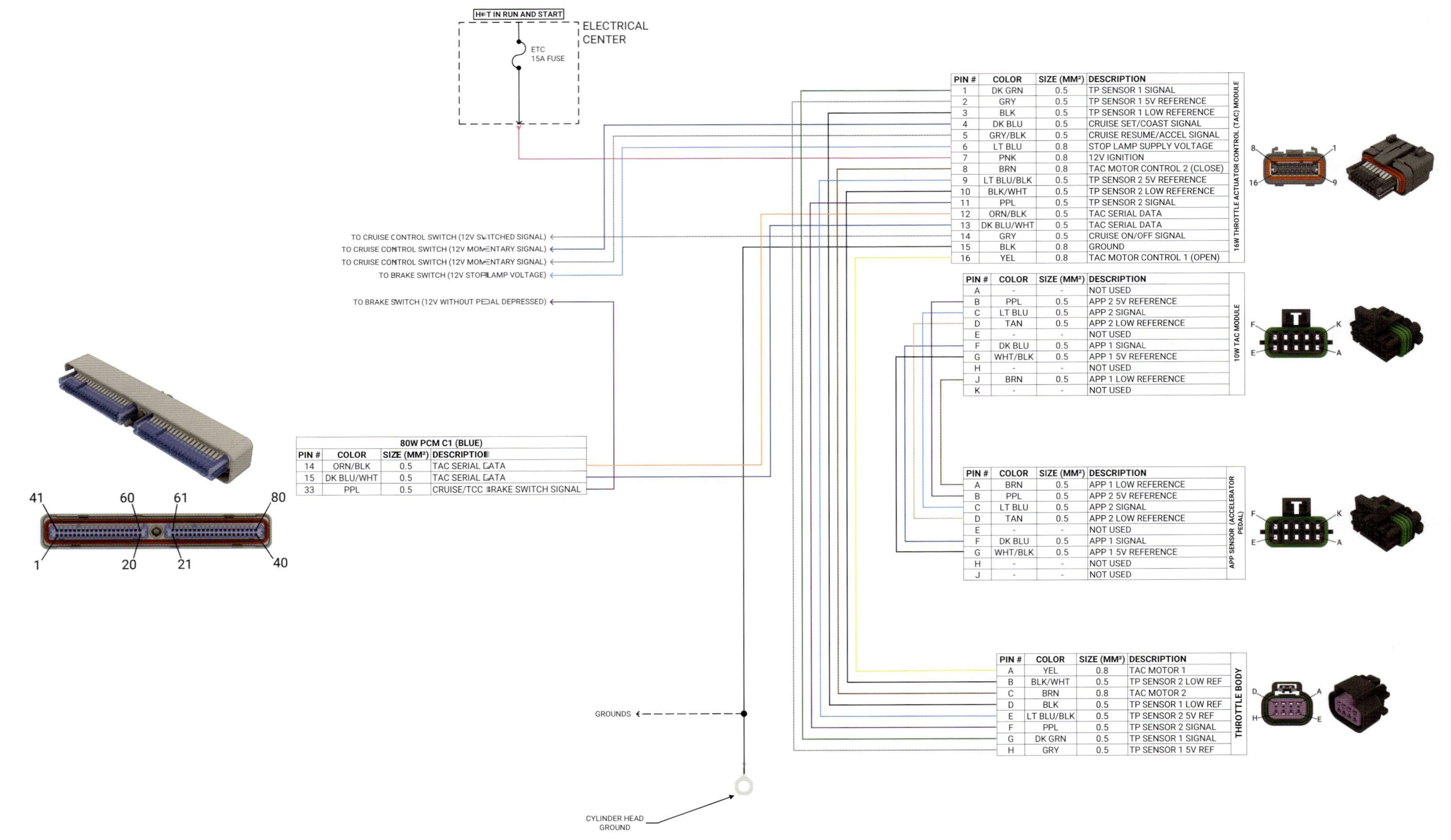

16W THROTTLE ACTUATOR CONTROL (TAC) MODULE

PIN #	COLOR	SIZE (MM²)	DESCRIPTION
1	DK GRN	0.5	TP SENSOR 1 SIGNAL
2	GRY	0.5	TP SENSOR 1 5V REFERENCE
3	BLK	0.5	TP SENSOR 1 LOW REFERENCE
4	DK BLU	0.5	CRUISE SET/COAST SIGNAL
5	GRY/BLK	0.5	CRUISE RESUME/ACCEL SIGNAL
6	LT BLU	0.8	STOP LAMP SUPPLY VOLTAGE
7	PNK	0.8	12V IGNITION
8	BRN	0.8	TAC MOTOR CONTROL 2 (CLOSE)
9	LT BLU/BLK	0.5	TP SENSOR 2 5V REFERENCE
10	BLK/WHT	0.5	TP SENSOR 2 LOW REFERENCE
11	PPL	0.5	TP SENSOR 2 SIGNAL
12	ORN/BLK	0.5	TAC SERIAL DATA
13	DK BLU/WHT	0.5	TAC SERIAL DATA
14	GRY	0.5	CRUISE ON/OFF SIGNAL
15	BLK	0.8	GROUND
16	YEL	0.8	TAC MOTOR CONTROL 1 (OPEN)

10W TAC MODULE

PIN #	COLOR	SIZE (MM²)	DESCRIPTION
A	-	-	NOT USED
B	PPL	0.5	APP 2 5V REFERENCE
C	LT BLU	0.5	APP 2 SIGNAL
D	TAN	0.5	APP 2 LOW REFERENCE
E	-	-	NOT USED
F	DK BLU	0.5	APP 1 SIGNAL
G	WHT/BLK	0.5	APP 1 5V REFERENCE
H	-	-	NOT USED
J	BRN	0.5	APP 1 LOW REFERENCE
K	-	-	NOT USED

80W PCM C1 (BLUE)

PIN #	COLOR	SIZE (MM²)	DESCRIPTION
14	ORN/BLK	0.5	TAC SERIAL DATA
15	DK BLU/WHT	0.5	TAC SERIAL DATA
33	PPL	0.5	CRUISE/TCC BRAKE SWITCH SIGNAL

APP SENSOR (ACCELERATOR PEDAL)

PIN #	COLOR	SIZE (MM²)	DESCRIPTION
A	BRN	0.5	APP 1 LOW REFERENCE
B	PPL	0.5	APP 2 5V REFERENCE
C	LT BLU	0.5	APP 2 SIGNAL
D	TAN	0.5	APP 2 LOW REFERENCE
E	-	-	NOT USED
F	DK BLU	0.5	APP 1 SIGNAL
G	WHT/BLK	0.5	APP 1 5V REFERENCE
H	-	-	NOT USED
J	-	-	NOT USED

THROTTLE BODY

PIN #	COLOR	SIZE (MM²)	DESCRIPTION
A	YEL	0.8	TAC MOTOR 1
B	BLK/WHT	0.5	TP SENSOR 2 LOW REF
C	BRN	0.8	TAC MOTOR 2
D	BLK	0.5	TP SENSOR 1 LOW REF
E	LT BLU/BLK	0.5	TP SENSOR 2 5V REF
F	PPL	0.5	TP SENSOR 2 SIGNAL
G	DK GRN	0.5	TP SENSOR 1 SIGNAL
H	GRY	0.5	TP SENSOR 1 5V REF

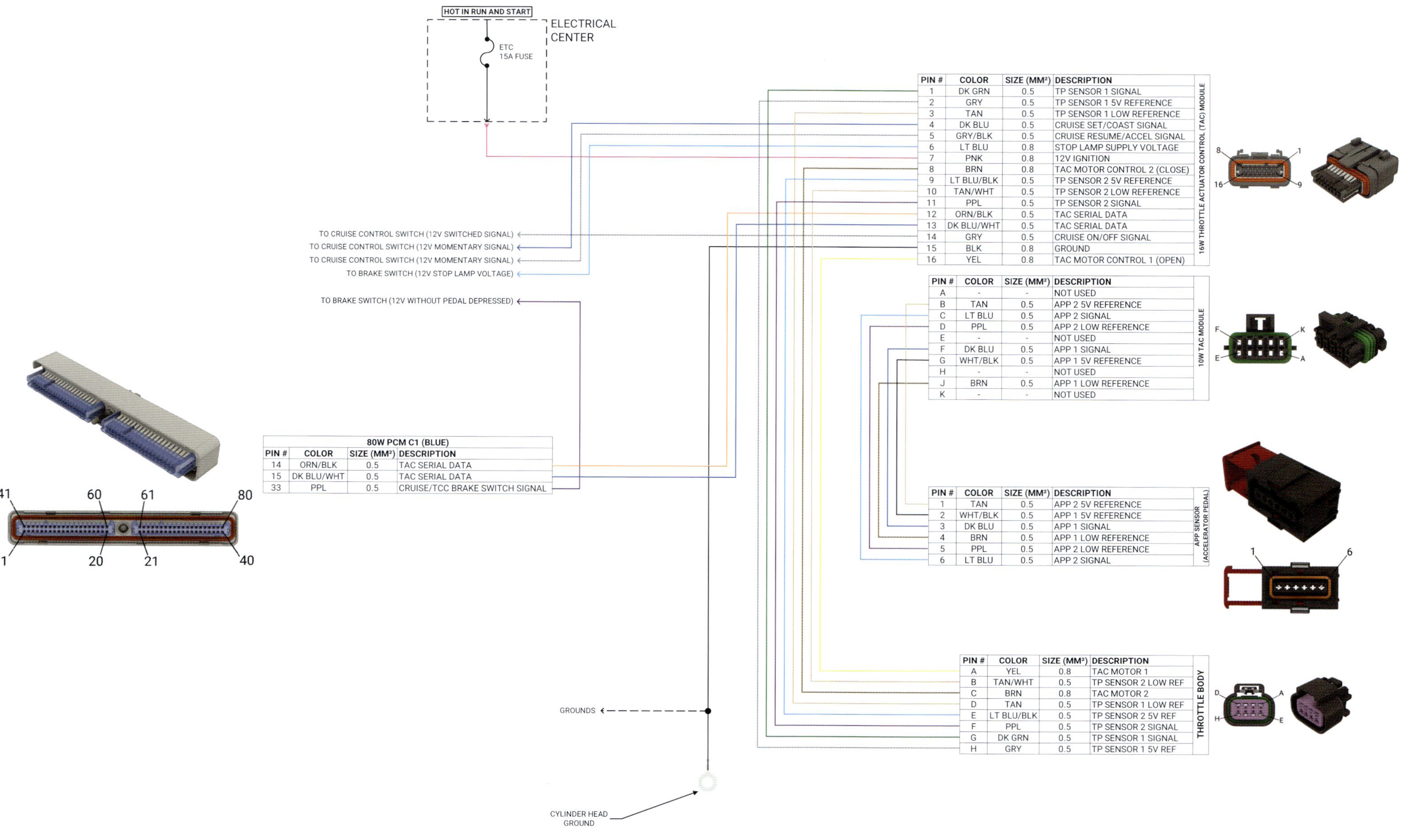

16W THROTTLE ACTUATOR CONTROL (TAC) MODULE

PIN #	COLOR	SIZE (MM²)	DESCRIPTION
1	DK GRN	0.5	TP SENSOR 1 SIGNAL
2	GRY	0.5	TP SENSOR 1 5V REFERENCE
3	TAN	0.5	TP SENSOR 1 LOW REFERENCE
4	DK BLU	0.5	CRUISE SET/COAST SIGNAL
5	GRY/BLK	0.5	CRUISE RESUME/ACCEL SIGNAL
6	LT BLU	0.8	STOP LAMP SUPPLY VOLTAGE
7	PNK	0.8	12V IGNITION
8	BRN	0.8	TAC MOTOR CONTROL 2 (CLOSE)
9	LT BLU/BLK	0.5	TP SENSOR 2 5V REFERENCE
10	TAN/WHT	0.5	TP SENSOR 2 LOW REFERENCE
11	PPL	0.5	TP SENSOR 2 SIGNAL
12	ORN/BLK	0.5	TAC SERIAL DATA
13	DK BLU/WHT	0.5	TAC SERIAL DATA
14	GRY	0.5	CRUISE ON/OFF SIGNAL
15	BLK	0.8	GROUND
16	YEL	0.8	TAC MOTOR CONTROL 1 (OPEN)

10W TAC MODULE

PIN #	COLOR	SIZE (MM²)	DESCRIPTION
A	-	-	NOT USED
B	TAN	0.5	APP 2 5V REFERENCE
C	LT BLU	0.5	APP 2 SIGNAL
D	PPL	0.5	APP 2 LOW REFERENCE
E	-	-	NOT USED
F	DK BLU	0.5	APP 1 SIGNAL
G	WHT/BLK	0.5	APP 1 5V REFERENCE
H	-	-	NOT USED
J	BRN	0.5	APP 1 LOW REFERENCE
K	-	-	NOT USED

80W PCM C1 (BLUE)

PIN #	COLOR	SIZE (MM²)	DESCRIPTION
14	ORN/BLK	0.5	TAC SERIAL DATA
15	DK BLU/WHT	0.5	TAC SERIAL DATA
33	PPL	0.5	CRUISE/TCC BRAKE SWITCH SIGNAL

APP SENSOR (ACCELERATOR PEDAL)

PIN #	COLOR	SIZE (MM²)	DESCRIPTION
1	TAN	0.5	APP 2 5V REFERENCE
2	WHT/BLK	0.5	APP 1 5V REFERENCE
3	DK BLU	0.5	APP 1 SIGNAL
4	BRN	0.5	APP 1 LOW REFERENCE
5	PPL	0.5	APP 2 LOW REFERENCE
6	LT BLU	0.5	APP 2 SIGNAL

THROTTLE BODY

PIN #	COLOR	SIZE (MM²)	DESCRIPTION
A	YEL	0.8	TAC MOTOR 1
B	TAN/WHT	0.5	TP SENSOR 2 LOW REF
C	BRN	0.8	TAC MOTOR 2
D	TAN	0.5	TP SENSOR 1 LOW REF
E	LT BLU/BLK	0.5	TP SENSOR 2 5V REF
F	PPL	0.5	TP SENSOR 2 SIGNAL
G	DK GRN	0.5	TP SENSOR 1 SIGNAL
H	GRY	0.5	TP SENSOR 1 5V REF

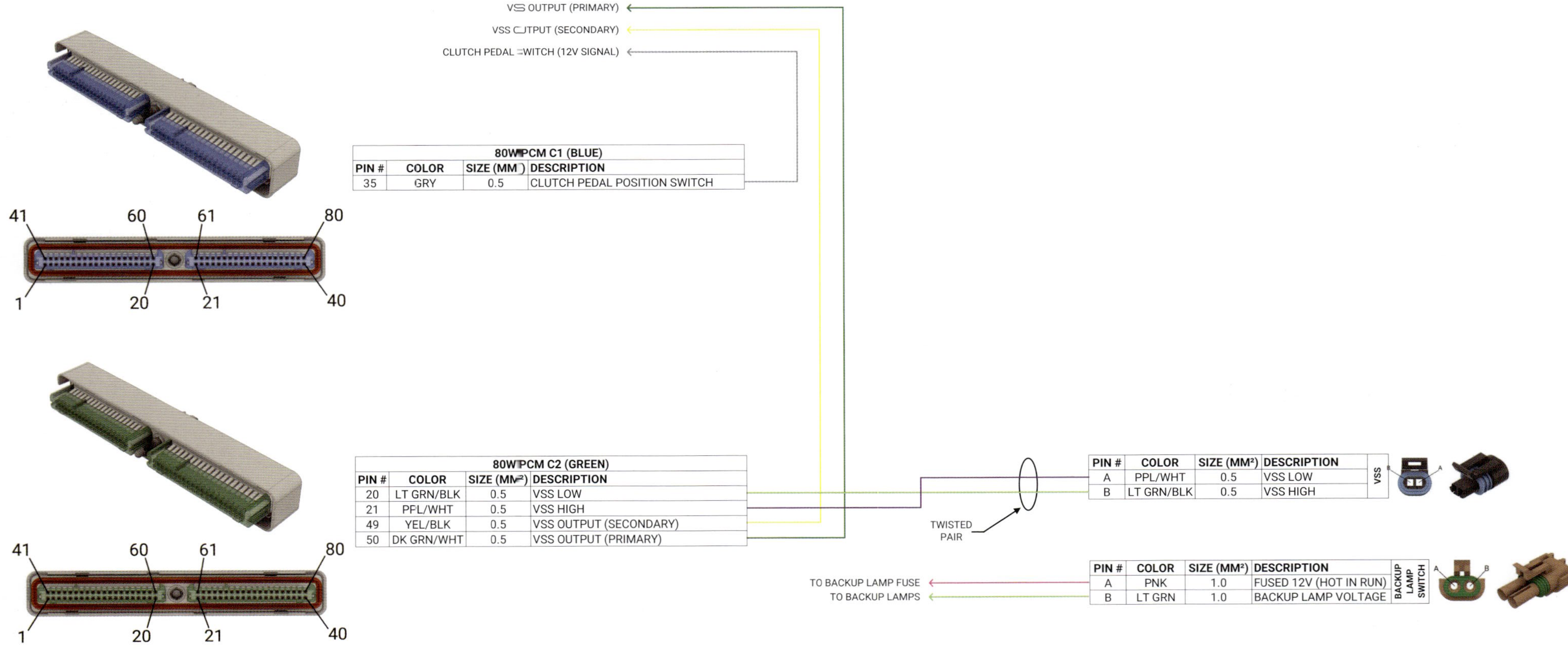

80W PCM C1 (BLUE)			
PIN #	COLOR	SIZE (MM²)	DESCRIPTION
35	GRY	0.5	CLUTCH PEDAL POSITION SWITCH

80W PCM C2 (GREEN)			
PIN #	COLOR	SIZE (MM²)	DESCRIPTION
20	LT GRN/BLK	0.5	VSS LOW
21	PFL/WHT	0.5	VSS HIGH
49	YEL/BLK	0.5	VSS OUTPUT (SECONDARY)
50	DK GRN/WHT	0.5	VSS OUTPUT (PRIMARY)

PIN #	COLOR	SIZE (MM²)	DESCRIPTION
A	PPL/WHT	0.5	VSS LOW
B	LT GRN/BLK	0.5	VSS HIGH

PIN #	COLOR	SIZE (MM²)	DESCRIPTION
A	PNK	1.0	FUSED 12V (HOT IN RUN)
B	LT GRN	1.0	BACKUP LAMP VOLTAGE

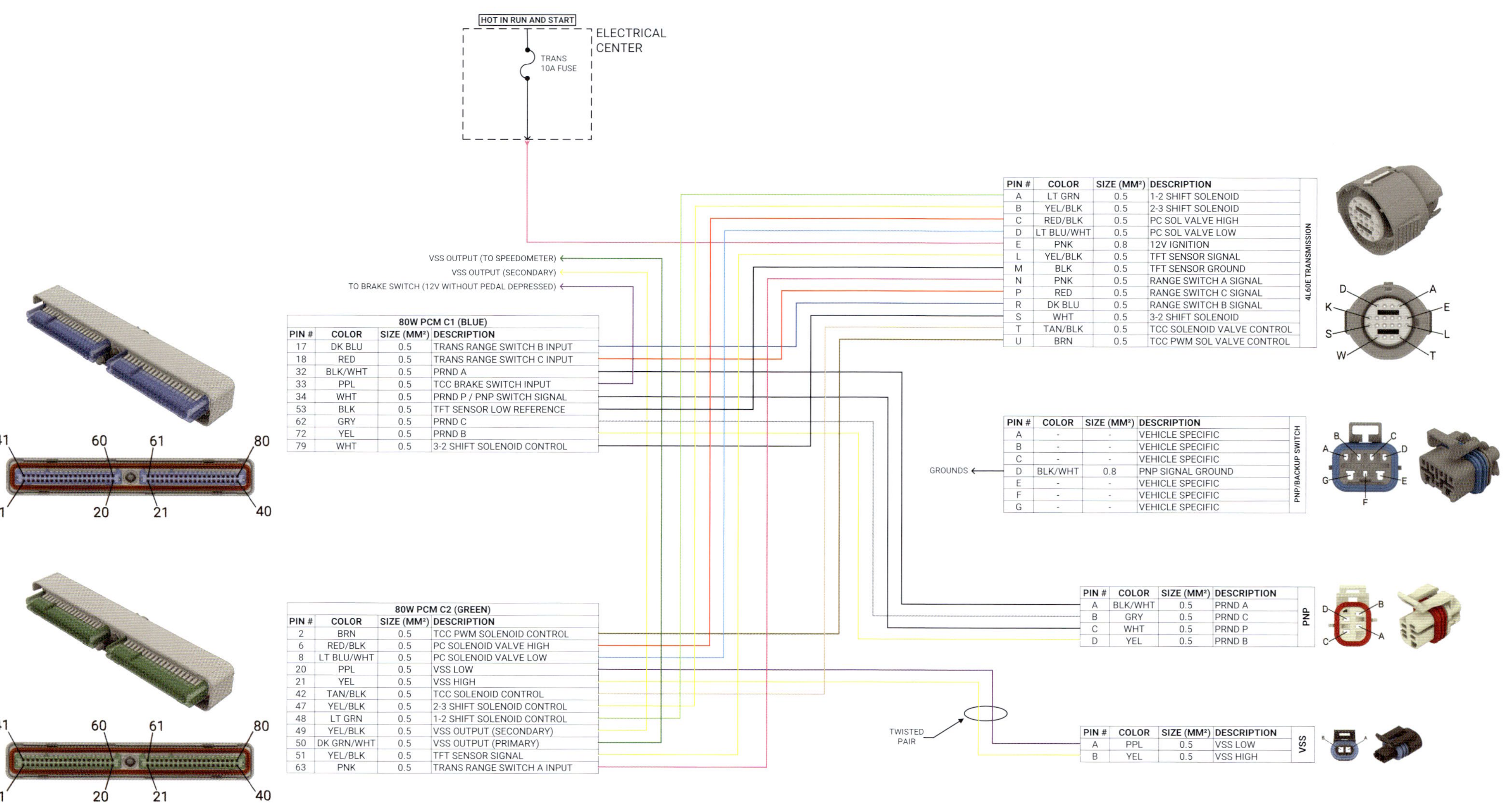

4L60E TRANSMISSION

PIN #	COLOR	SIZE (MM²)	DESCRIPTION
A	LT GRN	0.5	1-2 SHIFT SOLENOID
B	YEL/BLK	0.5	2-3 SHIFT SOLENOID
C	RED/BLK	0.5	PC SOL VALVE HIGH
D	LT BLU/WHT	0.5	PC SOL VALVE LOW
E	PNK	0.8	12V IGNITION
L	YEL/BLK	0.5	TFT SENSOR SIGNAL
M	BLK	0.5	TFT SENSOR GROUND
N	PNK	0.5	RANGE SWITCH A SIGNAL
P	RED	0.5	RANGE SWITCH C SIGNAL
R	DK BLU	0.5	RANGE SWITCH B SIGNAL
S	WHT	0.5	3-2 SHIFT SOLENOID
T	TAN/BLK	0.5	TCC SOLENOID VALVE CONTROL
U	BRN	0.5	TCC PWM SOL VALVE CONTROL

PNP/BACKUP SWITCH

PIN #	COLOR	SIZE (MM²)	DESCRIPTION
A	-	-	VEHICLE SPECIFIC
B	-	-	VEHICLE SPECIFIC
C	-	-	VEHICLE SPECIFIC
D	BLK/WHT	0.8	PNP SIGNAL GROUND
E	-	-	VEHICLE SPECIFIC
F	-	-	VEHICLE SPECIFIC
G	-	-	VEHICLE SPECIFIC

PNP

PIN #	COLOR	SIZE (MM²)	DESCRIPTION
A	BLK/WHT	0.5	PRND A
B	GRY	0.5	PRND C
C	WHT	0.5	PRND P
D	YEL	0.5	PRND B

VSS

PIN #	COLOR	SIZE (MM²)	DESCRIPTION
A	PPL	0.5	VSS LOW
B	YEL	0.5	VSS HIGH

80W PCM C1 (BLUE)

PIN #	COLOR	SIZE (MM²)	DESCRIPTION
17	DK BLU	0.5	TRANS RANGE SWITCH B INPUT
18	RED	0.5	TRANS RANGE SWITCH C INPUT
32	BLK/WHT	0.5	PRND A
33	PPL	0.5	TCC BRAKE SWITCH INPUT
34	WHT	0.5	PRND P / PNP SWITCH SIGNAL
53	BLK	0.5	TFT SENSOR LOW REFERENCE
62	GRY	0.5	PRND C
72	YEL	0.5	PRND B
79	WHT	0.5	3-2 SHIFT SOLENOID CONTROL

80W PCM C2 (GREEN)

PIN #	COLOR	SIZE (MM²)	DESCRIPTION
2	BRN	0.5	TCC PWM SOLENOID CONTROL
6	RED/BLK	0.5	PC SOLENOID VALVE HIGH
8	LT BLU/WHT	0.5	PC SOLENOID VALVE LOW
20	PPL	0.5	VSS LOW
21	YEL	0.5	VSS HIGH
42	TAN/BLK	0.5	TCC SOLENOID CONTROL
47	YEL/BLK	0.5	2-3 SHIFT SOLENOID CONTROL
48	LT GRN	0.5	1-2 SHIFT SOLENOID CONTROL
49	YEL/BLK	0.5	VSS OUTPUT (SECONDARY)
50	DK GRN/WHT	0.5	VSS OUTPUT (PRIMARY)
51	YEL/BLK	0.5	TFT SENSOR SIGNAL
63	PNK	0.5	TRANS RANGE SWITCH A INPUT

2004-2007 P59 PCM (TRANSMISSION – 4L60E AUTOMATIC LATE PRNDL)

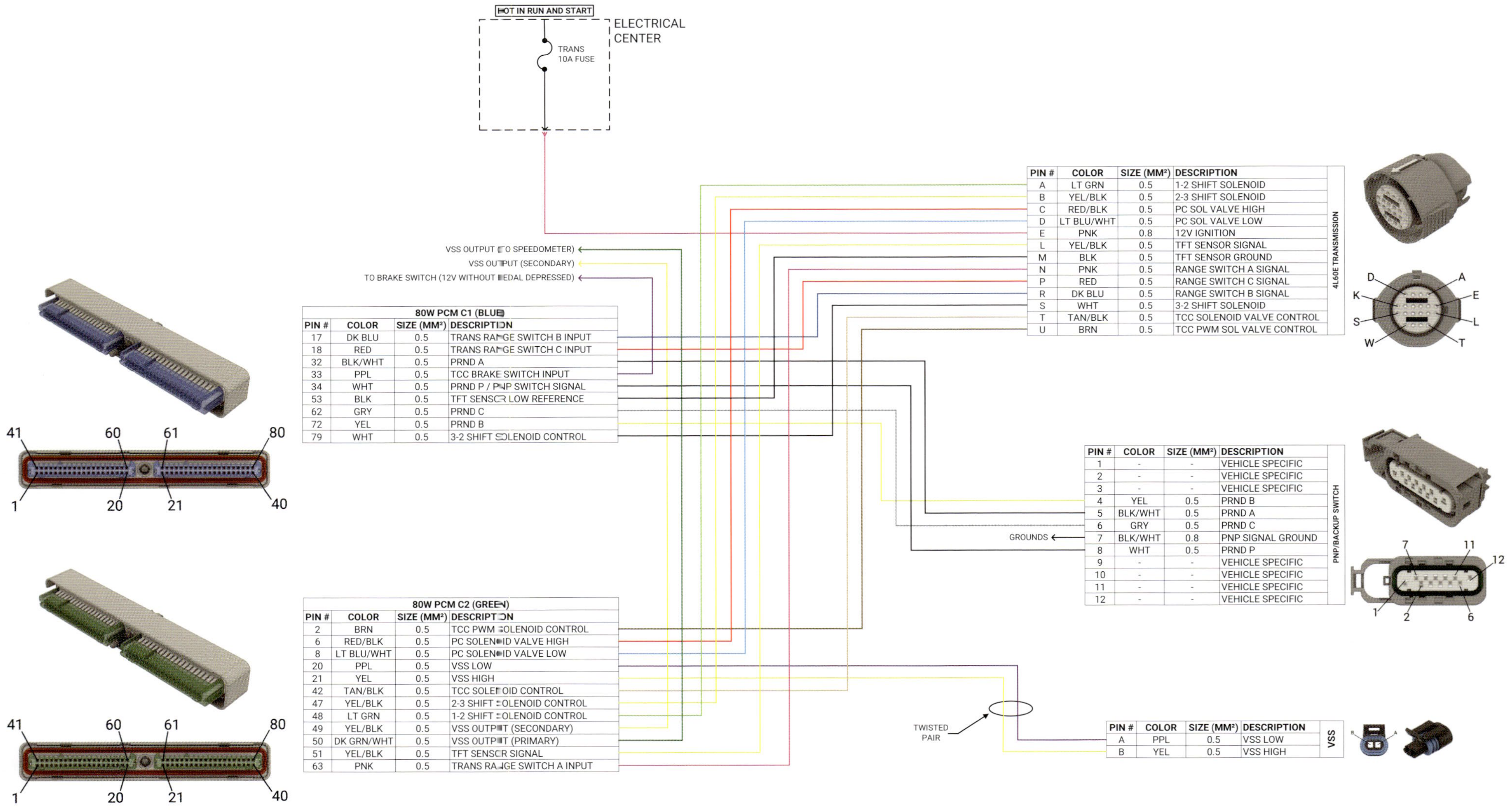

HOT IN RUN AND START

ELECTRICAL CENTER

TRANS 10A FUSE

VSS OUTPUT (TO SPEEDOMETER)
VSS OUTPUT (SECONDARY)
TO BRAKE SWITCH (12V WITHOUT PEDAL DEPRESSED)

GROUNDS

TWISTED PAIR

4L60E TRANSMISSION

PIN #	COLOR	SIZE (MM²)	DESCRIPTION
A	LT GRN	0.5	1-2 SHIFT SOLENOID
B	YEL/BLK	0.5	2-3 SHIFT SOLENOID
C	RED/BLK	0.5	PC SOL VALVE HIGH
D	LT BLU/WHT	0.5	PC SOL VALVE LOW
E	PNK	0.8	12V IGNITION
L	YEL/BLK	0.5	TFT SENSOR SIGNAL
M	BLK	0.5	TFT SENSOR GROUND
N	PNK	0.5	RANGE SWITCH A SIGNAL
P	RED	0.5	RANGE SWITCH C SIGNAL
R	DK BLU	0.5	RANGE SWITCH B SIGNAL
S	WHT	0.5	3-2 SHIFT SOLENOID
T	TAN/BLK	0.5	TCC SOLENOID VALVE CONTROL
U	BRN	0.5	TCC PWM SOL VALVE CONTROL

80W PCM C1 (BLUE)

PIN #	COLOR	SIZE (MM²)	DESCRIPTION
17	DK BLU	0.5	TRANS RANGE SWITCH B INPUT
18	RED	0.5	TRANS RANGE SWITCH C INPUT
32	BLK/WHT	0.5	PRND A
33	PPL	0.5	TCC BRAKE SWITCH INPUT
34	WHT	0.5	PRND P / PNP SWITCH SIGNAL
53	BLK	0.5	TFT SENSOR LOW REFERENCE
62	GRY	0.5	PRND C
72	YEL	0.5	PRND B
79	WHT	0.5	3-2 SHIFT SOLENOID CONTROL

PNP/BACKUP SWITCH

PIN #	COLOR	SIZE (MM²)	DESCRIPTION
1	-	-	VEHICLE SPECIFIC
2	-	-	VEHICLE SPECIFIC
3	-	-	VEHICLE SPECIFIC
4	YEL	0.5	PRND B
5	BLK/WHT	0.5	PRND A
6	GRY	0.5	PRND C
7	BLK/WHT	0.8	PNP SIGNAL GROUND
8	WHT	0.5	PRND P
9	-	-	VEHICLE SPECIFIC
10	-	-	VEHICLE SPECIFIC
11	-	-	VEHICLE SPECIFIC
12	-	-	VEHICLE SPECIFIC

80W PCM C2 (GREEN)

PIN #	COLOR	SIZE (MM²)	DESCRIPTION
2	BRN	0.5	TCC PWM SOLENOID CONTROL
6	RED/BLK	0.5	PC SOLENOID VALVE HIGH
8	LT BLU/WHT	0.5	PC SOLENOID VALVE LOW
20	PPL	0.5	VSS LOW
21	YEL	0.5	VSS HIGH
42	TAN/BLK	0.5	TCC SOLENOID CONTROL
47	YEL/BLK	0.5	2-3 SHIFT SOLENOID CONTROL
48	LT GRN	0.5	1-2 SHIFT SOLENOID CONTROL
49	YEL/BLK	0.5	VSS OUTPUT (SECONDARY)
50	DK GRN/WHT	0.5	VSS OUTPUT (PRIMARY)
51	YEL/BLK	0.5	TFT SENSOR SIGNAL
63	PNK	0.5	TRANS RANGE SWITCH A INPUT

VSS

PIN #	COLOR	SIZE (MM²)	DESCRIPTION
A	PPL	0.5	VSS LOW
B	YEL	0.5	VSS HIGH

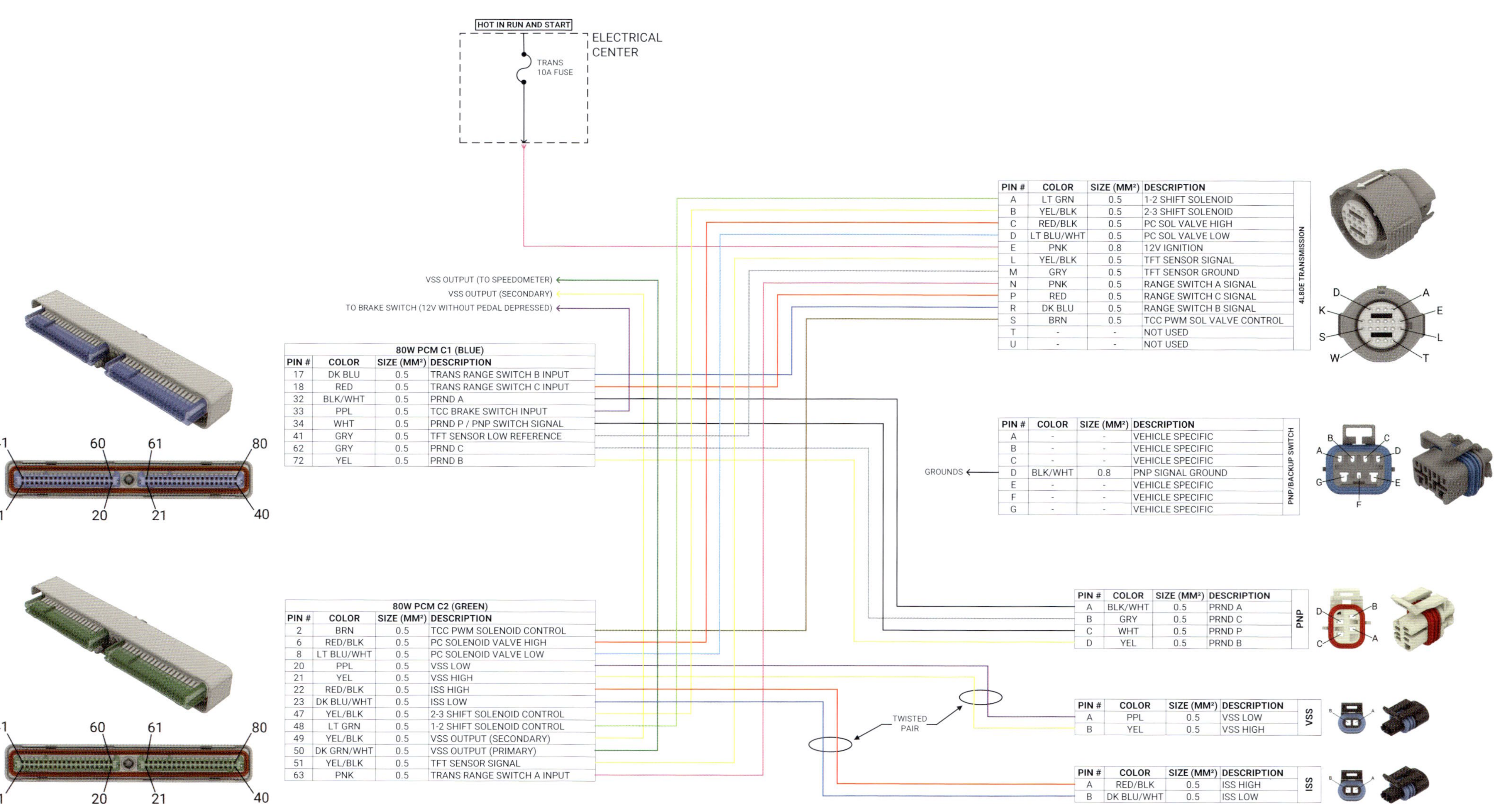

4L80E TRANSMISSION

PIN #	COLOR	SIZE (MM²)	DESCRIPTION
A	LT GRN	0.5	1-2 SHIFT SOLENOID
B	YEL/BLK	0.5	2-3 SHIFT SOLENOID
C	RED/BLK	0.5	PC SOL VALVE HIGH
D	LT BLU/WHT	0.5	PC SOL VALVE LOW
E	PNK	0.8	12V IGNITION
L	YEL/BLK	0.5	TFT SENSOR SIGNAL
M	GRY	0.5	TFT SENSOR GROUND
N	PNK	0.5	RANGE SWITCH A SIGNAL
P	RED	0.5	RANGE SWITCH C SIGNAL
R	DK BLU	0.5	RANGE SWITCH B SIGNAL
S	BRN	0.5	TCC PWM SOL VALVE CONTROL
T	-	-	NOT USED
U	-	-	NOT USED

PNP/BACKUP SWITCH

PIN #	COLOR	SIZE (MM²)	DESCRIPTION
A	-	-	VEHICLE SPECIFIC
B	-	-	VEHICLE SPECIFIC
C	-	-	VEHICLE SPECIFIC
D	BLK/WHT	0.8	PNP SIGNAL GROUND
E	-	-	VEHICLE SPECIFIC
F	-	-	VEHICLE SPECIFIC
G	-	-	VEHICLE SPECIFIC

PNP

PIN #	COLOR	SIZE (MM²)	DESCRIPTION
A	BLK/WHT	0.5	PRND A
B	GRY	0.5	PRND C
C	WHT	0.5	PRND P
D	YEL	0.5	PRND B

VSS

PIN #	COLOR	SIZE (MM²)	DESCRIPTION
A	PPL	0.5	VSS LOW
B	YEL	0.5	VSS HIGH

ISS

PIN #	COLOR	SIZE (MM²)	DESCRIPTION
A	RED/BLK	0.5	ISS HIGH
B	DK BLU/WHT	0.5	ISS LOW

80W PCM C1 (BLUE)

PIN #	COLOR	SIZE (MM²)	DESCRIPTION
17	DK BLU	0.5	TRANS RANGE SWITCH B INPUT
18	RED	0.5	TRANS RANGE SWITCH C INPUT
32	BLK/WHT	0.5	PRND A
33	PPL	0.5	TCC BRAKE SWITCH INPUT
34	WHT	0.5	PRND P / PNP SWITCH SIGNAL
41	GRY	0.5	TFT SENSOR LOW REFERENCE
62	GRY	0.5	PRND C
72	YEL	0.5	PRND B

80W PCM C2 (GREEN)

PIN #	COLOR	SIZE (MM²)	DESCRIPTION
2	BRN	0.5	TCC PWM SOLENOID CONTROL
6	RED/BLK	0.5	PC SOLENOID VALVE HIGH
8	LT BLU/WHT	0.5	PC SOLENOID VALVE LOW
20	PPL	0.5	VSS LOW
21	YEL	0.5	VSS HIGH
22	RED/BLK	0.5	ISS HIGH
23	DK BLU/WHT	0.5	ISS LOW
47	YEL/BLK	0.5	2-3 SHIFT SOLENOID CONTROL
48	LT GRN	0.5	1-2 SHIFT SOLENOID CONTROL
49	YEL/BLK	0.5	VSS OUTPUT (SECONDARY)
50	DK GRN/WHT	0.5	VSS OUTPUT (PRIMARY)
51	YEL/BLK	0.5	TFT SENSOR SIGNAL
63	PNK	0.5	TRANS RANGE SWITCH A INPUT

2003-2007 P59 PCM (TRANSMISSION – 4L80E AUTOMATIC LATE PRNDL)

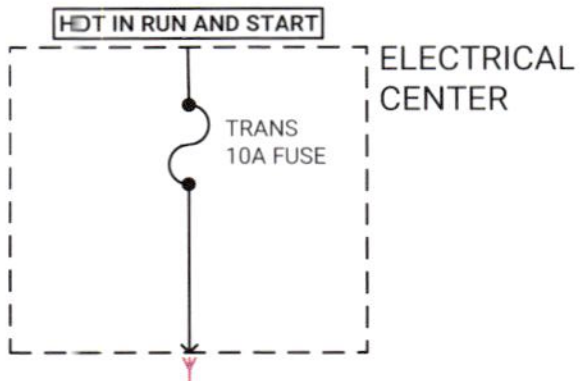

VSS OUTPUT (TO SPEEDOMETER)
VSS OUTPUT (SECONDARY)
TO BRAKE SWITCH (12V WITHOUT PEDAL DEPRESSED)

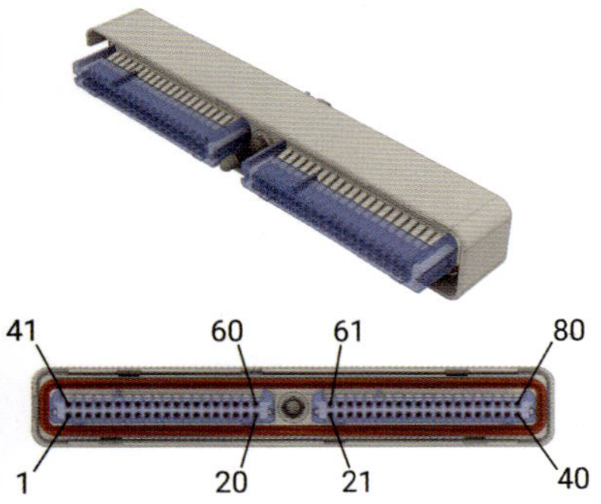

80W PCM C1 (BLUE)			
PIN #	COLOR	SIZE (MM²)	DESCRIPTION
17	DK BLU	0.5	TRANS RANGE SWITCH B INPUT
18	RED	0.5	TRANS RANGE SWITCH C INPUT
32	BLK/WHT	0.5	PRND A
33	PPL	0.5	TCC BRAKE SWITCH INPUT
34	WHT	0.5	PRND P / PUP SWITCH SIGNAL
41	GRY	0.5	TFT SENSOR LOW REFERENCE
62	GRY	0.5	PRND C
72	YEL	0.5	PRND B

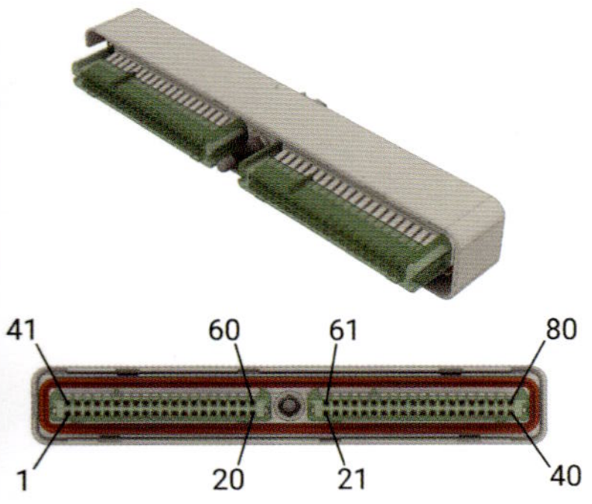

80W PCM C2 (GREEN)			
PIN #	COLOR	SIZE (MM²)	DESCRIPTION
2	BRN	0.5	TCC PWM SOLENOID CONTROL
6	RED/BLK	0.5	PC SOLENOID VALVE HIGH
8	LT BLU/WHT	0.5	PC SOLENOID VALVE LOW
20	PPL	0.5	VSS LOW
21	YEL	0.5	VSS HIGH
22	RED/BLK	0.5	ISS HIGH
23	DK BLU/WHT	0.5	ISS LOW
47	YEL/BLK	0.5	2-3 SHIFT SOLENOID CONTROL
48	LT GRN	0.5	1-2 SHIFT SOLENOID CONTROL
49	YEL/BLK	0.5	VSS OUTPUT (SECONDARY)
50	DK GRN/WHT	0.5	VSS OUTPUT (PRIMARY)
51	YEL/BLK	0.5	TFT SENSOR SIGNAL
63	PNK	0.5	TRANS RANGE SWITCH A INPUT

4L80E TRANSMISSION

PIN #	COLOR	SIZE (MM²)	DESCRIPTION
A	LT GRN	0.5	1-2 SHIFT SOLENOID
B	YEL/BLK	0.5	2-3 SHIFT SOLENOID
C	RED/BLK	0.5	PC SOL VALVE HIGH
D	LT BLU/WHT	0.5	PC SOL VALVE LOW
E	PNK	0.8	12V IGNITION
L	YEL/BLK	0.5	TFT SENSOR SIGNAL
M	GRY	0.5	TFT SENSOR GROUND
N	PNK	0.5	RANGE SWITCH A SIGNAL
P	RED	0.5	RANGE SWITCH C SIGNAL
R	DK BLU	0.5	RANGE SWITCH B SIGNAL
S	BRN	0.5	TCC PWM SOL VALVE CONTROL
T	-	-	NOT USED
U	-	-	NOT USED

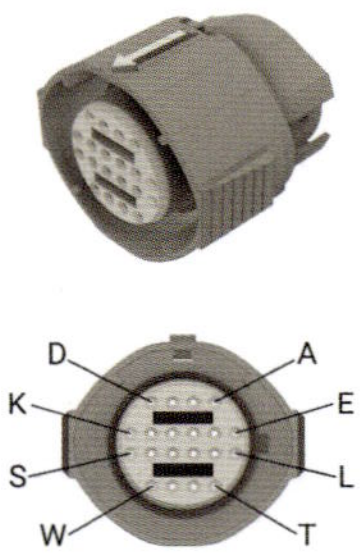

PNP/BACKUP SWITCH

PIN #	COLOR	SIZE (MM²)	DESCRIPTION
1	-	-	VEHICLE SPECIFIC
2	-	-	VEHICLE SPECIFIC
3	-	-	VEHICLE SPECIFIC
4	YEL	0.5	PRND B
5	BLK/WHT	0.5	PRND A
6	GRY	0.5	PRND C
7	BLK/WHT	0.8	PNP SIGNAL GROUND
8	WHT	0.5	PRND P
9	-	-	VEHICLE SPECIFIC
10	-	-	VEHICLE SPECIFIC
11	-	-	VEHICLE SPECIFIC
12	-	-	VEHICLE SPECIFIC

GROUNDS

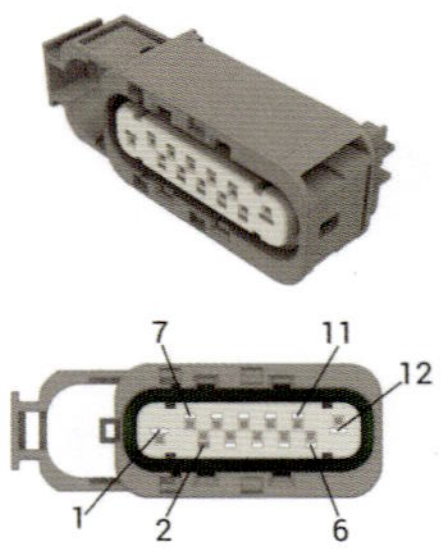

TWISTED PAIR

VSS

PIN #	COLOR	SIZE (MM²)	DESCRIPTION
A	PPL	0.5	VSS LOW
B	YEL	0.5	VSS HIGH

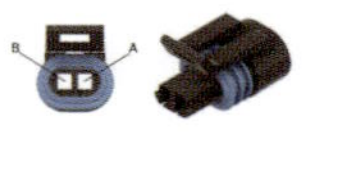

ISS

PIN #	COLOR	SIZE (MM²)	DESCRIPTION
A	RED/BLK	0.5	ISS HIGH
B	DK BLU/WHT	0.5	ISS LOW

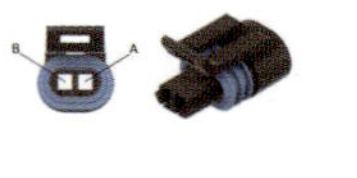

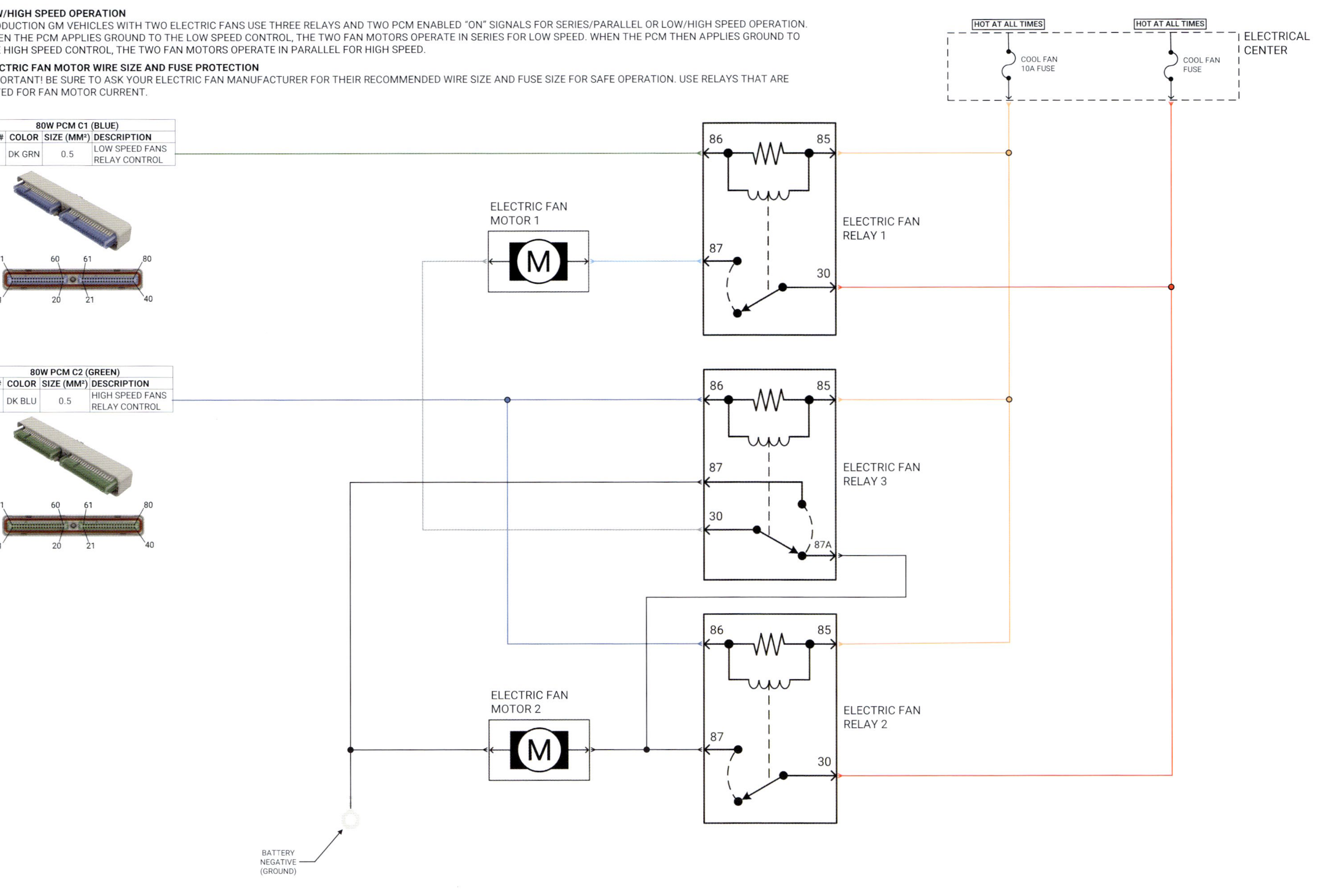

LOW/HIGH SPEED OPERATION
PRODUCTION GM VEHICLES WITH TWO ELECTRIC FANS USE THREE RELAYS AND TWO PCM ENABLED "ON" SIGNALS FOR SERIES/PARALLEL OR LOW/HIGH SPEED OPERATION.
WHEN THE PCM APPLIES GROUND TO THE LOW SPEED CONTROL, THE TWO FAN MOTORS OPERATE IN SERIES FOR LOW SPEED. WHEN THE PCM THEN APPLIES GROUND TO
THE HIGH SPEED CONTROL, THE TWO FAN MOTORS OPERATE IN PARALLEL FOR HIGH SPEED.
ELECTRIC FAN MOTOR WIRE SIZE AND FUSE PROTECTION
IMPORTANT! BE SURE TO ASK YOUR ELECTRIC FAN MANUFACTURER FOR THEIR RECOMMENDED WIRE SIZE AND FUSE SIZE FOR SAFE OPERATION. USE RELAYS THAT ARE
RATED FOR FAN MOTOR CURRENT.
HOT AT ALL TIMES
HOT AT ALL TIMES
ELECTRICAL CENTER
COOL FAN 10A FUSE
COOL FAN FUSE
80W PCM C1 (BLUE)
PIN # COLOR SIZE (MM²) DESCRIPTION
42 DK GRN 0.5 LOW SPEED FANS RELAY CONTROL
41 60 61 80 1 20 21 40
80W PCM C2 (GREEN)
PIN # COLOR SIZE (MM²) DESCRIPTION
33 DK BLU 0.5 HIGH SPEED FANS RELAY CONTROL
41 60 61 80 1 20 21 40
ELECTRIC FAN MOTOR 1
M
ELECTRIC FAN MOTOR 2
M
ELECTRIC FAN RELAY 1
ELECTRIC FAN RELAY 3
ELECTRIC FAN RELAY 2
86 85 87 30 87A
BATTERY NEGATIVE (GROUND)

INDEPENDENT ON/OFF OPERATION
TWO ELECTRIC FANS CAN BE INDEPENDENTLY CONTROLLED THROUGH THE USE OF TWO RELAYS FOR ON/OFF (HIGH SPEED) OPERATION.

ELECTRIC FAN MOTOR WIRE SIZE AND FUSE PROTECTION
IMPORTANT! BE SURE TO ASK YOUR ELECTRIC FAN MANUFACTURER FOR THEIR RECOMMENDED WIRE SIZE AND FUSE SIZE FOR SAFE OPERATION. USE RELAYS THAT ARE RATED FOR FAN MOTOR CURRENT.

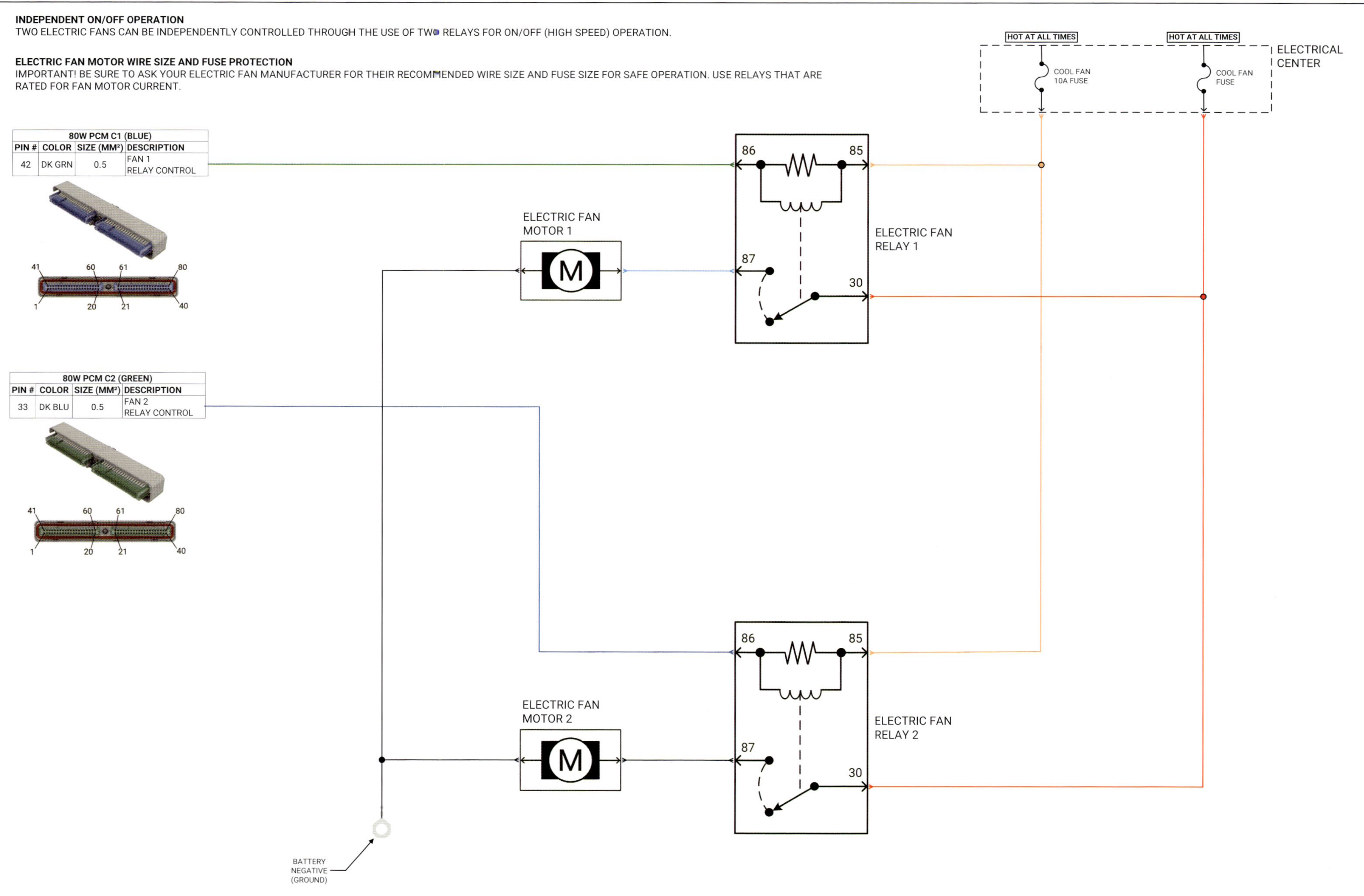

80W PCM C1 (BLUE)			
PIN #	COLOR	SIZE (MM²)	DESCRIPTION
42	DK GRN	0.5	FAN 1 RELAY CONTROL

80W PCM C2 (GREEN)			
PIN #	COLOR	SIZE (MM²)	DESCRIPTION
33	DK BLU	0.5	FAN 2 RELAY CONTROL

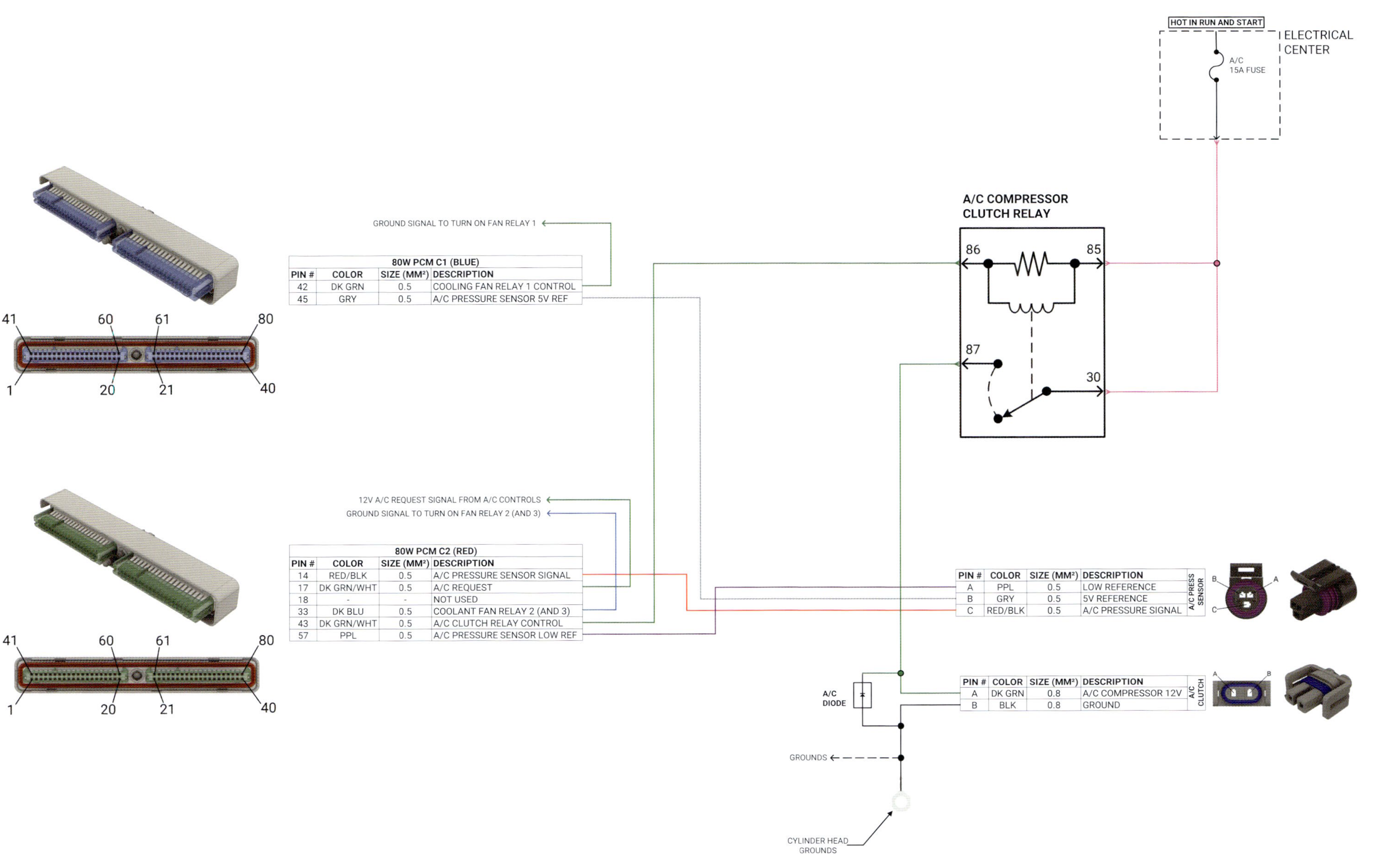

80W PCM C1 (BLUE)

PIN #	COLOR	SIZE (MM²)	DESCRIPTION
42	DK GRN	0.5	COOLING FAN RELAY 1 CONTROL
45	GRY	0.5	A/C PRESSURE SENSOR 5V REF

80W PCM C2 (RED)

PIN #	COLOR	SIZE (MM²)	DESCRIPTION
14	RED/BLK	0.5	A/C PRESSURE SENSOR SIGNAL
17	DK GRN/WHT	0.5	A/C REQUEST
18	-	-	NOT USED
33	DK BLU	0.5	COOLANT FAN RELAY 2 (AND 3)
43	DK GRN/WHT	0.5	A/C CLUTCH RELAY CONTROL
57	PPL	0.5	A/C PRESSURE SENSOR LOW REF

A/C PRESS SENSOR

PIN #	COLOR	SIZE (MM²)	DESCRIPTION
A	PPL	0.5	LOW REFERENCE
B	GRY	0.5	5V REFERENCE
C	RED/BLK	0.5	A/C PRESSURE SIGNAL

A/C CLUTCH

PIN #	COLOR	SIZE (MM²)	DESCRIPTION
A	DK GRN	0.8	A/C COMPRESSOR 12V
B	BLK	0.8	GROUND

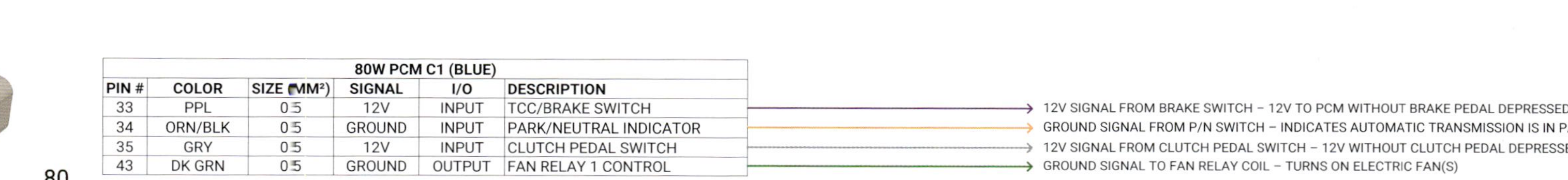

80W PCM C1 (BLUE)					
PIN #	COLOR	SIZE (MM²)	SIGNAL	I/O	DESCRIPTION
33	PPL	0.5	12V	INPUT	TCC/BRAKE SWITCH
34	ORN/BLK	0.5	GROUND	INPUT	PARK/NEUTRAL INDICATOR
35	GRY	0.5	12V	INPUT	CLUTCH PEDAL SWITCH
43	DK GRN	0.5	GROUND	OUTPUT	FAN RELAY 1 CONTROL

- 12V SIGNAL FROM BRAKE SWITCH – 12V TO PCM WITHOUT BRAKE PEDAL DEPRESSED
- GROUND SIGNAL FROM P/N SWITCH – INDICATES AUTOMATIC TRANSMISSION IS IN PARK OR NEUTRAL
- 12V SIGNAL FROM CLUTCH PEDAL SWITCH – 12V WITHOUT CLUTCH PEDAL DEPRESSED
- GROUND SIGNAL TO FAN RELAY COIL – TURNS ON ELECTRIC FAN(S)

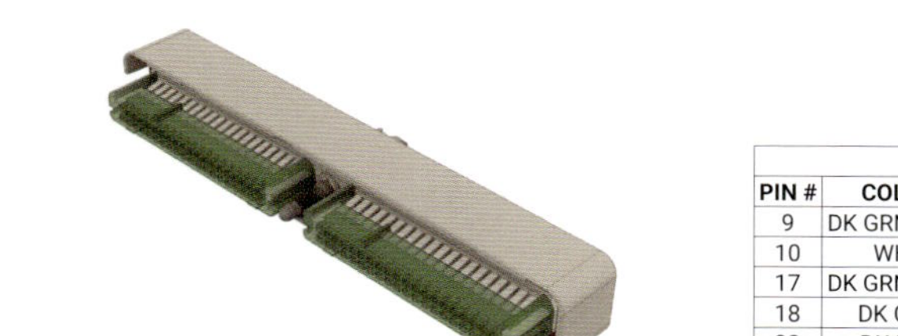

80W PCM C2 (RED)					
PIN #	COLOR	SIZE MM²	SIGNAL	I/O	DESCRIPTION
9	DK GRN/WHT	0.5	12V	OUTPUT	FUEL PUMP RELAY CONTROL
10	WHT	0.8	-	OUTPUT	ENGINE SPEED OUTPUT
17	DK GRN/WHT	0.5	12V	INPUT	A/C REQUEST
18	DK GRN	0.8	12V	INPUT	A/C STATUS
33	DK BLU	0.5	GROUND	OUTPUT	FAN RELAY 2 (AND 3) CONTROL
43	DK GRN/WHT	0.5	GROUND	OUTPUT	A/C RELAY CONTROL
46	BRN/WHT	0.5	GROUND	OUTPUT	MALFUNCTION INDICATOR LAMP
49	YEL/BLK	0.5	-	OUTPUT	VSS OUTPUT (SECONDARY)
50	DK GRN/WHT	0.5	-	OUTPUT	VSS OUTPUT (PRIMARY)

- 12V SIGNAL TO FUEL PUMP RELAY COIL – TURNS ON FUEL PUMP
- ENGINE SPEED SIGNAL FOR TACHOMETER – CONFIGURABLE WITHIN PCM CALIBRATION
- 12V SIGNAL FROM A/C CONTROLS – INDICATES A/C IS REQUESTED ON BY OPERATOR
- 12V SIGNAL FROM A/C COMPRESSOR CLUTCH – INDICATES A/C CLUTCH HAS 12V
- GROUND SIGNAL TO FAN RELAY COIL (CONTROLS HIGH/LOW SPEED W/ THREE RELAYS)
- GROUND SIGNAL TO A/C CLUTCH RELAY COIL – ENGAGES A/C COMPRESSOR CLUTCH
- GROUND SIGNAL TO MIL LAMP – ILLUMINATES 12V LAMP WHEN DTC(S) ARE PRESENT
- VEHICLE SPEED SIGNAL – PULSE COUNT CONFIGURABLE WITHIN PCM CALIBRATION
- VEHICLE SPEED SIGNAL FOR SPEEDOMETER – PULSE COUNT CONFIGURABLE WITHIN PCM CALIBRATION

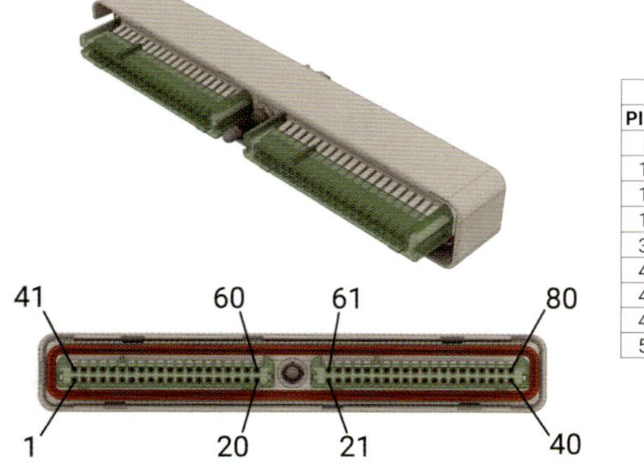

CONNECTOR END VIEWS

GM service manuals contain harness connector end views within their respective chapters. Connector end views are commonly presented as line drawings with basic information based on the vehicle that's represented. I've taken this detail a bit further by drawing and presenting color 3D renderings of each connector (with possible variations) and usage across the Gen III PCMs. These renderings are near spot-on representations of the actual connectors. With a harness connector in your hand, you will have no question that the reference information in the following pages match.

You will notice that the wire colors and wire sizes are not mentioned. GM did not always use the same wire colors or sizes across every year, make, model, engine size, and transmission type. A good best practice is to use the wire colors that GM used in the production vehicle that your PCM was pulled from or that matches the base calibration loaded in your PCM. Because any custom harness contains lengths other than what was used in a production GM vehicle, the GM service manual's wire sizes should only be used as reference. I recommend consulting with a trusted engine harness builder to determine wire size based on your harness length.

While all illustrations and tables are my own, a significant amount of this data came from the study of GM's service system at acdelcotds .com Should you need additional information about your particular application, I recommend purchasing a subscription to GM's service system and beginning your search by vehicle year, make, and model.

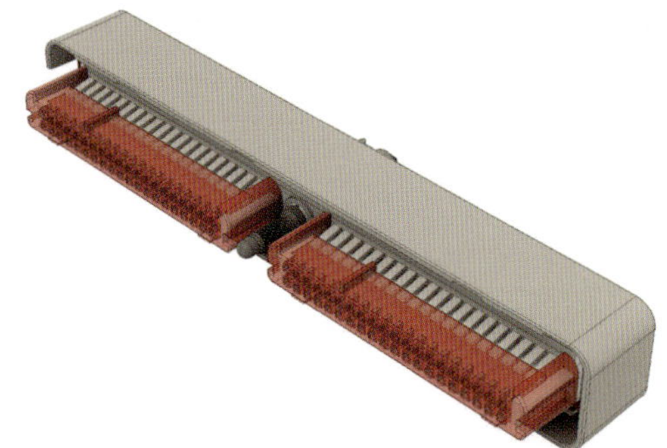

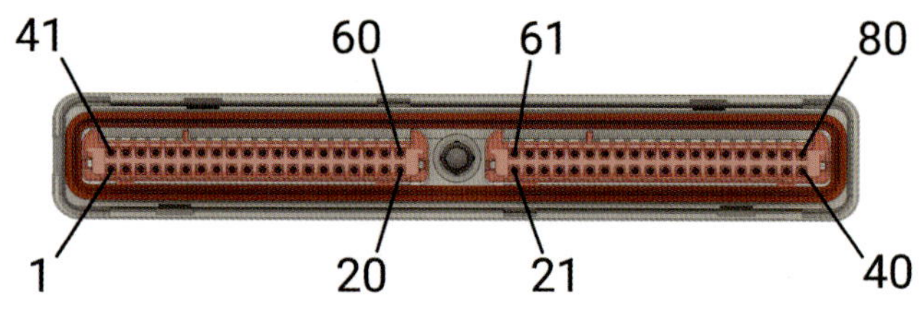

Pin	Color	Function
3	White	EVAP Canister Vent Solenoid Valve Control
4	Brown/White	Camshaft Position (CMP) Sensor Signal
7	Yellow	Vehicle Speed Sensor (VSS) Signal High
9	Pink/Black	Fuel Injector #3 Control
11	Dark Blue	Vehicle Antitheft System (VATS) Fuel Enable
12	Light Blue/Black	Fuel Injector #4 Control
13	Red/White	Ignition Coil #2 Control
14	Dark Green	A/C Status (12V Compressor Clutch Voltage)
15	Black/White	Fuel Injector #5 Control
18	Yellow/Black	Fuel Injector #6 Control
21	Purple	Intake Air Temperature (IAT) Sensor Low Reference
22	Dark Blue	Transmission Range Signal B
23	Light Green/Black	Fuel Injector #2 Control
24	Black/White	Sensor Ground Jumper
25	Pink	Transmission Range Signal A
26	Black/White	Transmission (PRND) Switch A
27	Red/Black	Fuel Injector #7 Control
30	Gray/Black	Spark Retard Signal
31	Dark Blue/White	Fuel Injector #8 Control
32	Orange/Black	Park/Neutral Position (PNP) Switch Signal
32	White	Transmission PRND Switch P
33	Blk	Fuel Injector #1 Control
34	Gray	Skip Shift Solenoid (Manual Transmission)
34	White	3-2 Shift Solenoid (Automatic Transmission)
35	Light Green	1-2 Shift Solenoid
36	Dark Blue	Fuel Gauge Output Control
37	Brown/White	Malfunction Indicator Lamp (MIL) Control
39	Dark Green/White	A/C Clutch Relay Control
40	White	Skip Shift Lamp Control (Manual Transmission)
40	Yellow/Black	2-3 Shift Solenoid (Automatic Transmission)

Pin	Color	Function
41	Brown/White	Low Oil Level Indicator Lamp Control
41	Pink/White	PCM Chassis Pitch Output Circuit
42	Light Green	Reverse Inhibit (Or Lockout) Solenoid Control
43	Dark Green	Electric Cooling Fan Relay #1 Control
44	Yellow	Crankshaft Position (CKP) Sensor Signal
45	Dark Green/White	EVAP Canister Purge Valve Control
46	Orange/Black	Desired Torque
47	Dark Green/White	A/C Request Signal
48	Yellow	Mass Airflow (MAF) Sensor Signal
49	Purple	Ignition Coil #1 Control
52	Purple/White	Ignition Coil #8 Control
53	Red	Ignition Coil #7 Control
54	Light Blue/White	Ignition Coil #6 Control
55	Dark Green/White	VSS Output Signal
56	Dark Green	Ignition Coil #5 Control
57	Dark Green/White	Ignition Coil #4 Control
58	Light Blue	Ignition Coil #3 Control
59	Brown/White	Ignition Coils Bank 2 Low Reference
60	Brown	Ignition Coils Bank 1 Low Reference
61	Red	Transmission Range Signal C
62	Black	EGR Pintle Position Ground
63	Black	A/C Refrigerant Pressure Sensor Ground
64	Black	Engine Oil Pressure (EOP) Sensor Low Reference
65	Gray	Transmission PRND Switch C
66	Yellow	Transmission PRND Switch B
68	Gray	Clutch Switch Signal
69	Brown	EVAP Purge Vacuum Switch Signal
71	Purple	VSS Signal Low
72	Black	PCM Ground
73	Gray	Extended Travel Brake Switch Signal
75	Gray	Fuel Tank Level Sensor Ground
76	Black	PCM Ground
77	Purple	TCC/Brake Switch Signal

1997–1998 LS1 PCM Connector C1 (Red)

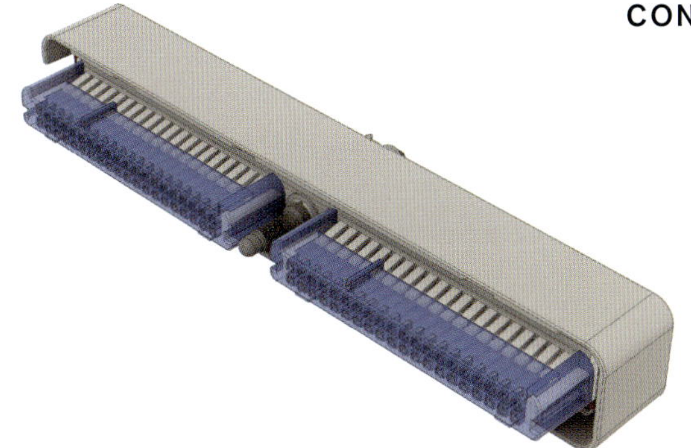

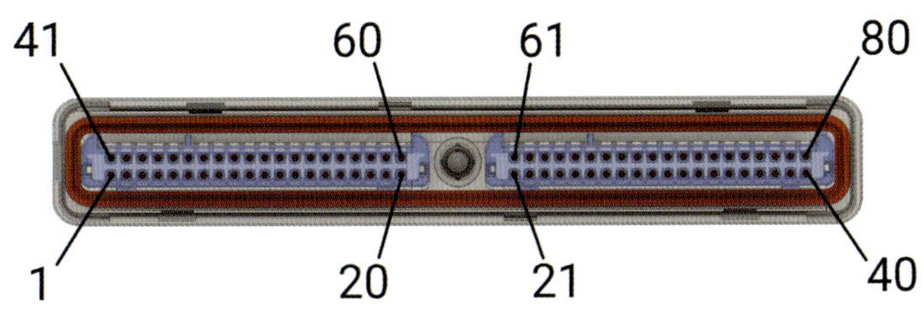

1997–1998 LS1 PCM Connector C2 (Blue)

Pin	Color	Function
1	Tan	HO$_2$S Signal Low Bank 2 Sensor 2
2	Tan/White	HO$_2$S Signal Low Bank 1 Sensor 2
3	Tan	Serial Data (UART)
4	Red	Camshaft Position (CMP) Sensor 12V Reference
5	Tan	HO$_2$S Signal Low Bank 2 Sensor 1
6	Tan/White	HO$_2$S Signal Low Bank 1 Sensor 1
7	Red/Black	A/C Refrigerant Pressure Sensor Signal
8	Tan	Intake Air Temperature (IAT) Sensor Signal
9	Brown	EGR Pintle Position Sensor Signal
10	Purple	Fuel Level Sensor Signal
11	Gray	Generator F Terminal
12	Dark Blue	Throttle Position (TP) Sensor Signal
13	Yellow/Black	Transmission Fluid Temp Sensor Signal
14	Orange/Black	Transmission Fluid Temp Sensor Low Reference
19	Pink	Pcm 12V Ignition
20	Orange	Pcm 12V Battery
21	Black	Pcm Ground
22	Yellow/Black	Crankshaft Position (CKP) Sensor Low Reference
23	Black	Throttle Position (TP) Sensor Low Reference
24	Black/White	Sensor Ground Jumper
25	Brown	Engine Coolant Temp (ECT) Low Reference
26	Orange/Black	Manifold Absolute Pressure (MAP) Sensor Low Ref
28	Dark Blue	Engine Cooling Fan Relay #2 and #3 Control
30	Brown	Air Pump Relay Control
31	Purple	Air Solenoid Relay Control
32	Tan/Black	TCC Enable Solenoid
33	Brown	TCC (PWM) Solenoid Valve Control
34	Gray	EGR Valve Ground
35	White	Engine Speed Output (Tachometer)
36	Light Blue/White	Trans Fluid Pressure Control Solenoid Control Low
37	Dark Green/White	Fuel Pump Relay Control
38	Light Blue	EGR Valve Control Circuit
39	Red/Black	Transmission Fluid Pressure Control Solenoid Control High
40	Tan/Black	Torque Delivered
41	Purple	HO$_2$S Signal High Bank 2 Sensor 2

1997–1998 LS1 PCM Connector C2 (Blue)

Pin	Color	Function
42	Purple/White	HO$_2$S Signal High Bank 1 Sensor 2
43	Gray	Throttle Position (TP) Sensor 5V Reference
44	Gray	Fuel Level Sensor 5V Reference
45	Gray	Engine Oil Pressure (EOP) Sensor 5V Reference
46	Purple	HO$_2$S Signal High Bank 2 Sensor 1
47	Purple/White	HO$_2$S Signal High Bank 1 Sensor 1
48	Light Green	Manifold Absolute Pressure (MAP) Sensor Signal
49	Yellow	Engine Coolant Temp (ECT) Sensor Signal
52	Dark Green	Fuel Tank Pressure Sensor Signal
53	Tan/White	Engine Oil Pressure (EOP) Sensor Signal
54	Light Green/Black	Idle Air Control (IAC) Coil B Low
55	Light Blue/Black	IAC Coil A Low
56	Light Blue/White	IAC Coil A High
57	Light Green/White	IAC Coil B High
58	Purple	Class 2 Serial Data (OBD-II DLC)
60	Black	PCM Ground
61	Orange	PCM 12V Battery
62	Light Green	Crankshaft Position (CKP) Sensor 12V Reference
64	Gray	Manifold Absolute Pressure (MAP) Sensor 5V Ref
65	Gray	EGR Pintle Position Sensor 5V Reference
66	Gray	A/C Refrigerant Pressure Sensor 5V Reference
67	Gray	Fuel Tank Pressure Sensor 5V Reference
68	Light Blue	Knock Sensor (Ks) Rear Signal
69	Dark Blue	Knock Sensor (Ks) Front Signal
70	Pink/Black	Camshaft Position (CMP) Sensor Low Reference
71	Tan	Tac Module Serial Data
72	Orange/Black	Tac Module Serial Data
76	Brown	Oil Level Sensor Signal
77	Red	Generator L Terminal

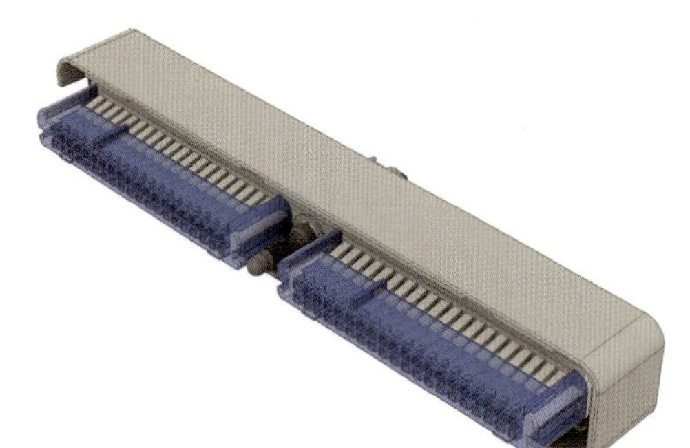

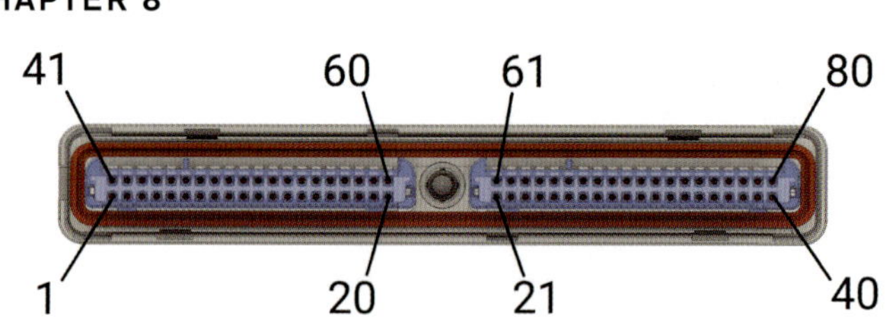

Pin	Color	Function
1	Black	PCM Ground
2	Light Green	Crankshaft Position (CKP) Sensor 12v Reference
3	Pink/Black	Fuel Injector #3 Control
4	Light Green/Black	Fuel Injector #2 Control
7	Gray	Engine Oil Pressure (EOP) Sensor 5v Reference
8	Gray	Throttle Position (TP) Sensor 5V Reference
11	Light Blue	Knock Sensor (KS) Rear Signal
12	Dark Blue/White	Crankshaft Position (CKP) Sensor Signal
13	Orange/Black	Requested Torque Signal
14	Tan	Throttle Actuator Control (TAC) Serial Data
15	Orange/Black	Throttle Actuator Control (TAC) Serial Data
17	Dark Blue	Transmission Range Signal B
18	Red	Transmission Range Signal C
19	Pink	PCM 12V Ignition
20	Orange	PCM 12V Battery
21	Yellow/Black	Crankshaft Position (CKP) Sensor Low Reference
23	Gray	Fuel Tank Pressure Sensor/Sender Low Reference
25	Tan	HO$_2$S Signal Low Bank 2 Sensor 2
26	Tan	HO$_2$S Signal Low Bank 2 Sensor 1
28	Tan/White	HO$_2$S Signal Low Bank 1 Sensor 2
29	Tan/White	HO$_2$S Signal Low Bank 1 Sensor 1
32	Gray	Clutch Pedal Position (CPP) Switch Signal (F-Body)
32	Black/White	Transmission PRND A Input Signal
33	Purple	TCC Brake Switch
34	Orange/Black	PNP Switch Signal
34	White	Transmission PRND P Input Signal
35	Gray	Clutch Pedal Position (CPP) Switch Signal (Except F-Body)
36	Black	Fuel Injector #1 Control
37	Yellow/Black	Fuel Injector #6 Control
38	Pink/White	Powertrain Induced Chassis Pitch Signal
40	Black	PCM Ground
41	Black	EGR Pintle Position Sensor Low Reference
42	Dark Green	Engine Cooling Fan Relay 1 Control
43	Red/Black	Fuel Injector #7 Control

Pin	Color	Function
44	Light Blue/Black	Fuel Injector #4 Control
45	Gray	A/C Refrigerant Pressure Sensor 5V Reference
46	Gray	Fuel Tank Pressure Sensor 5V Reference
47	Gray	EGR Pintle Position Sensor 5V Reference
48	Gray	Manifold Absolute Pressure (MAP) Sensor 5V Ref
51	Dark Blue	Knock Sensor (KS) Front Signal
53	Black	Transmission Temperature Sensor Low Reference
54	Orange/Black	Manifold Absolute Pressure (MAP) Sensor Low Ref
55	Brown	EGR Pintle Position Sensor Signal
57	Orange	PCM 12V Battery
58	Dark Green	Class 2 Serial Data (OBD-II DLC)
59	Yellow	Class 2 Serial Data
60	Black	Throttle Position (TP) Sensor Low Reference
61	Pink/Black	Camshaft Position (CMP) Sensor Low Reference
62	Gray	Extended Travel Brake Switch Signal
63	Black	Engine Oil Pressure (EOP) Sensor Low Reference
65	Purple	HO$_2$S Signal High Bank 2 Sensor 2
66	Purple	HO$_2$S Signal High Bank 2 Sensor 1
68	Purple/White	HO$_2$S Signal High Bank 1 Sensor 2
69	Purple/White	HO$_2$S Signal High Bank 1 Sensor 1
70	Brown	Low Oil Level Switch Signal
72	Yellow	Transmission PRND B Input Signal
73	Brown/White	Camshaft Position (CMP) Sensor Signal
74	Yellow	Engine Coolant Temperature (ECT) Sensor Signal
76	Blacl/White	Fuel Injector #5 Control
77	Dark Blue/White	Fuel Injector #8 Control
79	Gray	Skip Shift Solenoid Control (Manual Transmission)
79	White	3-2 Shift Solenoid Control (Automatic Transmission)
80	Black	Engine Coolant Temperature (ECT) Low Reference

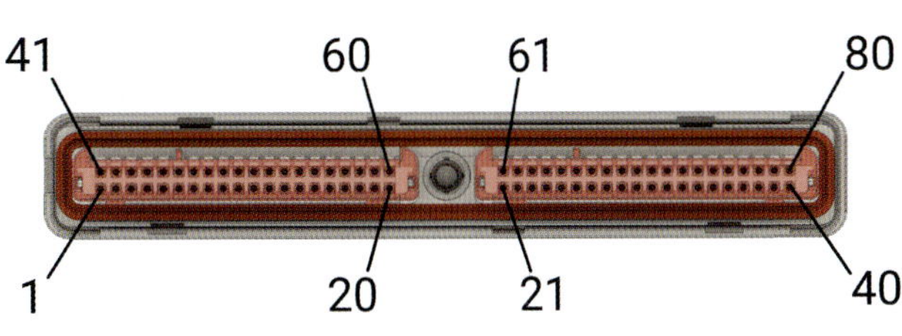

1999–2002 P01 PCM Connector C2 (Red)

Pin	Color	Function
1	Black	PCM Ground
2	Brown	TCC Solenoid Control
4	Purple	Air Solenoid Relay Control
5	Tan/Black	Torque Delivered
6	Red/Black	Transmission Fluid Pressure Control Solenoid High
7	Red	EGR Control
8	Light Blue/White	Transmission Fluid Pressure Control Solenoid Low
9	Dark Green/White	Fuel Pump Relay Control
10	White	Engine Speed Output Signal (Tachometer)
11	Dark Blue	Secondary A/C High Pressure Switch
13	White	Cruise Control Enable Signal
14	Red/Black	A/C Refrigerant Pressure Sensor Signal
15	Red	Generator L Terminal
16	Gray/Black	Four-Wheel Drive Switch Signal Low
17	Dark Green/White	A/C Request Signal
18	Dark Green	A/C Status Signal (12V Compressor Clutch Voltage)
19	Black/White	Four-Wheel Drive Front Axle Switch
20	Purple	Vehicle Speed Sensor (VSS) Low
21	Yellow	Vehicle Speed Sensor (VSS) Signal
22	Red/Black	Input Shaft Speed (ISS) Sensor Signal (4L80E)
23	Dark Blue/White	Input Shaft Speed (ISS) Sensor Low (4l80E)
24	Dark Blue	Throttle Position (TP) Sensor Signal
25	Tan	Intake Air Temperature (IAT) Sensor Signal
26	Purple	Ignition Coil #1 Control
27	Red	Ignition Coil #7 Control
28	Light Blue/White	Ignition Coil #6 Control
29	Dark Green/White	Ignition Coil #4 Control
30	Dark Blue	VATS Fuel Enable Signal
31	Yellow	Mass Airflow (MAF) Sensor Signal
32	Light Green	Manifold Air Pressure (MAP) Sensor Signal
33	Dark Blue	Engine Cooling Fan Relay 2 And 3 Control
33	Dark Green	HVAC Recirculation Door Control

1999–2002 P01 PCM Connector C2 (Red)

Pin	Color	Function
34	Dark Green/White	EVAP Canister Purge Valve Control
36	Brown	Air Pump Relay Control
37	Dark Green	Cruise Control Inhibit
39	Red	Camshaft Position (CMP) Sensor 12V Reference
40	Black	PCM Ground
41	Gray	EGR Position Sensor Ground
42	Tan/Black	TCC Enable Circuit
43	Dark Green/White	A/C Clutch Relay Control
44	Light Green	Reverse Inhibit (Lockout) Solenoid Control
45	White	EVAP Canister Vent Valve Control
46	Brown/White	Malfunction Indicator Lamp (MIL) Control
47	Yellow/Black	Transmission Shift Solenoid B
48	Light Green	Transmission Shift Solenoid A
49	Yellow/Black	Vehicle Speed Output Signal (Secondary)
50	Dark Green/White	Vehicle Speed Output Signal (Primary)
51	Yellow/Black	Transmission Temperature Sensor Signal
52	Gray	Generator F Terminal
53	Gray/Black	Spark Retard Signal
54	Purple	Fuel Level Sensor Signal
55	Dark Green	A/C Compressor Cyling Switch Signal
57	Purple	Intake Air Temperature (IAT) Sensor Low Reference
58	Tan/White	Engine Oil Pressure (EOP) Sensor Signal
60	Brown	Ignition Coils Bank 1 Low Reference
61	Brown/White	Ignition Coils Bank 2 Low Reference
62	Gray	Transmission PRND C Input Signal
63	Pink	Transmission Range Signal A
64	Dark Green	Fuel Tank Pressure Sensor Signal
66	Purple/White	Ignition Coil #8 Control
67	Red/White	Ignition Coil #2 Control
68	Dark Green	Ignition Coil #5 Control
69	Light Blue	Ignition Coil #3 Control
73	Light Blue	Fuel Level Sensor Signal (Secondary)
76	Light Green/White	IAC Coil B High
77	Light Green/Black	IAC Coil B Low
78	Light Blue/Black	IAC Coil A Low
79	Light Blue/White	IAC Coil A High

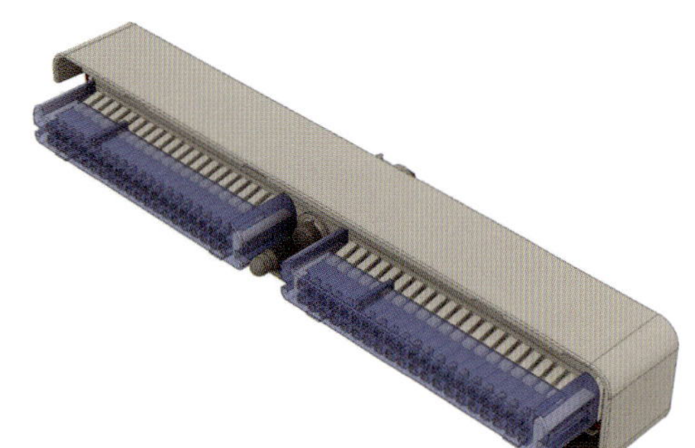
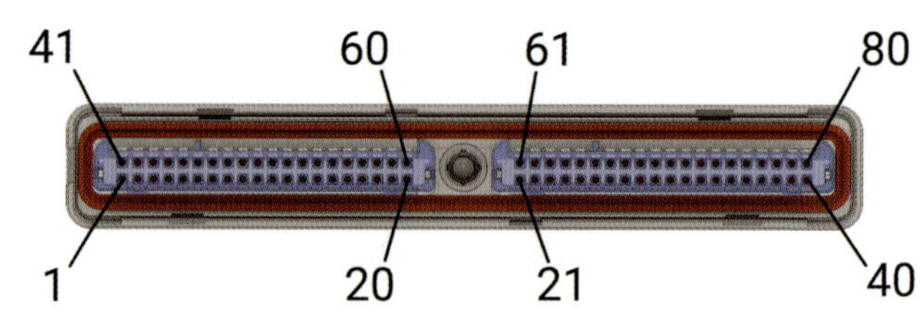

2003–2007 P59 PCM Connector C1 (Blue)		
Pin	Color	Function
1	Black/White	PCM Ground
2	Light Green	Crankshaft Position (CKP) Sensor 12V Reference
3	Pink/Black	Fuel Injector #3 Control
4	Light Green/Black	Fuel Injector #2 Control
7	Gray	Engine Oil Pressure (EOP) Sensor 5v Reference
8	Gray	Throttle Position (TP) Sensor 5v Reference
11	Light Blue	Knock Sensor (KS) Rear Signal
12	Dark Blue/White	Crankshaft Position (CKP) Sensor Signal
13	Orange/Black	Requested Torque Signal
14	Orange/Black	Throttle Actuator Control (TAC) Serial Data
15	Dark Blue/White	Throttle Actuator Control (TAC) Serial Data
17	Dark Blue	Transmission Range Signal B
18	Red	Transmission Range Signal C
19	Pink	PCM 12V Ignition
20	Orange	PCM 12V Battery
21	Yellow/Black	Crankshaft Position (CKP) Sensor Low Reference
23	Gray	Fuel Tank Pressure Sensor/Sender Low Reference
24	Black/White	Ground
25	Tan	HO$_2$S Signal Low Bank 2 Sensor 2
26	Tan	HO$_2$S Signal Low Bank 2 Sensor 1
27	Black/White	Ground
28	Tan/White	HO$_2$S Signal Low Bank 1 Sensor 2
29	Tan/White	HO$_2$S Signal Low Bank 1 Sensor 1
30	Light Green	Coolant Level Switch Signal
32	Black/White	Transmission PRND A Input Signal
33	Purple	TCC Brake Switch
34	White	Transmission PRND P Input Signal
35	Gray	Clutch Pedal Position (CPP) Switch Signal
36	Black	Fuel Injector #1 Control
37	Yellow/Black	Fuel Injector #6 Control
38	Pink/White	Damping Lift/Dive Signal
39	Yellow/Black	Starter Enable Relay Control
40	Black/White	PCM Ground
42	Dark Green	Engine Cooling Fan Relay 1 Control
43	Red/Black	Fuel Injector #7 Control

2003–2007 P59 PCM Connector C1 (Blue)		
Pin	Color	Function
44	Light Blue/Black	Fuel Injector #4 Control
45	Gray	A/C Refrigerant Pressure Sensor 5V Reference
46	Gray	Fuel Tank Pressure Sensor 5V Reference
48	Gray	Manifold Absolute Pressure (MAP) Sensor 5V Ref
51	Dark Blue	Knock Sensor (KS) Front Signal
53	Black	Transmission Temperature Sensor Low Reference
54	Orange/Black	Manifold Absolute Pressure (MAP) Sensor Low Ref
57	Orange	PCM 12V Battery
58	Dark Green	Class 2 Serial Data (OBDII DLC)
59	Yellow	Class 2 Serial Data
60	Black	Throttle Position (TP) Sensor Low Reference
61	Pink/Black	Camshaft Position (CMP) Sensor Low Reference
62	Gray	Extended Travel Brake Switch Signal
63	Black	Engine Oil Pressure (EOP) Sensor Low Reference
64	Black/White	Ground
65	Purple	HO$_2$S Signal High Bank 2 Sensor 2
66	Purple	HO$_2$S Signal High Bank 2 Sensor 1
67	Black/White	Ground
68	Purple/White	HO$_2$S Signal High Bank 1 Sensor 2
69	Purple/White	HO$_2$S Signal High Bank 1 Sensor 1
70	Brown	Low Oil Level Switch Signal
72	Yellow	Transmission PRND B Input Signal
73	Brown/White	Camshaft Position (CMP) Sensor Signal
74	Yellow	Engine Coolant Temperature (ECT) Sensor Signal
75	Pink	Off/Run/Crank Voltage
76	Black/White	Fuel Injector #5 Control
77	Dark Blue/White	Fuel Injector #8 Control
79	Gray	Skip Shift Solenoid Control (Manual Transmission)
79	White	3-2 Shift Solenoid Control (Automatic Transmission)
80	Black	Engine Coolant Temperature (ECT) Low Reference

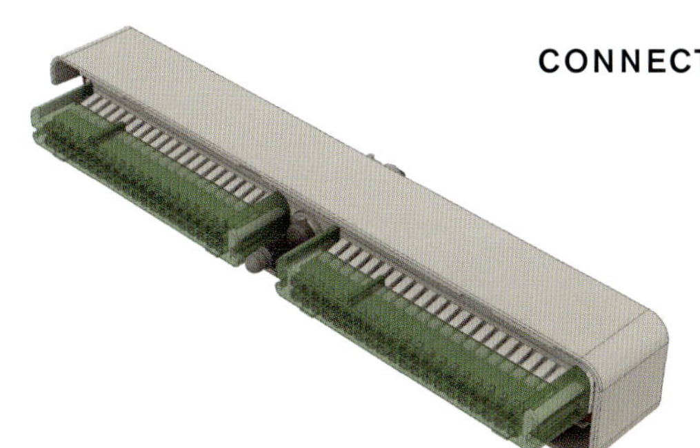

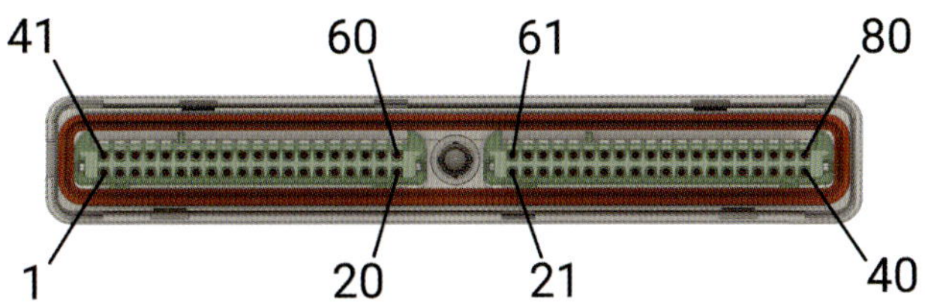

2003–2007 P59 PCM Connector C2 (Green)		
Pin	Color	Function
1	Black	PCM Ground
2	Brown	TCC Solenoid Control
3	Tan	Fuel Pump Relay Control (Secondary)
4	Purple	Air Solenoid Relay Control
5	Tan/Black	Torque Delivered
6	Red/Black	Transmission Fluid Pressure Control Solenoid High
8	Light Blue/White	Transmission Fluid Pressure Control Solenoid Low
9	Dark Green/White	Fuel Pump Relay Control
10	White	Engine Speed Output Signal (Tachometer)
14	Red/Black	A/C Refrigerant Pressure Sensor Signal
15	Red	Generator L Terminal
16	Gray/Black	4 Wheel Drive Switch Signal Low
17	Dark Green/White	A/C Request Signal
18	Dark Green	Clutch Start Switch Signal
19	Black/White	4 Wheel Drive Front Axle Switch
20	Purple	Vehicle Speed Sensor (VSS) Low
21	Yellow	Vehicle Speed Sensor (VSS) Signal
22	Red/Black	Input Shaft Speed (ISS) Sensor Signal (4l80E)
23	Dark Blue/White	Input Shaft Speed (ISS) Sensor Low (4l80e)
24	Dark Blue	Throttle Position (TP) Sensor Signal
25	Tan	Intake Air Temperature (IAT) Sensor Signal
26	Purple	Ignition Coil #1 Control
27	Red	Ignition Coil #7 Control
28	Light Blue/White	Ignition Coil #6 Control
29	Dark Green/White	Ignition Coil #4 Control
31	Yellow	Mass Airflow (MAF) Sensor Signal
32	Light Green	Manifold Air Pressure (MAP) Sensor Signal
33	Dark Blue	Engine Cooling Fan Relay 2 and 3 Control
34	Dark Green/White	EVAP Canister Purge Valve Control
35	White	Engine Speed Signal (with Hybrid)
36	Brown	Air Pump Relay Control
39	Red	Camshaft Position (CMP) Sensor 12V Reference
40	Black	PCM Ground
41	Gray	EGR Position Sensor Ground
42	Tan/Black	TCC Enable Circuit

2003–2007 P59 PCM Connector C2 (Green)		
Pin	Color	Function
43	Dark Green/White	A/C Clutch Relay Control
44	Light Green	Reverse Inhibit (Lockout) Solenoid Control
45	White	EVAP Canister Vent Valve Control
46	Brown/White	Malfunction Indicator Lamp (MIL) Control
47	Yellow/Black	Transmission Shift Solenoid B
48	Light Green	Transmission Shift Solenoid A
49	Yellow/Black	Vehicle Speed Output Signal (Secondary)
50	Dark Green/White	Vehicle Speed Output Signal (Primary)
51	Yellow/Black	Transmission Temperature Sensor Signal
52	Brown	HO$_2$S Heater Low Control
53	Red/White	HO$_2$S Heater Low Control
54	Purple	Fuel Level Sensor Signal
55	Dark Green	A/C Compressor Cycling Switch Signal
57	Purple	Intake Air Temperature (IAT) Sensor Low Reference
58	Tan/White	Engine Oil Pressure (EOP) Sensor Signal
59	Purple	Crank Voltage
60	Brown	Ignition Coils Bank 1 Low Reference
61	Brown/White	Ignition Coils Bank 2 Low Reference
62	Gray	Transmission PRND C Input Signal
63	Pink	Transmission Range Signal A
64	Dark Green	Fuel Tank Pressure Sensor Signal
66	Purple/White	Ignition Coil #8 Control
67	Red/White	Ignition Coil #2 Control
68	Dark Green	Ignition Coil #5 Control
69	Light Blue	Ignition Coil #3 Control
70	Tan/White	High Speed GMLAN Serial Data (+) (with Hybrid)
71	Tan	High Speed GMLAN Serial Data (-) (with Hybrid)
72	Black/White	HO$_2$S Heater Low Control
73	Light Blue	Fuel Level Sensor Signal (Secondary)
74	Light Green	HO$_2$S Heater Low Control
75	Gray	Generator F Terminal
76	Light Green/White	IAC Coil B High
77	Light Green/Black	IAC Coil B Low
78	Light Blue/Black	IAC Coil A Low
79	Light Blue/White	IAC Coil A High
80	Black	A/C Refrigerant Pressure Sensor Low Reference

Accelerator Pedal Position (APP) Sensor
1997–2004 Corvette

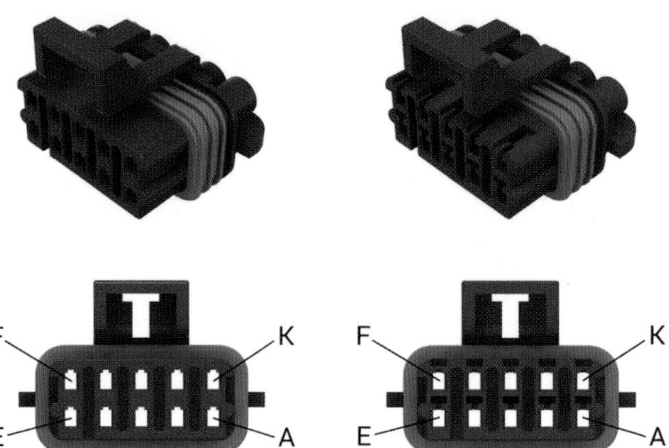

Pin	Function	1997–2004 Corvette TAC	2004–2005 CTS-V TAC
A	APP Sensor 3 Low Ref	C1-A	C1-A
B	APP Sensor 2 Low Ref	C1-E	C1-E
C	APP Sensor 2 Signal	C1-C	C1-C
D	APP Sensor 2 5V Ref	C1-D	C1-D
E	APP Sensor 3 5V Ref	C1-E	C1-E
F	APP sensor 1 Signal	C1-F	C1-F
G	APP Sensor 1 5V Ref	C1-G	C1-G
H	-	-	-
J	APP Sensor 1 Low Ref	C1-J	C1-J
K	APP Sensor 3 Signal	C1-K	C1-K

Accelerator Pedal Position (APP) Sensor
1994–2000 Truck 6.5L Diesel

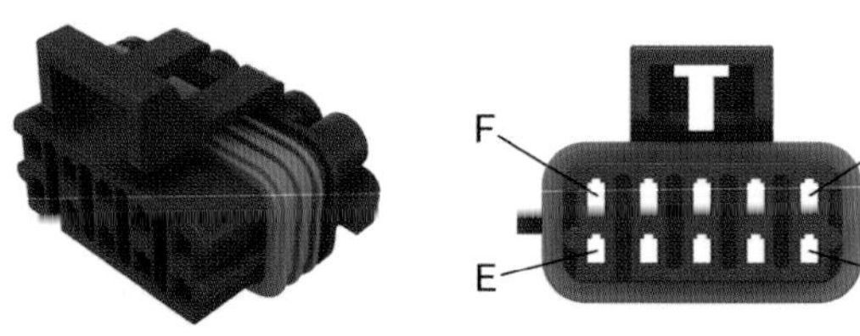

Pin	Function	2003–2007 Truck/SUV TAC
A	APP Sensor 1 Low Ref	C2-J
B	APP Sensor 2 Low Ref	C2-B
C	APP Sensor 2 Signal	C2-C
D	APP Sensor 2 5V Ref	C2-D
E	-	-
F	APP Sensor 1 Signal	C2-F
G	APP Sensor 1 5V Ref	C2-G
H	-	-
J	-	-
K	-	-

• While this is not a production GM implementation, it is confirmed that the 1994–2000 6.5L pedal works with the 2003–2007 truck TAC modules. The 6.5L pedal bolt pattern matches the firewall of the popular 1988–2000 old body style (OBS) full-size trucks and SUVs.

Accelerator Pedal Position (APP) Sensor
2000-2005 Truck/SUV

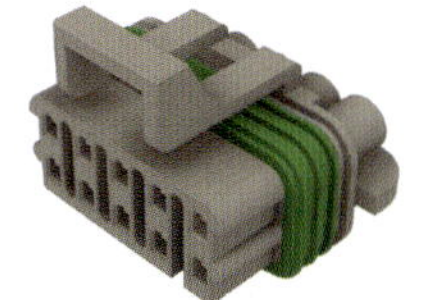 

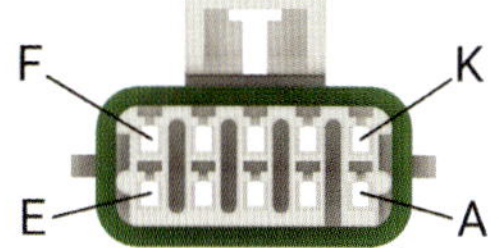

Pin	Function	2000–2002 Truck/SUV TAC	2003–2004 Truck/SUV TAC	2005–2007 Truck/SUV TAC
A	APP Sensor 3 Low Ref APP Sensor 3 5V Ref	C2-A -	- C2-A	-
B	APP Sensor 2 Low Ref APP Sensor 2 5V Ref	C2-B -	- C2-B	- C2-B
C	APP Sensor 2 Signal	C2-C	C2-C	C2-C
D	APP Sensor 2 5V Ref APP Sensor 2 Low Ref	C2-D -	- C2-D	- C2-D
E	APP Sensor 1 Low Ref	C2-J	C2-J	C2-J
F	APP Sensor 1 Signal	C2-F	C2-F	C2-F
G	APP Sensor 1 5V Ref	C2-G	C2-G	C2-G
H	-	-	-	-
J	APP Sensor 3 5V Ref APP Sensor 3 Low Ref	C2-E	C2-E	-
K	APP Sensor 3 Signal	C2-K	C2-K	-

• The 2003-2007 TAC does not actually use the APP sensor 3 signal.

Accelerator Pedal Position (APP) Sensor
2004–2005 Cadillac CTS-V

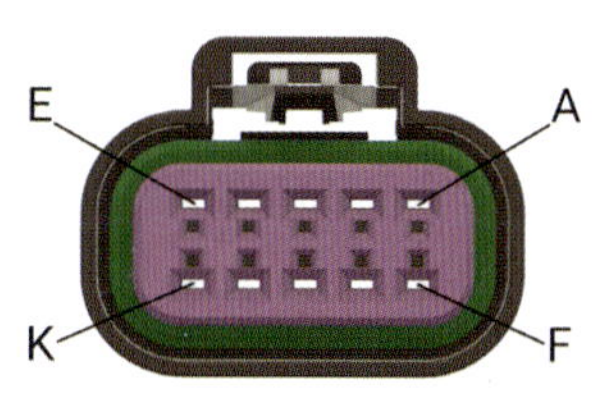

Pin	Function	1997–2004 Corvette TAC	2004–2005 CTS-V TAC
A	APP Sensor 3 Signal	C2-K	C2-K
B	APP Sensor 3 5V Ref	C2-E	C2-E
C	-	-	-
D	APP Sensor 1 5V Ref	C2-G	C2-G
E	APP Sensor 1 Signal	C2-F	C2-F
F	APP Sensor 3 Low Ref	C2-A	C2-A
G	APP Sensor 2 Low Ref	C2-B	C2-B
H	APP Sensor 2 Signal	C2-C	C2-C
J	APP Sensor 2 5V Ref	C2-D	C2-D
K	APP Sensor 1 Low Ref	C2-J	C2-J

Air-Conditioning A/C Pressure Sensor

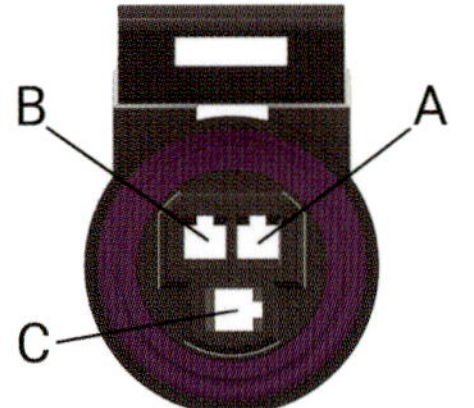
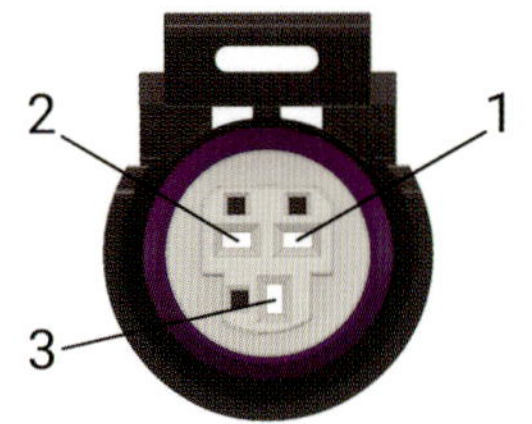

Pin	Function	1997–1998 PCM	P01/P59 PCM
A or 1	Low Reference	C1-63	C2-57
B or 2	5V Reference	C2-66	C1-45
C or 3	A/C Pressure Signal	C2-7	C2-14

Air-Conditioning A/C Compressor Clutch

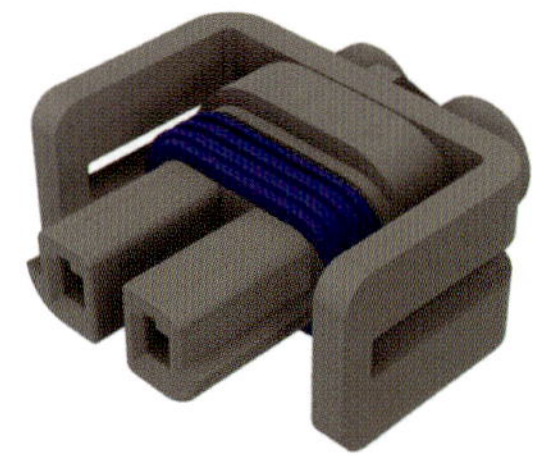
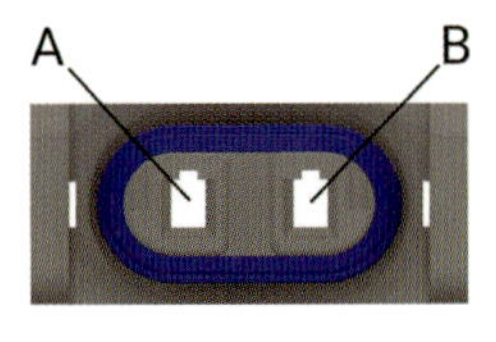

Pin	Function
A	A/C Compressor Clutch Supply Voltage
B	Ground

Backup Lamp Switch
With Manual Transmissions

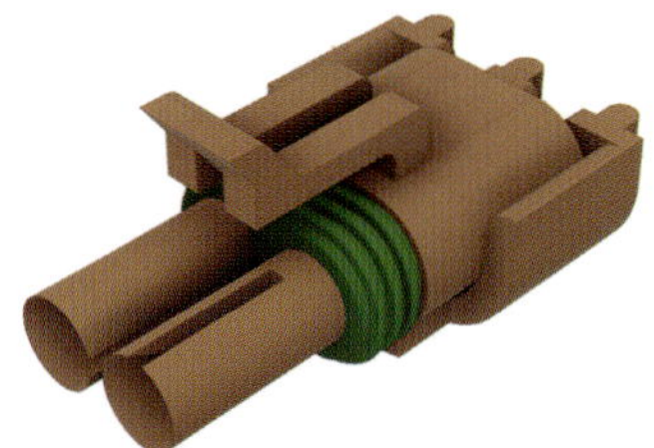

Pin	Function
A	Fused Ignition Voltage
B	Output To Backup Lamps

Camshaft Position (CMP) Sensor
With 1x CMP Behind Intake Manifold Only

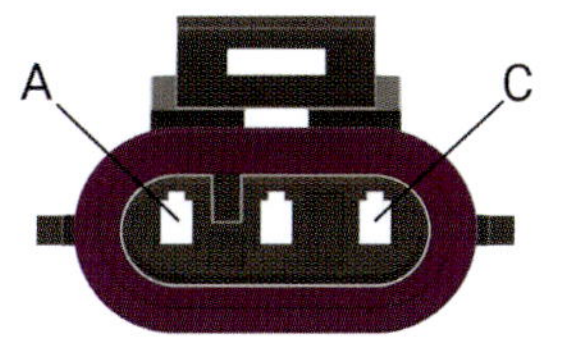

Pin	Function	1997–1998 PCM	P01/P59 PCM
A	CMP Signal	C1-4	C1-73
B	Low Ref	C2-70	C1-61
C	12V Supply	C2-4	C2-39

Camshaft Position (CMP) Sensor
With 1x in Timing Cover Only

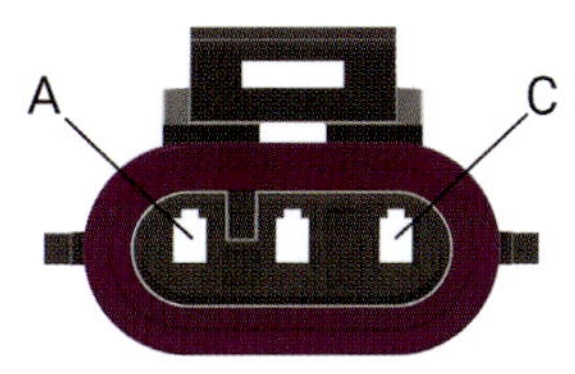

Pin	Function	1997–1998 PCM	P01/P59 PCM
A	5V or 12V Supply	C2-4	C2-39
B	Low Ref	C2-70	C1-61
C	CMP Signal	C1-4	C1-73

LS2 engines are fitted with a 1x camshaft timing sprocket.

Clutch Pedal Position (CPP) Switch
GM Part Number 10180569

Pin	Function
A	CPP Switch Signal
B	12V Switched Ignition
C	CPP Switch Signal
D	Ground

Clutch Pedal Starter Safety Switch
GM Part Number 14094368

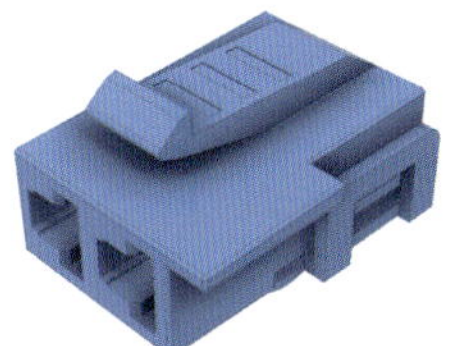

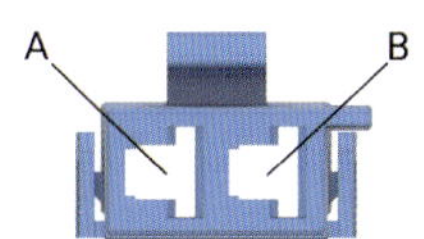

Pin	Function
A	Starter S Terminal
B	Ignition Switch (Crank)

Crankshaft Position (CKP) Sensor
With 24x CKP–Equipped Engines Only

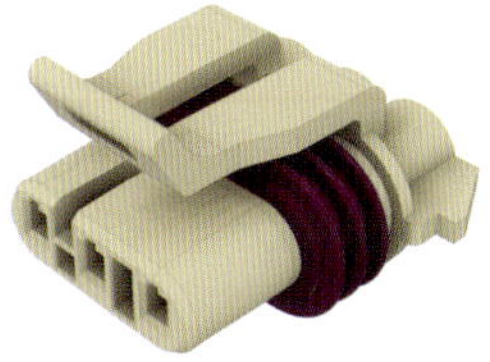

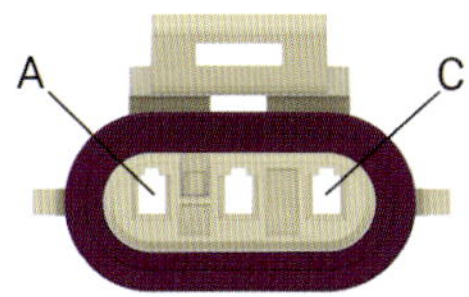

Pin	Function	1997–1998 PCM	P01/P59 PCM
A	CKP Signal	C1-44	C1-12
B	Low Ref	C2-22	C1-21
C	12V Supply	C2-62	C1-2

Cruise Control Brake and Clutch Switch

GM Part Number 22620888

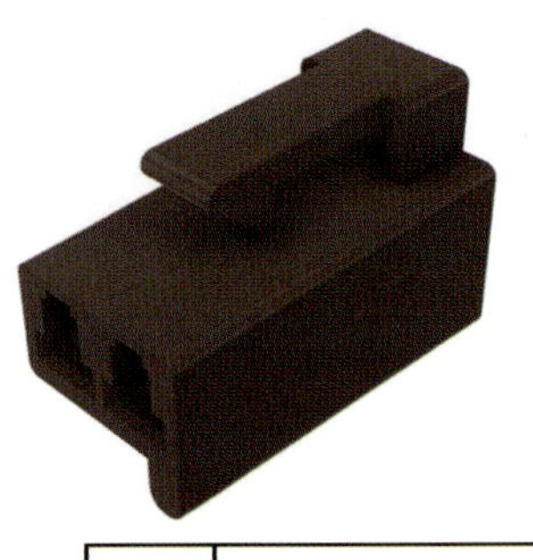

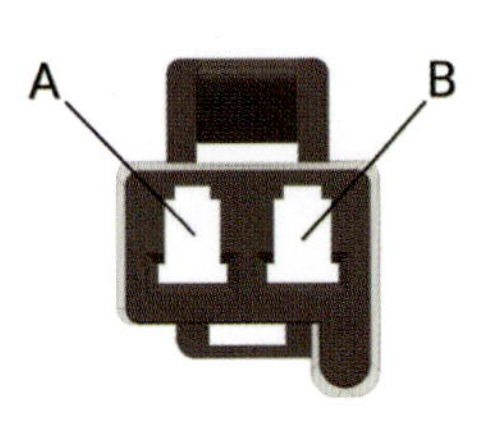

Pin	Function
A	Cruise Control Release Signal
B	12V Switched Ignition

Electric Fan Motor

1997–2004 Corvette
1998–2002 Camaro and Firebird

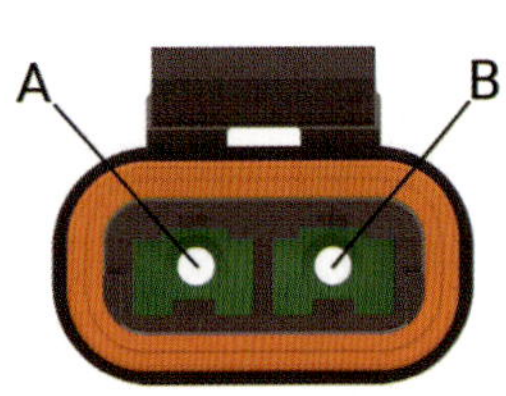

Pin	Function
A	Ground
B	12V Switched from Relay

Engine Coolant Temperature (ECT) Sensor

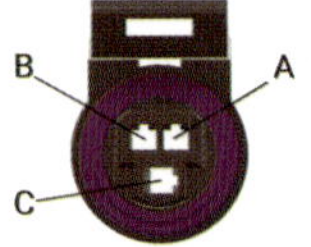 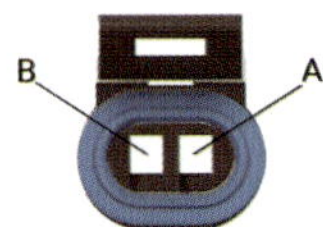 

Pin	Function	1997–1998 PCM	P01/P59 PCM
A	Low Ref	C2-25	C1-80
B	ECT Signal	C2-49	C1-74
C	Temp Gauge 1998 F-Body	-	-

• The 1998 F-Body coolant temperature output (cavity C) is compatible with many early GM gauges.

Exhaust Gas Recirculation (EGR) Valve

1998–2000 Camaro and Firebird
1999–2002 Truck, Van, and SUV

 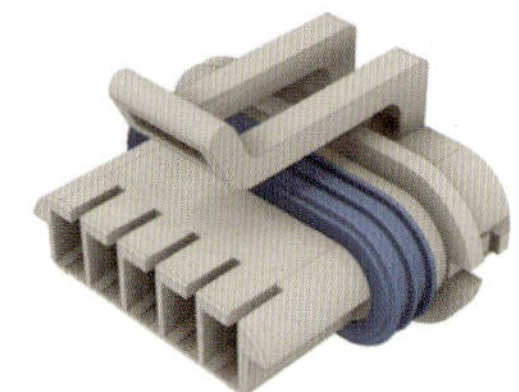

 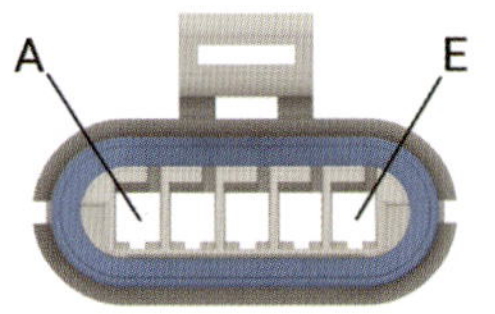

Pin	Function	1997–1998 PCM	P01 PCM
A	EGR Valve Ground	C2-34	C2-41
B	EGR Sensor Ground	C1-62	C1-41
C	EGR Pintle Position	C2-9	C1-55
D	EGR 5V Reference	C2-65	C1-47
E	EGR Valve Control	C2-38	C2-7

Electric Fan Motor

2003–2007 Truck/SUV

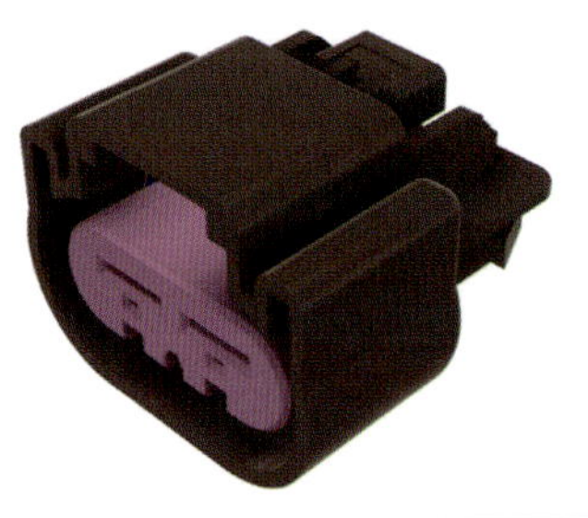

Pin	Function
A	Ground
B	12V Switched from Relay

Engine Oil Level Switch

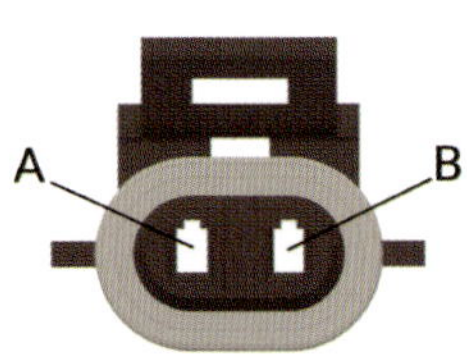

Pin	Function	1997–1998 PCM	P01/P59 PCM
A	Oil Level Signal	C2-76	C1-70
B	Ground	-	-

Engine Oil Pressure Sending Unit

Camaro/Firebird Gauges

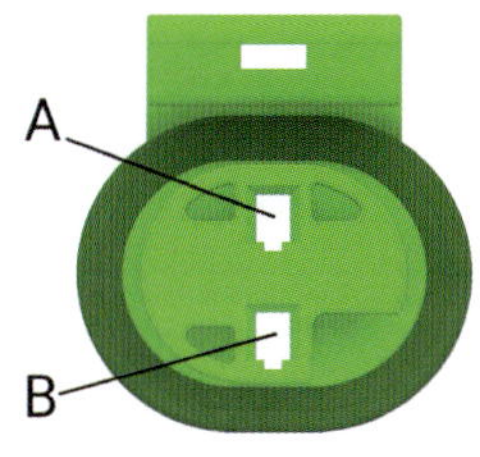

Pin	Function
A	Oil Pressure Indicator Control
B	Not Used

Evaporative Emissions (EVAP) Canister Purge Solenoid Valve

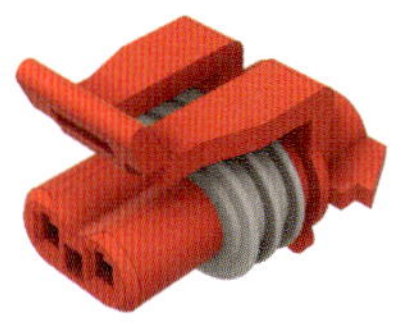
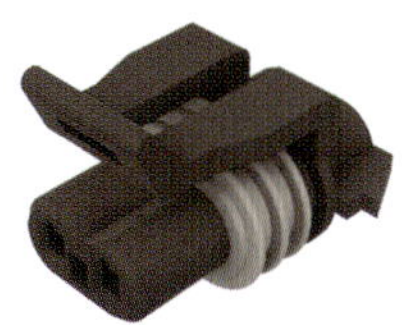

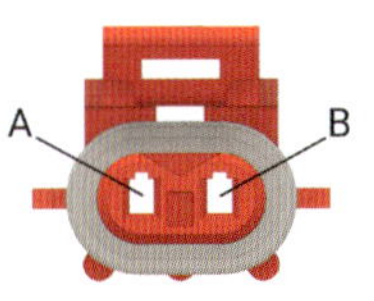
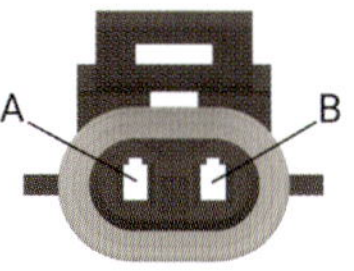

Pin	Function	1997–1998 PCM	P01/P59 PCM
A	12V Ignition	-	-
B	Solenoid Control	C1-45	C2-34

Evaporative Emissions (EVAP) Canister Vent Solenoid Valve

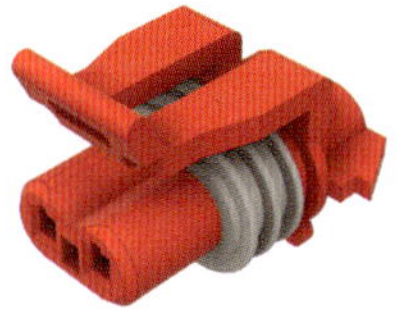

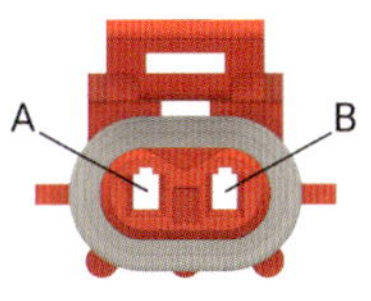
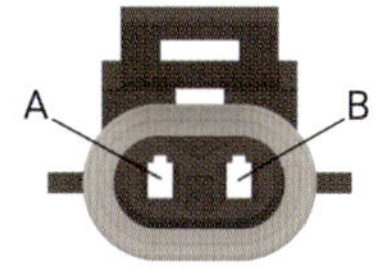

Pin	Function	1997–1998 PCM	P01/P59 PCM
A	12V Battery	-	-
B	Solenoid Control	C1-3	C2-45

Engine Oil Pressure (EOP) Sensor

With GM Part Number 12616646 EOP

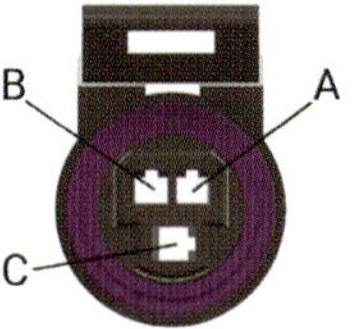
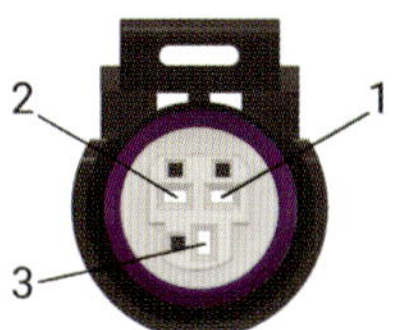

Pin	Function	1997–1998 PCM	P01/P59 PCM
A or 1	Low Ref	C1-64	C1-63
B or 2	5V Ref	C2-45	C1-7
C or 3	EOP Signal	C2-53	C2-58

Fuel Injectors

EV1 Injectors

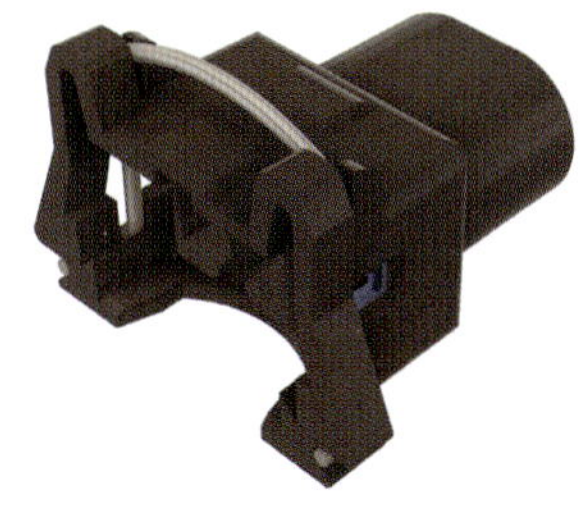
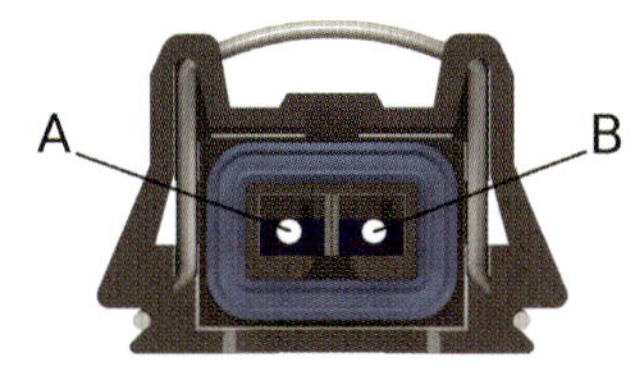

PIN	FUNCTION	1997–1998 PCM	P01/P59 PCM
A	12V Ignition	-	-
B	Fuel Injector 1	C1-33	C1-36
	Fuel Injector 2	C1-23	C1-4
	Fuel Injector 3	C1-9	C1-3
	Fuel Injector 4	C1-12	C1-44
	Fuel Injector 5	C1-15	C1-76
	Fuel Injector 6	C1-18	C1-37
	Fuel Injector 7	C1-27	C1-43
	Fuel Injector 8	C1-31	C1-77

Fuel Injectors

With Multec 2 (Truck) Injectors

 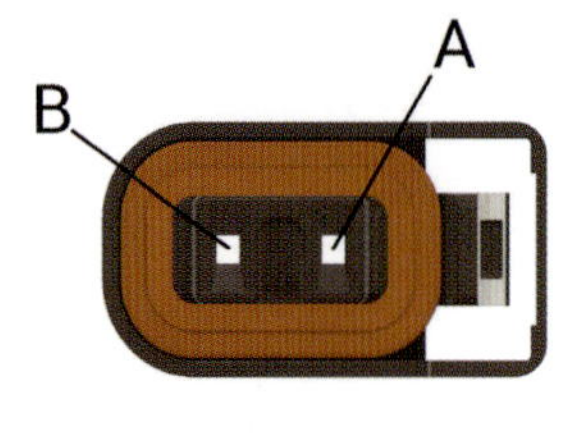

Pin	Function	1997–1998 PCM	P01/P59 PCM
A	Fuel Injector 1 Fuel Injector 2 Fuel Injector 3 Fuel Injector 4 Fuel Injector 5 Fuel Injector 6 Fuel Injector 7 Fuel Injector 8	C1-33 C1-23 C1-9 C1-12 C1-15 C1-18 C1-27 C1-31	C2-36 C2-4 C2-3 C2-44 C2-76 C2-37 C2-43 C2-77
B	12V Ignition	-	-

Generator

2004 GTO

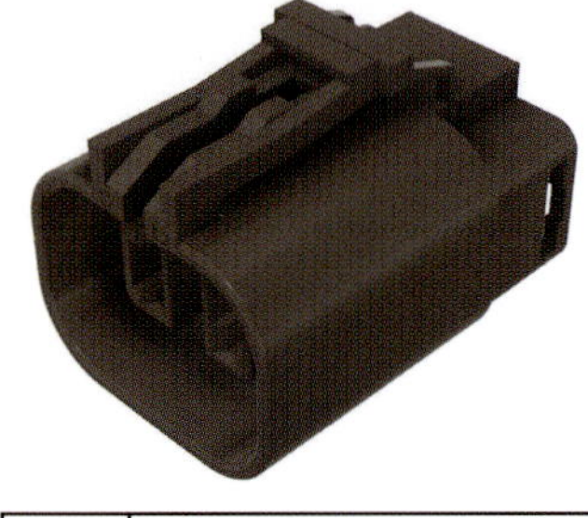 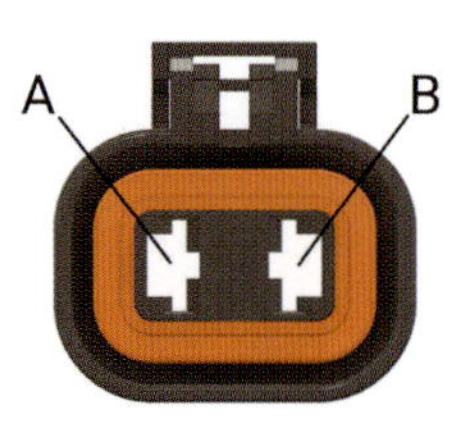

Pin	Function
A	Fused B+ Voltage
B	Charge Indicator Lamp Output/Turn on Signal (L Terminal)

Generator

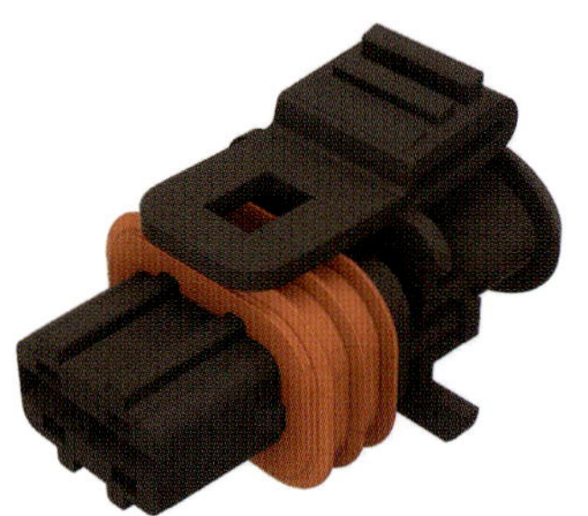 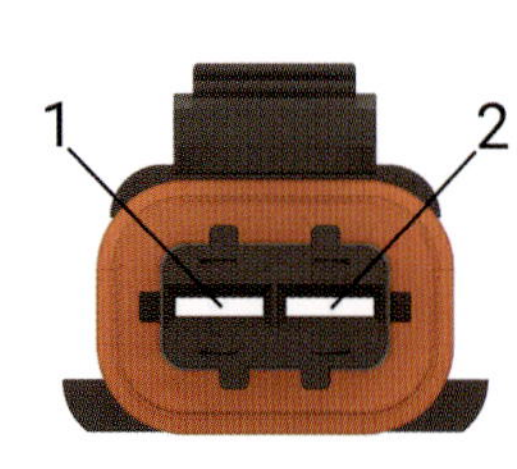

Pin	Function	1997–1998 PCM	P01 PCM	P59 PCM
1	Charge Indicator Lamp Output/ Turn on Signal (L Terminal)	C2-77	C2-15	C2-15
2	Generator Field Duty Cycle Signal (F Terminal)	C2-11	C2-52	C2-75

Generator

 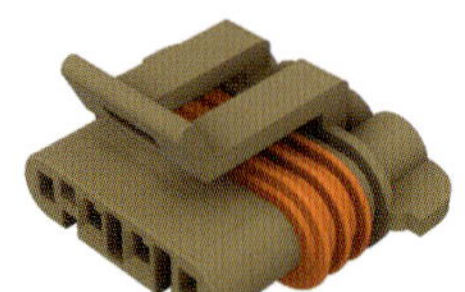 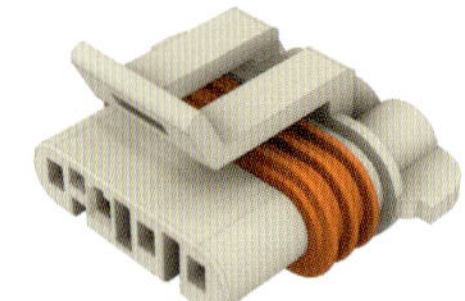

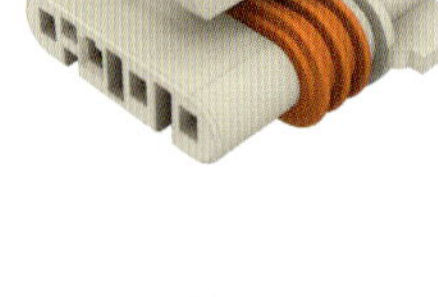

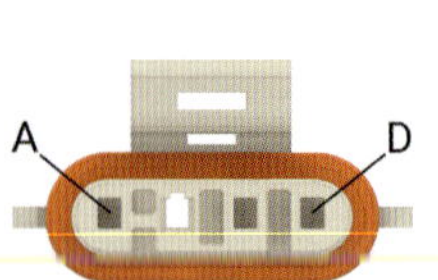

Pin	Function	1997–1998 PCM	P01 PCM	P59 PCM
A	-	-	-	-
B	Charge Indicator Lamp Output/ Turn on Signal (L Terminal)	C2-77	C2-15	C2-15
C	Generator Field Duty Cycle Signal (F Terminal)	C2-11	C2-52	C2-75
D	Used Battery	-	-	-

Idle Air Control (IAC) Valve

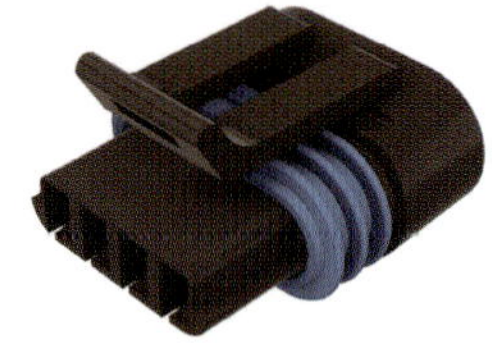 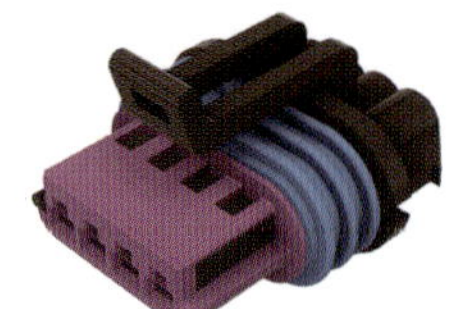

 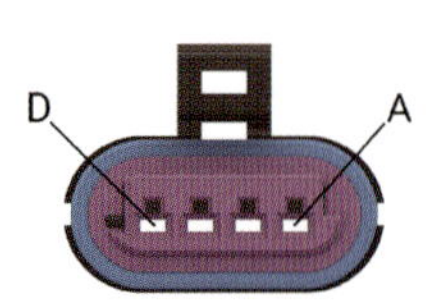

Pin	Function	1997–1998 PCM	P01/P59 PCM
A	Coil B Low	C2-54	C2-77
B	Coil B High	C2-57	C2-76
C	Coil A Low	C2-55	C2-78
D	Coil A High	C2-56	C2-79

Ignition Coil Sub-Harness

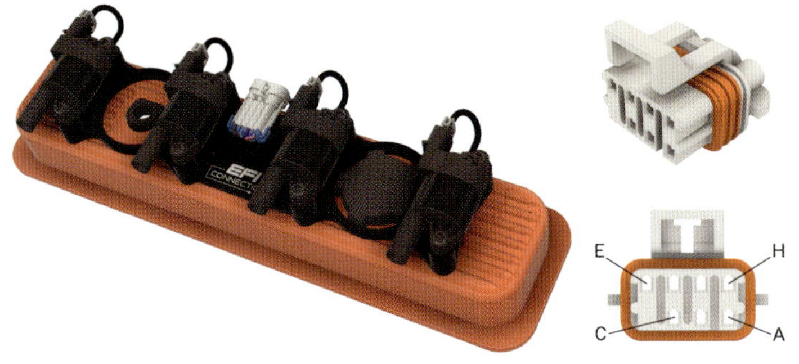

Pin	Function
A	Ground
B	Ignition Control Signal Cylinder 2 or Cylinder 7
C	Ignition Control Signal Cylinder 4 or Cylinder 5
D	-
E	PCM or ECM Low Reference
F	Ignition Control Signal Cylinder 6 or Cylinder 3
G	Ignition Control Signal Cylinder 8 or Cylinder 1
H	12V Ignition

Ignition Coil (IC) - LS1 and LS6 Only

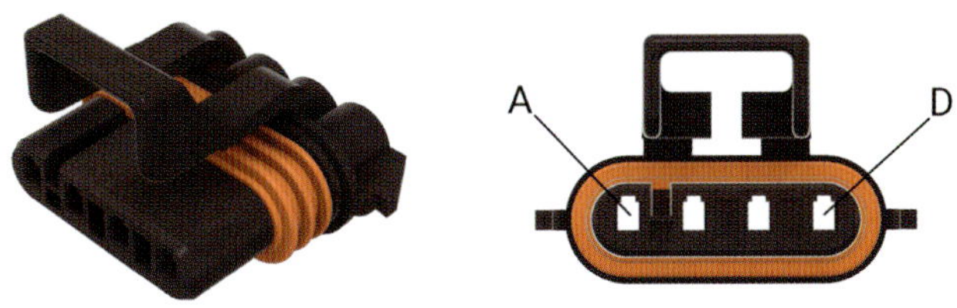

Pin	Function	1997–1998 PCM	P01/P59 PCM
A or 1	Ground	-	-
B or 2	Low Ref 1,3,5,7 Low Ref 2,4,6,8	C1-60 C1-59	C2-60 C2-61
C or 3	IC 1 IC 2 IC 3 IC 4 IC 5 IC 6 IC 7 IC 8	C1-49 C1-13 C1-58 C1-57 C1-56 C1-54 C1-53 C1-52	C2-26 C2-67 C2-69 C2-29 C2-68 C2-28 C2-27 C2-66
D or 4	12V Ignition	-	-

Ignition Coil (IC) - Except LS1 and LS6

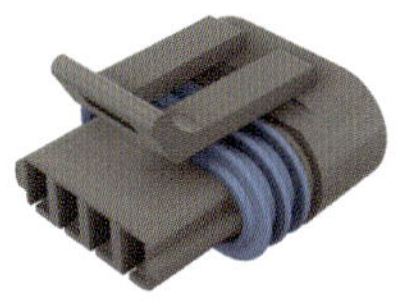

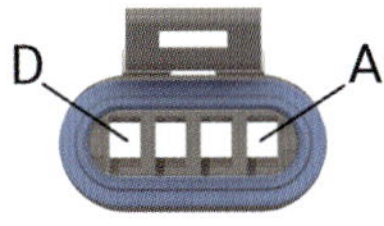

Pin	Function	97-98 PCM	P01/P59 PCM
A or 1	Ground	-	-
B or 2	Low Ref 1,3,5,7 Low Ref 2,4,6,8	C1-60 C1-59	C2-60 C2-61
C or 3	IC 1 IC 2 IC 3 IC 4 IC 5 IC 6 IC 7 IC 8	C1-49 C1-13 C1-58 C1-57 C1-56 C1-54 C1-53 C1-52	C2-26 C2-67 C2-69 C2-29 C2-68 C2-28 C2-27 C2-66
D or 4	12V Ignition	-	-

Intake Air Temperature (IAT) Sensor

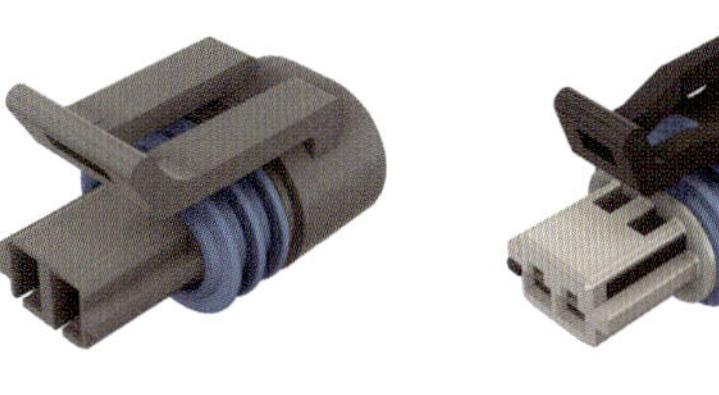

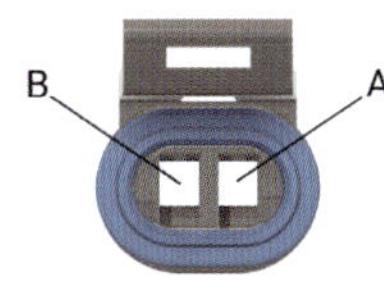

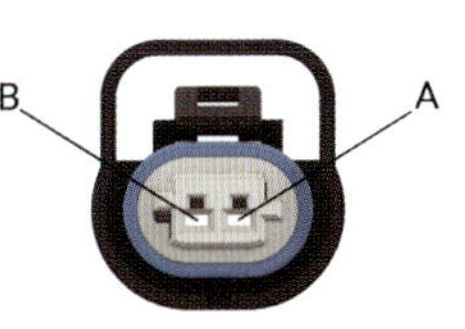

Pin	Function	1997–1998 PCM	P01/P59 PCM
A	Low Ref	C1-21	C2-57
B	IAT Signal	C2-8	C2-25

- Engines fitted with a five-wire MAF sensor do not have an external IAT sensor.
- Engines converted to speed density will need to use this IAT connector.

Knock Sensor Harness Connection
Inline Connection With Gen III LS-Series Engines

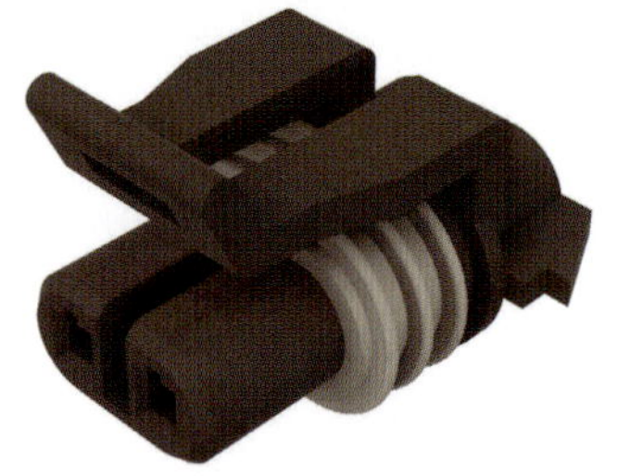

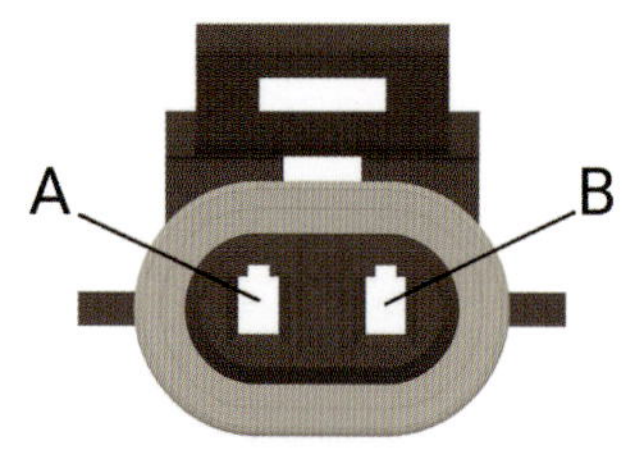

Pin	Function	1997–1998 PCM	P01/P59 PCM
A	Knock Sensor 1 Signal (Front)	C2-69	C1-51
B	Knock Sensor 2 Signal (Rear)	C2-68	C1-11

Knock Sensor (KS) - Resonant
Gen III LS-Series Knock Sensors
Located Below Intake Manifold

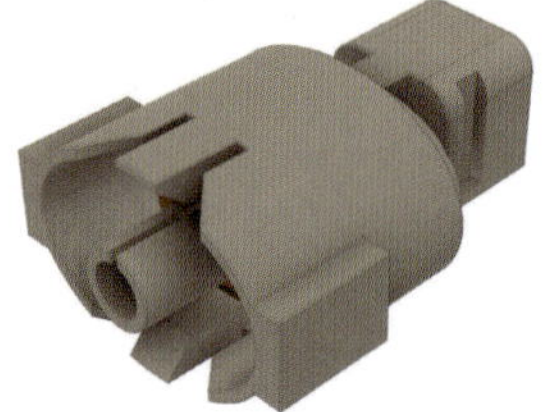

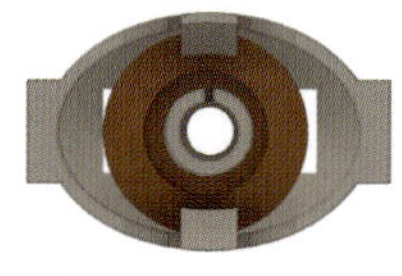

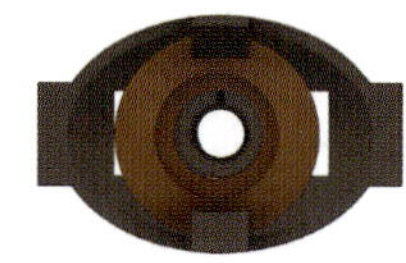

Pin	Function	1997–1998 PCM	P01/P59 PCM
-	Signal Front Signal Rear	C2-69 C2-68	C1-51 C1-11

Manifold Absolute Pressure (MAP) Sensor
With Delphi Map

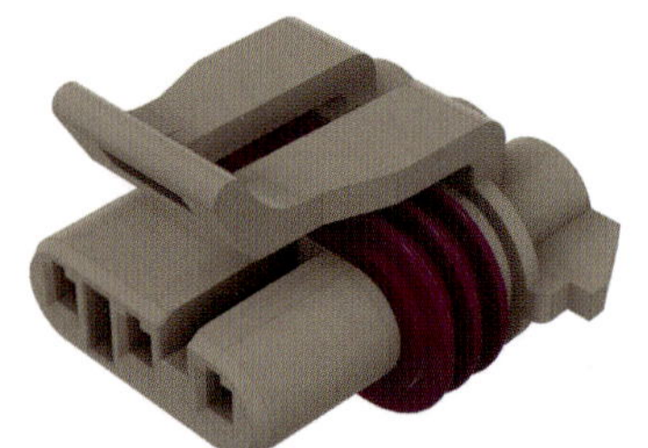

Pin	Function	1997–1998 PCM	P01/P59 PCM
A	Low Ref	C2-26	C1-54
B	MAP Signal	C2-48	C2-32
C	5V Ref	C2-64	C1-48

Mass Air Flow (MAF) Sensor
Five-Wire Round 85-mm MAF

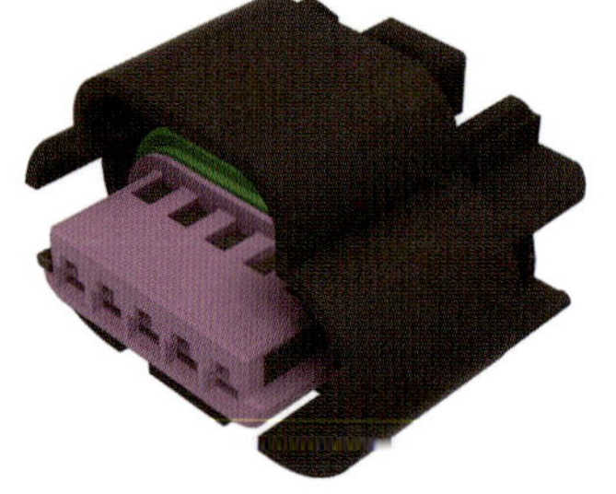

Pin	Function	1997–1998 PCM	P01/P59 PCM
A	IAT Low Reference	C1-21	C2-57
B	IAT Sensor Signal	C2-8	C2-25
C	Ground	-	-
D	12V Ignition	-	-
E	MAF Signal	C1-48	C2-31

Mass Air Flow (MAF) Sensor
Three-Wire LS1 MAF

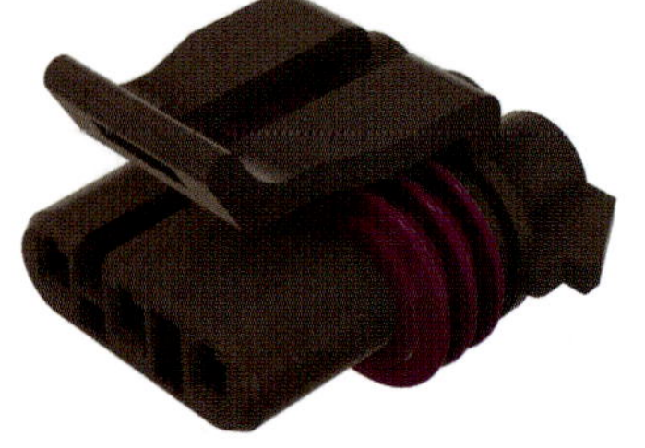

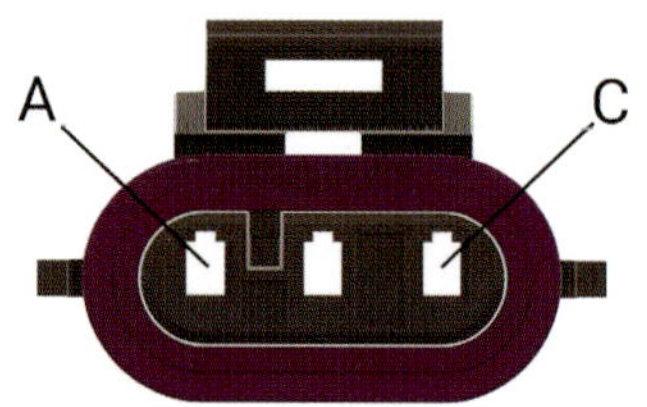

Pin	Function	1997–1998 PCM	P01/P59 PCM
A	MAF Signal	C1-48	C2-31
B	Ground	-	-
C	12V Ignition	-	-

Heated Oxygen Sensor (HO$_2$S)

Covers All LS-Series Applications

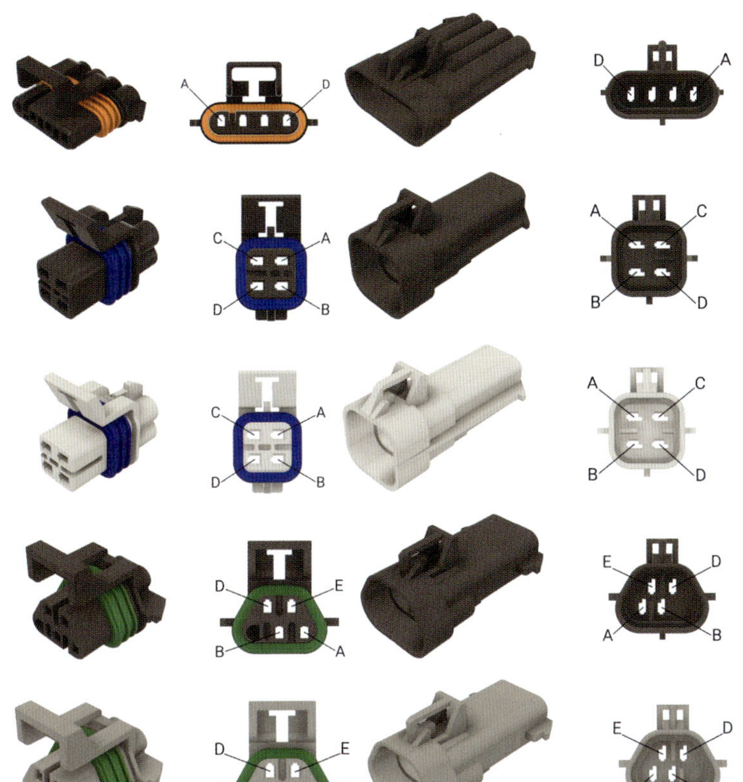

Pin	Function	1997–1998 PCM	P01/P59 PCM
A	Bank 1 Sensor 1 (Left Front) - Low Bank 2 Sensor 1 (Right Front) - Low Bank 1 Sensor 2 (Left Rear) - Low Bank 2 Sensor 2 (Right Rear) - Low	C2-6 C2-5 C2-2 C2-1	C1-29 C1-26 C1-28 C1-25
B	Bank 1 Sensor 1 (Left Front) - High Bank 2 Sensor 1 (Right Front) - High Bank 1 Sensor 2 (Left Rear) - High Bank 2 Sensor 2 (Right Rear) - High	C2-47 C2-46 C2-42 C2-41	C1-69 C1-66 C1-68 C1-65
C			
D	HO$_2$S heater wiring varies by application; See GM schematics for year/make/model/engine.		
E			

Park/Neutral Position (PNP) Switch

1999–2003 4-Speed Automatic Transmissions

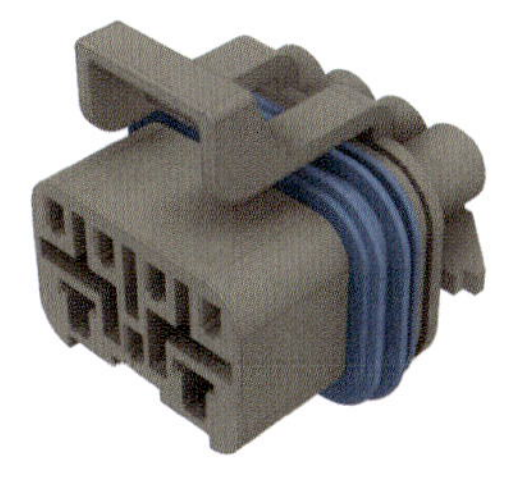
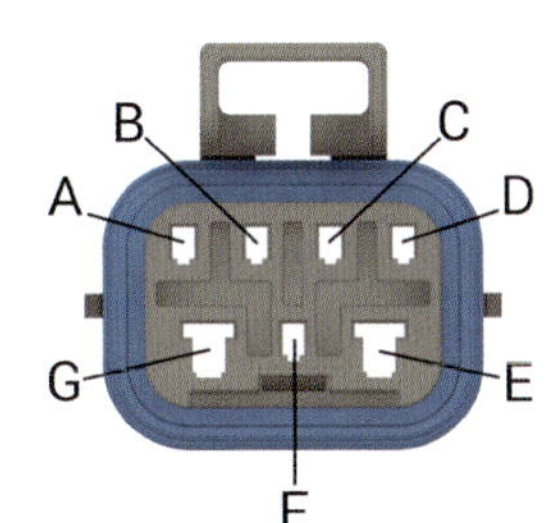
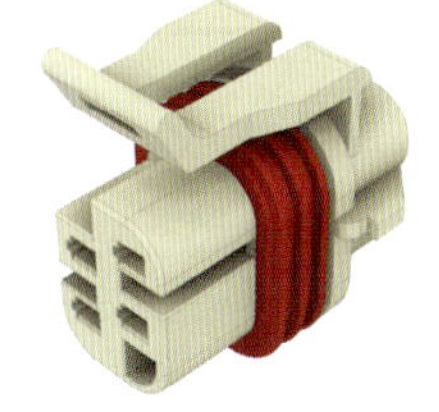
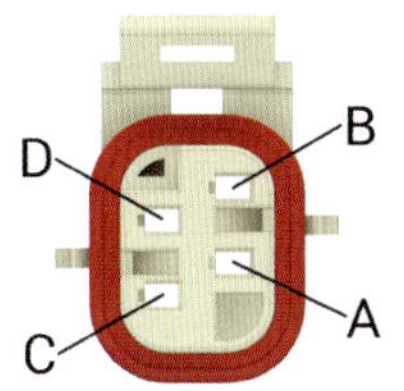

Pin	Function	1997–1998 PCM	P01/P59 PCM
C1-A	-	-	-
C1-B	Neutral Safety Switch Park Signal	-	-
C1-C	Ignition Voltage	-	-
C1-D	Ground	-	-
C1-E	-	-	-
C1-F	Backup Lamp Supply Voltage	-	-
C1-G	-	-	-
C2-A	Transmission Position Switch Signal A	-	C1-32
C2-B	Transmission Position Switch Signal C	-	C2-62
C2-C	Transmission Position Switch Signal P	-	C1-34
C2-D	Transmission Position Switch Signal B	-	C1-72

• Implementations vary. See GM schematics for year/make/model/engine.

Park/Neutral Position (PNP) Switch
2003–2007 4-Speed Automatic Transmissions

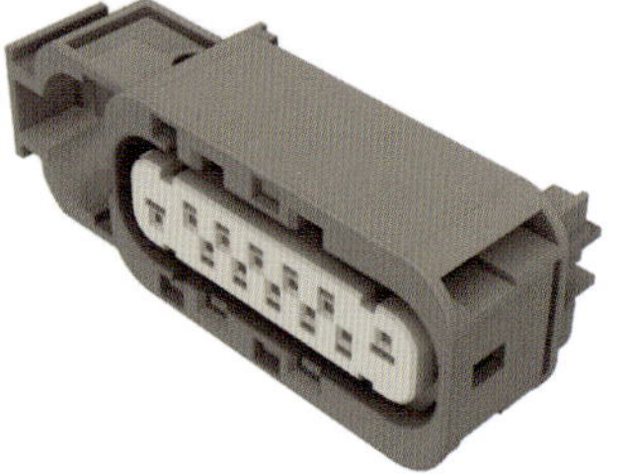
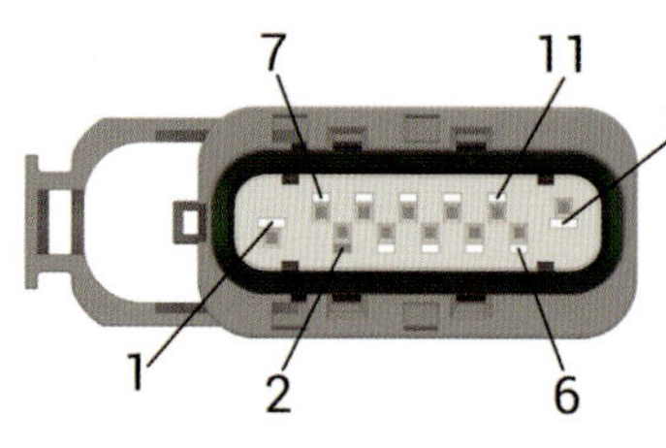

Pin	Function	1997–1998 PCM	P01/P59 PCM
1	-	-	-
2	-	-	-
3	-	-	-
4	Transmission Position Switch Signal B	-	C1-72
5	Transmission Position Switch Signal A	-	C1-32
6	Transmission Position Switch Signal C	-	C2-62
7	Ground	-	-
8	Transmission Position Switch Signal P	-	C1-34
9	-	-	-
10	Backup Lamp Supply Voltage	-	-
11	12V Ignition Voltage	-	-
12	-	-	-

• Implementations vary. See GM schematics for year/make/model/engine.

OBD-II Diagnostic Connector

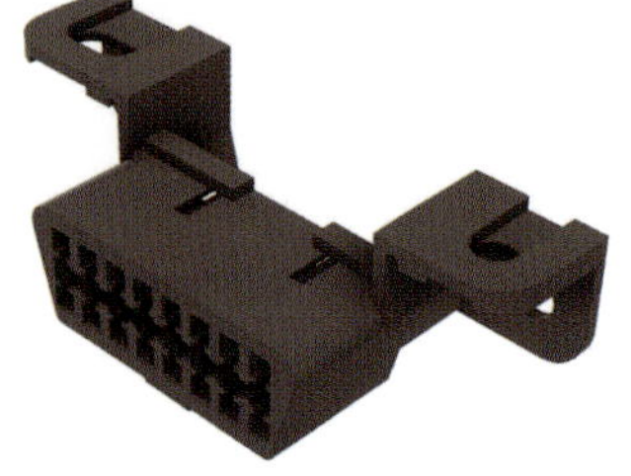
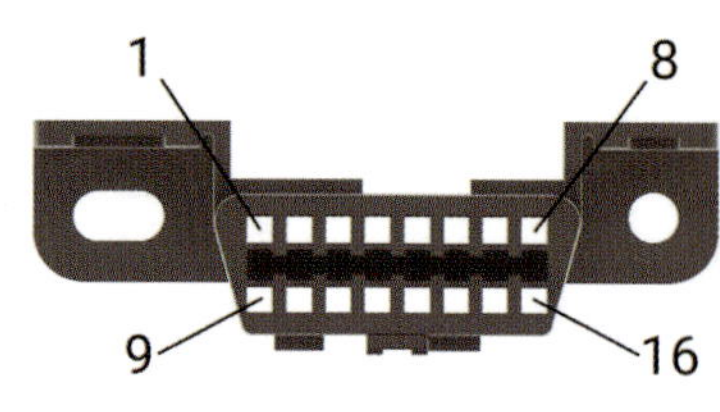

Pin	Function	1997–1998 PCM	P01/P59 PCM
2	Serial Data	C2-58	C1-58
4	Ground	-	-
5	Ground	-	-
6	CAN Bus (+)	-	-
14	CAN Bus (-)	-	-
16	Fused B+	-	-

Reverse Lockout Solenoid
Tremec 6-Speed Manual Transmission

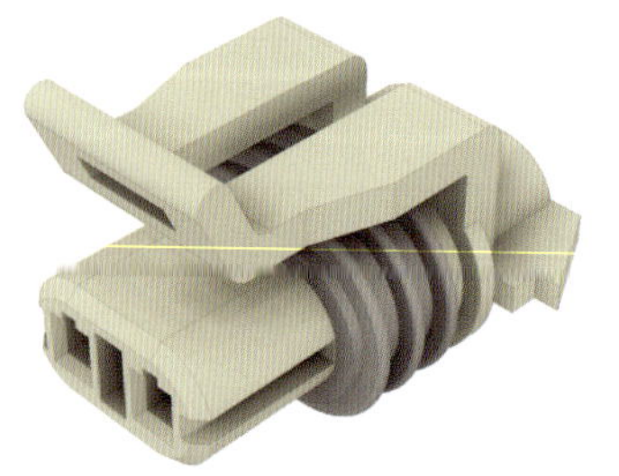
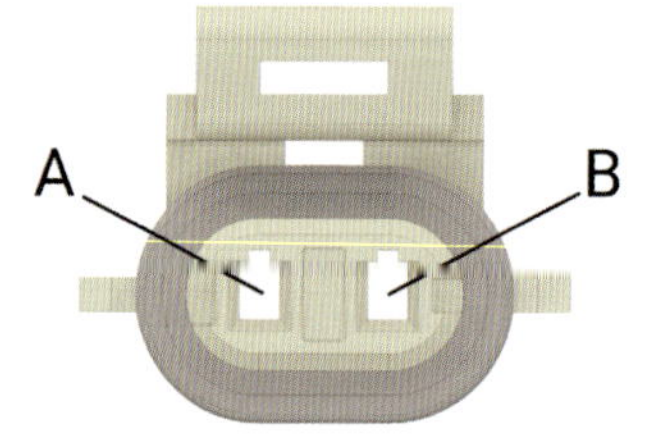

Pin	Function	1997–1998 PCM	P01/P59 PCM
A	Solenoid Control	C1-42	C2-44
B	12V Ignition	-	-

Secondary Air Injection Reaction (AIR) Bleed Valve Solenoid
1998–1999 Camaro Firebird

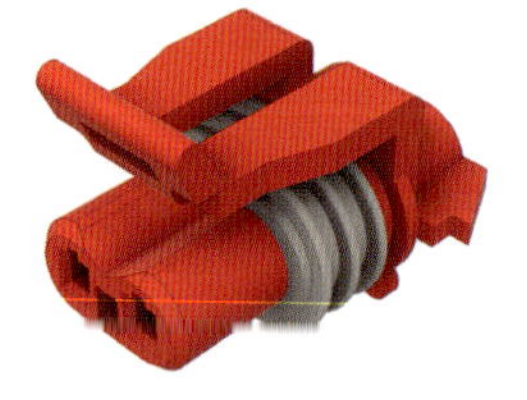

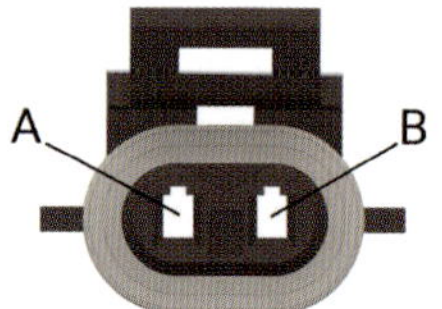

Pin	Function
A	Secondary AIR Injection Bleed Valve Solenoid Feed (Switched B+ from Relay)
B	Ground

Secondary Air Injection Reaction (AIR) Bypass Valve Solenoid

2000–2002 Camaro Firebird

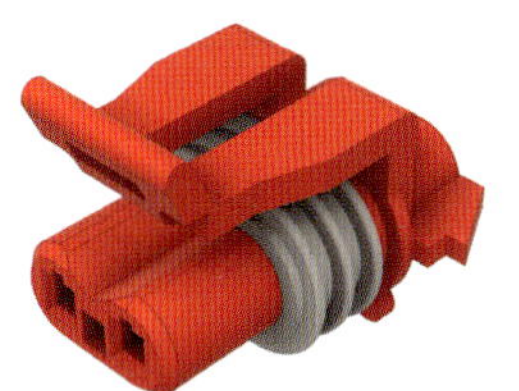

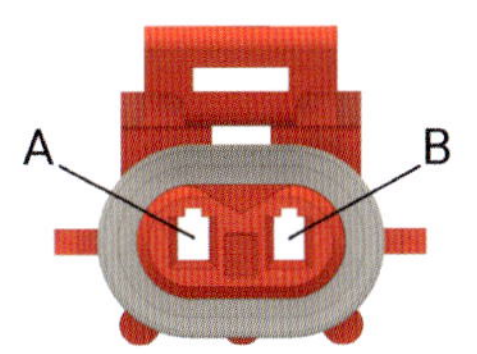

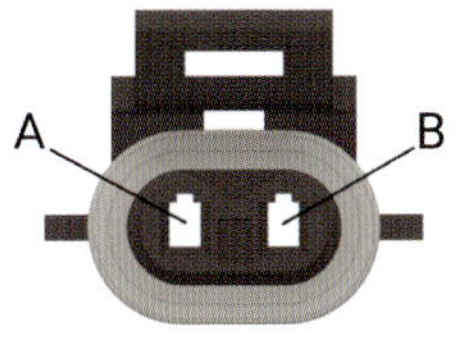

Pin	Function
A	Battery Positive
B	AIR Bypass Valve Control

Secondary Air Injection Reaction (AIR) Pump

1997–1999 Corvette
1998–1999 Camaro Firebird

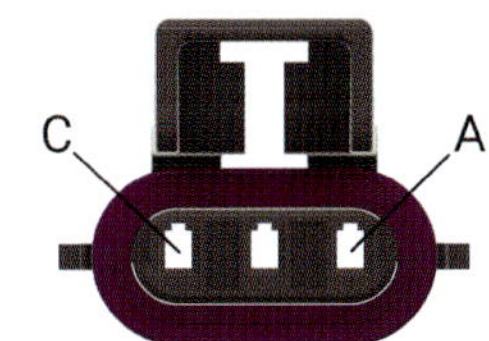

Pin	Function
A	AIR Injection Reaction Pump Motor Feed (Switched B+ from Relay)
B	Secondary AIR Injection Solenoid Feed (Switched B+ from Relay)
C	Ground

Secondary Air Injection Reaction (AIR) Solenoid

2000–2004 Corvette

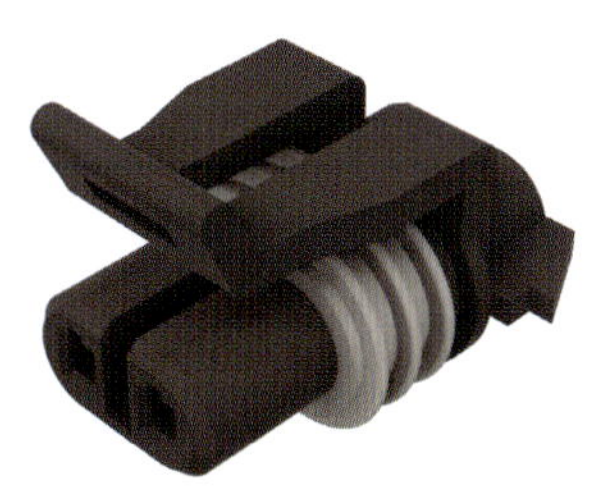

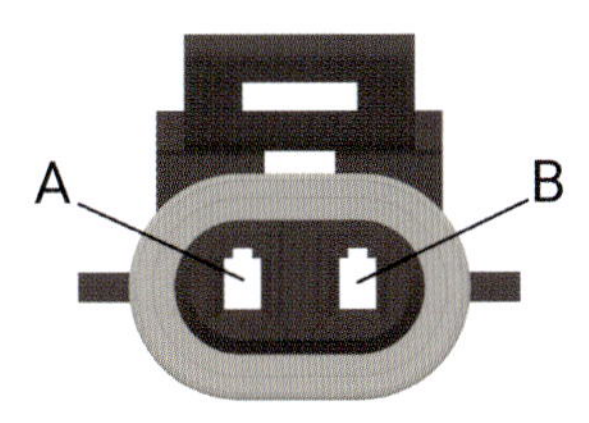

Pin	Function
A	12V Ignition
B	AIR Solenoid Control

Secondary Air Injection Reaction (AIR) Solenoid

1999–2001 Truck/SUV

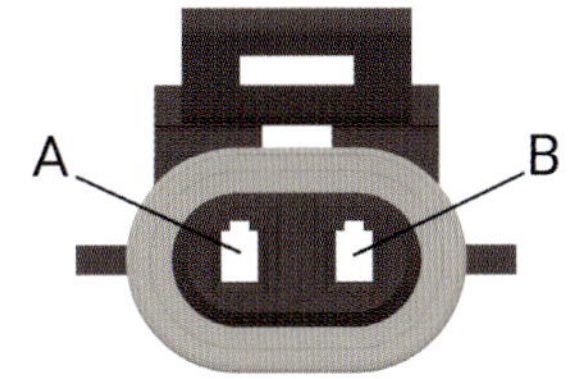

Pin	Function
A	Secondary AIR Injection Bleed Valve Solenoid Feed (Switched B+ from Relay)
B	Ground

Secondary Air Injection Reaction (AIR) Pump

2000–2002 Camaro and Firebird
2000–2004 Corvette
1999–2001 Truck/SUV

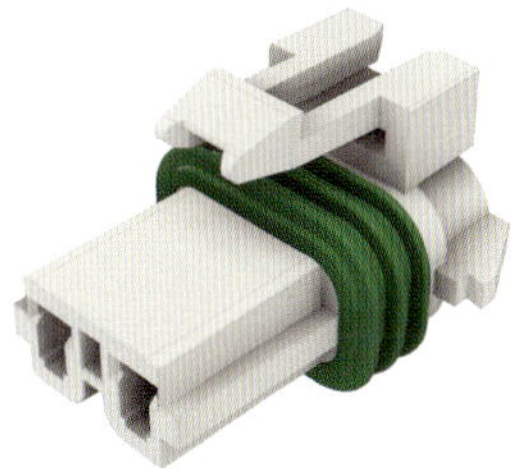

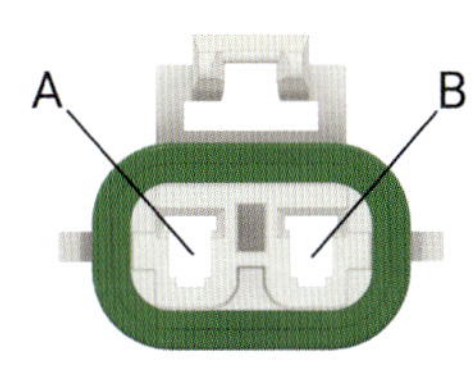

Pin	Function
A	AIR Injection Reaction Pump Motor Feed (Switched B+ from Relay)
B	Ground

Starter
Inline Connection to Many Starters

 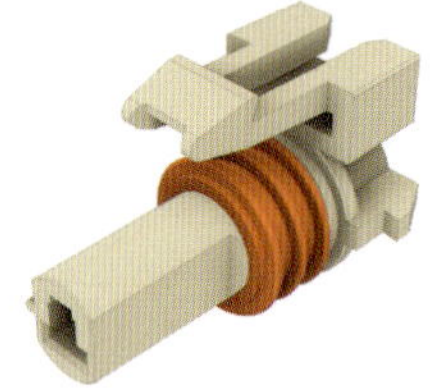 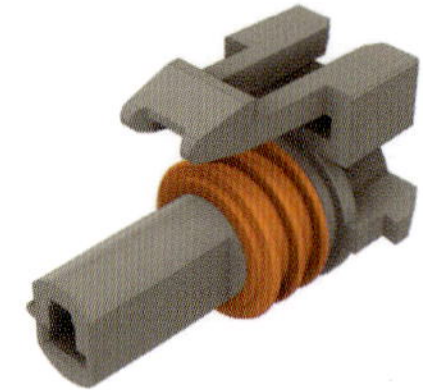

 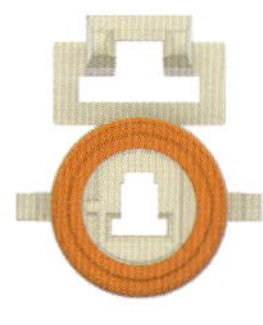 

PIN	FUNCTION
-	Starter S Terminal (Crank)

Skip Shift Solenoid
Tremec 6-Speed Manual Transmission

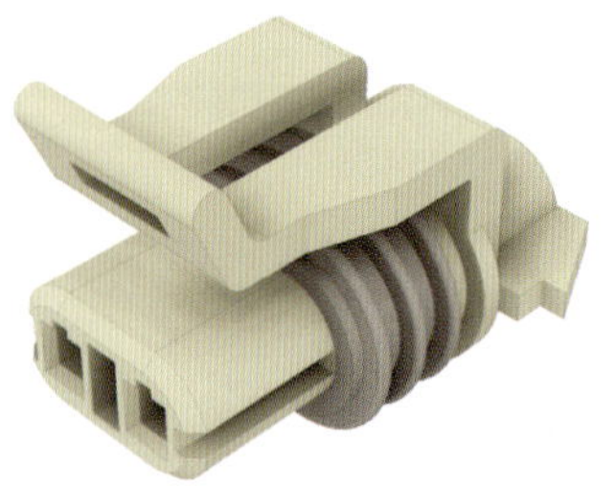 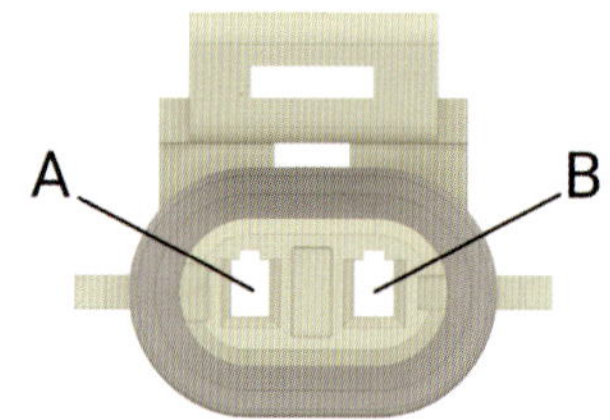

Pin	Function	1997–1998 PCM	P01/P59 PCM
A	Solenoid Control	C1-34	C1-79
B	12V Ignition	-	-

Stop Lamp Switch
GM Part Number 10170430

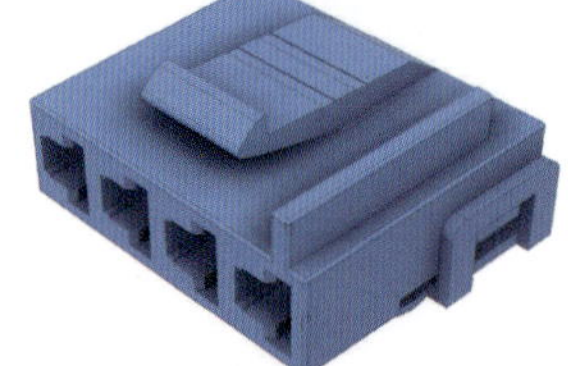 

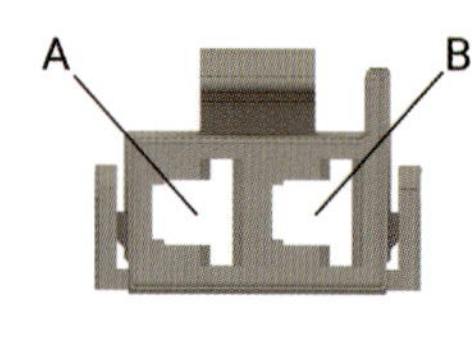

Pin	Function
4W-A	12V Ignition (With 4L60E)
4W-B	A/T Shift Lock Solenoid Supply Voltage (With 4L60E)
4W-C	12V Ignition
4W-D	TCC Brake Switch Signal
2W-A	Battery Positive Voltage
2W-B	Stop Lamp Supply Voltage

Throttle Actuator Control (TAC) Module
10W Connector
1997–2004 Corvette
2004–2005 Cadillac CTS-V

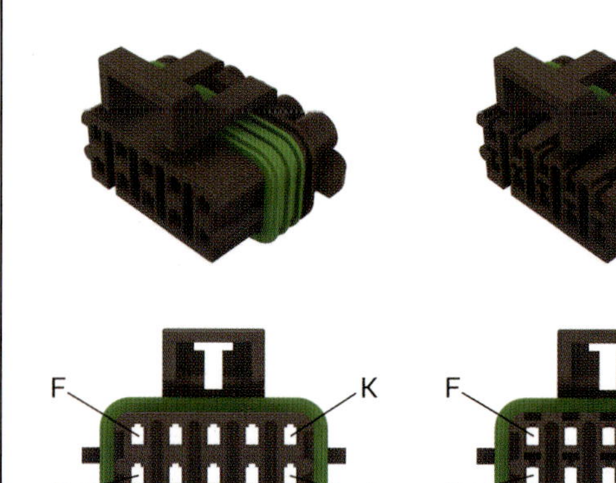 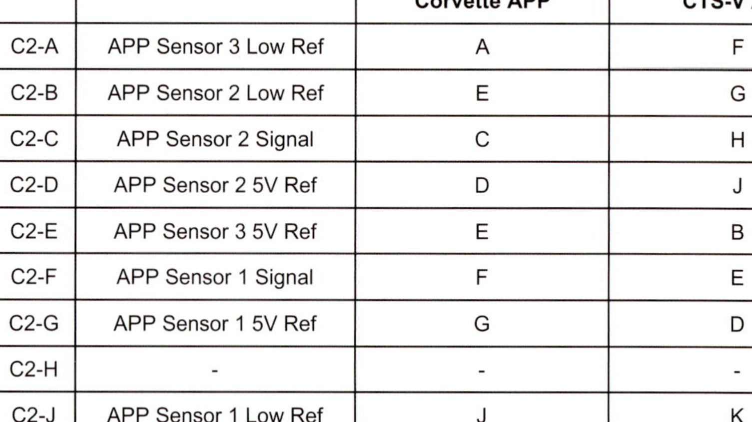

Pin	Function	1997–2004 Corvette APP	2004–2005 CTS-V APP
C2-A	APP Sensor 3 Low Ref	A	F
C2-B	APP Sensor 2 Low Ref	E	G
C2-C	APP Sensor 2 Signal	C	H
C2-D	APP Sensor 2 5V Ref	D	J
C2-E	APP Sensor 3 5V Ref	E	B
C2-F	APP Sensor 1 Signal	F	E
C2-G	APP Sensor 1 5V Ref	G	D
C2-H	-	-	-
C2-J	APP Sensor 1 Low Ref	J	K
C2-K	APP Sensor 3 Signal	K	A

Throttle Actuator Control (TAC) Module

10W Connector
2000–2002 Truck/SUV

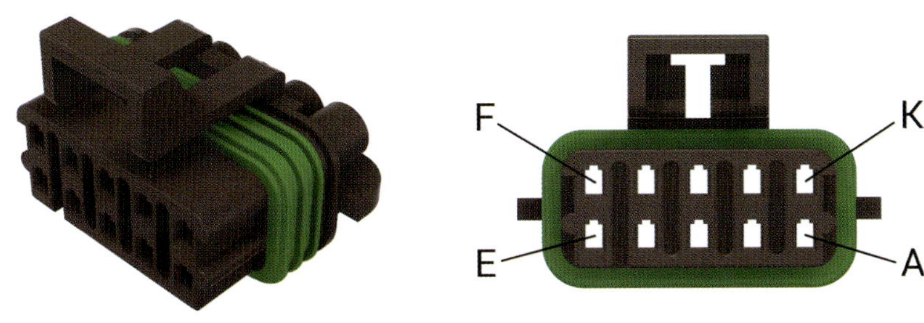

Pin	Function	2000–2005 Truck/SUV APP
C2-A	APP Sensor 3 Low Ref	A
C2-B	APP Sensor 2 Low Ref	B
C2-C	APP Sensor 2 Signal	C
C2-D	APP Sensor 2 5V Ref	D
C2-E	APP Sensor 3 5V Ref	J
C2-F	APP Sensor 1 Signal	F
C2-G	APP Sensor 1 5V Ref	G
C2-H	-	-
C2-J	APP Sensor 1 Low Ref	E
C2-K	APP Sensor 3 Signal	K

Throttle Actuator Control (TAC) Module

10W Connector
2003–2007 Truck/SUV/Van

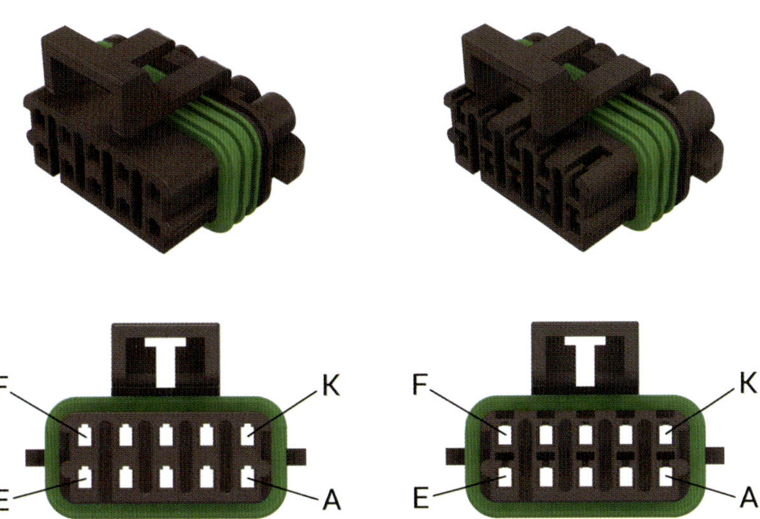

Pin	Function	2003–2004 Truck APP	2005 Truck APP	2006–2007 Truck APP
C2-A	APP Sensor 3 Low Ref	A	-	-
C2-B	APP Sensor 2 Low Ref	B	B	3
C2-C	APP Sensor 2 Signal	C	C	2
C2-D	APP Sensor 2 5V Ref	D	D	1
C2-E	APP Sensor 3 5V Ref	J	-	-
C2-F	APP Sensor 1 Signal	F	F	5
C2-G	APP Sensor 1 5V Ref	G	G	4
C2-H	-	-	-	-
C2-J	APP Sensor 1 Low Ref	E	E	6
C2-K	APP Sensor 3 Signal	K	-	-

• The 2003–2007 TAC does not actually use the APP sensor 3 signal.

Throttle Actuator Control (TAC) Module
16W Connector

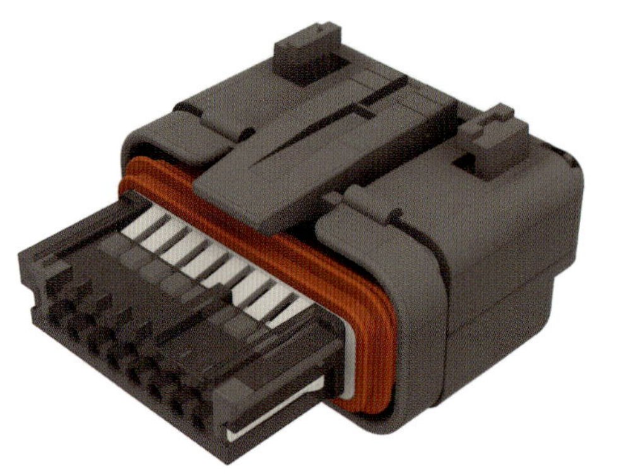

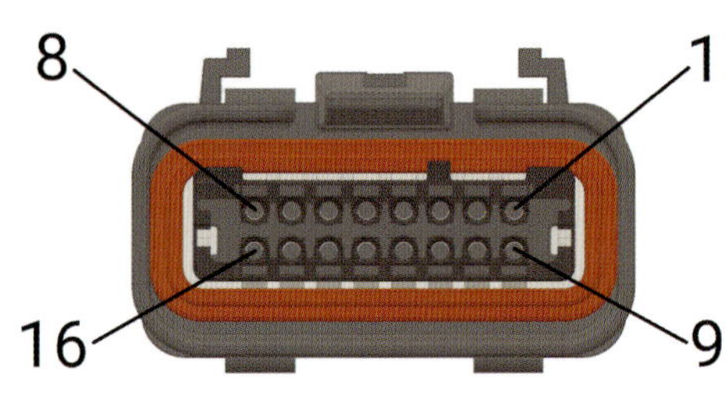

Pin	Function	1997–1998 PCM	P01/P59 PCM	LS1/LS6 Throttle	2000–2002 Truck Throttle	2003-2007 Truck/Van Throttle
1	TP Sensor 1 Signal	-	-	6W-C	6W-C	8W-G
2	TP Sensor 1 5V Ref	-	-	6W-A	6W-A	8W-H
3	TP Sensor 1 Low Ref	-	-	6W-B	6W-B	8W-D
4	Cruise Set/Coast Signal	-	-	-	-	-
5	Cruise Resume/Accel Signal	-	-	-	-	-
6	Stop Lamp Supply Voltage	-	-	-	-	-
7	12V Ignition	-	-	-	-	-
8	TAC Motor Control - 2 (Close)	-	-	2W-B	2W-A	8W-C
9	TP Sensor 2 5V Ref	-	-	6W-D	6W-D	8W-E
10	TP Sensor 2 Low Ref	-	-	6W-E	6W-E	8W-B
11	TP Sensor 2 Signal	-	-	6W-F	6W-F	8W-F
12	TAC Serial Data	C2-71	C1-14	-	-	-
13	TAC Serial Data	C2-72	C1-15	-	-	-
14	Cruise On/Off Signal	-	-	-	-	-
15	Ground	-	-	-	-	-
16	TAC Motor Control - 1 (Open)	-	-	2W-A	2W-B	8W-A

• The Truck/Van TAC module is not interchangeable with Corvette TAC module.
• The 2000–2002 Truck TAC module is not interchangeable with 2003–2007 Truck/Van TAC module.

Throttle Body
LS1/LS6 Corvette and CTS-V

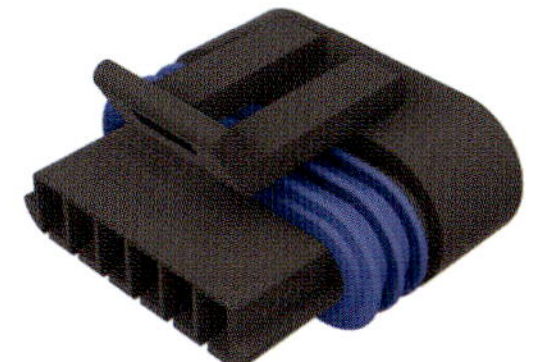
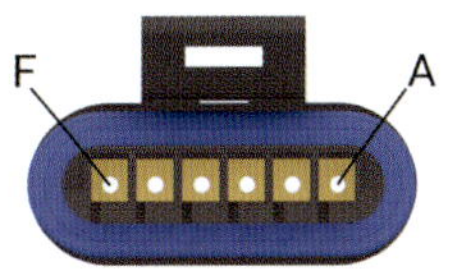

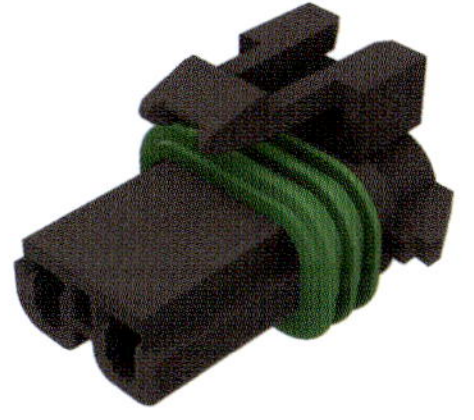
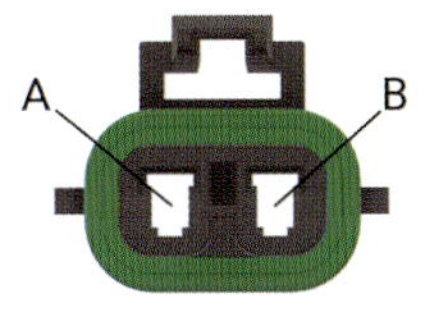

Pin	Function	1997–2004 Corvette TAC Module	2004–2005 CTS-V TAC Module
6W-A	TP Sensor 1 5V Ref	16W-2	16W-2
6W-B	TP Sensor 1 Low Ref	16W-3	16W-3
6W-C	TP Sensor 1 Signal	16W-1	16W-1
6W-D	TP Sensor 2 5V Ref	16W-9	16W-9
6W-E	TP Sensor 2 Low Ref	16W-10	16W-10
6W-F	TP Sensor 2 Signal	16W-11	16W-11
2W-A	TAC Motor Control - 1 (Open)	16W-16	16W-16
2W-B	TAC Motor Control - 2 (Close)	16W-8	16W-8

• The 1997–2004 Corvette and 2004–2005 CTS-V TAC modules are interchangeable.

Throttle Body
2000–2002 Truck

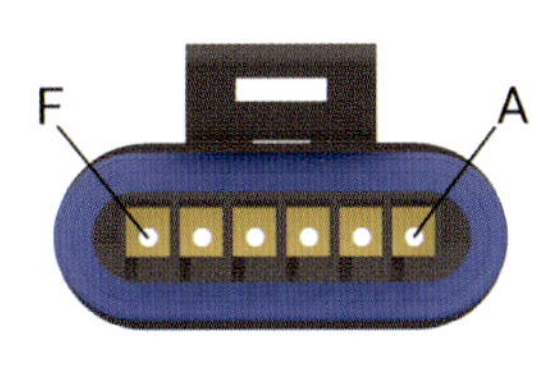

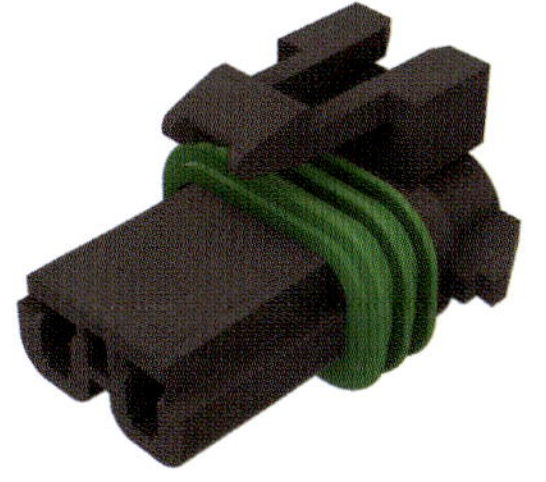
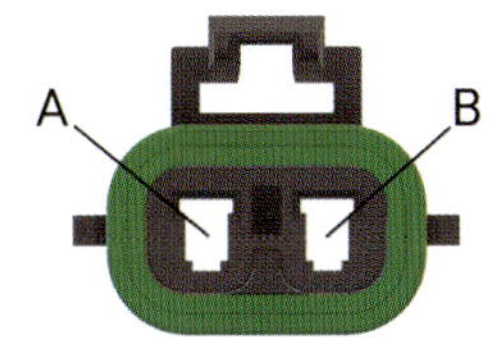

Pin	Function	2000–2002 Truck TAC Module
6W-A	TP Sensor 1 5V Ref	16W-2
6W-B	TP Sensor 1 Low Ref	16W-3
6W-C	TP Sensor 1 Signal	16W-1
6W-D	TP Sensor 2 5V Ref	16W-9
6W-E	TP Sensor 2 Low Ref	16W-10
6W-F	TP Sensor 2 Signal	16W-11
2W-A	TAC Motor Control - 2 (Close)	16W-8
2W-B	TAC Motor Control - 1 (Open)	16W-16

Transmission: 4-Speed Automatic
4L60E/4L65E/4L70E Transmissions

Throttle Body
Gen III 8 Wire

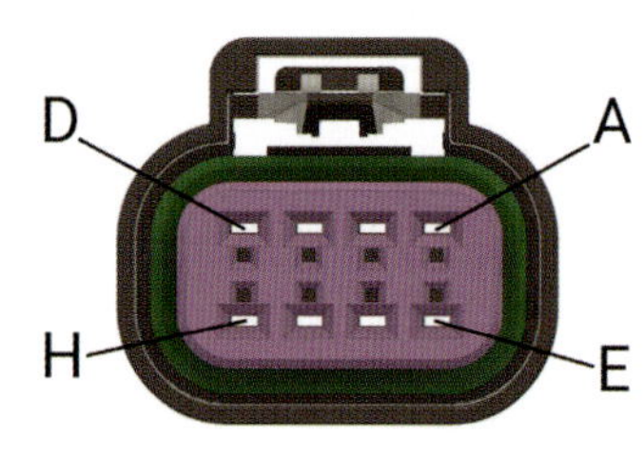

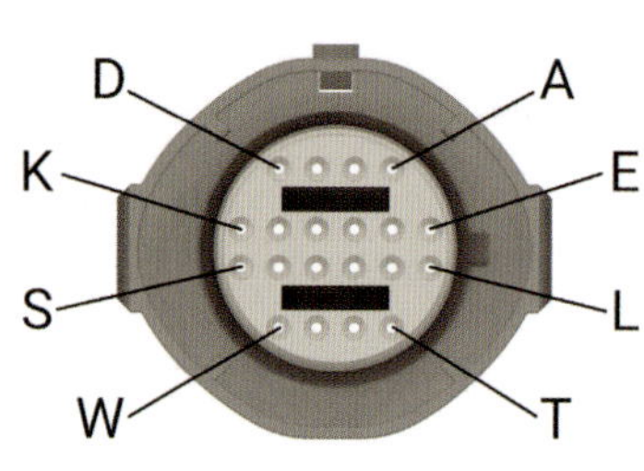

Pin	Function	2003–2007 SUV/Truck/Van TAC
A	TAC Motor Control - 1 (Open)	16W-16
B	TP Sensor 2 Low Reference	16W-10
C	TAC Motor Control - 2 (Close)	16W-8
D	TP Sensor 1 Low Reference	16W-3
E	TP Sensor 2 5V Reference	16W-9
F	TP Sensor 2 Signal	16W-11
G	TP Sensor 1 Signal	16W-1
H	TP Sensor 1 5V Reference	16W-2

Pin	Function	1997–1998 PCM	P01/P59 PCM
A	1-2 Shift Solenoid Valve	C1-35	C2-48
B	2-3 Shift Solenoid Valve	C1-40	C2-47
C	Pressure Control Solenoid Valve Hi	C2-39	C2-6
D	Pressure Control Solenoid Valve Lo	C2-36	C2-8
E	12V Ignition	-	-
K	Input Speed Sensor (ISS) Signal	-	-
L	Fluid Temperature Sensor Signal	C2-13	C2-51
M	Low Reference	C2-14	C1-53
N	Transmission Range A Input	C1-25	C2-63
P	Transmission Range C Input	C1-61	C1-18
R	Transmission Range B Input	C1-22	C1-17
S	3-2 Shift Solenoid Valve	C1-34	C1-79
T	TCC Solenoid Valve	C2-32	C2-42
U	TCC PWM Solenoid Valve	C2-33	C2-2
V	Input Speed Sensor (ISS) Low Ref	-	-

• Input speed sensor (ISS) with 4L70E only.

Vehicle Speed Sensor (VSS)
Output Shaft Speed (OSS) Sensor
4L60E/4L65E/4L70E/4L80E/4L85E/Manual Transmissions

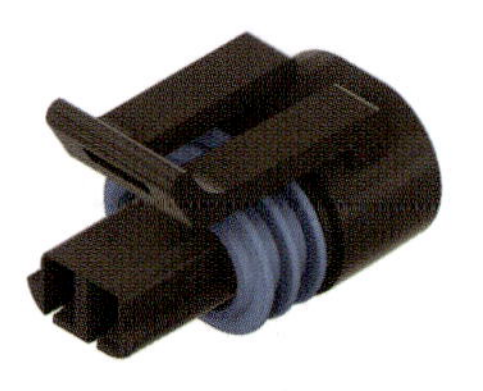

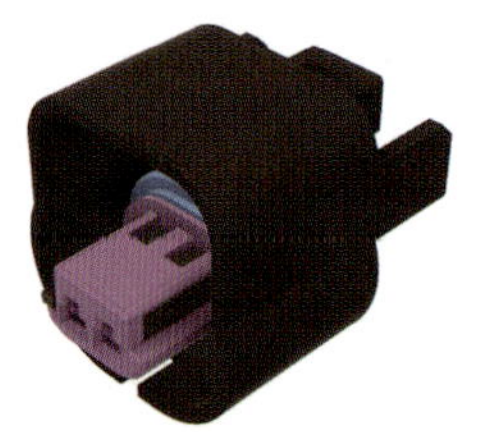

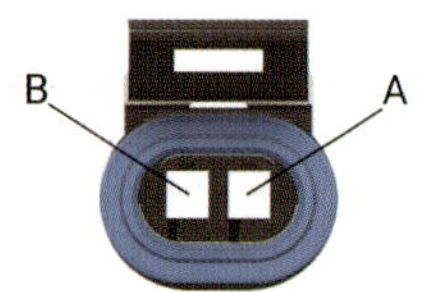

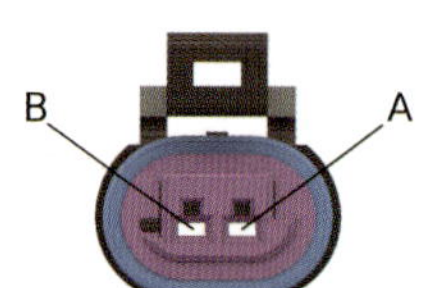

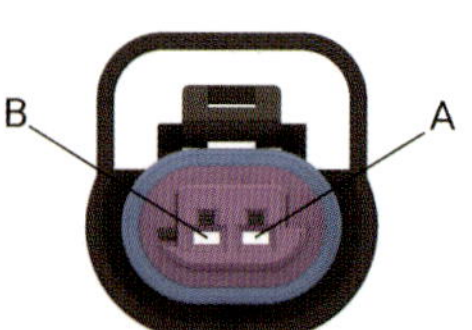

Pin	Function	1997–1998 PCM	P01/P59 PCM
A	VSS Low Signal	C2-71	C2-20 or C2-21
B	VSS High Signal	C2-7	C2-21 or C2-20

Transmission: 4-Speed Automatic
4L80E/4L85E Transmissions

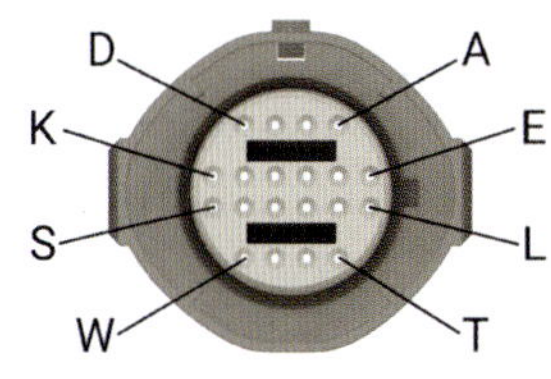

Pin	Function	P01/P59 PCM
A	1-2 Shift Solenoid Valve	C2-48
B	2-3 Shift Solenoid Valve	C2-47
C	Pressure Control Solenoid Valve Hi	C2-6
D	Pressure Control Solenoid Valve Lo	C2-8
E	12V Ignition	-
L	Fluid Temperature Sensor Signal	C2-51
M	Low Reference	C1-41
N	Transmission Fluid Pressure Switch Signal A	C2-63
P	Transmission Fluid Pressure Switch Signal C	C1-18
R	Transmission Fluid Pressure Switch Signal B	C1-17
S	TCC PWM Solenoid Valve Control	C2-2

4L80E/4L85E Input Shaft Speed (ISS) Sensor

PIN	FUNCTION	P01/P59 PCM
A	Input Shaft Speed Sensor High Signal	C2-22
B	Input Shaft Speed Sensor Low Signal	C2-23

CONTROL MODULE PROGRAMMING (TUNING)

Control module programming is so closely related to engine wiring that I felt it necessary to touch on the basics of setting up GM control modules for stand-alone operation. My intention for this chapter is to reveal initial calibration programming (base calibration) and provide options for updating parameters and tables within the base calibration.

First, let's get a few definitions out of the way, as I'll be referring to these electronic control modules by their common acronym names.

ECU

The electronic control unit (ECU) is a generic name that represents any electronic module within a vehicle.

PCM

The powertrain control module (PCM) is the reprogrammable electronic control module that controls engine and transmission functions. It is sometimes referred to as a vehicle control module (VCM).

ECM

The engine control module (ECM) is the reprogrammable electronic control module that controls only engine functions.

TCM

The transmission control module (TCM) is the reprogrammable electronic control module that controls only transmission functions.

FSCM

The fuel system control module (FSCM) is the reprogrammable electronic control module used with some GM Gen IV LS-series vehicles to control fuel pressure via pulse width modulation of the fuel pump.

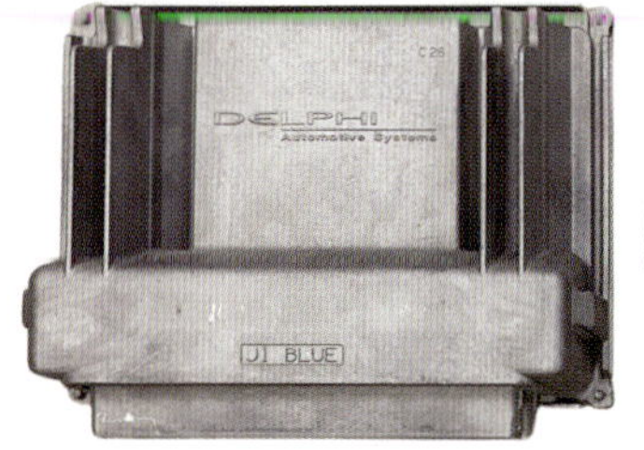

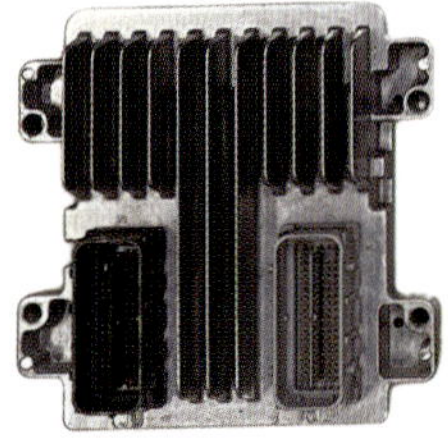

GM Gen III systems include a PCM (top left) and TAC module (top middle). Gen IV systems use an ECM (bottom left), TCM (bottom right), BCM (bottom middle), and sometimes an FSCM (top right). While production vehicles sometimes rely on a BCM for crank/start, cruise control, and tap shift functions, the BCM is never necessary for stand-alone engine and transmission operation.

TAC

The throttle actuator control (TAC) module is the electronic control module that communicates with a PCM to control the throttle body motor and cruise control functions within GM Gen III LS-series vehicles. The TAC module cannot be reprogrammed. Be sure to use a TAC module compatible with the PCM's base calibration. A mismatch will likely result in an unresponsive throttle and stored DTCs.

BCM

The body control module (BCM) is the electronic control module responsible for monitoring and controlling many vehicle functions. Most notably, in some applications, the BCM communicates with the ECM to operate the air-conditioning and cruise control functions.

Base Calibration

Most GM LS-series electronic control modules are flash programmable through the vehicle's 16 cavity diagnostic connector using a programming interface tool and supporting software. Not to be misunderstood as a starter calibration for an LS engine

swap, a PCM's base calibration is the as-stock calibration loaded into the PCM for intended use with a production vehicle. A base calibration will completely match GM's defined parameters and table values.

For the enthusiast who is simply upgrading his or her existing LS-equipped vehicle for more performance, the base calibrations are the current calibrations, as created by GM, loaded in the vehicle's various PCMs. These calibrations are VIN (vehicle identification number)-specific and generally should not be changed to base calibrations of a different vehicle. Introducing a PCM with a different base calibration or flashing in a different base calibration will likely result in set DTCs, communication errors, and possibly a no-start condition.

For the enthusiast who purchased a drivetrain takeout from a salvaged LS-equipped vehicle, the base calibration is considered to be the calibration within the related PCM as it was in the original GM vehicle. Because drivetrain takeouts are usually intended for early retrofit installations, there may be good reasons to change the base calibration within the PCM to support a desired feature related to an auxiliary system such as air-conditioning or electric fans.

The OBD-II diagnostic link connector was introduced in the OBD-I 1995 Camaro, Firebird, and Corvette—one year prior to the implementation of OBD-II in 1996. Often missing from a drivetrain and wire harness takeout, this 16-cavity connector is necessary to make a physical connection to the vehicle using an OBD-II compatible diagnostic scan tool. While you can source a used OBD-II connector from any 1996-and-newer vehicle, be careful because there are several different connector manufacturers, and each manufacturer variation uses its own proprietary terminal.

Finally, the enthusiast who is piecing together an LS-series drivetrain for an early muscle car, street rod, or truck is starting from scratch and must first consider the requirements of the project and installed components before choosing a base calibration for the PCM involved. This book does not go into exhaustive detail about all calibration options available among the many different GM vehicles. It is best to hire an experienced performance shop or tuner to help you navigate the initial PCM base calibrations for your LS-swap project.

Dealer-Level Programming Interfaces and Software

The following section discusses several pieces of equipment that are used for diagnostics and servicing.

GM Tech 2, CANdi Module, and TIS 2000 Software

The GM Tech 2 is a bidirectional interface used to perform dealer-level diagnostics and service programming. This tool was the GM service department standard from 1996 until the release of the MDI tool in 2010. Vehicle coverage includes all GM OBD-II makes and models, including cars, trucks, and vans from 1996 to 2013. While not covered in this book, the Tech 2 also supports some earlier OBD-I applications.

As a handheld unit, the Tech 2 allows the operator to retrieve DTCs, clear DTCs, read ECU data, perform dealer-level bidirectional functions, and more. While connected to a PC via the serial port, the Tech 2 can perform ECU service programming. Service programming is VIN-based and only allows for GM-defined calibrations. The Tech 2 cannot be used to

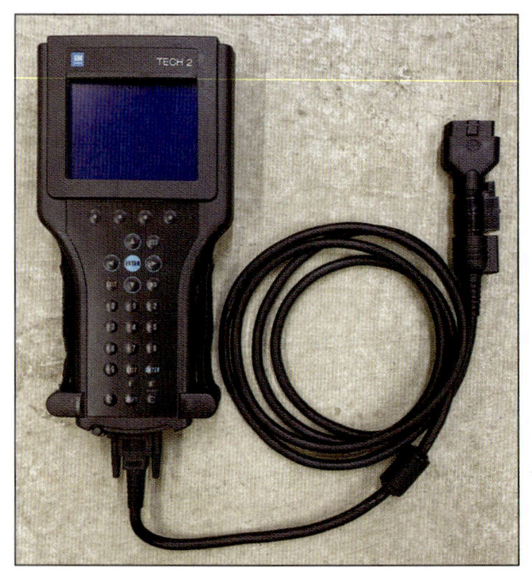

The GM Tech 2 handheld interface was the GM dealer-level service department diagnostic tool for all Gen III LS-series-equipped vehicles. This powerful tool can be used to perform advanced, bidirectional service and diagnostic procedures. The Tech 2 continues to serve LS enthusiasts as a J2534 programming device, OBD-II diagnostic tool, and through its ability to perform the bidirectional crankshaft position variation learn procedure.

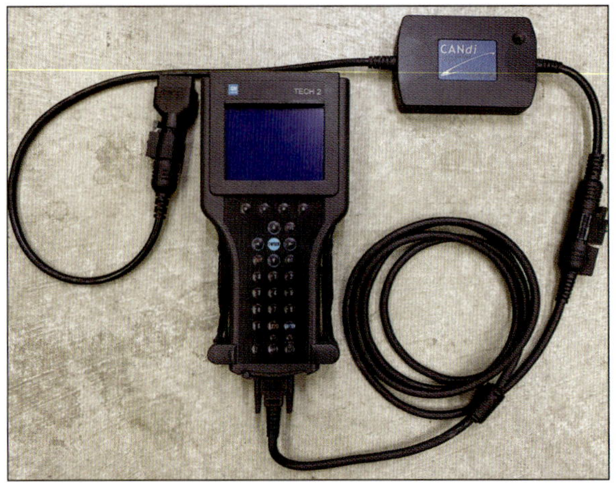

GM's Tech 2 was not designed for CAN bus communications, so GM released a pass-through CANdi module for Tech 2 CAN bus support. By connecting the CANdi module inline with the 16-cavity OBD-II diagnostic connector, the Tech 2 can be used to perform service, diagnostics, and programming on the Gen IV CAN bus ECUs.

Before GM service software was available through the internet, the Tech 2 was used with GM service Techline Information System software TIS2000. Professional tuners still rely on this Microsoft Windows–based software to perform service programming of 2007-and-older ECUs. With this software being long out of service, those determined to have it may be on the lookout for a used GM dealership service laptop or Panasonic Toughbook.

disable the vehicle antitheft system (VATS), remove emissions, change electric fan on/off temperatures, or perform any custom programming. While there are countless OBD-II scan tools on the market, very few offer some Tech 2 features, such as "Crankshaft Position Variation Learn" or service programming.

Vehicles that communicate via controller area network (CAN) bus are not directly compatible with the Tech 2. CAN bus communication requires the addition of GM's Controller Area Network Diagnostic Interface (CANdi) module. The CANdi module is connected in line with the Tech 2's OBD-II cable. Practically speaking, this means that Gen IV LS-series applications require the use of a CANdi module when using the Tech 2.

GM's Techline Information System software (TIS 2000) was often installed on Microsoft Windows-based Panasonic Toughbook laptop computers and used by GM service technicians in conjunction with the Tech 2. TIS 2000 software does not connect to the internet, so software updates were a manual effort as new vehicle support and updated calibrations were released. Service programming involves retrieving vehicle data using the Tech 2 through the vehi-

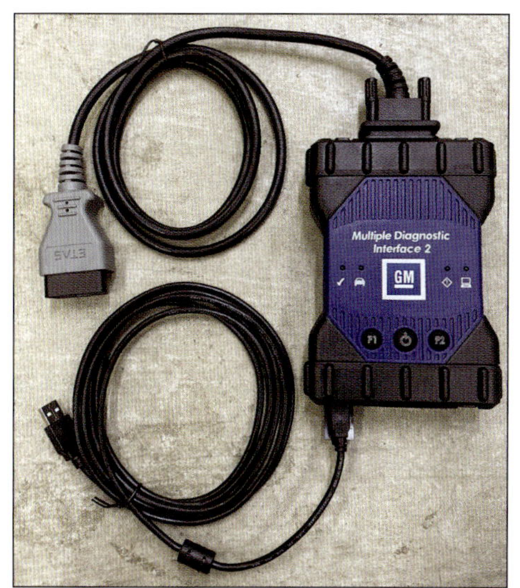

The GM multiple diagnostic interface (MDI) tool was the successor to the Tech 2. Paired with GM's online service software TIS2Web, the MDI and newer MDI 2 are used for service, diagnostics, and programming. The MDI 2 features USB and WiFi connectivity capabilities. Lacking a display, the MDI and MDI 2 can be used with the TIS2Web software Tech2Win to emulate the Tech 2 on a Windows-based PC.

GM MDI and TIS2Web Software

The successor to the Tech 2 was the GM multiple diagnostic interface (MDI) tool, which was followed by the release of the faster, WiFi-capable, MDI 2 tool. The MDI tools lack a display, so for vehicle diagnostics, they must be used with GM's Global Diagnostics System (GDS 2) software. For vehicles not supported by GDS 2, the MDI interface can be used with GM's Tech2Win software to emulate the Tech 2 on a PC.

Service programming is now an online subscription-based service that is available through the ACDelco Technical Delivery System called TIS2Web. Technicians must first create an account and then purchase a 24-month subscription to a vehicle (or vehicles) based on each vehicle's VIN. The 24-month access allows the registered user access to service the programming of all available onboard programmable modules. The intended use of TIS2Web is limited to technicians working directly with the vehicle and its 16-cavity diagnostic connector. Off-board programming is not within TIS2Web's terms of use and is strictly prohibited by GM.

The onboard programming limitation of TIS2Web creates a significant hurdle for the enthusiast who is piecing together an LS drivetrain using 2008-and-newer ECUs. For example, sourcing a 6L90E transmission from a 2010 Silverado to mate to a 2010 Corvette LS3 engine in a street rod will result in an ECM/TCM mismatch. Ideally, the TCM needs to be programmed with the 2010 Corvette calibration. TIS2Web will not allow this activity. Moreover, in many cases, TIS2Web requires ECM and TCM sequence programming, which means that you may not be able to

Performing as J2534 pass-through devices, the Drew Technologies CarDAQ and Mongoose devices are aftermarket alternatives to GM's expensive Tech 2 and MDI devices when using TIS2Web. CarDAQ supports programming for all makes and models, while Mongoose is limited to its intended automotive makes. With more than 20 years of experience in J2534 diagnostics and reprogramming solutions, Drew Technologies is an industry leader.

program the TCM independently. An ECM/TCM mismatch may be a showstopper.

The impractical workaround would be to temporarily install these modules in a 2010 Corvette and use TIS2Web to program both ECM and TCM. With that being unrealistic, these sorts of scenarios are best left to companies who refurbish ECUs and offer VIN-specific programming so that the ECU(s) you receive will be ready for the next step: custom programming using packages, such as EFILive or HP Tuners.

SAE J2534 Pass-Through Devices

The Society of Automotive Engineers (SAE) J2534 standard requires all automakers to allow the use of non-GM pass-through interface tools to be used for diagnostics and service programming. What this means

cle's OBD-II diagnostic connector, and then a serial port connection to the laptop to load the desired TIS 2000 calibration into the Tech 2, and finally another trip to the vehicle's OBD-II diagnostic connector to program or reprogram onboard modules.

Technicians (or enthusiasts) who desire unlimited GM module service programming for 1996–2007 vehicles may eliminate current GM service system subscription costs by sourcing a Tech 2 and TIS 2000 software. A used or knockoff Tech 2 and used GM service laptop, depending on availability, may quickly pay for themselves when compared to only a handful of vehicle subscriptions for GM's online service system.

All LS-series PCMs are programmed to expect a signal from an antitheft module to allow the engine to start and run. Early LS-equipped vehicles contained a resistor in the ignition key that was used to satisfy the security system and allow the PCM to run the engine. LS-series PCMs are capable of several types of VATS implementations, but fortunately these systems can be easily turned off or overridden by custom programming software. While eBay and some well-respected businesses offer VATS disable modules for some LS PCMs, they're really more of a gimmick because any LS swap requires additional custom programming anyway. Save your money and eliminate VATS through the PCM calibration.

is that you aren't required to buy highly expensive GM tools to use GM TIS2Web software. Moreover, you can buy a J2534 device, such as the DrewTech CarDAQ, and have service programming capabilities for most vehicle manufacturers.

Custom Calibration and Starter Calibration

Any change to the original GM-defined parameters or tables within an ECU are considered to be custom. A custom calibration is required to prevent a no-start condition when swapping any LS drivetrain into another vehicle. In the very least, custom calibration changes include the elimination of the VATS.

More commonly, a starter calibration has modified GM's original programming to also eliminate irrelevant diagnostic trouble codes (DTCs), eliminate emissions equipment, and change electric fan on/off temperature settings. An ECU's programming may only be changed at the custom level by using a performance-level programming interface and related PC-based software.

Performance-Level Programming Interfaces and Software

There are very few options when it comes to choosing a custom programming solution for 1996-and-newer GM ECUs. While there are some free and lesser-known open source options for custom programming LS-based ECUs, I'm only going to provide an overview of the two industry-leading tuning suites that are well-established and relatively easy to learn.

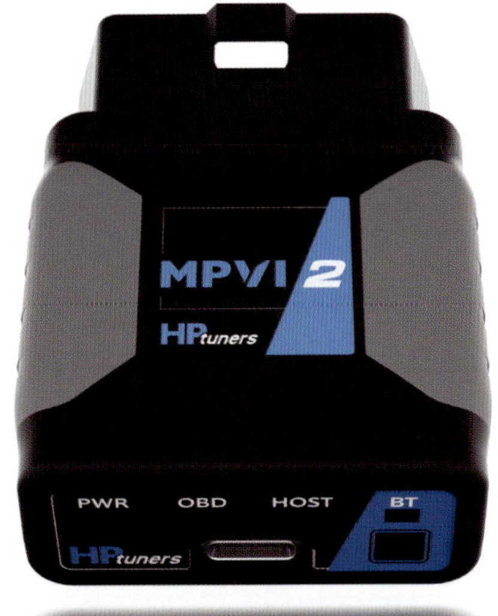

HP Tuners

As enthusiasts began swapping used LS1 and early LS-series drivetrains, HP Tuners emerged to simplify and improve on early programming software, such as LS1-edit, which was used for off-board programming. HP Tuners now offers what it calls the VCM Suite, which consists of ECU editor software (VCM Editor) and ECU scanner software (VCM Scanner). The PC-based software communicates with the vehicle's ECU through a multipurpose vehicle interface (MPVI).

Twelve years after the release of its first MPVI interface, the MPVI2 became the standard interface used to connect to the vehicle's 16-cavity OBD-II diagnostic connector. The MPVI2 is a Bluetooth-capable device with an expansion port that allows for connecting external devices such as a wideband oxygen sensor. With the MPVI2 attached to a vehicle's OBD-II diagnostic connector, the user simply connects a USB cable to the MPVI2 and his or her laptop PC to begin data logging or tuning.

The MPVI2 and VCM Suite retail for as little as $299.99, which is a very attractive price to data log and

Enthusiasts and professionals have been using HP Tuners products over the years to scan, log, and tune all LS-series ECUs. VCM Suite includes software capable of advanced data logging and custom tuning features fully sufficient for any stand-alone LS electronics implementation. Their MPVI interface handles communication between a PC and onboard ECUs through a vehicle's 16-cavity diagnostic connector. The introductory price of HP Tuners has long been attractive to enthusiasts who have very few vehicles to work with.

EFILive's Scan & Tune package includes its handheld FlashScan interface, which is a powerful device that handles communication between a PC and onboard ECUs through a vehicle's 16-cavity diagnostic connector. The EFILive solution for GM applications supports all LS-series ECUs and is fully capable of programming your ECUs for stand-alone operation. The introductory price to work with FlashScan is among the highest in the industry, but EFILive's long list of features and capabilities do not disappoint.

tune your own LS-series controllers. Costs increase as additional features and credits are added. While scanning and data logging features are included with the base price, programming a control module requires a license activation that must be purchased using credits. For example, to work with a 2002 Camaro Z28, HP Tuners requires a one-time use of two credits ($49.99 each) to license the PCM and the calibration file retrieved from the PCM. This is considered a single vehicle license that allows the user unlimited programming access to that 2002 Camaro Z28 calibration file and PCM. The user may also be presented with the option to buy a year/model license or unlimited vehicle group license for additional credits.

EFILive

In the early days of LS engine swaps, EFILive was another company to quickly emerge as an industry leader for scanning, data logging, and custom programming. The key component, or PC-to-vehicle interface, to the EFILive solution is called FlashScan. By using FlashScan, the user can scan and data log using the included Scan Tool software and then perform custom programming changes using the included Tuning Tool software.

The USB interface cable first released was called FlashScan (now FlashScan V1). This interface performs as a connection between a PC computer and the vehicle's OBD-II diagnostic connector. FlashScan V1 supports external inputs for adding devices such as a wideband oxygen sensor. FlashScan V2 was introduced to add support for the CAN bus ECUs introduced in the 2005 model year with the E40 ECM and T42 TCM. In November 2020, EFILive replaced FlashScan V2 with FlashScan V3.

While the EFILive solution is among the highest priced in the industry, it offers attractive features that may best align with the user. Professionals may link their FlashScan device to the integration-ready AutoCal device to offer remote scanning, data logging, and tuning. What this means is that the FlashScan owner can send an AutoCal device to a customer anywhere in the world to receive logged vehicle data and send customized calibration files via email. The customer simply uses AutoCal to record data and flash new calibrations using the vehicle's OBD-II diagnostic connector. Remote custom tuning doesn't get much easier than this!

The EFILive Scan Tool software is included with the purchase of FlashScan (and with AutoCal). While the Tuning Tool software is also included, the ability to program an ECU is dependent on a VIN license activation. FlashScan/AutoCal VIN licenses sell for $125. The activation of a VIN license will fill one of the available 600 VIN slots and give the user programming access to the licensed ECM and TCM. For vehicles that do not contain a TCM, only the ECM (or PCM) will be licensed.

Professionals and enthusiasts who source used ECUs with the intent to reprogram as a different vehicle type, will find EFILive licensing to be more desirable than HP Tuners licensing because FlashScan licenses the ECU hardware while HP Tuners licenses the ECU and vehicle type. Let's unload that statement with a common example. Let's say you are looking for a 2001–2002 GM# 12200411 PCM for a Camaro LS1 engine and 4L60E transmission project. You buy a used 12200411 PCM through eBay, and after communicating with the PCM, the retrieved VIN indicates it was last used in a 2002 Chevrolet S10 Pickup with a 4.3L V-6 engine. EFILive allows you to license this PCM as the 2002 Chevrolet S10 pickup and to flash in any supporting calibration file without the use of an additional license. Your project requires a 2002 Camaro LS1 with 4L60E calibration, so you acquire and flash the PCM with the 2002 Camaro LS1 with 4L60E calibration without activating an additional VIN license. This activity with HP Tuners costs you a second license activation. Now, let's say that you want to change the operating system to add another feature to your project such as electronic throttle (drive by wire). With EFILive, you can use the same PCM to flash in a 2002 Corvette LS1 with 4L60E calibration without activating an additional VIN license. This same activity with HP Tuners will cost you a third license activation.

Base Calibration Walk-Through

Let's take a look at the work involved to set up brand new or used PCMs with a base calibration containing the complete operat-

The most trusted way to load a base calibration into a Gen III PCM is to use GM's TIS2000 software to load the most current calibration that GM has to offer for the particular vehicle year/make/model/engine you want to work with. Gen III PCMs can receive a new base calibration (operating system and all calibration segments) by using EFILive's Tune software and any FlashScan interface. By choosing to full flash the PCM with the intended (PCM hardware compatible) calibration, you can avoid the use of a Tech 2 and TIS2000 software.

ing system (OS) and calibration data. The base calibration should be sourced from a vehicle that best matches the equipment you are working with (engine type, throttle type, transmission type, etc.). New PCMs require loading a base calibration. The calibration found in a refurbished or used PCM may not be trustworthy because you likely won't know the history of the PCM. The stored VIN can be changed independent of calibration and it's always possible that someone has made custom changes to the stored calibration.

Gen III LS-Series PCMs

The easiest way to flash a base calibration into a Gen III PCM is to use GM's service programming system (SPS) through TIS 2000 software or TIS2Web online. If, for example, you know that your LS engine build has a cable throttle system and a 4L60E transmission, and you have a GM number 12200411 PCM, then you may search the internet for a 2002 Camaro Z28 VIN from a vehicle having the same equipment. Using a Tech 2 and SPS, you can retrieve and flash the 2002 Camaro Z28 calibration into your PCM. At this point, the PCM is as it would be if removed from the production vehicle.

With certain caution, it is possible to use EFILive or HP Tuners to establish a different base calibration into Gen III PCMs. First, the hardware service number must be compatible with the PCM service number that GM used for the base calibration you have chosen. Secondly, not all Gen III PCMs contain idle air control (IAC) driver hardware for cable throttle support, so it is possible to flash in a cable throttle calibration but the PCM not be able

to control the IAC motor. Lastly, you may have to activate more licenses than you intended for this activity, especially with HP Tuners.

Additionally, EFILive and HP Tuners did not develop their software with this programming activity in mind, so proceed with caution at your own risk. EFILive and HP Tuners have enormous user communities online through their message forums to share questions, solutions, and even calibration files.

Starter (or Custom) Calibration Walk-Through

The focus of this book is related to GM LS-series wiring. Mere mention of "starter calibration" may generate a hopeful expectation that this book will show you how to tune your PCM. There are books written, DVDs available, endless message forum content, and countless YouTube videos that discuss tuning. This book will not go into great detail on the topic of custom tuning. The following content is intended for the beginner who knows very little about what it will take to use a GM PCM for an engine and transmission swap project.

I've received enough emails through the years with the question, "Can you remove VATS from my PCM?" to know that the average enthusiast doesn't know that there is so much more involved for a starter calibration. By the way, a starter calibration is just that—so you can expect less-than-desirable performance and maybe a few irrelevant stored DTCs until a professional tuner finishes the job. With that said, let's walk through the basic changes or at least considerations of a starter calibration.

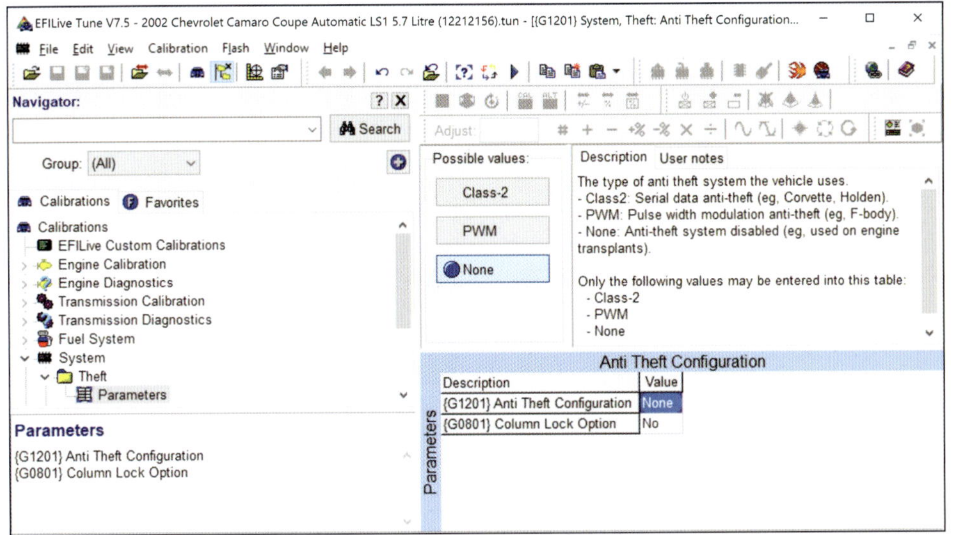

GM PCMs contain some method of antitheft protection to disable the engine from running in a suspected theft attempt. These antitheft features are integrated into production vehicles and need to be removed when using a GM PCM in a retrofitted vehicle. The easiest way to eliminate VATS is by using EFILive or HP Tuners to simply turn it off. These types of programming software are well-seasoned with all available LS-series PCMs in retrofitted applications to fully handle the behind-the-scenes steps that are necessary to overlook, or effectively disable, GM's security.

VATS

The first showstopper within any GM LS-series PCM calibration is VATS. Quite simply, when active, VATS prevents the fuel injectors from pulsing or delivering fuel during crank. This is nothing new, as the 1980s Corvette tuned port injection systems were the first to use this method of preventing the engine from running without a proper signal to the engine computer. While there are additional components to the VATS or GM Pass-Key/Passlock systems, all that is relevant for a starter calibration is to turn off this security feature.

Turning off VATS is very straightforward with Gen III PCMs. EFILive and HP Tuners have created their own patches to force the ECM into the decision to start. VATS disable settings are supported with both software packages to handle all Gen III and Gen IV LS-series PCMs/ECMs.

Fuel Injector Flow Rate

The PCM relies heavily on the values specified for fuel injector flow rate. For this reason, it is always necessary to be sure this table contains accurate values. Modifying other areas of the fuel delivery calibration may result in rework if you later find that you need to adjust the fuel injector flow rates. Consider that a fuel injector flows more or less fuel with varying rail pressure (top side of injector) and varying intake manifold pressure (bottom side of injector), so do your homework to determine what your fuel injectors are actually flowing based on the manufacturer's test data and your system's rail pressure. Stock engines with original injectors obviously

Consider that the primary intent of the engine control module is to deliver fuel to the engine so it can start and run. There are many tables and parameters related to fuel delivery calculations. The first table that should be corrected, if necessary, is the fuel injector flow rate table. Consider the rated injector flow rate and type of fuel system (referenced to vacuum or not) to determine the appropriate values within this table.

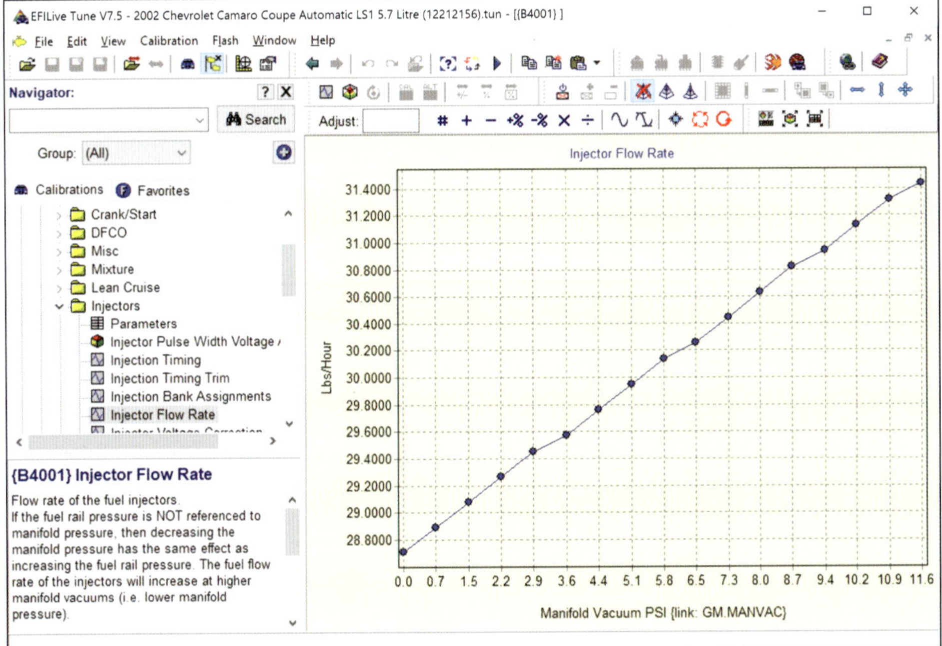

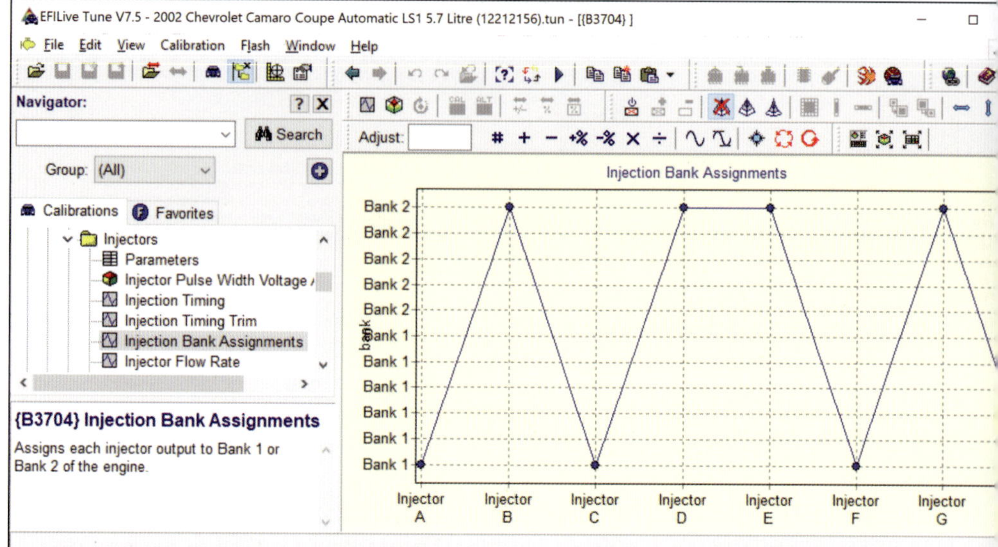

GM fuel systems using a vacuum-referenced fuel pressure regulator require constant values across the fuel injector flow rate table. When referenced to manifold vacuum through the small port in the top hat, the fuel rail pressure is held at a constant differential pressure relative to the pressure or vacuum in the engine's intake manifold. Excess fuel flows through the bottom of the regulator to the attached return line and back into the fuel tank. Many aftermarket fuel pressure regulators are adjustable with a top screw, allowing for higher fuel rail pressure by mechanically adding spring tension within the regulator hat.

The PCM is responsible for applying fuel trims during closed-loop operation. Being that there is only one oxygen sensor per side of the engine, to correctly add or remove fuel during engine operation, the PCM must know which fuel injectors are located in which bank of cylinders. GM V-8 engines assign cylinders 1, 3, 5, and 7 as Bank 1 and 2, 4, 6, and 8 as Bank 2 (cylinder 1 is located on the driver's side of the engine). The Injection Bank Assignments table represents the mapping of fuel injectors to engine banks. Should the wire harness be reworked at the PCM to change injector firing order, the Injection Bank Assignments table must be updated accordingly.

won't need adjustments to the fuel injector flow rates as long as the rail pressure hasn't changed.

Early multi-port fuel injection systems, such as the TPI and LT1 engines, are fitted with a return-style fuel system and vacuum-controlled/referenced fuel pressure regulator. The regulator housing contains a spring-actuated diaphragm that limits the fuel flow through the return fuel line. Manifold vacuum is used to adjust fuel pressure during engine operation. At idle, the fuel pressure drops as intake manifold vacuum releases spring pressure on the diaphragm within the regulator to return more fuel to the tank. Keep in mind that intake manifold vacuum is high as engine load is low. As engine load increases, the vacuum in the intake manifold decreases while allowing more spring pressure on the diaphragm within the regulator to increase fuel rail pressure. This activity changes the delivered fuel injector flow rate during engine operation. These early multi-port injected systems only specify a single fuel injector flow rate value. Varying flow rates across the intake manifold pressure range were naturally accounted for through the use of the vacuum referenced fuel pressure regulator. Some LS-series engines are equipped with a vacuum referenced fuel pressure regulator. In summary, a return-style fuel system requires constant values for the fuel injector flow rates.

Many LS-series engines use a returnless fuel system that does not contain a vacuum referenced regulator to adjust fuel pressure as the intake manifold vacuum, or engine load, changes. The Gen III PCMs account for this type of fuel system by defining fuel injector flow rates throughout the intake manifold pressure range. In summary, a returnless-style fuel system requires sloping values for the fuel injector flow rates.

Firing Order

There are two primary concerns when it comes to engine firing order: (1) the engine wire harness is pinned correctly at the PCM and (2) proper assignment of fuel injectors to each engine bank within the calibration. A quick look at how GM handled the firing order differences between the Gen I small-block Chevy (SBC) and Gen III LS1 with the GM number 12200411 PCM should provide some

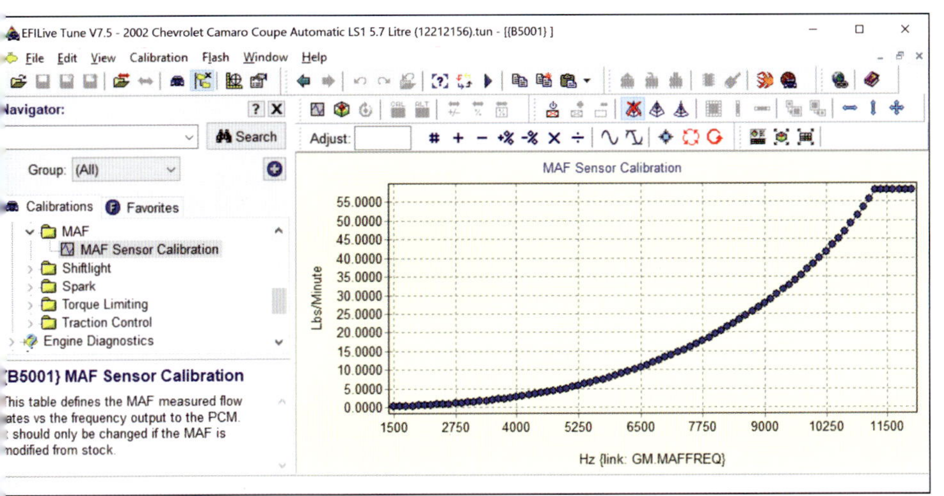

All LS-series engines are fitted with a mass airflow (MAF) sensor. GM used a variety of different sensors through the years. While any LS-series MAF sensor is electronically compatible with any LS-series PCM, the measured airflow rates in the calibration's MAF Sensor Calibration table are calibrated for the MAF size and related effects of intake air tubing for a particular GM vehicle. Any change to MAF size or air intake tubing, such as a cold-air intake upgrade, requires recalibration of the MAF Sensor Calibration table using feedback from a wideband oxygen sensor and setup of a MAF error graph to apply corrections to the defined values.

clarity (and reveal that a firing order change does not require any sort of "hack" to make the engine run as intended).

When you compare the fuel injector control pin assignments at the PCM between 2002 Express Van (Gen I SBC) and 2002 Camaro (Gen III LS1), you will see that GM swapped injectors 2 and 3 as well as 7 and 4 to address the actual engine firing order. Now for coil-per-cylinder ignition systems, you'll have to also swap ignition coil control wires 2 and 3 as well as 7 and 4 when using a Gen I SBC engine with a Gen III or Gen IV LS-series calibration. We're not quite done yet. The GM PCM calibrations contain a table that maps injectors to engine banks: bank 1 includes cylinders 1, 3, 5, and 7; and bank 2 includes cylinders 2, 4, 6, and 8. If this table does not accurately reflect the engine firing order and

PCM pin assignments of the injectors, the PCM incorrectly will apply fuel trims in closed-loop operation. The air/fuel mixture in the exhaust will reveal the PCMs confused state while the engine begins to stumble and likely stall.

MAF Sensor Calibration

Since the introduction of the 1994 LT1 engine management system, GM has used the hot wire principle through the MAF sensor with all V-8 gasoline engines to measure incoming air. Fitted with two sensing

GM's variety of electric fan implementations allow for many configurable options related to electric fan operation. Should your used LS drivetrain not be from a vehicle with electric fans, you can simply add the signal wire(s) to the PCM and update a few calibration settings to install one or two electric fans.

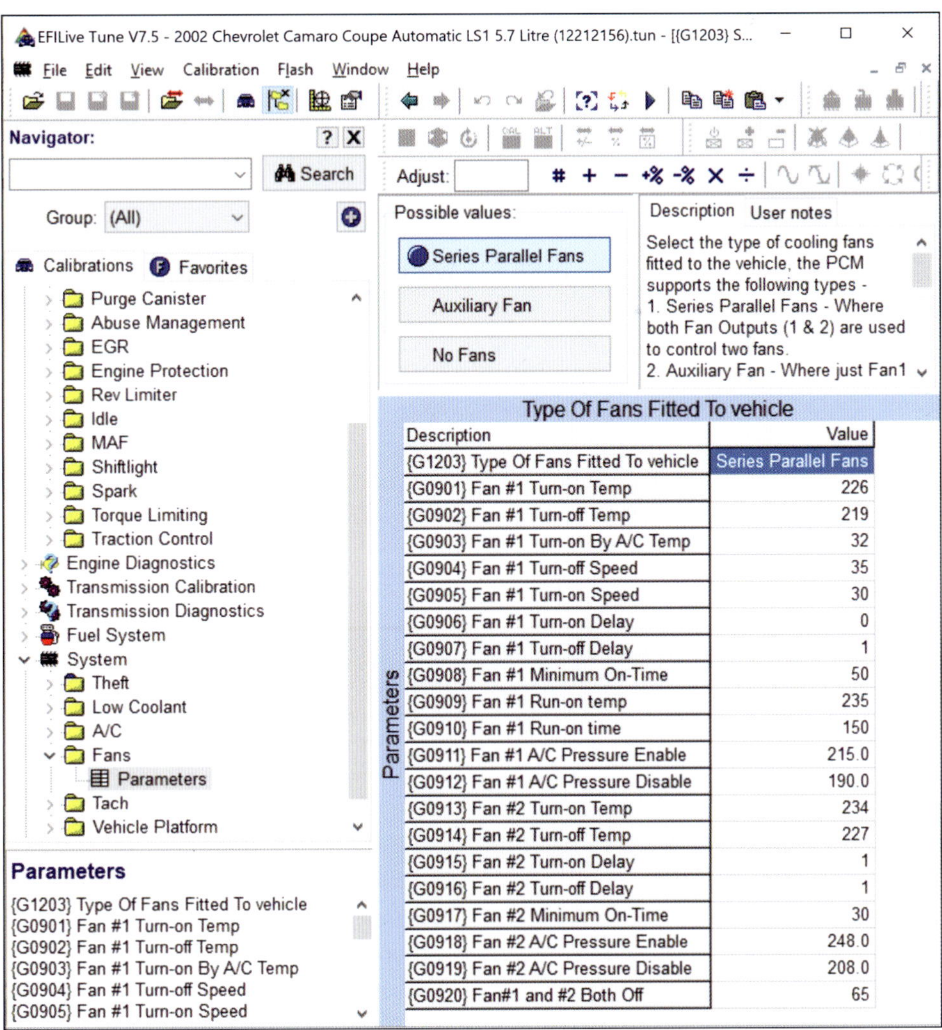

resistors (one hot and one cold) the MAF is used to compare ambient air (cold resistor) with airflow (hot resistor). The hot wire cools as air passes through the MAF housing, and the MAF automatically adjusts the hot wire current to compensate, the current is changed to a frequency that is read by the PCM to represent measured airflow.

MAF sensor placement must occur somewhere between the air filter and engine throttle body. Each established air intake configuration is uniquely tested by GM to determine the proper values within the PCM's MAF table. Any alteration to the MAF or intake pipe may require new values to be updated in the MAF table. All GM car, truck and van MAF sensors used since 1994 are generally compatible with any LS-series PCM.

Enthusiasts may choose to change the MAF due to MAF housing size or placement limitations within the engine bay. Before startup, caution should be taken to replace the MAF table values with those from a vehicle that best represent the MAF being used. Additionally, after the engine is ready for operation, the MAF table should be properly calibrated through data logging with the use of a wideband oxygen sensor to ensure correct values. Failure to properly calibrate the MAF table results in rich or lean operating conditions.

Electric Fans

PCM control of the electric fan, or in most cases multiple fans, is the best implementation. It is worth your time to understand electric fan control and implement accordingly. Electric fan installations using a manual control switch and relay (or relays) have several disadvantages:

- With the potential to forget to turn on the fans and oversight at some point being certain, there will be no warning light to remind the vehicle operator of the need to cool the radiator.
- As the vehicle accelerates, the increased airflow through the radiator becomes sufficient, and the electric fans are not needed. Unnecessary use of the fans and resistance caused by incoming air will only decrease the life of the fan motors.
- The A/C condenser, a heat exchanger found in front of the radiator, must be cooled during A/C operation. The electric fans are necessary for this purpose.

Not all LS-series PCMs are by default configured for electric fan control. Gen III PCMs have configurable settings related to the available two individual control circuits. The PCM grounds each electric fan control circuit based on electric fan calibration settings, such as coolant temperature, vehicle speed, A/C pressure, etc.

The early LS1 engines were fitted with an external intake air temperature (IAT) sensor ahead of the MAF sensor. Later systems moved the IAT sensor within the MAF sensor housing. When eliminating the MAF sensor in favor of speed density (MAP sensor only), the PCM continues to look for IAT sensor data. A simple IAT breakout harness is a plug-and-play solution to remove the MAF sensor and add an external LS1-style IAT sensor.

Speed Density (MAF-Less)

All LS-series PCMs by default rely on the mass airflow (MAF) sensor and manifold absolute pressure (MAP) sensor for fuel delivery calculations. The MAF sensor continually provides the ECU with measurements of incoming air mass while the MAP sensor continually provides the PCM with measurements of pressure within the intake manifold. When

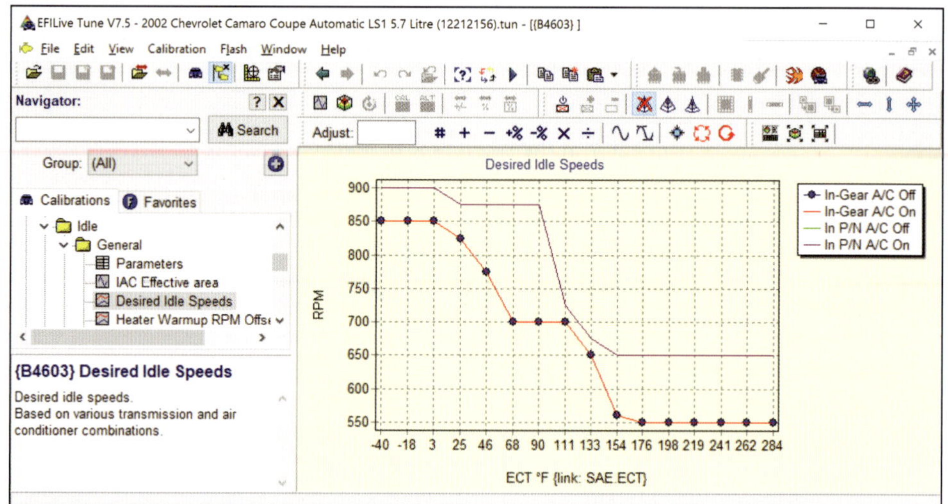

Performance engine builds may not be able to tolerate the low desired idle speeds commanded by default LS-series PCM calibrations. Should your engine not run stable at idle, you may need to increase the desired idle speeds for reliable engine performance.

the MAF is removed from the engine management system, the PCM is said to be operating in speed density mode, as air-density calculations are determined by MAP sensor data. An experienced tuner will be able to assist should you choose to remove the MAF sensor from your system. If you choose to tackle speed-density tuning on your own, there are books and online resources that go into great detail. The EFILive and HP Tuners message forums are also excellent resources to guide you through the process.

What does this have to do with wiring? When the MAF is eliminated, it is good practice to disconnect it from the PCM. Three-wire MAF sensors, which were used with LT1 and LS1 engines, can simply be disconnected from the engine harness. All five-wire MAF sensors include the intake air temperature (IAT) sensor. An IAT breakout harness (with external IAT sensor) is commonly used when converting to speed density.

Raising Desired Idle Speed

Modified engines may have difficulty maintaining the GM desired idle settings. When an engine first starts, the desired idle is high. As coolant temperature increases, the calibration is set to command a lower engine idle speed. Should your engine begin to stumble at low idle speed as it approaches operating temperature, you may need to increase the desired idle speeds until an experienced tuner can correct the calibration and determine appropriate idle speeds.

Open Loop and Closed Loop

Your engine's ECU will always start the engine without feedback from the front oxygen sensors. This is called open loop. The PCM works with preset calibration data to determine fuel delivery. When this data is appropriately calibrated for use with your engine, the engine runs as intended until the PCM switches to closed loop. When in closed loop, the PCM works with air/fuel data from the front two oxygen sensors to determine how much fuel to add or remove to keep the engine running at the defined air/fuel mixture. These applied fuel trims should only help an engine that needs minor PCM calibration changes. Updating the calibration to enter closed loop sooner than defined by GM may be necessary until an experienced tuner can dial in the fuel calibration with feedback from a wideband oxygen sensor.

Transmission

If your PCM was removed from a vehicle that used a different type of transmission than the one you

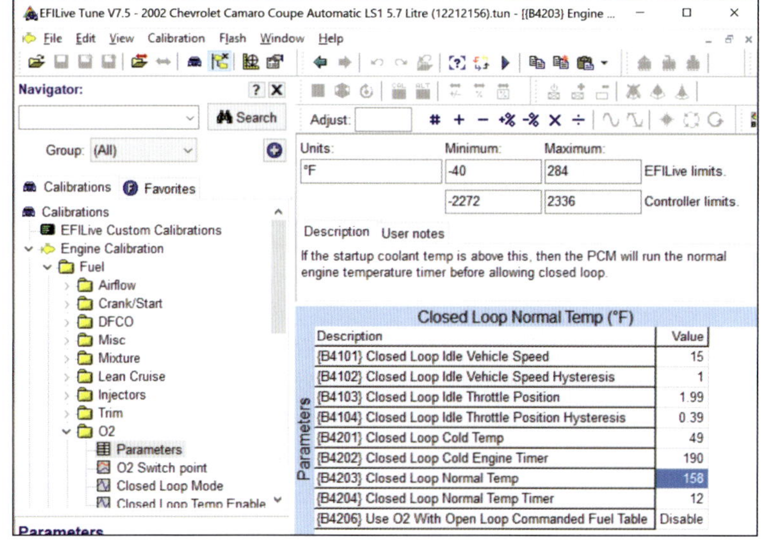

With so many different speedometer and tachometer choices, the LS-series PCM signals are not always compatible. Aftermarket solutions, such as the Dakota Digital SGI-100BT module, are capable of receiving many different types of speedometer and tachometer signals and then outputting configurable signals that can be used for your chosen GM or aftermarket speedometer and tachometer.

Closed Loop Normal Temp (°F)	
Description	Value
{B4101} Closed Loop Idle Vehicle Speed	15
{B4102} Closed Loop Idle Vehicle Speed Hysteresis	1
{B4103} Closed Loop Idle Throttle Position	1.99
{B4104} Closed Loop Idle Throttle Position Hysteresis	0.39
{B4201} Closed Loop Cold Temp	49
{B4202} Closed Loop Cold Engine Timer	190
{B4203} Closed Loop Normal Temp	158
{B4204} Closed Loop Normal Temp Timer	12
{B4206} Use O2 With Open Loop Commanded Fuel Table	Disable

GM's fueling strategy always includes the application of fuel trims during normal operating engine conditions. At startup, when an engine is cold, the PCM commands a richer fuel mixture and does not look at the oxygen sensor readings to apply fuel trims. This is considered open-loop operation. As the engine coolant temperature increases, the PCM soon begins to use oxygen-sensor readings to apply fuel trims to each bank of cylinders to maintain an ideal air/fuel mixture for normal engine operation. When receiving feedback from the oxygen sensors and applying fuel trims, the PCM is said to be in closed-loop operation. GM defines several parameters that affect the transition from open-loop to closed-loop operation.

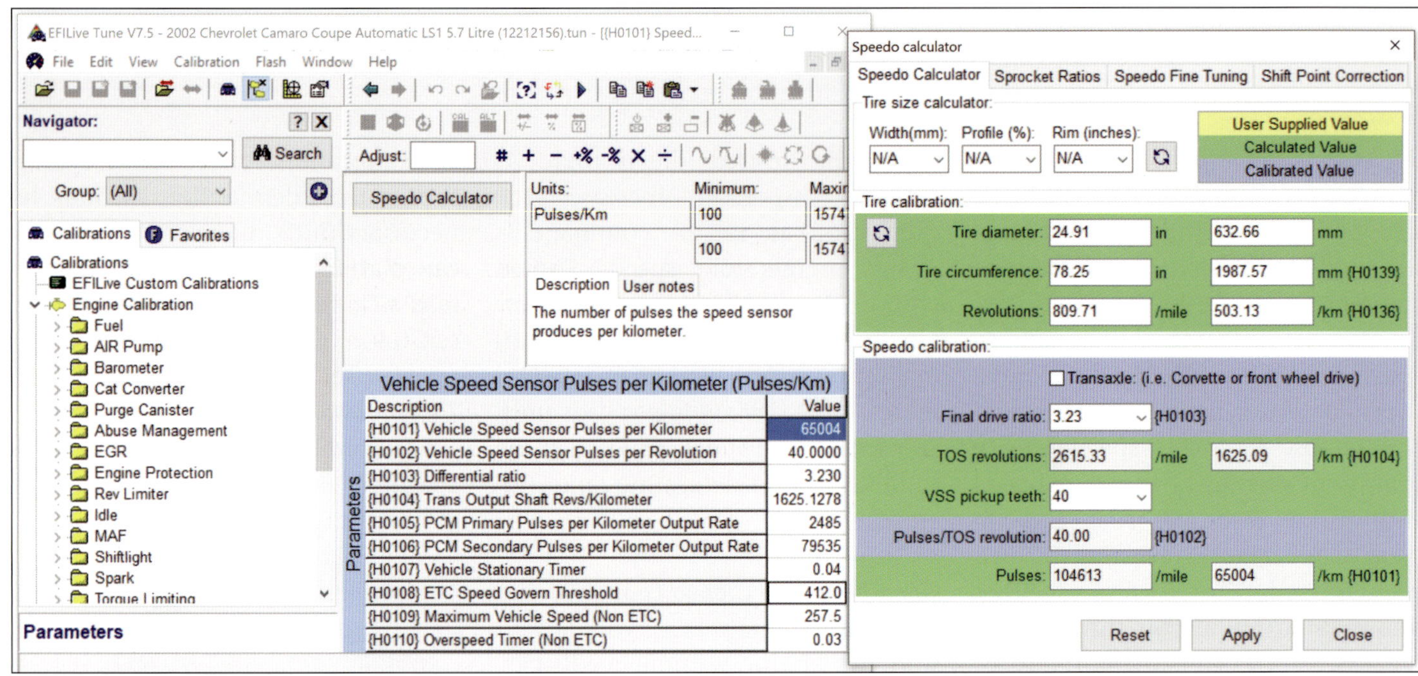

Functions such as deceleration fuel cut-off (DFCO) and electronic automatic transmission control require that the PCM is receiving accurate vehicle speed data. GM defines many configurable VSS parameters. EFILive makes the application of vehicle speed related parameters to automatic transmission shift settings a snap through the use of its Speedo calculator menus.

intend to use, load a base calibration into your PCM from a vehicle with the same transmission type that you will be using.

VSS output pulse count, tire size, and gear ratio are critical values that must accurately reflect the fitted VSS, vehicle's rear tire size, and differential gear ratio. GM PCMs receive vehicle speed as an AC sine wave through a 2-wire inductive variable reluctance (VR) sensor. If your (non-GM) transmission is fitted with a 3-wire Hall effect sensor, you will have to install an aftermarket interface (see Dakota Digital) to rework the square wave into a sine wave that can be read by the PCM.

GM 4-speed automatic transmissions, such as the 4L60E and 4L80E, contain shift solenoids that must be operated by the PCM. Any incorrect parameter (VSS pulse count, tire size, gear ratio) affects the transmission shift points and operation of the torque converter lockup solenoid. Manual T56 6-speed transmissions are not electronically controlled but

are fitted with a reverse lockout solenoid that is controlled based on vehicle speed.

Speedometer

The GM PCMs output one (sometimes two) configurable vehicle speed signals that may be used by many GM and aftermarket speedometers. Adding a terminated wire to the appropriate PCM connector cavity location will provide you with

a vehicle speed signal with which to work. If the VSS output signal cannot be used by your speedometer, count on a Dakota Digital speedometer interface module as a solution.

Eliminating Irrelevant DTCs

All GM LS-series PCMs are equipped with onboard diagnostics (OBD-II), which is a diagnostic reporting system that assists technicians to perform vehicle diagnostics,

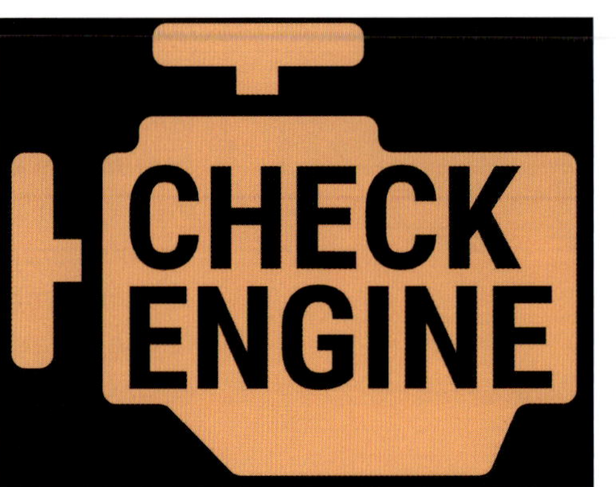

One of the perks to using a GM LS-series PCM is OBD-II diagnostics. Through the display of an illuminated telltale lamp, the vehicle operator can see the presence of a system fault. Countless aftermarket OBD-II scanners can be used through the vehicle's 16-cavity diagnostic connector to retrieve the stored fault codes or DTCs. Consider your retrofitted LS rig is on a **Hot Rod** *Power Tour and the check engine lamp turns on. You can simply pull into a nearby auto parts store or service shop to read the stored DTCs. Aftermarket systems rely on proprietary software and equipment to determine engine faults, often without the guidance of DTCs.*

BenchForce is the prominent bench programming solution for LS-series performance shops and many enthusiasts. By simplifying the vehicle's wiring and bringing the 16-cavity OBD-II connector to the bench, GM ECUs can be powered up for flash programming. The PowerBlock switch assembly is a CAN bus terminating device that receives plug-and-play ECU wire harnesses for trouble-free operation of ECU calibration tasks. Because of its use of the OBD-II diagnostic connector, the BenchForce solution is compatible with all GM and aftermarket programming interfaces.

service, and repairs. When a system fault or service request is present, a DTC is set, and the PCM applies a ground to the malfunction indicator lamp (MIL) to illuminate a bulb within the instrument panel cluster (IPC).

There are two parts within the calibration to address the DTCs: DTC processing enablers and MIL enablers. A quick look at a stock PCM's list of available DTCs reveals that many DTCs are not used or relevant for the vehicle calibration. For engine conversions, eliminate irrelevant DTCs (and turn off MIL enabling) so that you can be notified of a DTC only when it's important. In some cases, the presence of a DTC can prohibit PCM functionality of the electric fan control circuits, so modify the calibration accordingly before initial engine startup.

With so many enabled DTCs in a stock GM calibration, there's a very good possibility that you will overlook disabling a few irrelevant ones. Be sure that the MIL is wired correctly before initial startup, and then disable any additional irrelevant DTCs as they are reported.

BenchForce Off-Board Programming

When a PCM is removed from a vehicle and programmed on a table or bench, it is referred to as off-board programming. If you were to mail your PCM to a tuner for a starter calibration, your PCM will more than likely be programmed on a bench. All programming interface cables compatible with the LS-series ECUs include a cable that relies on the SAE J1962 standard defining a 16-pin OBD-II diagnostic connector that can typically be found just above the driver's feet and attached to the bottom of the dashboard.

BenchForce, a leading brand in off-board programming solutions, moves the 16-pin OBD-II diagnostic connector to the bench. Being a modular system, the core component to this solution is the PowerBlock switch assembly, which is a circuit board solution using GM-style header connections and a rugged anodized aluminum enclosure.

Adding an ECU to the bench is as straightforward as connecting an ECU-specific harness from the PowerBlock to the ECU. Adding additional ECUs to the bench (such as ECM and TCM) is accomplished by adding a Y-splitter harness. The scope of BenchForce far exceeds GM ECU support because other popular vehicle makes (such as Ford and Chrysler) are supported. Many heavy-duty J1939 applications are also supported.

Professional tuners using EFILive and HP Tuners have come to rely on the BenchForce off-board programming solution for their continued success. Acting as a CAN termination device, the PowerBlock enables tuners to communicate directly with TCMs that otherwise would require a connection with an ECM. Moreover, tuners who experience issues with production GM vehicles due to disruptive CAN bus communications may use BenchForce to temporarily remove the ECU from the vehicle for programming.

PROJECTS

This chapter features three projects: a P01 PCM Swap in a 1997 Camaro Z28 383-ci LT4 T56, a P59 PCM swap in 1990 K1500 GM Ram Jet 350 4L60E, and a P01 PCM swap in 1985 Camaro Z28 6.0L LS T56.

Project 1:
P01 PCM Swap in a 1997 Camaro Z28 383-ci LT4 T56

Several years ago, I purchased a beautiful 30th Anniversary Camaro Z28 as a shop vehicle for new product development. The stock 5.7L LT1 engine and T56 manual transmission were considered a performance drivetrain in its day, but compared to any newer Camaro, this car was lacking in performance. The rated 285 hp and 325 ft-lbs of torque gave this car moderate performance that produced satisfaction for only a short while. When the time was right, I knew this car would receive a crank and cam signal conversion that would eliminate the OptiSpark distributor and replace the original PCM with a modern coil-per-cylinder ignition system and more modern engine controller.

As the demand grew for Holley EFI systems, this car was used to prototype a direct-fit engine wire harness for Holley EFI ECUs. While the Holley Dominator ECU was certainly functional in this car, it was not able to provide me with a level of integration with which I was satisfied. I eventually removed Holley's $2,200-plus ECM and replaced it with a $50 salvage-yard GM P01 PCM for greater, yes greater, vehicle

I purchased this 30th Anniversary Camaro Z28 as a shop vehicle. It has the 5.7L LT1 engine and T56 manual transmission.

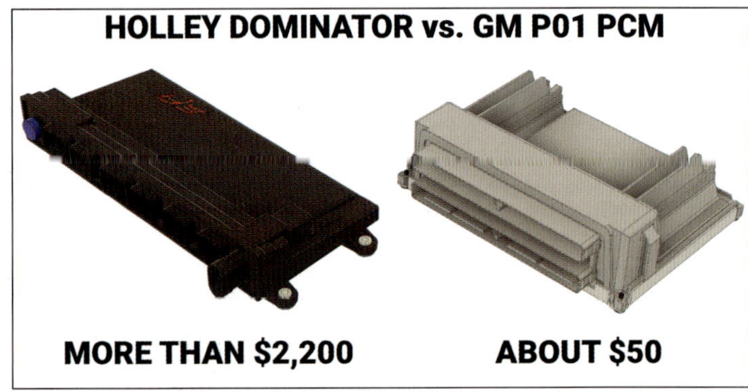

While many GM fuel injection enthusiasts have been flocking to Holley EFI systems, many still recognize the value and much lower expense of using a production GM PCM or ECM as their engine management system. Unless your project requires a second set of injectors, a second throttle body, or multiple configurable inputs and outputs, you will likely find that a GM engine management system is more than adequate and cost-friendly, too.

integration. This should not come as a surprise because aftermarket ECUs are designed and intended for use with off-road vehicles; this leaves them lacking some of the features that are found in production GM engine controllers.

383-ci LT4 Engine and Upgraded T56 Transmission

For a new powerplant, I reached out to Karl Ellwein of Ellwein Engines, who is one of the top LT1 engine builders in the world. Karl and I discussed my 383-ci engine and 500-hp (minimum) goal. Beginning with a 2-bolt block foundation, Karl drilled the block for the use of 4-bolt splayed main caps. With the recommendation to use a set of AFR LT4 cylinder heads, I provided Karl with a fresh GM LT4 intake manifold for porting, powder coating, and assembly. The piston rings were seated on an engine dyno, and the new 383ci LT4 exceeded my expectations by producing 556 hp and 515 ft-lbs of torque.

The T56 transmission that was removed from the car was in fine condition, but I felt it wise to have Tick Performance rebuild a T56 that would knowingly handle the new engine. Several weeks later, the upgraded T56 arrived with Tick's adjustable master cylinder and short-throw shifter. The power to the transmission is transferred through a SPEC Stage 2 Plus performance clutch.

24x/1x Crank/Cam Signal Conversion

Knowing I would use the P01 PCM, it was necessary for the engine to output a Gen III 24x crankshaft signal and 1x camshaft signal. I machined the appropriate crankshaft and camshaft signal components on my Haas CNC mill and shipped them to Karl Ellwein prior to the engine build.

While I could have used EFI Connection's most popular LT1 24x/1x crank/cam signal conversion, I wanted

Several years of customer feedback resulted in a prototype two-piece timing cover with a large 24x crankshaft reluctor and 1x camshaft signal within the camshaft timing sprocket (pictured left). The prototype became a more expensive production option to EFI Connection's popular lineup of 24x/1x crank/cam signal conversion kits (pictured right). All 24x/1x crank/cam signal conversion kits output the same GM Gen III LS-series crankshaft and camshaft signals. Variations of the product line allow for other considerations such as crank snout size, timing chain selection, and water pump drive type.

The best of the best: Ellwein Engines 383-ci LT4 engine and Tick Performance Stage 2 T56 transmission. This drivetrain combination delivers a street-menacing 556 hp and 515 ft-lbs of torque (and a lot of fun) while the GM P01 PCM number 12200411 provides manners and the drivability of a modern production vehicle.

to get some road time on my updated design that features a two-piece timing cover. Due to its size, the large 5.315-inch crankshaft reluctor has the perception of a cleaner signal, compared to the common 4.000-inch crankshaft reluctor, but an oscilloscope trace will reveal the same crankshaft signal output through the engine's RPM range.

The smaller crankshaft sensor was introduced with the updated production GM 4.3L engine in 2007 and requires a pull-up resistor for use with the P01 PCM. Cloyes, a performance timing set manufacturer, manufactures for EFI Connection a variation of its performance double-roller timing set. The unique timing set includes a camshaft sprocket that features a 360-degree raised ring that is machined by EFI Connection to create the desired camshaft signal to satisfy the PCM.

Electronic Throttle Equipment

As more of a novelty, I fitted the new engine with a 58-mm drive-by-wire throttle body. Many years ago, after developing the 24x/1x crank/cam signal conversions for SBC and LT1 engines, I contacted Tuned Port Induction Specialties (TPIS) to ask if it would be interested in manufacturing a drive-by-wire throttle body based on the LS1 Corvette.

Given that TPIS had already been manufacturing billet aluminum TPI/LT1 cable-operated throttle bodies and larger LS1 Corvette electronically operated throttle bodies, it was the ideal choice for this specialty product. The product line included 52-mm, 58-mm, and mono-blade TPI/LT1

A limited-production 58-mm drive-by-wire throttle body for LT1/LT4 intake manifolds is CNC machined to receive the TPS, motor, and internal gears of the LS1/LS6 Corvette/CTS-V throttle body. Supporting equipment includes the LS1/LS6 TAC module, CTS-V pedal assembly, and GM P01 PCM number 12200411.

drive-by-wire throttle bodies. Each throttle body requires the disassembly of a production GM LS1/LS6 throttle body to scavenge the TPS, motor assembly, and internal springs and gears. For this reason, they are among the most expensive throttle bodies available to GM enthusiasts.

The LS1/LS6 drive-by-wire throttle body requires the use of a TAC module for its operation, OBD-II diagnostics, safety, and cruise control. The TAC module is a small plastic box with two connections: one connection dedicated to the accelerator pedal position (APP) sensor and the other connection used for power, ground, PCM communications, cruise control, and throttle body operation and feedback. Compatible TAC modules include 1997–2004 Corvette and 2004–2005 Cadillac CTS-V.

While there are many GM electronic accelerator pedals, only a few are known to work with the LS1/LS6 TAC module. To have accurate pedal position data, the TAC module relies on signals from three potentiometers within the APP sensor housing. The TAC module provides reference voltage to the APP sensors and receives signal voltage sweeping from more than 0 toward 5 volts (sensor 1) and less than 5 toward 0 volts (sensor 2 and sensor 3). As a general rule, I tend to use the pedal GM intended for use with the TAC system that I'm working with. In this case, the 2004–2005 CTS-V pedal was the best fit in the Camaro, so I designed and manufactured an intermediate bracket to secure the pedal to the firewall.

Perhaps the greatest perk to GM's TAC system is integrated cruise control. When using the Holley Dominator ECU in this car, every touch of the turn signal multifunction lever was a reminder that cruise control was forever disabled, and that bothered me.

Bringing back cruise control required that I satisfied the P01 PCM and TAC module input requirements. Being a manual transmission, I looked at the 2002 Corvette factory schematics to see how GM implemented cruise control on the manual transmission–equipped Corvette. My Camaro had all of the necessary clutch and brake switches, so I simply had to repurpose them. To make this simple to understand while building the engine wire harness, I drew a wiring diagram that would represent my implementation.

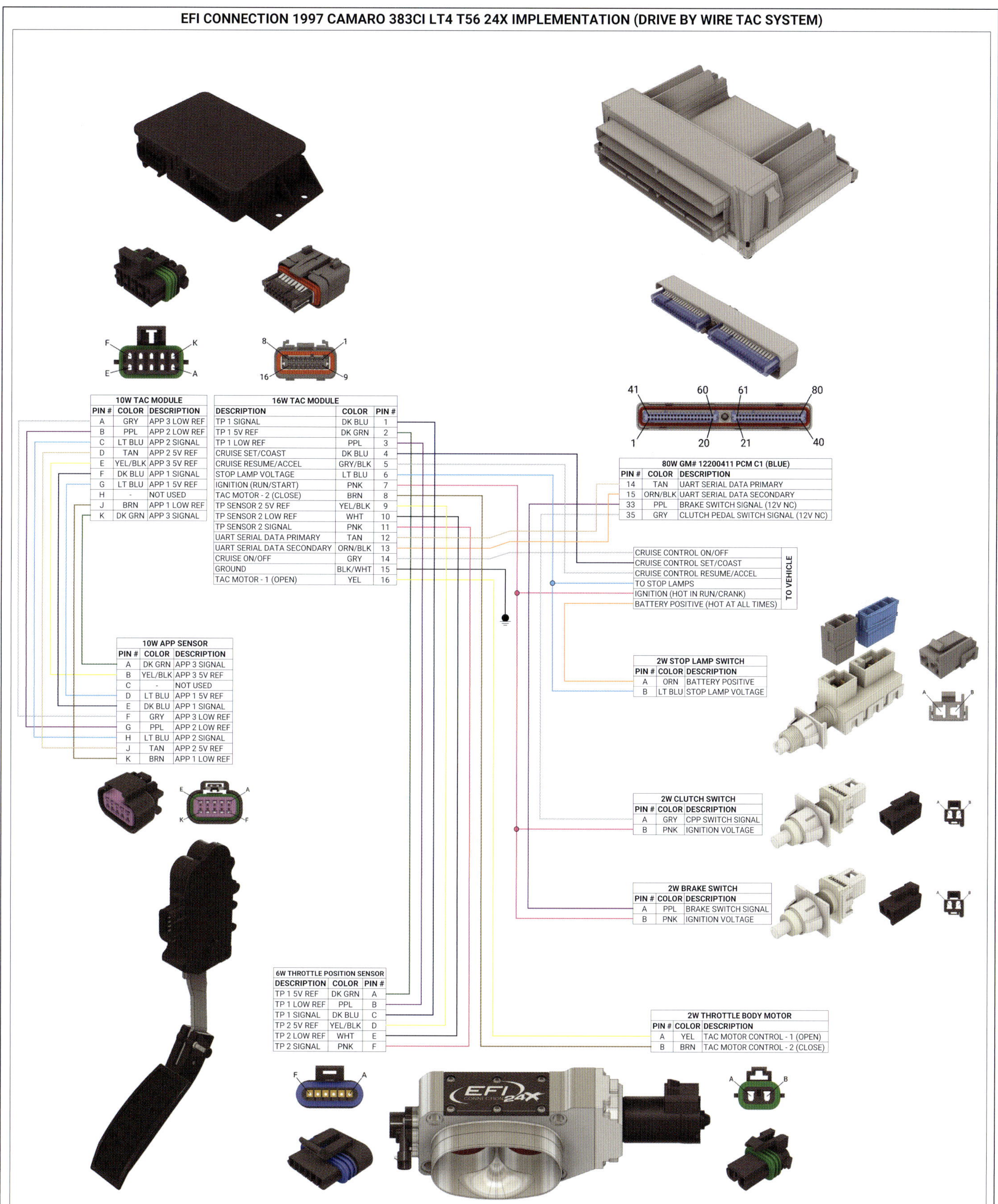

10W TAC MODULE

PIN #	COLOR	DESCRIPTION
A	GRY	APP 3 LOW REF
B	PPL	APP 2 LOW REF
C	LT BLU	APP 2 SIGNAL
D	TAN	APP 2 5V REF
E	YEL/BLK	APP 3 5V REF
F	DK BLU	APP 1 SIGNAL
G	LT BLU	APP 1 5V REF
H	-	NOT USED
J	BRN	APP 1 LOW REF
K	DK GRN	APP 3 SIGNAL

16W TAC MODULE

DESCRIPTION	COLOR	PIN #
TP 1 SIGNAL	DK BLU	1
TP 1 5V REF	DK GRN	2
TP 1 LOW REF	PPL	3
CRUISE SET/COAST	DK BLU	4
CRUISE RESUME/ACCEL	GRY/BLK	5
STOP LAMP VOLTAGE	LT BLU	6
IGNITION (RUN/START)	PNK	7
TAC MOTOR - 2 (CLOSE)	BRN	8
TP SENSOR 2 5V REF	YEL/BLK	9
TP SENSOR 2 LOW REF	WHT	10
TP SENSOR 2 SIGNAL	PNK	11
UART SERIAL DATA PRIMARY	TAN	12
UART SERIAL DATA SECONDARY	ORN/BLK	13
CRUISE ON/OFF	GRY	14
GROUND	BLK/WHT	15
TAC MOTOR - 1 (OPEN)	YEL	16

80W GM# 12200411 PCM C1 (BLUE)

PIN #	COLOR	DESCRIPTION
14	TAN	UART SERIAL DATA PRIMARY
15	ORN/BLK	UART SERIAL DATA SECONDARY
33	PPL	BRAKE SWITCH SIGNAL (12V NC)
35	GRY	CLUTCH PEDAL SWITCH SIGNAL (12V NC)

10W APP SENSOR

PIN #	COLOR	DESCRIPTION
A	DK GRN	APP 3 SIGNAL
B	YEL/BLK	APP 3 5V REF
C	-	NOT USED
D	LT BLU	APP 1 5V REF
E	DK BLU	APP 1 SIGNAL
F	GRY	APP 3 LOW REF
G	PPL	APP 2 LOW REF
H	LT BLU	APP 2 SIGNAL
J	TAN	APP 2 5V REF
K	BRN	APP 1 LOW REF

2W STOP LAMP SWITCH

PIN #	COLOR	DESCRIPTION
A	ORN	BATTERY POSITIVE
B	LT BLU	STOP LAMP VOLTAGE

2W CLUTCH SWITCH

PIN #	COLOR	DESCRIPTION
A	GRY	CPP SWITCH SIGNAL
B	PNK	IGNITION VOLTAGE

2W BRAKE SWITCH

PIN #	COLOR	DESCRIPTION
A	PPL	BRAKE SWITCH SIGNAL
B	PNK	IGNITION VOLTAGE

6W THROTTLE POSITION SENSOR

DESCRIPTION	COLOR	PIN #
TP 1 5V REF	DK GRN	A
TP 1 LOW REF	PPL	B
TP 1 SIGNAL	DK BLU	C
TP 2 5V REF	YEL/BLK	D
TP 2 LOW REF	WHT	E
TP 2 SIGNAL	PNK	F

2W THROTTLE BODY MOTOR

PIN #	COLOR	DESCRIPTION
A	YEL	TAC MOTOR CONTROL - 1 (OPEN)
B	BRN	TAC MOTOR CONTROL - 2 (CLOSE)

GM's electronic throttle control system involves very few parts, requiring the fourth-generation Camaro brake and clutch switch wiring be reworked to allow for a proper implementation. With cruise control integrated into the new TAC system, the existing brake and clutch switches are repurposed as PCM signal inputs. The stop lamp switch wiring is also reworked to break out 12V stop lamp voltage as an input to the TAC module.

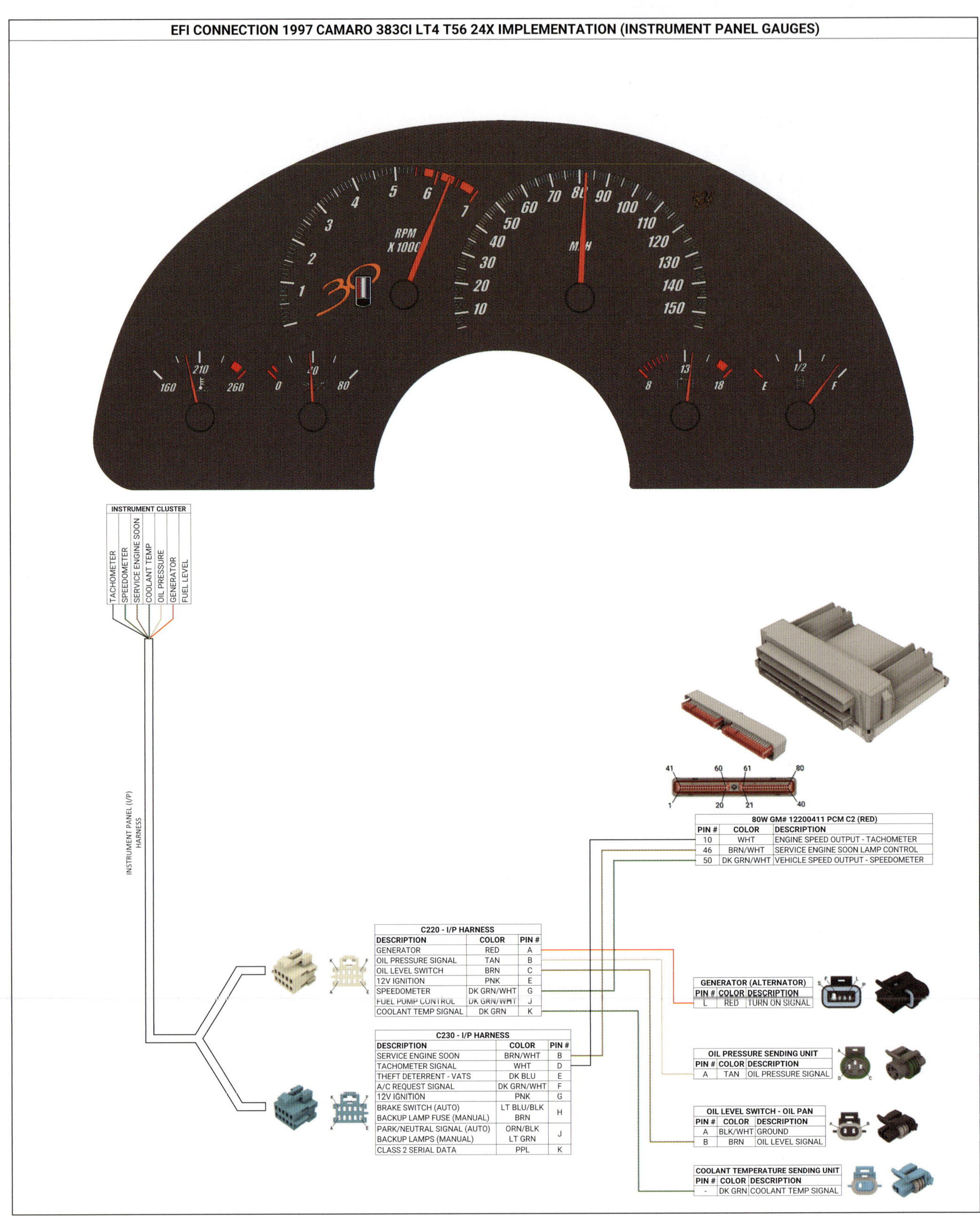

80W GM# 12200411 PCM C2 (RED)		
PIN #	COLOR	DESCRIPTION
10	WHT	ENGINE SPEED OUTPUT - TACHOMETER
46	BRN/WHT	SERVICE ENGINE SOON LAMP CONTROL
50	DK GRN/WHT	VEHICLE SPEED OUTPUT - SPEEDOMETER

C220 - I/P HARNESS		
DESCRIPTION	COLOR	PIN #
GENERATOR	RED	A
OIL PRESSURE SIGNAL	TAN	B
OIL LEVEL SWITCH	BRN	C
12V IGNITION	PNK	E
SPEEDOMETER	DK GRN/WHT	G
FUEL PUMP CONTROL	DK GRN/WHT	J
COOLANT TEMP SIGNAL	DK GRN	K

C230 - I/P HARNESS		
DESCRIPTION	COLOR	PIN #
SERVICE ENGINE SOON	BRN/WHT	B
TACHOMETER SIGNAL	WHT	D
THEFT DETERRENT - VATS	DK BLU	E
A/C REQUEST SIGNAL	DK GRN/WHT	F
12V IGNITION	PNK	G
BRAKE SWITCH (AUTO)	LT BLU/BLK	H
BACKUP LAMP FUSE (MANUAL)	BRN	H
PARK/NEUTRAL SIGNAL (AUTO)	ORN/BLK	J
BACKUP LAMPS (MANUAL)	LT GRN	J
CLASS 2 SERIAL DATA	PPL	K

GENERATOR (ALTERNATOR)		
PIN #	COLOR	DESCRIPTION
L	RED	TURN ON SIGNAL

OIL PRESSURE SENDING UNIT		
PIN #	COLOR	DESCRIPTION
A	TAN	OIL PRESSURE SIGNAL

OIL LEVEL SWITCH - OIL PAN		
PIN #	COLOR	DESCRIPTION
A	BLK/WHT	GROUND
B	BRN	OIL LEVEL SIGNAL

COOLANT TEMPERATURE SENDING UNIT		
PIN #	COLOR	DESCRIPTION
-	DK GRN	COOLANT TEMP SIGNAL

The fourth-generation F-Body instrument clusters are surprisingly easy to work with when using the GM number 12200411 PCM. No expensive interface modules are required to keep the speedometer and tachometer functional because the PCM's output signals are configurable within the PCM's calibration to make any necessary adjustments. The coolant temperature and oil pressure gauges are controlled by sending units already installed on the engine. Lastly, the service-engine-soon lamp is controlled by switched PCM ground. Very simply, the gauges are functional with the Gen III LS-series PCMs.

Instrument Cluster Compatibility

GM's 12200411 P01 PCM is directly compatible with the 1993–1997 Camaro and Firebird instrument clusters. When removing the Holley Dominator ECU from the vehicle, I was also able to remove the Dakota Digital speedometer and tachometer interface modules, which is an extra expense when using an aftermarket ECU. I'll briefly discuss speedometer and tachometer compatibility in more detail as I walk you through the calibration changes made within the PCM.

It's worth noting that I had minor difficulty with HP Tuners to update the Corvette speedometer settings to cooperate with the Camaro instrument cluster. I ultimately had to copy and paste settings from a Camaro LS1 T56 calibration into the Corvette calibration to get the speedometer to read correctly.

Additionally, the tachometer required me to use EFILive to enable the 12V pullup on the tach signal, as HP Tuners did not support this parameter for the Corvette operating system that I was working with. Out of curiosity, I temporarily installed a P59 PCM and loaded a 2005 Cadillac CTS-V calibration to see how the instrument cluster would cooperate.

While HP Tuners does support the 12V pullup setting for the CTS-V, the result was an unresponsive tachometer. While it took a little trial and error, the GM number 12200411 PCM was the best choice for the Camaro's instrument cluster.

Engine Wire Harness

An LS1 PCM conversion requires the removal of the original LT1 engine harness and installation of a replacement plug-and-play engine harness. For that, I used one of my

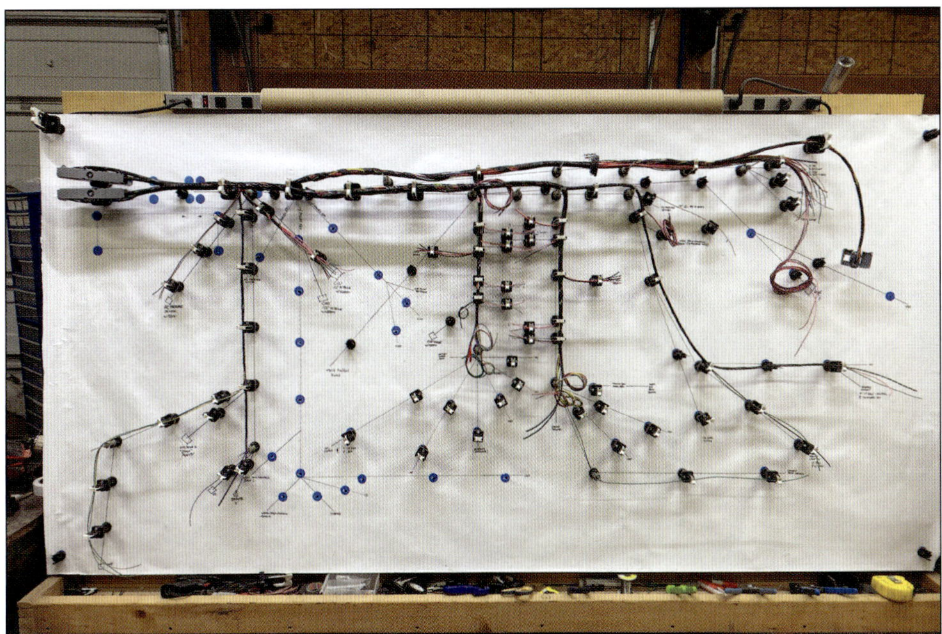

An engine wire harness is easiest to build when it is assembled on a template. With the LT1 engine sensor and devices layout staying the same, the original engine harness can be measured and the measurements transferred to a blank template for use with the new harness build. For a one-off harness build, consider using a sheet of plywood and nails to route wires where they are intended to go. There's far too much wire movement and wasted effort when attempting to build a harness on the engine.

existing harness board templates to begin assembly. The twist to this build was the electronic throttle body and TAC module wiring, which was a requirement rarely encountered in the 10-plus years I've been building these harnesses.

Careful attention is necessary to be sure wires are routed according to the year and transmission type of the car. The only two years of the LT1-engine-equipped Camaro and Firebird that share the same harness are 1996 and 1997. All other engine harnesses are specific to the year of the vehicle and do not interchange.

I begin at the PCM and run the precut lengths of wire to their appropriate location on the build template. Next, I add the spliced circuits to the template. The wires are then taped with a low-adhesive vinyl tape and trimmed to their appropriate lengths. I left the loose TAC module and cruise control–related wires extra-long so that I could neatly route the wires under the dash and trim them to length once in the car.

The PCM requires 12V signals from the brake and clutch anticipate switch. Those wires are bundled within 1/4 inch expandable sleeving. The TAC module requires stop lamp voltage and switched 12V cruise control signals. Those wires are bundled within 1/4-inch expandable sleeving. The APP sensor wires are bundled with 1/4-inch expandable sleeving. The three runs of bundled wires are routed under the dash and exit near the steering column.

The APP wiring was trimmed to comfortably fit and then terminated for the installation of the harness

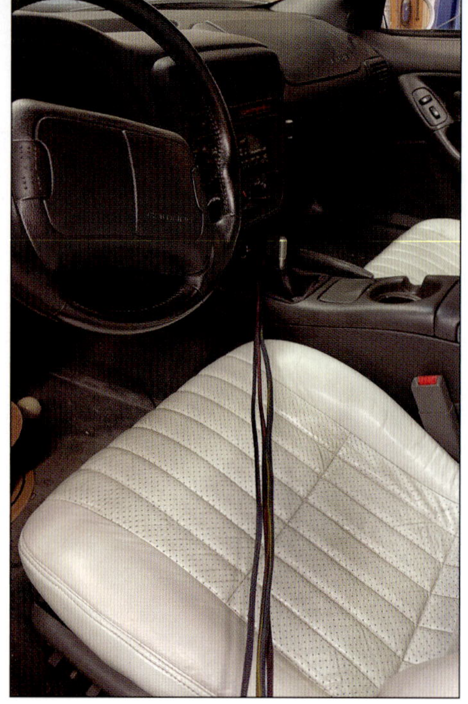

Getting wires to the interior driver's side of the vehicle is accomplished by breaking out the loose wires near the passenger-side firewall grommet and neatly routing them under the dash. Especially when many wires are involved, it's good practice to tape or install expandable sleeving on the bundle(s) of wires so that they stay together. Driver-side connections may include the accelerator pedal, brake switch, clutch anticipate switch, cruise control, and stop lamp signal.

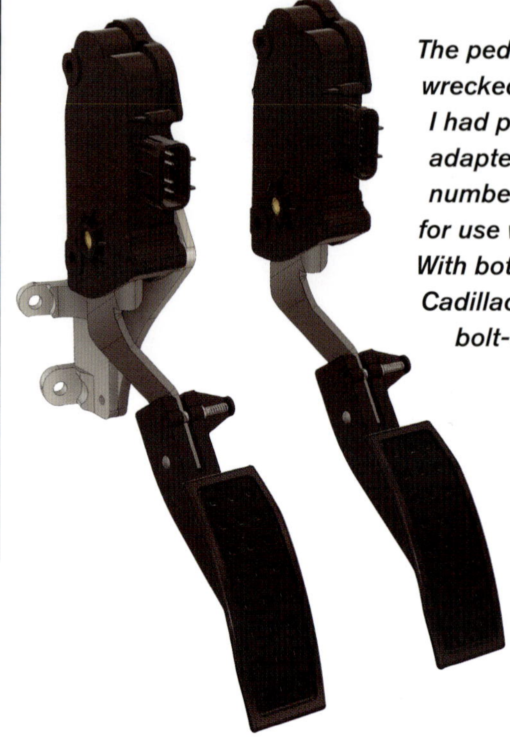

The pedal of choice was pulled from a wrecked 2004–2005 Cadillac CTS-V (left). I had previously manufactured a two-piece adapter bracket for the popular GM part number 10379038 pedal assembly (right) for use with the Holley Dominator EFI system. With both pedals being used in the 2004-2005 Cadillac CTS, the CTS-V pedal was a direct bolt-on to my aluminum bracket.

The cruise control interface connector is located on the steering column. Four of the included wires come down the steering column from the cruise control switches. With the original cruise control module removed from the engine bay, these wires simply stop at the cruise control module harness connector. This is the ideal location to get access to the cruise control signals.

connector. I designed a two-piece bracket to secure the accelerator pedal in its place. By taking careful measurements and 3-D printing a few prototypes, I determined the angle and proper location for the pedal. This design and prototyping process took several days before I was ready to machine several fixtures to make the final parts out of aluminum.

To make cruise control functional once again, the TAC module must receive 12V signals from the cruise control switches. By planning ahead, I bundled a 12V switched ignition wire with the three cruise control signal wires. Rather than cutting any wires under the dash, I located the long steering column connector containing the cruise control signal wires and simply replaced the four original cruise control module wires with the new TAC module and 12V ignition wires. The old cruise control wires were taped and tucked away.

In a similar way, I cut to length the PCM's brake switch and clutch anticipate switch wires before installing connectors and plugging them into the appropriate switches. The PCM requires these two 12V signals to allow or disable cruise control. The TAC module requires stop lamp voltage (opposite state of brake switch) to allow or disable cruise control, so I tapped into the stop lamp wire just below the steering column.

Back to the passenger's side of the dash, where the engine harness enters through the firewall, I make room for the TAC module. Tucked away behind the kick panel are the engine to dash harness interface connectors C210, C220, and C230. I found there to be just enough room behind the kick panel to put the TAC module. GM always installed the TAC module in the engine bay, but there was no convenient location in this car's engine bay. Moreover, keeping the TAC module out of sight but easily accessible was a good choice.

This engine has been fitted with

The 4th Gen F-Body doesn't offer many locations to mount the Corvette TAC module. The only obvious engine bay option was on the driver-side frame rail where the cruise control module used to be. This location would have resulted in rather long wire lengths. The other option was behind the passenger-side kick panel below the dash. GM left just enough room behind the kick panel to give me an interior-mounted TAC module solution.

Many LT1 engine enthusiasts eliminate the original mechanical driven water pump in favor of an aftermarket electric water pump. GM made no provision in the vehicle's electrical system for an electric water pump, so a new harness had to be made for water pump control. By tapping into the PCM's fuel pump relay control circuit and pulling battery power through a new relay, the water pump was wired to be on any time the engine is running. A clean installation involves mounting the relay near the battery and the fuse and water pump harness connector below the right engine cooling fan.

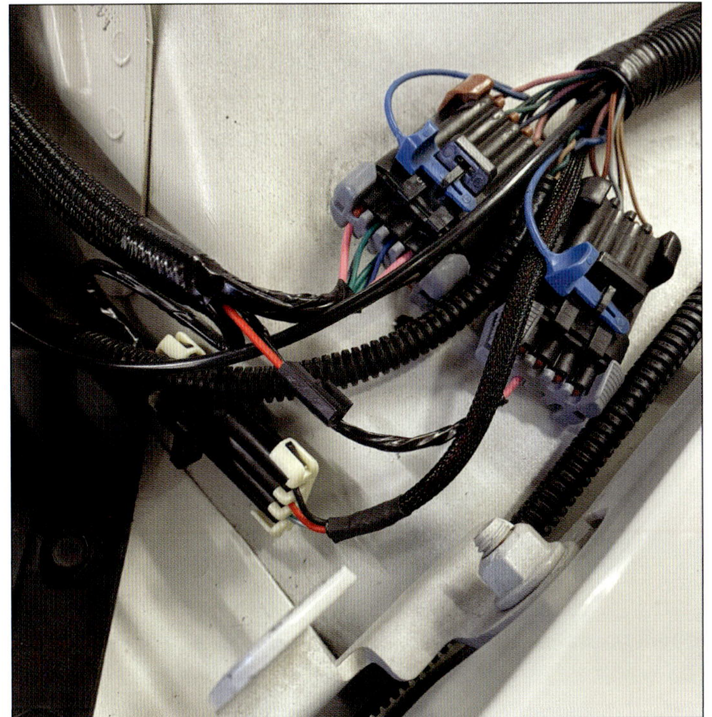

water pump has power. When the LED is off, the water pump fuse has blown. I installed a three-cavity Metri-Pack 150 connector near connectors C100 and C105 on the passenger-side strut tower to pass through the water pump relay control and water pump power and ground. A 12V LED was mounted in the vehicle so that the driver can always be aware of the water pump power status.

Should the electric water pump fuse blow, I want to know about it well before the lack of coolant flow causes the engine to overheat. A crafty solution is to break out the water pump power and ground wires and install a visible 12V LED. When the LED is on, the an aftermarket electric water pump. The pump simply requires 12V and ground for operation. Rather than throwing a switch to turn on the water pump, an easily forgetful and dangerous solution, I relied on the PCM's fuel pump relay control circuit to pick up a new relay that would switch fused battery power to the water pump. In this way, the water pump would always be on while the engine was running.

My remaining concern was that I wouldn't know if the water pump fuse had blown. My solution was to break out the water pump motor power and ground wires, route them inside the passenger compartment, and then install a 12V LED to let me know when the water pump was running.

PCM Calibration for Initial Start

My electronic throttle equipment and manual transmission persuaded me to begin with a GM number 12200411 P01 PCM with 2002 Corvette LS1 T56 base calibration. The custom twin 58-mm throttle body is essentially a 1997–2004 Corvette throttle body with a different housing and the 2004–2005 CTS-V shares the same throttle body and TAC module with the LS1 and LS6 Corvette, so my base calibration options were limited to these vehicles. Having previous experience with the 2002 Corvette base calibration, I knew my chances were excellent to pull off a successful implementation.

HP Tuners was my go-to company for creating the starter calibration. Should its software not support a parameter I need to rework, I can look at the calibration with EFILive software to see if support is available.

Using HP Tuners, I read the base calibration out of the PCM and saved the file on my laptop. I then applied HP Tuners credits toward the use of this PCM so that I could write my calibration changes as often as needed. My approach was to begin by changing known parameters and then adjusting several spark and fuel related tables. My engine builder, Karl Ellwein of Ellwein Engines, provided me with a calibration file from a similar engine he had built, so I copied several tables from his file into my own. I was thorough (to the best of my knowledge) to disable any irrelevant DTCs prior to the first start.

The engine fired up on the first attempt and settled on a nice lopey idle. I was careful to look for any leaks, listen for any unusual noises, and watch coolant temperature and oil pressure. Karl's spark and fuel tables were close, but there was plenty of MAF and VE tuning necessary before I would feel confident with extended amounts of driving.

While troubleshooting an idle issue in closed loop, I temporarily swapped the P01 PCM for a P59 PCM with 2005 CTS-V calibration. With the condition unchanging, I knew my issue was elsewhere. In short, the camshaft profile results in valve overlap that makes closed loop operation undesirable at idle. More noteworthy is that I was unable to get the P59 PCM with 2005 CTS-V calibration to cooperate at all with the tachometer. Since my idle condition was not related to a defective PCM, I reinstalled the P01 PCM to regain the function of the tachometer.

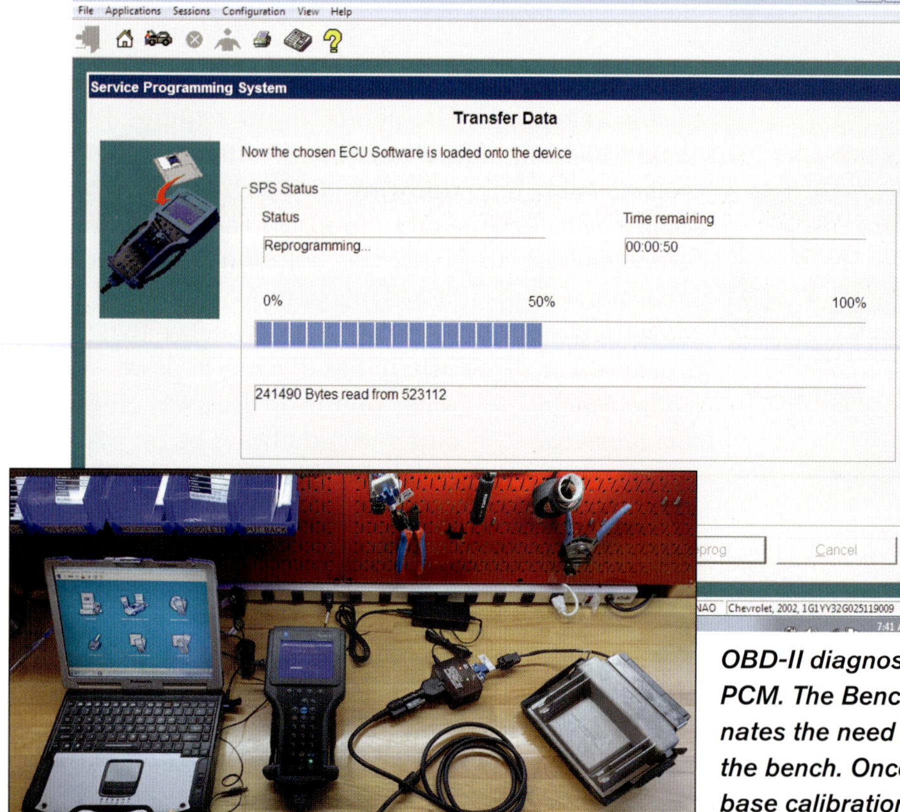

Using GM's TIS2000 software, I loaded a 2002 Corvette LS1 T56 calibration into my Tech 2. The calibration is retrieved from TIS2000 by providing a VIN from a 2002 Corvette fitted with the LS1 engine and T56 manual transmission. Having the latest version of TIS2000, I know that I'm receiving a base calibration free of any defects that may have been revealed when the 2002 Corvette was relatively new. After the Tech 2 is loaded with the base calibration, it is ready to program the PCM through the vehicle's OBD-II diagnostic connector.

After the Tech 2 has been loaded with a calibration for service programming, the Tech 2 is connected to the OBD-II diagnostic connector to communicate with the PCM. The BenchForce off-board harness system eliminates the need for the vehicle to allow programming on the bench. Once the PCM has been programmed with a base calibration, it is ready for custom calibration work in anticipation of the engine's first start.

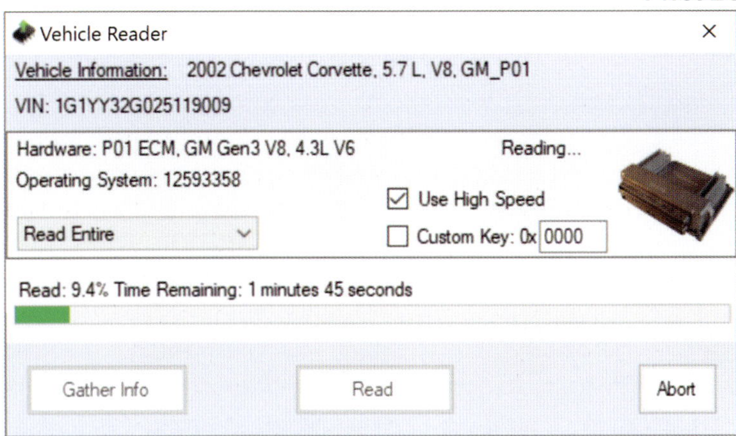

After a GM TIS2000 software base calibration was established in the PCM, the next step was to read the calibration with HP Tuners equipment. The process takes only a few minutes before presenting the available parameters and tables that can be changed.

Enabling PCM functions is accomplished by updating parameter values to represent realistic operating values. Conversely, disabling PCM functions is accomplished by updating parameter values to represent unrealistic operating values. For example, to disable AIR Pump control, the Disable ECT parameter is changed to an engine coolant temperature value that is so high that it will never be reached.

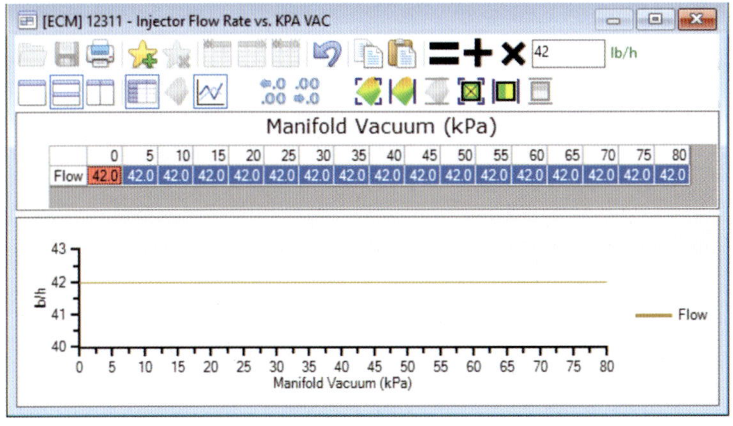

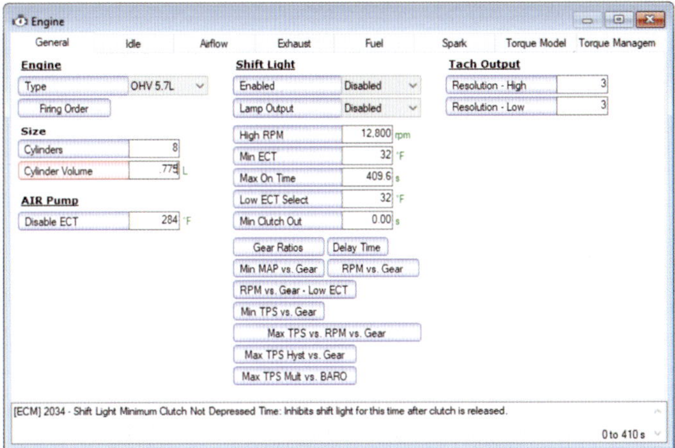

The PCM performs many real-time calculations during engine operation to properly deliver the correct amount of fuel and ignition timing. One of the important parameters to update when the engine size is something other than the base calibration's expectations is the cylinder volume. Because the engine for this application is now 383 ci, the cylinder volume is updated accordingly.

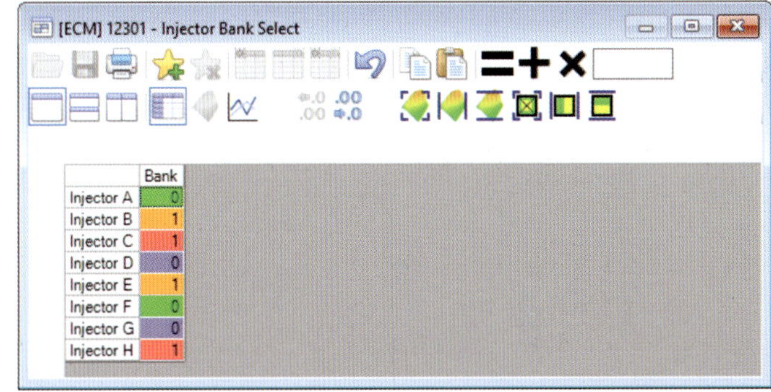

For proper closed-loop engine operation, the PCM must know which bank each injector is assigned to. When the PCM looks at the Injector Bank Select table, if a fuel injector is assigned to the wrong engine bank, that bank will be excessively rich or excessively lean as fuel trims are applied.

One of the critical values used when the PCM calculates fuel delivery is the fuel injector flow rate. Engines fitted with a fuel pressure regulator that is referenced to manifold vacuum require a constant flow rate across the Manifold Vacuum (kPa) range. When no manifold is applied to the fuel pressure regulator, the fuel injector flow rate values must be represented as sloping values across the Manifold Vacuum (kPa) range.

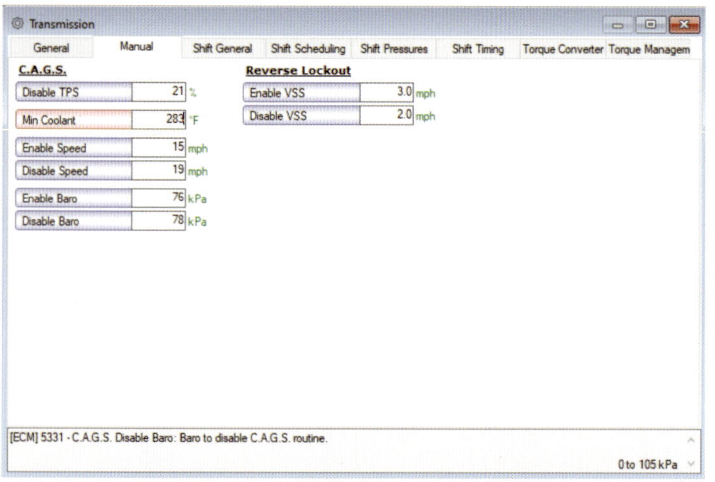

GM T56 6-speed manual transmissions are fitted with a solenoid that can block second and third gear, forcing the driver to either accelerate or shift from first to fourth gear. While the aftermarket offers a plug-in simulator to disable this feature, the better solution to eliminate this feature is to disable it from its source. One of the easiest ways to disable the skip shift feature is to update the Min Coolant parameter value to a coolant temperature so high that it will never be reached.

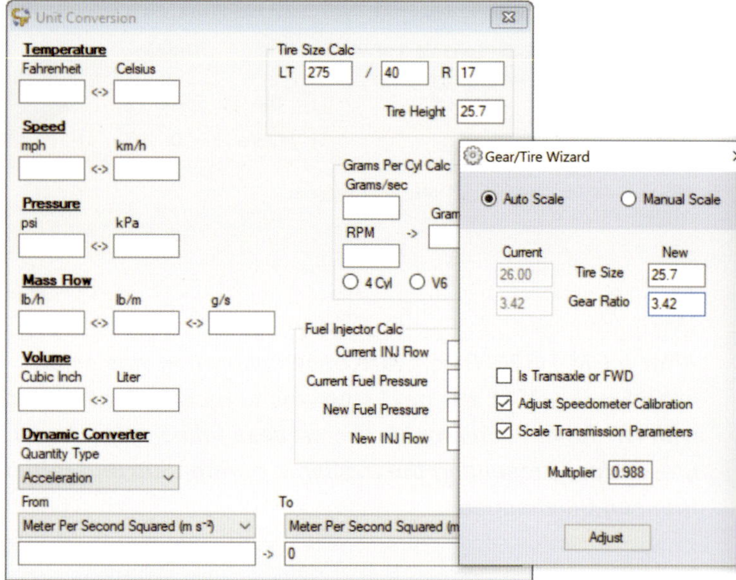

For the PCM to properly calculate vehicle speed, it must know the transmission output shaft pulses per revolution (17 for a GM T56 transmission), tire diameter, and rear-end gear ratio. Using the Unit Conversion utility, the tire height (or diameter) can be calculated. That value, and the vehicle's rear-end gear ratio, must be entered into the Gear/Tire Wizard to determine the adjusted multiplier.

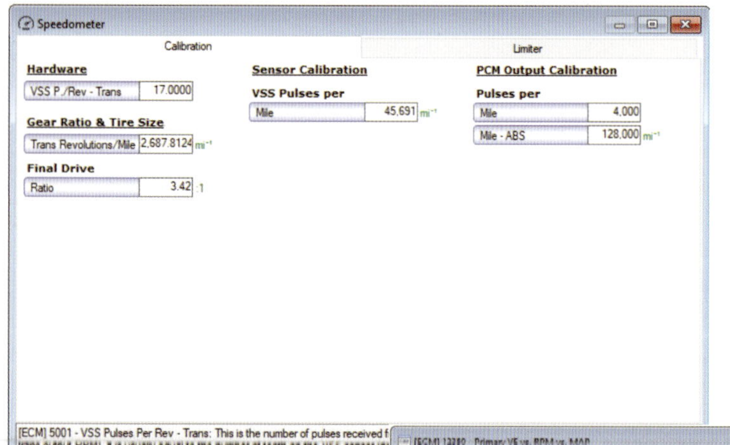

The speedometer calibration parameters may be adjusted to correct the actual vehicle speed that is seen during data logging. Adjust the PCM Output Calibration Pulses per Mile value to send the correct pulse count to the speedometer.

The volumetric efficiency table contains values used in the calculation of fuel delivery. A PCM tuner may rough in this table by data logging during driving or, ideally, using steady state values accomplished by using a chassis load bearing dynamometer. This is one of the important tables for engine operation and performance.

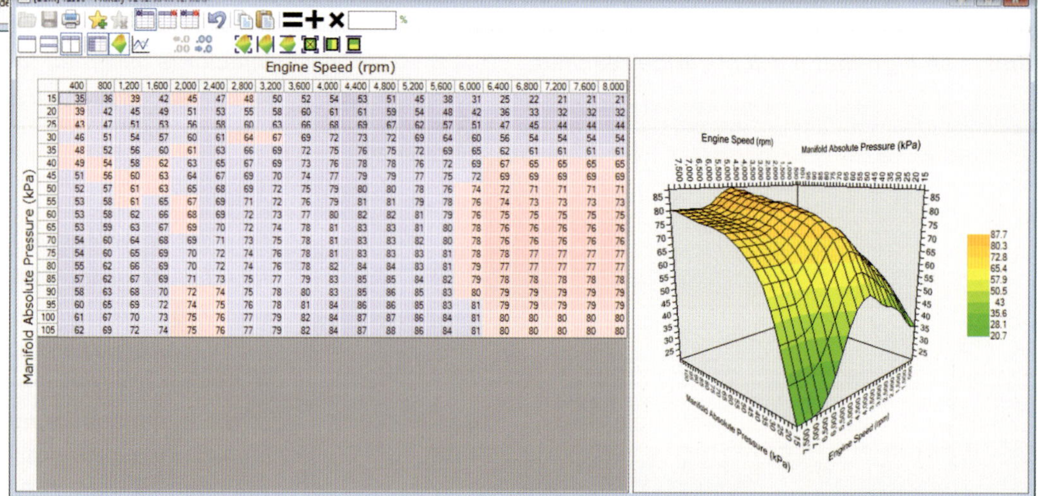

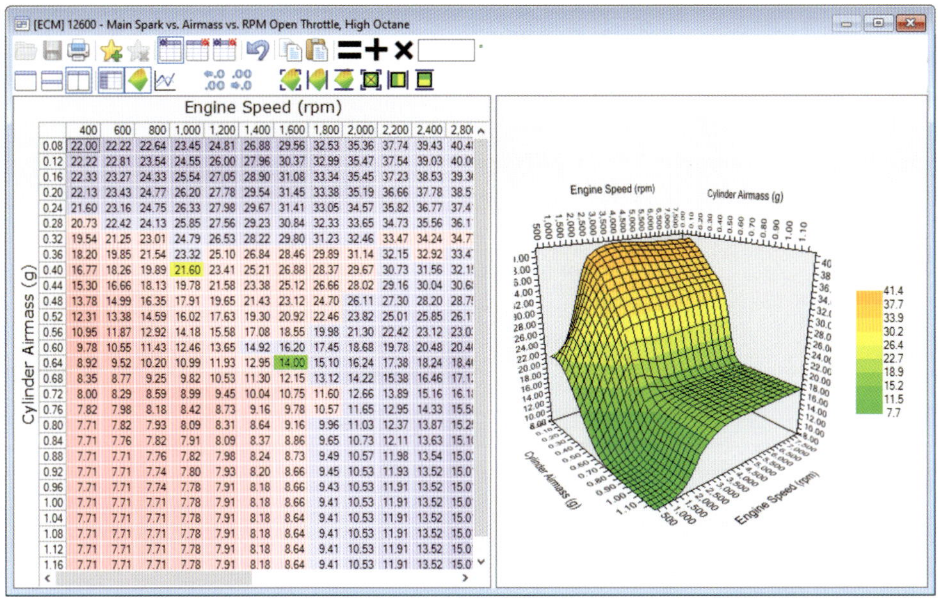

The main spark advance table has much to do with engine performance. Initial values are loaded based on the completed tuning of an engine of a similar build. This table is often finalized by using feedback from an engine or chassis dynamometer.

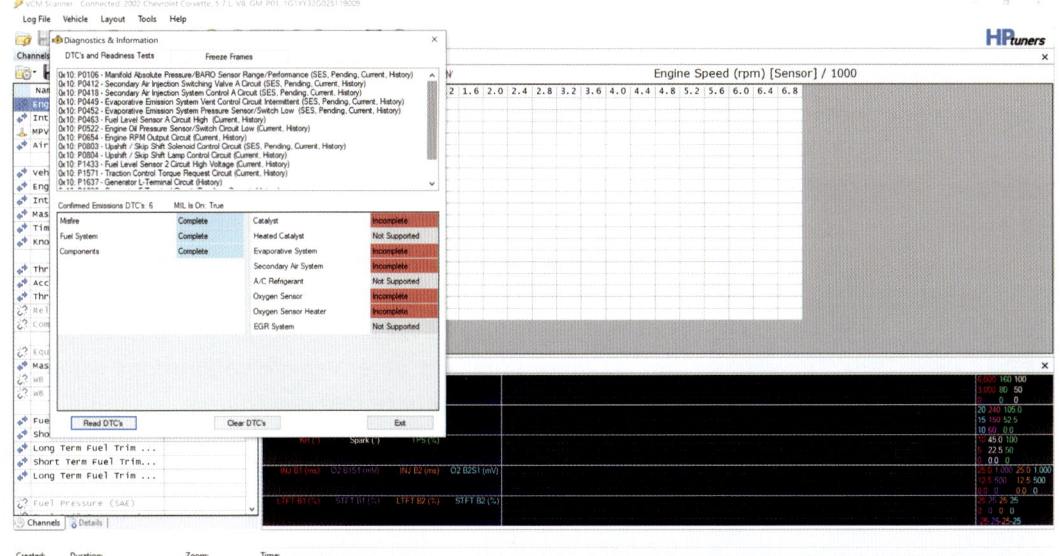

After a thorough walk through the PCM's calibration file, the parameters and tables have been updated to appropriate values that should allow the engine to start and run. There will likely be a long list of DTCs that are set after the initial engine start. All irrelevant DTCs can be noted and then disabled within the calibration file.

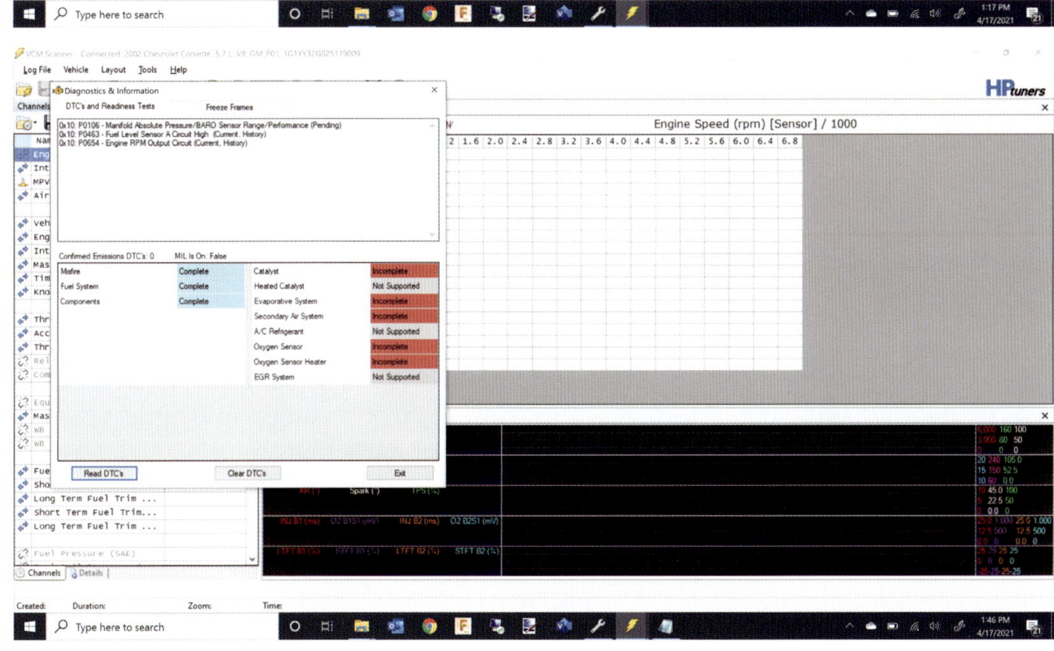

Some DTCs may not reveal themselves upon initial engine start. Expect at least several engine starts to catch the full list of DTCs that can be considered for being disabled. Be sure to deal with irrelevant DTCs sooner rather than later because they can prevent functions such as crankshaft variation relearn and electric fan operation.

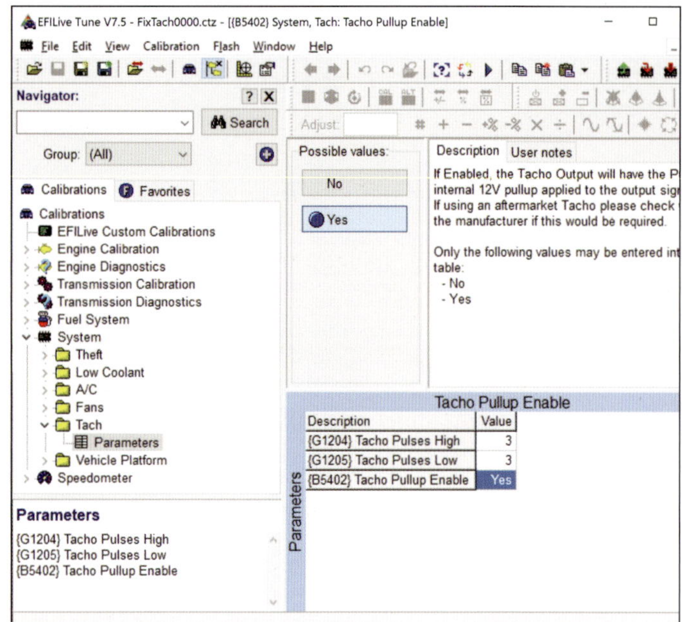

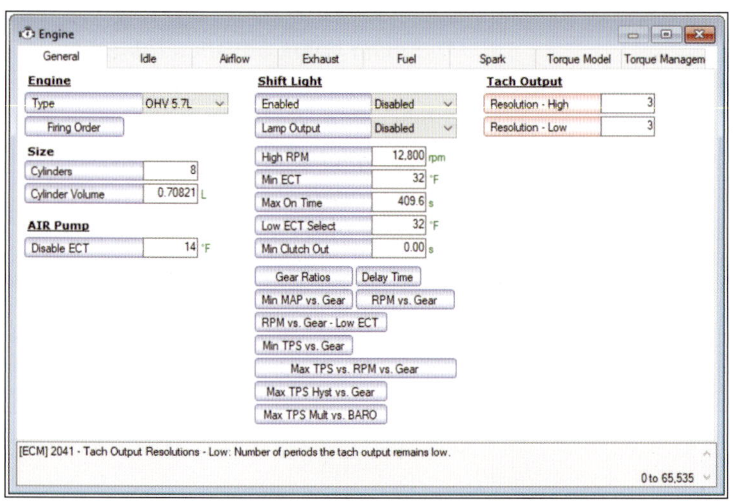

Typical tachometer output settings include the three parameters: Resolution - High, Resolution - Low, and 12V Pullup Enable. Not all calibrations present the option to change the 12V Pullup Enable value. This 2002 Corvette calibration is an example of one where HP Tuners software does not present the parameter. Unfortunately for the Camaro's tachometer, the default Corvette 12V Pullup setting (which is "No") prevents the tachometer from working at all.

This is a common question: "Which is better—EFILive or HP Tuners?" It's not a fair question because the answer depends on your usage. In general, it's best to consider which vehicles are supported. However, there are cases where EFILive offers a parameter that HP Tuners doesn't and vice versa. In the case of the 2002 Corvette calibration, HP Tuners software does not present the 12V tachometer pullup parameter. To enable the 12V tachometer pullup, EFILive can be used. This is not to say that HP Tuners never presents 12V tachometer pullup, as there are many other vehicle calibrations within HP Tuners software where this is available.

Boasting nearly 225 hp and 175 ft-lbs of torque more than the production 1996 Corvette LT4 engine, this Camaro is built to outperform most LS engines. EFI Connection's 24x/1x crank/cam signal conversion enables the use of the more-than-capable GM number 12200411 PCM to allow for a near seamless wiring integration into the vehicle. The novelty of the electronic 58-mm throttle body brings the added touch of GM's responsive cruise control system. Enthusiasts should count the costs and consider the capabilities of a GM engine management system before rushing to the aftermarket for what could be a lesser solution.

Final Impressions

This Camaro is impressive in so many ways, but what impresses me the most is the cleanliness of PCM integration into the vehicle's existing wiring, instrument cluster gauges, air-conditioning system, and cruise control switches. I wasn't able to say the same for the Holley Dominator ECU that was previously installed in the car.

GM's equipment is arguably cleaner, more reliable, just as capable, easier to troubleshoot, and far less expensive than what the aftermarket has to offer. As far as I'm concerned, and for what this vehicle requires for engine management, the GM number 12200411 PCM and related custom wiring were only an upgrade to the aftermarket equipment removed from the car.

Project 2:

P59 PCM Swap in a 1990 K1500 GM Ram Jet 350 4L60E

Who doesn't love a clean 1988–1998 Old Body Style (OBS) Chevrolet pickup truck with four-wheel drive? I found a local rust-free 1990 K1500 with a L19 7.4L TBI engine and 700R4 transmission while looking for a shop project.

The big-block engine was cleanly transplanted into this OBS by a previous owner, likely for towing purposes. While the engine ran well, there was nothing exciting about its performance. With a rated 230 hp and 380 ft-lbs torque, it does not

While browsing local online listings for Chevrolet BBC engines, I found a clean 1990 K1500 with a transplanted L19 7.4L TBI engine. The truck was an excellent buy to provide an L19 engine for new product development on the test stand and then as a roller ready for a more modern drivetrain and engine management system. With strong aftermarket support, any parts needed were simply an online search away.

While this truck came from the factory with a L05 5.7L TBI engine, the L19 7.4L TBI engine in the truck when I purchased it showed very few signs of engine wire harness rework, as the ECM required nothing more than an updated calibration in the PROM for the larger injectors and displacement. Any wire harness changes would have only been necessary to address length differences.

Prior to its installation in the truck, the Ram Jet 350 was mounted to the engine test stand with a coil-per-cylinder ignition system, P01 GM number 12200411 PCM, stand-alone harness, and 5.3L truck cable throttle body. An initial startup on the test stand was a fast way to check for any unforeseen problems. Dealing with issues after the engine is installed in the truck can be difficult to the point of having to remove for diagnosis and repair. With successful time on the engine test stand, the engine was ready for installation.

The P59 GM number 12576106 PCM is one of the Gen III LS-series controllers compatible with both electronic and cable throttle systems. Electronic throttle systems will require the use of a 2003-and-newer truck or van TAC module and pedal assembly. Cable throttle is supported due to the inclusion of IAC motor drivers on the main board. Used with many 2003-and-newer GM trucks and vans, this PCM is inexpensive, not hard to find, and suitable for most Gen III LS-series engine conversions.

no-brainer. This truck would experience better performance and drivability while allowing for PCM controlled shift points and firmness. A local transmission shop hooked me up with a fresh build and fresh 4x4 transfer case. With EFILive or HP Tuners, I would be able to adjust torque converter lockup and shift behavior.

With my engine and transmission details known, I then considered the LS-series PCM choices for this project. My go-to would typically be the ever-popular GM number 12200411 PCM, which is a P01 engine and transmission controller that supports the earliest GM electronic throttle systems (cable throttle is supported too). This would be fine, but the 2003-and-newer GM

truck electronic throttle equipment is plentiful and doesn't carry the high resale costs of the LS1 Corvette equipment. By using a P59 PCM from a 2003-and-newer GM truck, I was able to use the common and plentiful truck electronic throttle equipment, 4L60E transmission, integrated cruise control, and electric fan support.

The GM Ram Jet 350 crate engine includes a marine electronic fuel injection (MEFI 4) ECM. This basic batch-fire engine management system lacks the robustness of the LS-series PCMs/ECMs. Using a single coil and distributor ignition system from the mid-1980s, there was much to be gained by tossing this MEFI system aside in favor of a newer LS-series PCM for the added benefits of coil-per-cylinder ignition, electronic throttle, cruise control, and 4L60E transmission control.

	MEFI 4	P01	P59	E40	E38	E67	E78	Notes
Gen III 2003-and-up truck throttle body			X					Direct bolt-on Ram Jet 350; lowest cost
GM 6.5L diesel truck pedal		X	X					Direct bolt-on to 1988–1998 GM trucks
Discrete electric fans		X	X	X	X	X		2005 Chevrolet Avalanche fans
Fans on with A/C pressure		X	X	X	X	X		Add 0-5V A-C pressure sensor to high-pressure line
Integrated cruise control		X	X	X		X		Supports classic multi-function lever switches
4L60E transmission control		X	X	X	X	X		Requires 1996-and-up 4L60E for compatability

After knowing the engine and transmission components of my project, I considered my ECU choices. The MEFI 4 ECM bundled with the GM Ram Jet 350 crate engine totally strikes out. While the P01 has been a go-to through the years, my decision to use the 2003-and-up GM truck throttle body ultimately put me into a P59 PCM. The newer Gen IV ECMs either don't support direct cruise control signals or don't have known compatibility with the GM 6.5L diesel truck pedal; a direct bolt-on to my 1990 K1500 truck. The decision to use the P59 PCM further let me know that I'd be installing an EFI Connection 24x/1x crank/cam signal conversion on this Ram Jet 350 crate engine.

compare well with newer V-8 engines.

I've been a fan of the GM Ram Jet 350 crate engine and felt that this was an excellent engine choice because with 345 hp and 396 ft-lbs of torque, it easily outperforms the L19 engine. Being a Gen I SBC, the Ram Jet 350 was more of a bolt-in than an LS-series engine. An EFI Connection 24x/1x crank/cam signal conversion allows the use of any Gen III LS-series PCM and the Ram Jet 350 intake manifold's LS throttle body bolt pattern meant that I could simply remove the included cable throttle body and install any Gen III LS-series electronic throttle body.

The 700R4 transmission had to go. With Gen III LS-series PCM support, a 4L60E transmission is just a

24x/1x Crank/Cam Signal Conversion

The GM Ram Jet 350 crate engine does not contain the crankshaft and camshaft position signals required by the P59 PCM. Requiring the 24x crankshaft and 1x camshaft signals of the Gen III LS-series engines, an EFI Connection part number 120-00071 SBC 24x/1x crank/cam signal conversion hardware kit was installed.

EFI Connection has been the leader in Gen I SBC and Gen II LT1 crankshaft signal solutions for use with GM LS-series PCMs, ECMs, and many aftermarket ECUs. Featuring a GM-style design with a 24-tooth crankshaft reluctor that installs on the snout of the crankshaft, the engine timing cover hides the reluctor and receives a production GM Vortec crankshaft position sensor.

The 24-tooth crankshaft reluctor included in EFI Connection's kit is designed for use with the production 1996-and-newer GM SBC timing cover, which is the same timing cover that was originally installed on the Ram Jet 350. In fact, the Ram Jet 350 includes a production GM 4-tooth crankshaft reluctor that was simply removed and replaced with the 24-tooth crankshaft reluctor. After the timing cover reassembly, the engine was fitted with the crankshaft signal necessary to use the P59 PCM as if it were a Gen III LS-series engine!

The PCM must know more than crankshaft position to operate a sequential fire injection system. By adding the required 1x camshaft signal, the PCM will know engine stroke (intake or exhaust). The included 1x camshaft synchronizer serves the purpose of providing the Gen III LS-series 50-percent on/off camshaft position signal while driving the SBC engine oil pump. A clean aluminum dust cap sits on top of the cam sync, replacing the rotor and traditional distributor cap found on this 1996-and-newer Vortec distributor. GM used this same design, a modified Vortec distributor assembly, with the 24x-equipped L21 BBC engines in 1998.

EFI Connection's 1x SBC cam sync is more or less a 1996-and-newer production replacement GM Vortec distributor with high-voltage components removed in favor of an aluminum dust cap. During engine operation, the cam sync reluctor passes through a slot in the camshaft position sensor to generate a 50-percent duty cycle (signal high 50 percent and then low 50 percent) so that the PCM can determine on which stroke (intake or exhaust) the engine is. As an added benefit, this cam sync also serves the purpose of driving the engine's oil pump.

Engine Wire Harness Build

To many enthusiasts, the most intimidating part of any drivetrain swap is the wiring. The engine wire harness included with the GM Ram Jet 350 crate engine was not designed for this application and the original truck harness was configured for the L19 7.4L TBI engine, so a new harness would have to be made from scratch.

In addition, the truck's original engine bay wire harness included non-fuel injection functions, such as wipers, ABS, the starter, four-wheel drive, power to the interior fuse block, etc. A stand-alone harness build would satisfy the engine and transmission functions but leave the

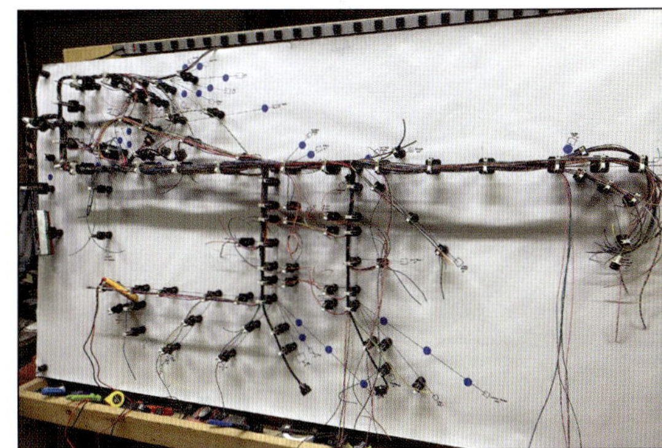

Engine wire harnesses are professionally built on template assembly boards that allow the assembler to route wires so that the finished assembly will properly fit the layout of the intended engine and transmission. Beginning with the PCM connectors, wires are added one at a time until the entire template has been populated. By using the original engine bay wire harness to create a template, the new harness assembly is sure to properly fit the truck with connections routed where they need to go. Once all of the wires have been applied to the template, the assembler moves on to the connector assembly and then final continuity check.

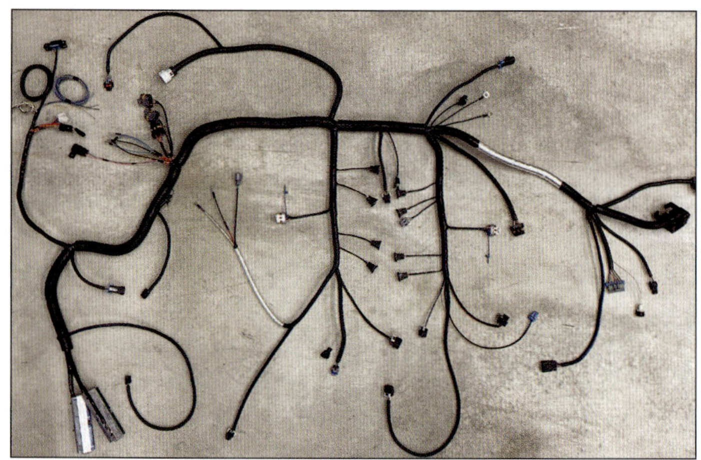

A completed OEM-quality engine wire harness assembly is the result of careful planning and meticulous detail. One-off engine wire harness builds may take more than one week to complete, as the assembler carefully studies the GM schematics of multiple vehicles to determine the correct components and connector pinout details. With high-temperature split loom and segments of reflective heat tape applied, this engine harness is ready for plug-and-play installation.

This K1500 was factory equipped with the larger heavy-duty radiator. For this, the 2005 Chevrolet Avalanche electric fan assembly is a near-perfect fit, requiring only minor trimming to cover the area between the radiator tanks. Trucks with the standard radiator can use the 2002 Camaro/Firebird electric fan assembly with minor modifications.

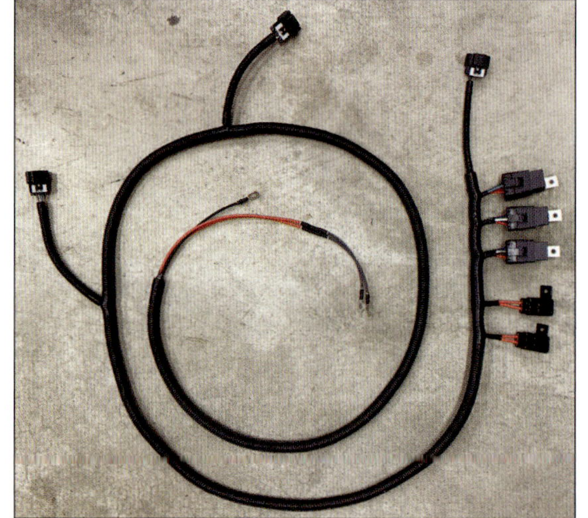

Electric fan harnesses must be constructed with wire sized appropriately for harness lengths and the current draw of the fans. Always consult the electric fan manufacturer for its wire size recommendation. An independent electric fan harness needs only relay coil power and relay coil grounds (control wires from PCM) from the main engine wire harness for operation. A three-relay configuration allows for the two fans to run in low and high speed operation as the third relay switches fan power from series to parallel. Alternatively, two relays can be used for independent on/off operation.

truck without the necessary wires for proper operation. A plug-and-play engine wire harness for a 1990 K1500 that has a Ram Jet 350 engine, electronic throttle, 4L60E transmission and P59 PCM is a tall order; it's not something you're going to find off the shelf.

Being a longtime engine wire harness builder and owning a production wire harness facility, I was definitely at an advantage to tackle this project. However, a patiently dedicated enthusiast could accomplish this work by reworking a stand-alone LS engine wire harness where necessary and grafting the assembly into a modified original truck engine bay wire harness. With proper techniques, much of the production equipment I had to my advantage could be substituted with hobbyist tools. Do-it-yourself online stores, such as www.eficonnection.com, offer the wire harness components necessary to make changes to your existing wire harness.

Electric Fan Installation

The 1988–1998 GM trucks did not receive electric fans but were fitted with an engine-driven fan. I opted to use a dual electric fan assembly from a 2005 Chevrolet Avalanche. This fan assembly was a clean fit (after very little trimming) to the heavy-duty radiator already installed in the truck. With the P59 PCM supporting up to two electric fans, this solution is fully sufficient to maintain engine coolant temperature.

Fuel Pump and Fuel Hoses

The GM TBI system uses a low-pressure fuel pump that is not capable of the fuel demands of any multi-port fuel injection manifold with eight independent fuel injectors. Being a direct bolt-on, I replaced the TBI pump on the 1990 K1500 fuel sending unit assembly with a fuel pump from a 1985–1992 Camaro L98 5.7L TPI.

The 42-psi fuel pressure within the Ram Jet 350 fuel system would exceed the TBI rubber hose pressure rating, so I also replaced the fuel lines with braided PTFE hose and -6 AN fittings. No wiring changes were necessary for the operation of the new fuel pump.

With the bed removed, the fuel pump sending unit assembly can be easily removed. For this Ram Jet 350 fuel system, a high-pressure fuel pump was required to supply 42 psi at the fuel rails. The 1985–1992 Camaro L98 5.7L TPI fuel pump is a direct replacement to the TBI pump mounted to the sending unit assembly within the fuel tank. Braided PTFE hoses and -6 AN fittings made quick work of upgrading the fuel lines for the higher fuel pressure.

PCM Base Calibration

I sourced a reconditioned P59 GM number 12576106 PCM through eBay for about $75 shipped. "Reconditioned" usually means that the case was bead blasted clean and then listed for sale. That was good enough

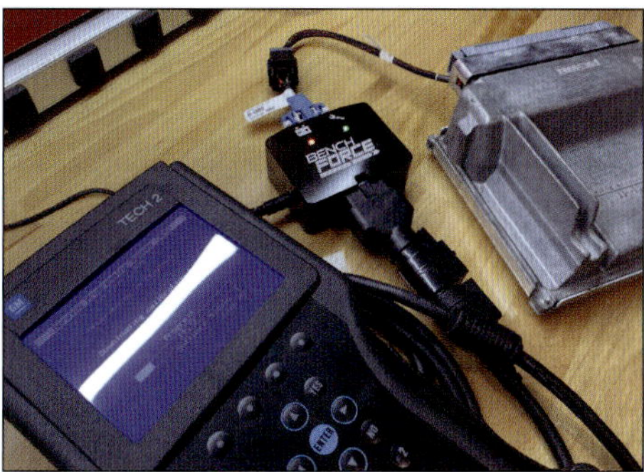

By using BenchForce off-board programming equipment with a GM Tech 2 and TIS2000 software, the P59 PCM can be loaded with the necessary base calibration for this 2003 Chevrolet Express 5.3L 4L60E application. The Tech 2 receives the correct calibration from TIS2000 based on the supplied VIN. Then, the Tech 2 is connected to the BenchForce PowerBlock switch assembly's OBD-II diagnostic connector to establish communication with the PCM for service programming. When the programming is complete, the PCM is as it would be if it were pulled from the 2003 Express.

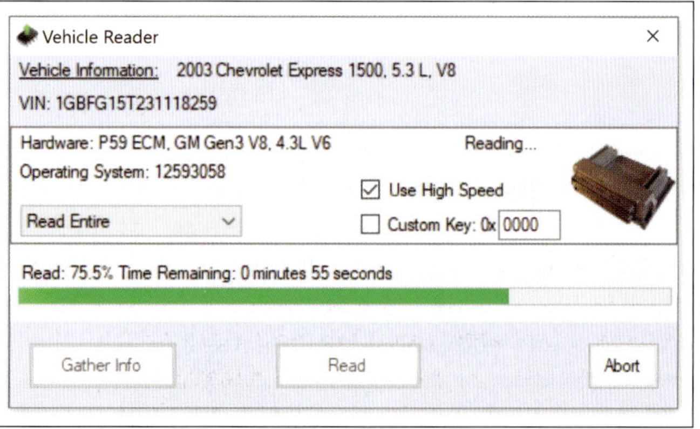

for me, as the reputable seller offered a one-year warranty.

Being used, the PCM was sure to contain an original GM calibration from the salvaged vehicle it was pulled from. The best base calibration suited for my engine and transmission requirements is found in the 2003 Chevrolet Express 5.3L 4L60E. This GM calibration is a perfect starting point for me to work with to accomplish PCM control of the engine, coil-per-cylinder ignition system, electronic throttle system, 4L60E transmission, electric fans, and cruise control. Using my BenchForce equipment, I connected my GM Tech 2 and TIS2000 laptop to flash in the 2003 Express Van calibration.

Custom Tuning for a Starter Calibration

With the appropriate base calibration loaded in the PCM, many calibration parameters and tables must be updated prior to the first engine start. In this case, the PCM expects to be controlling a stock 5.3L LS-series engine. The Ram Jet 350 engine will likely not run well with the 5.3L calibration. Using HP Tuners VCM Editor, I first read the calibration out of the PCM so that I could see the

To retrieve a PCM or ECM calibration file for editing purposes with the HP Tuners VCM Editor, the MPVI2 interface must first be connected to the vehicle's OBD-II diagnostic connector. By using the Read Vehicle function within the VCM Editor, the user selects the ECU type and begins the read process. When the Read Vehicle process is complete, the calibration file is ready to save and then open for the user to make any necessary changes.

calibration parameters and tables in an editor. Next, I'll walk through many of the calibration changes made prior to starting the engine in the truck.

Disabling PCM Generator Control

The System Options table presents engine-related options by vehicle type. Being that we are working with the 2003 Express, the represented vehicle is GMT610. The generator in the 1990 K1500 is not controlled by the ECM. I had a preference to keep it that way, so I updated the default Alt L-Term and Alt F-Term settings to values of 0.

Fuel Injector Flow Rate

By looking up the fuel injector part number for the Ram Jet 350, I found that the injectors are the same as were used with the Gen II LT1 engines. LT1 PCM calibration data reveals a flow rate of about 24 lbs/hr. Being that the Ram Jet 350 fuel pressure is referenced to manifold vacuum, I know to set the fuel injector flow rate to near 24 lbs/hr across the manifold vacuum range.

Injector Bank Select Table

For fuel trims to be applied correctly during closed-loop operation, the Injector Bank Select table must properly map fuel injectors to engine banks. Because the Ram Jet 350 is a Gen 1 SBC maintaining the traditional SBC firing order, my 5.3L LS calibration values must be changed to reflect the firing order of the Gen 1 SBC engine.

I've already swapped injectors (and coils) control outputs 2 and 3 as well as 7 and 4 at the PCM connectors within the engine wire harness, so now I swap values representing cylinders 2 and 3 as well as 7 and 4. A value of 0 represents Bank 1 (engine cylinders 1, 3, 5, and 7). A value of

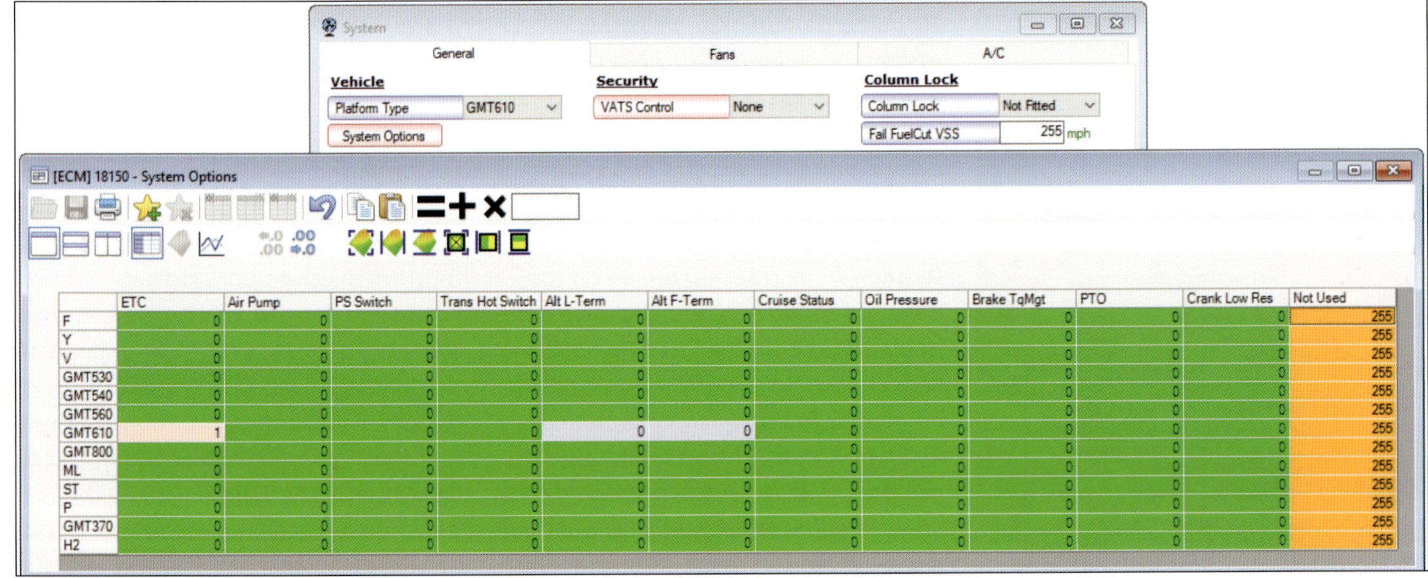

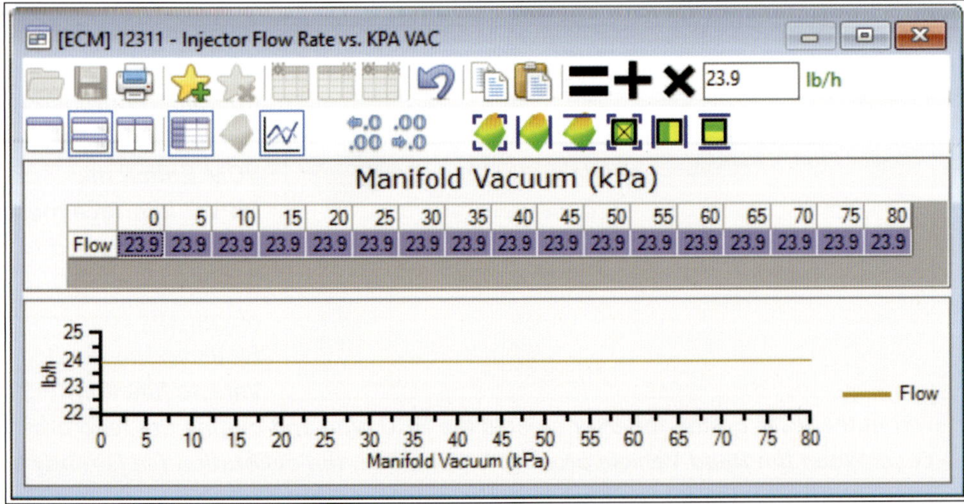

The System Options table is accessed in HP Tuners VCM Editor by clicking through the following path: System > General > (Vehicle) System Options.

The Injector Flow Rate table is accessed in HP Tuners VCM Editor by clicking through the following path: Engine > Fuel > General > (Flow Rate) Flow Rate vs. KPA.

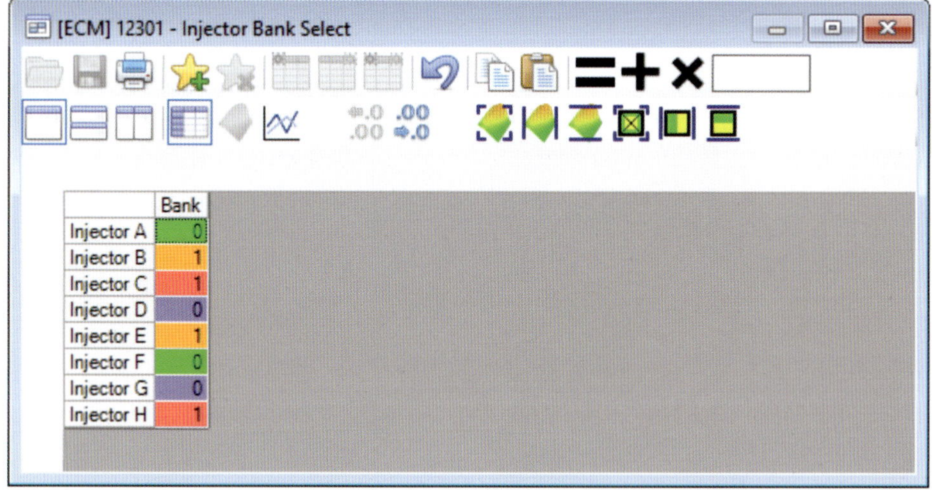

The Injector Bank Select table is accessed in HP Tuners VCM Editor by clicking through the following path: Engine > Fuel > General > (Injector Control) Injector Bank Select.

1 represents Bank 2 (engine cylinders 2, 4, 6, and 8). The alphabetic representation of injectors as ABCDEFGH = 18726543. Updating this table does not change the engine firing order. LS-series engines maintaining the LS-series firing order must use the default values within this table.

MAF Calibration Table

I chose to use the larger 85-mm round MAF sensor in the airstream ahead of the throttle body. I confirmed the 2003 Express was fitted with a smaller MAF sensor, so I had to update the MAF calibration table to more accurately reflect the sensor that is used. Many Gen III LS-series trucks are fitted with the 85-mm MAF, so I copied and pasted the values from a stock 2003 Silverado SS 6.0L calibration into my calibration. I expect minor modifications to this table to be necessary after installing a wideband oxygen sensor and monitoring the air/fuel mixture during engine operation.

Volumetric Efficiency Table

Additional fueling calculations are based on the volumetric efficiency table. This table represents the air-mass per cylinder and becomes the fail-safe table, relying on the MAP sensor when the MAF sensor has failed. While it's necessary to log actual air/fuel mixture with a wideband oxygen sensor to determine the calibration changes necessary to this table, I reached out to Jim Hall of TPIS for a calibration from a similar Ram Jet 350 engine he had tuned years ago to copy and paste initial values to start with. My dyno tuner will validate and adjust these table values as necessary on a load-bearing dyno. Known as "steady state" tuning, a load-bearing dyno allows the tuner to hold various RPM and Manifold Absolute Pressure cells to determine how rich or lean the engine runs at that state.

Spark Advance Table

The primary spark advance table, high octane, is used during normal engine operating conditions. the

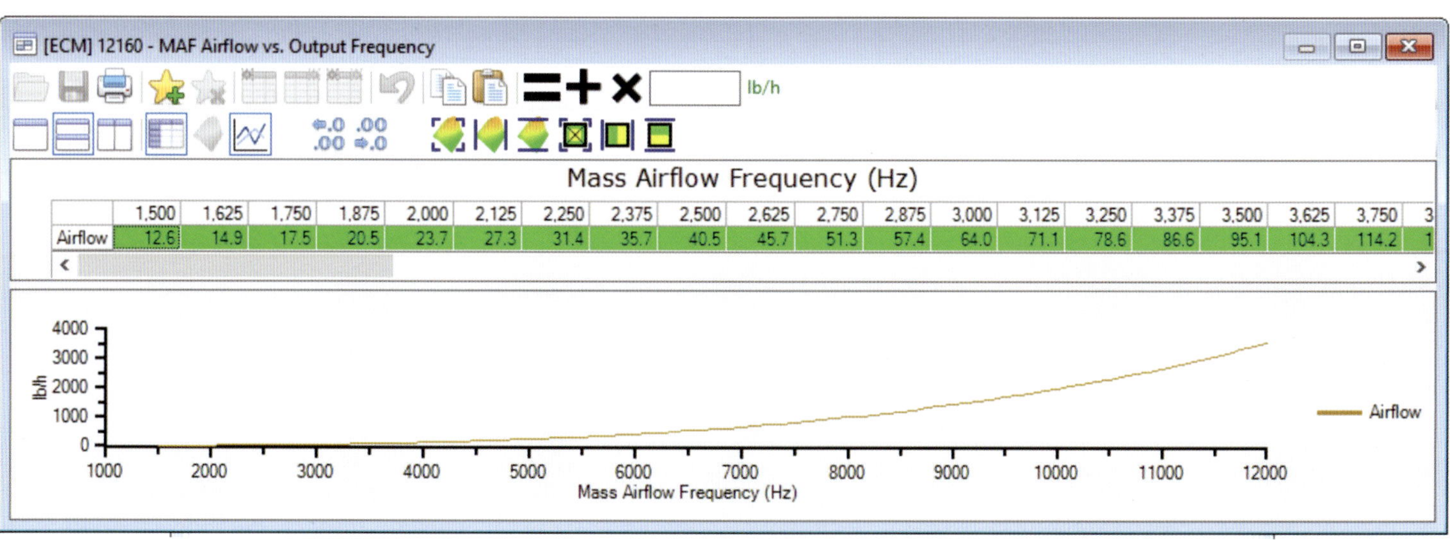

	1,500	1,625	1,750	1,875	2,000	2,125	2,250	2,375	2,500	2,625	2,750	2,875	3,000	3,125	3,250	3,375	3,500	3,625	3,750	3
Airflow	12.6	14.9	17.5	20.5	23.7	27.3	31.4	35.7	40.5	45.7	51.3	57.4	64.0	71.1	78.6	86.6	95.1	104.3	114.2	1

The MAF Calibration Airflow vs. Frequency table is accessed in HP Tuners VCM Editor by clicking through the following path: Engine > Airflow > General > (MAF Calibration) Airflow vs. Frequency.

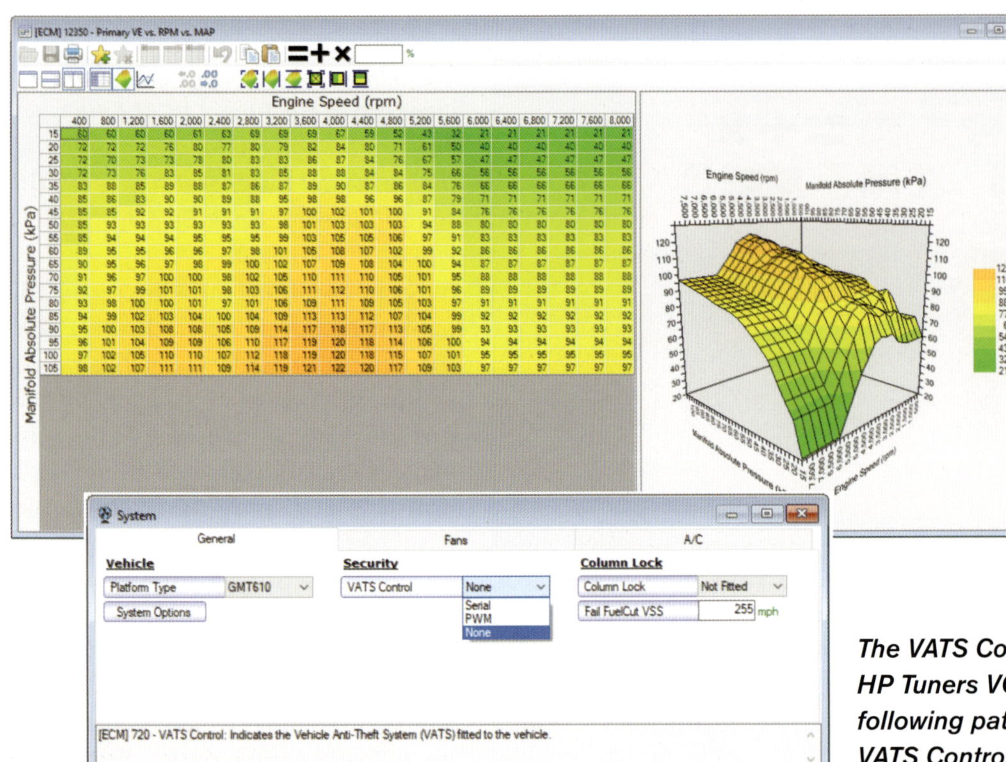

The Main VE table is accessed in HP Tuners VCM Editor by clicking through the following path: Engine > Airflow > General > (Main VE) Primary.

The VATS Control settings are accessed in HP Tuners VCM Editor by clicking through the following path: System > General > (Security) VATS Control.

low octane table contains safe spark advance values for reference during conditions where knock sensor activity is present. There are other calibration values that affect actual commanded spark advance, but for now, I will only update this table. As I have no prior experience with Ram Jet 350 tuning, I again look to Jim Hall's Ram Jet 350 calibration for copy-and-paste data into my startup calibration.

VATS

GM implemented a security system in the 2003 Express that prevents the PCM from allowing the engine to run. HP Tuners makes the removal of this security system as simple as changing one calibration setting. By choosing "None" for VATS Control, the PCM no longer looks for the okay signal prior to starting the engine.

Electric Fan Settings

The 2003 Express was not fitted with electric fans, so the PCM calibration needs quite a bit of work within the fans section to properly support the dual fan implementation in the truck. I simply copied and pasted the electric fan settings from a 2002 Camaro into the 2003 Express calibration and then lowered the on/off coolant temperature settings for each fan control.

Air-Conditioning Settings

For the dual electric fans to work correctly, I made one change to the A/C settings. Because the 2003 Express was not fitted with electric

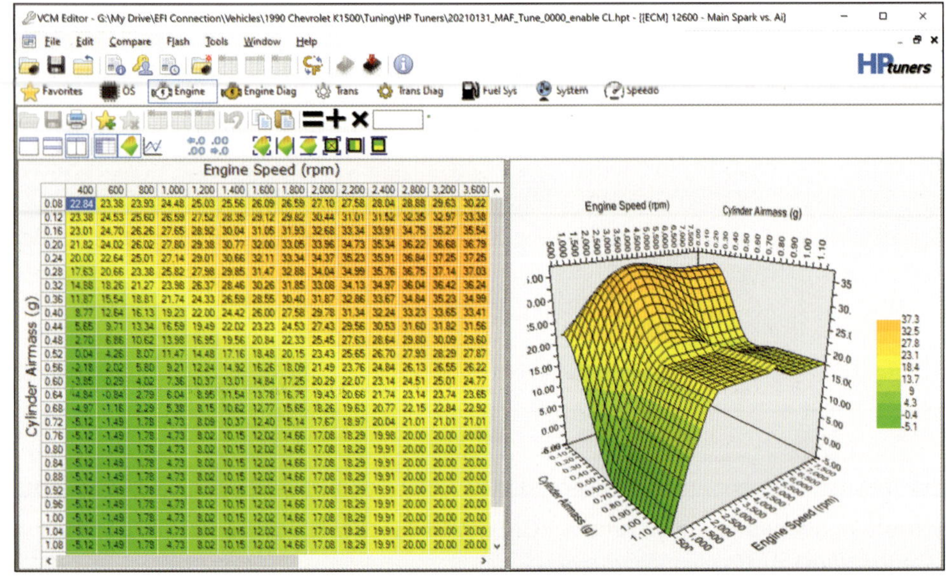

The primary Spark Advance table is accessed in HP Tuners VCM Editor by clicking through the following path: Engine > Spark > Advance > (Base) High Octane.

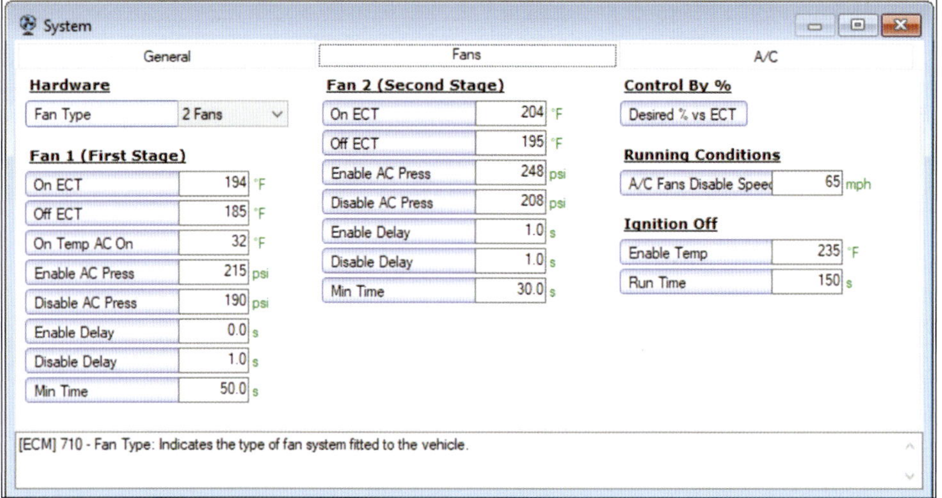

The electric fan settings are accessed in HP Tuners VCM Editor by clicking through the following path: System > Fans.

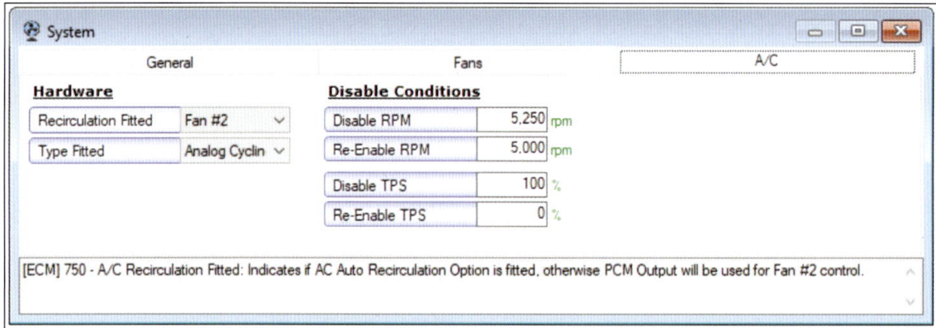

The air-conditioning settings are accessed in HP Tuners VCM Editor by clicking through the following path: System > A/C.

fans, PCM's Fan #2 control output is not set to control an electric fan relay. By changing Recirculation Fitted to a value of Fan #2, the PCM uses pin 33 of PCM Green connector for Fan #2 control. Additional settings related to Fan #2 are found in the Fans section of the same System window, which is just one tab to the left.

VSS Pulse Count, Tire Size, and Gear Ratio

At the very least, the PCM must have correct vehicle speed settings to properly shift the 4L60E transmission. A quick look at other PCM settings also reveals that vehicle speed is necessary. Three pieces of information are necessary for the PCM to

properly calculate vehicle speed: (1) the pulse count the PCM sees from the VSS mounted in the tail housing of the transmission (or in this case

NP241C transfer case), (2) tire size, and (3) gear ratio.

The NP241C transfer case is fitted with a 40-tooth reluctor on the output shaft, which produces a VSS signal of 40 pulses to the PCM per driveshaft revolution. The RPO sticker was missing from the glove box, but the original window sticker in the glove box revealed this truck is fitted with a 3.73 ratio gear set in the rear (and front) differential.

The truck received a brand new set of Goodyear Wrangler Fortitude HT 265/65R18 tires. We're going to need to know the actual tire height, so I used the convenient Unit Conversion utility (Tools > Unit Conversion) to determine the tire height in inches to be 31.6. I simply used the Gear/Tire Wizard (Edit > Gear/Tire Wizard) to input the new tire size and gear ratio and then click the Adjust button. Before calling this done, I navigate to the Speedometer section to verify that the VSS pulse count is set to 40.

That's all there is to it. The PCM is now configured correctly to accurately know vehicle speed. However, there is more work to be done in this truck to make the speedometer in

The Unit Conversion utility is accessed in HP Tuners VCM Editor by clicking the through the following path: Tools > Unit Conversion. The Gear/Tire Wizard is accessed in HP Tuners VCM Editor by clicking the following path: Edit > Gear/Tire Wizard.

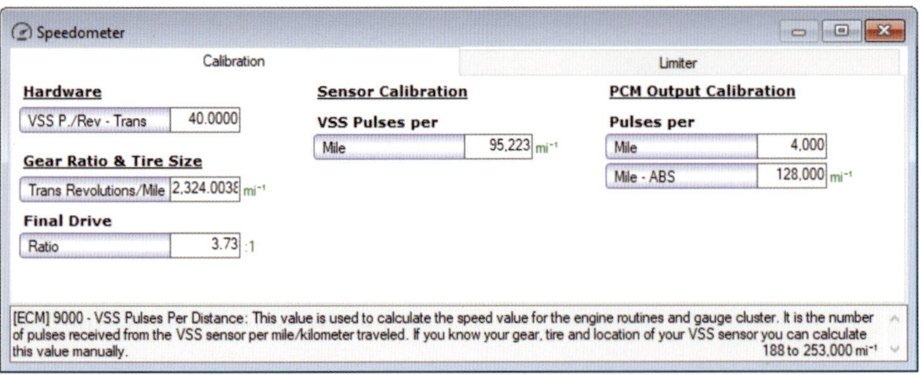

The VSS pulse count setting is accessed in HP Tuners VCM Editor by clicking through the following path: Speedo > Calibration > (Hardware) VSS P./Rev - Trans.

the instrument cluster read correctly. More on that later.

The First Start

Well, how did I do? I worked out any potential problems on the engine test stand prior to engine and transmission installation. I thoroughly studied the 1990 K1500 schematics and 2003 Express schematics to build a plug-and-play engine wire harness. The PCM has been loaded with a 2003 Express 5.3L 4L60E base calibration using GM's TIS2000 Service Programming System. Using HP Tuners VCM Editor, I updated several tables and parameters to better reflect the equipment I'm working with. I'm off to a great start, so now the true test is to start the engine and observe how it runs.

There's really no better way to determine if your engine is running with the proper air/fuel mixture than to monitor the exhaust with a good wideband oxygen sensor and controller. For that, I installed a wideband oxygen sensor ahead of the catalytic converter and connected my Innovate LM-2 Digital Air/Fuel Ratio Meter.

The initial startup revealed the engine is running near perfect. In a short time, and as coolant temperature rises, the PCM will go into closed loop and apply fuel trims to adjust the air/fuel mixture in an attempt to maintain the commanded stoichiometric air/fuel ratio.

While it is not covered in this book, I brought my wideband oxygen signal into HP Tuners VCM Scanner using the MPVI2 Pro Link cable so that I could monitor and log the air/fuel ratio with my laptop. This is especially useful when creating histograms that allow the tuner to copy and paste MAF and VE table error correction.

Cruise Control Wiring

The 1990 K1500 was fitted with a cable-driven cruise control module located on the firewall just above the brake booster. The wiring for the original cruise control module passes through a firewall grommet. Conveniently, the 2003 Truck TAC module can be bolted to the same

The 2003-and-up GM TAC module is designed to be mounted in the engine compartment. With the original cable-driven cruise control module removed from the truck, the TAC module is attached to the firewall using the three available bolt holes. The original firewall grommet was repurposed for the TAC to accelerator pedal harness. The second harness connection is used for power, cruise control, and throttle body functions.

A wideband oxygen sensor and controller are relatively inexpensive equipment to have in your shop toolbox. By monitoring the exhaust with a wideband oxygen sensor, you can determine how rich or lean the engine is running. Many controllers allow the user to choose between displaying air-to-fuel ratio or lambda. In the case of this application, the ideal stoichiometric air/fuel mixture of 14.7:1 will display as 1.00 lambda. As the lambda value increases, the mixture leans out. Values below 1.00 indicate a rich mixture.

1/4-20 threaded holes in the firewall. I pulled the original harness through the firewall into the cab and then used the original grommet with the TAC-to-accelerator pedal wiring for a clean installation.

All LS-series TAC modules expect 12V switched cruise control signals for operation. These signals are readily available within most early GM vehicles originally equipped with cruise control. Using the GM 1990 K1500 schematics, I determined that the original cruise control module harness contains the on/off, set/coast, and resume/accel signals.

With the cruise control harness now inside the vehicle, I simply wired in a mating connector on my engine wire harness for a plug-and-play solution. The TAC module must also see stop lamp supply voltage for cruise control operation; this is a 12V signal when the brake pedal is depressed.

Using the GM schematics, I easily identified the 18 AWG white wire that I was looking for coming down the instrument panel harness from the brake switch, cut and tapped into the circuit with a Weather-Pack connector, and broke out a loose wire to use with the TAC module brake circuit.

Speedometer Wiring

When planning this build, keeping a functional speedometer in the original instrument cluster appeared to be complicated. The 1990 K1500 instrument cluster has a direct connection to the two wire VSS and then outputs a speed signal to the original TBI ECM. The P59 PCM expects a dedicated connection to the VSS.

Experience has taught me that I cannot simply splice into the two VSS wires to share the signal. Mounting a second VSS was more work than I care to get involved with, so I had to rely on the VSS output signal from the P59 PCM on green connector pin 50. The instrument cluster expects a 40 pulse per driveshaft revolution signal and the 2003 Express calibration is factory set to output 4,000 pulses per mile.

Thinking ahead, I built the wire harness to easily add a Dakota Digital SGI-100BT speedometer module in the passenger's side of the dash. By using this speedometer interface, I worked with the PCM's speed output to fine adjust the speedometer.

Properly wiring the SGI-100BT can be intimidating if you don't know the requirements of your speedometer speed input signal. The module is clearly labeled, and Dakota Digital provides good instructions with several application scenarios. Switched ignition and ground are the easiest connections to make, so I began with those.

The P59 PCM speed output signal is provided on the dark green wire; that one gets connected to "INPUT." The purple and yellow twisted pair are coming from the instrument cluster.

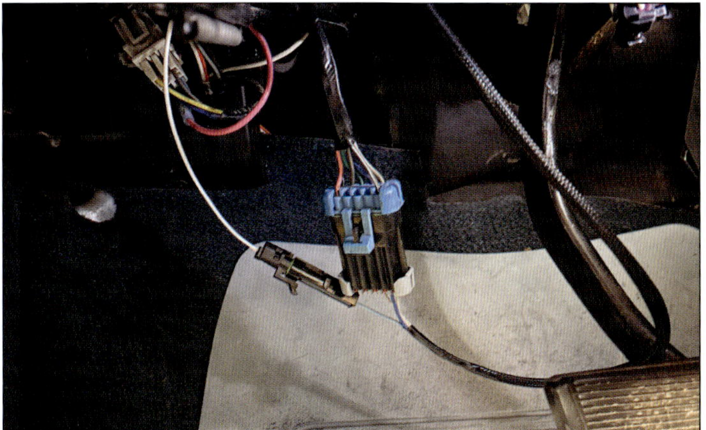

The TAC module requires 12V signals from the cruise control switch and 12V stop lamp supply voltage. By using the three cruise control switch signal circuits within the original cruise control module's 10-cavity blue Metri-Pack 150 female sealed connector, no wires had to be cut to make the connection. The 18 AWG white wire coming down from the brake switch provides 12V when the brake pedal is applied and satisfies the TAC module's brake switch requirement.

Dakota Digital's SGI-100BT module performs beautifully as a universal speedometer and tachometer signal interface; it allows you to input one type of signal and output another. This module can be used as a solution to many different engine swap and gauges scenarios. Requiring only power, ground, and a little knowledge of your input and output signals, you can make quick work of just about any speedometer and tachometer installation.

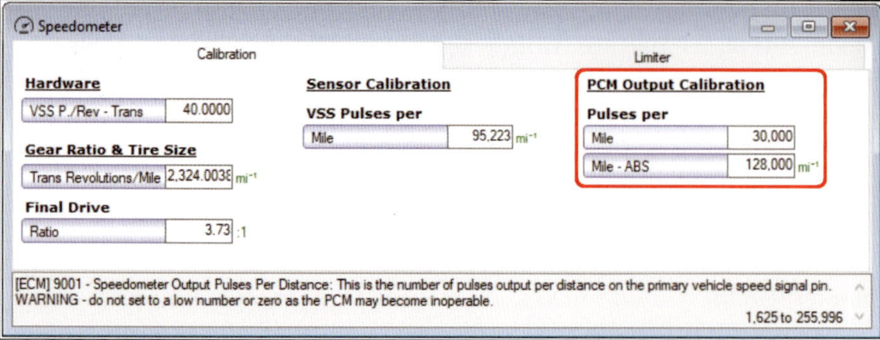

GM's LS-series PCMs allow you to change the default vehicle speed output signals. By default, you will see a value of 4,000 pulses per mile as the primary speed output. GM often uses this 4,000 pulse per mile signal to satisfy the speedometer in the instrument cluster. Using a Dakota Digital SGI-100BT interface module, you can get creative with the speed output signal to fine tune your speedometer.

Goodbye large round air cleaner! When you've seen one TBI system, you've seen them all. This beautiful Ram Jet 350 engine sparks high interest and excellent conversation. With ignition coil packs on the valve covers, enthusiasts have a double take and begin asking questions. With pride, I can explain that I exchanged a big-block for a Gen I small-block and wouldn't change a thing.

I looked at the GM service manual to identify the purple wire as VSS low and the yellow wire as VSS high. The purple wire gets connected to "SPD-" as sensor ground. Using Dakota Digital's instructions, I identify "OUT1" as a calibrated AC-type output signal that I know will be compatible with the instrument cluster. Being a universal interface, there are many other options and compatibilities with the SGI-100BT.

It was now time for a test drive to dial in the speedometer. Using Dakota Digital's instructions, I put the SGI-100BT in speedometer calibration mode and went for an easy drive. After increasing the displayed speed calibration value to the max value of 4.00, the truck's speedometer just peaked over 10 mph while vehicle speed was actually 60 mph.

By using the HP Tuners VCM Scanner, I watched actual vehicle speed with my laptop. I pulled to the side of the road, shut off the ignition, and then changed the PCM's speed output to 15,000 pulses per mile. After a quick PCM flash using HP Tuners VCM Editor, I was back on the road to repeat the test. Now, at 60 mph, the speedometer was reading about 30 mph. I was on the right track, so again I pulled to the side of the road to change the speed output to 30,000 pulses per mile. Back on the road again, the speedometer was reading just a little faster than actual speed, so I accelerated to 60 mph and set cruise control.

By decreasing the SGI-100BT displayed speed calibration value, which was previously set to 4.00, the speedometer approached nearer and nearer to actual vehicle speed. At a speed calibration value of 3.40, the speedometer accurately reflected logged vehicle speed. The speedometer calibration was then complete.

Final Impressions

This truck entered the shop as a heavy gas guzzler with disappointing acceleration for having a big-block under the hood. Diagnosing its constant open-loop condition with my AutoXray OBD-I scanner felt archaic. Working with the PROM-based ECM reminded me of an earlier time when I first got my feet wet with GM fuel injection systems. I put very few miles on the truck prior to pulling the drivetrain for its transformation.

The final results exceeded my expectations. I was rather surprised at how well this truck ran with my initial calibration; there was plenty of torque and excellent acceleration. The 4L60E transmission shift points were easily adjusted using HP Tuners, and no additional tuning was necessary to keep the PCM on its commanded air/fuel target.

The truck starts quickly every time, settles to a nice clean idle, and will get up and go as you'd expect from a Chevrolet Performance crate engine. It's a driver for sure with my favorite feature being the Gen III LS truck electronic throttle system. This truck drives so well with its Gen III LS electronics that I can't understand why GM didn't use the parts on hand when it was first introduced in the early 2000s to offer a similar package.

Many GM enthusiasts share a passion for the third-generation Camaro and Firebird. I've owned a few vehicles within this generation, but none of them compare well to the quality and detail I've seen in the garage of one of my customers. This particular customer had a desire to standardize the engine management systems used within his several F-Bodies. With much optimism, Holley EFI solutions were considered because the ECUs were gaining in popularity, several different GM ignition systems were supported, and the software was relatively easy to use.

With the installation of a GM Ram Jet 350 intake manifold on the engine in one of his third-generation Camaros, the original TBI ECM was replaced with a Holley HP ECM. All Holley EFI systems support the single coil and distributor ignition system found on the V-8 fuel injected TBI and TPI engines in the third-generation F-Bodies, so the Holley HP ECU was a promising solution.

Unfortunately, confirmed electromagnetic interference (EMI) resulted in intermittent ignition system failure that could be manipulated but not eliminated. After a lot of data logging and troubleshooting, the Holley HP ECU was removed and replaced with the once-popular PROM-based GM 1227730 ECM that can be found in the 1990–1992 Camaro and Firebird equipped with tuned port injection (TPI). This was a setback toward his ultimate goal of a standard engine management system, as the 1227730 ECM cannot control his LS engines.

GM used the 1227730 ECM in the 1990–1992 Camaro and Firebird to control the multi-port TPI system. Despite being PROM based, this ECM became tremendously popular among enthusiasts. Leading fuel injection businesses, such as Street & Performance and Tuned Port Injection Specialties, once relied heavily on this ECM to control just about any GM multi-port injection system installed on a traditional SBC or big-block Chevy engine.

As explained in my book, *How to Use and Upgrade to GM Gen III LS-Series Powertrain Control Systems,* a standard GM engine management system that supports both Gen I SBC and Gen III LS-series engines begins with the use of the ever-popular GM number 12200411 PCM.

While this P01 PCM won't control the TBI and TPI single coil and distributor ignition systems, a straightforward upgrade to the 1996-and-newer 5.7L Vortec single coil and distributor ignition system will allow the "0411" to be used with any multi-port Gen I SBC engine. With the GM number 12200411 PCM, my customer would have the standard engine management system he was looking for as long as any LS engine swap be fitted with the Gen III 24x/1x crank/cam signals.

In 2009, my customer installed a supercharged LS3 GM crate engine in his 1985 IROC-Z. The engine man-

During the rise of the LS-based GM number 12200411 PCM, Mike Noonan released a comprehensive book that was published by CarTech, covering the use of the still-popular 2001–2002 GM P01 PCM. This book covers the use of 1996-and-newer Vortec ignition systems and LS coil-per-cylinder ignition systems for Gen I SBC, Gen II LT1, and Gen VI BBC engines. The 24x crank signal–equipped LS-series engines and supported equipment are also covered in detail.

agement system included with GM's crate engine package was based on the E67 ECM. After several years of using HP Tuners to dial in and enjoy this drivetrain, a wayward piston put an abrupt end to all the fun. A replacement LS engine was prepped with Gen III 24x/1x crank/cam signals to get him going with his standard engine management system based on the GM number 12200411 P01 PCM.

While the change from a Gen IV ECM to a Gen III PCM may at first look like a downgrade, consider that both ECUs arguably offer the same engine performance. The LS-series ECUs are all very capable of supporting just about any LS engine. GM's 1996-and-newer OBD-II data monitoring parameter IDs (PIDs) are abundantly available for just about any data logging and tuning needs. EFILive and HP Tuners offer nearly the same Gen III PCM and Gen IV ECM support.

Two benefits of the Gen III system clearly make the GM number 12200411 PCM a winner: multiple ignition system support and full flash capability. Thinking of long-term service and replacement with GM's strict online service system terms of use, even an advanced enthusiast will have difficulty obtaining a GM base calibration for a used Gen IV ECM. Fortunately, HP Tuners and EFILive are capable of turning a used Gen III PCM into whatever supported vehicle application you desire.

The decision had been made: the GM number 12200411 PCM would be the foundation of my customer's standard engine management system. Not only is this PCM an excellent choice for his LS-swapped 1985 IROC-Z but it is also an excellent solution for any of his Camaros' Gen 1 SBC engines, as the Ram Jet 350 and TPI systems feature the supported eight fuel injectors and data sensors compatible with the P01 PCM. Through the use of a 1996-and-newer GM 4x/1x crank/cam signal solution, the "0411" can support single coil and distributor ignition. Through the use of EFI Connection's 24x/1x crank/cam signal solution(s), the "0411" can support coil-per-cylinder ignition.

Planning

The perception of difficulty increases as time spent planning decreases. I may be just as guilty of poor planning as the next guy and have often thought I'd be further along, or more advanced, with my working knowledge of GM engines and fuel injection systems if had I chosen to slow down and be patient through the learning and planning processes.

Fortunately for you, I chose to present this project in greater detail than I would have for just about any other harness build—except for my own projects. The time required to professionally draw and represent an engine wire harness as acceptable deliverables far exceeds the time it takes to manufacture one.

Many would scoff at the several-hundred-dollar price of an authentic GM service manual, and just about everyone would be appalled at the labor cost of a unique set of schematics to represent an engine wire harness and implementation. Even still, for the enthusiast, the planning is worth the time and expense.

Truth be told, I made several mistakes and omissions that required rework while creating the schematics you will see on the following pages. I'd rather my rework be done on paper (or electronically on my PC) than incur the cost of wasted materials and aggravation during assembly. Let's get to planning.

Requirements

My customer and I exchanged several messages by email to help me determine the scope of this project. For me to determine harness layout and the connectors involved, I simply look at the components installed on the engine and transmission.

A Gen III 6.0L LSX long-block lets me know that we're working with a 24x crankshaft reluctor and corresponding crankshaft position sensor. The knock sensors will be located below the intake manifold (rather than on the sides of the block) and require a connection to the knock sensor harness rather than direct connections to the knock sensors. The camshaft sensor will be located just behind the intake manifold (rather than in the Gen IV front engine timing cover).

An aftermarket FAST intake manifold means that I have to pay close attention to the location of the MAP sensor (front or rear) and fuel injector type (EV1, EV6, or Multec). I was provided with a photo of the engine that revealed an LS1-type MAP sensor in the front of the intake manifold with the connector end facing the driver side of the vehicle. The

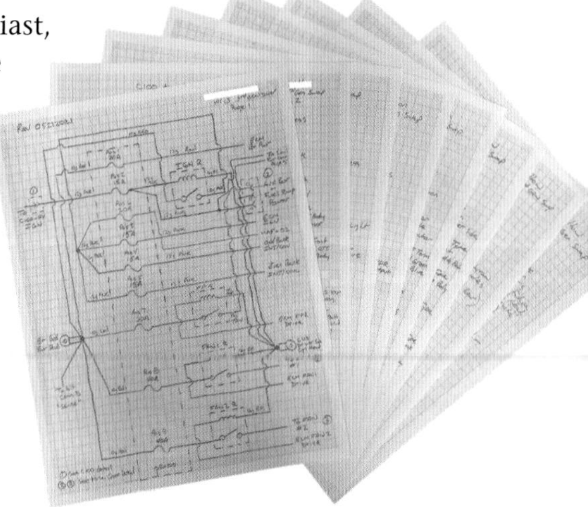

Save yourself from the aggravation of rework and give yourself something to reference once your project is complete by pulling out some graph paper and a pencil to sketch the work that lies ahead. You won't regret the time spent learning about the project, and you'll have greater confidence in your work.

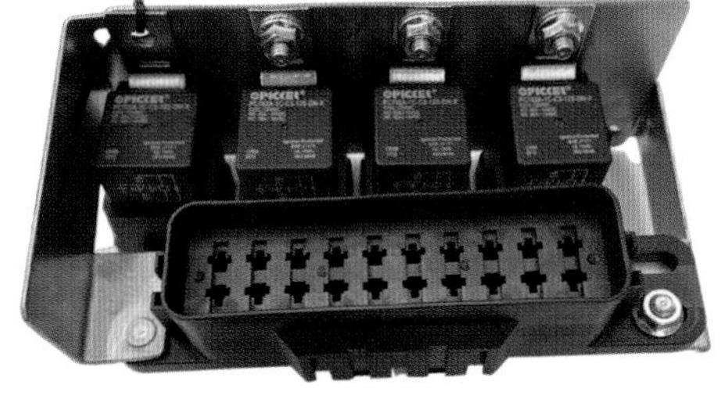
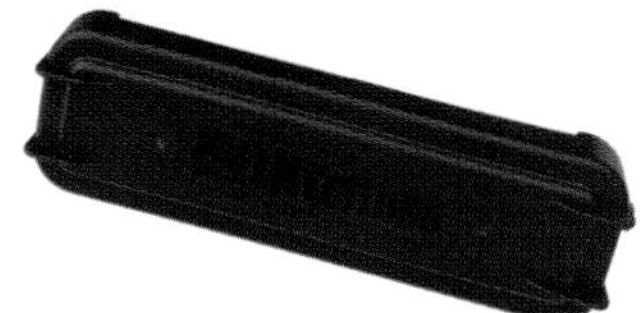

Littelfuse fuse holder (part number PDM61001ZXM) is a sealed fuse holder solution that is suitable for the engine bay. The base holds 10 fuses and includes a waterproof lid. Wires are inserted in the bottom side of the base and require single wire seals to prevent anything from contaminating the wire. When your electrical system requires additional circuits, this fuse holder is one of the better solutions available.

same photo revealed the installation of EV6 type fuel injectors (which require a different connector than the LS1's EV1-type fuel injectors).

The cable driven throttle body indicates the TPS and IAC valve are going to be located on the driver's side of the vehicle. No TAC module is necessary, as this engine does not have an electronic drive-by-wire throttle body.

Additional photos and written requirements indicate the use of a 2002 Camaro LS1 oil pressure sending unit (for the oil pressure gauge), a 1998 Camaro LS1 coolant temperature sensor/sending unit (for compatibility with the coolant temperature gauge), GM number 12611424 ignition coils (with direct connection to each coil rather than a traditional sub-harness), 2002 Camaro LS1 front oxygen sensors, an LS3-type MAF sensor, and an LS3 Corvette generator.

The T56 manual transmission lets me know that a backup lamp switch, reverse lockout solenoid, and vehicle speed sensor (VSS) are required in the harness. While the T56 trans-

mission also has a skip shift solenoid, it's unheard of for an enthusiast to keep this feature, as it's more of a nuisance to the driver. My customer also indicated that he will be using clutch anticipate switch GM number 10426455 so that the PCM will know when the clutch pedal is depressed.

A typical stand-alone or off-the-shelf engine harness would be fine for stand-alone engine operation but would not offer plug-and-play integration with the vehicle. My next focus would be the connections to the vehicle side harness based on the GM schematics for this 1985 IROC-Z a "G" as the eighth VIN digit.

Variations in these "integration" connections can be clearly observed when comparing 1982–1992 F-Body engine harnesses. While I won't cover these differences in detail, I can generally say that GM used the 15-cavity instrument panel (I/P) harness connector known in the GM service manual as connector "C207" to interface with the I/P harness running along the bottom of the dash.

In later years, GM used a 26-cavity bulkhead connector known in the GM service manual as connector "C100" to interface with the interior harness located above the driver's feet and fuse panel. Had this 1985 Camaro been fitted with the TPI system, a 6-cavity connector, referred to in the GM service manual as connector "C221," it would also be located near connector C207.

Rather than stressing the car's original electrical system, my customer made the wise choice of installing a separate fuse block and ignition relay so that he could add new fused circuits by pulling power from the battery. Had this been a fuel injected TPI car, he may have been able to get away with using the original electrical

system. With the addition of aftermarket electrical components that may pull additional current, it's better to be safe than sorry.

In addition to the new fuse block and ignition relay, he added a few additional connections you will see in the schematics that are labeled "C100 Interface," "Aux/Fuel," and "Local."

Diagrams and Schematics

See the page listed to view a diagram that goes with each section below.

Harness Layout Diagram
(See page 177)

With all requirements known, I created a harness layout diagram that represents the general layout and routing of the connectors within the harness. This layout is a top-down view that follows the typical harness routing within the third-generation F-Body engine bay.

The PCM is located inside the passenger compartment in the general area of the original ECM within the dash. Notice alphabetic reference points are established so that distances can be known. I also called out the general location of each splice point within the harness.

Vehicle Interface Connector Views
(See page 178)

Next, I created a connector view document that specifies for each connector cavity the wire size, wire color, and circuit function. In this way, I have a reference document to work with as I create actual schematics. I've previously made engine sensor and component connector views for just about every engine and transmission connection for GM fuel injected applications.

Spliced Circuits (See page 179)

This next part required careful consideration (and a little rework). It almost never fails that when I take on a custom harness job, I overlook something minor during the build that results in partial disassembly, rework, and scrapped materials. Those oversights can be avoided through careful, documented planning.

The most likely oversight will involve a spliced circuit. Harness professionals (should) create solder-less spliced circuits through an ultrasonic welding process. Spliced wire ends are stripped, loosely bundled together in an ultrasonic welding machine, and then compressed and vibrated at a frequency that bonds the copper together into what is referred to as a "nugget," which makes the application of solder unnecessary. In fact, that is the method used by OEMs today.

Whether it is ultrasonically welded or soldered, a spliced nugget should be covered with adhesive-lined shrink tube to provide a moisture resistant covering over the vulnerable copper strands. For clarity, I named each splice with an alphanumeric name beginning with "S" (for "splice") and then a numeric value.

I could go into greater detail to also present wire lengths, but I avoid that redundancy, as the harness build spreadsheet (not shown) and my wire processing machine call out all wire lengths.

Power and Grounds (See page 180)

A summary schematic of all power and ground circuits can be very helpful when it comes to troubleshooting or adding a new circuit someday in the future. The scope of my power and ground schematic is a bit larger than you'll see in a GM service manual, but the completeness of the schematic can be appreciated.

Notice the spliced circuits are represented by circles. Those circles do not imply a slice point but do indicate wires that are on the same circuit. It's

not uncommon to have more than one splice in a circuit, but I always keep splices to a minimum.

Starter and Charging
(See page 181)

While the starter is independent of PCM control, the starter crank circuit must be considered, as it belongs in connector C100. My customer's intentions were to keep the original battery power and starter circuits in the original C100 connector but to cut and terminate the other wires with a 6-cavity Weather-Pack connection.

I suppose there are several ways to go about this, but my customer's plan was solid. I've seen many third-generation F-Body harnesses with damaged battery power and starter wires (at the starter) that should simply be replaced.

Automotive wire has an intended lifespan that is affected by conditions such as temperature, abrasion, and fluid exposure. Always evaluate the condition of your used wiring before reuse. This car is now more than 36 years old; the original wiring has exceeded the manufacturer's recommended use.

Tachometer Pull-Up Resistor
(See page 182)

My customer has had enough experience with third-generation F-Body instrument clusters to identify a resistor that will cooperate with the tachometer circuit. He specified the use of a 470-ohm, 2-watt resistor. One end of the resistor is tapped into the tachometer circuit between the PCM and tachometer. The other end of the resistor receives fused 12V switched ignition power to "pull up" the signal.

Fuel Pump Control (See page 183)

It's well known that upgraded fuel pumps require larger wire to handle their current draw. It's interesting to note that within the fuel injected

third-generation F-Bodies, GM used 14 AWG wire to provide power to the fuel pump. The original wire size is just sufficient for the GM fuel pump. Rather than installing an add-on redundant fuel pump power relay that pulls battery power from the battery or alternator, my customer decided to upgrade the wire size to 10 AWG to eliminate any doubt about the fuel pump receiving all the power that it needs.

Fuel Injectors and Ignition Coils
(See pages 184 and 185)

It's common practice to combine power for each bank of fuel injectors and ignition coils on their own fused ignition circuit. It's also common to make use of GM's ignition coil harnesses, one per bank of coils. My customer requested that the ignition coil sub-harnesses be eliminated, meaning that there would be eight ignition coil connections rather than two ignition coil sub-harness connections. With several different connector types for fuel injectors and ignition coils, it was important to know that the engine was fitted with EV6-type fuel injectors and GM number 12611424 ignition coils.

Oxygen Sensors and MAF Sensor
(See page 186)

Another common practice is for the oxygen sensors and MAF sensor to share the same fused ignition circuit. Harness builders often label this as the "sensors" fuse. Most LS engine swaps eliminate the rear oxygen sensors, which are used to monitor the condition of the catalytic converters. Again, just like the fuel injectors and ignition coils, there are a variety of different connectors used to suit the oxygen sensors and MAF sensor being used. My customer chose to use 2002 Camaro oxygen sensors and an LS3-style MAF sensor.

Ignition Sensors (See page 187)

All Gen III LS-series crankshaft and camshaft sensors are powered by a 12V source through the PCM. Earlier GM systems and many aftermarket systems provide a fused 12V source to these sensors. The camshaft sensor is located at the back of the intake manifold.

Had my customer chosen to use a Gen IV 1x cam signal solution from within a Gen IV engine timing cover, the harness connector would be the same but the wires in cavities A and C would be swapped because the cam sensors are wired differently. Notice that the knock sensor connection is intended for a sub-harness that is installed under the intake manifold. This modular knock sensor solution is found with all Gen III LS-series engines.

Engine Sensors (See page 188)

The remaining engine data sensors include the TPS, IAC, MAP, and ECT. Again, there are a variety of sensor connectors from which to choose, so knowing which sensors were being used prior to the harness assembly saved me from rework.

While many Gen III LS-series engines feature Delphi Metri-Pack 150 connectors, later Gen III and Gen IV LS-series engines feature Delphi's GT 150 connector variants. I chose to use the GT 150 variants for ease of assembly and service. The chosen engine coolant temperature sensor was used only with the 1998 Camaro and Firebird, but is ideal for my customer's implementation because he can use the integrated sending unit rather than install a second coolant temperature sending unit in the cylinder head.

Manual Transmission (See page 189)

The manual transmission integration with the vehicle is minimal. The VSS provides tailshaft speed (17 pulses per driveshaft revolution) to the PCM so that it can control the state of the reverse lockout solenoid, buffer the signal for use with a Cable-X speedometer controller, and be used for other PCM functions, including deceleration fuel cut-off.

Some enthusiasts ask me if the VSS is required for a manual transmission. I always advise that they avoid shortcuts and make a way to give the PCM a vehicle speed signal. You'll also notice the clutch pedal anticipate switch is a ground signal (normally closed with foot off of the clutch pedal) to the PCM. It's worth noting that the Corvette also has a clutch anticipate signal, but it's a 12V signal and not on the same PCM pin as this Camaro PCM implementation.

Electric Fans (See page 190)

The prior installation of aftermarket electric fans made us question the sufficiency of the typical 12 AWG size wire GM uses for electric fan motors. We collectively decided to use a larger 10 AWG size wire.

In most cases, because current draw isn't often known at the time of purchase, stand-alone engine harness builds only include the fan relay coil control wires so that customers can work with the manufacturer of their electric fans to install appropriately sized power and ground wire, relays, and fuses. It's a safety best practice to install fusible links at the battery source; I appropriately installed 14 AWG fusible links onto the 10 AWG power wires.

Data Communications (See page 191)

It used to surprise me when customers would ask, "Does your engine wire harness include a diagnostic connector?" My response was, "Yes (of course—why wouldn't it?)."

I've been in this business long enough to see installations where the diagnostic connector is excluded or added for a small fee. Crazy. The diagnostic connector is absolutely necessary. You likely chose an OBD-II system because of popular tuning support (requiring a diagnostic connector) and advanced diagnostics (also requiring a diagnostic connector).

In this case, the P01 PCM communicates on the Class 2 serial data line on OBD-II connector pin 2. A 12V battery power source is necessary at the OBD-II diagnostic connector, so I spliced into the 20A fused PCM B+ source.

Gauges (See page 192)

Gauges are one of the top concerns when it comes to an LS engine swap. A closer look at the original engine harness or GM schematics quickly reveals that several gauges simply require sending units (fuel level, oil pressure, and coolant temperature) that are independent of the PCM's wiring.

The tachometer can receive the PCM's engine speed output signal with a 470-ohm pull-up resistor applied. The check-engine lamp is simply controlled by the PCM's switched ground signal. Being cable-driven, the speedometer is the tricky one in this car. I suppose there are a few invasive ways to tackle this, but the easiest way is to install Abbott Enterprises' Cable-X box.

I ordered my first Cable-X box more than 20 years ago, so time and experience reveals this to be a tried-and-true method of spinning a mechanical speedometer based on the PCM's vehicle speed output and the configuration of several dip switches.

Building a Trim-to-Fit Engine Harness

My work thus far has given me all the details I need to get started on the engine wire harness. My approach was to deliver to my customer an extra-long engine harness that we would trim to fit his engine and engine bay in the way he desires. With a few preliminary measurements of the engine and engine bay, I sketched a very basic layout on my harness template board and installed Panduit Quick-Build elastic retainers to hold the wires as I applied them to the board.

Here's a tip: When possible, begin at the PCM when building an engine harness. In that way, you can neatly bundle the wires together and trim the sensor and device ends before termination. It's nearly impossible to start with the sensor or device end and then determine the necessary cut length at the PCM—you'll surely end up with some wires that are too long and some that are too short.

The trim-to-fit harness went together rather quickly because it is missing all of the spliced circuits. With all of the sensor and device ends neatly bundled and taped or zip-tied, it was ready for my customer to work with.

I was thorough to clearly label all loose ends and include a second set of labels to be applied after he trimmed each end to his desired length. The returned harness was trimmed to fit

In exceptional cases, usually high-dollar builds, a partial engine harness is made with extra long lengths and then shipped to the customer to be laid out in the vehicle and then trimmed for a perfect fit. By labeling each loose end (and including another set of labels), the customer can cut the extra lengths and relabel the harness in preparation of its return for final assembly. What makes the harness partial is the missing spliced circuits, connectors, and final dress loom. This is typically not a cost-friendly process, as so many enthusiasts and speed shops have become familiar with subpar $250 stand-alone engine harnesses from China.

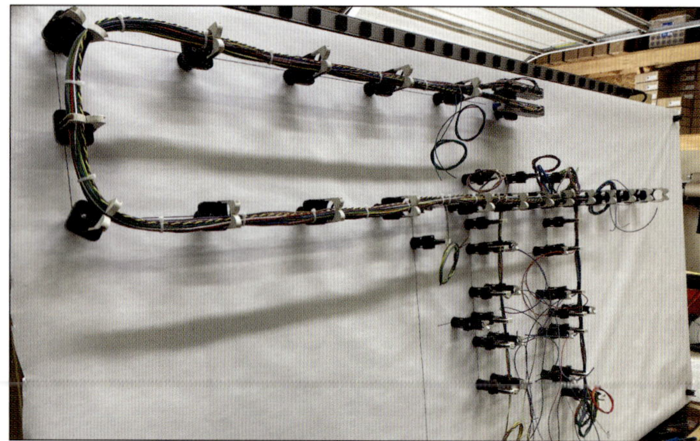

EFI Connection uses the Panduit Quick-Build harness board system during the construction of each engine wire harness. The Quick-Build grid tiles are fastened to a sheet of plywood, and a sheet of paper is cut to fit the area. Mounting pegs pierce the paper and twist to lock into the grid tiles. Mounting platforms and nail holders are compatible with the mounting pegs. Elastic retainers or custom manufactured fixtures can easily be fastened to the variety of available mounting platforms. This system is far too expensive for the average enthusiast, but DIYers can certainly come up with a few crafty ideas by observing how professionals do it.

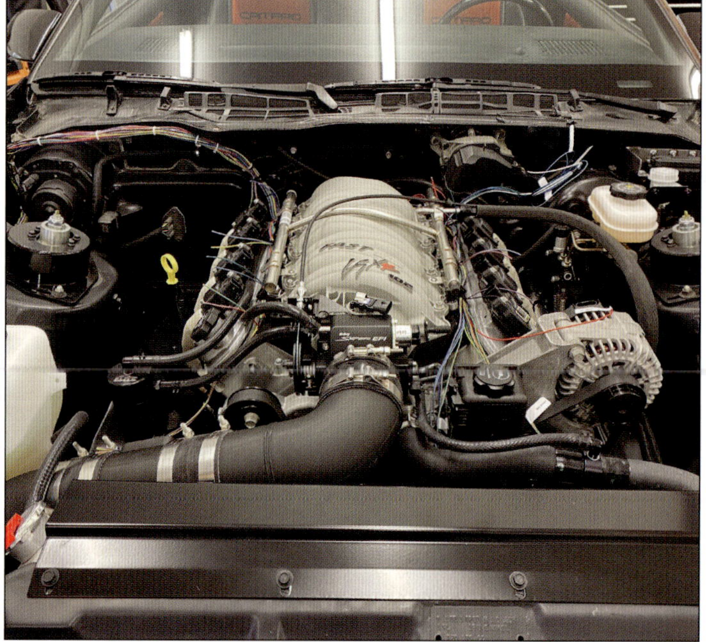

The engine bay in this car is very clean and organized. While a typical third-generation F-Body harness layout would have been okay, trimming the harness to best fit the engine and engine bay makes for an exceptional visual appearance. It's difficult for a remote customer to provide this level of length requirement details.

this 1985 IROC-Z and ready for me to update the harness layout diagram with measurements and my build spreadsheet with wire lengths for the spliced circuits.

Adding Spliced Circuits

Back on the template board and neatly routed using the Quick-Build elastic retainers, the harness needs only the spliced circuits and a few loose wires before being bundled with low-adhesive vinyl harness tape.

The low-adhesive tape prevents adhesive from oozing out as a result of the heat from the engine bay. With all wires in place, the harness receives a final trim to cut the spliced circuits to the precut lengths from the test fit on the car.

Installing Connectors

Now that the harness is neatly bundled and each sensor or device end is cut to final length, I'm ready to install the connectors. I chose to leave the harness on the build tem-plate for ease of accessibility. While this is not the most efficient way to build a large quantity of the same harness, it will be just fine for the sake of this build.

By following manufacturer guidelines for the size and application of cable seals, I stripped each wire end and applied cable seals where needed. In the same way, I followed manufacturer specifications to determine the correct terminal size for each wire and then used Rennsteig Tools hand-crimp tools to achieve OEM-quality crimp heights and widths to ensure the best possible connections. My schematics clearly indicate the proper connector cavity assignments to assist me in installing the connectors. Finally, I installed secondary locks on the connectors designed with this feature.

Continuity Quality Check

Being a one-off harness build, I don't have a mating test fixture and program to verify the accuracy of my work. The next best method is to simply use a digital multimeter to check for continuity from one end of each wire to the other. This process takes a bit of time but has the potential to save hours of rework should there be a defect once the harness has been installed.

I set my multimeter dial to the ohm-check function and press the buzzer button in preparation of my testing. By applying one test lead to one end of a terminated wire and the other test lead to the other end of the same wire, I listen for an audible beep to confirm continuity. This lets me know that I have at least inserted the wire into the correct connector cavity or cavities. Be aware that this method of continuity testing may provide a false positive result if the circuit is damaged. Load testing with a 12V test lamp is one way to stress the circuit to see if it can carry the required current.

Dressing the Completed Harness

The finishing touches for this

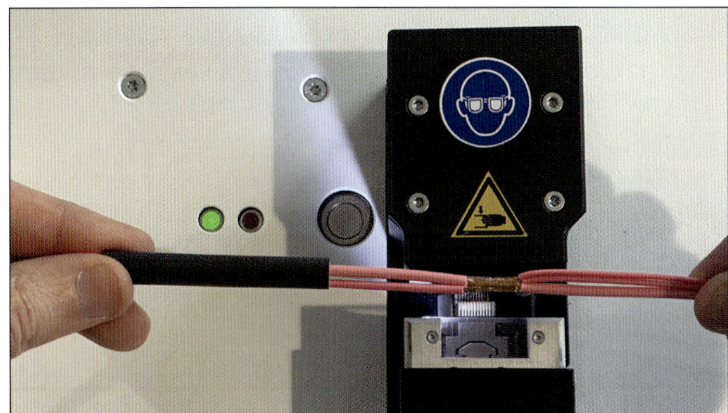

GM fuel injection harnesses have always contained spliced circuits. Splicing wires cannot be avoided, as multiple devices must share the same fused or ground source. The OEM quality of splices has come a long way since the introduction of electronic fuel injection systems in the 1980s. Long gone are the days of wrapping a soldered splice with cloth tape. Modern splices are now bonded with ultrasonic technology and protected by adhesive-lined heat shrink tubing.

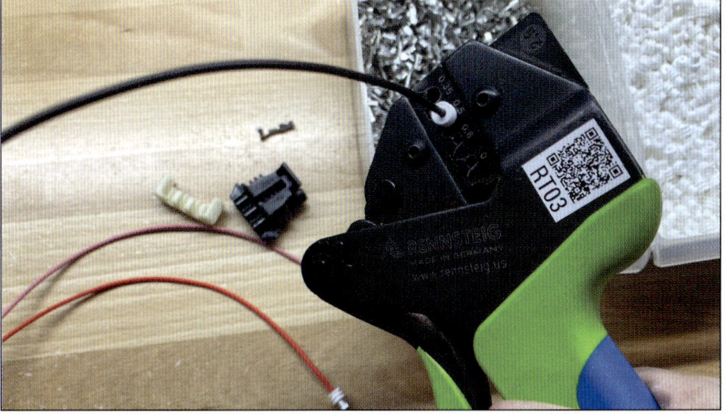

To manufacture a tidy engine wire harness assembly, connectors are typically installed late in the build process. To install connectors, each wire must first be terminated, and some wires require a cable seal prior to termination. Very simply, the end of the wire is stripped, receives a cable seal (where applicable), is terminated using a crimp tool, and then is inserted into the back side of the connector. Secondary locks are often used as a precautionary measure.

wire harness include Techflex Flexo PET expandable sleeving, Techflex Insultherm Tru-Fit high-temperature fiberglass sleeving, Techflex Flexo F6 braided split tube sleeving, and segments of Polyken aluminum foil laminated fiberglass cloth tape. For the cleanest look, I installed the expandable sleeving on loose harness ends prior to connector installation. Expandable sleeving has no split, so it must be installed prior to termination.

Next, I install fiberglass sleeving on the oxygen sensor wiring, as it has the potential to receive high heat from the exhaust headers. Braided split tube sleeving is then installed on the remaining segments of the harness. Finally, the aluminum foil laminated fiberglass cloth tape is used on areas of the harness that may receive high heat from the exhaust system.

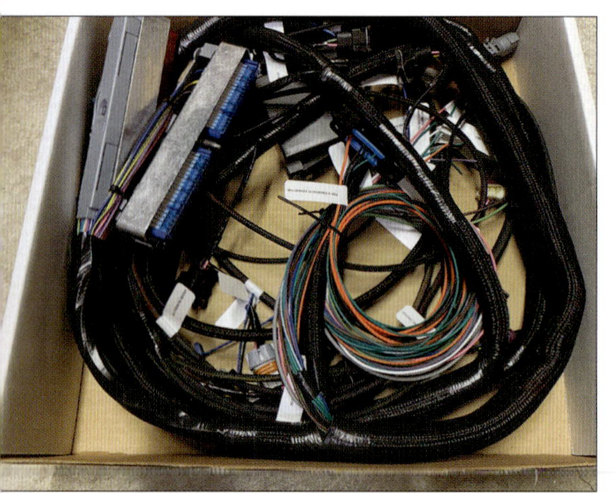

Many options are now available for covering and protecting engine wire harnesses. Because of its inexpensive cost and ease of installation, many manufacturers continue to use OEM-style high-temperature convoluted plastic split loom. Gaining popularity is the use of braided plastic loom because it reduces the bulky look of slit loom with improved form to fit. A variety of high-temperature vinyl and cloth tapes are available to seal and protect the remainder of harness assemblies.

Final Installation

The completed harness assembly is ready for installation. As a result of careful planning, the harness fits nicely in place. The C100 and C207 interface connections provide for a plug-and-play installation. The original harness bulkhead on the passenger side of the car is permanently installed on the original engine wire harness. While it is possible to carefully disassemble and modify with a larger hole (for the additional wires to pass), EFI Connection has designed and manufactured slick replacement bulkhead that allows for a clean installation and plenty of room for the larger harness bundle going into the passenger compartment. Finally, my customer made a custom bracket to hold the PCM nicely hidden behind the dash.

PCM Tuning Preparations

The details of the initial PCM calibration are similar to the details I've provided elsewhere in this book. For the sake of brevity, it is most important to note that I provided a GM number 12200411 PCM that I bench programmed using GM's TIS2000 software and Tech 2 interface. The ideal base calibration for this application was a 2002 Camaro LS1 T56.

By establishing this base calibration prior to my customer using his HP Tuners credits, it avoided him from having to apply credits twice toward the use of this PCM. Had he been using EFILive, he could have simply licensed the PCM once and loaded the base calibration from the 2002 Camaro. Using his HP Tuners equipment, he completed his startup calibration and began the tuning process with feedback from a wideband oxygen sensor.

The third-generation F-Bodies have a rectangular hole located in the body (just to the right of the passenger's feet) that is used for the engine harness to enter the vehicle and connect to the ECM and instrument panel harness. Protecting the harness from chafing on the opening is a hard-shell grommet that is permanently installed on the harness with adhesive. EFI Connection has designed and manufactures a replacement five-piece grommet that allows for a larger bundle of wires to pass through the body panel. This 3-D printed plastic grommet includes a new foam gasket to ensure an excellent seal to the body panel.

Final Thoughts

I really enjoyed working with my customer on his 1985 IROC-Z. This Gen III LS-series PCM solution is the first of several that are planned for his other third-generation F-Body projects. Now that I've documented the project in great detail, I'll be able to simply rework the C100 and C207 interface connections to follow the changes GM has made to these connectors through the years and models.

Plan carefully and document well. You'll thank yourself for your thorough dedication in due time.

1985 CAMARO 24X 6.0L LS T56 (HARNESS LAYOUT)

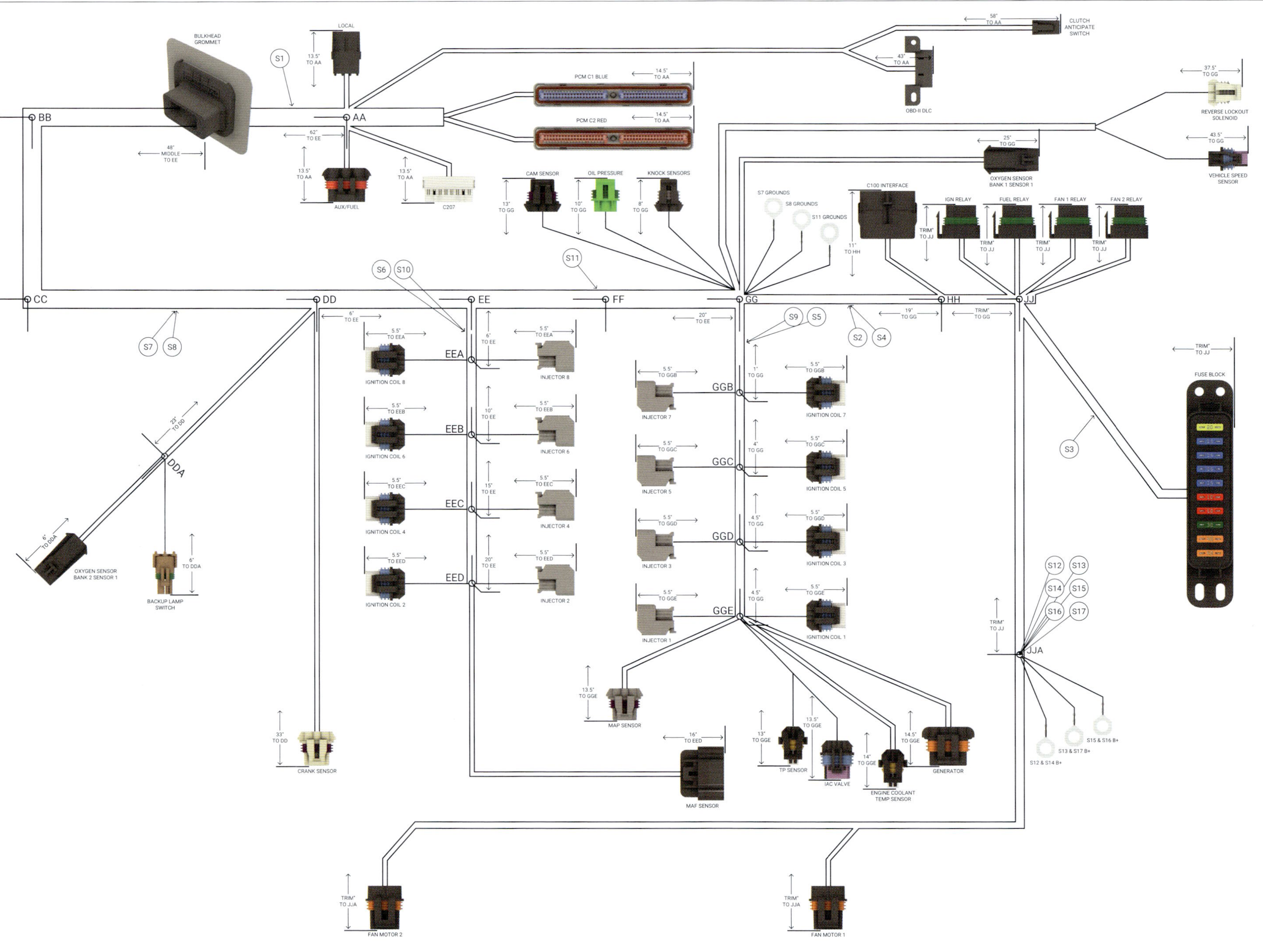

1985 CAMARO 24X 6.0L LS T56 (VEHICLE INTERFACE CONNECTOR VIEWS)

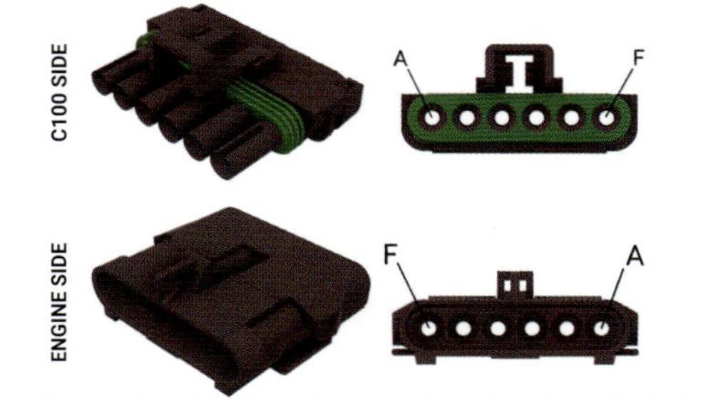

C100 (VIN G) - ENGINE HARNESS SIDE - GM IMPLEMENTATION

PIN #	COLOR	SIZE (MM²)	DESCRIPTION
A4	RED	5.0	POWER DISTRIBUTION (IGNITION SWITCH)
B4	PPL	5.0	STARTER S TERMINAL (CRANK)
C5	PPL	1.0	WIPER/WASHER
C6	DK GRN	1.0	WIPER/WASHER
C7	PNK	1.0	WIPER/WASHER
D5	GRY	1.0	WIPER/WASHER
D6	WHT	0.8	TACHOMETER
E5	TAN	0.8	OIL PRESSURE
F4	PNK	3.0	IGNITION
F5	DK GRN	0.8	COOLANT TEMP
F8	BRN	0.8	GENERATOR
G5	RED	3.0	POWER DISTRIBUTION (LIGHTS, FUSE BLOCK)

MM² TO AWG CONVERSION

SIZE (MM²)	AWG
0.35	22
0.5	20
0.8	18
1.0	16
2.0	14
3.0	12
5.0	10

C100 INTERFACE - CUSTOMER ADDITION

PIN #	COLOR	SIZE (MM²)	DESCRIPTION
A	PNK	3.0	12V IGNITION (WITH KEY ON AND CRANK)
B	WHT	0.8	TACHOMETER
C	TAN	0.8	OIL PRESSURE SIGNAL
D	DK GRN	0.8	COOLANT TEMPERATURE SIGNAL
E	BRN	0.8	GENERATOR
F	-	-	-

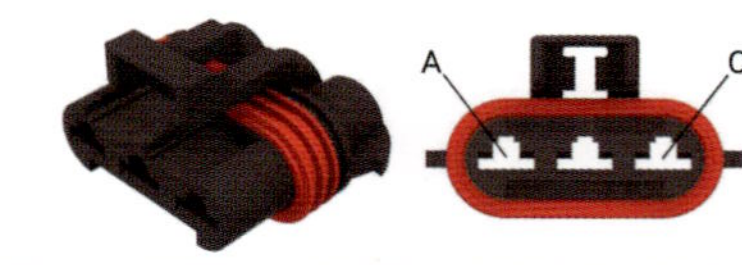

"AUX/FUEL" (LOCATED NEAR C207) - CUSTOMER ADDITION

PIN #	COLOR	SIZE (MM²)	DESCRIPTION
A	PNK	3.0	12V IGNITION (WITH KEY ON AND CRANK)
B	BLK	3.0	GROUND
C	RED	5.0	FUEL PUMP (12V POWER TO PUMP)

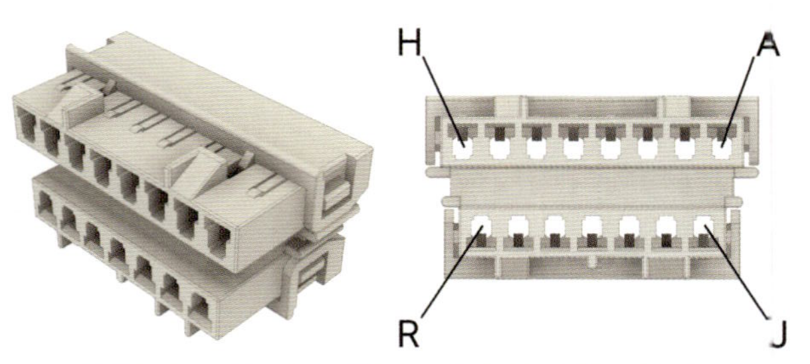

C207 (VIN G) - ENGINE HARNESS SIDE - GM IMPLEMENTATION

PIN #	COLOR	SIZE (MM²)	DESCRIPTION
B	LT GRN	1.0	BACKUP LIGHT (TO LIGHTS)
C	BRN/WHT	0.8	MIL CONTROL "CHECK ENGINE SOON"
G	DK BLU	1.0	BACKUP LIGHT (TO 20A TLRN B/U FUSE)
H	TAN	0.8	SHIFT LIGHT
L	RED	5.0	FUEL PUMP (12V TO POWER PUMP)

"LOCAL" (LOCATED NEAR C207) - CUSTOMER ADDITION

PIN #	COLOR	SIZE (MM²)	DESCRIPTION
A	DK GRN/WHT	0.8	PCM VSS OUTPUT SIGNAL
B	BLK	2.0	GROUND
C	PNK	2.0	12V IGNITION (WITH KEY ON AND CRANK)

1985 CAMARO 24X 6.0L LS T56 (ULTRASONIC SPLICES)

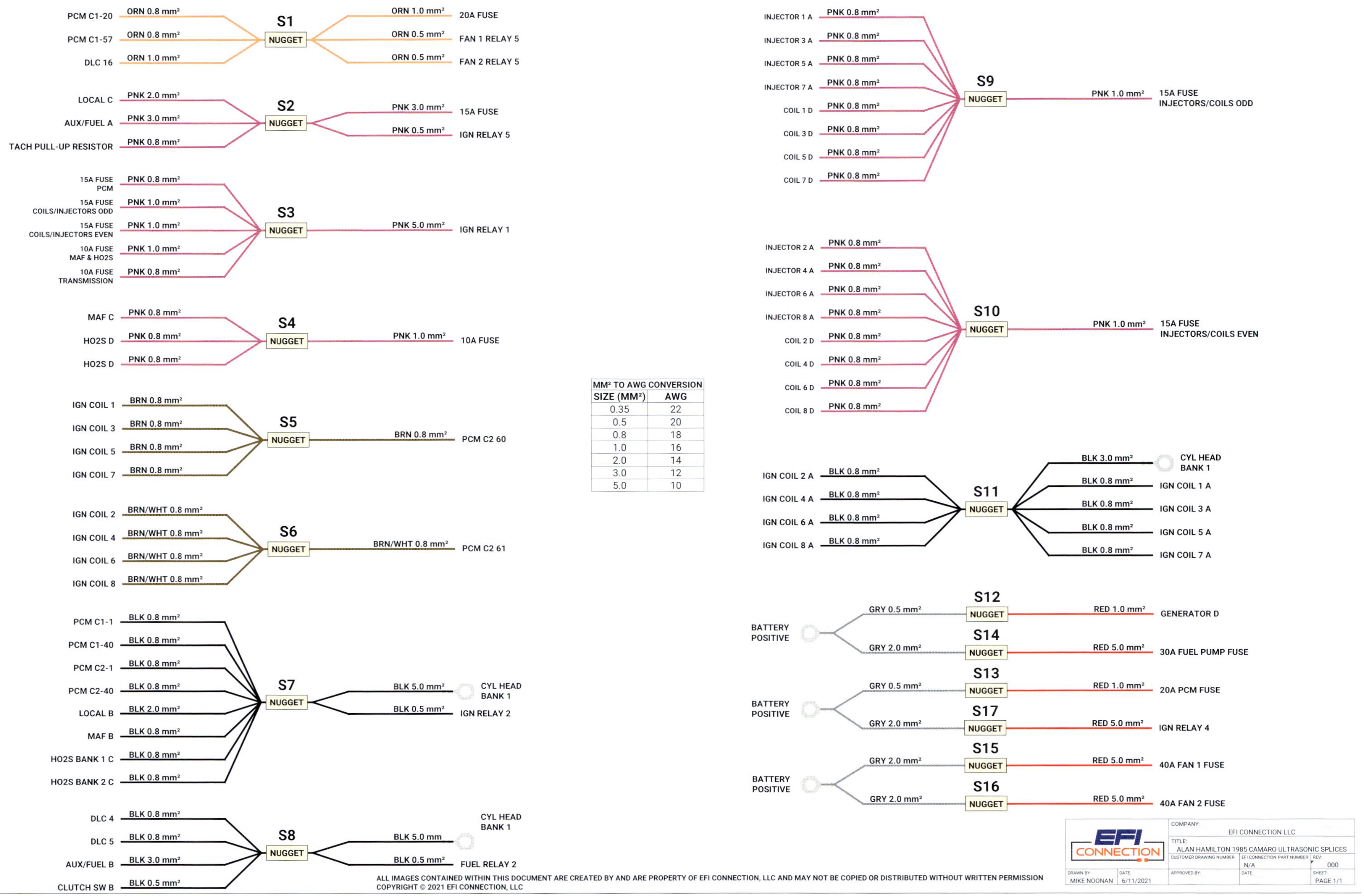

S1 — NUGGET
- PCM C1-20 — ORN 0.8 mm²
- PCM C1-57 — ORN 0.8 mm²
- DLC 16 — ORN 1.0 mm²
- ORN 1.0 mm² — 20A FUSE
- ORN 0.5 mm² — FAN 1 RELAY 5
- ORN 0.5 mm² — FAN 2 RELAY 5

S2 — NUGGET
- LOCAL C — PNK 2.0 mm²
- AUX/FUEL A — PNK 3.0 mm²
- TACH PULL-UP RESISTOR — PNK 0.8 mm²
- PNK 3.0 mm² — 15A FUSE
- PNK 0.5 mm² — IGN RELAY 5

S3 — NUGGET
- 15A FUSE PCM — PNK 0.8 mm²
- 15A FUSE COILS/INJECTORS ODD — PNK 1.0 mm²
- 15A FUSE COILS/INJECTORS EVEN — PNK 1.0 mm²
- 10A FUSE MAF & HO2S — PNK 1.0 mm²
- 10A FUSE TRANSMISSION — PNK 0.8 mm²
- PNK 5.0 mm² — IGN RELAY 1

S4 — NUGGET
- MAF C — PNK 0.8 mm²
- HO2S D — PNK 0.8 mm²
- HO2S D — PNK 0.8 mm²
- PNK 1.0 mm² — 10A FUSE

S5 — NUGGET
- IGN COIL 1 — BRN 0.8 mm²
- IGN COIL 3 — BRN 0.8 mm²
- IGN COIL 5 — BRN 0.8 mm²
- IGN COIL 7 — BRN 0.8 mm²
- BRN 0.8 mm² — PCM C2 60

S6 — NUGGET
- IGN COIL 2 — BRN/WHT 0.8 mm²
- IGN COIL 4 — BRN/WHT 0.8 mm²
- IGN COIL 6 — BRN/WHT 0.8 mm²
- IGN COIL 8 — BRN/WHT 0.8 mm²
- BRN/WHT 0.8 mm² — PCM C2 61

S7 — NUGGET
- PCM C1-1 — BLK 0.8 mm²
- PCM C1-40 — BLK 0.8 mm²
- PCM C2-1 — BLK 0.8 mm²
- PCM C2-40 — BLK 0.8 mm²
- LOCAL B — BLK 2.0 mm²
- MAF B — BLK 0.8 mm²
- HO2S BANK 1 C — BLK 0.8 mm²
- HO2S BANK 2 C — BLK 0.8 mm²
- BLK 5.0 mm² — CYL HEAD BANK 1
- BLK 0.5 mm² — IGN RELAY 2

S8 — NUGGET
- DLC 4 — BLK 0.8 mm²
- DLC 5 — BLK 0.8 mm²
- AUX/FUEL B — BLK 3.0 mm²
- CLUTCH SW B — BLK 0.5 mm²
- BLK 5.0 mm — CYL HEAD BANK 1
- BLK 0.5 mm² — FUEL RELAY 2

S9 — NUGGET
- INJECTOR 1 A — PNK 0.8 mm²
- INJECTOR 3 A — PNK 0.8 mm²
- INJECTOR 5 A — PNK 0.8 mm²
- INJECTOR 7 A — PNK 0.8 mm²
- COIL 1 D — PNK 0.8 mm²
- COIL 3 D — PNK 0.8 mm²
- COIL 5 D — PNK 0.8 mm²
- COIL 7 D — PNK 0.8 mm²
- PNK 1.0 mm² — 15A FUSE INJECTORS/COILS ODD

S10 — NUGGET
- INJECTOR 2 A — PNK 0.8 mm²
- INJECTOR 4 A — PNK 0.8 mm²
- INJECTOR 6 A — PNK 0.8 mm²
- INJECTOR 8 A — PNK 0.8 mm²
- COIL 2 D — PNK 0.8 mm²
- COIL 4 D — PNK 0.8 mm²
- COIL 6 D — PNK 0.8 mm²
- COIL 8 D — PNK 0.8 mm²
- PNK 1.0 mm² — 15A FUSE INJECTORS/COILS EVEN

S11 — NUGGET
- IGN COIL 2 A — BLK 0.8 mm²
- IGN COIL 4 A — BLK 0.8 mm²
- IGN COIL 6 A — BLK 0.8 mm²
- IGN COIL 8 A — BLK 0.8 mm²
- BLK 3.0 mm² — CYL HEAD BANK 1
- BLK 0.8 mm² — IGN COIL 1 A
- BLK 0.8 mm² — IGN COIL 3 A
- BLK 0.8 mm² — IGN COIL 5 A
- BLK 0.8 mm² — IGN COIL 7 A

S12 — NUGGET
- BATTERY POSITIVE — GRY 0.5 mm²
- RED 1.0 mm² — GENERATOR D

S14 — NUGGET
- BATTERY POSITIVE — GRY 2.0 mm²
- RED 5.0 mm² — 30A FUEL PUMP FUSE

S13 — NUGGET
- BATTERY POSITIVE — GRY 0.5 mm²
- RED 1.0 mm² — 20A PCM FUSE

S17 — NUGGET
- BATTERY POSITIVE — GRY 2.0 mm²
- RED 5.0 mm² — IGN RELAY 4

S15 — NUGGET
- BATTERY POSITIVE — GRY 2.0 mm²
- RED 5.0 mm² — 40A FAN 1 FUSE

S16 — NUGGET
- BATTERY POSITIVE — GRY 2.0 mm²
- RED 5.0 mm² — 40A FAN 2 FUSE

MM² TO AWG CONVERSION

SIZE (MM²)	AWG
0.35	22
0.5	20
0.8	18
1.0	16
2.0	14
3.0	12
5.0	10

COMPANY: EFI CONNECTION LLC
TITLE: ALAN HAMILTON 1985 CAMARO ULTRASONIC SPLICES
CUSTOMER DRAWING NUMBER: N/A
EFI CONNECTION PART NUMBER: N/A
REV: 000
DRAWN BY: MIKE NOONAN
DATE: 6/11/2021
APPROVED BY:
SHEET: PAGE 1/1

1985 CAMARO 24X 6.0L LS T56 (POWER, GROUND, VEHICLE INTERFACES)

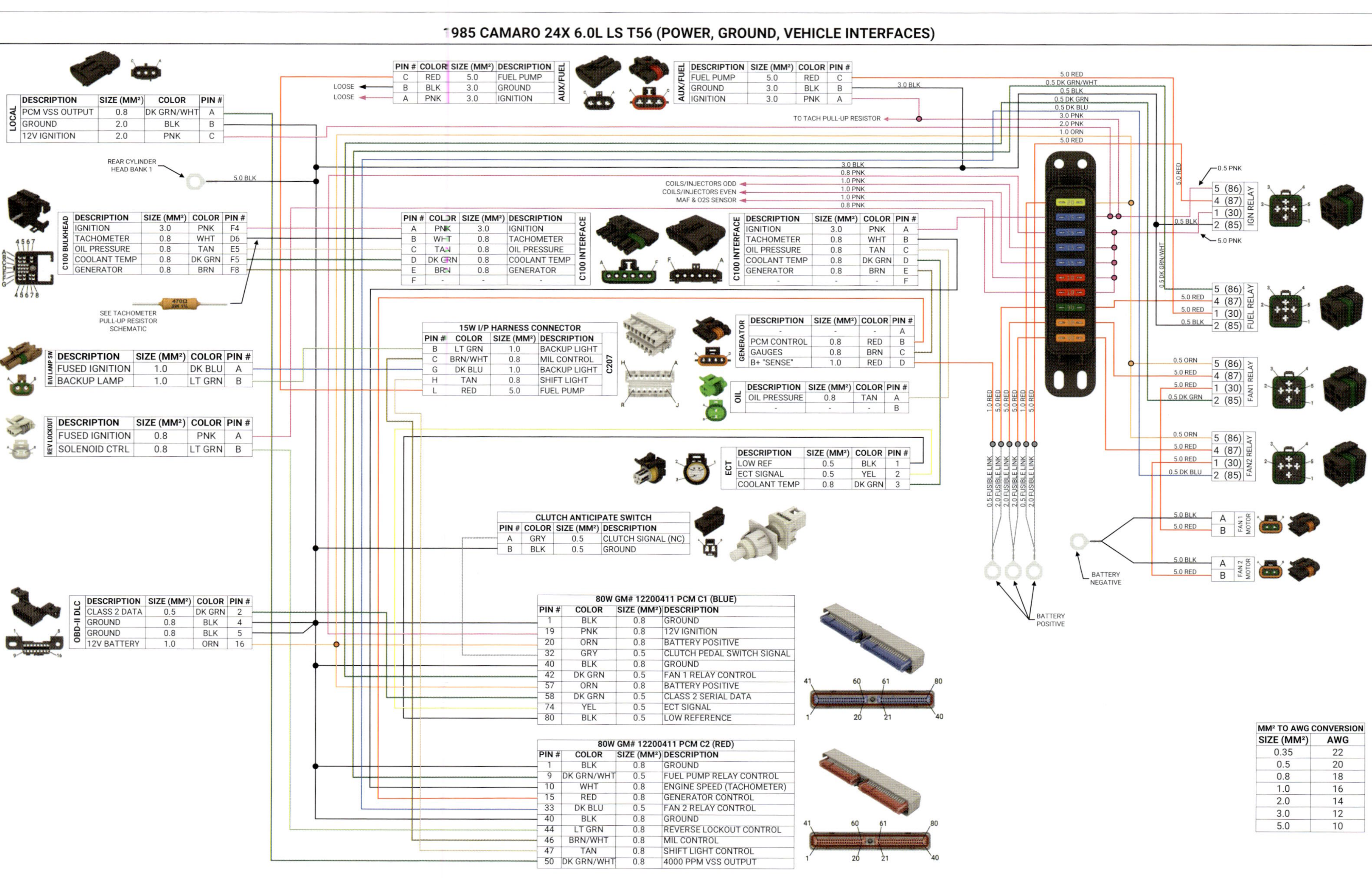

LOCAL

DESCRIPTION	SIZE (MM²)	COLOR	PIN #
PCM VSS OUTPUT	0.8	DK GRN/WHT	A
GROUND	2.0	BLK	B
12V IGNITION	2.0	PNK	C

AUX/FUEL

PIN #	COLOR	SIZE (MM²)	DESCRIPTION
C	RED	5.0	FUEL PUMP
B	BLK	3.0	GROUND
A	PNK	3.0	IGNITION

AUX/FUEL

DESCRIPTION	SIZE (MM²)	COLOR	PIN #
FUEL PUMP	5.0	RED	C
GROUND	3.0	BLK	B
IGNITION	3.0	PNK	A

C100 BULKHEAD

DESCRIPTION	SIZE (MM²)	COLOR	PIN #
IGNITION	3.0	PNK	F4
TACHOMETER	0.8	WHT	D6
OIL PRESSURE	0.8	TAN	E5
COOLANT TEMP	0.8	DK GRN	F5
GENERATOR	0.8	BRN	F8

C100 INTERFACE

PIN #	COLOR	SIZE (MM²)	DESCRIPTION
A	PNK	3.0	IGNITION
B	WHT	0.8	TACHOMETER
C	TAN	0.8	OIL PRESSURE
D	DK GRN	0.8	COOLANT TEMP
E	BRN	0.8	GENERATOR
F	-	-	-

C100 INTERFACE

DESCRIPTION	SIZE (MM²)	COLOR	PIN #
IGNITION	3.0	PNK	A
TACHOMETER	0.8	WHT	B
OIL PRESSURE	0.8	TAN	C
COOLANT TEMP	0.8	DK GRN	D
GENERATOR	0.8	BRN	E
-	-	-	F

15W I/P HARNESS CONNECTOR (C207)

PIN #	COLOR	SIZE (MM²)	DESCRIPTION
B	LT GRN	1.0	BACKUP LIGHT
C	BRN/WHT	0.8	MIL CONTROL
G	DK BLU	1.0	BACKUP LIGHT
H	TAN	0.8	SHIFT LIGHT
L	RED	5.0	FUEL PUMP

GENERATOR

DESCRIPTION	SIZE (MM²)	COLOR	PIN #
-	-	-	A
PCM CONTROL	0.8	RED	B
GAUGES	0.8	BRN	C
B+ "SENSE"	1.0	RED	D

OIL

DESCRIPTION	SIZE (MM²)	COLOR	PIN #
OIL PRESSURE	0.8	TAN	A
-	-	-	B

ECT

DESCRIPTION	SIZE (MM²)	COLOR	PIN #
LOW REF	0.5	BLK	1
ECT SIGNAL	0.5	YEL	2
COOLANT TEMP	0.8	DK GRN	3

B/U LAMP SW

DESCRIPTION	SIZE (MM²)	COLOR	PIN #
FUSED IGNITION	1.0	DK BLU	A
BACKUP LAMP	1.0	LT GRN	B

REV LOCKOUT

DESCRIPTION	SIZE (MM²)	COLOR	PIN #
FUSED IGNITION	0.8	PNK	A
SOLENOID CTRL	0.8	LT GRN	B

CLUTCH ANTICIPATE SWITCH

PIN #	COLOR	SIZE (MM²)	DESCRIPTION
A	GRY	0.5	CLUTCH SIGNAL (NC)
B	BLK	0.5	GROUND

OBD-II DLC

DESCRIPTION	SIZE (MM²)	COLOR	PIN #
CLASS 2 DATA	0.5	DK GRN	2
GROUND	0.8	BLK	4
GROUND	0.8	BLK	5
12V BATTERY	1.0	ORN	16

80W GM# 12200411 PCM C1 (BLUE)

PIN #	COLOR	SIZE (MM²)	DESCRIPTION
1	BLK	0.8	GROUND
19	PNK	0.8	12V IGNITION
20	ORN	0.8	BATTERY POSITIVE
32	GRY	0.5	CLUTCH PEDAL SWITCH SIGNAL
40	BLK	0.8	GROUND
42	DK GRN	0.5	FAN 1 RELAY CONTROL
57	ORN	0.8	BATTERY POSITIVE
58	DK GRN	0.5	CLASS 2 SERIAL DATA
74	YEL	0.5	ECT SIGNAL
80	BLK	0.5	LOW REFERENCE

80W GM# 12200411 PCM C2 (RED)

PIN #	COLOR	SIZE (MM²)	DESCRIPTION
1	BLK	0.8	GROUND
9	DK GRN/WHT	0.5	FUEL PUMP RELAY CONTROL
10	WHT	0.8	ENGINE SPEED (TACHOMETER)
15	RED	0.8	GENERATOR CONTROL
33	DK BLU	0.5	FAN 2 RELAY CONTROL
40	BLK	0.8	GROUND
44	LT GRN	0.8	REVERSE LOCKOUT CONTROL
46	BRN/WHT	0.8	MIL CONTROL
47	TAN	0.8	SHIFT LIGHT CONTROL
50	DK GRN/WHT	0.8	4000 PPM VSS OUTPUT

MM² TO AWG CONVERSION

SIZE (MM²)	AWG
0.35	22
0.5	20
0.8	18
1.0	16
2.0	14
3.0	12
5.0	10

1985 CAMARO 24X 6.0L LS T56 (STARTER AND CHARGING)

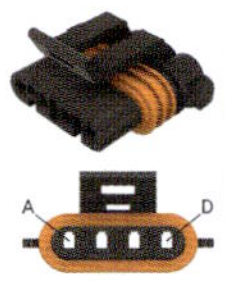

GENERATOR

DESCRIPTION	SIZE (MM²)	COLOR	PIN #
-	-	-	A
PCM CONTROL	0.8	RED	B
GAUGES	0.8	BRN	C
B+ "SENSE"	1.0	RED	D

80W GM# 12200411 PCM C2 (RED)

PIN #	COLOR	SIZE (MM²)	DESCRIPTION
15	RED	0.8	GENERATOR CONTROL

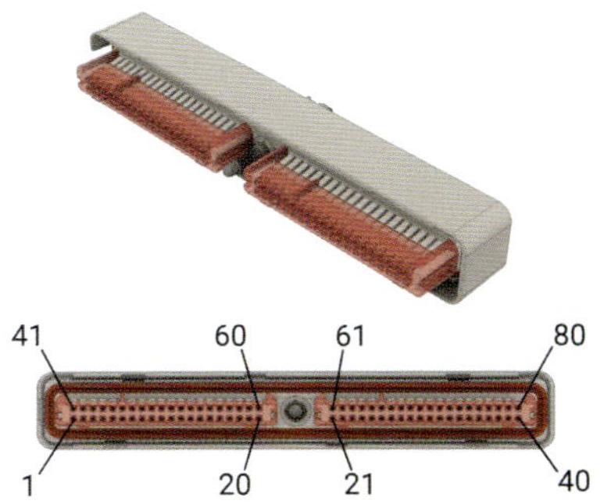

1.0 RED   0.5 FUSIBLE LINK

BATTERY POSITIVE

C100 BULKHEAD

PIN #	COLOR	SIZE (MM²)	DESCRIPTION
B4	PPL	5.0	STARTER
F4	PNK	3.0	IGNITION
D6	WHT	0.8	TACHOMETER
E5	TAN	0.8	OIL PRESSURE
F5	DK GRN	0.8	COOLANT TEMP
F8	BRN	0.8	GENERATOR

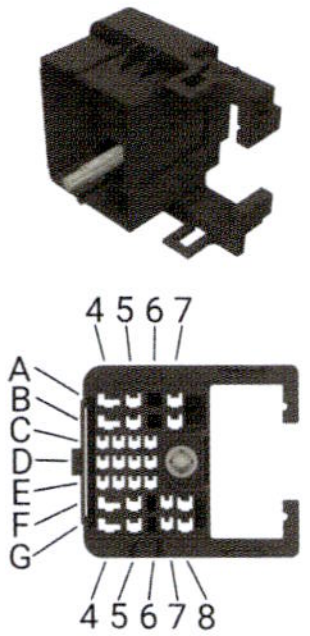

C100 BULKHEAD (INTERIOR)

DESCRIPTION	SIZE (MM²)	COLOR	PIN #
STARTER	5.0	PPL	B4
IGNITION	3.0	PNK	F4
TACHOMETER	0.8	WHT	D6
OIL PRESSURE	0.8	TAN	E5
COOLANT TEMP	0.8	DK GRN	F5
GENERATOR	0.8	BRN	F8

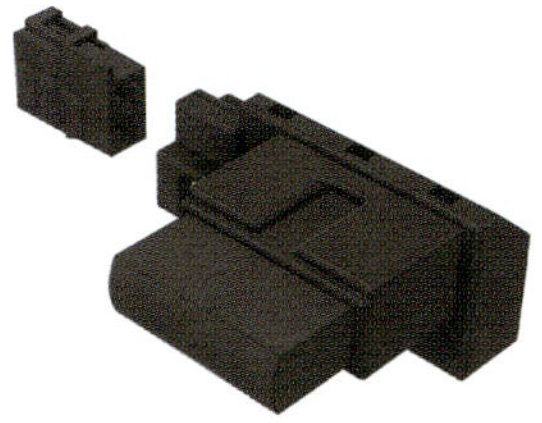

SEE TACHOMETER PULL-UP RESISTOR SCHEMATIC

470Ω 2W 1%

C100 INTERFACE

PIN #	COLOR	SIZE (MM²)	DESCRIPTION
A	PNK	3.0	IGNITION
B	WHT	0.8	TACHOMETER
C	TAN	0.8	OIL PRESSURE
D	DK GRN	0.8	COOLANT TEMP
E	BRN	0.8	GENERATOR
F	-	-	-

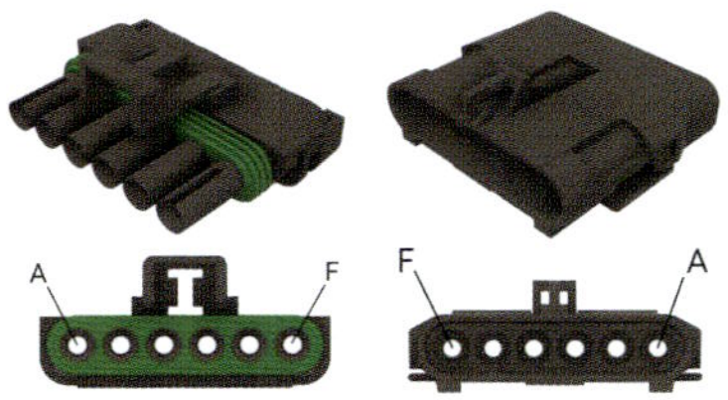

C100 INTERFACE

DESCRIPTION	SIZE (MM²)	COLOR	PIN #
IGNITION	3.0	PNK	A
TACHOMETER	0.8	WHT	B
OIL PRESSURE	0.8	TAN	C
COOLANT TEMP	0.8	DK GRN	D
GENERATOR	0.8	BRN	E
-	-	-	F

CLUTCH PEDAL STARTER SAFETY SWITCH

PIN #	COLOR	SIZE (MM²)	DESCRIPTION
A	PPL	5.0	STARTER S TERMINAL
B	YEL	5.0	IGNITION SWITCH (CRANK)

IGNITION SWITCH

STARTER 'S' TERMINAL

MM² TO AWG CONVERSION

SIZE (MM²)	AWG
0.35	22
0.5	20
0.8	18
1.0	16
2.0	14
3.0	12
5.0	10

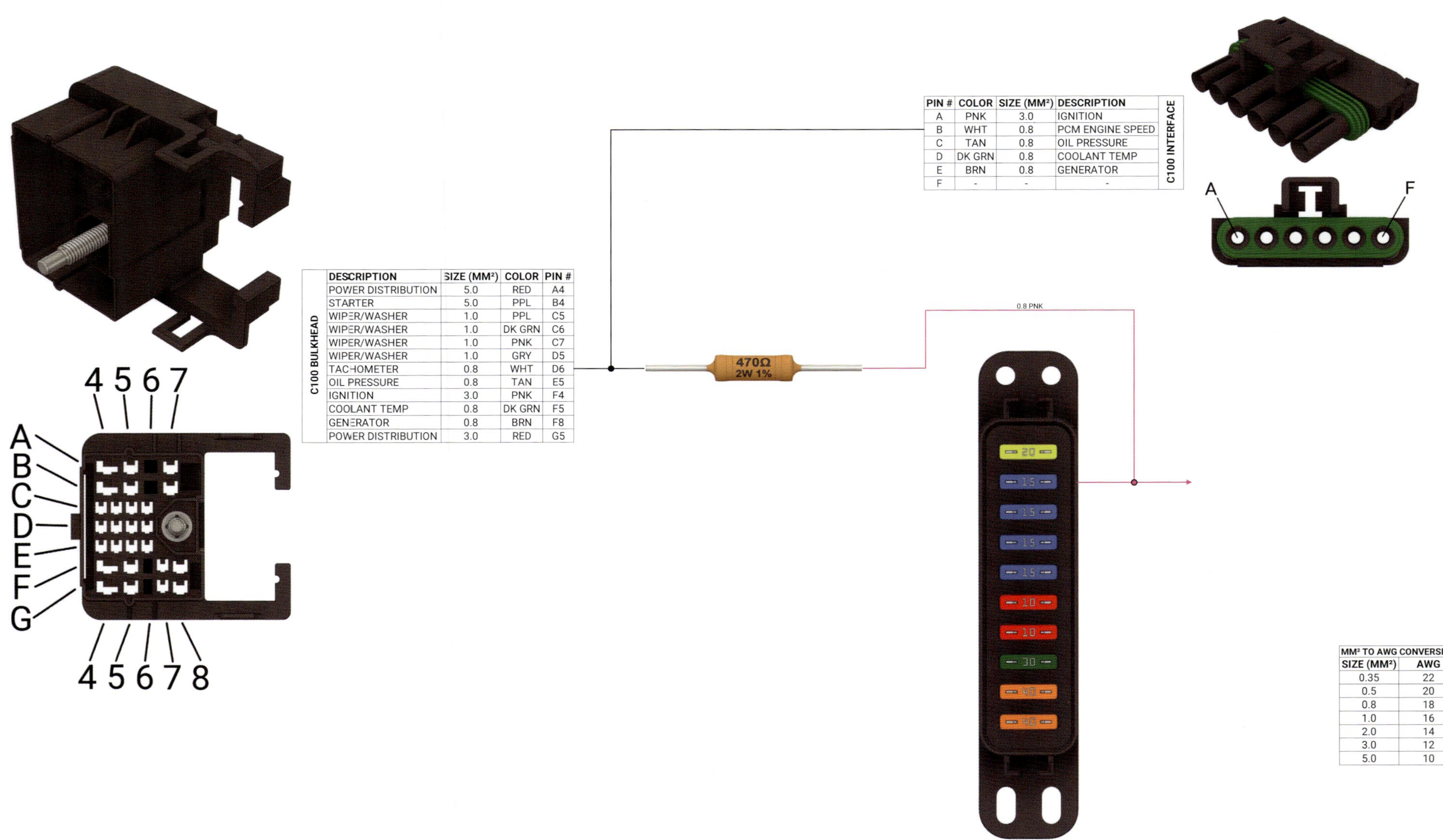

PIN #	COLOR	SIZE (MM²)	DESCRIPTION
A	PNK	3.0	IGNITION
B	WHT	0.8	PCM ENGINE SPEED
C	TAN	0.8	OIL PRESSURE
D	DK GRN	0.8	COOLANT TEMP
E	BRN	0.8	GENERATOR
F	-	-	-

C100 BULKHEAD

DESCRIPTION	SIZE (MM²)	COLOR	PIN #
POWER DISTRIBUTION	5.0	RED	A4
STARTER	5.0	PPL	B4
WIPER/WASHER	1.0	PPL	C5
WIPER/WASHER	1.0	DK GRN	C6
WIPER/WASHER	1.0	PNK	C7
WIPER/WASHER	1.0	GRY	D5
TACHOMETER	0.8	WHT	D6
OIL PRESSURE	0.8	TAN	E5
IGNITION	3.0	PNK	F4
COOLANT TEMP	0.8	DK GRN	F5
GENERATOR	0.8	BRN	F8
POWER DISTRIBUTION	3.0	RED	G5

MM² TO AWG CONVERSION	
SIZE (MM²)	AWG
0.35	22
0.5	20
0.8	18
1.0	16
2.0	14
3.0	12
5.0	10

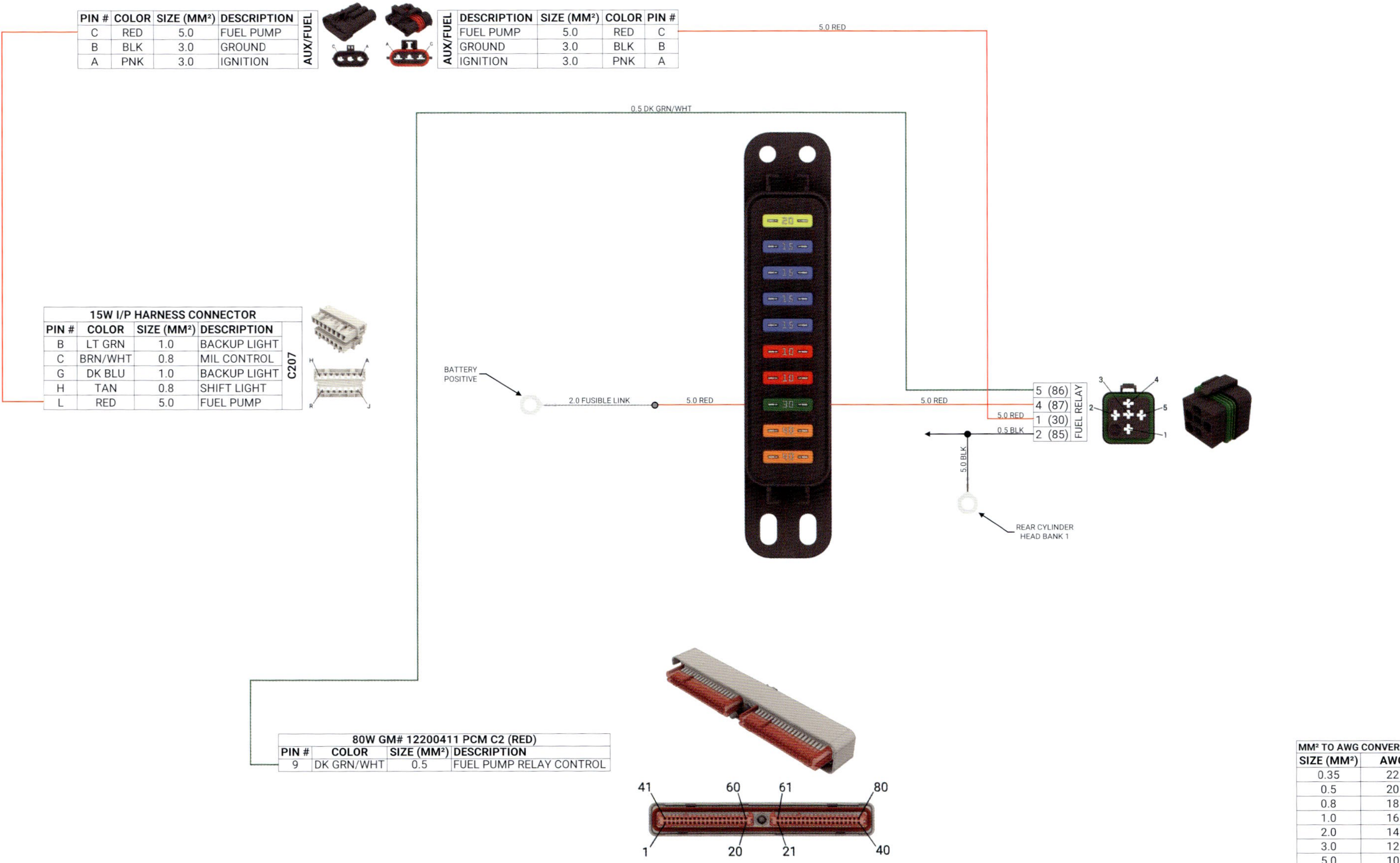

AUX/FUEL

PIN #	COLOR	SIZE (MM²)	DESCRIPTION
C	RED	5.0	FUEL PUMP
B	BLK	3.0	GROUND
A	PNK	3.0	IGNITION

AUX/FUEL

DESCRIPTION	SIZE (MM²)	COLOR	PIN #
FUEL PUMP	5.0	RED	C
GROUND	3.0	BLK	B
IGNITION	3.0	PNK	A

C207

15W I/P HARNESS CONNECTOR			
PIN #	COLOR	SIZE (MM²)	DESCRIPTION
B	LT GRN	1.0	BACKUP LIGHT
C	BRN/WHT	0.8	MIL CONTROL
G	DK BLU	1.0	BACKUP LIGHT
H	TAN	0.8	SHIFT LIGHT
L	RED	5.0	FUEL PUMP

80W GM# 12200411 PCM C2 (RED)			
PIN #	COLOR	SIZE (MM²)	DESCRIPTION
9	DK GRN/WHT	0.5	FUEL PUMP RELAY CONTROL

MM² TO AWG CONVERSION	
SIZE (MM²)	AWG
0.35	22
0.5	20
0.8	18
1.0	16
2.0	14
3.0	12
5.0	10

1985 CAMARO 24X 6.0L LS T56 (FUEL INJECTORS – EV6)

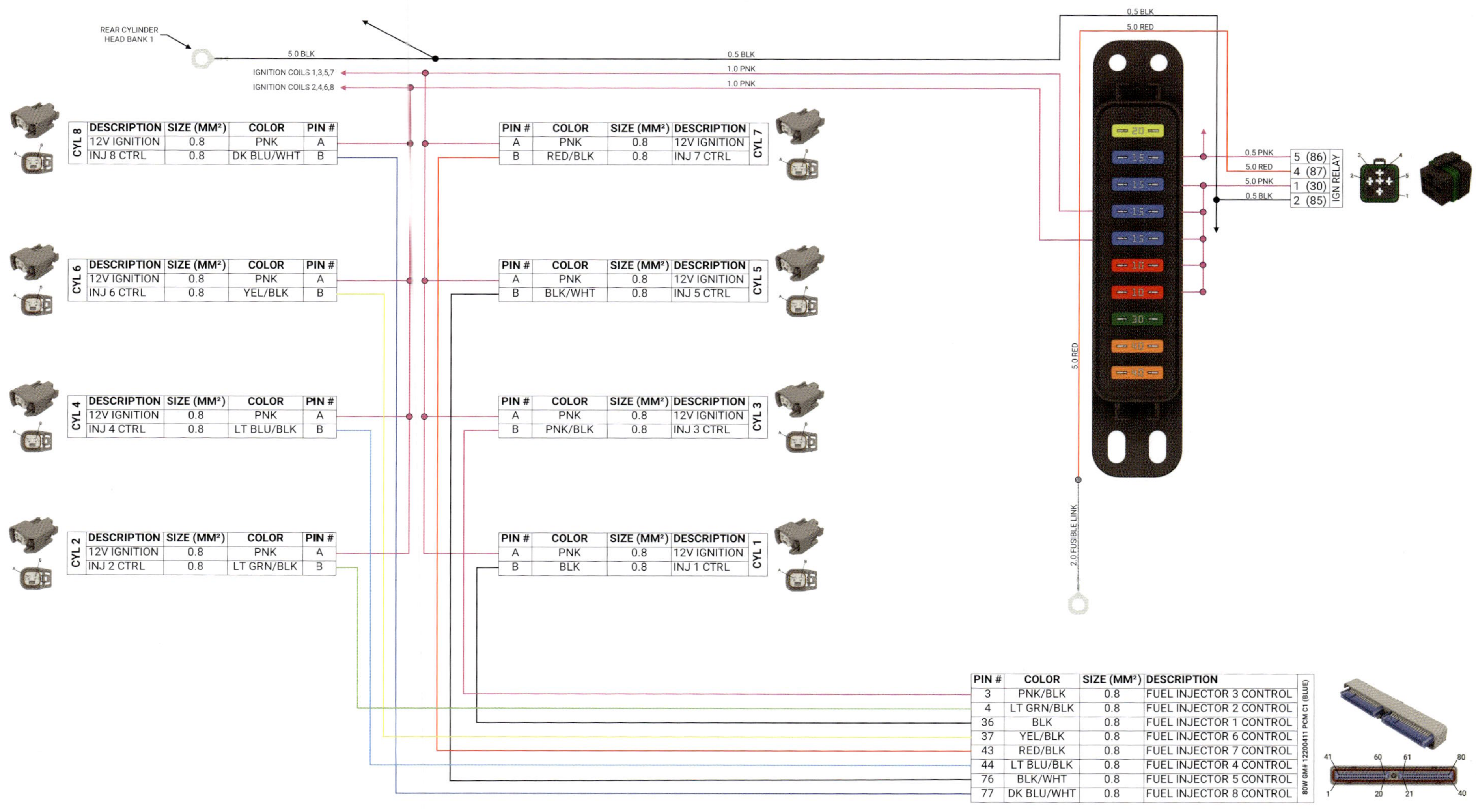

CYL 8

DESCRIPTION	SIZE (MM²)	COLOR	PIN #
12V IGNITION	0.8	PNK	A
INJ 8 CTRL	0.8	DK BLU/WHT	B

CYL 7

PIN #	COLOR	SIZE (MM²)	DESCRIPTION
A	PNK	0.8	12V IGNITION
B	RED/BLK	0.8	INJ 7 CTRL

CYL 6

DESCRIPTION	SIZE (MM²)	COLOR	PIN #
12V IGNITION	0.8	PNK	A
INJ 6 CTRL	0.8	YEL/BLK	B

CYL 5

PIN #	COLOR	SIZE (MM²)	DESCRIPTION
A	PNK	0.8	12V IGNITION
B	BLK/WHT	0.8	INJ 5 CTRL

CYL 4

DESCRIPTION	SIZE (MM²)	COLOR	PIN #
12V IGNITION	0.8	PNK	A
INJ 4 CTRL	0.8	LT BLU/BLK	B

CYL 3

PIN #	COLOR	SIZE (MM²)	DESCRIPTION
A	PNK	0.8	12V IGNITION
B	PNK/BLK	0.8	INJ 3 CTRL

CYL 2

DESCRIPTION	SIZE (MM²)	COLOR	PIN #
12V IGNITION	0.8	PNK	A
INJ 2 CTRL	0.8	LT GRN/BLK	B

CYL 1

PIN #	COLOR	SIZE (MM²)	DESCRIPTION
A	PNK	0.8	12V IGNITION
B	BLK	0.8	INJ 1 CTRL

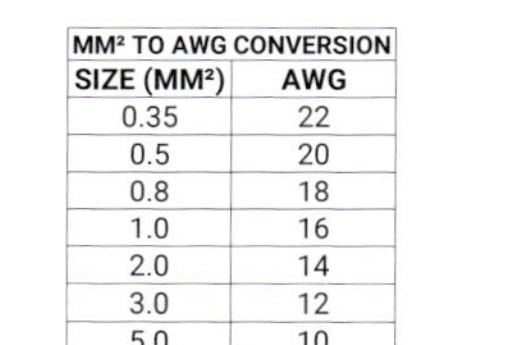

PIN #	COLOR	SIZE (MM²)	DESCRIPTION
3	PNK/BLK	0.8	FUEL INJECTOR 3 CONTROL
4	LT GRN/BLK	0.8	FUEL INJECTOR 2 CONTROL
36	BLK	0.8	FUEL INJECTOR 1 CONTROL
37	YEL/BLK	0.8	FUEL INJECTOR 6 CONTROL
43	RED/BLK	0.8	FUEL INJECTOR 7 CONTROL
44	LT BLU/BLK	0.8	FUEL INJECTOR 4 CONTROL
76	BLK/WHT	0.8	FUEL INJECTOR 5 CONTROL
77	DK BLU/WHT	0.8	FUEL INJECTOR 8 CONTROL

MM² TO AWG CONVERSION

SIZE (MM²)	AWG
0.35	22
0.5	20
0.8	18
1.0	16
2.0	14
3.0	12
5.0	10

1985 CAMARO 24X 6.0L LS T56 (IGNITION COILS)

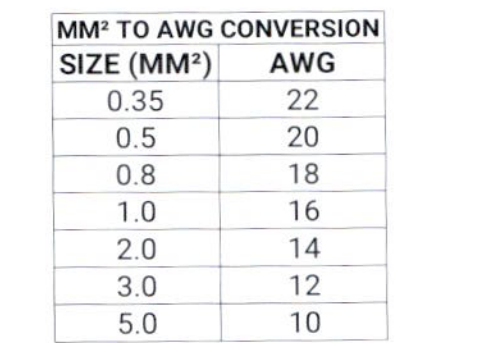

CYLINDER 8

DESCRIPTION	SIZE (MM²)	COLOR	PIN #
GROUND	0.8	BLK	A
LOW REFERENCE	0.8	BRN/WHT	B
IC 8 CONTROL	0.8	PPL/WHT	C
12V IGNITION	0.8	PNK	D

CYLINDER 6

DESCRIPTION	SIZE (MM²)	COLOR	PIN #
GROUND	0.8	BLK	A
LOW REFERENCE	0.8	BRN/WHT	B
IC 6 CONTROL	0.8	LT BLU/WHT	C
12V IGNITION	0.8	PNK	D

CYLINDER 4

DESCRIPTION	SIZE (MM²)	COLOR	PIN #
GROUND	0.8	BLK	A
LOW REFERENCE	0.8	BRN/WHT	B
IC 4 CONTROL	0.8	DK GRN/WHT	C
12V IGNITION	0.8	PNK	D

CYLINDER 2

DESCRIPTION	SIZE (MM²)	COLOR	PIN #
GROUND	0.8	BLK	A
LOW REFERENCE	0.8	BRN/WHT	B
IC 2 CONTROL	0.8	RED/WHT	C
12V IGNITION	0.8	PNK	D

CYLINDER 7

PIN #	COLOR	SIZE (MM²)	DESCRIPTION
A	BLK	0.8	GROUND
B	BRN	0.8	LOW REFERENCE
C	RED	0.8	IC 7 CONTROL
D	PNK	0.8	12V IGNITION

CYLINDER 5

PIN #	COLOR	SIZE (MM²)	DESCRIPTION
A	BLK	0.8	GROUND
B	BRN	0.8	LOW REFERENCE
C	DK GRN	0.8	IC 5 CONTROL
D	PNK	0.8	12V IGNITION

CYLINDER 3

PIN #	COLOR	SIZE (MM²)	DESCRIPTION
A	BLK	0.8	GROUND
B	BRN	0.8	LOW REFERENCE
C	LT BLU	0.8	IC 3 CONTROL
D	PNK	0.8	12V IGNITION

CYLINDER 1

PIN #	COLOR	SIZE (MM²)	DESCRIPTION
A	BLK	0.8	GROUND
B	BRN	0.8	LOW REFERENCE
C	PPL	0.8	IC 1 CONTROL
D	PNK	0.8	12V IGNITION

80W GM# 12200411 PCM C1 (RED)

PIN #	COLOR	SIZE (MM²)	DESCRIPTION
26	PPL	0.8	IGNITION CONTROL 1
27	RED	0.8	IGNITION CONTROL 7
28	LT BLU/WHT	0.8	IGNITION CONTROL 6
29	DK GRN/WHT	0.8	IGNITION CONTROL 4
60	BRN	0.8	LOW REFERENCE (ODD)
61	BRN/WHT	0.8	LOW REFERENCE (EVEN)
66	PPL/WHT	0.8	IGNITION CONTROL 8
67	RED/WHT	0.8	IGNITION CONTROL 2
68	DK GRN	0.8	IGNITION CONTROL 5
69	LT BLU	0.8	IGNITION CONTROL 3

MM² TO AWG CONVERSION

SIZE (MM²)	AWG
0.35	22
0.5	20
0.8	18
1.0	16
2.0	14
3.0	12
5.0	10

IGN RELAY

1985 CAMARO 24X 6.0L LS T56 (MAF AND OXYGEN SENSORS)

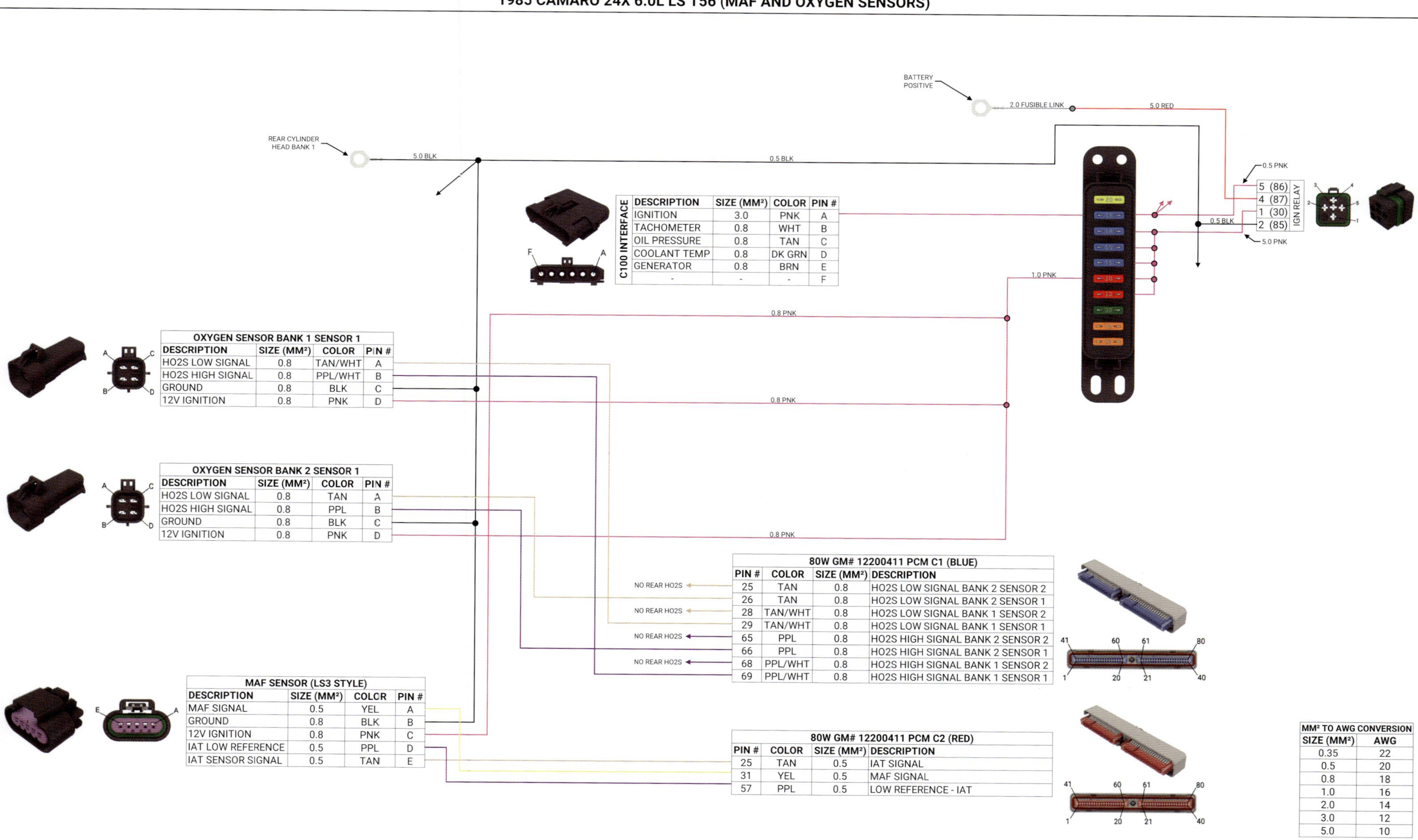

C100 INTERFACE

DESCRIPTION	SIZE (MM²)	COLOR	PIN #
IGNITION	3.0	PNK	A
TACHOMETER	0.8	WHT	B
OIL PRESSURE	0.8	TAN	C
COOLANT TEMP	0.8	DK GRN	D
GENERATOR	0.8	BRN	E
-	-	-	F

OXYGEN SENSOR BANK 1 SENSOR 1

DESCRIPTION	SIZE (MM²)	COLOR	PIN #
HO2S LOW SIGNAL	0.8	TAN/WHT	A
HO2S HIGH SIGNAL	0.8	PPL/WHT	B
GROUND	0.8	BLK	C
12V IGNITION	0.8	PNK	D

OXYGEN SENSOR BANK 2 SENSOR 1

DESCRIPTION	SIZE (MM²)	COLOR	PIN #
HO2S LOW SIGNAL	0.8	TAN	A
HO2S HIGH SIGNAL	0.8	PPL	B
GROUND	0.8	BLK	C
12V IGNITION	0.8	PNK	D

MAF SENSOR (LS3 STYLE)

DESCRIPTION	SIZE (MM²)	COLCR	PIN #
MAF SIGNAL	0.5	YEL	A
GROUND	0.8	BLK	B
12V IGNITION	0.8	PNK	C
IAT LOW REFERENCE	0.5	PPL	D
IAT SENSOR SIGNAL	0.5	TAN	E

80W GM# 12200411 PCM C1 (BLUE)

PIN #	COLOR	SIZE (MM²)	DESCRIPTION
25	TAN	0.8	HO2S LOW SIGNAL BANK 2 SENSOR 2
26	TAN	0.8	HO2S LOW SIGNAL BANK 2 SENSOR 1
28	TAN/WHT	0.8	HO2S LOW SIGNAL BANK 1 SENSOR 2
29	TAN/WHT	0.8	HO2S LOW SIGNAL BANK 1 SENSOR 1
65	PPL	0.8	HO2S HIGH SIGNAL BANK 2 SENSOR 2
66	PPL	0.8	HO2S HIGH SIGNAL BANK 2 SENSOR 1
68	PPL/WHT	0.8	HO2S HIGH SIGNAL BANK 1 SENSOR 2
69	PPL/WHT	0.8	HO2S HIGH SIGNAL BANK 1 SENSOR 1

80W GM# 12200411 PCM C2 (RED)

PIN #	COLOR	SIZE (MM²)	DESCRIPTION
25	TAN	0.5	IAT SIGNAL
31	YEL	0.5	MAF SIGNAL
57	PPL	0.5	LOW REFERENCE - IAT

MM² TO AWG CONVERSION

SIZE (MM²)	AWG
0.35	22
0.5	20
0.8	18
1.0	16
2.0	14
3.0	12
5.0	10

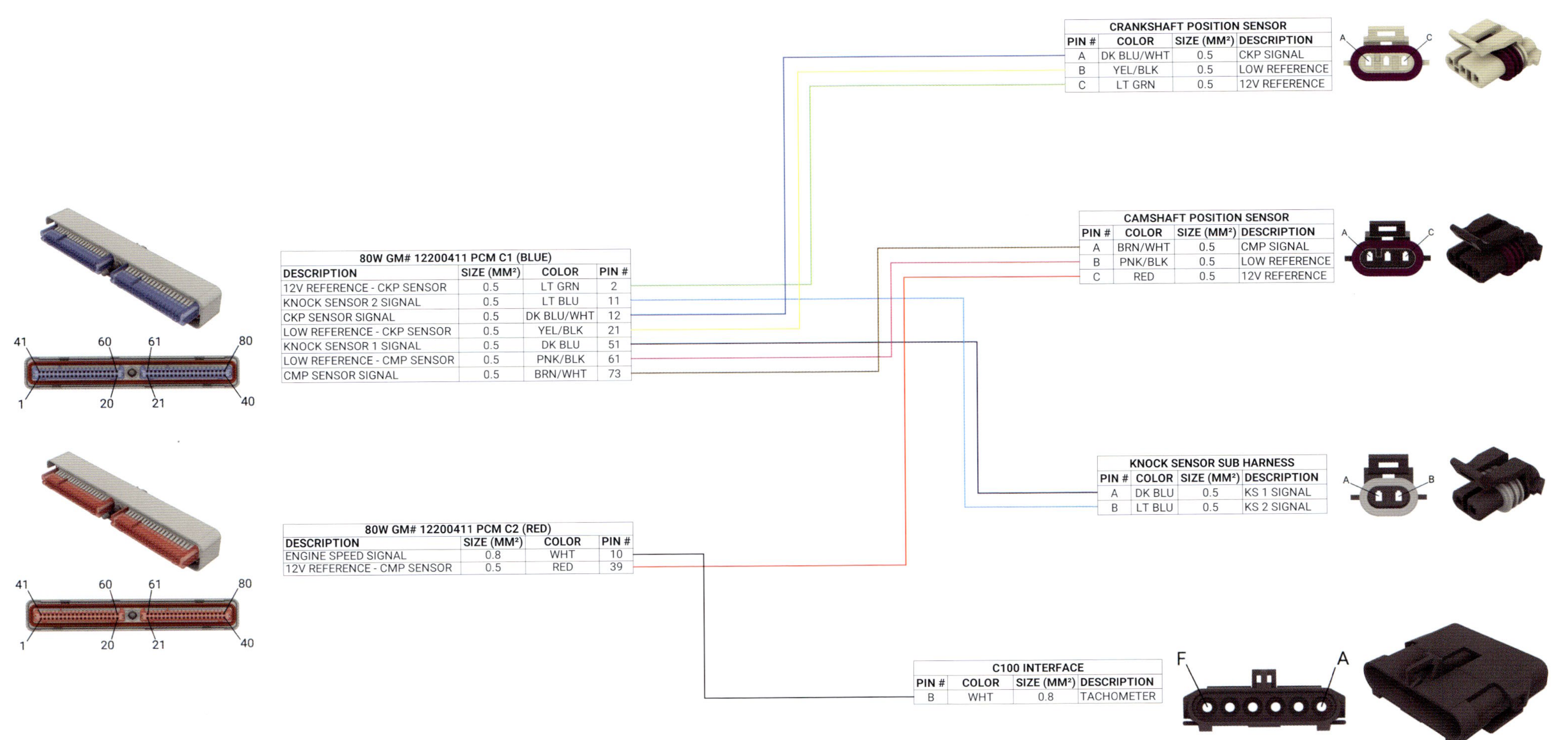

CRANKSHAFT POSITION SENSOR

PIN #	COLOR	SIZE (MM²)	DESCRIPTION
A	DK BLU/WHT	0.5	CKP SIGNAL
B	YEL/BLK	0.5	LOW REFERENCE
C	LT GRN	0.5	12V REFERENCE

CAMSHAFT POSITION SENSOR

PIN #	COLOR	SIZE (MM²)	DESCRIPTION
A	BRN/WHT	0.5	CMP SIGNAL
B	PNK/BLK	0.5	LOW REFERENCE
C	RED	0.5	12V REFERENCE

KNOCK SENSOR SUB HARNESS

PIN #	COLOR	SIZE (MM²)	DESCRIPTION
A	DK BLU	0.5	KS 1 SIGNAL
B	LT BLU	0.5	KS 2 SIGNAL

80W GM# 12200411 PCM C1 (BLUE)

DESCRIPTION	SIZE (MM²)	COLOR	PIN #
12V REFERENCE - CKP SENSOR	0.5	LT GRN	2
KNOCK SENSOR 2 SIGNAL	0.5	LT BLU	11
CKP SENSOR SIGNAL	0.5	DK BLU/WHT	12
LOW REFERENCE - CKP SENSOR	0.5	YEL/BLK	21
KNOCK SENSOR 1 SIGNAL	0.5	DK BLU	51
LOW REFERENCE - CMP SENSOR	0.5	PNK/BLK	61
CMP SENSOR SIGNAL	0.5	BRN/WHT	73

80W GM# 12200411 PCM C2 (RED)

DESCRIPTION	SIZE (MM²)	COLOR	PIN #
ENGINE SPEED SIGNAL	0.8	WHT	10
12V REFERENCE - CMP SENSOR	0.5	RED	39

C100 INTERFACE

PIN #	COLOR	SIZE (MM²)	DESCRIPTION
B	WHT	0.8	TACHOMETER

MM² TO AWG CONVERSION

SIZE (MM²)	AWG
0.35	22
0.5	20
0.8	18
1.0	16
2.0	14
3.0	12
5.0	10

1985 CAMARO 24X 6.0L LS T56 (ENGINE SENSORS)

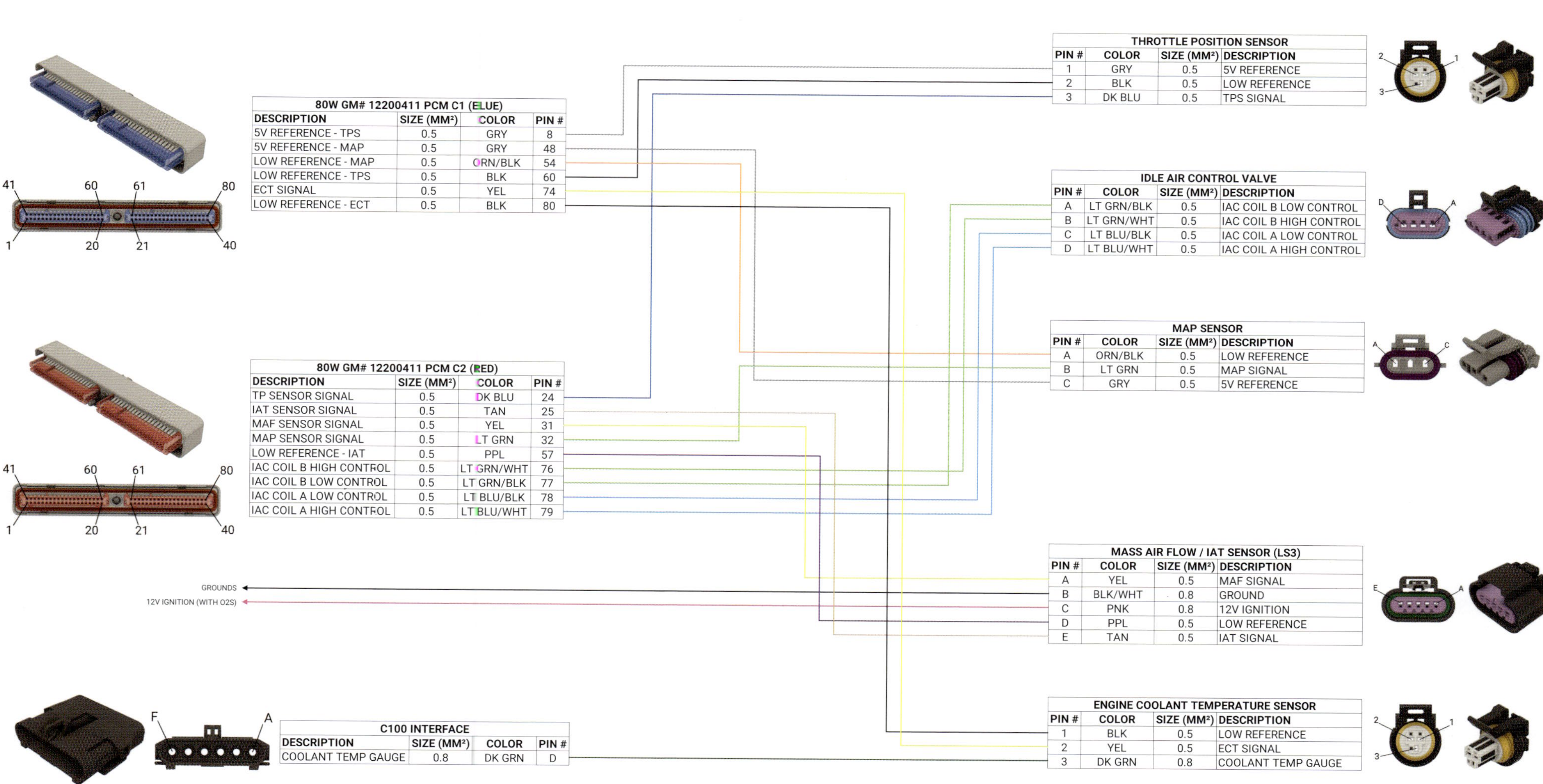

80W GM# 12200411 PCM C1 (BLUE)

DESCRIPTION	SIZE (MM²)	COLOR	PIN #
5V REFERENCE - TPS	0.5	GRY	8
5V REFERENCE - MAP	0.5	GRY	48
LOW REFERENCE - MAP	0.5	ORN/BLK	54
LOW REFERENCE - TPS	0.5	BLK	60
ECT SIGNAL	0.5	YEL	74
LOW REFERENCE - ECT	0.5	BLK	80

80W GM# 12200411 PCM C2 (RED)

DESCRIPTION	SIZE (MM²)	COLOR	PIN #
TP SENSOR SIGNAL	0.5	DK BLU	24
IAT SENSOR SIGNAL	0.5	TAN	25
MAF SENSOR SIGNAL	0.5	YEL	31
MAP SENSOR SIGNAL	0.5	LT GRN	32
LOW REFERENCE - IAT	0.5	PPL	57
IAC COIL B HIGH CONTROL	0.5	LT GRN/WHT	76
IAC COIL B LOW CONTROL	0.5	LT GRN/BLK	77
IAC COIL A LOW CONTROL	0.5	LT BLU/BLK	78
IAC COIL A HIGH CONTROL	0.5	LT BLU/WHT	79

THROTTLE POSITION SENSOR

PIN #	COLOR	SIZE (MM²)	DESCRIPTION
1	GRY	0.5	5V REFERENCE
2	BLK	0.5	LOW REFERENCE
3	DK BLU	0.5	TPS SIGNAL

IDLE AIR CONTROL VALVE

PIN #	COLOR	SIZE (MM²)	DESCRIPTION
A	LT GRN/BLK	0.5	IAC COIL B LOW CONTROL
B	LT GRN/WHT	0.5	IAC COIL B HIGH CONTROL
C	LT BLU/BLK	0.5	IAC COIL A LOW CONTROL
D	LT BLU/WHT	0.5	IAC COIL A HIGH CONTROL

MAP SENSOR

PIN #	COLOR	SIZE (MM²)	DESCRIPTION
A	ORN/BLK	0.5	LOW REFERENCE
B	LT GRN	0.5	MAP SIGNAL
C	GRY	0.5	5V REFERENCE

MASS AIR FLOW / IAT SENSOR (LS3)

PIN #	COLOR	SIZE (MM²)	DESCRIPTION
A	YEL	0.5	MAF SIGNAL
B	BLK/WHT	0.8	GROUND
C	PNK	0.8	12V IGNITION
D	PPL	0.5	LOW REFERENCE
E	TAN	0.5	IAT SIGNAL

C100 INTERFACE

DESCRIPTION	SIZE (MM²)	COLOR	PIN #
COOLANT TEMP GAUGE	0.8	DK GRN	D

ENGINE COOLANT TEMPERATURE SENSOR

PIN #	COLOR	SIZE (MM²)	DESCRIPTION
1	BLK	0.5	LOW REFERENCE
2	YEL	0.5	ECT SIGNAL
3	DK GRN	0.8	COOLANT TEMP GAUGE

MM² TO AWG CONVERSION

SIZE (MM²)	AWG
0.35	22
0.5	20
0.8	18
1.0	16

1985 CAMARO 24X 6.0L LS T56 (MANUAL TRANSMISSION)

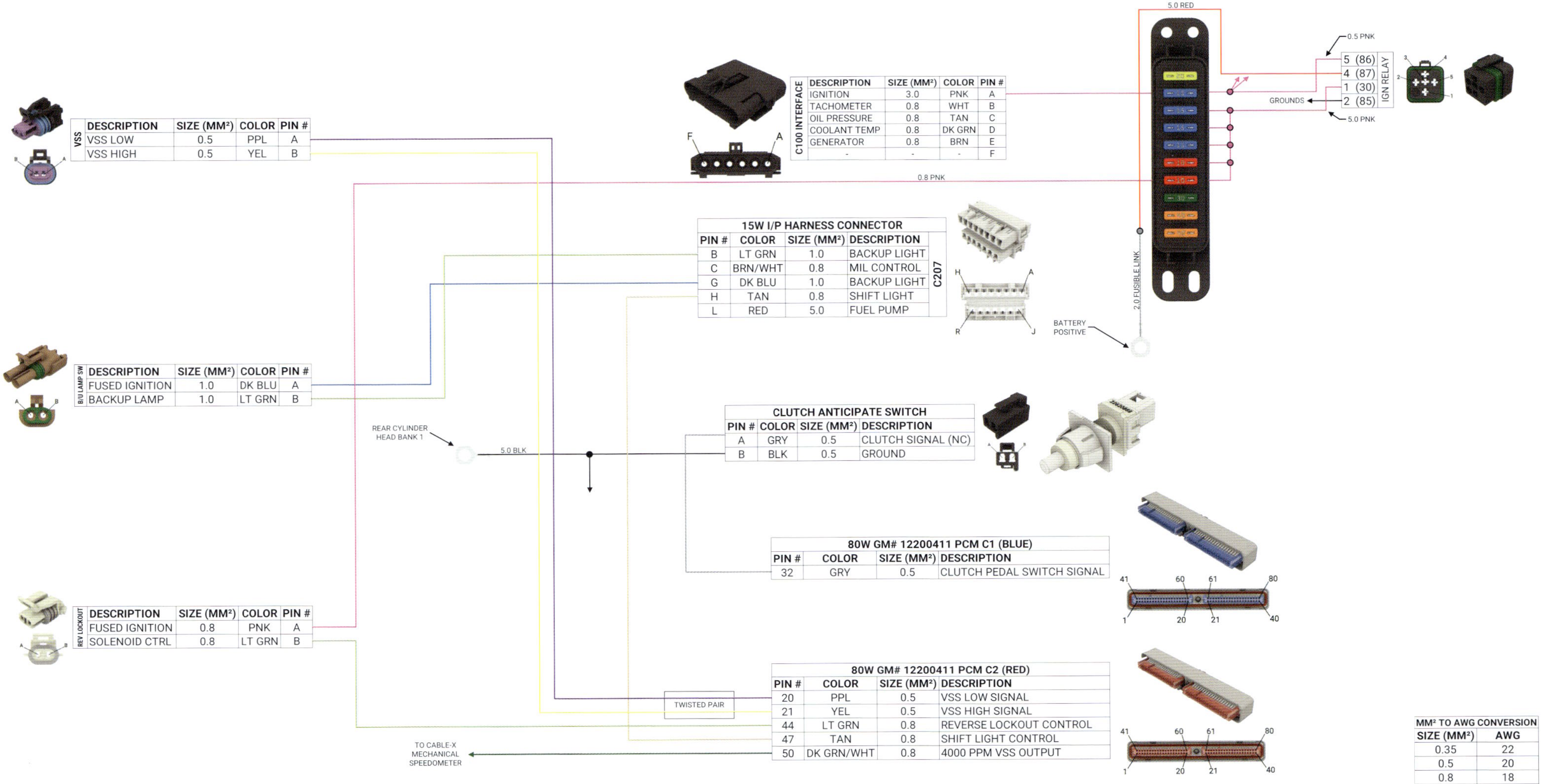

MM² TO AWG CONVERSION

SIZE (MM²)	AWG
0.35	22
0.5	20
0.8	18
1.0	16
2.0	14
3.0	12
5.0	10

C100 INTERFACE

DESCRIPTION	SIZE (MM²)	COLOR	PIN #
IGNITION	3.0	PNK	A
TACHOMETER	0.8	WHT	B
OIL PRESSURE	0.8	TAN	C
COOLANT TEMP	0.8	DK GRN	D
GENERATOR	0.8	BRN	E
-	-	-	F

15W I/P HARNESS CONNECTOR — C207

PIN #	COLOR	SIZE (MM²)	DESCRIPTION
B	LT GRN	1.0	BACKUP LIGHT
C	BRN/WHT	0.8	MIL CONTROL
G	DK BLU	1.0	BACKUP LIGHT
H	TAN	0.8	SHIFT LIGHT
L	RED	5.0	FUEL PUMP

CLUTCH ANTICIPATE SWITCH

PIN #	COLOR	SIZE (MM²)	DESCRIPTION
A	GRY	0.5	CLUTCH SIGNAL (NC)
B	BLK	0.5	GROUND

80W GM# 12200411 PCM C1 (BLUE)

PIN #	COLOR	SIZE (MM²)	DESCRIPTION
32	GRY	0.5	CLUTCH PEDAL SWITCH SIGNAL

80W GM# 12200411 PCM C2 (RED)

PIN #	COLOR	SIZE (MM²)	DESCRIPTION
20	PPL	0.5	VSS LOW SIGNAL
21	YEL	0.5	VSS HIGH SIGNAL
44	LT GRN	0.8	REVERSE LOCKOUT CONTROL
47	TAN	0.8	SHIFT LIGHT CONTROL
50	DK GRN/WHT	0.8	4000 PPM VSS OUTPUT

VSS

DESCRIPTION	SIZE (MM²)	COLOR	PIN #
VSS LOW	0.5	PPL	A
VSS HIGH	0.5	YEL	B

B/U LAMP SW

DESCRIPTION	SIZE (MM²)	COLOR	PIN #
FUSED IGNITION	1.0	DK BLU	A
BACKUP LAMP	1.0	LT GRN	B

REV LOCKOUT

DESCRIPTION	SIZE (MM²)	COLOR	PIN #
FUSED IGNITION	0.8	PNK	A
SOLENOID CTRL	0.8	LT GRN	B

1985 CAMARO 24X 6.0L LS T56 (ELECTRIC FANS)

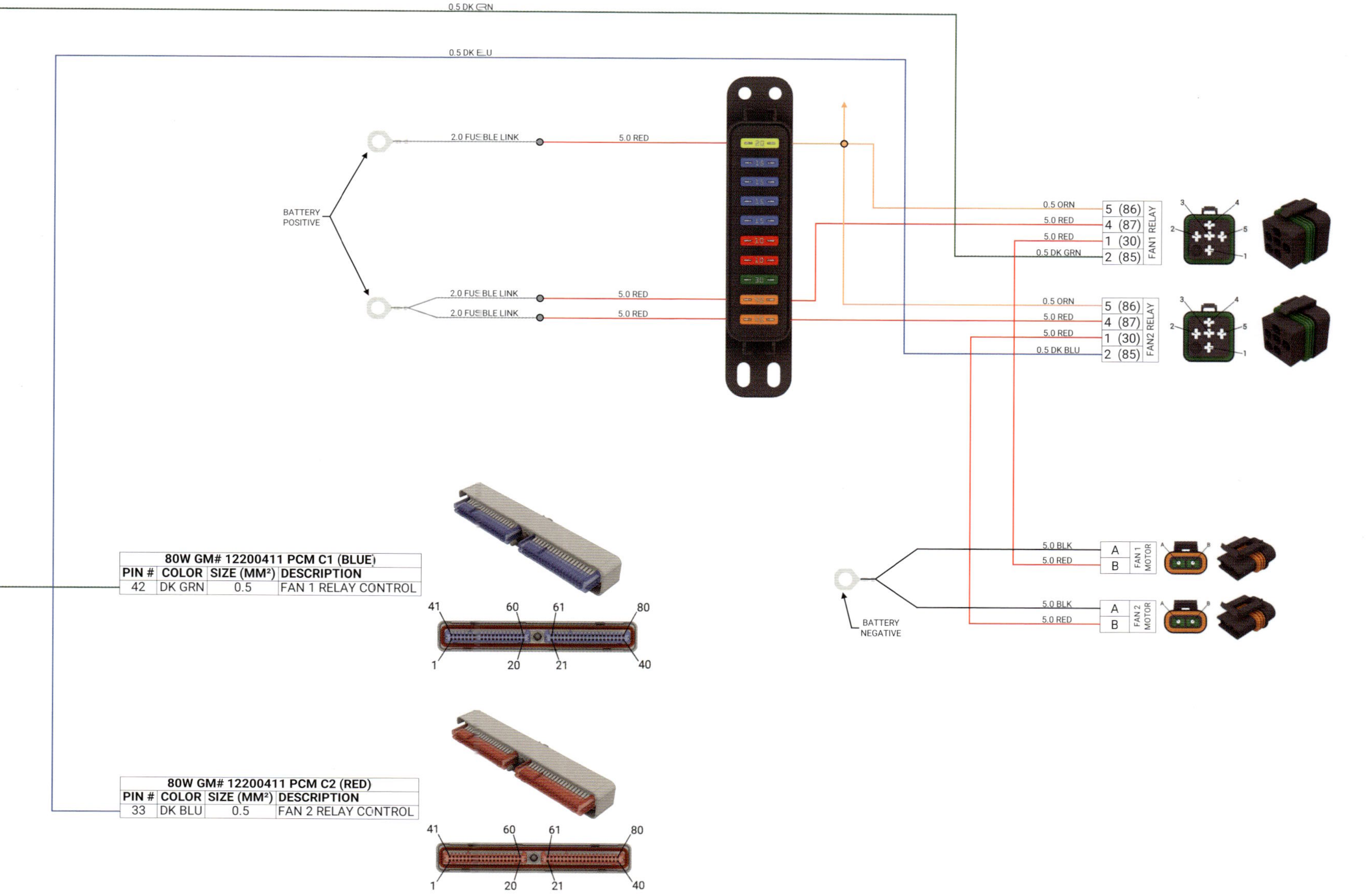

80W GM# 12200411 PCM C1 (BLUE)			
PIN #	COLOR	SIZE (MM²)	DESCRIPTION
42	DK GRN	0.5	FAN 1 RELAY CONTROL

80W GM# 12200411 PCM C2 (RED)			
PIN #	COLOR	SIZE (MM²)	DESCRIPTION
33	DK BLU	0.5	FAN 2 RELAY CONTROL

MM² TO AWG CONVERSION	
SIZE (MM²)	AWG
0.35	22
0.5	20
0.8	18
1.0	16
2.0	14
3.0	12
5.0	10

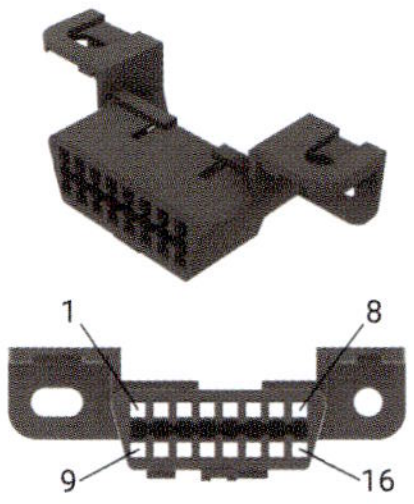

OBD-II DLC

DESCRIPTION	SIZE (MM²)	COLOR	PIN #
CLASS 2 DATA	0.5	DK GRN	2
GROUND	0.8	BLK	4
GROUND	0.8	BLK	5
12V BATTERY	1.0	ORN	16

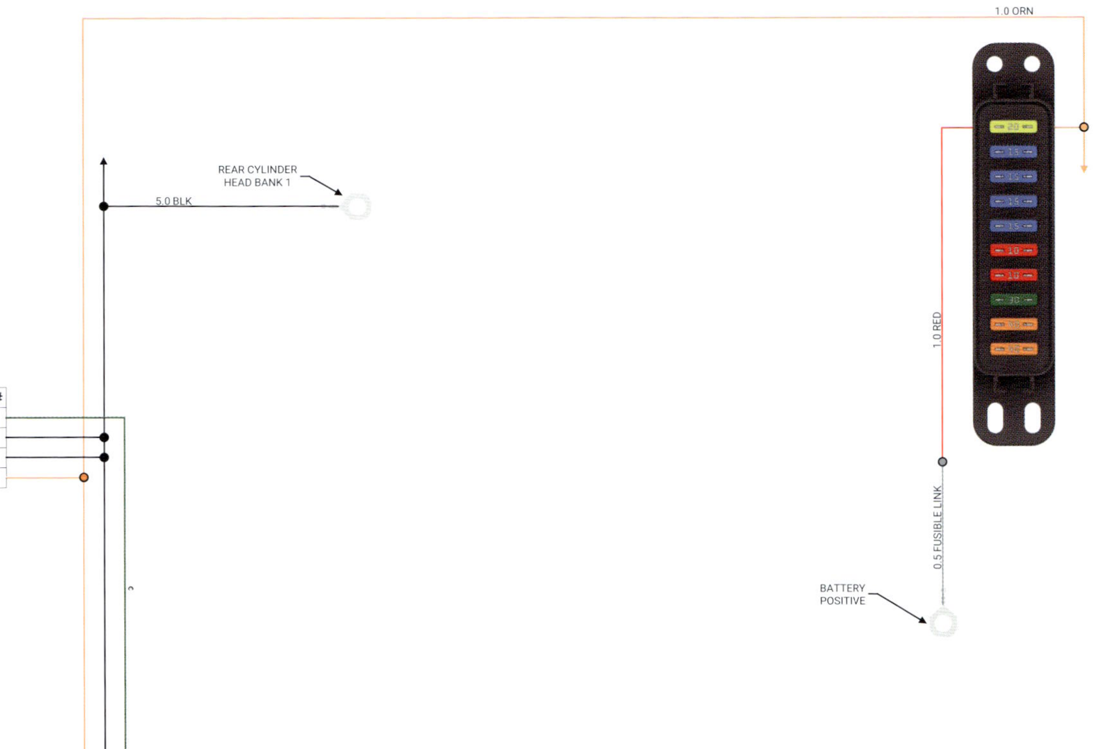

80W GM# 12200411 PCM C1 (BLUE)			
PIN #	COLOR	SIZE (MM²)	DESCRIPTION
1	BLK	0.8	GROUND
19	PNK	0.8	12V IGNITION
20	ORN	0.8	BATTERY POSITIVE
40	BLK	0.8	GROUND
57	ORN	0.8	BATTERY POSITIVE
58	DK GRN	0.5	CLASS 2 SERIAL DATA

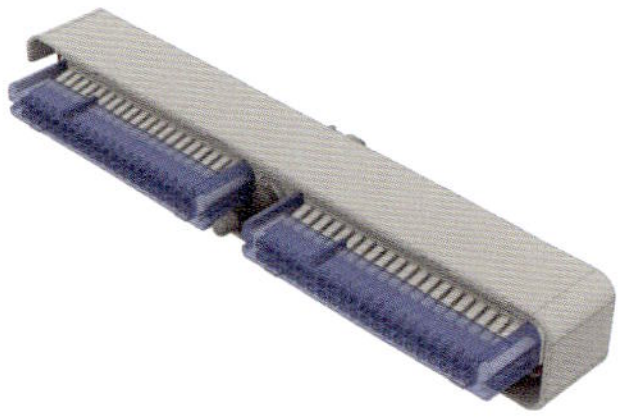

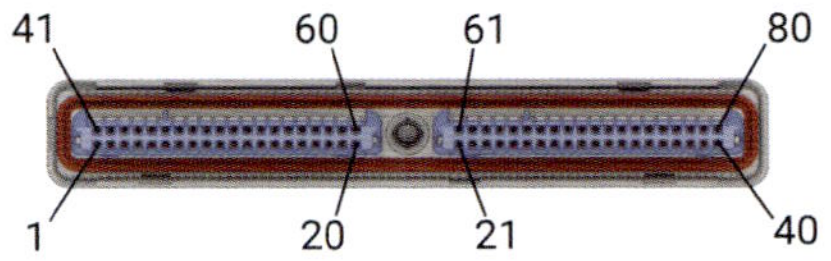

MM² TO AWG CONVERSION	
SIZE (MM²)	AWG
0.35	22
0.5	20
0.8	18
1.0	16
2.0	14
3.0	12
5.0	10

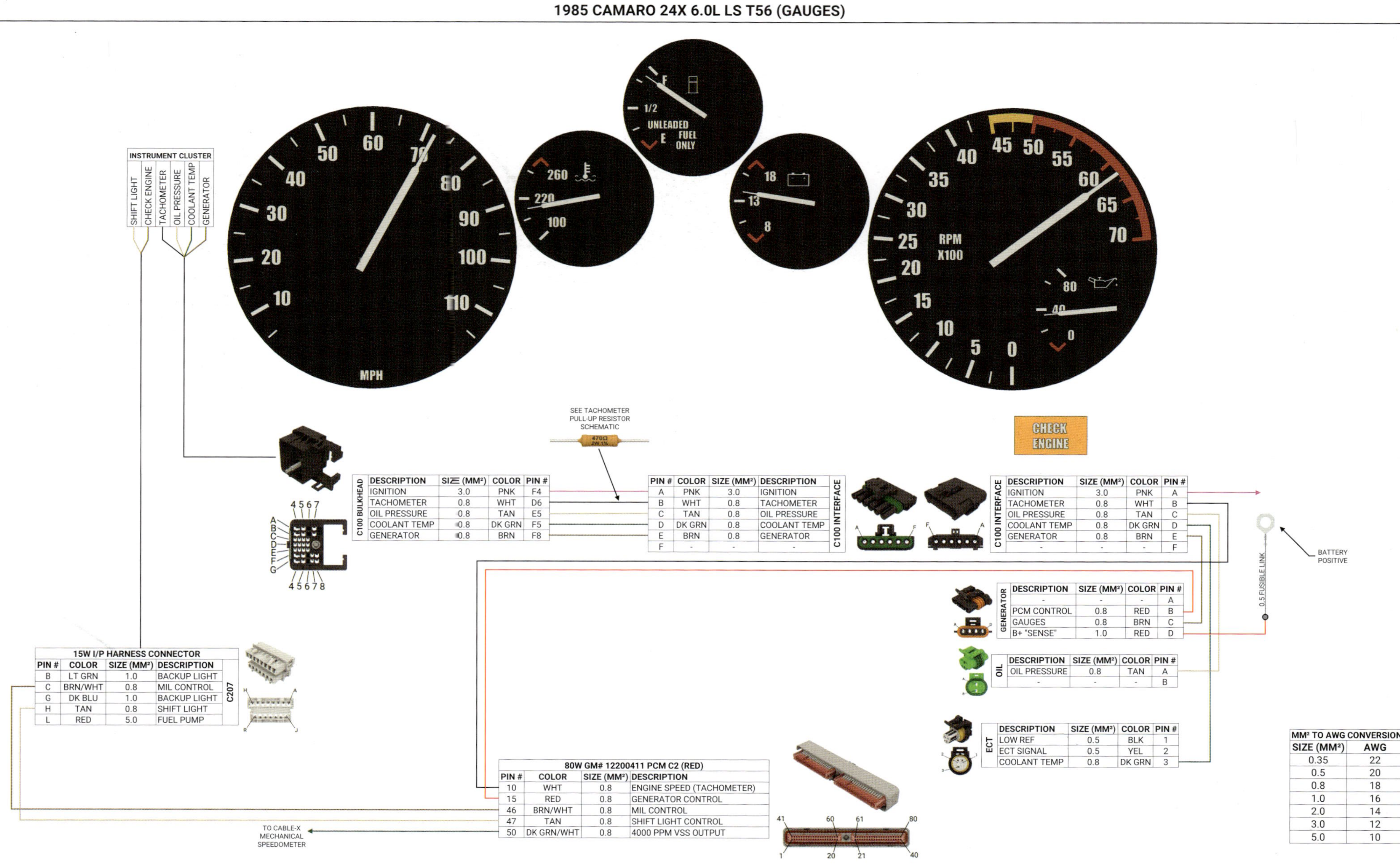

C100 BULKHEAD

DESCRIPTION	SIZE (MM²)	COLOR	PIN #
IGNITION	3.0	PNK	F4
TACHOMETER	0.8	WHT	D6
OIL PRESSURE	0.8	TAN	E5
COOLANT TEMP	0.8	DK GRN	F5
GENERATOR	0.8	BRN	F8

C100 INTERFACE

PIN #	COLOR	SIZE (MM²)	DESCRIPTION
A	PNK	3.0	IGNITION
B	WHT	0.8	TACHOMETER
C	TAN	0.8	OIL PRESSURE
D	DK GRN	0.8	COOLANT TEMP
E	BRN	0.8	GENERATOR
F	-	-	-

C100 INTERFACE

DESCRIPTION	SIZE (MM²)	COLOR	PIN #
IGNITION	3.0	PNK	A
TACHOMETER	0.8	WHT	B
OIL PRESSURE	0.8	TAN	C
COOLANT TEMP	0.8	DK GRN	D
GENERATOR	0.8	BRN	E
-	-	-	F

GENERATOR

DESCRIPTION	SIZE (MM²)	COLOR	PIN #
-	-	-	A
PCM CONTROL	0.8	RED	B
GAUGES	0.8	BRN	C
B+ "SENSE"	1.0	RED	D

OIL

DESCRIPTION	SIZE (MM²)	COLOR	PIN #
OIL PRESSURE	0.8	TAN	A
-	-	-	B

ECT

DESCRIPTION	SIZE (MM²)	COLOR	PIN #
LOW REF	0.5	BLK	1
ECT SIGNAL	0.5	YEL	2
COOLANT TEMP	0.8	DK GRN	3

15W I/P HARNESS CONNECTOR

PIN #	COLOR	SIZE (MM²)	DESCRIPTION
B	LT GRN	1.0	BACKUP LIGHT
C	BRN/WHT	0.8	MIL CONTROL
G	DK BLU	1.0	BACKUP LIGHT
H	TAN	0.8	SHIFT LIGHT
L	RED	5.0	FUEL PUMP

C207

80W GM# 12200411 PCM C2 (RED)

PIN #	COLOR	SIZE (MM²)	DESCRIPTION
10	WHT	0.8	ENGINE SPEED (TACHOMETER)
15	RED	0.8	GENERATOR CONTROL
46	BRN/WHT	0.8	MIL CONTROL
47	TAN	0.8	SHIFT LIGHT CONTROL
50	DK GRN/WHT	0.8	4000 PPM VSS OUTPUT

MM² TO AWG CONVERSION

SIZE (MM²)	AWG
0.35	22
0.5	20
0.8	18
1.0	16
2.0	14
3.0	12
5.0	10